HOSTELLING
INTERNATIONAL

Europe2000

Welcome
Bienvenue
Willkommen
Bienvenido

Hostelling International is the brand name of the International Youth Hostel Federation, the organization that represents Youth Hostel Associations, worldwide.

For budget accommodation you can trust, look for the blue triangle symbol.

The information in this Guide has been supplied by the Youth Hostel Associations of each country represented. Every effort has been made to ensure that it is correct, and Hostelling International can accept no responsibility for any inaccuracies or for changes subsequent to publication.

ISBN 0 901496 54 5

Évora Youth Hostel - Portugal
Rotherhithe Youth Hostel - London, England
Af Chapman Youth Hostel - Stockholm, Sweden

How to Use This Guide

Liège Youth Hostel - Belgium

Welcome to the world of Hostelling International - a unique network of accommodation centres where you can enjoy a good night's sleep in friendly surroundings at an affordable price.

This Guide provides details of the facilities available at Youth Hostels that are registered with the

INTERNATIONAL YOUTH HOSTEL FEDERATION.

You will find these details listed alphabetically by country and city.

In this introductory section we provide some general information about Hostelling International, its services for guests, its membership benefits, and its commitment to a level of assured standards which all hostels must work to achieve.

If you require any information about hostels worldwide you can
either:

Contact your local Youth Hostel Association (YHA) prior to departure
or:

Visit our Internet home page at **www.iyhf.org**

An Introduction to Hostelling International

The Youth Hostel movement was founded in Germany in the early years of this century, and spread rapidly between the Wars, especially in Europe.

Today, Hostelling International offers you a choice of nearly 4,500 accommodation centres in more than 60 countries worldwide.

At Youth Hostels in Europe, Asia, Africa, the Americas and the Pacific we hope to offer you a consistently high service - a good night's sleep in friendly surroundings at an affordable price.

This Guide provides details of the hostels that you can choose from. Today it is possible to book a bed up to 6 months in advance using the International Booking Network (IBN) system - you can find details about IBN within this guide.

No Age Limit

Despite their name, Youth Hostels are open to people of all ages in virtually every country where they are located. A small number of German hostels have a maximum age restriction, which is a requirement of local legislation.

Guests under 14 years of age should be accompanied by an adult, and many hostels now offer family rooms.

Most hostels accept group bookings and the majority now offer a variety of accommodation options - you can find single, double and dormitory rooms in most major hostels.

Privileges of Membership

To stay at a Youth Hostel you must become a member of your national Youth Hostel Association (YHA). Additional to your membership, you will receive certain special services and benefits, including access to thousands of discounts worldwide. The details of some of these discounts are listed in this Guide. You can get the details of other discounts by contacting the YHA of the country you are visiting.

Or you can visit our discount database at our web page at **www.iyhf.org.**

If you do not have a national YHA in your country, you can purchase a Hostelling International Card or a "welcome stamp" when you arrive at your chosen hostel.

St Pancras Youth Hostel - London, England

Assured Standards

Hostelling International recognizes that consistent quality and service are important to budget travellers. That is why we have introduced our Assured Standards Scheme, to ensure that you can rely on a consistent level of services and facilities wherever you stay in our hostels.

What do Assured Standards at hostels mean to you?

Welcome

Hostels are open to everyone, irrespective of age, sex, culture, race or religion. If you do not already have membership, you will be able to take out full or short-term membership at the hostel you stay at.

You will be able to reserve a bed in advance, by telephone, fax, email, post or through the IBN system.

You are normally able to check-in (or out) between 0700 hrs and 1000 hrs and 1700 hrs and 2230 hrs at most hostels.

Above all, welcoming you will be the priority of the hostel staff and they will be committed to providing the support and information that you need to get the most out of your stay.

Comfort

You can expect a good, comfortable night's sleep, sufficient showers, WCs and washing facilities, plus a good supply of hot water. Where it is not included in the overnight charge, freshly laundered linen will be available for hire if you require it.

Although meals are generally available, where only self-catering is provided you will normally be able to buy basic food supplies in the hostel or close by. These hostels will provide food storage, preparation, cooking and washing up areas for you to use.

Cleanliness

Wherever you travel you can expect the highest standards of cleanliness and hygiene from Hostelling International.

Security

Hostel staff will make every endeavour to ensure your personal security, and the security of your possessions during your stay. Lockers will be available to store your own luggage and valuables.

Privacy

The Assured Standards Scheme promises privacy in showers, washing areas and toilets. The vast majority of hostels offer accommodation in single sex dormitories, although some hostels, on request, might offer mixed sex dormitory rooms to people travelling together. However, single sex dormitories will always be made available.

Locarno Youth Hostel - Switzerland

4

A Commitment to our Environment

Whitepark Bay Youth Hostel - N Ireland

Environmental Charter

In addition to these Assured Standards, hostels will also adhere to the IYHF Environmental Charter which lays down the criteria for the consumption and conservation of resources, waste disposal and recycling, nature conservation and the provision of environmental education.

For many people the essence of simple hostels is that they are found in remote, unusual locations and are often very special buildings. We must admit though, that it is hard to apply the same standards across all locations - in the middle of a rain forest or in a remote shepherd's hut. Because of these variations we do make some exceptions to standards for small hostels and those with simple facilities where you may find limited staffing and shorter opening hours. This type of hostel is clearly indicated as a **simple hostel.**

Standards are monitored by Hostelling International and by you, the user. **There are comment forms at the back of this Guide to help you contact us.**

The International Booking Network (IBN)

Book Ahead Through IBN

Our computerized booking system offers you a simple and cheap advance booking option for nearly 300 key hostels in 47 countries worldwide.

Wherever you see this IBN symbol **IBN** in the Guide, it means that you can book a bed up to 6 months in advance of your stay (depending on availability). The hostels in the network are listed within each of the country sections and highlighted in blue.

The IBN hostels offer a service which is unique in the budget accommodation sector.

- You can pay for reservations in the local currency from where you are making the booking, before your departure.
- You can make reservations during your travels from any IBN hostel or local IBN Booking Centre. **The list of Booking Centres is found on pages 43 to 54.**
- In many cases you can pay by credit card.
- In many countries you can call a single Central Reservations Office (see listing on page 7) to book a series of overnight stays in several hostels in advance.

Stirling Youth Hostel - Scotland

Luxembourg City Youth Hostel - Luxembourg

OTHER BOOKING INFORMATION

You can arrive at a hostel without a reservation, but in busy times we advise strongly that you reserve ahead of time to avoid disappointment.

- Family rooms are soon occupied and groups should also book ahead of time.
- You can book hostel beds by sending a fax or letter to the hostel of your choice.
- If you book by letter, be sure to enclose an international postal reply coupon (available at most post offices) and a self-addressed envelope. If you make an advance booking without paying a deposit you will usually be required to arrive at the hostel by 1800 hours, unless a different time is agreed.

We know you will enjoy the hostel experience. You will certainly be able to afford it. We look forward to meeting you.

MAKE YOUR CREDIT CARD BOOKINGS AT THESE CENTRES	
Australia	☎ (2) 9261 1111
Canada	☎ (1) (800) 663 5777
England & Wales	☎ (1629) 581 418
France	☎ (1) 44 89 87 27
Northern Ireland	☎ (1232) 324 733
Republic of Ireland	☎ (1) 830 1766
New Zealand	☎ (9) 303 9524
Scotland	☎ (541) 553 255
Switzerland	☎ (1) 360 14 14
USA	☎ (202) 783 6161

Commission Free Currency Exchange

A SPECIAL OFFER FOR HOSTELLING INTERNATIONAL MEMBERS.

TRAVELEX - the world's largest airport and passenger terminal bureau de change - has offered Hostelling International members a very special service to reduce the cost of international travel.

By showing your membership card you can enjoy Commission Free Currency Exchange at any of the 300 Travelex offices worldwide. The list of their offices can be found on the Travelex website at **www.travelexgrp.com.**

This fabulous service will save you a significant amount, especially when you are planning to visit more than one country.

Exclusive Travelex Buy Back Plus: *for a nominal fee, Travelex will buy back any unused currency at exactly the same rate that you bought it, commission free!*

These offers are not available for the exchange of one Euro legacy currency into another (eg the offer is not available for the exchange of Belgium Francs into Deutsche Marks or Italian Lira).

Travelex

Den Haag Youth Hostel - Netherlands

3 1833 01996 8699

Comment vous servir de ce Guide...

Kalundborg Youth Hostel - Denmark

Bienvenue au monde d'Hostelling International - un réseau unique d'hébergement où vous pouvez passer une bonne nuit de sommeil dans un milieu accueillant et à des prix abordables.

Ce guide détaille et liste les services proposés dans les Auberges de Jeunesse affiliées à la

INTERNATIONAL YOUTH HOSTEL FEDERATION.

Vous les trouverez par **ordre alphabétique, par pays et par ville.**

Dans cette introduction, nous vous proposons des renseignements généraux sur Hostelling International - les services et les avantages offerts aux adhérents, ainsi que notre engagement à garantir des normes minimales, que chaque auberge devra s'efforcer d'atteindre.

Si vous avez besoin de renseignements sur les auberges du monde entier, vous pouvez **soit:**

- Contacter l'Association d'auberges de jeunesse de votre pays avant votre départ
  soit:
- Consulter notre site Internet à **www.iyhf.org.**

Hostelling International - Introduction

Le mouvement des Auberges de Jeunesse a été fondé en Allemagne au début du siècle et s'est rapidement étendu à d'autres pays entre les deux guerres, principalement en Europe.

Aujourd'hui, Hostelling International vous propose un choix de 4 500 centres d'hébergement dans plus de 60 pays disséminés de par le monde entier.

Dans nos auberges d'Europe, d'Asie, d'Afrique, d'Amérique et du Pacifique, nous espérons vous offrir un service constant et de haute qualité - une bonne nuit de sommeil dans un milieu accueillant, à un prix abordable.

Ce guide est un recueil de renseignements sur toutes les auberges qui sont à votre disposition. Il est maintenant possible de réserver un lit jusqu'à six mois à l'avance en utilisant le système de réservation IBN - International Booking Network - Voir les pages suivantes pour de plus amples renseignements.

Pas de limite d'âge

Malgré leur nom, les Auberges de Jeunesse sont ouvertes à tous les âges, dans pratiquement tous les pays où elles sont implantées. Un nombre limité d'auberges allemandes imposent un âge limite et ce, en raison des contraintes de la législation locale.

Les jeunes de moins de 14 ans devront être accompagnés par un adulte et d'ailleurs, nombreux sont nos établissements qui proposent des chambres familiales.

La plupart des auberges acceptent les groupes et la majorité, surtout dans les grandes villes, mettent à disposition un choix d'hébergement, c'est à dire, des chambres individuelles, des chambres pour couples ou bien encore des dortoirs.

Les Privilèges de l'Adhésion

Afin d'être admis à séjourner dans une auberge de jeunesse, il vous faudra devenir membre de l'Association d'Auberges de Jeunesse de votre pays. Votre carte d'adhérent vous permettra en outre de bénéficier de certains services et avantages exclusifs, notemment de nombreuses réductions dans votre pays et à l'étranger. Ce guide vous en donne un avant-goût en listant quelques-uns de ces avantages mais pour en savoir plus, contactez l'Association d'AJ du pays que vous désirez visiter. Vous pouvez également faire un tour sur notre site Web **(www.iyhf.org)** où vous trouverez notre base de données des réductions.

S'il n'existe pas d'Association nationale dans votre pays, vous pouvez acheter une carte ou un Timbre de Bienvenue (Welcome Stamp) à votre arrivée à l'auberge.

Ambleside Youth Hostel - England

Normes Garanties

Hostelling International reconnaît qu'un service et des installations de qualité constante, d'une auberge à l'autre, importent beaucoup aux gens qui voyagent avec un budget limité. Le Plan pour la Garantie des Normes en Auberges a été mis en place précisément pour vous assurer cette constance dans nos prestations, quelle que soit l'auberge où vous séjournez.

Qu'est-ce que les Normes Garanties vous apportent?

Accueil

Les auberges sont ouvertes à tous, quel que soit votre âge, sexe, culture, race ou religion. Si vous n'avez pas déjà l'avantage d'être membre, vous aurez la possibilité d'aquérir, à l'auberge où vous comptez séjourner, une adhésion complète ou partielle.

Vous pouvez réserver un lit à l'avance, par téléphone, fax, e-mail, courrier ordinaire ou via le système IBN.

En principe, il vous sera possible d'arriver entre 7h et 10h et entre 17h et 22h30 dans la plupart des auberges.

Mais surtout, vous accueillir sera la priorité du personnel de l'auberge qui s'engagera à vous fournir l'aide et l'information dont vous aurez besoin pour tirer un maximum de votre séjour.

Confort

Vous pouvez compter passer une bonne nuit de sommeil confortablement et trouver un nombre suffisant de douches et de sanitaires, ainsi qu'une bonne réserve d'eau chaude!

Là où ce n'est pas compris dans le prix de la nuité, il vous sera possible de louer des draps propres, si besoin est.

Bien qu'elles servent en général des repas, certaines auberges peuvent n'être aménagées que d'une cuisine individuelle. Dans ces cas-là, vous devriez être en mesure d'acheter des denrées de base, soit à l'auberge, soit à proximité. Ces auberges mettront à votre disposition une reserve pour denrées, une surface de préparation et de cuisson et un évier pour la vaisselle.

Propreté

Où que vous soyez, vous êtes en droit d'attendre des auberges et de leur personnel un haut degré de propreté et d'hygiène.

Sécurité

Le personnel des auberges fera tout son possible pour garantir votre sécurité personnelle et celle de vos biens pendant votre séjour. Des consignes fermant à clé seront à votre disposition pour y déposer bagages et objets de valeur.

Intimité

Le Plan de Garantie des Normes vous promet votre intimité dans les douches, salles de bain et toilettes. La vaste majorité des auberges proposent un hébergement dans des dortoirs non-mixtes bien qu'il soit possible que certains établissements offrent, sur demande, des chambres ou dortoirs mixtes à des groupes de personnes voyageant ensemble. Cependant, des dortoirs non-mixtes devront toujours être disponibles.

Notre Engagement envers l'Environnement

Annecy Youth Hostel - France

Charte de l'Environnement

Outre ces Normes Garanties, les auberges s'engagent à adhérer à la Charte Environnementale de l'IYHF qui dicte les critères de consommation et de préservation des ressources, d'élimination des déchets et de recyclage, de défense de l'environnement et prévoit également que les auberges devront jouer un rôle dans l'éducation écologique.

Pour beaucoup de gens, ce qui caractérise l'ajisme ce sont des endroits perdus, isolés et insolites et des bâtiments très spéciaux.

Nous devons admettre, cependant, qu'il nous est difficile d'appliquer ces mêmes normes partout - au milieu de la forêt tropicale ou dans une cabane de berger isolée, par exemple.

C'est pourquoi nous avons fait une exception de quelques petites auberges plus simplement equipées, où le personnel, ainsi que les périodes d'ouverture, peuvent être limités. Ce type d'auberge sera indiqué clairement dans le guide sous l'appellation Auberge Simple (ou Simple Hostel).

La présence de ces normes dans les auberges seront contrôlées par Hostelling International et par vous, les usagers. N'hésitez pas à utiliser les cartes ou fiches-commentaires que vous trouverez dans ce guide et qui vous permettront de nous contacter plus facilement.

Le Réseau International de Réservation (IBN)

Réservez à l'avance grâce à IBN

Notre réseau international de réservation (IBN) vous offre une solution simple et économique pour réserver à l'avance et à peu de frais dans plus de 300 sites-clés, répartis dans 47 pays à travers le monde.

Un symbole IBN **(IBN)** apposé au nom d'une auberge vous signale qu'il vous sera possible d'y réserver un lit jusqu'à 6 mois avant votre départ (selon les disponibilités).

Ces auberges IBN sont répertoriées par pays dans chacune des sections consacrées aux diverses Associations nationales et apparaissent en bleu. Elles vous offrent un service unique dans le secteur de l'hébergement économique.

IBN vous permet:

● de régler votre séjour dans la devise du pays où vous effectuez votre réservation, avant votre départ.

● d'effectuer des réservations au cours de vos périples depuis l'auberge ou centre de réservation IBN le plus proche. **Vous trouverez la liste de ces centres de réservation IBN aux pages 43 - 54.**

● dans la plupart des cas, de payer par carte de crédit

● dans de nombreux pays, d'appeler une seule centrale de réservation (voir ci-dessous) pour réserver une série de nuitées dans plusieurs auberges.

AUTRES METHODES DE RESERVATION

Vous pouvez vous présenter à l'auberge sans réservation, mais en saison, nous vous recommandons vivement de réserver à l'avance pour vous éviter une déception.

● Les chambres familiales sont très demandées. Quant aux groupes, ils devront toujours faire une réservation au préalable.

● Il est également possible de réserver en envoyant un fax ou un courrier directement à l'auberge concernée.

● Si vous réservez par courrier, n'oubliez pas de joindre un coupon-réponse international (que vous obtiendrez dans les bureaux de poste) ainsi qu'une enveloppe à vos nom et adresse. N'oubliez pas cependant, si vous réservez sans verser d'arrhes, que vous devrez arriver à l'auberge avant 18h, à moins d'avoir convenu avec l'auberge d'une heure différente pour votre arrivée. **Nous sommes sûrs que votre expérience des auberges sera agréable. Elle sera de toutes façons abordable. Nous sommes impatients de faire votre connaissance.**

RESERVEZ PAR CARTE DE CREDIT AUPRES DES CENTRES SUIVANTS	
Angleterre & Pays de Galles	☎ **(1629) 581 418**
Australie	☎ **(2) 9261 1111**
Canada	☎ **(1) (800) 663 5777**
Écosse	☎ **(541) 553 255**
États-Unis	☎ **(202) 783 6161**
France	☎ **(1) 44 89 87 27**
Irlande du Nord	☎ **(1232) 324 733**
Nouvelle-Zélande	☎ **(9) 303 9524**
République d'Irlande	☎ **(1) 830 1766**
Suisse	☎ **(1) 360 14 14**

Change Sans Commission

UNE OFFRE SPECIALE RESERVEE AUX MEMBRES HOSTELLING INTERNATIONAL

TRAVELEX - la chaîne de bureaux de change la plus prédominante dans les aéroports et autres terminaux passagers - offre aux membres Hostelling International un service très exclusif qui leur permet de réduire les frais de leurs voyages transfrontaliers.

Sur simple présentation de votre carte d'adhérent, vous pouvez changer des devises sans commission à n'importe lequel des bureaux Travelex dans le monde. Pour une liste de leurs établissements, consultez le site Web Travelex à l'adresse suivante: **www.travelexgrp.com.**

Cette offre unique vous permettra d'économiser des sommes considérables, surtout si vos voyages vous emmènent dans plus d'un pays.

Le Buy Back Plus, une offre exclusive de Travelex: moyennant une somme modique , nous rachèterons toutes les devises étrangères que vous n'aurez pas utilisées exactement au même taux qu'à l'achat, et ce, sans commission!

Cette offre n'est pas valable lorsque le change s'effectue entre les devises nationales de pays faisant partie de l'Union Monétaire et Economique européenne (Zone Euro) (par exemple, pour changer des francs belges en marks allemands ou lires italiennes).

Rome Youth Hostel - Italy

Wie Sie diesen Führer benutzen

Vienna Brigittenau Youth Hostel - Austria

Willkommen in der Welt von Hostelling International - dem einmaligen Netz von Unterkünften für eine gute Nachtruhe in freundlicher Umgebung - zu einem Preis, den Sie sich leisten können.

Wie Sie diesen Führer benutzen

Der Führer enthält Informationen über die Ausstattungen und Leistungen der Jugendherbergen, die in der

INTERNATIONAL YOUTH HOSTEL FEDERATION

zusammengeschlossen sind.

Die Angaben sind nach Ländern und Orten alphabetisch geordnet.

In der Einführung finden Sie die wichtigsten Auskünfte über Hostelling International - den angebotenen Gästeservice, die Vorteile für Mitglieder und die allen Herbergen auferlegte Verpflichtung, vorgegebene Standards zu gewährleisten.

Falls Sie weitere Informationen über Herbergen in aller Welt wünschen, können Sie sich

entweder

● vor Ihrer Abreise an den Jugendherbergsverband Ihres Landes wenden

oder

● unsere Internet Home Page **www.iyhf.org** besuchen.

Eine Einführung zu Hostelling International

Die Jugendherbergsbewegung wurde am Anfang dieses Jahrhunderts in Deutschland gegründet und hat sich während des Krieges insbesondere in Europa schnell verbreitet.

Heute bietet Hostelling International eine Auswahl von nahezu 4.500 Herbergen in 60 Ländern in aller Welt an.

In den Jugendherbergen Europas, Asiens, Afrikas, Nord- und Südamerikas und des pazifischen Raums wollen wir Ihnen einen gleichbleibenden guten Service anbieten - eine erfrischende Nachtruhe in freundlicher Umgebung und preiswert dazu.

Dieser Führer enthält Angaben über die Herbergen, die Ihnen zur Wahl stehen. Heute ist es möglich, eine Übernachtung 6 Monate im voraus zu buchen unter Benutzung des "International Booking Network (IBN) Systems" - Einzelheiten dazu auf den folgenden Seiten.

Würzburg Youth Hostel - Germany

Keine Altersbegrenzung

Jugendherbergen sind trotz ihres Namens in quasi jedem Land für alle Altersgruppen offen. Nur eine kleine Anzahl von Herbergen in Deutschland hat eine obere Altersgrenze aufgrund örtlicher Vorschriften.

Gäste unter 14 Jahren sollten von einem Erwachsenen begleitet sein, und viele Herbergen bieten heute Familienzimmer an. Reisegruppen werden in den meisten Herbergen aufgenommen mit einer Auswahl an Unterbringungsmöglichkeiten: Sie finden Einzel, Doppel- und Mehrbettzimmer in den meisten größeren Herbergen.

Vorteile für Mitglieder

Um Unterkunft in einer Jugendherberge zu bekommen, müssen Sie Mitglied des Jugendherbergsverbandes (YHA) Ihres Landes sein. Zusätzlich zu Ihrer Mitgliedskarte bekommen Sie neben tausenden von Preisvergünstigungen weltweit so manchen speziellen Service und Vorteil. In diesem Führer sind die wichtigsten der international erhältlichen Vergünstigungen aufgeführt. Zusätzliche Rabatte können Sie bei dem Jugendherbergsverband des besuchten Landes in Erfahrung bringen. Oder besuchen Sie die Datenbank zu Preisvergünstigungen auf unserer Web-Seite **www.iyhf.org.**

Falls Ihr Land keinen eigenen Jugendherbergsverband hat, können Sie bei der Ankunft in der von Ihnen ausgewählten Herberge entweder eine "Hostelling International Card" oder einzelne "Welcome Stamps" erwerben.

Zugesicherte Standards

Hostelling International weiß, daß gleichbleibende Qualität und guter Service für den preisbewußten Gast von Bedeutung sind. Um diese Leistungen zu erreichen, haben wir das Konzept der "Zugesicherten Standards" eingeführt, damit Ihnen überall in unseren Herbergen ein annehmbarer Service und entsprechende Ausstattungen angeboten werden.

Was bedeuten diese Zugesicherten Standards für Sie?

Empfang

In unseren Herbergen sind alle Besucher willkommen, unabhängig von Alter, Geschlecht, Kulturkreis, Rasse oder Religion. Wenn Sie der Herbergsbewegung noch nicht angehören, so können Sie in jeder Herberge die volle oder zeitlich begrenzte Mitgliedschaft erwerben.

Sie können Ihre Unterkunft entweder per Telefon, Fax, Post oder e-mail oder durch das IBN-System im voraus buchen. **Normalerweise kann man in allen Herbergen zwischen 07.00 und 10.00 sowie 17.00 und 22.30 Uhr ein- bzw. auschecken.**

Am allerwichtigsten ist jedoch die herzliche Aufnahme durch das Herbergspersonal. Alle Mitarbeiter werden bemüht sein, Ihnen mit Auskünften zu helfen und Sie so zu beraten, daß Ihr Aufenthalt ein voller Erfolg wird.

Aalborg Youth Hostel - Denmark

Komfort

Sie können eine gute und komfortable Nachtruhe erwarten, genügend Duschen, WC's und Waschgelegenheiten sowie ausreichend warmes Wasser.

In einigen Herbergen ist frische Bettwäsche nicht im Übernachtungspreis enthalten, kann jedoch, wenn erwünscht, ausgeliehen werden. In den meisten Herbergen werden Mahlzeiten angeboten. Dort, wo nur Selbstversorgung möglich ist, können Sie normalerweise Ihre Grundnahrungsmittel in der Herberge oder nahebei kaufen. In diesen Herbergen werden Ihnen alle notwendigen Einrichtungen, wie zur Nahrungsmittelaufbewahrung, zur Essensvorbereitung, zum Kochen und Abwaschen, zur Verfügung stehen.

Sauberkeit

Wo immer Sie auch reisen, in unseren Herbergen können Sie höchste Sauberkeits- und Hygienestandards erwarten.

Sicherheit

Unser Personal wird bemüht sein, während Ihres Aufenthaltes Ihre Sicherheit und die Ihres persönlichen Eigentums zu gewährleisten. Es gibt Schließfächer für Ihr Gepäck und Ihre Wertsachen.

Privatsphäre

Die Zugesicherten Standards versprechen Ihnen Privatsphäre in Duschen, Waschräumen und WC's. Die Mehrheit der Herbergen bietet Unterkünfte in Schlafräumen für Gäste desselben Geschlechts. Es gibt aber auch solche, die Gästen, die zusammen reisen, auf deren Anfrage Unterkünfte in einem gemischten Zimmer anbieten. Jedoch werden Schlafräume für Gäste desselben Geschlechts immer zur Verfügung stehen.

Killarney Youth Hostel - Republic of Ireland

Umweltcharta

Zusätzlich zu den Zugesicherten Standards befolgen unsere Herbergen die IYHF-Umweltcharta. Diese schreiben die Kriterien zur Nutzung und zum Sparen von Ressourcen, zur Vermeidung von Abfall und zum Einsatz von Recycling vor, wie man die natürliche Umwelt schützt und wie man durch Erziehung das Umweltbewußtsein fördern kann.

Für viele Besucher hat eine einfache Herberge, wie man sie in abgelegenen Gegenden oder in ungewöhnlichen Gebäuden findet, einen besonderen Reiz. Wir müssen zugeben, daß es schwierig ist, den gleichen Standard in den verschiedensten Herbergen - in der Mitte eines Regenwaldes oder in einer einsam gelegenen Schäferhütte - zu erreichen. Es gibt daher Ausnahmen für kleine Herbergen, die nur eine einfache Ausstattung, wenig Personal und kürzere Öffnungszeiten haben. Diese Herbergen haben wir deutlich als **einfache Herbergen** gekennzeichnet.

Die Standards werden von Hostelling International und von Ihnen, unseren Gästen, überwacht. **Die Antwortkarten im hinteren Teil dieses Führers helfen Ihnen, uns zu informieren.**

Gebührenfreier Devisenverkauf

EIN SONDERANGEBOT FÜR MITGLIEDER VON HOSTELLING INTERNATIONAL

TRAVELEX - die weltweit größte Spezialbank mit Wechselstuben in Flughäfen und Terminals, bietet Hostelling International Mitgliedern einen Sonderservice an, mit dem Sie bei internationalen Reisen Kosten sparen können.

Bei der Vorlage Ihres Herbergsausweises können Sie den Service des gebührenfreien Devisentausches in den 300 weltweit existierenden Travelex-Geschäftsstellen in Anspruch nehmen. Eine Liste dazu finden Sie auf der Travelex-Web-Seite **www.travelexgrp.com.**

Dieser super Service spart Ihnen viel Geld, besonders wenn Sie planen, mehrere Länder zu besuchen.

Exklusives Travelex Rückkauf-Angebot: Für eine Minimalgebühr kauft Travelex unbenutzte Devisen zum Einkaufspreis zurück, ohne Kommission!

Diese Angebote gelten nicht für den Umtausch von Währungen der Nationen, die der Europäischen Währungsunion (EURO-ZONE) angehören (z.B. nicht für den Umtausch von Belgischen Franken in Deutsche Mark oder Italienische Lire).

Travelex

Solothurn Youth Hostel - Switzerland

Das International Booking Network (IBN)

Vorausbuchungen durch IBN

Mit unserem Computer-Buchungssystem IBN können Sie einfach und preiswert Reservierungen in ca. 300 der wichtigsten Herbergen in 47 Ländern weltweit vornehmen.

Überall dort, wo Sie das IBN-Symbol (IBN) im Führer sehen, können Sie eine Unterkunft 6 Monate im voraus buchen (vorausgesetzt es sind Betten frei). Die Herbergen, die in diesem Netzwerk zusammengeschlossen sind, werden innerhalb des jeweiligen Landes aufgeführt und in blau hervorgehoben.

Die IBN-Herbergen bieten damit einen Service an, der für den preisbewußten Übernachtungssektor einmalig ist.

- Sie können in der Währung des jeweiligen Landes, von dem aus Sie die Reservierung vor Ihrer Abreise vornehmen, bezahlen.
- Sie können während Ihrer Reise von jeder IBN-Herberge oder lokalem IBN-Buchungszentrum aus reservieren. **Die Liste zu den Buchungszentren finden Sie auf Seite 43-54.**
- In vielen Fällen können Sie mit Kreditkarten bezahlen.
- In vielen Ländern können Sie eine einzelne Zentrale Buchungsstelle (siehe Übersicht auf Seite 25) anrufen, um im voraus mehrere Übernachtungen für verschiedene Herbergen zu reservieren.

Wastwater Youth Hostel - England

WEITERE BUCHUNGSINFORMATIONEN

Sie können ohne Vorausbestellung einer Unterkunft in jeder Herberge eintreffen: Wir raten jedoch dringend - besonders in den Hauptreisezeiten - zu reservieren, um Enttäuschungen zu vermeiden.

- Dies ist besonders wichtig für Gruppenreisen und für Familienzimmer, die oft schnell vergeben sind.

- Sie können Unterkünfte in den von Ihnen ausgewählten Herbergen per Fax oder Brief buchen.

- Falls Sie schriftlich buchen, legen Sie bitte einen internationalen Postcoupon, den man in den meisten Postämtern erhält, und einen Briefumschlag mit Ihrer Anschrift bei. Falls Sie ohne Anzahlung gebucht haben und keine andere Zeit vereinbart wurde, wird normalerweise erwartet, daß Sie vor 18.00 Uhr in der Herberge eintreffen.

Wir sind überzeugt, daß Ihnen Ihr Herbergsaufenthalt gefallen wird. Auf jeden Fall können Sie sich diesen leisten! Wir freuen uns auf Ihren Besuch.

Gent Youth Hostel - Belgium

RESERVIEREN SIE PER KREDITKARTE BEI DIESEN ZENTREN:	
Australien	☎ (2) 9261 1111
England & Wales	☎ (1629) 581 418
Frankreich	☎ (1) 44 89 87 27
Irland	☎ (1) 830 1766
Kanada	☎ (1) (800) 663 5777
Neuseeland	☎ (9) 303 9524
Nordirland	☎ (1232) 324 733
Schottland	☎ (541) 553 255
Schweiz	☎ (1) 360 14 14
USA	☎ (202) 783 6161

Deutsch

Cómo Utilizar Esta Guía

Venice Youth Hostel - Italy

Bienvenido al mundo de Hostelling International - una red de centros de alojamiento sin igual, en los que usted pasará una buena noche en un ambiente acogedor y a precios asequibles.

Esta guía contiene información sobre las instalaciones y prestaciones de los albergues juveniles afiliados a la

INTERNATIONAL YOUTH HOSTEL FEDERATION (IYHF)

(Federación Internacional de Albergues Juveniles)

Los albergues se encuentran listados alfabéticamente por país y por ciudad.

En esta introducción encontrará información general sobre Hostelling International: los servicios que ofrecemos a nuestros huéspedes, las ventajas de que disfrutan nuestros socios y nuestro compromiso de garantizar unas normas mínimas que todos los albergues deben esforzarse en cumplir.

Si desea obtener información suplementaria sobre cualquier albergue del mundo, usted puede:

Contactar con la Asociación de Albergues Juveniles de su país antes de salir de viaje

o bien:

Consultar nuestra página Internet en la dirección siguiente: **www.iyhf.org**

Hostelling International - Introducción

El alberguismo juvenil fue fundado en Alemania a principios de siglo y se extendió con rapidez, dentro de Europa especialmente, durante el periodo de entreguerras.

Actualmente, Hostelling International le propone una gama de casi 4,500 centros de alojamiento repartidos por más de 60 países del mundo.

En los albergues juveniles de Europa, Asia, Africa, las Américas y el Pacífico, esperamos ofrecerle un servicio uniforme de primera calidad - una buena noche en un ambiente acogedor y a precios asequibles.

Esta guía contiene información detallada sobre los albergues a su disposición. Ahora es posible reservar una cama con hasta 6 meses de antelación a través de la red internacional de reservas IBN (International Booking Network), de la que encontrará una descripción más adelante.

Para Jóvenes de todas las Edades

A pesar de su nombre, los albergues juveniles están abiertos a personas de todas las edades en prácticamente todos los países. Sólo en un pequeño número de albergues alemanes existe un límite máximo de edad impuesto por la legislación regional.

Los menores de 14 años deberán ir acompañados de un adulto y muchos albergues hoy día ofrecen habitaciones familiares. La mayoría aceptan grupos y disponen de varios tipos de habitación - usted encontrará habitaciones individuales, dobles y grandes dormitorios en casi todos los principales albergues.

Afiliación - Sus Privilegios

Para alojarse en un albergue juvenil, es necesario hacerse socio de la Asociación de Albergues Juveniles del país donde uno viva. Además de ser socio, usted disfrutará de ciertos servicios y ventajas especiales que incluyen miles de descuentos a nivel internacional. En esta guía se detallan algunos de ellos y, contactando con la Asociación del país que piensa visitar, averiguará de qué otros descuentos puede beneficiarse en dicho país. O bien, consulte la base de datos de descuentos de nuestra página Internet en **www.iyhf.org.**

Si no existe una Asociación de Albergues Juveniles en su país, usted tendrá la oportunidad de adquirir una tarjeta Hostelling International o un "sello de bienvenida" a su llegada al albergue elegido.

Bilbao Youth Hostel - Spain

Normas Garantizadas

Hostelling International es consciente de la importancia que tiene un nivel de calidad y servicio constante para los viajeros con presupuesto limitado. Por este motivo, hemos instituido nuestro Plan de Normas Garantizadas, para que usted pueda contar con instalaciones y prestaciones de un grado uniforme cuando se aloje en cualquiera de nuestros albergues.

¿Qué representan para usted las Normas Garantizadas de los albergues?

Recibimiento

Los albergues están abiertos a todos, sin distinción de edad, sexo, cultura, raza ni religión. Si usted no es aún socio, podrá hacerse socio de pleno derecho o afiliarse a corto plazo en el albergue mismo.

Puede reservar una cama por teléfono, correo, fax, correo electrónico o a través del sistema IBN.

Generalmente, el horario de la recepción es de 7 h. a 10 h. y de 17 h. a 22.30 h. como mínimo en casi todos los albergues.

Ante todo, la prioridad del personal será acogerle y hacer todo lo posible por asistirle y darle la información que necesite para disfrutar de su estancia al máximo.

Comodidad

Usted puede estar seguro de que pasará una buena y confortable noche, y de que dispondrá de un número adecuado de duchas, servicios y lavabos, así como de suficiente agua caliente.

En los casos en que no esté incluida en el precio de la pernoctación, será posible alquilar ropa blanca recién lavada si la necesita.

Aunque los albergues suelen servir comidas, en los que sólo sea posible cocinar uno mismo se podrán generalmente comprar alimentos básicos en el albergue mismo o cerca de él. Estos albergues dispondrán de un lugar donde guardar los alimentos, encimeras para la preparación de comidas, una cocina para guisar y una pila para lavar la vajilla.

Limpieza

Adondequiera que viaje, Hostelling International le garantiza las más rigurosas normas de limpieza e higiene.

Seguridad

El personal del albergue hará todo lo posible por proteger tanto a usted como sus efectos personales durante su estancia y el establecimiento dispondrá de armarios con cerrojo para su equipaje y objetos de valor.

Intimidad

Nuestro Plan de Normas Garantizadas le asegura su intimidad en los cuartos de baño, duchas y aseos. En la gran mayoría de los albergues, el alojamiento consiste en dormitorios separados para hombres y mujeres, aunque es posible que algunos de ellos dispongan de habitaciones mixtas para quienes viajen juntos y soliciten este servicio. No obstante, siempre existirá la posibilidad de alojarse en dormitorios para hombres o mujeres solamente.

Zermatt Youth Hostel - Switzerland

Nuestro Compromiso Ecológico

Normas Medioambientales

Además de estas Normas Garantizadas, los albergues se comprometen a cumplir con las Normas Medioambientales de la IYHF. Estas establecen los criterios relativos al consumo y conservación de recursos, a la eliminación de residuos y su reciclaje, a la protección de la naturaleza y a la provisión de educación medioambiental.

Los albergues sencillos atraen a muchas personas por encontrarse en lugares aislados y poco corrientes y, a menudo, en edificios muy especiales. No obstante, tenemos que admitir que es difícil mantener las mismas normas en todas partes - por ejemplo, en medio de là selva tropical o en una remota cabaña de pastor. Debido a estas diferencias, aplicamos algunas de nuestras normas de forma menos rigurosa en ciertos albergues pequeños y en aquellos que sólo poseen instalaciones básicas, en los que usted podrá encontrarse con un número de empleados y un horario de apertura limitado. Este tipo de albergue se halla indicado claramente con la denominación **"simple hostel"** *(albergue sencillo)*.

Las normas son objeto de un seguimiento por parte de Hostelling International y también por parte de usted, el usuario. **Con este fin y para ayudarle a contactar con nosotros, al final de esta guía encontrará impresos en los que puede enviarnos sus comentarios.**

La Red Internacional de Reservas - IBN

Reserve con antelación a través de IBN.

Nuestro sistema informatizado de reservas constituye una forma sencilla y barata de reservar antes de salir de viaje en más de 300 albergues clave repartidos por 47 países.

Dondequiera que usted vea el símbolo **IBN** en esta guía, podrá reservar una cama hasta 6 meses antes de su estancia (siempre y cuando haya plazas disponibles). Bajo cada país encontrará los albergues conectados a la red IBN impresos en color azul.

Los albergues IBN ofrecen un servicio sin igual en el sector del alojamiento económico, a saber:

- IBN le permite abonar sus reservas en la moneda del país en el que efectúe las mismas, antes de su viaje.
- Usted podrá hacer reservas durante el transcurso de su viaje desde cualquier albergue IBN o el Centro de Reservas IBN más cercano **(véase la lista de centros en las páginas 43-54).**
- Generalmente, será posible pagar con tarjeta de crédito.
- En muchos países existe la posibilidad de llamar a una sola Oficina Central de Reservas (véase la lista de oficinas en la página 31) para reservar varias pernoctaciones en diferentes albergues.

Eilat Youth Hostel - Israel

RESERVAS - INFORMACIÓN SUPLEMENTARIA

Es posible llegar a un albergue sin reserva previa, pero, en temporada alta, le instamos a que reserve con antelación para no llevarse desilusiones.

- Las habitaciones familiares en particular se ocupan con rapidez y los grupos también deben reservar con tiempo.
- Usted puede realizar sus reservas enviando un fax o una carta al albergue deseado.
- Si reserva por correo, no se olvide de adjuntar un cupón internacional de respuesta pagada (en venta en la mayoría de las oficinas de correos) y un sobre con su nombre y dirección. Si realiza una reserva sin abonar un depósito, normalmente deberá llegar al albergue antes de las 18 h., a menos que haya concertado previamente otra hora de llegada.

Estamos seguros de que disfrutará de su estancia en nuestros albergues y de que no le saldrá cara la experiencia. Esperamos tener el agrado de su visita.

RESERVE CON TARJETA DE CRÉDITO EN LOS SIGUIENTES CENTROS:	
Australia	☎ (2) 9261 1111
Canadá	☎ (1) (800) 663 5777
Escocia	☎ (541) 553 255
Estados Unidos	☎ (202) 783 6161
Francia	☎ (1) 44 89 87 27
Inglaterra y Gales	☎ (1629) 581 418
Irlanda del Norte	☎ (1232) 324 733
Nueva Zelanda	☎ (9) 303 9524
República de Irlanda	☎ (1) 830 1766
Suiza	☎ (1) 360 14 14

Cambio de Divisas Gratuito

UNA OFERTA ESPECIAL PARA LOS SOCIOS DE HOSTELLING INTERNATIONAL

TRAVELEX, la compañía de cambio de divisas con el mayor número de oficinas en aeropuertos y terminales de pasajeros del mundo, ofrece a los socios de Hostelling International un servicio muy especial destinado a reducir el coste de sus viajes internacionales.

Presentando su carnet de socio, usted podrá cambiar divisas sin pagar comisión en cualquiera de las 300 sucursales internacionales de Travelex listadas en su página Internet en **www.travelexgrp.com.**

Gracias a esta fabulosa oferta, logrará importantes ahorros, sobre todo si tiene previsto viajar a más de un país.

"Buy Back Plus" - una oferta exclusiva de Travelex: *Por una pequeña cantidad, Travelex vuelve a comprar las divisas extranjeras no utilizadas al mismo tipo de cambio aplicado en el momento de la compra, y ¡sin comisión!*

Estas ofertas no son válidas para el cambio de divisas entre las monedas nacionales de los países pertenecientes a la Unión Económica y Monetaria Europea (p.ej. dichas ofertas no se aplican al cambio de francos belgas en marcos alemanes o en liras italianas).

Travelex

Zaragoza Youth Hostel - Spain

Money From Home In Minutes.

If you're stuck for cash on your travels, don't panic. Millions of people trust Western Union to transfer money in minutes to 165 countries and over 50,000 locations worldwide. Our record of safety and reliability is second to none. For more information, call Western Union: USA 1-800-325-6000, Canada 1-800-235-0000. Wherever you are, you're never far from home.

www.westernunion.com

WESTERN UNION | MONEY TRANSFER

The fastest way to send money worldwide.

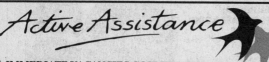

AFRICA, AMERICAS, ASIA, PACIFIC

Youth Hostels outside of Europe are listed in the Hostelling International Guide - Africa, Americas, Asia and the Pacific. The addresses of the full member Associations are given below:

Les Auberges de jeunesse en dehors de l'Europe figurent dans le Hostelling International Guide - Afrique, Amériques, Asie et le Pacifique. Les adresses des Associations membres à part entière sont données ci-dessous:

Die Jugendherbergen ausserhalb von Europa werden im Hostelling International Guide - Afrika, Amerika, Asien und de Pazifik, aufgeführt. Die Adressen der vollberechtigten Mitgliedsverbände sind unten angegeben:

Los Albergues Juveniles fuera de Europa se incluyen en la Hostelling International Guide - Africa, Américas, Asia y el Pacífico. A continuación se encuentran las direcciones de las Asociaciones miembros de pleno derecho:

ALGERIA:

Fédération Algérienne des Auberges de Jeunesse, 213 Rue Hassiba Ben Bouali, BP 15 El-Annasser, 16015 Alger.
t (2) 683049 **f** (2) 683049

AUSTRALIA:

Australian Youth Hostels Association, Inc, Level 3, 10 Mallett St, Camperdown, 2050 New South Wales.
t (2) 9565 1699 **f** (2) 9565 1325
e yha@yha.au
www.yha.com.au

BAHRAIN:

Bahrain Youth Hostels Society, PO Box 2455, H No. 1105 R No. 4225 Block 342, Manama.
t (973) 727170 **f** (973) 729919

BRAZIL:

Federação Brasileira dos Albergues de Juventude, Rua General Dionisio 63, Botafogo, CEP: 22271-050, Rio de Janeiro.
t (21) 2860303 **f** (21) 2865652
e info@hostel.org.br
www.hostel.org.br

CANADA:

Hostelling International - Canada, 205 Catherine St, Suite 400, Ottawa, Ontario K2P 1C3.
t (613) 237-7884 **f** (613) 237-7868
e info@hostellingintl.ca
www.hostellingintl.ca

CHILE:

Asociación Chilena de Albergues Turísticos Juveniles, Hernando de Aguirre 201 Of 602, Santiago.
t (2) 2333220 **f** (2) 2332555
e achatj@hostelling.co.cl
www.hostelling.co.cl

CHINA (People's Republic of):

Guangdong Youth Hostels Association of China, 185 Huanshi Xi Road, Guangzhou
t (86) (20) 86677422
f (86) (20) 86665039
e youthhostel_gd@21cn.com

Hong Kong Youth Hostels Association,
Room 225, Block 19, Shek Kip Mei Estate,
Sham Shui Po, Kowloon, Hong Kong.
🆃 27881638 🅵 27883105
🅴 hkyha@datainternet.com
www.yha.org.hk

COSTA RICA:

Red Costarricense de Albergues Juveniles, PO
Box 1355-1002 P E, Ave Central, Calles 29 y 31,
San José.
🆃 2348186 🅵 2244085
🅴 recajhi@sol.racsa.co.cr
www.hostels.com/cr.html

ECUADOR:

Asociación Ecuatoriana de Albergues, Pinto
325 y Reina Victoria, Quito.
🆃 (2) 550911 🅵 (2) 508221
🅴 ecuatori@pi.pro.ec

EGYPT:

Egyptian Youth Hostels Association, 1
El-Ibrahimy St, Garden City, Cairo.
🆃 (2) 3561448, 3540527 🅵 (2) 3550329
🅴 eyhahi@idsci.gov.eg

INDIA:

Youth Hostels Association of India, 5 Nyaya
Marg, Chanakyapuri, New Delhi 110 021.
🆃 (11) 6871969, 6110250 🅵 (11) 6113469
🅴 yhostel@del2.vsnl.net.in

JAPAN:

Japan Youth Hostels Inc, Suidobashi Nishiguchi
Kaikan, 2-20-7 Misaki-cho, Chiyoda-ku, Tokyo
101-0061.
🆃 (3) 3288-1417,1424 🅵 (3) 3288 1248
🅴 jyh@znet.or.jp
www.znet.or.jp/~jyh

KENYA:

Kenya Youth Hostels Association, PO Box
48661, Ralph Bunche Road, Nairobi.
🆃 (2) 721765 🅵 (2) 724862
🅴 kyha@africaonline.co.ke

S. KOREA:

Korea Youth Hostels Association, Rm 408,
Juksun Hyundai Bldg 80, Juksun-Dong,
Jongro-Ku, Seoul 110-052.
🆃 (2) 7253031 🅵 (2) 7253113
🅴 inform@kyha.or.kr
www.kyha.or.kr

LIBYA:

Libyan Youth Hostel Association, 69 Amr Ben
Al-Aas Street, PO Box 10322, Tripoli,
Al-Jamahiriya.
🆃 (21) 4445171 🅵 (21) 3330118

MALAYSIA:

Malaysian Youth Hostels Association, KL
International Youth Hostel, 21 Jalan Kg. Attap,
50460 Kuala Lumpur.
🆃 (3) 22736870/71 🅵 (3) 22741115
🅴 myha@pd.jaring.my

MOROCCO:

*Fédération Royale Marocaine des Auberges de
Jeunes*, BP 15998, Parc de la Ligue Arabe, Casa
Principale, Casablanca 21000.
🆃 (2) 470952 🅵 (2) 227677

NEW ZEALAND:

*Youth Hostels Association of New Zealand
Inc*, PO Box 436, 193 Cashel St, 3rd Floor,
Union House, Christchurch.
🆃 (3) 3799970 🅵 (3) 3654476
🅴 info@yha.org.nz
www.yha.org.nz

PAKISTAN:

Pakistan Youth Hostels Association, Shaheed-e-Millat Rd, Aabpara, Sector G-6/4, Islamabad.

📞 (51) 826899 📠 (51) 9206417

PERU:

Asociación Peruana de Albergues Turisticos Juveniles, Avda Casimiro Ulloa 328, San Antonio, Miraflores, Lima 18.

📞 (1) 2423068 📠 (1) 4448187

📧 hostell@mail.cosapidata.com.pe

PHILIPPINES:

Youth & Student Hostel Foundation of the Philippines, 4227-9 Tomas Claudio St, Baclaran, Parañaque 1700, Metro Manila.

📞 (2) 8320680, 8322112 📠 (2) 8322263

QATAR:

Qatar Youth Hostels Association, PO Box 9660, Doha.

📞 867180, 866402 📠 863968

SAUDI ARABIA:

Saudi Arabian Youth Hostels Association, Alshehab Alghassni St, Alnmouzajiyah District, North Almurabb'h, PO Box 2359, Riyadh 11451.

📞 (1) 4055552, 4051478 📠 (1) 4021079

SOUTH AFRICA:

Hostels Association of South Africa, 3rd Floor St Georges House, 73 St Georges Mall, Cape Town 8001.

📞 (21) 4242511 📠 (21) 4244119

📧 info@hisa.org.za

www.hisa.org.za

SUDAN:

Sudanese Youth Hostels Association, PO Box 1705, House 66, Street No 47 Khartoum East, Khartoum.

📞 (11) 722087 📠 (11) 780308

THAILAND:

Thai Youth Hostels Association, 25/14 Phitsanulok Road, Thay-Wej Market, Dusit, Bangkok 10300.

📞 (2) 628-7413 📠 (2) 628-7416

📧 bangkok@yha.org

www.tyha.org

TUNISIA:

Association Tunisienne des Auberges de Jeunesse, 10 Rue Ali Bach Hamba, BP 320, 1015 Tunis RP.

📞 (1) 353277 📠 (1) 352172

📧 ataj@planet.tn

www.cybertunisia.com/ataj

UNITED ARAB EMIRATES:

United Arab Emirates Youth Hostel Association, Al Qusaiss Road, Near Al Ahli Club, PO Box 19536, Dubai.

📞 (4) 2988151 📠 (4) 2988141

USA:

American Youth Hostels, Inc, 733 15th Street N.W, Suite 840, Washington DC 20005.

📞 (202) 7836161 📠 (202) 7836171

📧 hiayhserv@hiayh.org

www.hiayh.org

URUGUAY:

Asociación de Alberguistas del Uruguay, Pablo de María 1583/008, PC 11200, PO Box 10680, Montevideo.

📞 (2) 4004245, 4000581 📠 (2) 4001326

📧 aau@adinet.com.uy

www.internet.com.uy/aau

INTERNATIONAL TELEPHONE CODES AND EMERGENCY CONTACT NUMBERS
INDICATIFS TÉLÉPHONIQUES INTERNATIONAUX ET NUMÉROS D'URGENCE

Country	GMT	Int Code	Country Code	Medical	Police	Fire
Algeria	+1	00	+213			
Argentina	-4	00	+5411	107	101	100
Australia	+8/+10	0011	+61	000	000	000
Austria	+1	00	+43	144	133	122
Bahrain	+3	0	+973	999	999	999
Bangladesh	+6	00	+880			
Belgium	+1	00	+32	100	101	100
Brazil	-2/-5	00	+55	192	190	193
Canada	-3/-11	00	+1	911	911	911
Chile	-6	00	+56	131	133	132
China - Guangdong	+8	00	+86	120	110	119
China - Hong Kong	+8	00	+852	999	999	999
Colombia	-5	009	+57	132	112	119
Costa Rica	-6	00	+506	911	117	118
Croatia	+1	00	+385	94	92	93
Cyprus	+2	00	+357	199/112	199/122	199/122
Czech Republic	+1	00	+420	155	158	150
Denmark	+1	00	+45	112	112	112
Ecuador	-5	00	+593	131	101	102
Egypt	+2	00	+20	123	122	125
Estonia	+2	800	+372	003	002	001
Faeroe Islands	GMT	00	+298	000	000	000
Finland	+2	999	+358	112	10022	112
France	+1	00	+33	15	17	18
Germany	+1	00	+49	112	110	112
Greece	+2	00	+30	166	100	199
Guatemala	-6	00	+502	125/128	120/110	123/122
Hungary	+1	00	+36	104	107	105
Iceland	GMT	00	+354	112	112	112
India	+5.5	00	+91	102	100	101
Indonesia	+7/+9	001	+62	118	110	113
Ireland - Republic	GMT	00	+353	999	999	999
Israel	+2	00	+972	101	100	102
Italy	+1	00	+39	118	112	115
Japan	+9	001	+81	119	110	119
Kenya	+3	0196	+254	999	999	999
Libya	+2	00	+218	191	193	190
Lithuania	+1	8-10	+370	03	02	01
Luxembourg	+1	00	+352	112	113	112

Country	GMT	Int Code	Country Code	Medical	Police	Fire
Macedonia	+1	99	+389	94	92	93
Malaysia	+8	00	+60	999	999	994
Malta	+1	00	+356	196	191	199
Mexico	-6/8	00	+52	080	080	080
Morocco	GMT	00	+212	19	19	19
Nepal	+5.45	00	+977	102	100	101
Netherlands	+1	00	+31	112	112	112
New Caledonia	+10	00	+687	15	17	18
New Zealand	+12	00	+64	111	111	111
Nicaragua	+6	001	+505	128	118	115
Norway	+1	00	+47	113	112	110
Pakistan	+5	00	+92	15	16	16
Peru	-5	00	+51	105	105	116
Philippines	+8	00	+63			
Poland	+1	0	+48	999	997	998
Portugal	+1	00	+351	112	112	112
Qatar	+3	00	+974	999	999	999
Russia	+2/+12	00	+7	02	01	03
Saudi Arabia	+3	00	+966	977	999	998
Singapore	+8	001	+65	995	999	995
Slovakia	+1	00	+42	155	158	150
Slovenia	+1	00	+386	112	113	112
South Africa	+2	01	+27	10177	10111	10111
South Korea	+9	001/002	+82	119	112	119
Spain	+1	00	+34	061	091	080
Sudan	+2	00	+249			
Sweden	+1	009	+46	112	112	112
Switzerland	+1	00	+41	144	117	118
Taiwan	+8	00	+886			
Thailand	+7	001	+66	1155	191	199
Tunisia	+1	00	+216	190	197	198
Turkey	+2	00	+90	112	155	110
UAE	+4	00	+971	999	292222	669999
United Kingdom	GMT	00	+44	999	999	999
Uruguay	-3	00	+598	105	109	104
USA	-6/9	011	+1	911	911	911
Venezuela	-4	00	+58	171	171	171
Yugoslavia	+1	00	+381			

Net Savings @ Hostelling International

The advantages are clear

X-RAY VISION

HOSTELLING INTERNATIONAL®

netsavings@hostellinginternational.org.uk

INTERNATIONAL BOOKING NETWORK [IBN] BOOKING CENTRES

The International Booking Network (IBN) enables you to book a bed up to 6 months in advance of your stay (depending on availability) at nearly 300 key hostels around the world. The locations listed below all offer outward bookings by IBN. The hostels in the network are listed within each of the country sections and highlighted in blue. They are also indicated with the symbol [IBN].

CENTRES DE RESERVATION [IBN] (INTERNATIONAL BOOKING NETWORK)

Le réseau international de réservation (International Booking Network - IBN) vous permet de réserver un lit jusqu'à six mois à l'avance (selon les disponibilités), dans près de 300 auberges à travers le monde. Les sites listés ci-dessous vous offrent tous la possibilité d'effectuer des réservations par le biais d'IBN. Les auberges appartenant au réseau IBN sont indiquées en bleu dans le listing des auberges de chaque pays et également par le symbole [IBN].

INTERNATIONAL BOOKING NETWORK [IBN] BUCHUNGSZENTREN

International Booking Network (IBN) ermöglicht Ihnen das Buchen einer Unterkunft bis zu 6 Monaten im voraus (in Abhängigkeit von der Verfügbarkeit) in ca. 300 der wichtigsten Herbergen rund um den Globus. Die unten aufgelisteten Herbergen bieten alle Buchungen durch IBN. Die im Netzwerk zusammengeschlossenen Herbergen sind innerhalb jeder Ländersektion aufgeführt und blau hervorgehoben. Sie sind auch mit dem Symbol [IBN] gekennzeichnet.

INTERNATIONAL BOOKING NETWORK [IBN] CENTROS DE RESERVAS

La Red Internacional de Reservas IBN le permite reservar una cama hasta 6 meses antes de su estancia (siempre y cuando haya camas disponibles) en casi 300 albergues claves del mundo. Los centros relacionados a continuación ofrecen todos ellos la posibilidad de realizar reservas a través de IBN. Los albergues que pertenecen a la red IBN aparecen impresos en color azul en las listas de albergues de cada país y llevan, además, el símbolo [IBN].

(IBN)

ARGENTINA

Red Argentina de Alojamiento para Jóvenes
Buenos Aires – National Office
Florida 835, 3rd Floor Of.319,
1005 Buenos Aires
☏ (54) (11) 4511-8712
✆ (54) (11) 4312-0089
✉ raaj@hostels.org.ar

AUSTRALIA

Australian Youth Hostels Association
Adelaide – YHA South Australia
38 Sturt Street, Adelaide, South Australia 5000
☏ (61) (8) 82315583
✆ (61) (8) 82314219
✉ yhasa@ozemail.com.au

Brisbane – YHA Queensland
154 Roma Street, Brisbane, Queensland 4000
☏ (61) (7) 3236-1680
✆ (61) (7) 3236-0647
✉ travel@yhaqld.org

Cairns – YHA Queensland
20-24 McLeod Street, Cairns, Queensland 4870
☏ (61) (7) 4051-0772
✆ (61) (7) 4031-3158
✉ cnsyha@yhaqld.org

Canberra – YHA New South Wales
191 Dryandra Street, O'Connor,
Canberra, ACT 2602
☏ (61) (2) 6248-9155
✆ (61) (2) 6249-1731
✉ canberra@yhansw.org.au

Darwin - YHA Northern Territory
69 Mitchell Street, Darwin, NT 0801
☏ (61) (8) 8981-6344
✆ (61) (8) 8981-6674
✉ yhant@yhant.org.au

Melbourne – YHA Victoria
83-85 Hardware Lane, Melbourne, Victoria 3000
☏ (61) (3) 9670-7991
✆ (61) (3) 9640-0540
✉ membership@yhavic.org.au

Perth – YHA Western Australia
236 William Street, Northbridge, Perth,
Western Australia 6003
☏ (61) (8) 9227-5122
✆ (61) (8) 9227-5123
✉ inquiries@yhawa.com.au

Sydney – YHA New South Wales
GPO Box 5276, 422 Kent St, Sydney,
New South Wales 2001
☏ (61) (2) 9261-1111
✆ (61) (2) 9261-1969
✉ yha@yhansw.org.au

Sydney - travel.com.au
80 Clarence Street, Sydney 2000
☏ (61) (2) 9249-5400
✆ (61) (2) 9279-2221

AUSTRIA

Österreichischer Jugendherbergsverband
Graz – ÖJHV YGH
Idlhofgasse 74, A-8020 Graz
☏ (43) (316) 9083
✆ (43) (316) 9083-88
✉ jgh-graz@jgh.at

Graz –Logo Youth Information Service
Karmeliterplatz1, A-8010 Graz
☏ (43) (316) 1799
✆ (43) (316) 877 4900
✉ info@logo.at

Klagenfurt – ÖJHV Regional Office
Neckheimgasse 6, 9020 Klagenfurt
☏ (43) (463) 230019
✆ (43) (463) 230022

Vienna – ÖJHV National Office
1010 Wien, Schottenring 28
☏ (43) (1) 5321660
🖷 (43) (1) 5350861
✉ oejvh-wien-travel-service@oejhv.or.at

Österreichisches Jugendherbergswerk
Vienna – ÖJHW National Office
1010 Wien, Helferstorferstrasse 4
☏ (43) (1) 5331833
🖷 (43) (1) 533183385
✉ oejhw@oejhw.or.at

BELGIUM

Belgium - Les Auberges de Jeunesse
Brussels – Les AJ National Office
Rue de la Sablonnière 28, B-1000 Bruxelles
☏ (32) (2) 219 5676
🖷 (32) (2) 219 1451
✉ info@laj.be

Belgium - Vlaamse Jeugdherbergcentrale
Antwerp – VJH National Office
Van Stralenstraat 40, B-2060 Antwerpen
☏ (32) (3) 232-7218
🖷 (32) (3) 231-8126
✉ vjh@vjh.be

BRAZIL

Federaçao Brasiliera dos Albergues da Juventude
Curitiba – Regional Office
Rua Padre Agostinho 645, Mercês, Curitiba,
Paraná CEP - 80430-050
☏ (55) (41) 233-2746
🖷 (55) (41) 233-2834
✉ ajcwb@uol.com.br

Porto Alegre – Regional Office
Rua Dos Andradas, 1137 S. 1318,
Centro - Porto Alegre, RS CEP: 90020-008
☏ (55) (51) 226-5380
🖷 (55) (51) 226-5380
✉ turjovem@zaz.com.br

Rio de Janeiro – Regional Office
Rua da Assembleia No 10, Sala 1616,
Centro-CEP:20011-000, Rio de Janeiro
☏ (55) (21) 5312234
🖷 (55) (21) 5311943
✉ albergue@microlink.com.br

São Paulo – Regional Office
Rua Sete de Abril, 386 Cj. 22, CEP 01044-908,
Sao Paulo - SP
☏ (55) (11) 2580388
🖷 (55) (11) 2580388
✉ info@alberguesp.com.br

CANADA

Canadian Hostelling Association
Edmonton – Travel Shop
10926 - 88 Avenue, Edmonton, Alberta T6G 0Z1
☏ (1) (780) 439-3089
🖷 (1) (780) 433-7781
✉ travelshop@hostellingintl.ca

Montréal – Tourism Jeunesse
4545 Pierre de Coubertin, C P 1000,
Succursale M, Montréal, Quebec H1V 3R2
☏ (1) (514) 252-3117
🖷 (1) (514) 252-3119

Ottawa – National Office
400-205 Catherine Street, Ottawa, Ontario,
K2P 1C3
☏ (1) (613) 237-7884
🖷 (1) (613) 237-7868
✉ info@hostellingintl.ca

Vancouver – Regional Office
134 Abbott Street, Suite 402, Vancouver,
British Colombia, V6B 2K4
☏ (1) (604) 684-7101
🖷 (1) (604) 684-7181

IBN

CHILE

Asociación Chilena de Albergues Turísticos Juveniles
Santiago – National Office
Hernando de Aguirre 201,OF 602, Providencia
☏ (56) (2) 2333220
🖷 (56) (2) 2332555
✉ achatj@hostelling.co.cl

CHINA

Guangdong Youth Hostels Association of China
Guangzhou – National Office
185 Huanshi xi Road, Guangzhou,
Guangdong Province
☏ (86) (20) 86677422
🖷 (86) (20) 86665039
✉ youthhostel_gd@21cn.com

Hong Kong Youth Hostels Association
Hong Kong – National Office
Room 225, Block 19, Shek Kip Mei Estate,
Shamshuipo, Kowloon, Hong Kong
☏ (852) 27881638
🖷 (852) 27883105
✉ hkyha@datainternet.com

CROATIA

Croatian Youth Hostel Association
Zagreb – National Office
Dezmanova 9, 10000 Zagreb
☏ (385) (1) 484-7474
🖷 (385) (1) 484-7472
✉ hfhs-cms@zg.tel.hr

CZECH REPUBLIC

KMC Club of Young Travellers
Prague – National Office
KMC - Travel Service Booking Centre, Praha 1,
Karolíny Světlé 30, 110 00 Prague
☏ (420) (2) 22221328
🖷 (420) (2) 8550013
✉ kmc@kmc.cz

DENMARK

Danhostel
Copenhagen – National Office
Hostelling International Denmark,
Vesterbrogade 39, DK1620, Copenhagen V
☏ (45) 33313612
🖷 (45) 33313626
✉ ldv@danhostel.dk

ECUADOR

Idiomas s.a.
Guayaquil –
Junin 203 y Panama, Floor 2, Office 4, Guayaquil
☏ (593) (4) 56-4488
🖷 (593) (4) 56-6939
✉ idiomasl@idiomas.com.ec

ENGLAND & WALES

Youth Hostels Association (England & Wales)
Credit/Debit Card Reservations only –
PO Box 67, Matlock, Derbyshire DE4 3YX
☏ (44) (1629) 581418
🖷 (44) (1629) 581062

1st Western Air Travel
Totnes –
1st Western Air Travel, Bickham, Totnes, Devon,
TQ9 7NJ
☏ (44) (1548) 821665
🖷 (44) (1548) 821614
✉ info@westernair.co.uk

ESTONIA

Estonian Youth Hostels Association
Tallin – National Office
Tatari 39-310, 10134 Tallinn
☏ (372) 6461455
🖷 (372) 6461595
✉ eyha@online.ee

FINLAND

Suomen Retkeilymajajärjestö-SRM
Helsinki – National Office
Yrjönkatu 38 B 15, 00100 Helsinki
☏ (358) (9) 694-0377
📠 (358) (9) 693-1349
✉ info@srm.inet.fi

FRANCE

Fédération Unie des Auberges de Jeunesse
Paris – National Office
27 rue Pajol, 75018 Paris
☏ (33) 44898727
📠 (33) 44898710
✉ fuaj@fuaj.org

Paris – FUAJ Beaubourg
9 Rue Brantome, 75003 Paris
☏ (33) 4804 7040
📠 (33) 4277 0329

GERMANY

Deutsches Jugendherbergswerk
Berlin – Brandenburg Regional Office
Tempelhofer Ufer 32, D-10963 Berlin
☏ (49) (30) 2649520
📠 (49) (30) 2620437
✉ djh-berlin-brandenburg@jugendherberge.de

Detmold – National Office
Deutsches Jugendherbergswerk, Service GmbH,
32754 Detmold
☏ (49) (5231) 7401-0
📠 (49) (5231) 740149
✉ service@djh.de

Dresden - Sachsen Regional Office
Maternistrasse 22, 01067 Dresden
☏ (351) 4942211
📠 (351) 4942213
✉ servicecenter@djh-sachsen.de

Düsseldorf – Rheinland Regional Office
Postfach 110301, 40503 Düsseldorf
☏ (49) (211) 57703-20/-49
📠 (49) (211) 5770350
✉ service-center@djh-rheinland.de

Hamburg – Nordmark Regional Office
Rennbahnstrasse 100, 22111 Hamburg
☏ (49) (40) 655995-0
📠 (49) (40) 655995-52
✉ service@djh-nordmark.de

Munich – YH München Booking Center
Wendl-Dietrich-Strasse 20, 80634 München
☏ (49) (89) 131156
📠 (49) (89) 1678745
✉ jhmuenchen@djh-bayern.de

HUNGARY

Magyarorszagi Ifjusagi Szallasok
Budapest – Express Travel
Express Office No. 204, 1052 Budapest V.,
Semmelweis u. 4.
☏ (36) (1) 317-8600
📠 (36) (1) 317-6823

IRELAND - NORTHERN

Hostelling International - Northern Ireland
Belfast – National Office
22 Donegall Road, Belfast, BT12 5JN
☏ (44) (28) 90315435
📠 (44) (28) 90439699
✉ info@hini.org.uk

IRELAND - REPUBLIC

An Oige
Dublin – Booking Centre
61 Mountjoy Street, Dublin 7
☏ (353) (1) 8301766
📠 (353) (1) 8301600
✉ anoige@iol.ie

IBN

ISRAEL

Israel Youth Hostels Association
Jerusalem – National Office
Jerusalem 1 Shazar St,
International Convention Center, PO Box 6001,
Jerusalem 91060
📞 (972) (2) 655-8400
📠 (972) (2) 655-8432
📧 iyhytb@netvision.net.il

ITALY

Assoc Italiana Alberghi per la Gioventu
Bologne – Regional Office
Via dell' Unione n.6/a, 40126 Bologna
📞 (39) (051) 224913
📠 (39) (051) 224913

Catania – Local Office
Via Andrea Costa 34/B, 95129 Catania
📞 (39) (095) 539853
📠 (39) (095) 539853

Florence – Regional Office
Viale Augusto Righi 2/4, Florence
📞 (39) (055) 600315
📠 (39) (055) 610300

Genoa – Regional Office
Salita Salvatore Viale n 1, Genova
📞 (39) (010) 586407
📠 (39) (010) 586407

Naples – Regional Office
Salita della Grotta a Piedigrotta 23, 80122 Naples
📞 (39) (081) 7612346
📠 (39) (081) 761 2391

Palermo – Regional Office
Via Houel 5, 90138 Palermo, Sicily
📞 (39) (091) 336595
📠 (39) (091) 336595

Rome – National Office
Via Cavour 44, 00184 Rome
📞 (39) (06) 4871152
📠 (39) (06) 4880492
📧 aig@uni.net

Venice – Regional Office
Calle Castelforte S. Rocco, 3101 San Polo,
Venezia
📞 (39) (041) 5204414
📠 (39) (041) 5204034

JAPAN

Japan Youth Hostels Inc
Kyoto – Kyoto Youth Hostel Association
29 Uzumasa-Nakayamacho, Ukyo-ku,
Kyoto 616-8191
📞 (81) (75) 462-9185
📠 (81) (75) 462-2289
📧 utano-yh@mbox.kyoto-inet.or.jp

Nagoya-Aichi – Aichi Youth Hostel Association
Aichiken Seinen Kaikan, 18-8 Sakae 1 chome,
Naka-ku, Nagoya-shi 460-0008
📞 (81) (52) 221-6080
📠 (81) (52) 221-6057

Osaka – Osaka Youth Hostel Association
Nankai-Nihonbashi Bdg.2F, 1-3-19,
Nihonbashi-Nishi, Naniwa-ku, Osaka 556-0004
📞 (81) (6) 6633-8621
📠 (81) (6) 6634-0751
📧 yhaosaka@osk3.3web.ne.jp

Tokyo – National Office (JYH)
Suidobashi Nishiguchi Kaikan, 2-20-7,
Misaki-cho, Chiyoda-ku, Tokyo 101-0061
📞 (81) (3) 3288-1417
📠 (81) (3) 3288-1248
📧 info@jyh.or.jp

Tokyo – Tokyo Youth Hostels Association
Saiwai Building, 4 Gobancho, Chiyoda-Ku,
Tokyo 102-0076
📞 (81) (3) 3261-0191
📠 (81) (3) 3261-0190

Tokyo-Yoyogi – Tokyo-Yoyogi Youth Hostel
3-1 Yoyogi-Kamizono-cho, Shibuya-ku,
Tokyo 151-0052
📞 (81) (3) 3467-9163
📠 (81) (3) 3467-9417

KOREA - SOUTH

Korea Youth Hostels Association
Seoul – National Office
Rm 408, Juksun Hyundai Bldg 80, Juksun-Dong,
Jongro-Ku, Seoul 110-052
☎ (82) (2) 725-3031
✆ (82) (2) 725-3113
✉ inform@kyha.or.kr

LITHUANIA

Lithuanian Youth Hostels
Vilnius – National Office
Filaretai Youth Hostel
Filaretu Street 17,
2007 Vilnius
☎ (370) (2) 254627/262660
✆ (370) (2) 220149
✉ filaretai@post.omnitel.net

MALAYSIA

Malaysian Youth Hostels Association
Kuala Lumpur – MSL Travel Centre
66, Jalan Putra, 50350 Kuala Lumpur
☎ (60) (3) 4424722
✆ (60) (3) 4433707
✉ msl@po.jaring.my

MALTA

NSTS Student & Youth Travel
Valletta –
220 St Paul Street, Valletta VLT07
☎ (356) 244983
✆ (356) 230330
✉ nsts@nsts.org

MEXICO

Red Mexicana de Alojamiento para Jóvenes
Mexico City – Mundo Joven Travel Shop
Insurgentes sur #1510-D, Mexico City DF 03920
☎ (52) (5) 6628244
✆ (52) (5) 6631556
✉ hostellingmexico@remaj.com

NETHERLANDS

Stichting Nederlandse Jeugdherberg Centrale
Amsterdam – National Office
Professor Tulpstraat 2, 1018 HA Amsterdam
☎ (31) (20) 5513155
✆ (31) (20) 6390199

NEW ZEALAND

Auckland – USIT Beyond Travel Centre
18 Shortland Street, Auckland
☎ (64) (9) 379-4224
✆ (64) (9) 366-6275
✉ enquiries@usitbeyond.co.nz

Youth Hostels Association of New Zealand
Christchurch - National Office
P O Box 436, Level 3, Union House,
193 Cashel Street, Christchurch
☎ (64) (3) 3799970
✆ (64) (3) 3654476
✉ info@yha.org.nz

NORWAY

Norske Vandrerhjem
Oslo – National Office
Dronningensgate 26, PB 364 Sentrum,
N-0102 Oslo
☎ (47) (23) 139300
✆ (47) (23) 139350
✉ hostels@online.no

PERU

*Asociación Peruana de Albergues Turísticos
Juveniles*
Lima – National Office
AJ Turistico Internacional, Av Casimiro Ulloa 328,
Lima 18
☎ (51) (1) 2423068
✆ (51) (1) 4448187
✉ hostell@mail.cosapidata.com.pe

IBN

PORTUGAL

Movijovem
Lisbon – National Office
Av Duque de Avila 137, 1069-017 Lisbon
- (351) 3138820
- (351) 3521466 / 3528621
- movijovem@mail.telepac.pt

RUSSIA

St Petersburg – Russian Youth Hostels,
Sindbad Travel
3rd Sovetskaya Ulitsa 28, St Petersburg
- (7) (812) 327-8384
- (7) (812) 329-8019
- ryh@ryh.ru

Moscow – Blue Chip Travel
Chistoprudny Blvd. 12A, Suite 628,
101000 Moscow
- (7) (095) 9169364
- (7) (095) 9244968

Moscow – STAR Travel
Leningradskypr. 80/21, 3rd Floor, Moscow
- (7) (095) 797-9555
- (7) (095) 797-9554
- star@glasnet.ru

SCOTLAND

Scottish Youth Hostels Association
Stirling – National Office
7 Glebe Crescent, Stirling, FK8 2JA
- (44) (8701) 553255
- (44) (1786) 891350
- info@syha.org.uk

SINGAPORE

Singapore – STA Travel Pte Ltd
33A Cuppage Road, Cuppage Terrace, Singapore
229458
- (65) 7377188
- (65) 7372591
- sales@statravel.com.sg

SLOVAKIA

CKM SYTS
Bratislava – CKM 2000 Travel
Vysoka 32, 814 45 Bratislava
- (421) (7) 52731024
- (421) (7) 52731025
- ckm2000@ckm.sk

SOUTH AFRICA

Hostels Association of South Africa
Cape Town – National Office
3rd Floor, St Georges House, 73 St Georges Mall,
Cape Town, 8001
- (27) (21) 242511
- (27) (21) 244119
- info@hisa.org.za

Durban – Africa Wonderland Tours
19 Smith Street, Durban 4001, Natal
- (27) (31) 3324944
- (27) (31) 332-4551

Johannesburg – Africa Wonderland Tours
Inchanga Ranch, Inchanga Road, Witkoppen,
4 Ways, Johannesburg
- (27) (11) 708-1459
- (27) (11) 708-1464
- ivi@pixie.co.za

SPAIN

Red Española de Albergues Juveniles
Barcelona/TUJUCA
C. Calabria, 147, 08015 Barcelona
- (34) (93) 4838341
- (34) (93) 4838347
- tujcom@usa.net

Madrid – TIVE Office
C/Fernando el Catolico 88, 28015 Madrid
- (34) (91) 5437412
- (34) (91) 5440062
- tive.juventud@comadrid.es

Valencia – Turivaj
c/ Hospital, 11, 46001 Valencia
☎ (34) (96) 3869700
✆ (34) (96) 3869903
✉ turivaj@ivaj.gva.es

SWEDEN

Swedish Touring Club
Stockholm – National Office
Box 25, 101 20 Stockholm
☎ (46) (8) 4632270
✆ (46) (8) 6781958
✉ info@stfturist.se

SWITZERLAND

Schweizer Jugendherbergen
Zurich – National Office
Schaffhauserstrasse 14, Postfach, CH-8042 Zurich
☎ (41) (1) 360-1414
✆ (41) (1) 360-1460
✉ bookingoffice@youthhostel.ch

TAIWAN

Kaohsiung City –
Kaohsiung International Youth Hostel
120 Wen wu First Street, Kaohsiung
☎ (886) (7) 2012477
✆ (886) (7) 2156322
✉ jumper@flash.net.tw

Taipei – Chinese Taipei Youth Hostel Association
12F-10-Nº50, Chung Hsiao West Road,
Sec 1, Taipei
☎ (886) (2) 2331 8366
✆ (886) (2) 2388 9093

Taipei – Federal Vacation
7F, 41 Tung-Hsin Rd, Taipei 110
☎ (886) (2) 87681133
✆ (886) (2) 87681515
✉ tci@tptsl.seed.net.tw

Taipei –
Kang Wen Culture & Education Foundation
1208A/12F, 142, Chung-Hsiao E Rd, Sec 4, Taipei
☎ (886) (2) 27751138
✆ (886) (2) 27212784
✉ gftours@tptsl.seed.net.tw

THAILAND

Thai Youth Hostels Association
Bangkok – National Office
25/14 Phitsanulok Road, Thay-wej, BKK 10300
☎ (66) (2) 628-7413, 7414, 7415
✆ (66) (2) 628-7416
✉ bangkok@tyha.org

UNITED STATES

Hostelling International – American Youth Hostels
Boston –
Eastern New England Council Travel Centre
1105 Commonwealth Avenue, Boston, MA 02215
☎ (1) (617) 779-0900
✆ (1) (617) 779-0904
✉ admin_hienec@juno.com

Boulder –
Rocky Mountain Council Travel Centre
1310 College Avenue, Suite 315, Boulder,
Colorado 80302
☎ (1) (303) 442-1166
✆ (1) (303) 442-4453
✉ hi-rocky@indra.com

Chicago – Metro Chicago Council Travel Centre
2232 West Roscoe Street, Chicago, IL 60618
☎ (1) (773) 327-8327
✆ (1) (773) 327-4287
✉ hiayhchigo@aol.com

Los Angeles – Los Angeles Council Travel Centre
1434 Second Street, Santa Monica, CA 90401
☎ (1) (310) 393-3413
✆ (1) (310) 393-1769
✉ hiayhla@aol.com

IBN

New York – HI-New York Hostel Shop
891 Amsterdam Avenue, New York, NY 10025
☎ (1) (212) 932-2300
✆ (1) (212) 932-2574
✉ reserve@hinewyork.org

Philadelphia –
Delaware Valley Council Travel Centre
624 South 3rd Street, Philadelphia, PA 19147
☎ (1) (215) 925-6004
✆ (1) (215) 925-4874
✉ hidvc@hi-dvc.org

San Francisco –
Golden Gate Council Travel Centre
425 Divisadero Street, Suite 307, San Francisco,
CA 94117
☎ (1) (415) 701-1320
✆ (1) (415) 863-3865
✉ hiayh@norcalhostels.org

St Louis – Gateway Council Travel Centre
7187 Manchester Road, St Louis,
MO 63143-2450
☎ (1) (314) 644-4660
✆ (1) (314) 644-6192
✉ info@gatewayhiayh.org

Washington DC – HI-AYH National Office
733 15th Street N W, Suite 840,
Washington DC 20005
☎ (1) (202) 783-6161
✆ (1) (202) 783-6171
✉ hiayhserv@hiayh.org

URUGUAY

Asociacion de Alberguistas del Uruguay
Montevideo – National Office
Pablo del Maria 1583/008, 11200 Montevideo
☎ (598) (2) 400-4245
✆ (598) (2) 400-1326
✉ aau@adinet.com.uy

> **The world is a book, and those who do not travel read only one page.**
>
> Le monde est un livre et ceux qui ne voyagent pas n'en lisent qu'une seule page.
>
> **Die Welt ist ein Buch, und die, die nicht reisen, lesen nur eine Seite.**
>
> El mundo es un libro y los que no viajan sólo leen una página.
>
> **St Augustine**

Austria

AUTRICHE
ÖSTERREICH
AUSTRIA

(V) **Österreichischer Jugendherbergsverband, Hauptverband, 1010 Wien, Schottenring 28, Austria.**

t (43) (1) 5335353, 5335354
f (43) (1) 5350861
e oejhv-zentrale@oejhv.or.at
e oejvh-wien-travel-service@oejhv.or.at
www.oejhv.or.at

Office Hours: Monday-Thursday, 09.00-17.00hrs
Friday 09.00-15.00hrs

Travel Service, GmbH: Österreichischer Jugendherbergsverband, Gonzagagasse 22, 1010 Wien, Austria.

t (43) (1) 5321660
f (43) (1) 5350861
e oejhv-wien-travel-service@oejhv.or.at

A copy of the Hostel Directory for (V) & (W) can be obtained from: Hauptverband, 1010 Wien, Schottenring 28, Austria.

(W) **Österreichisches Jugendherbergswerk, 1010 Wien, Helferstorferstrasse 4, A 1010 Wien, Austria.**

t (43) (1) 5331833
f (43) (1) 5331833 Ext 85
e oejhw@oejhw.or.at
www.oejhw.or.at/oejhw

Office Hours: Monday-Friday, 09.30-18.00hrs

Travel Section: Supertramp, 1010 Wien, Helferstorferstrasse 4, Austria

t (43) (1) 5335137
f (43) (1) 5331833 Ext 81
e travel@supertramp.co.at
www.supertramp.co.at

Capital:	Vienna	**Population:**	8,025,000
Language:	German	**Size:**	83,849 sq km
Currency:	AS (Schilling)	**Country Code:**	43

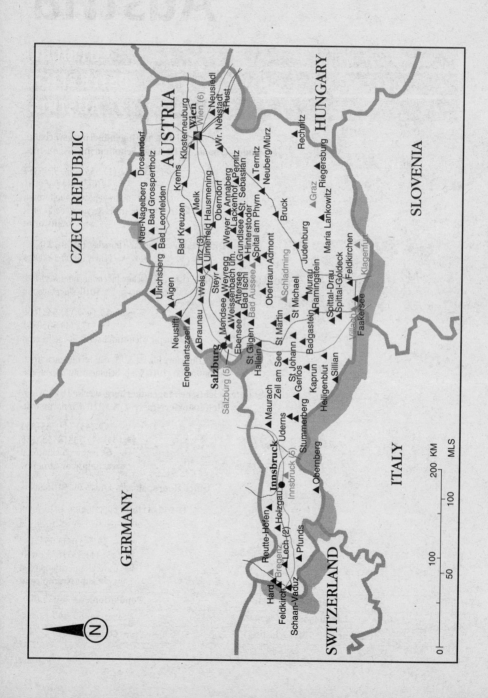

English

AUSTRIAN HOSTELS

Youth Hostels in Austria are controlled by two Associations which operate independently, ÖJHV (Ⓥ) and ÖJHW (Ⓦ). Both Associations are participating in Hostelling International's Assured Standards Scheme see page 4 for details. Many hostels have facilities for skiing, see individual entries for details.

Hostels are generally open 07.00-22.00hrs (07.00-24.00hrs in cities). Few have self-catering facilities and where they do exist you may be charged for use, but most serve meals.

Expect to pay in the region of 150-250 AS (11.00-18.20 Euros) including breakfast and linen hire, unless otherwise stated.

HEALTH

In case of an accident or emergency which requires a stay in hospital full payment has to be made for treatment and medication received. Also general practioners' fees have to be paid in full. It is therefore advisable to take out private insurance before travelling.

BANKING HOURS

Generally 08.00-12.30 and 13.30-15.00hrs on Monday, Tuesday, Wednesday and Friday; 08.00-12.30 and 13.30-17.30hrs on Thursday. All banks are closed Saturday and Sunday.

The exchange counters at airports and main railway stations are usually open from the first to last plane or train, ie 08.00-22.00hrs every day.

POST OFFICES

Post offices are open Monday to Friday 08.00-12.00 and 14.00-18.00hrs. (Monetary transactions only up to 17.00hrs).

SHOPPING HOURS

Weekdays 08.00-18.30hrs and Saturday 08.00-17.00hrs. Many shops close for two hours at midday.

Refund on Value-Added Tax: Ask for leaflet "Tax-Free Shopping".

TRAVEL

Rail

Rail travel in Austria is extremely developed. Special offers are available via the Austrian Federal Railways (information at main railway stations).

Bus

Developed regional network.

Driving

It is advisable to have an international driving licence; third party insurance is obligatory. The wearing of seat-belts is compulsory and children under 12 are not allowed in front seats. Dipped headlights can be used at all times. Tolls are payable on a number of mountain roads and road tunnels. A compulsory permit must be purchased in order to use motorways..

All major international car-hire firms have offices in Austria.

Français

AUBERGES DE JEUNESSE AUTRICHIENNES

Les auberges de jeunesse autrichiennes sont administrées par deux Associations indépendantes l'une de l'autre, l'ÖJHV (Ⓥ) et l'ÖJHW (Ⓦ). De nombreuses auberges sont équipées pour le ski, se reporter à la liste des auberges pour plus de détails. Toutes les auberges participent au Plan Hostelling

International pour la Garantie des Normes en auberges - voir page 13 pour plus de détails.

Les auberges sont en général ouvertes de 7h à 22h (de 7h à 24h dans les grandes villes). Quelques-unes seulement sont équipées d'une cuisine pour les touristes, dans quel cas il pourra vous être demandé une contribution financière, mais la plupart servent des repas.

Une nuit, petit déjeuner et location de draps compris (sauf indication contraire), coûte entre 150 et 250 SCH (11.00-18.20 ECU) environ.

SOINS MEDICAUX

En cas d'accident ou d'urgence nécessitant une hospitalisation, le patient sera tenu d'acquitter la totalité des frais relatifs aux soins et médicaments reçus, ainsi que les honoraires des médecins généralistes. Il vous est par conséquent recommandé de souscrire à une police d'assurances avant votre départ.

HEURES D'OUVERTURE DES BANQUES

En général, les banques sont ouvertes de 8h à 12h30 et de 13h30 à 15h les lundi, mardi, mercredi et vendredi. Le jeudi, elles ouvrent de 8h à 12h30 et de 13h30 à 17h30. Toutes les banques sont fermées le samedi et le dimanche.

Les bureaux de change situés dans les aéroports et les gares principales sont d'habitude ouverts entre les heures de départ ou d'arrivée du premier et du dernier avion ou train, c'est-à-dire de 8h à 22h tous les jours.

BUREAUX DE POSTE

Les bureaux de poste sont ouverts du lundi au vendredi de 8h à 12h et de 14h à 18h. (Les transactions monétaires sont possibles jusqu'à 17h seulement).

HEURES D'OUVERTURE DES MAGASINS

En semaine, les magasins sont ouverts de 8h à 18h30 et le samedi, de 8h à 17h. De nombreux magasins ferment entre midi et deux heures.

Remboursement de la TVA: procurez-vous le dépliant "Les achats hors-taxes".

DEPLACEMENTS

Trains
Les services ferroviaires sont très développés en Autriche. Des offres spéciales sont disponibles auprès des Chemins de fer fédéraux autrichiens (renseignements dans les gares principales).

Autobus
Réseau régional développé.

Automobiles
Un permis de conduire international est conseillé et l'assurance au tiers est obligatoire. Le port des ceintures de sécurité est également obligatoire et il est interdit aux enfants de moins de 12 ans de voyager à l'avant de la voiture. Les codes peuvent être utilisés en permanence. Un certain nombre de routes de montagne et de tunnels routiers sont à péage, ainsi que les autoroutes.

Toutes les grandes agences internationales de location de voitures possèdent des bureaux en Autriche.

Deutsch

ÖSTERREICHISCHE JUGENDHERBERGEN

Für Jugendherbergen gibt es in Österreich zwei unabhängige Vereine, den ÖJHV (Ⓥ) und das ÖJHW (Ⓦ). Viele Jugendherbergen bieten Möglichkeiten zum Skilaufen - siehe jeweilige Angaben. Alle Jugendherbergen sind an dem 'Plan garantierter Standards' beteiligt (siehe Seite 20 für Einzelheiten).

Die Herbergen sind im allgemeinen von 07.00-22.00 Uhr (in Städten von 07.00-24.00 Uhr) geöffnet. Wenige Jugendherbergen haben Selbstversorgungsmöglichkeiten und einige berechnen dafür. In den meisten Jugendherbergen sind Mahlzeiten erhältlich.

Es ist mit einem Preis von 150-250 S (11.00-18.20 ECU), einschließlich Frühstück und Miete von Bettwäsche, zu rechnen (sofern nicht anders angegeben).

GESUNDHEIT

Bei Unfällen oder dringenden Krankheitsfällen, die einen Krankenhausaufenthalt erfordern, muß für die empfangene Behandlung und Arzneimittel voll bezahlt werden. Auch Arztrechnungen müssen voll bezahlt werden. Es empfiehlt sich daher, vor Antritt der Reise eine Privatversicherung abzuschließen.

GESCHÄFTSSTUNDEN DER BANKEN

Im allgemeinen montags, dienstags, mittwochs und freitags 08.00-12.30 und 13.30-15.00 Uhr; donnerstags 08.00-12.30 und 13.30-17.30 Uhr. Samstags und sonntags sind alle Banken geschlossen.

Die Devisenschalter auf Flughäfen und großen Bahnhöfen sind im allgemeinen vom ersten bis zum letzten Flugzeug bzw. Zug, d.h. täglich von 08.00-22.00 Uhr geöffnet.

POSTÄMTER

Postämter sind montags bis freitags von 08.00-12.00 und von 14.00-18.00 Uhr geöffnet (Geldgeschäfte nur bis 17.00 Uhr).

LADENÖFFNUNGSZEITEN

Werktags 08.00-18.30 Uhr und samstags 08.00-17.00 Uhr. Viele Geschäfte sind um die Mittagszeit zwei Stunden geschlossen.

Mehrwertsteuer-Rückerstattung: Lassen Sie sich den Prospekt "Steuerfreies Einkaufen" geben.

REISEN

Eisenbahn

Der Eisenbahnverkehr ist in Österreich außerordentlich gut ausgebaut. Über die Österreichischen Bundesbahnen sind Sonderangebote erhältlich (Auskunft auf den größeren Bahnhöfen).

Busse

Gut ausgebautes regionales Netz.

Autofahren

Es ist ratsam, sich einen internationalen Führerschein zu beschaffen. Haftpflichtversicherung ist Pflicht. Das Tragen von Sicherheitsgurten ist obligatorisch und Kinder unter 12 dürfen sich nicht auf den vorderen Sitzen befinden. Man muß immer mit Abblendlicht fahren. Bei Benutzung mehrerer Bergstraßen und Straßentunneln ist eine Maut zahlbar. Die Benutzung der Autobahnen ist kostenpflichtig!

Alle großen internationalen Mietwagen-Unternehmen haben Niederlassungen in Österreich.

Español

ALBERGUES JUVENILES AUSTRIACOS

Los albergues juveniles austriacos están administrados por dos asociaciones que funcionan independientemente la una de la otra, la ÖJHV (Ⓥ) y la ÖJHW (Ⓦ). Ambas Asociaciones participan en el Plan de Normas Garantizadas de Hostelling International (véase la página 28 para más información). Muchos albergues están equipados para el esquí (véase la información sobre cada uno de ellos).

Generalmente, los albergues están abiertos de 7 h. a 22 h. (de 7 h. a 24 h. en las ciudades). Pocos disponen de cocina para huéspedes y los que la tengan posiblemente le cobren por su uso, pero la mayoría sirven comidas.

Los precios oscilan entre 150 y 250 chelines austriacos (11,00-18,20 Euros) incluyendo desayuno y sábanas, a no ser que se indique lo contrario.

INFORMACIÓN SANITARIA

En caso de accidente o urgencia que requiera hospitalización, Ud. tendrá que abonar el importe total del tratamiento médico y medicamentos. También tendrá que pagar las consultas de los médicos de cabecera en su totalidad. Por lo tanto, le aconsejamos se haga un seguro privado antes de viajar.

HORARIO DE LOS BANCOS

Generalmente, los bancos abren de 8 h. a 12.30 h. y de 13.30 h. a 15 h. los lunes, martes, miércoles y viernes; de 8 h. a 12.30 h. y de 13.30 h. a 17.30 h. los jueves. Todos los bancos cierran los sábados y domingos.

Las ventanillas de cambio de divisas en los aeropuertos y principales estaciones ferroviarias suelen estar abiertas desde el primer avión o tren hasta el último, es decir, de 8 h. a 22 h. todos los días.

OFICINAS DE CORREOS

Las oficinas de correos abren de lunes a viernes, de 8 h. a 12 h. y de 14 h. a 18 h. (Transacciones monetarias sólo hasta las 17 h.)

HORARIO COMERCIAL

Entre semana las tiendas abren de 8 h. a 18.30 h. y los sábados de 8 h. a 17 h. Muchas tiendas cierran durante dos horas al mediodía.

Reembolso del I.V.A. (Impuesto sobre el Valor Añadido): Solicite el folleto "Tax-Free Shopping" (Compras Libres de Impuestos).

DESPLAZAMIENTOS

Tren
El sistema ferroviario de Austria está muy desarrollado. Se pueden conseguir ofertas especiales a través de la compañía de Ferrocarriles Federales Austriacos (información en las principales estaciones de tren).

Autobús
Red regional desarrollada.

Automóvil
Es aconsejable tener un permiso de conducir internacional; el seguro contra terceros es obligatorio. También es obligatorio ponerse el cinturón de seguridad y no está permitido a los niños menores de 12 años viajar en el asiento delantero. Es obligatorio llevar las luces de cruce siempre encendidas. Algunas carreteras de montaña, túneles y autopistas son de peaje.

Todas las principales compañías internacionales de alquiler de coches tienen oficinas en Austria.

Bad Gastein ⓦ

5640 Bad Gastein,
Ederplatz 2,
Salzburg.
☎ (6434) 2080
🖷 (6434) 50688
✉ hostel.badgastein@salzburg.co.at

Open Dates:	🗓12
Open Hours:	07.00-11.00hrs; 17.00-22.00hrs
Reservations:	Ⓡ ⊂CC⊐
Price Range:	AS 190.00-230.00 € 13.80-16.70 BB inc 🍽
Beds:	150 - 10x²🛏 43x⁴🛏
Facilities:	👪 53x 👫 🍴 (BD) 👥 📺 📖 🧺 2 x 🍷 🕐 🖼 🅿 ℹ ♿ ⚟ ♻ 🪑 ⛺ 🏠

Directions:

✈	Salzburg Wolfgang Amadeus 80km
🚆	Bad Gastein 400m
Attractions:	🚡 ⛰ 🚵 🏊 ⛷ 🚶 ∪5km ⚲4km ⛵400m

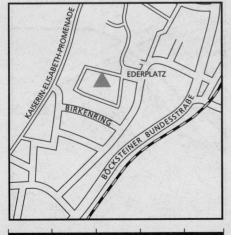

Bregenz ⓥ

Mehrerauerstraße 3-5,
6900 Bregenz,
Vorarlberg.
☎ (5574) 42867
🖷 (5574) 42867-88
✉ bregenz@jgh.at

Open Dates:	🗓12
Open Hours:	07.00-22.00hrs
Reservations:	Ⓡ ⌊IBN⌋ ⊂CC⊐
Price Range:	AS 180.00-270.00 € 13.10-19.60 BB inc 🍽
Beds:	128 - 4x²🛏 4x⁴🛏 4x⁵🛏 14x⁶🛏 1x⁶🛏
Facilities:	👪 👫 🍴 👥 📺 4 x 🍷 🕐 ⬆ ℹ 🍼 ♿ ⚟ 🪑 ⛽

Directions:

✈	Altenrhein CH 20km
A🚌	20m
🚆	300m
Attractions:	⛰ 🄌300m 🚶 ⚲ ⛵200m

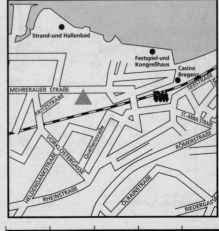

Graz ⓥ

A-8020 Graz,
Idlhofgasse 74,
Steiermark.
- ☏ (316) 714876
- ✆ (316) 714876-88
- ✉ jgh.graz@jgh.at

Open Dates:	01.01-23.12; 30-31.12
Open Hours:	07.00-10.00; 17.00-22.00hrs
Reservations:	Ⓡ [IBN] [CC]
Price Range:	AS 220.00-320.00 € 16.00-23.30 [BB]inc 🍽
Beds:	96 - 9x² 15x⁴ 1x⁶ 2x⁶
Facilities:	� 5x ♥♥♥ ⑩ 💾 TV 📺4 x 🔌 ▣ 🖼 ⑧ P 🚿 ♻ ⛰ 🔄 🔍 🏢 🏠
Directions:	[2SW] from city centre
✈	Thalerhof 7km
A🚌	500m
🚂	Hauptbahnhof Graz 500m
🚌	#31,32,33,50 150m
🚋	300m
Attractions:	U5km ✗4km ⚓3km

Innsbruck ⓦ

6020 Innsbruck,
Reichenauerstrasse 147,
Tirol.
- ☏ (512) 346179, 346180
- ✆ (512) 346179 Ext 12
- ✉ yhibk@tirol.com

Open Dates:	01.01-23.12; 27-31.12
Open Hours:	07.00-10.00hrs; 17.00-23.00hrs
Reservations:	Ⓡ [IBN]
Price Range:	AS 155.00-260.00 € 11.26 - 18.90 [BB]inc
Beds:	178 - 5x¹ 5x² 6x⁴ 24x⁶
Facilities:	♥♥♥ 6x ♥♥♥ ⑩ (BD) 🎒 TV 2 x 🔌 🖼 ⑧ P ⓘ 🚿 ♻ ⛰ 🔄 🔍 🏢
Directions:	[2NE] from city centre
✈	Innsbruck 5km
A🚌	Innsbruck Hauptbahnhof 2km
🚌	Bus O, 2km ap König Laurinstrasse
Attractions:	🏊 ⛰ 🚴 ⛷ 3000m ⛸ 🎿 U500m ✗50m ⚓1km

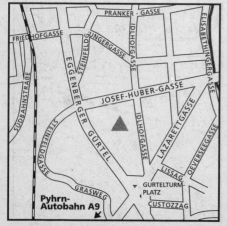

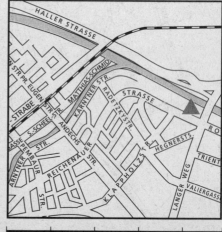

Kaprun Ⓥ

A-5710 Kaprun,
Nikolaus Gassnerstrasse 448,
Salzburg.
☎ (6547) 8507
🖷 (6547) 8507 Ext 3
📧 oejhv-salzburg@oejhv.or.at

Open Dates:	🔟
Open Hours:	07.00-22.00hrs
Reservations:	Ⓡ
Price Range:	AS 185.00-275.00 € 13.45 - 19.99 BB inc 🍴
Beds:	150 - 2x¹ 4x² 4x³ 9x⁴ 13x⁶ 2x⁶
Facilities:	♒ 9x ♒ 🍽 🛏 📺 3 x🍴 🅿 ⓘ 🐾 ♨ 🏔 ⊙ 🔍 ⛰ 🏠
Directions:	
🚂	Zell am See 6km
Attractions:	⛳ ⛰ 🔍 🏊 2000m ⛸ 🎿 ⚒ 🚡 700m

Klagenfurt Ⓥ

JGH,
A-9020 Klagenfurt,
Universitätsviertel,
Neckheimg. 6
☎ (463) 230020
🖷 (463) 230020 Ext: 20
📧 oejhv-kaernten@oejhv.or.at

Open Dates:	🔟
Open Hours:	06.00-10.00hrs; 17.00-23.00hrs
Reservations:	Ⓡ IBN
Price Range:	AS 210 € 15.26 BB inc 🍴
Beds:	3x² 35x⁴
Facilities:	♿ ♒ 35x ♒ 🍽 🛏 📺 4 x🍴 🔲 🧳 ⓘ 🐾 ♨
Directions:	
✈	Klagenfurt-Wörthersee 12km
🚂	Klagenfurt 4km
🚌	#10 or #12 200m
Attractions:	⛳ ♒ 🚴 🏊 1500-2000m ⛳5km ⚒100m 🚡1km

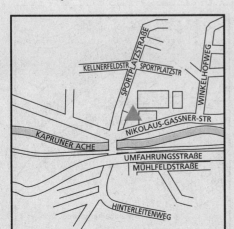

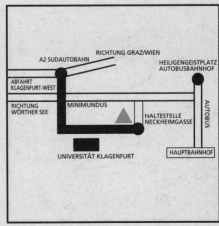

Linz ⓥ - Stanglhofweg

4020 Linz,
Stanglhofweg 3,
Oberösterreich: (near the stadium,
1km to centre)
📞 (732) 664434
📠 (732) 664434 Ext. 75
📧 jgh.linz@oejhv.or.at

Open Dates:	10.01-17.12
Open Hours:	07.30-16.00; 18.00-21.00 hrs (Mon-Thur); 7.30-12.00; 18.00-21.00 hrs (Fri), 18.00-21.00 hrs (Sat & Sun)
Reservations:	Ⓡ
Price Range:	AS 173.00-303.00 € 12.57 - 22.01 BBinc 🍴
Beds:	170 - 24x² 4x³ 28x⁴
Facilities:	††† 28x ††† ⁙ 🖵 📺 4 x 🍽 📷 🎱 🅿 ⓘ 🛝 ⛰ 🔍 🏢 🏨

Directions:

✈	Linz 10km
⛴	Linz-Schiffsanlegestelle 4km
🚇	Linzer 2km
🚌	#17 500m, #19 500m, #45 500m ap Leondingerstr
🚃	#1 2km, #3 2km ap Goethekreuzung
Attractions:	⚒ 🏊 3km

Salzburg ⓥ

JGH,
A-5020 Salzburg Nonntal,
Josef-Preis Allee 18.
📞 (662) 8426700
📠 (662) 841101
📧 oejhv-sbg-jgh-nonntal@oejhv.or.at

Open Dates:	🗓
Open Hours:	07.00-24.00hrs
Reservations:	Ⓡ ⟨IBN⟩ ⟨CC⟩
Price Range:	AS 167.00 (8 Bed/room), AS 217.00 (4 Bed/room), AS 267.00 (2 Bed/room) € 12.14 (8 Bed/room), 15.77 (4 Bed/room), 19.41 (2 Bed/room) BBinc 🍴
Beds:	390 - 21x² 5x³ 19x⁴ 2x⁵ 32x⁶
Facilities:	♿ ††† 19x ††† ⁙ 🖵 📺 📷 🎱 ⁙ 5 x 🍽 🔲 📷 🏧 🎱 🔁 🅿 ⓘ 🛝 ⛰ 🔍 🏢

Directions:

	⟨1 SW⟩ from city centre
✈	Salzburg Maxglan 5km
A🚌	#77 to station, #5 to Justizgebäude
🚇	Salzburg 3km
🚌	#5 ap Justizgebäude
🚃	#5 150m
Attractions:	⛳ ⛰ 🚴 ⛷ 1400m 🏊 🎿 ∪ 1km ⚒ 1.5km 🏊 1.5km

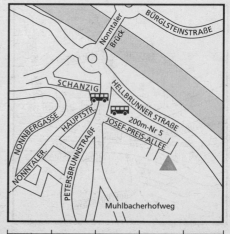

Salzburg ⓦ -
Eduard Heinrich Haus

5020 Salzburg - Josefiau,
Eduard-Heinrich Str 2.
☏ (662) 625976
🖷 (662) 627980
📧 hostel.eduard-heinrich@salzburg.co.at

Open Dates:	🗓12
Open Hours:	07.00-10.00hrs; 17.00-24.00hrs
Reservations:	Ⓡ ⒾⒷ⒩ ⒸⒸ
Price Range:	AS 180.00-220.00 € 13.10 - 16.00 BB inc 🍽
Beds:	120 - 4x² 4x³ 1x⁴ 16x⁶
Facilities:	👪 21x 👫 🍴 (BD) 🛏 📺 🧺 2 x 🍷 🔲 🖼 🅿 ℹ 🎿 ⛰ 🔍 🎣 🏕
Directions:	3SW from city centre
✈	Salzburg Wolfgang Amadeus 6km
🚉	Salzburg 4km
🚌	500m ap Bundespolizeidirektion 1km
Attractions:	⛲ ⛰ 🚴 🏊 🎣 ∪2km 🐚2km 🛥2km

Schladming ⓥ

8970 Schladming,
Coburgstrasse 253,
Steiermark.
☏ (3687) 24531
🖷 (3687) 24531 Ext 88
📧 jgh.schladming@jgh.at

Open Dates:	01.01-31.10; 24-31.12
Open Hours:	08.00-13.00hrs; 17.00-22.00hrs
Reservations:	Ⓡ ⒾⒷ⒩ ⒸⒸ
Price Range:	AS 180.00-310.00 € 13.10 - 22.50 BB inc 🍽
Beds:	198 - 2x¹ 10x² 3x³ 20x⁴ 1x⁵ 16x⁶
Facilities:	👪 7x 👫 🍴 🛏 📺 🧺 2 x 🍷 🖼 ♿ 8 🅿 ℹ 🎿 🎣 ⛰ 🔍 🍴
Directions:	
✈	Salzburg 89km
🚉	Schladming 1.5km
🚌	Rathausplatz 100m
Attractions:	⛲ ⛰ 🏊 🎣 🎿 ∪1km 🐚500m 🛥500m

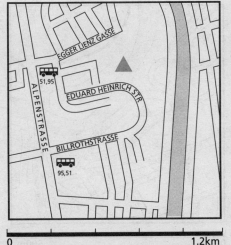

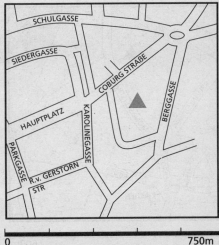

0   1.2km

0   750m

St Gilgen [Ⓥ] -
JGH Schafbergblick

YGH,
5340 St Gilgen,
Mondseerstraße 7-11,
Salzburg.
☎ (6227) 2365
✆ (6227) 2365 Ext 75
✉ jgh.stgilgen@oejhv.or.at

Open Dates:	24.01-16.12
Open Hours:	08.00-13.00hrs(Mon-Fri), 17.00-19.00hrs(daily)
Reservations:	**Ⓡ**
Price Range:	AS 155-275 € 11.26 - 19.98 ᴮᴮⁱⁿᶜ 🗐
Beds:	128 - 12x² 26x⁴
Facilities:	♦♦♦ 26x ♦♦♦ ⦿ ≞ TV 2 x 🍴 🔟 P ⓘ 🧺 ♨ 🏔 🚿 🔍 ♠ 🏠

Directions:

✈	Salzburg 40km
🚆	Salzburg 30km
🚌	ap St. Gilgen 500m
Attractions:	🐾 ⛰ 🔍 ⛷ 1522m 🎿 🎿 ∪20km ⚲300m 🏊

Villach [Ⓥ]

9500 Villach,
St Martin,
Dinzlweg 34,
Kärnten.
☎ (4242) 56368
✆ (4242) 56368-20
✉ jgh.villach@oejhv.or.at

Open Dates:	🗓12
Open Hours:	06.00-10.00hrs; 17.00-22.00hrs
Reservations:	**Ⓘ B N**
Price Range:	AS 190.00 € 13.81 ᴮᴮⁱⁿᶜ 🗐
Beds:	144 - 3x² 28x⁵
Facilities:	♦♦♦ 28x ♦♦♦ ⦿ ≞ TV 🗐3 x 🍴 P ⓘ 🧺 ♨ 🏔 🚿 🔍

Directions:

✈	Klagenfurt Wörthersee 45km
🚆	Villach 1.5km
🚌	St. Martin 300m
Attractions:	🐾 ⛰ 🔍 🚴 🎿 1000-2000m 🎿 🎿 ⚲ 🏊2.5km

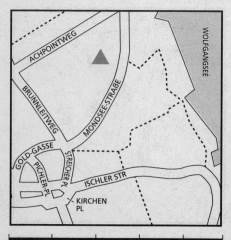

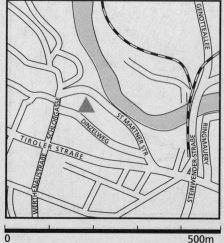

Wien ⱽ - Brigittenau

1200 Wien,
Friedrich Engelsplatz 24.
☏ (1) 33282940, 3300598
🖷 (1) 3308379
🖃 jgh.1200wien@chello.at

Open Dates:	01.01-05.02; 20.02-31.12
Open Hours:	◷
Reservations:	Ⓡ IBN
Price Range:	AS 170-215 € 12.35 - 15.62 BBinc 🍽
Beds:	434 - 103x² 12x³ 36x⁴ 4x⁶ 1x⁶
Facilities:	♿ ♦ 155x ♦ ⦿ (BD) 🚍 📺 4 x ⛾ ⬚ ⬛ ⬗ 🏧 Ⓟ ⬚ ⚘
Directions:	4NW from city centre
✈	Wien-Schwechat 20km
A🚌	Südbahnhof, then S1, S2 or S3
⛴	Wien-Reichsbrücke 2.5km
🚆	W 6km, S 7km, Handelskai 500m
🚌	11A, 5A ap Friedrich Engels Platz 50m
🚃	N, 31, 33 ap Friedrich Engels Platz 50m
Ⓤ	U6 Handelskai 500m
Attractions:	⚘ 1km ⚘ ⚘ 1km ⚘ 1km

Wien ⱽ - Hütteldorf

1130 Wien,
Schlossberggasse 8.
☏ (1) 8771501, 8770263
🖷 (1) 8770263 Ext 2
🖃 jgh@wigast.com

Open Dates:	🄱2
Open Hours:	07.00-24.00hrs
Reservations:	Ⓡ IBN CC
Price Range:	AS 158.00-205.00 € 11.48-14.90 BBinc 🍽
Beds:	295 - 4x¹ 11x² 2x³ 11x⁴ 1x⁵ 24x⁶ 7x⁶
Facilities:	♦ 23x ♦ ⦿ (BD) 🚍 📺 🖥 ⬚ ⬛ ⬗ ⬘ Ⓟ ⓘ ⬚ ⚘ ⛺ 🔍 🏠
Directions:	10W from city centre
✈	Vienna International 30km
🚆	Wien Hütteldorf 500m
🚌	53b 20m
Ⓤ	U4 Hütteldorf 500m
Attractions:	⚘ ⚘ ⚘ 500m ⚘ 1km

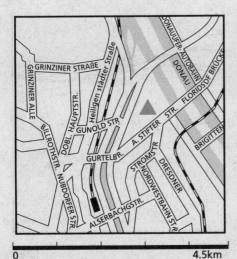

0   4.5km

0   1.2km

Wien ⓦ - Myrthengasse

1070 Wien,
Myrthengasse 7,
Neustiftgasse 85.
☎ (1) 52363160
✆ (1) 5235849
🖂 hostel@chello.at

Open Dates:	🗓️
Open Hours:	07.00-01.00hrs
Reservations:	Ⓡ ⟦IBN⟧
Price Range:	AS 170-210 € 12.35-15.26 BB inc 🍽️
Beds:	241 - 16x² 8x³ 32x⁴ 3x⁵ 7x⁶
Facilities:	♿ ⵜⵜⵜ 67x ⵜⵜⵜ 🍴 🛏️ 📺 1 x 🍸 📷 💼 🚿 🔒 ⓘ 🧺 🎴
Directions:	2W from city centre
✈	Wien-Schwechat 20km
A🚌	Vienna ✈ lines 20km
🚂	Westbahnhof 3km, Südbahnhof 8km
🚌	#48A 1.2km; #13A 5km ap For 48A Burggasse; for 13A Südbahnhof
Ⓤ	U2, U3 Volkstheater; U6 Burggasse

Zell am See ⓦ

5700 Zell am See,
Haus der Jugend,
Seespitzstrasse 13,
Salzburg.
☎ (6542) 57185
✆ (6542) 571854
🖂 hostel.zell-see@salzburg.co.at

Open Dates:	01.12-31.10
Open Hours:	07.00-10.00hrs; 16.00-22.00hrs
Reservations:	Ⓡ ⟦CC⟧
Price Range:	AS 155.00-195.00 € 11.30-14.20 BB inc 🍽️
Beds:	106 - 7x² 17x⁴ 4x⁶
Facilities:	ⵜⵜⵜ 28x ⵜⵜⵜ 🍴 🛏️ 📺 📷 🧺 💼 🅿 ⓘ ⚘ ⛰️ 🔍 🌲
Directions:	
✈	Salzburg Wolfgang Amadeus 100km
🚌	Zell am See 2km
Attractions:	⚘ ⛰️ 🔍 🚵 ⛷️ 🎿 🚶 ∪1km 🎣1km ⛴️2km

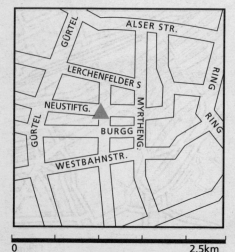

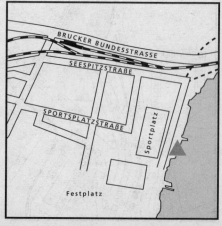

Location/Address	Telephone No. Fax No.	Beds	Opening Dates	Facilities
▲ Admont Ⓦ 8911 Admont-Schloss Röthelstein, Aigen 32 Steiermark. 🄴 jgh.admont@jgh.at	☎ (3613) 2432 🛂 (3613) 279583	104	01.01–31.10; 27–31.12	♦♦♦ ⑩ ⓡ 🄲🄲 🅿
▲ Aigen Ⓥ 4160 Aigen im Mühlkreis, Adalbert-Stifter-Landesjugendherberge, Oberösterreich.	☎ (7281) 6283 🛂 (7281) 6283-4	80	01.01–31.08; 23.09–31.12	⑩ ⓡ 🅿
▲ Annaberg Ⓦ 3222 Annaberg, Annarotte 77, Niederösterreich. 🄴 jugendherberge-annaberg@telecom.at	☎ YH (2728) 8496 🛂 (2728) 8442	116	🗓12	♦♦♦ ⑩ ⓡ 🅿
▲ Bad Aussee Ⓥ 〔IBN〕 A-8990 Bad Aussee, Jugendherbergsstr 148, Steiermark. 🄴 jgh.badaussee@jgh.at	☎ (3622) 52238 🛂 (3622) 52238-88	145	01.01–31.10; 25–31.12	♦♦♦ ⑩ ⓡ 🄲🄲 🅿 ▣
▲ Bad Gastein Ⓦ **5640 Bad Gastein, Ederplatz 2, Salzburg.** 🄴 hostel.badgastein@salzburg.co.at	☎ (6434) 2080 🛂 (6434) 50688	150	🗓12	♦♦♦ ⑩ ⓡ 🄲🄲 🅿 ▣
▲ Bad Großpertholz Ⓦ 3972 Bad Großpertholz, Bad Großpertholz 177, Niederösterreich.	☎ (2857) 2965 🛂 (2857) 2965	52	15.04–15.10	♦♦♦ ⑩ ⓡ 🅿
▲ Bad Ischl Ⓥ - JGH Bad Ischl YGH 4820 Bad Ischl, Am Rechensteg 5, Oberösterreich. 🄴 jgh.badischl@oejhv.or.at	☎ (6132) 26577 🛂 (6132) 26577 Ext 75	122	24.01–30.11	♦♦♦ ⑩ ♿ 🅿
△ *Bad Kreuzen* Ⓦ *Oberösterreich, 4362 Bad Kreuzen,* *Neuaigen 14, Burg.*	☎ *(7266) 6686*	*45*	*01.04–31.10*	⑩ ☞ 🅿
△ *Bad Leonfelden* Ⓦ *Passauer Strasse 3, 4190 Bad Leonfelden*	☎ *(7213) 8109* 🛂 *(7213) 634213*	*44*	🗓12	⑩ ☞
▲ Braunau Ⓥ 5280 Braunau am Inn, Osternbergerstr 57, Oberösterreich.	☎ (7722) 81638 🛂 (7722) 81638, 6313614	52	01.03–31.10	ⓡ ♿
▲ Bregenz Ⓥ 〔IBN〕 **Mehrerauerstraße 3-5, 6900 Bregenz,** **Vorarlberg.** 🄴 bregenz@jgh.at	☎ (5574) 42867 🛂 (5574) 42867-88	128	🗓12	♦♦♦ ⑩ ⓡ 🄲🄲 ▣
▲ Bruck an der Mur Ⓥ Stadtwaldstrasse 1, A-8600 Bruck 🄴 jgh.bruck@jgh.at	☎ (3862) 58448 🛂 (3862) 58448-88	92	🗓12	♦♦♦ ⑩ ⓡ ♿ 🄲🄲 🅿 ▣ ☕ 🍴
▲ Drosendorf Ⓦ 2095 Drosendorf an der Thaya, Badstrasse 25.	☎ (2915) 2257 🛂 (2915) 2257	63	15.04–15.10	♦♦♦ ⑩ ⓡ 🅿
▲ Ebensee Ⓦ 4802 Ebensee-Rindbach, Rindbachstrasse 15, Oberösterreich.	☎ (6133) 6698 🛂 (6133) 669885	80	01.04–31.10	♦♦♦ ⑩ ⓡ ♿ 🅿
▲ Engelhartszell Ⓦ Bike Hostel, 4090 Engelhartszell 68.	☎ (7717) 8115 🛂 (7717) 8115-13	38	01.05–31.10	♦♦♦ ⑩ ⓡ

Location/Address	Telephone No. Fax No.	Beds	Opening Dates	Facilities
△ *Faak - See - Scheiber* Ⓦ 9583 Faak - See - Scheiber	❶ (4254) 2301 ❻ (4254) 46464	51	🗓12	⑩ ☛ P
△ *Feldkirch* Ⓦ 6805 Feldkirch-Levis, Reichstrasse 111, Vorarlberg.	❶ (5522) 73181 ❻ (5522) 79399	96	01.01–10.11; 11–31.12	ⅲ ⑩ Ⓡ ♿ P ☐
△ *Feldkirchen* Ⓥ 9560 Kärnten, Briefelsdorf 7, Am Maltschachersee.	❶ (4277) 2644	38	25.04–04.10	⑩ P ☐
▲ **Gerlos** Ⓥ - JH Enzian Nr. 172, A-6281 Gerlos (Alt 1250-2500m)	❶ (5284) 5277 ❻ (5284) 54104	50	01.05–30.10; 01.12–30.04	ⅲ P
▲ **Graz** Ⓥ (IBN) A-8020 Graz, Idlhofgasse 74, Steiermark. ❷ jgh.graz@jgh.at	❶ (316) 714876 ❻ (316) 714876-88	96	01.01–23.12; 30–31.12	ⅲ ⑩ Ⓡ 2SW ᶜᶜ P ☐ ☕
▲ **Grundlsee** Ⓥ A-8993 Grundlsee, Wienern-Gössl 149. ❷ bookingcenter@jgh.at	❶ (3622) 8629 ❻ (3622) 8629-4	60	01.05–31.10	⑩ Ⓡ P
▲ **Hallein** Ⓥ A-5400 Hallein, Schloss Wispach-Esterhazy, Salzburg. ❷ oejhv-salzburg@oejhv.or.at	❶ (6245) 80397 ❻ (6245) 80397 Ext 3	112	01.04–30.09	⑩ P
△ *Hard* Ⓥ 6971 Hard, Allmendstr. 87, Vorarlberg (1,5km from Bregenz).	❶ (5574) 79716 ❻ (5574) 79716	22	🗓12	Ⓡ P
▲ **Heiligenblut** Ⓥ 9844 Heiligenblut, Hof 36, Kärnten.	❶ (4824) 2259 ❻ (4824) 2259	87	05.12.99–15. 10.2000	ⅲ ⑩ P
▲ **Hinterstoder** Ⓦ 4573 Hinterstoder 33, Oberösterreich.	❶ (7564) 5227 ❻ (7564) 522711	96	🗓12	ⅲ ⑩ Ⓡ P
▲ **Holzgau** Ⓦ - Holzgauerhof 6654 Holzgau 66	❶ (5633) 5250 ❻ (5633) 5250-4	53	15.12–15.05; 15.06–01.11	ⅲ ⑩ Ⓡ P ☕
▲ **Innsbruck** Ⓦ (IBN) 6020 Innsbruck, Reichenauerstrasse 147, Tirol. ❷ yhibk@tirol.com	❶ (512) 346179, 346180 ❻ (512) 346179 Ext 12	178	01.01–23.12; 27–31.12	⑩ Ⓡ 2NE P
△ *Innsbruck* Ⓦ - "Fritz Prior - Schwedenhaus" 6020 Innsbruck, Rennweg 17b, Tirol. ❷ youth.hostel@tirol.com	❶ (512) 585814 ❻ (512) 585814-4	75	01.07–31.08	ⅲ ⑩ 2NE P
▲ **Innsbruck** Ⓥ 6020 Innsbruck, Volkshaus, Radetzkystr 47.	❶ (512) 395882, (663) 9156214 ❻ (512) 395882/ 4	52	🗓12	P
▲ **Judenburg** Ⓥ YGH Judenburg, Kaserngasse 22, A-8750 Judenburg. ❷ jgh.judenburg@jgh.at	❶ (3572) 87355 ❻ (3572) 87355-88	98	01.01–31.10; 25–31.12	ⅲ ⑩ Ⓡ ♿ ᶜᶜ P ☐ ☕
▲ **Kaprun** Ⓥ A-5710 Kaprun, Nikolaus Gassnerstrasse 448, Salzburg. ❷ oejhv-salzburg@oejhv.or.at	❶ (6547) 8507 ❻ (6547) 8507 Ext 3	150	🗓12	ⅲ ⑩ Ⓡ P

Location/Address	Telephone No. Fax No.	Beds	Opening Dates	Facilities
▲ Klagenfurt Ⓥ ⒤ⒷⓃ JGH, A-9020 Klagenfurt, Universitätsviertel, Neckheimg. 6 ⓔ oejhv-kaernten@oejhv.or.at	❶ (463) 230020 ❺ (463) 230020 Ext: 20	🛏12		††† ⓮ Ⓡ ♿ ☞ 🅾
▲ Klagenfurt Ⓦ - Kolping JGH 9020 Klagenfurt, Enzenbergstrasse 26, Kärnten.	❶ (463) 56965 ❺ (463) 5696532	200	10.07–10.09	⓮ 🅿
△ *Klosterneuburg* Ⓦ *3400 Klosterneuburg-Gugging, Hüttersteig 8, Niederösterreich.*	❶ *(2243) 83501* ❺ *(2243) 83501*	*65*	*01.05–01.09*	⓮ ☞ 🅿
▲ Krems Ⓥ 3500 Krems an der Donau, Ringstrasse 77, Niederösterreich. ⓔ oejhv-noe@oejhv.or.at	❶ (2732) 83452 ❺ (2732) 83452	52	01.04–31.10	††† ⓮ Ⓡ 🅿
▲ Lackenhof Ⓦ 3295 Lackenhof am Ötscher, Ötscherweg 3, Niederösterreich.	❶ (7480) 5251 ❺ (7480) 5338	137	🛏12	††† ⓮ Ⓡ
▲ Lech Ⓥ 6764 Vorarlberg, Arlberger Taxizentrale, Lech 428. ⓔ taxi@lech.at	❶ (5583) 2501 ❺ (5583) 32586	45	15.06–15.09	††† ☞
▲ Lech-Stubenbach Ⓦ Jugendheim Lech-Stubenbach, A-6764 Lech am Arlberg, Stubenbach 244.	❶ (5583) 2419 ❺ (5583) 24194	64	01.07–31.08; 01.12–30.04.	††† ⓮ Ⓡ
▲ Linz Ⓥ - Stanglhofweg 4020 Linz, Stanglhofweg 3, Oberösterreich: (near the stadium, 1km to centre) ⓔ jgh.linz@oejhv.or.at	❶ (732) 664434 ❺ (732) 664434 Ext. 75	170	10.01–17.12	††† ⓮ Ⓡ 🅿
▲ Linz Ⓥ - Blütenstr Landesjugendherberge Linz im Lentia 2000, 4040 Linz, Blütenstr 23.	❶ (732) 737078 ❺ (732) 737078-15	106	01.01–22.12; 26–31.12	⓮ 🅿
▲ Linz Ⓦ - Kapuzinerstr 4020 Linz, Kapuzinerstr 14, Oberösterreich.	❶ (732) 778777 ❺ (732) 7817894	36	01.03–30.10	††† ⓮ Ⓡ 🅾
▲ Maria Lankowitz Ⓥ A 8591 Maria Lankowitz, Am See 2, Styria. ⓔ jgh.marialankowitz@jgh.at	❶ (3144) 71700 ❺ (3144) 71700-88	124	01.01–31.10; 25–31.12	††† Ⓡ ♿ ⒸⒸ 🅿 ☕
△ *Maurach am Achensee* Ⓥ *Dr Stumpf Jugendherberge, 6212 Maurach-Lärchenwiese. (Tirol)*	❶ *(5243) 5239* ❺ *(5243) 5239*	*200*	*01.01–31.03; 01.05–31.10; 01–31.12*	††† ⓮ ⒸⒸ 🅿
▲ Melk Ⓦ 3390 Melk an der Donau, Abt-Karl-Strasse 42, Niederösterreich.	❶ (2752) 52681 ❺ (2752) 54257	104	15.03–31.10	††† ⓮ Ⓡ 🅿
▲ Mondsee Ⓥ 5310 Mondsee, Krankenhausstrasse 9, Oberösterreich. ⓔ jgh.mondsee@oejhv.or.at	❶ (6232) 2418 ❺ (6232) 2418 Ext 75	80	01.02–16.12	††† ⓮ 🅿
▲ Murau Ⓦ 8850 Murau, St. Leonhardsplatz 4 Steiermark. ⓔ jgh.murau@jgh.at	❶ (3532) 2395 ❺ (3532) 2395	126	01.05–31.12	††† ⓮ Ⓡ ♿ ⒸⒸ 🅿 ☕

Location/Address	Telephone No. Fax No.	Beds	Opening Dates	Facilities
▲ Neuberg ⓥ 8692 Neuberg an der Mürz, Kaplanweg 8, Steiermark. ⓔ bookingcenter@jgh.at	☎ (3857) 8495 🖷 (3857) 8495-4	50	01.01–31.03; 01.05–31.10; 25–31.12	⑪ Ⓡ Ⓟ
▲ Neu-Nagelberg ⓥ 3871 Neu-Nagelberg 114. ⓔ oejhv-noe@oejhv.or.at	☎ (2859) 7476 🖷 (2859) 7476	39	11.01–23.12	⑪ Ⓡ Ⓟ
▲ Neusiedl ⓦ 7100 Neusiedl am See, Herbergsgasse 1, Burgenland.	☎ (2167) 2252 🖷 (2167) 2252	86	01.03–30.11	⑪⑪ ⑪ Ⓡ Ⓟ
△ Neustift ⓦ 4143 Neustift im Mühlkreis 71, Rannahof, Oberösterreich. ⓔ jugendherberge@vpn.at	☎ (7284) 8196 🖷 (7284) 8396	100	🗓12	⑪⑪ ⑪ Ⓟ
▲ Obernberg ⓦ Jugendheim am Brenner, Obernberg 49, 6156 Obernberg. ⓔ spot.obernberg@alpenverein.at	☎ (5274) 87475 🖷 (5274) 87475	85	01.01–15.04; 01.06–30.09; 27–31.12 (⑪⑪ Only)	⑪ Ⓟ
▲ Oberndorf ⓥ 6372 Oberndorf, bei Kitzbühel/Tirol, Eberharting 1.	☎ (05352) 63651 🖷 (05352) 65201	104	01.01–31.10; 15–31.12	⑪⑪ ⑪ 6N Ⓟ ⑤
▲ Obertraun ⓦ 4831 Obertraun, Winkl 26, Oberösterreich.	☎ (6131) 360 🖷 (6131) 3604	160	🗓12	⑪⑪ ⑪ Ⓡ Ⓟ
△ Pernitz ⓦ 2763 Pernitz, Hauptstr 79, Niederösterreich.	☎ (2632) 72373	45	01.04–31.10	🚲
▲ Pfunds ⓥ JGH Dangl, A-6542 Pfunds 347, Tirol.	☎ (5474) 5244 🖷 (5474) 5244-4	60	01.05–20.10; 15.12–20.04	⑪⑪ ⑪ Ⓡ 🚲 Ⓟ
△ Ramingstein ⓥ - Burg Finstergrün 5591 Ramingstein, Wald 65	☎ (06475) 228 🖷 (06475) 228	160	01.05–15.10	⑪ Ⓟ
△ Rechnitz ⓥ Burgenland, 7471 Rechnitz, Hochstrasse 1	☎ (3363) 79245 🖷 (3363) 79245	52	🗓12	⑪ 🚲 Ⓟ
▲ Reutte-Höfen ⓥ 6600 Reutte, JGH am Graben 1, Tirol. ⓔ jgh-hoefen@tirol.com	☎ (5672) 626440 🖷 (5672) 626444	58	01.01–02.11; 15–31.12	⑪⑪ ⑪ Ⓡ
△ Riegersburg ⓦ 8333 Riegersburg 3, "Im Cillitor", Steiermark. ⓔ bookingcenter@jgh.at	☎ (3153) 8217 🖷 (3153) 8217-88	53	01.05–31.10	⑪ Ⓡ Ⓟ
▲ Rust ⓦ - JGH Rust 7071 Rust, Conradplatz 1.	☎ (2685) 591 🖷 (2685) 591-4	58	🗓12	⑪⑪ ⑪ Ⓡ ⒸⒸ Ⓟ 🐾
▲ Salzburg ⓥ ⒾⒷⓃ JGH, A-5020 Salzburg Nonntal, Josef-Preis Allee 18. ⓔ oejhv-sbg-jgh-nonntal@oejhv.or.at	☎ (662) 8426700 🖷 (662) 841101	390	🗓12	⑪⑪ ⑪ Ⓡ 1SW ♿ ⒸⒸ 🚲 Ⓟ ⑤
▲ Salzburg ⓦ - Aigner Strasse 5026 Salzburg, Aigner Strasse 34.	☎ (662) 623248 🖷 (662) 623248	105	01.07–31.08	⑪⑪ ⑪ 2NW Ⓟ

Location/Address	Telephone No. Fax No.	Beds	Opening Dates	Facilities
▲ **Salzburg** Ⓦ - Eduard Heinrich Haus (IBN) **5020 Salzburg - Josefiau,** **Eduard-Heinrich Str 2.** ⊖ hostel.eduard-heinrich@salzburg.co.at	☏ (662) 625976 ℻ (662) 627980	120	🄻	♦♦ 🍴 ⓡ 3SW ⒸⒸ P 🄶
▲ **Salzburg** Ⓦ 5071 Salzburg-Walserfeld, Schulstrasse 18	☏ (662) 851377 ℻ (662) 853301	156	01.07–25.08	♦♦ 🍴 P
▲ **Schladming** Ⓥ (IBN) **8970 Schladming, Coburgstrasse 253,** **Steiermark.** ⊖ jgh.schladming@jgh.at	☏ (3687) 24531 ℻ (3687) 24531 Ext 88	198	01.01–31.10; 24–31.12	♦♦ 🍴 ⓡ ⒸⒸ P
▲ **Sillian** Ⓦ 9920 Sillian-Arnbach 37, Tirol.	☏ (4842) 6321 ℻ (4842) 6321-20	37	01.05–31.10	✇
▲ **Spital am Pyhrn** Ⓦ 'Lindenhof', 4582 Spital am Pyhrn 77, Oberösterreich.	☏ (7563) 214	140	01.01–31.10; 01–31.12	♦♦ 🍴 P
▲ **Spittal an der Drau** Ⓥ 9800 Spittal an der Drau, Stadiongelände, zur Seilbahn 2 neben Goldecktalstation, Kärnten.	☏ (4762) 3252 ℻ (4762) 3252 Ext 4	69	🄻	🍴 P
▲ **Spittal/Goldeck** Ⓦ 9800 Spittal/Goldeck, Kärnten.	☏ (4762) 2701	45	26.12.99–24. 03.2000; 28.06–20.09	♦♦ 🍴 ⓡ
△ *Steyr* Ⓥ *4400 Steyr, Josef Hafnerstrasse 14,* *Oberösterreich.*	☏ *(7252) 45580* ℻ *(7252) 45580*	*45*	*06.01–22.12*	🍴 ✇ P
△ *Stummerberg* Ⓦ *6272 Kaltenbach/Stumm, Zillertal,* *Stummerberg 68, Tirol.*	☏ *(5283) 3577*	*40*	🄻	♦♦ 🍴 ✇ P
▲ **St Gilgen** Ⓥ - JGH Schafbergblick **YGH, 5340 St Gilgen,** **Mondseerstraße 7-11, Salzburg.** ⊖ jgh.stgilgen@oejhv.or.at	☏ (6227) 2365 ℻ (6227) 2365 Ext 75	128	24.01–16.12	♦♦ 🍴 ⓡ P
▲ **St Johann im Pongau** Ⓥ 5600 St Johann im Pongau, JH Weitenmoos, Salzburg. ⊖ rohrmoser@weitenmoos.at	☏ (6412) 6222 ℻ (6412) 6222 Ext 4	150	02.12–14.10	♦♦ 🍴 P
▲ **St Martin am Tennengebirge** Ⓥ JH Sonnrain, A-5522 St Martin Nr 100, Salzburg. ⊖ oejhv-salzburg@oejhv.or.at	☏ (6463) 7318 ℻ (6463) 7318 Ext 3	126	01.01–17.04; 11.05–30.09; 16–31.12	♦♦ 🍴 4SE P
▲ **St Michael im Lungau** Ⓥ A-5582 Herbergsgasse 348, Salzburg. ⊖ oejhv-salzburg@oejhv.or.at	☏ (6477) 8630 ℻ (6477) 8630-3	188	01.01–17.04; 11.05–30.09; 16–31.12	♦♦ 🍴 4SE ✇ P
▲ **St Sebastian/Mariazell** Ⓥ - Sportzentrum Mariazellerland A-8630 St. Sebastian/ Mariazell. ⊖ jgh.mariazellerland@jgh.at	☏ (3882) 2669 ℻ (3882) 2669-88	136	🄻	♿ ⒸⒸ 🄶 ☕

Location/Address	Telephone No. Fax No.	Beds	Opening Dates	Facilities
△ *Ternitz* Ⓥ *2630 Ternitz, Straße des 12. Februar 38.*	☎ *(2630) 38483* 🖷 *(2630) 38483-4*	*30*	*01.01–31.01;* *15.02–15.10;* *15.11–31.12*	⑩ 🅿
▲ Uderns Ⓥ 6271 Uderns, Finsing 73, YGH "Finsingerhof".	☎ (5288) 62010, (6644) 109514 🖷 (5288) 62866	89	🔲12	�037 ⑩ Ⓡ 🅿
▲ Ulmerfeld-Hausmening Ⓥ 3363 Ulmerfeld-Hausmening Burgweg 1 Schloss, Niederösterreich. ✉ oejhv-noe@oejhv.or.at	☎ (7475) 54080	62	01.04–31.10	♂♀ ⑩ Ⓡ 🅿 ⓐ
▲ Ulrichsberg Ⓦ 4161 Ulrichsberg, Falkensteinstr.1.	☎ (7288) 7046 🖷 (7288) 7046-20	34	🔲12	♂♀ ⑩ Ⓡ ♿
Vienna/Vienne/Viena ☞ Wien				
▲ **Villach** Ⓥ 〔IBN〕 **9500 Villach, St Martin, Dinzlweg 34,** **Kärnten.** ✉ jgh.villach@oejhv.or.at	☎ **(4242) 56368** 🖷 **(4242)** **56368-20**	**144**	🔲12	♂♀ ⑩ 🅿
△ *Weissenbach am Attersee* Ⓥ *-* *Europacamp* *Franz von Schönthanallee 42,* *4854 Weissenbach, Oberösterreich.*	☎ *(7663) 220* 🖷 *(7663) 220-14*	*118*	*29.05–30.08*	⑩ 🅿 ⓐ 🍴
▲ Wels Ⓥ 4600 Wels, Dragonerstr.22.	☎ (7242) 235757, 67284 🖷 (7242) 235756	50	07.01–23.12	⑩ 🅿
▲ Weyer Ⓦ 3335 Weyer, Mühlein 56, Oberösterreich.	☎ (7355) 6284 🖷 (7355) 62844	136	🔲12	♂♀ ⑩ Ⓡ ♿ 🅿
▲ Weyregg Ⓦ 4852 Weyregg 3, Oberösterreich.	☎ (7664) 2780 🖷 (7664) 27804	42	01.05–31.10	♂♀ ⑩ Ⓡ 🅿
△ *Wien* Ⓥ *Ruthensteiner JH, 1150 Wien,* *Robert Hamerling 24.* ✉ *hostel.ruthensteiner@telecom.at*	☎ *(1) 8934202,* *8932796* 🖷 *(1) 8932796*	*77*	🔲12	♂♀ ⑩ 〔5W〕 ☞
▲ Wien Ⓥ 〔IBN〕 Schloßherberge am Wilhelminenberg, 1160 Wien, Savoyenstrasse 2. ✉ shb@wigast.com	☎ (1) 4858503700 🖷 (1) 4858503702	164	🔲12	♂♀ ⑩ Ⓡ 〔10W〕 〔CC〕 🅿 ⓐ
▲ Wien Ⓥ - Brigittenau 〔IBN〕 **1200 Wien, Friedrich Engelsplatz 24.** ✉ jgh.1200wien@chello.at	☎ (1) 33282940, 3300598 🖷 (1) 3308379	434	01.01-05.02; 20.02-31.12	♂♀ ⑩ Ⓡ 〔4NW〕 ♿ 🅿 ⓐ
▲ Wien Ⓥ - Hütteldorf 〔IBN〕 **1130 Wien, Schlossberggasse 8.** ✉ jgh@wigast.com	☎ (1) 8771501, 8770263 🖷 (1) 8770263 Ext 2	295	🔲12	♂♀ ⑩ Ⓡ 〔10W〕 〔CC〕 🅿 ⓐ
▲ Wien Ⓦ - Myrthengasse 〔IBN〕 **1070 Wien, Myrthengasse 7,** **Neustiftgasse 85.** ✉ hostel@chello.at	☎ (1) 52363160 🖷 (1) 5235849	241	🔲12.	♂♀ ⑩ Ⓡ 〔2W〕 ♿ ⓐ
△ *Wien* Ⓦ *- Turmherberge Don Bosco* *1030 Wien, Lechnerstrasse 12.*	☎ *(1) 7131494*	*53*	*01.03–30.11*	〔3SE〕

Location/Address	Telephone No. Fax No.	Beds	Opening Dates	Facilities
▲ **Wiener Neustadt** Ⓥ 2700 Wiener Neustadt, Europahaus, Promenade 1, Niederösterreich. (50km SE of Wien) e oejhv-noe@oejhv.or.at	t (2622) 29695 f (2622) 642103	36	01.07–31.08	R P
▲ **Zell am See** Ⓦ **5700 Zell am See, Haus der Jugend, Seespitzstrasse 13, Salzburg.** e hostel.zell-see@salzburg.co.at	t (6542) 57185 f (6542) 571854	106	01.12–31.10	R CC P

Travel, instead of broadening the mind, often merely lengthens the conversation.

Voyager, plutôt que d'élargir l'esprit a tendance simplement à rallonger la conversation.

Anstatt zu bilden, bietet Reisen oft lediglich mehr Stoff zur Unterhaltung.

A menudo, en vez de ampliar los horizontes de las personas, lo único que hacen los viajes es alargar la conversación.

Elizabeth Drew

HOSTELLING
INTERNATIONAL

Make your credit card bookings at these centres
Réservez par carte de crédit auprès des centres suivants
Reservieren Sie per Kreditkarte bei diesen Zentren
Reserve con tarjeta de crédito en los siguientes centros

English

Australia	☎ (2) 9261 1111
Canada	☎ (1) (800) 663 5777
England & Wales	☎ (1629) 581 418
France	☎ (1) 44 89 87 27
Northern Ireland	☎ (1232) 324 733
Republic of Ireland	☎ (1) 830 1766
New Zealand	☎ (9) 303 9524
Scotland	☎ (541) 553 255
Switzerland	☎ (1) 360 1414
USA	☎ (202) 783 6161

Français

Angleterre & Pays de Galles	☎ (1692) 581 418
Australie	☎ (2) 9261 1111
Canada	☎ (1) (800) 663 5777
Écosse	☎ (541) 553 255
États-Unis	☎ (202) 783 6161
France	☎ (1) 44 89 87 27
Irlande du Nord	☎ (1232) 324 733
Nouvelle-Zélande	☎ (9) 303 9524
République d'Irlande	☎ (1) 830 1766
Suisse	☎ (1) 360 1414

Deutsch

Australien	☎ (2) 9261 1111
England & Wales	☎ (1629) 581 418
Frankreich	☎ (1) 44 89 87 27
Irland	☎ (1) 830 1766
Kanada	☎ (1) (800) 663 5777
Neuseeland	☎ (9) 303 9524
Nordirland	☎ (1232) 324 733
Schottland	☎ (541) 553 255
Schweiz	☎ (1) 360 1414
USA	☎ (202) 783 6161

Español

Australia	☎ (2) 9261 1111
Canadá	☎ (1) (800) 663 5777
Escocia	☎ (541) 553 255
Estados Unidos	☎ (202) 783 6161
Francia	☎ (1) 44 89 87 27
Inglaterra y Gales	☎ (1629) 581 418
Irlanda del Norte	☎ (1232) 324 733
Nueva Zelanda	☎ (9) 303 9524
República de Irlanda	☎ (1) 830 1766
Suiza	☎ (1) 360 1414

IBN INTERNATIONAL BOOKING NETWORK

Belgium

BELGIQUE
BELGIEN
BELGICA

Ⓥ **Vlaamse Jeugdherbergcentrale,**
Van Stralenstraat 40,
B-2060 Antwerp, Belgium.

☎ (32) 03 2327218
🖷 (32) 03 2318126
✉ info@vjh.be
www.vjh.be

Office Hours: Monday-Friday 09.00-18.00hrs. Saturday (Easter-15.09) 09.00-13.00hrs.

Ⓛ **Les Auberges de Jeunesse,**
Rue de la Sablonnière 28 B-1000, Brussels, Belgium.

☎ (32) 02 2195676
🖷 (32) 02 2191451
✉ info@laj.be
www.laj.be

Office Hours: Monday-Friday, 09.00-12.30hrs/13.00-17.00hrs

A copy of the Hostel Directory for this Country can be obtained from:
The National Office.

Capital:	Brussels	**Population:**	10,000,100
Language:	Dutch, French, German	**Size:**	30,515 sq km
Currency:	BEF (Belgian franc)	**Telephone Country Code:**	32

NETHERLANDS

Ostende ▲Blankenberge
Oostende ▲Dudzele   Antwerpen   ▲Zoersel
Oostduinkerke ▲Brugge-Europa
              ▲Maldegem   ▲Nijlen
                      ▲Gent   Westerlo   Bokrijk-Genk ▲
Kortrijk ▲   ▲Diest
         Brussels ▲ Brussels (3)
Geraardsbergen ▲   ▲Tongeren
Tournai ▲ Huizingen ▲   ▲St Martens-Voeren
                                Liège ●Liège
                        Namur ▲   ▲Tilff ▲Malmedy
                                    Sankt Vith

GERMANY

BELGIUM

              ▲Champlon
      Bouillon ▲

FRANCE

Ⓝ

```
 0  |____50____100____150 KM
          50        MLS
```

English

BELGIAN HOSTELS

The 'Vlaamse Jeugdherbergcentrale', hostels marked Ⓥ, runs hostels in the northern region. 'Les Auberges de Jeunesse' (LAJ) hostels marked Ⓛ, operate in the southern part of the country. Both Associations have hostels in the capital-city of Brussels.

Hostels are open 08.00-23.00hrs and in Brussels 07.00-02.00hrs. Some hostels close reception during the day between 10.00 and 17.00hrs or during the winter for one night a week.

Expect to pay 420-495 BF per night including breakfast plus bed linen hire if required. Special prices are available to families with children. Most hostels have family rooms which you should book in advance.

PASSPORTS AND VISAS

An identity card is sufficient for nationals of EU countries. In any other case, please contact Belgian Embassy or Consulate in your country of residence.

BANKING HOURS

Banks are open Monday to Friday, 09.00-16.00hrs.

POST OFFICES

Post Offices are open Monday to Friday, 09.00-17.00hrs.

SHOPPING HOURS

Shops are normally open 09.00-18.00hrs, Monday to Saturday.

TRAVEL

Rail

Rail travel is extremely good especially with a Benelux Tourrail Pass. The "Go-Pass" for young people up to 26 years and the "Multipass" for small groups offer cheap tickets.

Bus

Brussels has a metro system, buses and trams. All larger cities have good local buses. There is also a national bus company for longer distances.

Ferry

Ferry services are available from Oostende to Ramsgate and Zeebrugge to Hull.

Driving

Driving is on the right-hand side. Speed limits range from 50-120kmph. There is a good highway network.

Français

AUBERGES DE JEUNESSE BELGES

La 'Vlaamse Jeugdherbergcentrale', auberges indiquées Ⓥ, gère les auberges situées dans la région du nord. 'Les Auberges de Jeunesse', auberges indiquées Ⓛ, gère celles qui se trouvent dans la partie sud. Les deux associations possèdent des auberges dans la capitale, Bruxelles.

Les auberges sont ouvertes de 8h à 23h et, à Bruxelles, de 7h à 2h. Pour certaines auberges, l'accueil ferme dans la journée entre 10h et 17h. En outre, en hiver, quelques-unes ferment une nuit par semaine.

Une nuit avec petit-déjeuner coûte de 420 à 495 FB, plus location de draps, éventuellement. Dans les auberges belges, des tarifs spéciaux sont proposés pour les familles avec enfants. La plupart des auberges peuvent offrir des chambres familiales qui doivent être réservées à l'avance.

PASSEPORTS ET VISAS

Une carte d'identité suffit pour les citoyens des pays de l'Union Européenne. Dans tous les autres cas, veuillez contacter l'Ambassade ou le Consulat de Belgique dans votre propre pays.

HEURES D'OUVERTURE DES BANQUES

Les banques sont ouvertes du lundi au vendredi, de 9h à 16h.

BUREAUX DE POSTE

Les bureaux de poste sont ouverts du lundi au vendredi, de 9h à 17h.

HEURES D'OUVERTURE DES MAGASINS

Les magasins sont en général ouverts de 9h à 18h, du lundi au samedi.

DEPLACEMENTS

Trains

Les déplacements en train sont excellents, surtout si vous avez une carte Bénélux Tourrail. Les cartes "Go-Pass" pour les jeunes jusqu'à 26 ans et "Multipass" pour les petits groupes permettent d'obtenir des billets à bas prix.

Autobus

Bruxelles possède un réseau de métro, de bus et de trams. Toutes les grandes villes ont un bon service d'autobus. Il existe également une compagnie d'autobus nationale pour les longs parcours.

Ferry-boats

Les traversées s'effectuent d'Ostende à Ramsgate et de Zeebrugge à Hull.

Automobiles

La conduite est à droite. Les limitations de vitesse vont de 50 à 120km/h. Le réseau autoroutier est très développé.

Deutsch

BELGISCHE JUGENDHERBERGEN

Die mit Ⓥ gekennzeichneten Herbergen in der nördlichen Region werden von der 'Vlaamse Jeugdherbergcentrale' betrieben. 'Les Auberges de Jeunesse' (LAJ), mit Ⓛ gekennzeichnete Herbergen, im südlichen Landesteil tätig. Beide Verbände haben Herbergen in der Hauptstadt Brüssel.

Die Herbergen sind von 08.00-23.00 Uhr und in Brüssel von 07.00-02.00 Uhr geöffnet. Einige Herbergen schließen ihren Empfang während des Tages zwischen 10.00 und 17.00 Uhr. Einige Herbergen schließen im Winter für eine Nacht pro Woche.

Es ist mit einem Preis von 420-495 bfr pro Nacht plus Frühstück und, bei Bedarf, einer Gebühr für die Miete von Bettwäsche zu rechnen. Für Familien mit Kindern werden Sonderpreise angeboten. Die meisten Herbergen haben Familienzimmer, die vorbestellt werden sollten.

PÄSSE UND VISA

Für Staatsangehörige der EU-Länder genügt ein Personalausweis. Andere Personen wenden sich bitte an die Belgische Botschaft oder das Belgische Konsulat in dem Land, in dem sie ihren Wohnsitz haben.

GESCHÄFTSSTUNDEN DER BANKEN

Die Banken sind montags bis freitags von 09.00-16.00 Uhr geöffnet.

POSTÄMTER

Postämter sind montags bis freitags von 09.00-17.00 Uhr geöffnet.

LADENÖFFNUNGSZEITEN

Die Geschäfte sind im allgemeinen montags bis samstags von 09.00-18.00 Uhr geöffnet.

REISEN

Eisenbahn

Der Eisenbahnverkehr ist außerordentlich gut, besonders mit einem Benelux Tourrail Pass. Der "Go-Pass" für junge Leute bis zu 26 Jahren und der "Multipass" für kleine Gruppen ermöglichen preisgünstiges Eisenbahnfahren.

Busse

Brüssel hat ein U-Bahn-Netz, Busse und Straßenbahnen. Alle größeren Städte haben gute Nahverkehrsbusse. Es gibt auch ein überregionales Busunternehmen für längere Strecken.

Fähren

Von Oostende nach Ramsgate und von Seebrügge nach Hull gibt es einen Fährverkehr.

Autofahren

Es herrscht Rechtsverkehr. Das Tempolimit reicht von 50 - 120 km/h. Es gibt ein gutes Straßennetz.

Español

ALBERGUES JUVENILES BELGAS

La "Vlaamse Jeugdherbergcentrale" (albergues con el símbolo Ⓥ), es responsable de los albergues de la región norte. "Les Auberges de Jeunesse" (LAJ) (albergues con el símbolo Ⓛ), administran los albergues del sur del país. Ambas Asociaciones tienen albergues en la capital, Bruselas.

Los albergues están abiertos de 8 h. a 23 h. y, en Bruselas, de 7 h. a 2 h. La recepción de algunos de ellos cierra durante el día entre las 10 h. y las 17 h. y, en invierno, ciertos albergues cierran una noche a la semana.

El precio por noche con desayuno oscila entre 420 y 495 francos belgas y las sábanas, si las necesita, se cobran aparte. Los albergues belgas ofrecen tarifas especiales para las familias con niños. La mayoría disponen de habitaciones familiares que es necesario reservar con antelación.

PASAPORTES Y VISADOS

Los ciudadanos de los países pertenecientes a la Unión Europea sólo necesitan su carnet de identidad. En los demás casos, infórmese en la embajada o consulado belgas de su país.

HORARIO DE LOS BANCOS

Los bancos abren de lunes a viernes, de 9 h. a 16 h.

OFICINAS DE CORREOS

Las oficinas de correos abren de lunes a viernes, de 9 h. a 17 h.

HORARIO COMERCIAL

Las tiendas suelen abrir de 9 h. a 18 h., de lunes a sábado.

DESPLAZAMIENTOS

Tren

La red ferroviaria es excelente, especialmente con la tarjeta "Benelux Tourrail". Las tarjetas "Go-Pass" para jóvenes de hasta 26 años y "Multipass" para grupos pequeños permiten conseguir billetes a precios reducidos.

Autobús

Bruselas cuenta con una red de metro, autobuses y tranvías. Todas las grandes ciudades disfrutan de un buen servicio de autobuses. Existe también una compañía nacional de autobuses de largo recorrido.

Ferry

Existe un servicio de ferrys entre Ostende y Ramsgate, y entre Zeebrugge y Hull.

Automóvil

Se conduce por la derecha. Los límites de velocidad oscilan entre 50 y 120 km/h. La red de carreteras es buena.

Antwerpen [Ⓥ] -
Op Sinjoorke

2020 Antwerpen,
Eric Sasselaan 2.
☏ 03 2380273
ℹ 03 2481932

Open Dates:	07.01-15.12
Open Hours:	07.00-10.00; 16.00-24.00hrs (night access)
Reservations:	IBN CC
Price Range:	BEF 420 € 10.41 BB inc ⌟
Beds:	126 - 2x¹ 2x² 8x⁴ 10x⁶ 3x⁶
Facilities:	♿ ⏱ 8x ⏱ 🍽 ☕ 🏠 📺 📋 2 x 🍷 ⬜ 🖼 8 🅿 🚲 ♨ ⛰ 🔍
Directions:	4S from city centre
✈	Brussels 45km; Antwerp 5km
🚂	Antwerp Central 5km, Antwerp South 500m
🚌	27 Central Station, 25 Groenplaats (direction Bouwcentrum) 100m
U	2 Central Station (direction Hoboken U Bouwcentrum) 100m

Brugge [Ⓥ] - Europa

8310 Brugge 4/Assebroek,
Baron Ruzettelaan 143.
☏ 050 352679
ℹ 050 353732

Open Dates:	09.01-15.12
Open Hours:	07.30-10.00; 13.00-23.00hrs (night access)
Reservations:	IBN CC
Price Range:	BEF 420-495 € 10.41-12.27 BB inc ⌟
Beds:	212 - 4x¹ 22x⁴ 20x⁶
Facilities:	♿ 22x ⏱ 🍽 ☕ 🏠 📺 2 x 🍷 🖼 8 🅿 🚲 ♨ 🔍
Directions:	2SE from city centre
✈	Brussels 85km
🚂	Brugge 1.5km
🚌	2 300m; 749 100m

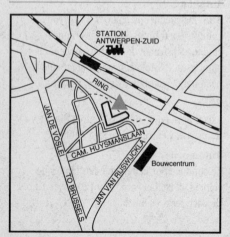

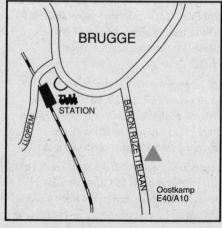

Brussels Ⓛ - Generation Europe

4 Rue de l'Eléphant,
1080 Bruxelles.
☎ 02 4103858
🖷 02 4103905
✉ brussels.europe@laj.be

Open Dates:	16.01-30.12
Open Hours:	07.30-01.00hrs
Reservations:	(IBN) ⊂CC⊃
Price Range:	BEF 420-800 € 10.41-19.83 BBinc 🛏
Beds:	160 - 10x² 24x⁴ 2x⁶ 4x⁶
Facilities:	♿ �203 26x 👫 🍽 ≗ 📺 🕮 4 x🍷 🔥 🖼 ♒ 🔢 💲 Ⓟ ⒤ 📶 🐾 🏎 🌐 🔍 🏠 🏬

Directions:	
✈	Zaventem 15km
⛴	Zeebrugge 125km
🚎	South Station 2km
🚃	18 500m ap Porte de Flandres
Ⓤ	Comte de Flandre 300m

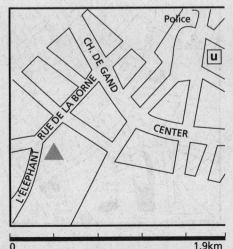

Brussels Ⓛ - Jacques Brel

Rue de la Sablonnière 30,
1000 Bruxelles.
☎ 02 2180187
🖷 02 2172005
✉ brussels.brel@laj.be

Open Dates:	01.01-16.12
Open Hours:	07.30-01.00hrs
Reservations:	(IBN) ⊂CC⊃
Price Range:	BEF 420-800 € 10.41-19.83 BBinc 🛏
Beds:	173 - 2x¹ 21x² 5x³ 11x⁴ 6x⁶ 3x⁶
Facilities:	♿ �203 16x 👫 🍽 ≗ 📱 🕮 4 x🍷 🔥 🖼 ♒ ⊜ ⒤ 📶 🔍 🏬

Directions:	1NE from city centre
✈	Brussels 20km
A🚐	BH, BZ 200m
⛴	Zeebrugge 125km
🚎	Gare Bruxelles Nord 2km
🚌	61 200m ap Botanique
🚃	92, 93, 94 200m ap Botanique
Ⓤ	Madou 200m; Botanique 200m

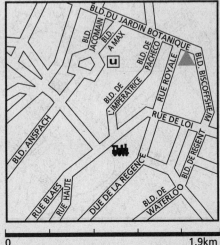

Brussels Ⓥ - Bruegel

1000 Brussels,
Heilig Geeststraat 2. (Corner:
Keizerslaan-Kapellekerk/Eglise de la
Chapelle)
☎ 02 5110436
📠 02 5120711
📧 jeugdherberg.bruegel@ping.be

Open Dates:	🗓️
Open Hours:	07.00-02.00hrs
Reservations:	(CC)
Price Range:	BEF 420-800 € 10.40-19.83 [BB]inc 🍽️
Beds:	136 - 5x¹ 21x² 2x³ 9x⁴ 1x⁵ 1x⁶ 3x⁶
Facilities:	♿ ⛹ 31x ⛹ 🍴 ☕ 🏛️ 📺 3 x🍷 📷 🔟 🛄 🚲 ⛰️ ⊘
Directions:	1S from city centre
✈	Brussels 15km
🚂	Central Station 300m
🚌	20 Midi Station 50m ap Chapelle
Ⓤ	Central Station 300m

Gent Ⓥ - De Draecke

9000 Gent,
St Widostraat 11.
☎ 09 2337050
📠 09 2338001
📧 youthhostel.gent@skynet.be

Open Dates:	🗓️
Open Hours:	07.00-23.00hrs (night Access)
Reservations:	(IBN) (CC)
Price Range:	BEF 420-585 € 10.41-14.50 [BB]inc 🍽️
Beds:	106 - 6x² 3x³ 10x⁴ 3x⁵ 5x⁶
Facilities:	⛹ 27x ⛹ 🍴 ☕ 🏛️ 📺 📷 1 x🍷 📷 🔟 🛄 🚲
Directions:	
✈	Brussel 65km
🚢	Oostende 55km
🚂	Gent St Pieters 4km
🚊	No. 1, 10, 11, 12, 13 200m ap Gravensteen (Castle)

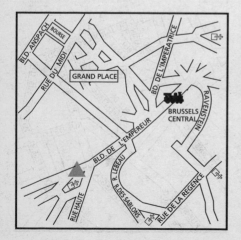

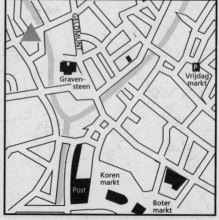

Liège [Ⓛ] -
Georges Simenon

**Rue Georges Simenon 2,
4020 Liège.**
- ☎ 04 3445689
- ✆ 04 3445687
- ✉ liège@laj.be

Open Dates:	01-08.01; 12.02-31.12
Open Hours:	07.30-01.00hrs
Reservations:	IBN CC
Price Range:	BEF 495-800 € 12.27-19.83 BBinc SH
Beds:	204 - 16x⁴ 12x⁵ 4x⁶
Facilities:	♿ ⚥ 40x ⚥ ⛏ ⛴ 📺 📖4 x 🍷 ▣ ▣ 8 ⚡ ⓘ 🔌 ♨

Directions:

✈	Brussels 100km
🚆	Liège Guillemins 2km
🚌	No. 4 300m
Attractions:	⛵500m

Oostende [Ⓥ] -
De Ploate

**8400 Oostende,
Langestraat 82.**
- ☎ 059 805297
- ✆ 059 809274
- ✉ deploate@online.be

Open Dates:	02.01-01.12; 15-22.12; 25-30.12
Open Hours:	07.30-24.00hrs (night access)
Reservations:	CC
Price Range:	BEF 465 € 11.52 BBinc
Beds:	124 - 3x³ 4x⁴ 3x⁵ 2x⁶ 9x⁶
Facilities:	⚥ 21x ⚥ ⛏ 🍷 ⛴ 📺 📖 🧺 1 x🍷 ▣ 8 ⓘ ♨

Directions:

✈	Oostende 5km
A🚐	Line 6 Airport 5km
⛴	Oostende 2km
🚆	Oostende 2km

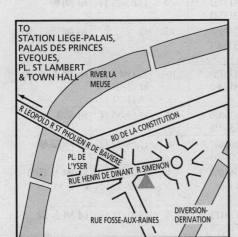

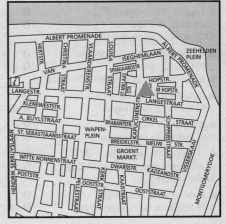

0 ━━━━━━━━━━━━━━━ 1.9km

Location/Address	Telephone No. / Fax No.	Beds	Opening Dates	Facilities
▲ **Antwerpen** Ⓥ - Op Sinjoorke [IBN] 2020 Antwerpen, Eric Sasselaan 2.	☎ 03 2380273 📠 03 2481932	126	07.01–15.12	ᛁᛁᛁ �𝍈 [4S] ♿ CC P 🏠 🍵
▲ **Blankenberge** Ⓥ - De Wullok 8370 Blankenberge, Ruitersstraat 9.	☎ 050 415307 📠 050 426014	79	[12]	ᛁᛁᛁ �𝍈 ♿ 🧺 P 🍵
▲ **Bokrijk/Genk** Ⓥ - De Roerdomp 3600 Bokrijk/Genk, Boekrakelaan 30.	☎ 089 356220 📠 089 303980	112	27.02–05.11	ᛁᛁᛁ �𝍈 ♿ P 🍵
▲ **Bouillon** Ⓛ - Sur La Hauteur Chemin du Christ 16, 6830 Bouillon. ✉ bouillon@laj.be	☎ 061 468137 📠 061 467818	136	01–08.01; 12.02–29.11; 16–31.12	ᛁᛁᛁ ⟨⟩ Ⓡ CC 🧺 P 🏠 🍵
▲ **Brugge** Ⓥ - Europa [IBN] 8310 Brugge 4/Assebroek, Baron Ruzettelaan 143.	☎ 050 352679 📠 050 353732	212	09.01–15.12	ᛁᛁᛁ ⟨⟩ [2SE] ♿ CC P 🍵
▲ **Brugge** Ⓥ - Brugge/Dudzele "Herdersbrug" 8380 Dudzele/Brugge, Louis Coiseaukaai 46.	☎ 050 599321 📠 050 599349	106	15.01–15.12	ᛁᛁᛁ ⟨⟩ ♿ P 🏠 🍵
▲ **Brussels** Ⓛ - Generation Europe [IBN] 4 Rue de l'Eléphant, 1080 Bruxelles. ✉ brussels.europe@laj.be	☎ 02 4103858 📠 02 4103905	160	16.01–30.12	ᛁᛁᛁ ⟨⟩ ♿ CC P 🏠
▲ **Brussels** Ⓛ - Jacques Brel [IBN] Rue de la Sablonnière 30, 1000 Bruxelles. ✉ brussels.brel@laj.be	☎ 02 2180187 📠 02 2172005	173	01.01–16.12	ᛁᛁᛁ ⟨⟩ [1NE] ♿ CC 🏠
▲ **Brussels** Ⓥ - Bruegel 1000 Brussels, Heilig Geeststraat 2. (Corner: Keizerslaan-Kapellekerk/ Eglise de la Chapelle) ✉ jeugdherberg.bruegel@ping.be	☎ 02 5110436 📠 02 5120711	136	[12]	ᛁᛁᛁ ⟨⟩ [1S] ♿ CC 🍵
▲ **Champlon** Ⓛ - Barriere De Champlon Rue de la Gendarmerie 6, Barrière de Champlon, 6971 Champlon. ✉ champlon@laj.be	☎ 084 455294 📠 084 457045	72	01–08.01; 12.02–29.11; 16–31.12	⟨⟩ Ⓡ CC 🧺 P 🏠 🍵
▲ **Diest** Ⓥ - Den Drossaard 3290 Diest, St Jansstraat 2 (Warande).	☎ 013 313721 📠 013 313721	70	15.02–15.11	ᛁᛁᛁ ⟨⟩ 🍵
▲ **Gent** Ⓥ - De Draecke [IBN] 9000 Gent, St Widostraat 11. ✉ youthhostel.gent@skynet.be	☎ 09 2337050 📠 09 2338001	106	[12]	ᛁᛁᛁ ⟨⟩ CC 🍵
▲ **Geraardsbergen** Ⓥ - 'T Schipke 9500 Geraardsbergen, Kampstraat 59. (Recreatiedomein 'De Gavers').	☎ 054 416189 📠 054 419461	104	[12] (ᛁᛁᛁ 01.01–01.04; 08.11–31.12)	ᛁᛁᛁ ⟨⟩ ♿ 🧺 🍵
▲ **Huizingen** Ⓥ - 'T Golvende Brabant 1654 Huizingen, Prov Domein.	☎ 02 3830026 📠 02 3830026	58	15.02–30.11	ᛁᛁᛁ Ⓡ 🧺
▲ **Kortrijk** Ⓥ - Groeninghe 8500 Kortrijk, Passionistenlaan 1A.	☎ 056 201442 📠 056 204663	96	17.01–22.12	ᛁᛁᛁ ⟨⟩ P 🍵
▲ **Liège** Ⓛ - Georges Simenon [IBN] Rue Georges Simenon 2, 4020 Liège. ✉ liège@laj.be	☎ 04 3445689 📠 04 3445687	204	01–08.01; 12.02–31.12	ᛁᛁᛁ ⟨⟩ ♿ CC 🧺 🏠
▲ **Maldegem** Ⓥ - Die Loyale 9990 Maldegem, Gentsesteenweg 124.	☎ 050 713121 📠 050 719070	74	15.02–15.11	ᛁᛁᛁ ⟨⟩ ♿ P

Location/Address	Telephone No. Fax No.	Beds	Opening Dates	Facilities
▲ **Malmédy** Ⓛ - Hautes Fagnes 4960 Malmédy, Bévercé 8a. 🅔 malmedy@laj.be	☎ 080 338386 🖷 080 770504	178	01.01–02.09; 25.09–24.11; 01–31.12	♦♦♦ ⦿ Ⓡ 1N ♿ ⒸⒸ ☞ Ⓟ ⊡ ☕
▲ **Namur** Ⓛ - Felicien Rops [IBN] 5000 Namur, Ave Félicien Rops, 8 La Plante. 🅔 namur@laj.be	☎ 081 223688 🖷 081 224412	100	01–08.01; 12.02–31.12	♦♦♦ ⦿ ♿ ⒸⒸ ☞ Ⓟ ⊡ ☕
▲ **Nijlen** Ⓥ - 'T Pannenhuis 2560 Nijlen, Wijngaardberg 42.	☎ 03 4110733 🖷 03 4110725	64	15.02–15.11	♦♦♦ ⦿ ☞ ☕
▲ **Oostduinkerke** Ⓥ - De Peerdevisser 8670 Oostduinkerke, Duinparklaan 41	☎ 058 512649 🖷 058 522880	135	15.01–15.12	♦♦♦ ⦿ ♿ ☕
▲ **Oostende** Ⓥ - De Ploate **8400 Oostende, Langestraat 82.** 🅔 deploate@online.be	☎ 059 805297 🖷 059 809274	124	02.01–01.12; 15–22.12; 25–30.12	♦♦♦ ⦿ ⒸⒸ ☕
▲ **Sankt-Vith** Ⓥ - Ardennen-Eifel 4780 St Vith, Rodterstrasse 13A.	☎ 080 229331 🖷 080 229332	90	01.01–23.12; 27–31.12	♦♦♦ ⦿ ♿ Ⓟ ☕
▲ **Tilff** Ⓛ - Ferme du Château 4130 Tilff, Esplanade de L'abeille 9. 🅔 tilff@laj.be	☎ 04 3882100 🖷 04 3445687	35	01–08.01; 12.02–31.12	Ⓡ ☞ Ⓟ
▲ **Tongeren** Ⓥ - Begeinhof 3700 Tongeren, St Ursulastraat 1.	☎ 012 391370 🖷 012 391348	82	🗓	♦♦♦ ⦿ ♿ Ⓟ ☕
▲ **Tournai** Ⓛ 7500 Tournai, Rue Saint-Martin 64. 🅔 tournai@laj.be	☎ 069 216136 🖷 069 216140	100	01–08.01; 12.02–29.11; 16–31.12	♦♦♦ ⦿ Ⓡ ♿ ⒸⒸ ☞ ☕
▲ **Voeren** Ⓥ - De Veurs 3790 St Martens Voeren, Comberg 29B.	☎ 04 3811110 🖷 04 3811313	90	06.03–15.11; 23–31.12	♦♦♦ ⦿ ☕
▲ **Westerlo** Ⓥ - Boswachtershuis 2260 Westerlo, Papendreef 1.	☎ 014 547938 🖷 014 547938	82	01.03–13.11 (For ♦♦♦ 01.03–23.12)	♦♦♦ ⦿ Ⓟ ☕
▲ **Zoersel** Ⓥ - Gagelhof 2980 Zoersel, Gagelhoflaan 18.	☎ 03 3851642 🖷 03 3851642	62	01.06–30.09 (For ♦♦♦ 🗓 Ⓡ)	♦♦♦ ⦿ Ⓡ ☞ Ⓟ ☕

International Booking Network

The advantages are clear

 INTERNATIONAL BOOKING NETWORK

netsavings@hostellinginternational.org.uk

Croatia

CROATIE
KROATIEN
CROACIA

**Hrvatski Ferijalni i Hostelski Savez
(Croatian Youth Hostel Association),
Savska cesta 5/1
10000 Zagreb, Croatia.**

t (385) 4829294
f (385) 4829296
e hfhs@zg.tel.hr
www.ncomp.com/hfhs

Office hours: Mon 08.00-18.00hrs; Tues-Fri 08.00-16.00hrs

Travel Section: HFHS Travel Section,
Dežmanova 9, 10000 Zagreb, Croatia.

t (385) (1) 4847474
f (385) (1) 4847472
e hfhs-cms@zg.tel.hr

Office hours: Mon-Fri 08.00-16.00hrs.

A copy of the Hostel Directory for this Country can be obtained from:
The National Office.

Capital:	Zagreb	**Population:**	4,784,265
Language:	Croatian	**Size:**	56,538 sq km.
Currency:	Kuna (Kn)	**Telephone Country Code:**	385

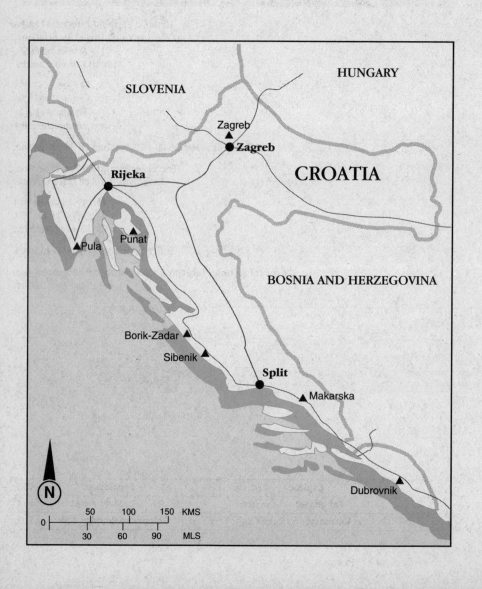

English

CROATIAN HOSTELS

Croatian Youth Hostels are situated in famous historical cities and areas with many interesting monuments, museums and galleries. Information about events, festivals, popular attractions, recreation, sports and other facilities for hostellers is available at Youth Hostels.

Hostels are generally open 08.00-23.00hrs. As Zagreb, Dubrovnik and Pula are the only hostels open all year, check individual entries carefully for opening dates. Expect to pay in the region of 16-20 DEM (58.00-80.00 kn) per night including visitors tax.

PASSPORTS AND VISAS

An Entrance Visa is necessary for citizens of all African and Latin American countries (except Chile), Asian and Pacific countries, USA, Canada, Luxembourg, Belgium, Netherlands, Albania, Greece and all countries of the former Soviet Union. Visas can be issued in Croatian Embassies, Consulates or at Croatian border offices.

HEALTH

Vaccinations are not required.

Reciprocal agreements on health care exist between Croatia and certain countries, entitling visitors to treatment on the same basis as Croatians. Enquire about obtaining a certificate before you travel. Other visitors are required to pay for treatment, but charges are very moderate in most cases.

BANKING HOURS

Monday-Friday 08.00-19.00hrs; Saturday 08.00-12.00hrs.

POST OFFICES

Monday-Friday 07.00-20.00hrs; Saturday 07.00-13.00hrs.

SHOPPING HOURS

Monday-Friday 08.00-20.00hrs; Saturday 08.00-13.00hrs.

TRAVEL

Air

Croatia Airlines run internal services linking major cities. The best air connections are via Zagreb.

Rail

Rail travel is good.

Bus

Coach services connect all towns. There are good bus services in the main towns.

Ferry

Coastal ferry routes link certain islands along the Adriatic Coast.

Driving

All towns are connected with good roads. Car hire is available in bigger towns.

Road assistance is organized by HAK (Croatian Auto-Club) and it operates on major roads and in towns by dialing 987. Drivers should have valid documents for themselves and the vehicle, as well as a green or blue insurance card.

Français

AUBERGES DE JEUNESSE CROATES

Les auberges de jeunesse croates sont situées dans des villes célèbres d'importance historique et dans des lieux où se trouvent des monuments intéressants, des musées et des galeries d'art. Elles vous renseigneront sur les événements, festivals, attractions populaires, loisirs, sports et autres services à l'intention des voyageurs les utilisant.

Les auberges sont en général ouvertes de 8h à 23h. Celles de Zagreb, de Dubrovnik et de Pula sont les seules à être ouvertes toute l'année; il est donc prudent de consulter la liste avec soin pour leurs dates d'ouverture. Une nuit vous coûtera entre 16-20 DEM (58,00-80,00 kn), taxe de séjour comprise.

PASSEPORTS ET VISAS

Un visa d'entrée est nécessaire pour les citoyens de tous les pays africains et latino-américains (sauf le Chili), les pays d'Asie et du Pacifique, les Etats-Unis, le Canada, le Luxembourg, la Belgique, les Pays-Bas, l'Albanie, la Grèce et tous les pays de l'ancienne Union Soviétique. Les visas peuvent être obtenus dans les Ambassades et Consulats croates ou dans les bureaux douaniers croates.

SOINS MEDICAUX

Aucune vaccination n'est requise.

Des accords médicaux réciproques ont été passés entre la Croatie et certains pays, permettant aux citoyens de ces pays de bénéficier des mêmes soins que ceux prodigués aux Croates. Renseignez-vous sur l'obtention d'un certificat avant votre départ. Les autres visiteurs devront payer tous frais médicaux encourus, mais ces derniers sont minimes dans la plupart des cas.

HEURES D'OUVERTURE DES BANQUES

Les banques sont ouvertes de 8h à 19h, du lundi au vendredi, et de 8h à 12h le samedi.

BUREAUX DE POSTE

Les bureaux de poste sont ouverts du lundi au vendredi, de 7h à 20h et le samedi de 7h à 13h.

HEURES D'OUVERTURE DES MAGASINS

Les magasins sont ouverts de 8h à 20h du lundi au vendredi et de 8h à 13h le samedi.

DEPLACEMENTS

Avions

La compagnie aérienne Croatia Airlines relie les villes principales par des vols intérieurs. Les meilleures correspondances aériennes passent par Zagreb.

Trains

Le service ferroviaire est bon.

Autobus

Les villes sont reliées par des services de cars. De bons services d'autobus desservent les villes principales.

Ferry-boats

Des services côtiers relient certaines îles le long de la côte adriatique.

Automobiles

Toutes les villes sont reliées par de bonnes routes. Il est possible de louer des voitures dans les grandes villes.

L'automobile-club croate, HAK, organise les dépannages sur les routes principales et dans les villes; appelez le 987. Les conducteurs doivent être munis de documents valides, pour eux-mêmes et pour leur véhicule, ainsi qu'une carte verte ou bleue (pour l'assurance).

Deutsch

KROATISCHE JUGENDHERBERGEN

Die kroatischen Jugendherbergen liegen in berühmten historischen Städten und Gegenden, wo es viele interessante Denkmäler, Museen und Galerien gibt. Die Jugendherbergen erteilen Auskünfte über Veranstaltungen, Feste, beliebte Sehenswürdigkeiten, Unterhaltungs- und Sportmöglichkeiten sowie andere Einrichtungen.

Die Herbergen sind im allgemeinen von 08.00-23.00 Uhr geöffnet. Da es nur in Zagreb,

Dubrovnik und Pula eine ganzjährig geöffnete Herberge gibt, sind die in den einzelnen Einträgen stehenden Öffnungstermine genau zu beachten. Es ist mit einem Preis von 16-20 DM (58,00-80,00 Kn) pro Nacht, einschließlich Gästesteuer, zu rechnen.

PÄSSE UND VISA

Staatsbürger aus allen afrikanischen und lateinamerikanischen Ländern (außer Chile) sowie aus allen asiatischen und pazifischen Ländern, den USA, Kanada, Luxemburg, Belgien, den Niederlanden, Albanien, Griechenland und allen Ländern der ehemaligen Sowjetunion benötigen ein Einreisevisum. Visa werden in Botschaften und Konsulaten Kroatiens und an den kroatischen Grenzstellen ausgestellt.

GESUNDHEIT

Es sind keine Impfungen erforderlich.

Zwischen Kroatien und gewissen Ländern bestehen beiderseitige Verträge über die Gesundheitspflege, die ausländischen Reisenden Anspruch auf die gleiche Behandlung wie Kroatiern zusichern. Erkundigen Sie sich vor Ihrer Abreise, wie Sie sich eine entsprechende Bescheinigung beschaffen können. Reisende aus den verbleibenden Ländern müssen für ihre Behandlung selbst bezahlen, aber in den meisten Fällen sind die Kosten nicht sehr hoch.

GESCHÄFTSSTUNDEN DER BANKEN

Montags-freitags 08.00-19.00 Uhr, samstags 08.00-12.00 Uhr.

POSTÄMTER

Montags-freitags 07.00-20.00 Uhr, samstags 07.00-13.00 Uhr.

LADENÖFFNUNGSZEITEN

Montags-freitags 08.00-20.00 Uhr, samstags 08.00-13.00 Uhr.

REISEN

Flugverkehr
Croatia Airlines bietet einen Inlandsverkehr zwischen größeren Städten. Die besten Flugverbindungen führen über Zagreb.

Eisenbahn
Die Eisenbahnverbindungen sind gut.

Busse
Zwischen allen Städten gibt es Busverbindungen. In den größeren Städten wird ein guter Busverkehr geboten.

Fähren
Küstenfähren verkehren zwischen gewissen Inseln an der adriatischen Küste.

Autofahren
Alle Städte verbindet ein gutes Straßennetz. In größeren Städten können Autos gemietet werden.

HAK (der kroatische Automobil-Club) bietet auf Hauptverkehrsstraßen und in Städten einen Pannendienst, der über die Nr. 987 gerufen werden kann. Der Fahrer muß im Besitz gültiger Papiere für sich und das Fahrzeug sein und eine grüne oder blaue Versicherungskarte vorweisen können.

Español

ALBERGUES JUVENILES CROATAS

Los albergues juveniles croatas se encuentran en ciudades de fama histórica y en lugares sembrados de monumentos interesantes, de museos y de galerías de arte. Los albergues mismos le proporcionarán información sobre espectáculos, fiestas, atracciones populares, actividades de esparcimiento y deportivas y otras prestaciones.

Los albergues suelen abrir de 8 h. a 23 h. En vista de que los de Zagreb, Dubrovnik y Pula son los únicos que abren todo el año, le recomendamos que averigüe cuándo están abiertos los demás en la lista de albergues. Los precios oscilan entre 16 y 20 DEM (58-80 kn) por noche, incluyendo el impuesto de visitante.

PASAPORTES Y VISADOS

Los visitantes procedentes de todos los países africanos y latinoamericanos (excepto Chile), de los países asiáticos y del Pacífico, de los Estados Unidos, Canadá, Luxemburgo, Bélgica, Países Bajos, Albania, Grecia y de todos los países de la antigua Unión Soviética necesitan visado de entrada. Los visados pueden obtenerse en las embajadas y consulados croatas o en las aduanas croatas.

INFORMACIÓN SANITARIA

No es necesaria ninguna vacuna.

Existen acuerdos recíprocos entre Croacia y algunos países que dan derecho a los visitantes procedentes de dichos países a recibir la misma asistencia médica que los croatas. Consiga un certificado antes de salir de viaje. Los demás visitantes deberán abonar todos los gastos médicos, pero éstos suelen ser módicos.

HORARIO DE LOS BANCOS

De lunes a viernes de 8 h. a 19 h. Sábados de 8 h. a 12 h.

OFICINAS DE CORREOS

De lunes a viernes de 7 h. a 20 h. Sábados de 7 h. a 13 h.

HORARIO COMERCIAL

De lunes a viernes de 8 h. a 20 h. Sábados de 8 h. a 13 h.

DESPLAZAMIENTOS

Avión
Croatia Airlines ofrece vuelos nacionales entre las principales ciudades. Las mejores conexiones aéreas son vía Zagreb.

Tren
Croacia cuenta con una buena red ferroviaria.

Autobús
Existen líneas de autocar que enlazan todas las ciudades y un buen servicio de autobuses urbanos en las ciudades principales.

Ferry
Las líneas costeras de ferry enlazan algunas islas de la costa adriática.

Automóvil
Todas las ciudades están bien comunicadas por carretera. En las ciudades más importantes se pueden alquilar coches.

El club croata del automóvil HAK se encarga de la asistencia en carretera en las principales carreteras y poblaciones marcando el 987. Los conductores deberán llevar documentos en regla tanto personales como del vehículo, así como una tarjeta de seguro verde o azul.

Dubrovnik

Bana Jelačića 15-17,
20000 Dubrovnik.
📞 (20) 423241
📠 (20) 412592

Open Dates:	🗓️
Open Hours:	🕐
Reservations:	**R**
Price Range:	$10-12
	BB inc 🖥️
Beds:	80 - 1x² 🛏️ 14x⁴ 🛏️ 4x⁶ 🛏️
Facilities:	👪 2x 👪 🍽️ 🚿 👥 📺 1 x 🍷
	📷 ℹ️ 🎴

Directions:

✈️	Dubrovnik 10km
A🚌	Gruž Station 500m
⛴️	Gruž-Luka 1km
🚌	#4 & 5 100m ap Montovijerna

Attractions: 🔍

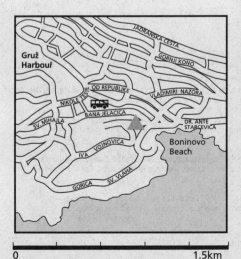

> **Two roads diverged in a wood, and I, I took the one less travelled by, and that has made all the difference.**

Deux routes divergeaient dans le bois, et moi... moi, j'ai pris la moins utilisée et c'est ce qui a tout changé.

Im Wald traf ich auf eine Weggabelung, und ich - ich nahm den weniger betretenen Pfad, und seitdem ist alles anders.

De un camino, en el bosque, salían dos senderos, y yo... yo tomé el menos usado. Y esto lo ha cambiado todo.

Robert Frost, The Road Not Taken

Location/Address	Telephone No. Fax No.	Beds	Opening Dates	Facilities
▲ **Borik-Zadar** YH Borik, Obala Kneza Trpimira 76, 23 000 Zadar.	❶ (23) 331145 ❸ (23) 331190	330	01.04–30.11	� ⑩ Ⓡ Ⓟ
▲ **Dubrovnik** **Bana Jelačića 15-17, 20000 Dubrovnik.**	❶ (20) 423241 ❸ (20) 412592	80	ⓑ	♜ ⑩ Ⓡ ☞
▲ **Pula** Zaljev Valsaline 4, 52 000 Pula. ❺ hfhs-pula@pu.tel.hr	❶ (52) 210002/ 210003 ❸ (52) 212394	145	ⓑ	♜ ⑩ Ⓡ Ⓟ

Zadar ☞ **Borik-Zadar**

YOUTH HOSTEL ACCOMMODATION
OUTSIDE THE ASSURED STANDARDS SCHEME

Makarska - Popotnik-Makarska Ivana Gorana Kovačića BB, 2 (Celjsko Ljetovalište), 21000 Makarska, Croatia.	❶ (386) 63 484110/ 484111 ❸ (386) 63 442870	130	10.06–15.09	♜ ⑩ Ⓡ 1.NW ᴄᴄᶜ Ⓟ Ⓟ
Punat, Island KRK YH Punat 51 521 Punat, Otok KRK.	❶ (51) 854037 ❸ (1) 4841269	125	01.06–30.09	♜ ⑩ Ⓡ Ⓟ
Šubićevac-Šibenik YH Šubićevac, Put Luguša 1, 22 000 Šibenik.	❶ (22) 216410 ❸ (22) 216410	40	01.04–31.10	♜ Ⓡ Ⓟ
Zagreb Petrinjska 77, 10 000 Zagreb.	❶ (1) 4841261 ❸ (1) 4841269	210	ⓑ	♜ Ⓡ Ⓟ

A traveller must have the back of an ass to bear all, a tongue like the tail of a dog to flatter all, the mouth of a hog to eat what is set before him, the ear of a merchant to hear all and say nothing.

Un voyageur doit avoir le dos d'un baudet pour tout porter, une langue pareille à une queue de chien pour flatter tout le monde, la gueule d'un cochon pour manger ce qu'on lui sert, l'oreille d'un marchand pour tout entendre et ne rien dire.

Ein Reisender muß die Haut eines Elefanten haben, um alles zu ertragen, eine zuckersüße Zunge, um allen zu schmeicheln, den Appetit einer neunköpfigen Raupe, um alles zu essen, was man ihm vorsetzt, das Ohr eines treuen Dieners, der alles hört aber nichts sagt.

El que viaja debe tener la espalda de un mulo para cargar con todo, una lengua como la cola de un perro para alabar a todos, una boca como el hocico de un cerdo para comer todo lo que le pongan, y los oídos de un mercader para oírlo todo y no decir nada.

Thomas Nashe (1567-1601)

Cyprus

CHYPRE
ZYPERN
CHIPRE

**Cyprus Youth Hostel Association,
34 Th Theodotou Street,
PO Box 21328, Nicosia, Cyprus.**

☎ (357) (2) 670027
🖷 (357) (2) 672896
📧 montis@logos.cy.net

Office Hours: Su 08.00-13.00hrs; 16.11-18.30
Wi 08.00-13.00hrs; 14.30-17.30

A copy of the Hostel Directory for this Country can be obtained from:
The National Office.

Capital:	Nicosia		**Population:**	700,000
Language:	Greek		**Size:**	9,251 sq km
Currency:	C£ (Cyprus pound)		**Telephone Country Code:**	357

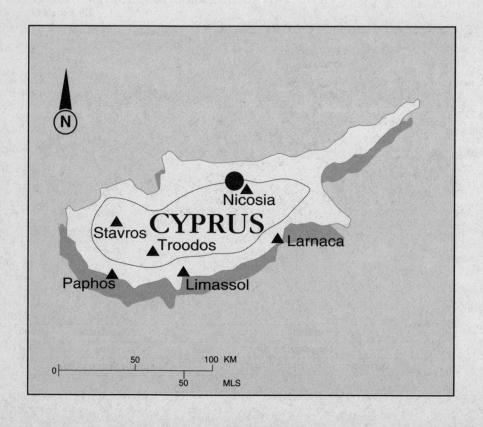

English

CYPRUS HOSTELS

5 hostels, each offering unique locations, and all with family rooms.

All hostels are open 24 hours and with the exception of Stavros all have self-catering facilities. Expect to pay C£ 3.50-C£ 6.50, plus sheet hire if needed at C£ 1.00.

PASSPORTS AND VISAS

Visitors from most countries need only a valid passport for visits of up to three months, but it is advisable to check visa requirements before travelling.

HEALTH

There are no vaccination requirements to enter Cyprus.

BANKING HOURS

Banks are open Monday to Friday 08.15-12.30hrs. Centrally located Banks provide an "afternoon tourist service" on weekdays except for Tuesday afternoons.

POST OFFICES

Post Offices are open Monday to Friday 07.30-13.30hrs and Thursday 15.00-18.00hrs.

Additional to the above the District Post Offices in Nicosia, Larnaca, Limassol and Paphos, the Branch Post Office of Eleftheria Square in Nicosia, the City Central Post Office in Limassol and the Post Office in Paralimni are also open Monday, Tuesday and Thursday for the following hours: October-April, 15.30-17.30hrs and May-September, 16.00-18.00hrs. They are also open Saturdays, all year 09.00-11.00hrs.

All Post Offices are closed on Sundays and Public Holidays.

SHOPPING HOURS

During the winter period (1 October-30 April) shops are open Monday, Tuesday, Thursday, Friday 08.00-13.00hrs and 14.30-17.30hrs. On Wednesday and Saturday they are only open 08.00-13.00hrs.

In summer (1 May-30 September) they are open Monday, Tuesday, Thursday, Friday 08.00-13.00hrs and 16.00-19.00hrs. Wednesday and Saturday are the same as for winter.

TRAVEL

Travel is very easy along the main highways between larger cities. Smaller roads in mountainous areas are more difficult. There is very little public transport after 19.00hrs. Taxis are cheap and easy to find.

Rail

There is no rail network in Cyprus.

Bus

Transurban buses: Various bus companies link all major towns with daily routes at specified intervals.

Rural buses: Almost all villages are connected to the nearest town by local buses. Bus operation is limited to once or twice a day. Regional bus companies, formed recently, will provide more routes.

Urban buses: Operate frequently during the day and in certain tourist areas during the summer their routes are extended till midnight.

Driving

Fairly good surfaced roads complying with international traffic requirements link the towns and villages. Four lane motorways connect the capital, Nicosia, with the coastal towns of Limassol and Larnaca. Minor and forest roads are still largely unsurfaced but in good to fair condition.

Visitors can drive in Cyprus as long as they are in possession of either a valid international driving licence, or their national driving licence, provided this is valid for the class of vehicle they wish to drive. A six month Temporary Driving Licence is available to visitors at a cost of C£3.00.

Self drive car rental firms have offices in all towns, and at Larnaca International Airport, with English speaking personnel. Daily rates vary from C£13.00, for a small car to C£23.00 for larger cars.

Français

AUBERGES DE JEUNESSE CYPRIOTES

Il y a 5 auberges à Chypre, chacune occupant un site unique. Elles offrent toutes des chambres familiales.

Toutes les auberges sont ouvertes 24h sur 24 et, à l'exception de celle de Stavros, disposent de cuisines pour les touristes. Le prix d'une nuit se situe entre 3.50 et 6.50 livres cypriotes, plus location de draps le cas échéant (1 livre cypriote).

PASSEPORTS ET VISAS

Un passeport en règle est requis pour la plupart des visiteurs pour un séjour de trois mois maximum, mais il est préférable de s'assurer avant le départ qu'un visa n'est pas nécessaire.

SOINS MEDICAUX

Aucune vaccination n'est requise pour Chypre.

HEURES D'OUVERTURE DES BANQUES

Les banques sont ouvertes du lundi au vendredi de 8h15 à 12h30. Les banques situées dans les centres-villes offrent un "service pour touristes l'après-midi" tous les jours sauf le mardi.

BUREAUX DE POSTE

Les bureaux de poste sont ouverts du lundi au vendredi de 7h30 à 13h30 et le jeudi de 15h à 18h.

En outre, les bureaux de poste régionaux de Nicosie, Lárnaka, Limassol et Paphos, le bureau de poste local situé sur la Place Eleftheria à Nicosie, le bureau de poste central de Limassol et celui de Paralimni sont également ouverts les lundi, mardi et jeudi aux heures suivantes: d'octobre à avril, de 15h30 à 17h30 et de mai à septembre, de 16h à 18h. Ils sont aussi ouverts le samedi, toute l'année, de 9h à 11h.

Tous les bureaux de poste sont fermés le dimanche et les jours fériés.

HEURES D'OUVERTURE DES MAGASINS

En hiver (du 1er octobre au 30 avril), les magasins sont ouverts les lundi, mardi, jeudi et vendredi de 8h à 13h et de 14h30 à 17h30. Le mercredi et le samedi, ils ne sont ouverts qu'entre 8h et 13h.

En été (du 1er mai au 30 septembre), ils sont ouverts les lundi, mardi, jeudi et vendredi de 8h à 13h et de 16h à 19h. Le mercredi et le samedi, les horaires sont les mêmes qu'en hiver.

DEPLACEMENTS

Il est très facile de se déplacer sur les routes principales reliant les grandes villes. Les petites routes desservant les régions montagneuses sont plus difficiles.

Les transports publics sont très réduits après 19h. Les taxis sont bon marché et faciles à trouver.

Trains
Il n'y a pas de chemin de fer à Chypre.

Autobus
Autobus interurbains: Diverses compagnies d'autobus relient toutes les villes principales au moyen de trajets journaliers à intervalles spécifiés.

Autobus ruraux: Presque tous les villages sont reliés à la ville la plus proche par des autobus locaux qui toutefois ne passent qu'une ou deux fois par jour. Les compagnies d'autobus régionales, qui existent depuis peu de temps, offriront davantage d'itinéraires.

Autobus urbains: Ils sont fréquents pendant la journée et, dans certaines régions touristiques, ils continuent à fonctionner jusqu'à minuit en été.

Automobiles

D'assez bonnes routes conformes aux exigences internationales de la circulation relient villes et villages. Des autoroutes à quatre voies relient la capitale, Nicosie, aux villes côtières de Limassol et Lárnaka. Les petites routes et les routes forestières sont en grande partie non goudronnées mais sont dans un état allant de bon à assez bon.

Les visiteurs ont le droit de conduire à Chypre à condition d'être munis d'un permis de conduire international en règle ou de leur permis de conduire national pourvu qu'il soit valable pour la catégorie de véhicule qu'ils souhaitent conduire. Il est possible de se procurer un permis de conduire valable six mois moyennant 3 livres cypriotes.

Les agences de location de voitures possèdent des bureaux dans toutes les villes ainsi qu'à l'aéroport international de Lárnaka, qui dispose de personnel parlant anglais. Les tarifs journaliers vont de 13 livres cypriotes pour une petite voiture à 23 livres cypriotes pour les voitures plus importantes.

Deutsch

ZYPRIOTISCHE JUGENDHERBERGEN

Fünf Jugendherbergen, wovon jede einmalig gelegen ist; alle mit Familienräumen.

Alle Herbergen sind 24 Stunden am Tag geöffnet und, außer der Herberge in Stavros, haben alle Einrichtungen für Selbstversorger. Es ist mit einem Preis von 3,50-6,50Z£ plus, bei Bedarf, Lakenmiete (1,00Z£) zu rechnen.

PÄSSE UND VISA

Für einen Aufenthalt bis zu drei Monaten brauchen Besucher aus den meisten Ländern nur einen gültigen Reisepaß. Es empfiehlt sich jedoch, sich vor Antritt der Reise nach den Visumsvorschriften zu erkundigen.

GESUNDHEIT

Die Einreise nach Zypern unterliegt keinen Impfvorschriften.

GESCHÄFTSSTUNDEN DER BANKEN

Die Banken sind montags bis freitags von 08.15-12.30 Uhr geöffnet. Zentral gelegene Banken bieten werktags, außer am Dienstagnachmittag, einen "Nachmittagsservice für Touristen".

POSTÄMTER

Postämter sind montags bis freitags von 07.30-13.30 Uhr und donnerstags von 15.00-18.00 Uhr geöffnet.

Abgesehen davon sind die Bezirks-Postämter in Nikosia, Larnaka, Limassol und Paphos, die Postfiliale auf dem Eleftheria Square in Nikosia, das Postamt im Stadtzentrum von Limassol und das Postamt in Paralimni auch montags, dienstags und donnerstags zu folgenden Zeiten geöffnet: Oktober-April 15.30-17.30 Uhr und Mai-September 16.00-18.00 Uhr. Sie sind auch samstags ganzjährig von 09.00-11.00 Uhr geöffnet.

Alle Postämter sind sonn- und feiertags geschlossen.

LADENÖFFNUNGSZEITEN

Im Winter (1. Oktober-30. April) sind die Geschäfte montags, dienstags, donnerstags und freitags von 08.00-13.00 Uhr und von 14.30-17.30 Uhr geöffnet. Mittwochs und samstags sind sie nur von 08.00-13.00 Uhr geöffnet.

Im Sommer (1. Mai-30. September) sind sie montags, dienstags, donnerstags und freitags von 08.00-13.00 Uhr und von 16.00-19.00 Uhr geöffnet. Die Öffnungszeiten für mittwochs und samstags sind gleich wie im Winter.

REISEN

Auf den Hauptverkehrsstraßen zwischen den größeren Städten ist das Reisen sehr einfach. Kleinere Straßen im Gebirge sind schwieriger. Nach 19.00 Uhr gibt es kaum noch öffentliche Verkehrsmittel. Taxis sind billig und leicht zu finden.

Eisenbahn
In Zypern gibt es kein Eisenbahnnetz.

Busse
Transurbaner Busverkehr: Verschiedene Busunternehmen bieten zu bestimmten Zeiten einen täglichen Verkehr zwischen allen größeren Städten.
Busverkehr auf dem Land:
Nahverkehrsbusse verkehren zwischen fast allen Dörfern und der nächsten Stadt. Die Busse fahren nur ein oder zweimal am Tag. Vor kurzem gegründete regionale Busunternehmen werden auf weiteren Strecken verkehren.
Städtische Busse: Während des Tages wird ein häufiger Verkehr geboten, und in gewissen Fremdenverkehrsgebieten fahren die Busse im Sommer bis Mitternacht.

Autofahren
Ziemlich gute Straßen, für die die internationalen Verkehrsvorschriften gelten, verbinden die Städte und Dörfer. Vierspurige Autobahnen verbinden die Hauptstadt, Nikosia, mit den Küstenstädten Limassol und Larnaka. Neben- und Waldstraßen sind oft noch unbefestigt, aber in gutem bis annehmbarem Zustand.

Besucher können in Zypern autofahren, sofern sie im Besitz eines gültigen internationalen Führerscheines oder eines in ihrem Land ausgestellten Führerscheines sind, der für ihre Fahrzeugklasse gilt. Gegen Bezahlung einer Gebühr von 3,00Z£ wird für Besucher ein vorübergehender Führerschein ausgestellt, der sechs Monate gültig ist.

Mietwagen-Unternehmen haben Niederlassungen in allen Städten und auf dem Internationalen Flughafen von Larnaka. Das Personal spricht Englisch. Die Tagessätze liegen zwischen 13,00Z£ für einen Kleinwagen und 23,00Z£ für größere Fahrzeuge.

Español

ALBERGUES JUVENILES CHIPRIOTAS

Existen 5 albergues en Chipre. Todos ellos están ubicados en emplazamientos excepcionales y ofrecen habitaciones familiares.

Todos los albergues están abiertos las 24 horas del día y tienen cocina para huéspedes, excepto el de Stavros. Suelen costar entre 3,50 y 6.50 C£ (libras chipriotas), más sábanas (1 libra chipriota), si las necesita.

PASAPORTES Y VISADOS

Los visitantes de la mayoría de los países sólo necesitan un pasaporte válido para visitas de hasta tres meses de duración, pero recomendamos que averigüe si necesita visado antes de viajar.

INFORMACIÓN SANITARIA

No es necesaria ninguna vacuna para Chipre.

HORARIO DE LOS BANCOS

Los bancos abren de lunes a viernes, de 8.15 h. a 12.30 h. Los más céntricos ofrecen además un "servicio de tarde para los turistas" los días laborables, excepto el martes por la tarde.

OFICINAS DE CORREOS

Las oficinas de correos abren de lunes a viernes de 7.30 h. a 13.30 h. y el jueves de 15 h. a 18 h.

Además de este horario, las oficinas de correos regionales de Nicosía, Lárnaca, Limassol y Paphos, la sucursal de la Plaza Eleftheria de Nicosía, la oficina central de Limassol y la oficina de Paralimni también abren el lunes, martes y jueves con el siguiente horario: de octubre a abril, de 15.30 h. a 17.30 h. y de mayo a septiembre, de 16 h. a 18 h. También abren los sábados de 9 h. a 11 h. durante todo el año.

Todas las oficinas de correos cierran los domingos y festivos.

HORARIO COMERCIAL

En invierno (del 1º de octubre al 30 de abril), las tiendas abren los lunes, martes, jueves y viernes de 8 h. a 13 h. h. y de 14.30 h. a 17.30 h. Los miércoles y sábados sólo abren de 8 h. a 13 h.

En verano (del 1º de mayo al 30 de septiembre) abren los lunes, martes, jueves y viernes de 8 h. a 13 h. y de 16 h. a 19 h. Los miércoles y sábados, el horario es el mismo que en invierno.

DESPLAZAMIENTOS

Es muy fácil desplazarse por las carreteras principales que enlazan las ciudades más grandes. Las carreteras más pequeñas de las zonas montañosas resultan más difíciles. Los transportes públicos son muy escasos después de las 19 h., pero los taxis son baratos y fáciles de encontrar.

Tren
No existe una red ferroviaria en Chipre.

Autobús
Autobuses interurbanos: Varias líneas de autobuses enlazan las principales ciudades, con servicios diarios y un horario fijo.

Autobuses rurales: Casi todos los pueblos se comunican con la ciudad más cercana por medio de autobuses locales, los cuales sólo tienen servicios una o dos veces al día. Las compañías regionales de autobuses, formadas recientemente, ofrecerán más itinerarios.

Autobuses urbanos: Hay autobuses frecuentes durante el día y, en algunas zonas turísticas, en verano, el servicio continúa hasta la medianoche.

Automóvil
Carreteras asfaltadas bastante buenas y que cumplen con las normas internacionales de circulación enlazan las ciudades y los pueblos. Autopistas de cuatro carriles enlazan la capital, Nicosía, con las ciudades costeras de Limassol y Lárnaca. Las carreteras secundarias y forestales siguen en gran parte sin asfaltar, pero están en buenas o bastante buenas condiciones.

Se permite a los visitantes conducir en Chipre siempre y cuando tengan un permiso de conducir internacional en regla o su permiso nacional que sea válido para el tipo de vehículo que deseen conducir. Los visitantes pueden obtener un Permiso de Conducir Provisional válido seis meses, al precio de 3 libras chipriotas.

Las compañías de alquiler de coches sin conductor tienen oficinas en todas las ciudades y en el aeropuerto internacional de Lárnaca, con personal que habla inglés. Las tarifas diarias oscilan entre 13 libras chipriotas para un coche pequeño y 23 libras chipriotas para uno más grande.

YOUTH HOSTEL ACCOMMODATION
OUTSIDE THE ASSURED STANDARDS SCHEME

Location/Address	Telephone No. Fax No.	Beds	Opening Dates	Facilities
Larnaca 27 Nicolaou Rossou St, Larnaca: near Ayios Lazaros church.	☎ (4) 621188 📠 (2) 672896	70	📠	🚻 🛁 🅿
Nicosia 5 Hadjidakis St, Off Them. Dervis St, Nicosia.	☎ (2) 674808 📠 (2) 672896	50	📠	🚻 Ⓡ 2SW 🛁 🅿
Paphos 37 Eleftherios Venizelos Ave, Paphos.	☎ (6) 232588 📠 (2) 672896	22	📠	🚻 🍽 Ⓡ 🛁 🅿
Stavros Government Rest House (Ministry of Agriculture, Forestry Dept), Forest Centre, Stavros, Psoka.	☎ (6) 722338	14	📠	🚻 🍽 Ⓡ 🅿
Troodos Ex-Olympus Hotel, Mount Troodos.	☎ (5) 420200 📠 (2) 672896	22	📠	🚻 🍽 Ⓡ 🛁 🅿

Happiness is not a station you arrive at, but a manner of travelling.

Le bonheur n'est pas une gare à laquelle on arrive, plutôt une façon de voyager.

Glück ist nicht die Endstation, sondern die Reise selbst.

La felicidad no es una estación a la que uno llega, sino una forma de viajar.

Margaret Lee Runbeck

Czech Republic

LA REPUBLIQUE TCHEQUE
DIE TSCHECHISCHE REPUBLIK
LA REPUBLICA CHECA

**KMC Club of Young Travellers,
Karolíny Světlé 30, 11000 Praha 1,
Czech Republic.**

☎ (420) (2) 22220081, 22220347, 22221328
📠 (420) (2) 22220347, 22221328

Office Hours: Monday-Friday, 09.00-17.00hrs

A copy of the Hostel Directory for this Country can be obtained from:
The National Office.

Capital:	Prague (Czech Republic)	**Population:**	10,500,000
Language:	Czech	**Size:**	78,864 sq km
Currency:	Kč (Czech Koruna)	**Telephone Country Code:**	420

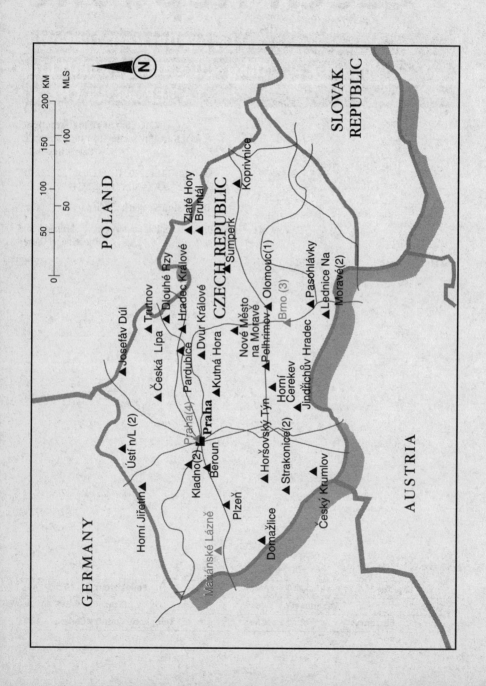

English

CZECH HOSTELS

Take time to visit this rapidly changing country and make sure you see the countryside as well as the big cities. With 5 hostels in Prague and a network of 38 hostels in total, Youth Hostels are the best way to see them.

In Prague and other big cities hostels are open 24hrs, elsewhere they are open 06.00-22.00hrs, although dormitories are closed 10.00-17.00hrs, except for shelter in bad weather.

Expect to pay in the region of Kč 150-500, including sheet hire. All bookings should be made through the national office.

PASSPORTS AND VISAS

Visitors from most European countries and the USA generally do not require visas. When necessary visas can be obtained at Czech missions before arrival.

HEALTH

Visitors to the Czech Republic should take out private insurance before they travel.

BANKING HOURS

Banks are open 08.00-17.00hrs Monday - Friday.

POST OFFICES

Normal opening hours are 08.00-19.00hrs Monday - Friday. In Prague the main post office offers 24-hour service.

SHOPPING HOURS

09.00-19.00hrs Monday - Friday; 09.00-15.00hrs Saturday.

TRAVEL

Air
The national airline CSA offers some discounts.

Rail
Rail travel is cheap and Inter-Rail cards are valid.

Bus
The CSAD bus company offers a fast service but it is more expensive than rail travel.

Français

AUBERGES DE JEUNESSE TCHEQUES

Prenez le temps de visiter ce pays en pleine transformation, et faites en sorte d'explorer la campagne autant que les grandes villes. Avec 5 auberges à Prague et un réseau qui compte 38 auberges au total, les auberges de jeunesse représentent la meilleure façon de découvrir ce pays.

A Prague et dans d'autres grandes villes, les auberges sont ouvertes 24 heures sur 24. Ailleurs, elles sont ouvertes de 6h à 22h, bien que les dortoirs soient fermés entre 10h et 17h, à part un abri en cas de mauvais temps.

Une nuit vous coûtera entre 150 et 500 Kč, location de draps comprise. Toute réservation doit être faite en passant par le bureau national.

PASSEPORTS ET VISAS

En principe, les visiteurs en provenance de la plupart des pays européens et des Etats-Unis n'ont pas besoin de visa. Le cas échéant, vous pouvez obtenir un visa dans une mission tchèque avant votre arrivée.

SOINS MEDICAUX

Il est conseillé aux voyageurs se rendant à la République Tchèque de souscrire à une police d'assurance avant leur voyage.

HEURES D'OUVERTURE DES BANQUES

Les banques sont ouvertes de 8h à 17h du lundi au vendredi.

BUREAUX DE POSTE

Les bureaux de poste sont normalement ouverts de 8h à 19h, du lundi au vendredi. A Prague, la poste principale est ouverte 24 heures sur 24.

HEURES D'OUVERTURE DES MAGASINS

Les magasins sont ouverts de 9h à 19h du lundi au vendredi, et de 9h à 15h le samedi.

DEPLACEMENTS

Avions
La ligne aérienne nationale CSA offre certaines réductions.

Trains
Le train est bon marché et les cartes Inter-Rail sont valides.

Autobus
La compagnie d'autobus CSAD assure un service rapide mais plus cher que le train.

Deutsch

TSCHECHISCHE JUGENDHERBERGEN

Lassen Sie sich Zeit, um dieses Land zu besuchen, in dem so viele Änderungen stattfinden. Dabei sollten Sie nicht nur die großen Städte besuchen, sondern auch aufs Land hinaus fahren. In Prag gibt es 5 Herbergen, und das ganze Netz besteht aus 38 Herbergen. Diese Art des Reisens bietet Ihnen die beste Möglichkeit, alles genau zu besichtigen.

In Prag und anderen großen Städten sind die Herbergen 24 Stunden geöffnet. An anderen Orten sind sie von 06.00-22.00 Uhr geöffnet. Obwohl die Schlafräume von 10.00-17.00 Uhr geschlossen sind, dienen sie bei schlechtem Wetter als Unterstand.

Es ist mit einem Preis von ca. 150-500 Kč zu rechnen, in dem eine Gebühr für die Miete von Laken bereits enthalten ist. Alle Buchungen sind über die Landesgeschäftsstelle vorzunehmen.

PÄSSE UND VISA

Reisende aus den meisten europäischen Ländern und den USA brauchen im allgemeinen kein Visum. Bei Bedarf kann man sich vor der Ankunft in einer tschechischen Mission ein Visum besorgen.

GESUNDHEIT

Wer in die Tschechische Republik reist, sollte vor Antritt der Reise eine private Versicherung abschließen.

GESCHÄFTSSTUNDEN DER BANKEN

Banken sind montags bis freitags von 08.00-17.00 Uhr geöffnet.

POSTÄMTER

Die normalen Öffnungszeiten sind montags bis freitags von 08.00-19.00 Uhr. In Prag bietet die Hauptpost einen 24-Stunden-Service.

LADENÖFFNUNGSZEITEN

Montags - freitags von 09.00-19.00 Uhr, samstags von 09.00-15.00 Uhr.

REISEN

Flugverkehr
Die staatliche Fluggesellschaft CSA bietet gewisse Ermäßigungen.

Eisenbahn
Das Eisenbahnfahren ist billig, und es gelten auch Inter-Rail-Karten.

Busse
Das Busunternehmen CSAD bietet einen schnellen Busverkehr. Die Busse sind aber teurer als die Eisenbahn.

Español

ALBERGUES JUVENILES CHECOS

Tómese tiempo para visitar este país que tanto está cambiando y no deje de explorar tanto el campo como las grandes ciudades. Con 5 albergues en Praga y una red de 38 albergues en total, la forma ideal de conocer el país es alojándose en albergues juveniles.

En Praga y otras grandes ciudades, los albergues están abiertos las 24 horas del día. En otros lugares, abren de 6 h. a 22 h., aunque los dormitorios están cerrados entre las 10 h. y las 17 h., excepto como refugio cuando hace mal tiempo.

El precio de una noche es de alrededor de 150 a 500 Kč (corunas checas), sábanas incluidas. Todas las reservas deben hacerse a través de la oficina nacional.

PASAPORTES Y VISADOS

Generalmente, los visitantes procedentes de la mayoría de los países europeos y de los Estados Unidos no necesitan visado. De ser necesario, éste puede obtenerse en las misiones checas antes de llegar al país.

INFORMACIÓN SANITARIA

Se recomienda a los visitantes hacerse un seguro privado antes de salir de viaje para la República Checa.

HORARIO DE LOS BANCOS

Los bancos abren de 8 h. a 17 h. de lunes a viernes.

OFICINAS DE CORREOS

El horario normal es de 8 h. a 19 h. de lunes a viernes. En Praga, la central de correos abre las 24 horas del día.

HORARIO COMERCIAL

Las tiendas abren de 9 h. a 19 h. de lunes a viernes y de 9 h. a 15 h. los sábados.

DESPLAZAMIENTOS

Avión
La compañía aérea nacional CSA ofrece algunos descuentos.

Tren
Viajar en tren es económico y valen las tarjetas de Inter-Rail.

Autobús
La compañía de autobuses CSAD ofrece un servicio rápido, aunque es más caro que el tren.

Praha - Hotel Beta

Roškotova 1225/I,
14700 Praha 4 - Krč.
☎ (2) 61262158
📠 (2) 61261202
✉ beta@alphanet.cz

Open Dates:	01.01-22.12; 26-31.12
Open Hours:	🕙
Reservations:	Ⓡ ⒾⒷⓃ ⒸⒸ
Price Range:	CSK 400-430 BB inc 🖥
Beds:	250 - 40x² 🛏 30x³ 🛏 20x⁴ 🛏
Facilities:	♿ ♦♦♦ 5x ♦♦♦ 🍽 ♨ 📺 🎬 ⛪ 🅿 Ⓘ

Directions:

✈	Praha-Ruzyně 20km
🚂	Praha-Hlavní nádraží 9km
🚌	124,205 50m ap U Statku
Ⓤ	U-Line - Budějovická

Attractions: ⚲2km 🏊3km

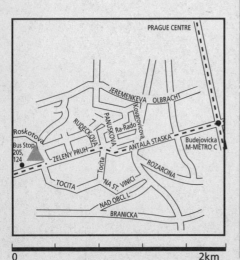

PRAGUE CENTRE
JEREMENKEVA OLBRACHT
Kovarovicova
Roškotova
RUDECKOVA PANUSKOVA Ra-Rado
Bus Stop ZELENY PRUH ANTALA STASKA Budejovicka
205, M-METRO C
124 Tocita
ROZARCINA
TOCITA NA ST. VINICI
NAD OBCL I
BRANICKA
0   2km

> The service we render to others is really the rent we pay for our room on this earth. It is obvious that man is himself a traveller; that the purpose of this world is not "to have and to hold" but "to give and serve." There can be no other meaning.
>
> Le service que l'on rend aux autres est vraiment le loyer que nous payons pour notre chambre sur cette terre. Il est évident que l'homme est lui-même un voyageur; que le but de ce monde n'est pas "d'avoir et de posséder" mais "de donner et servir". Il ne peut y avoir d'autre intention.
>
> Den Dienst, den wir für andere leisten, ist im Grunde die Miete für unseren Platz auf dieser Erde. Offensichtlich ist der Mensch selbst ein Reisender; der Zweck besteht nicht in "besitzen und behalten" sondern "geben und dienen". Eine andere Auslegung gibt es nicht.
>
> El servicio que prestamos a nuestros semejantes es, en realidad, el alquiler que pagamos por nuestra morada en esta tierra. Está claro que el hombre en sí es un viajero; que la razón de ser del mundo no es "tener y guardar", sino "dar y prestar servicio". La vida no puede tener ningún otro sentido.
>
> **Sir Wilfred T. Grenfell**

Location/Address	Telephone No. Fax No.	Beds	Opening Dates	Facilities
△ **Beroun** - Hotel Barbora Garni Na Podolí 740, Beroun.	☎ (311) 25442 ✆ (311) 612500	26	🗓12	♟ ⦿ ⓡ ⚲ 🅿 ☕
▲ **Brno** - Hotel Interservis [IBN] Lomená 48, 61700 Brno-Komárov. ⊜ youth.hostel@iol.cz	☎ (5) 45234232, 45233165 ✆ (5) 45234232, 45233165	150	🗓12	♟ ⦿ ⓡ ⚲ 🅿 ☕
▲ **Brno** - Koleje Jana Taufera MZLU Jana Babáka 3/5, 61600 Brno.	☎ (5) 41321335 ✆ (5) 41248966	30	🗓12	♟ ⦿ ⓡ ⚲ ♂ 🅿
▲ **Brno** - Penzion Palacký Kolejní 2, 61200 Brno.	☎ (5) 41321263 ✆ (5) 757301	80	🗓12	♟ ⦿ ⓡ ⚲ 🅿 ☕
△ **Bruntál** - Hotel Slezan Revoluční 20, 79201 Bruntál.	☎ (646) 711907 ✆ (646) 711913	161	🗓12	♟ ⦿ ⚲ 🅿
△ **Česká Lípa** - Vila Adéla Česká Lípa, 47001 Česká Lípa, Děčínská 1414.	☎ (425) 52786, 52831	26	🗓12	♟ ⓡ ♂
△ **Český Krumlov** - Travellers Hostel Soukenická 43, 38101 Český Krumlov	☎ (337) 711345	45	🗓12	♟ ⦿ ⓡ ♂ 🅿 ☕
△ **Dlouhé Rzy v Orlických Horách** -Astra Rekreační zařízení.	☎ (443) 95051	160	01.06–30.09	♟ ⦿ ⚲ 🅿
△ **Domažlice** - Domov mládeže Obchodníakademie 34401 Domažlice, Boženy Němcové 116.	☎ (189) 722386	96	🗓12	♟ ⦿ ⓡ ♂
△ **Dvůr Králové nad Labem** - Hostel Student E. Krásnohorské 2069, 54401 Dvůr Králové nad Labem.	☎ (437) 820184 ✆ (437) 820194	200	🗓12	♟ ⦿ ⓡ ⚲ ♂ 🅿
△ **Horní Jiřetín** - Zámek 43543 Horní Jiřetín, Zámek Jezeří.	☎ (35) 93338	15	🗓12	♟ ⓡ ♂ 🅿
△ **Horšovský Týn** - Domov mládeže SZŠ 34601 Horšovský Týn, Nádražní ulice 43.	☎ (188) 2319, 2432	45	🗓12	♟ ⦿ ⓡ ♂
△ **Hříběcí.u Horní Cerekve** - Ubytovna Domu Dětí a Mládeže 39403 Horní Cerekev.	☎ (366) 26411 ✆ (366) 26411	38	01.06–15.09	♟ ⦿ 🅿
▲ **Hradec Králové** - Hotel Garni Na Kotli 1147, 50296 Hradec Králové.	☎ (49) 5763600 ✆ (49) 5763111	67	🗓12	♟ ⦿ 🅿
△ **Jindřichův Hradec** - Pension uTkadlen, Pod Hradem 7/IV., Jindřichův Hradec	☎ (331) 321348 ✆ (331) 26076	20	🗓12	♟ ⦿ ⓡ 🅿
△ **Josefův Důl** - Sportcentrum Peklo 46844 Josefův Důl 960.	☎ (428) 381068 ✆ (428) 381103	126	🗓12	♟ ⦿ ⓡ 🅿 ☕
△ **Kladno** - Domov mládeže SOŠ, SOU a U 27201 Kladno 2, ul 5, května 1870.	☎ (312) 623165 ✆ (312) 623166	80	🗓12	♟ ⦿ ⓡ
△ **Kladno** - Domov mládeže SOŠ, SOU a U K Nemocnici 2007, 27203 Kladno, Dubská.	☎ (312) 627416 ✆ (312) 628598	130	🗓12	♟ ⦿ ⓡ ⚲ ♂ 🅿
△ **Kopřvnice** - Turistická ubytovna Pod lesem Komenského 622, 74221 Kopřivnice.	☎ (656) 721357 ✆ (656) 811064	150	🗓12	♟ ⦿ ⓡ ⚲ ♂ 🅿
△ **Kutná Hora** - O-KČT TJ Turista Národního odboje 56, 28401 Kutná Hora.	☎ (327) 512960 ✆ (327) 514961	36	🗓12	♟ ⓡ ⚲ ♂ 🅿

Location/Address	Telephone No. Fax No.	Beds	Opening Dates	Facilities
△ **Lednice na Moravě** - Koleje MZLU Petra Bezruče Valtická 538, 69144 Lednice na Moravě.	☏ (627) 340161 ℻ (627) 340983	220	🛏12	⇋ ⁙ Ⓡ ♿ ☕ P
▲ **Mariánské Lázně** - Hotel Krakonos (IBN) 35334 Mariánské Lázně. ✉ krankonoš.ml@iol.cz	☏ (165) 622624 ℻ (165) 622383	250	🛏12	⁙ Ⓡ
△ **Nové Město na Moravě** - Hotelová ubytovna DUO 59231 Nové Město na Moravě, Masarykova 1493.	☏ (616) 916245	150	🛏12	⇋ ⁙ Ⓡ ☕
△ **Olomouc** - Univerzita Palackého Šmeralova 12, 77111 Olomouc.	☏ (608) 5226057 ℻ (608) 5226057	66	🛏12	⇋ ⁙ Ⓡ ♿ ☕ P
▲ **Pardubice** - Harmony Club Hotely Bělehradská 458, 53009 Paradubice.	☏ (40) 6435020 ℻ (40) 6435025	90	🛏12	⇋ ⁙ Ⓡ ♿ ⊂CC⊃ ☕ P ⚐
△ **Pasohlávky** - Turist Unimo 69122 Pasohlávky 60.	☏ (626) 427712 ℻ (626) 427712	90	🛏12	⇋ ⁙ Ⓡ ♿ ☕ P ⚐
△ **Pelhřimov** - JENA Ubytovna Pražská 1541, 39301 Pelhřimov.	☏ (366) 22045	66	🛏12	⇋ ⁙ Ⓡ ♿ ☕ P
△ **Plzeň** - Hostel SOU č.4 Vejprnická 56, 31802 Plzeň.	☏ (19) 286443 ℻ (19) 286443	80	🛏12	⇋ ⁙ Ⓡ 3W P
▲ **Praha** - Hostel Advantage Sokolská 11-13, 12000 Praha 2.	☏ (2) 24914062 ℻ (2) 24914067	96	🛏12	⇋ ⁙ Ⓡ ♿ ⚐
▲ **Praha** - Hotel Beta (IBN) **Roškotova 1225/I, 14700 Praha 4 - Krč.** ✉ beta@alphanet.cz	☏ (2) 61262158 ℻ (2) 61261202	250	01.01-22.12; 26-31.12	⇋ ⁙ Ⓡ ♿ ⊂CC⊃ P
△ **Praha** - Hotel Standart Vodní Stavby, 17000 Praha 7 - Holešovice, Přístavní 2.	☏ (2) 875258 or 875674 ℻ (2) 806752	150	🛏12	⇋ ⁙ Ⓡ
△ **Praha** - Travellers Hostel Dlouhá 33, 11000 Praha 1	☏ (2) 24826663; 24826662 ℻ (2) 24826665	127	🛏12	⇋ ⁙ Ⓡ 0.5N ♿ P ⊡ ☕
▲ **Strakonice** - Domov mládeže Želivského 291, 38642 Strakonice.	☏ (342) 23281	70	🛏12	⇋ ⁙ Ⓡ ♿ ☕ P
▲ **Strakonice** - Hotel Garnet Dr.J.Fifky 186, 38602 Strakonice.	☏ (342) 321984 ℻ (342) 28231	104	🛏12	⇋ ⁙ Ⓡ ♿ P ☕ ⚐
△ **Trutnov** - Pension Ùsvit M.Gorkého 421, 54101 Trutnov.	☏ (439) 811405 ℻ (439) 826406	200	🛏12	⇋ ⁙ Ⓡ P
△ **Ústí n/L** - Ubytovna Junior 40000 Ústí n/L, Kosmonautù 571/1.	☏ (47) 62215	15	🛏12	⇋ ⁙ Ⓡ
▲ **Ústí nad Labem-Nestěmice** - Hotel Český Lev Sibiřská 560, 40331 Ústí nad Labem-Nestěmice.	☏ (47) 60356, (47) 60901 ℻ (47) 69477	150	🛏12	⇋ ⁙ Ⓡ ♿ P ⚐
▲ **Zlaté Hory** - Areál Bohema Travel Market, Areál Bohema, 79376 Zlaté Hory.	☏ (645) 425177 ℻ (645) 425069	520	🛏12	⇋ ⁙ Ⓡ ♿ ⊂CC⊃ P ☕ ⚐

Denmark

DANEMARK

DÄNEMARK

DINAMARCA

DANHOSTEL Danmarks Vandrerhjem
Vesterbrogade 39, DK-1620 Copenhagen V,
Denmark.

☎ (45) 33313612
✆ (45) 33313626
✉ ldv@danhostel.dk
www.danhostel.dk

Office Hours: Monday-Thursday 09.00-16.00hrs and Friday 09.00-15.00hrs.

A copy of the Hostel Directory for this Country can be obtained from: The National Office and all hostels.

Capital:	Copenhagen	
Language:	Danish	
Currency:	kr (1 Krone = 100 øre)	

Population:	5,170,000
Size:	43,069 sq km
Telephone Country Code:	45

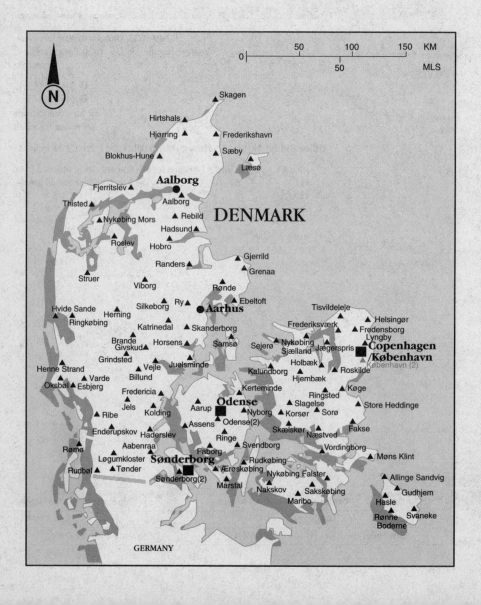

50   100   150   KM

0

50   MLS

N

Skagen

Hirtshals

Hjørring   Frederikshavn

Sæby

Blokhus-Hune   Læsø

Fjerritslev   **Aalborg**

Thisted   Aalborg   **DENMARK**

Nykøbing Mors   Rebild

Hadsund

Roslev   Hobro

Struer   Randers   Gjerrild

Viborg   Grenaa

Rønde

Hvide Sande   Ry   **Aarhus**   Ebeltoft   Tisvildeleje

Herning   Silkeborg   Helsingør

Ringkøbing   Frederiksværk   Fredensborg

Katrinedal   Skanderborg   Lyngby

Brande   Horsens   Samsø   Sejerø Nykøbing   **Copenhagen**

Givskud   Sjælland Jægerspris **/København**

Grindsted   Juelsminde   København (2)

Henne Strand   Vejle   Kalundborg   Holbæk   Roskilde

Oksbøl Varde Billund   Hjembæk

Esbjerg   Fredericia   Kerteminde   Ringsted   Køge

Jels   Aarup   **Odense**   Nyborg Slagelse   Store Heddinge

Ribe   Kolding   Odense(2)   Korsør Sorø

Assens   Skælskør   Fakse

Enderupskov Haderslev   Ringe   Svendborg   Næstved

Aabenraa   Faborg   Vordingborg

Rømø   Løgumkloster **Sønderborg**   Rudkøbing   Møns Klint

Rudbøl   Tønder   Ærøskøbing Nykøbing Falster

Sønderborg(2)   Marstal   Nakskov Sakskøbing   Allinge Sandvig

Maribo   Gudhjem

Hasle   Svaneke

Rønne

Boderne

GERMANY

English

DANISH HOSTELS

Youth Hostels in Denmark have excellent facilities for families.

Most Danish hostels are primarily open 08.00-12.00hrs and 16.00-20.00hrs. The two hostels in Copenhagen are open 24hrs. There is access to common areas the whole day. If you are not able to claim your bed by 17.00hrs, you must warn the hostel in advance. Reservations are essential from 1.9-15.5 (individuals), 1.1-31.12 (groups). Most Danish hostels accept group bookings. Contact national office or directly to hostel.

Danish hostels have prices for private rooms and prices for beds in sharing rooms/dormitory. The price for a private room fluctuates between DKK 200-600 for 2-6 persons per night. The maximum price for a bed per night is DKK 100. No charge for children under 2 years. Notify the hostel on reservation. All hostels have self-catering facilities with pots and pans, but you need to provide your own cutlery and crockery. Many hostels also provide meals at reasonable prices., primarily breakfast.

DANHOSTEL is in the process of introducing environmental approved hostels. This is done in co-operation with the official body called The Green Key. So far The Green Key has now been awarded to 13 hostels but more are on the way. Look out for The Green Key Flag which indicates an environmentally friendly hostel.

PASSPORTS AND VISAS

Please contact Danish Embassy or Consulate in your country of residence.

BANKING HOURS

Business Hours: Monday-Friday 09.30-16.00hrs, Thursday 09.30-18.00hrs.

Many branches at airports, harbours and railway stations are open longer hours for exchange of currency. The hours may have slight local variations. The red cash dispensers "Kontanten" accept Visa Euro, Master and Cirrus cards for drawing Danish currency. "Kontanten" dispensers are always open. Please note that Danish banks may refuse to exchange large foreign bank notes.

POST OFFICES

Normally weekdays 09.00/10.00-17.00/17.30hrs and Saturday 09.00-12.00hrs. All post offices are closed on Sundays.

SHOPPING HOURS

In general shops are open Monday-Friday 09.00-17.30hrs and Saturday 09.00-13.00hrs. However supermarkets and department stores often stay open until 19.00hrs on weekdays and until 17.00hrs on Saturdays.

TRAVEL

Air

Copenhagen Airport is the hub of the domestic routes. Domestic airports Aalborg, Copenhagen, Tirstrup/Åarhus, Billund and Odense are located so that they serve several towns. The flight times are minimal. There are numerous discounted domestic air fares, including the so called "green departures" as well as child, youth and group reductions.

Rail

Intercity services are the cornerstone of the DSB network and they link most towns in Denmark. On the principal routes there are regular services every hour. Seats must be reserved on these trains.

An electrified metropolitan S-Train railway network connects Copenhagen city centre with the outskirts and the Copenhagen airport, at intervals of 10-20 minutes.

A number of international trains link up with the internal services to form a very comprehensive rail network.

Bus

Many local bus connections. Further information at the railway stations.

Ferry

Surrounded by water and with nowhere more than 55km from the sea, Denmark is a country of many inhabited islands. These are linked by an extensive network of ferry routes.

All vessels are part of the country's integrated transport system and are punctual and reliable.

"Storebaeltsbroen", The Great Belt Bridge between Funen and Zealand. After 12 years of intensive construction work, H.M. Queen Margrethe II of Denmark inaugurated on 14 June 1998, what had then become the largest engineering project in the history of Denmark, The Great Belt Fixed Link. Fares by passenger cars are DKK 210 and motorbikes DKK 105 single crossing.

Driving

Your driving licence must clearly indicate that it applies to a vehicle of the type being used. A green card is not compulsory but recommended. A warning triangle is obligatory as is the wearing of seat belts. Dipped headlights are compulsory 24 hours a day. Right hand drive cars must have black adhesive triangles often supplied by ferry companies or car shops.

Français

AUBERGES DE JEUNESSE DANOISES

Les auberges de jeunesse au Danemark sont très bien équipées pour les familles.

La plupart des auberges danoises ouvrent en général de 8h à 12h et de 16h à 20h. Les deux auberges de Copenhague restent ouvertes 24h/24. L'accès aux salles collectives est possible toute la journée. S'il vous est impossible de prendre possession de votre lit à 17h au plus tard, vous êtes prié d'en informer l'auberge à l'avance. Il est essentiel de réserver entre 1/9 et 15/5 (pour les individuels) et entre 1/1 et 31/12 (pour les groupes). La plupart des auberges danoises acceptent les réservations de groupes. Veuillez contacter le bureau national ou directement l'auberge en question.

Les auberges danoises pratiquent des prix différents pour les chambres privées et pour les lits en chambres collectives ou dortoirs. Le prix d'une chambre privée varie entre 200 et 600 couronnes pour 2 à 6 personnes par nuit. Le prix maximum pour un lit et une nuit est de 100 couronnes. La nuitée est gratuite pour les enfants de moins de 2 ans. Prévenez-en l'auberge au moment de la réservation. Toutes les auberges ont des cuisines à la disposition des touristes, avec batterie de cuisine, mais il vous faudra fournir vos couverts et votre vaisselle. De nombreuses auberges servent des repas, principalement le petit déjeuner, à des prix raisonnables.

DANHOSTEL travaille également à l'homologation d'auberges dites écologiques. Ce projet est réalisé en collaboration avec un organisme officiel dénommé "La Clef Verte". Jusqu'à présent, la Clef Verte a été attribuée à 13 auberges et d'autres devraient suivre bientôt. Essayez de repérer le drapeau de la Clef Verte qui indique une auberge qui respecte l'environnement.

PASSEPORTS ET VISAS

Veuillez contacter l'ambassade ou le consulat danois de votre pays de résidence.

HEURES D'OUVERTURE DES BANQUES

Heures d'ouverture des guichets:

Du Lundi au Vendredi: 9h30-16h00 Jeudi: 9h30-18h00. De nombreuses agences dans les aéroports, gares maritimes et ferrovières sont ouvertes plus longtemps pour assurer un service de change. Les heures d'ouverture peuvent varier quelque peu selon l'endroit. Les distributeurs rouges d'argent liquide 'Kontanten' acceptent les cartes Visa, Euro, Master et Cirrus pour le retrait de devises danoises. Ces distributeurs 'Kontanten' sont ouverts en permanence. Veuillez prendre note que les banques danoises sont susceptibles de refuser de changer les billets de banque étrangers de grosses dénominations.

BUREAUX DE POSTE

Ils sont en général ouverts en semaine de 9h/10h à 17h/17h30 et le samedi de 9h à 12h. Tous les bureaux de poste sont fermés le dimanche.

HEURES D'OUVERTURE DES MAGASINS

En général, les magasins sont ouverts de 9h à 17h30 du lundi au vendredi et de 9h à 13h le samedi. Cependant, les supermarchés et les grands magasins sont souvent ouverts jusqu'à 19h en semaine et jusqu'à 17h le samedi.

DEPLACEMENTS

Avions

L'aéroport de Copenhague assure les vols intérieurs. Les aéroports nationaux (Aalborg, Copenhagen, Tirstrup/Åarhus, Billund et Odense) sont situés de façon à desservir plusieurs villes. Les temps de vol sont minimes. Les tarifs des vols intérieurs faisant l'objet de réductions sont nombreux, parmi lesquels les "départs verts", en plus de réductions pour enfants, jeunes adultes et groupes.

Trains

Les services interurbains représentent la pierre angulaire du réseau DSB et relient la plupart des villes danoises. Les lignes principales jouissent de services réguliers toutes les heures.

Il est essentiel de réserver vos places dans ces trains.

Un réseau ferroviaire métropolitain électrifié S-Train relie le centre de Copenhague à la banlieue et l'aéroport de Copenhague toutes les 10 à 20 minutes.

Plusieurs trains internationaux sont reliés au service intérieur pour former un réseau ferroviaire très complet.

Autobus

De nombreuses liaisons locales sont assurées par un service de bus. Pour plus d'informations, adressez-vous aux guichets des gares ferroviaires.

Ferry-boats

Le Danemark est un pays entouré d'eau et aucun endroit n'est à plus de 55km de la mer. Les nombreuses îles habitées sont reliées par un vaste réseau de services maritimes. Tous les bateaux font partie du système de transport intégré du pays et sont ponctuels et fiables.

Le "Storebaeltsbroen", le pont de la "Grand Belt" entre l'île de Fyn et celle de Sjaeland: après 12 ans de travaux intensifs, sa Majesté la Reine Marguerite II du Danemark a inauguré le 14 juin 1998, ce qui est devenu le plus grand projet de génie civil jamais entrepris dans toute l'histoire du Danemark. Un aller et retour coûte 210 couronnes pour les voitures et les motos, 105 pour une simple traversée.

Automobiles

Votre permis de conduire doit indiquer clairement le type de véhicule auquel il se rapporte. La carte verte n'est pas obligatoire mais conseillée. Le triangle est obligatoire de même que le port des ceintures de sécurité. Il est obligatoire de rouler en codes 24h sur 24. Les véhicules avec conduite à droite doivent avoir des triangles noirs adhésifs que l'on peut souvent obtenir auprès des compagnies de ferry ou dans les magasins d'articles pour automobiles.

Deutsch

DÄNISCHE JUGENDHERBERGEN

Jugendherbergen in Dänemark haben ausgezeichnete Einrichtungen für Familien.

Die meisten Jugendherbergen sind von 08.00-12.00 Uhr und von 16.00-20.00 Uhr geöffnet. Die zwei Jugendherbergen in Kopenhagen sind 24 Stunden am Tag geöffnet. Die Gemeinschaftsbereiche sind ganztägig zugänglich. Wenn Sie Ihr Bett nicht bis spätestens 17.00 Uhr in Anspruch nehmen, müssen Sie die Herberge im voraus verständigen. Reservierungen sind vom 1.9-15.5 (Einzelreisende) und vom 1.1-31.12 (Gruppen) unerläßlich. Die meisten Jugendherbergen akzeptieren Reservierungen von Gruppen. Bitte erkundigen Sie sich beim Nationalverband oder direkt bei der Jugendherberge.

Dänische Jugendherbergen haben verschiedene Preise für Privatzimmer und Betten in geteilten Schlafsälen. Für ein Privatzimmer für 2-6 Personen ist mit einem Preis zwischen 200-600 DKK pro Nacht zu rechnen. Der Höchstpreis für ein Bett ist 100 DKK pro Nacht. Setzen Sie die Herberge bei der Reservierung in Kenntnis, wenn Kinder unter 2 Jahren mitreisen. Die Übernachtung ist für sie kostenlos. Alle Herbergen haben Einrichtungen für Selbstversorger, einschließlich Töpfe und Pfannen. Sie müssen aber Ihr eigenes Besteck und Geschirr mitbringen. Viele Herbergen stellen Mahlzeiten zur Verfügung und sind sehr preiswert, insbesondere das Frühstück.

DANHOSTEL ist gerade dabei, Jugendherbergen unter dem Aspekt des Umweltschutzes einzustufen. Dies geschieht in Zusammenarbeit mit der offiziellen Organisation "The Green Key". Bisher ist der "Grüne Schlüssel" nur 13 Herbergen verliehen worden, weitere Herbergen werden jedoch bald folgen. Eine umweltfreundliche Herberge ist an der Flagge mit dem grünen Schlüssel zu erkennen.

PÄSSE UND VISA

Bitte setzen Sie sich mit der dänischen Botschaft oder dem Konsulat in Ihrem Land in Verbindung.

GESCHÄFTSSTUNDEN DER BANKEN

Montags bis freitags 09.30-16.00 Uhr, donnerstags 09.30-18.00 Uhr. Viele Fillialen auf Flughäfen, Bahnhöfen und an Häfen sind zum Geldumtausch länger geöffnet. Öffnungszeiten sind von Ort zu Ort unterschiedlich. Bitte beachten Sie, daß dänische Banken sich weigern können, ausländische Banknoten mit einem hohen Nennwert zu wechseln.

Rote Bankautomaten "Kontanten" akzeptieren Visa Euro, Master und Cirrus, um dänisches Bargeld zu erhalten. "Kontanten"-Automaten sind immer zugänglich.

POSTÄMTER

Im allgemeinen werktags von 09.00/10.00-17.00/17.30 Uhr und samstags von 09.00-12.00 Uhr. Alle Postämter sind sonntags geschlossen.

LADENÖFFNUNGSZEITEN

Im allgemeinen sind die Geschäfte montags bis freitags von 9.00 bis 17.30 Uhr, und samstags von 9.00 bis 13.00 Uhr geöffnet. Die Geschäftszeit von Supermärkten und Warenhäusern ist jedoch an Wochentagen oft bis 19.00 Uhr und samstags bis 17.00 Uhr.

REISEN

Flugverkehr

Kopenhagen ist der Hauptflughafen für den Inlandsverkehr. Die Flughäfen für den Inlandsverkehr Aalborg, Kopenhagen, Tirstrup/Åarhus, Billund und Odense sind so gelegen, daß sie mehreren Städten dienen. Die Flugzeiten sind minimal. Es gibt zahlreiche

Nachlässe auf Inlandsflüge, darunter die sogenannten "grünen Abflüge" sowie Ermäßigungen für Kinder, Jugendliche und Gruppen.

Eisenbahn

Der Intercity-Verkehr ist die Hauptstütze des DSB-Netzes. Diese Züge verkehren zwischen den meisten Städten in Dänemark. Auf den Hauptstrecken verkehrt jede Stunde ein Zug. In diesen Zügen muß man einen Platz reservieren lassen.

Ein elektrifiziertes S-Bahn-Netz verbindet das Stadtzentrum von Kopenhagen mit den Außenbezirken und dessen Flughafen. Die Züge verkehren alle 10-20 Minuten.

Mehrere internationale Züge haben Anschluß an den Inlandsverkehr, so daß ein sehr umfangreiches Eisenbahnnetz geboten wird.

Busse

Es gibt viele örtliche Busverbindungen. Weitere Informationen sind auf den Bahnhöfen erhältlich.

Fähren

Da Dänemark von Wasser umgeben und an keiner Stelle mehr als 55 km vom Meer entfernt ist, gibt es viele bewohnte Inseln, die durch ein umfangreiches Fährnetz miteinander verbunden sind.

Alle Schiffe gehören zu dem Verkehrsverbundsystem des Landes. Sie sind pünktlich und zuverlässig.

Am 14. Juni 1998 wurde nach 12 Jahren intensiver Bauarbeiten das bis dahin größte Bauprojekt in der Geschichte Dänemarks - "Storebaeltsbroen", die Brücke über dem Großen Belt, die Fünen und Seeland miteinander verbindet - von Seiner Majestät Königin Margrethe II von Dänemark eingeweiht. Die Gebühren pro Überquerung belaufen sich auf 210 DKK für ein Kfz und 105 DKK für ein Motorrad.

Autofahren

Ihr Führerschein muß deutlich angeben, daß er für ein Fahrzeug des benutzten Typs gilt. Eine grüne Versicherungskarte ist nicht obligatorisch, aber empfehlenswert. Ein Warndreieck und das Tragen eines Sicherheitsgurtes sind Pflicht. 24 Stunden am Tag muß mit Abblendlicht gefahren werden. Autos mit Rechtssteuerung müssen ein schwarzes Dreieck tragen, das in Geschäften, die mit Kfz-Zubehör handeln, und Fährbootunternehmen erhältlich ist.

Español

ALBERGUES JUVENILES DANESES

Los albergues juveniles de Dinamarca son excelentes para viajar en familia. La mayoría abren de 8 h. a 12 h. y de 16 h. a 20 h., pero los dos albergues de Copenhague están abiertos las 24 horas del día. Es posible acceder a las zonas comunes todo el día. Usted deberá avisar al albergue de antemano si no puede registrarse antes de las 17 h. Es imprescindible reservar con antelación para estancias entre el 1/9 y el 15/5 (individuos) y entre el 1/1 y el 31/12 (grupos). Casi todos los albergues aceptan reservas para grupos. Rogamos se pongan en contacto con la oficina nacional o directamente con el albergue.

Las tarifas son distintas para las habitaciones privadas y los dormitorios compartidos: las habitaciones privadas para 2-6 personas cuestan entre 200 y 600 DKK (coronas danesas) por noche y el precio máximo de una cama es de 100 coronas por noche. El alojamiento es gratuito para los niños menores de 2 años: avise al albergue al hacer su reserva. Es posible cocinar uno mismo en todos los albergues, pero, aunque estos disponen de utensilios de cocina, usted tendrá que traerse su propia vajilla y cubertería. Muchos albergues además sirven comidas, principalmente el desayuno, a precios razonables.

DANHOSTEL está implementando un sistema de reconocimiento de los albergues que protegen el medio ambiente en colaboración con un organismo oficial llamado "La Llave Verde". Actualmente, la Llave Verde ha sido adjudicada a 13 albergues, pero se están procesando varias más. Busque la Banderilla de La Llave Verde que señala un albergue ecológico.

PASAPORTES Y VISADOS

Rogamos se ponga en contacto con la embajada o el consulado daneses del país donde resida.

HORARIO DE LOS BANCOS

Horario de atención al público: de lunes a viernes, de 9.30 h. a 16 h.; jueves de 9.30 h. a 18 h. Muchas de las sucursales de los aeropuertos, puertos y estaciones de tren abren hasta más tarde para cambiar divisas. Es posible que el horario varíe un poco según la localidad. Los cajeros automáticos rojos "Kontanten" aceptan las tarjetas Visa Euro, Master y Cirrus para retirar moneda danesa y están siempre abiertos. Importante: los bancos daneses a veces se niegan a cambiar los billetes extranjeros de alta denominación.

OFICINAS DE CORREOS

Normalmente abren los días laborables de 9 h./10 h. a 17 h./17.30 h. y los sábados de 9 h. a 12 h. Todas las oficinas de correos cierran los domingos.

HORARIO COMERCIAL

Generalmente, las tiendas abren de lunes a viernes de 9 h. a 17.30 h. y los sábados de 9 h. a 13 h., pero muchos supermercados y grandes almacenes están abiertos hasta las 19 h. los días laborables y hasta las 17 h. los sábados.

DESPLAZAMIENTOS

Avión

El aeropuerto de Copenhague es el eje de las rutas nacionales. Los aeropuertos nacionales de Aalborg, Copenhague, Tirstrup/Åarhus, Billund y Odense están situados de manera que puedan ser utilizados por varias poblaciones. La duración de los vuelos es mínima. Existen muchas tarifas reducidas, entre ellas las "salidas verdes", así como descuentos para niños, jóvenes y grupos.

Tren

Los servicios rápidos interurbanos son el pilar de la red DSB y enlazan la mayoría de las ciudades danesas. Las líneas principales tienen servicios regulares cada hora. Es necesario reservar asiento en estos trenes.

El centro de Copenhague se comunica con las afueras de la ciudad y con el aeropuerto de Copenhague mediante la red ferroviaria metropolitana electrificada "S-Train" que tiene trenes cada 10-20 minutos.

Varios trenes internacionales tienen conexiones con los servicios nacionales, formando así una red ferroviaria muy amplia.

Autobús

Existen muchas líneas de autobuses locales. Infórmese en las estaciones de tren.

Ferry

Dinamarca es un país rodeado de agua y ningún lugar se encuentra a más de 55 kilómetros del mar. Las numerosas islas habitadas se comunican mediante una amplia red de líneas de ferry.

Todos los barcos forman parte del sistema de transporte integrado del país y son puntuales y fiables.

El "Storebaeltsbroen", el Puente del Gran Belt, que une la isla de Fionia con la de Sjaelland: después de 12 años de trabajos intensivos, el 14 de junio de 1998 su Majestad la Reina

Margarita II de Dinamarca inauguró lo que entonces se había convertido en la obra de ingeniería de más envergadura de toda la historia de Dinamarca, el "Enlace Fijo del Gran Belt".

Automóvil

Su permiso de conducir debe indicar claramente que es válido para el tipo de vehículo que usted conduzca. No es obligatoria la carta verde, pero sí recomendable. Es obligatorio transportar un triángulo de advertencia, llevar los cinturones de seguridad abrochados y circular con las luces de cruce encendidas las 24 horas del día. Los coches con volante a la derecha deben estar provistos de triángulos negros adhesivos, que suelen poderse adquirir en las tiendas de las compañías de ferry o en las de automóviles.

'Hope is the last thing that dies in man; and though it be exceedingly deceitful, yet it is of this good use to us, that while we are travelling through life it conducts us in a easier and more pleasant way to our journey's end.

L'espérance est la dernière chose à mourir chez l'homme; et bien qu'elle soit des plus fourbes, elle nous est cependant bien utile, car tout au long du chemin de la vie, elle nous mène plus aisément et plus agréablement vers la fin du voyage.

Hoffnung ist das Letzte, was in einem Menschen stirbt; und obwohl äußerst betrügerisch von gutem Nutzen für uns, begleitet sie uns doch auf einfachere und angenehmere Weise bis an's Ende unseres Weges.

La esperanza es lo último que pierde el hombre; y, aunque es sumamente ilusoria, nos es de gran utilidad, pues, a lo largo de nuestra vida, nos facilita el camino y nos lleva de forma más placentera hacia nuestro destino.

François, Duc de la Rochefoucauld

Aalborg -
Aalborg Vandrerhjem

'Fjordparken',
Skydebanevej 50,
9000 Aalborg.
☎ 98116044
✆ 98124711

Open Dates: 20.01-15.12

Open Hours: 08.00-12.00; 16.00-21.00 hrs

Reservations: **R**

Price Range: DKK 100.00 🏧

Beds: 140 - 35x🛏

Facilities: ♿ 35x 👪 🍴 (B) 🛡 🚻 📺 📖
2 x🍽 🔲 🅿 🧺 ⁄⃔ ⬛

Directions:

✈ Aalborg 10km

A🚌 4km

🚂 3km

🚌 #8 200m

Attractions: ∪600m ⚲500m ⚓500m

Århus - Pavillonen

Marienlundsvej 10,
8240 Risskov.
☎ 86167298
✆ 86105560
e danhostel.aarhus@get2net.dk

Open Dates: 20.01-15.12

Open Hours: 07.00-11.00; 16.00-22.00 hrs

Reservations: **R**

Price Range: DKK 85.00-95.00
(Rooms 255-380 DKK) 🏧

Beds: 150 - 20x🛏 2x🛏 12x🛏

Facilities: ♿ 👪 20x 👪 🍴 (B) 🛡 🚻 📺
🔲 🎱 🔲 🅿 🛈 🧺 🐾 ⁄⃔

Directions: ③N from city centre

✈ Tirstrup - Aarhus 30km

🚢 Aarhus 3km

🚌 1 - 6 - 9 - 56 to Marienlund

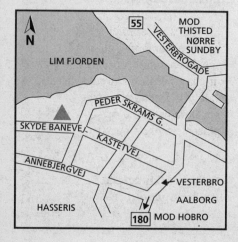

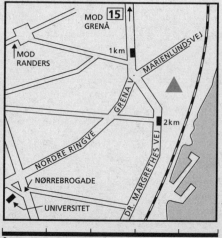

Billund -
Billund Vandrerhjem

Ellehammers Alle 2,
7190 Billund.
☏ 75332777
✆ 75332877
e billund@danhostel.dk

Open Dates: 🗓

Open Hours: 08.00-12.00; 15.00-20.00 hrs

Reservations: **R** **CC**

Price Range: DKK 100 (Rooms 325-450 DKK) 🍴

Beds: 228 - 22x⁴ 22x⁵ 2x⁶

Facilities: ♿ ♟ 44x ♟ 🍽 ☕ 🛏 📺 📖 🧺3 x 🍴 🗄 💻 ♨ 8 🅿 🛈 📶 🎿 🎢 ☎

Directions:

✈ Billund 500m

A🚌 Billund 500m

⛴ Esbierg 60km

🚂 Vejle 25km

🚌 44 & 912F 500m

Attractions: 🏞 🚴 ⛳ 🎣500m ⛵500m

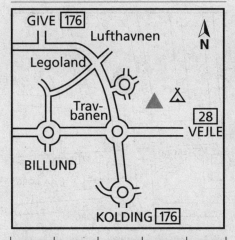

Copenhagen -
Copenhagen Amager

Vejlands Allé 200,
2300 København S.
☏ 32522908
✆ 32522708
e copenhagen-amager@danhostel.dk

Open Dates: 15.01-01.12

Open Hours: 🕐

Reservations: **R** **IBN**

Price Range: DKK 90.00-120.00 🍴

Beds: 528 - 64x² 80x⁵

Facilities: ♿ ♟ 144x ♟ 🍽 ☕ 🛏 📺 2 x 🍴 🗄 ♨ 🅿 🛈 📶 🎿 🎢 ☎

Directions: **4SE** from city centre

✈ Copenhagen 4km

A🚌 100S + 250S

⛴ Copenhagen 4km

🚂 Copenhagen Central Station 5km

🚌 46, 100S & 250S

Attractions: 🏞 ⛵2km

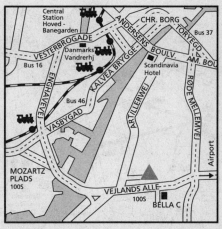

Copenhagen -
Copenhagen Bellahøj

Herbergvejen 8,
2700 Brønshøj.
☎ 38289715
🖷 38890210
✉ bellahoej@danhostel.dk

Open Dates:	01.03-15.01
Open Hours:	🕐
Reservations:	**R** **IBN**
Price Range:	DKK 90.00-120.00 (Rooms DKK 250-640) 🔟
Beds:	252 - 7x⁴🛏 31x⁶🛏 3x⁶🛏
Facilities:	♿ 🛉 7x 🛉 🍽 🛋 🏨 📺 🖼 3 x🍴 🔲 📷 🏧 🔟 Ⓟ 🍴 ♻ ⚠ 🔍

Directions:	5NW from city centre
✈	Kastrup-Copenhagen 15km
A🚌	250S 800m
⛴	Copenhagen 5km
🚃	Copenhagen Central 4km
🚌	11 or 2 200m ap Bellahøj or Brønshøj
Ⓤ	Grøndal 500m
Attractions:	⚓500m

Fjerritslev

Brøndumvej 14-16,
9690 Fjerritslev.
☎ 98211190
🖷 98212522

Open Dates:	🔟
Open Hours:	07.00-22.00 hrs
Reservations:	**R** **CC**
Price Range:	DKK 100.00 (Rooms 200-500 DKK) 🔟
Beds:	178 - 2x²🛏 2x³🛏 38x⁴🛏 1x⁶🛏
Facilities:	♿ 🛉 40x 🛉 🍽 🛋 📺 🖼 3 x🍴 📷 🔟 ⊜ Ⓟ 🅸 🍴 ♻ ⚠ ♻ 🔍 ⊞

Directions:	
✈	Aalborg 45km
A🚌	200m
⛴	10km
🚃	50km
🚌	100m
Attractions:	⚘ ⚘ 5km 🚴 🚶 ∪ 2km ⚲ ⚓

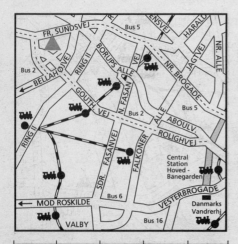

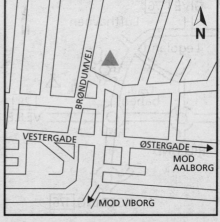

Helsingør - "Villa Moltke"

**Ndr Strandvej 24,
3000 Helsingør.**
☎ 49211640
✆ 49211399
℮ helsingoer@danhostel.dk

Open Dates:	01.02-30.11
Open Hours:	08.00-12.00; 15.00-21.00hrs (01.05-30.09); 08.00-12.00; 15.00-20.00hrs (01.10-30.04)
Reservations:	**R**
Price Range:	DKK 90.00 🍴
Beds:	180 - 3x² 2x³ 19x⁴ 7x⁵ 3x⁶ 6x⁶
Facilities:	♿ ⅲ 38x ⅲ 🍽 (B) ♂ ⚑ 📺 ▤ ☒3 x🍷 🖾 ♨ 🅿 ℹ 🧺 ⚡ ⋀ 🔍 🏠
Directions:	1.5NW from city centre
✈	Copenhagen 60km
⛴	Helsingborg-Helsingør 2km
🚌	Helsingør 2km
🚐	340 200m ap Højstrup 200m
🚃	Højstrup 200m ap Højstrup 200m
Attractions:	⛳ 🔍 🎿 ∪2km ⚲100m ≋100m

Odense - The Hans Christian Andersen

**Kragsbjerggården,
Kragsbjergvej 121,
5230 Odense M.**
☎ 66130425
✆ 65912863
℮ odensehostel@mailhost.net

Open Dates:	15.02-01.12
Open Hours:	08.00-12.00; 16.00-20.00hrs
Reservations:	**R**
Price Range:	DKK 92.00 (ⅲ DKK 250-360) 🍴
Beds:	170 - 4x² 15x⁴ 1x⁵ 12x⁶
Facilities:	ⅲ 32x ⅲ 🍽 ♂ ⚑ 📺 ☒ 3 x🍷 ▣ 🖾 ♨ 🅿 ℹ 🧺 ⚡ ⋀ 🔍 🏠
Directions:	2 SE from city centre
✈	Billund 75km
A🚐	2.5km
🚌	Odense 2.5km
🚐	61; 62; 63; 64 200m ap Munkebjerg Plads
Attractions:	🚴 ≋2.5km

There are 2 hostels in Odense. See following pages.

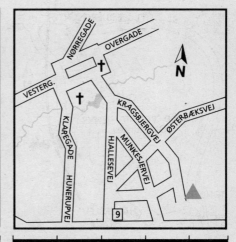

Ribe

Sct Pedersgade 16,
6760 Ribe.
☎ 75420620
✆ 75424288
✉ ribehanh@post5.tele.dk

Open Dates:	01.02-30.11
Open Hours:	08.00-12.00; 16.00-18.00hrs
Reservations:	**R**
Price Range:	DKK 100.00-250.00 🔟
Beds:	140 - 4x² 18x⁴ 12x⁵
Facilities:	♿ ♦♦♦ 34x ♦♦♦ � (B) ☎ ♨ 📺 📠 🗄4 x ☍ ☐ 🖼 8 P ⓘ ⊠ ♨ ⋔ ▨ ❀ ⊞ ⌂

Directions:

✈	Billund 55km
⛴	Esbjerg 35km
🚌	Ribe 500m
🚌	Ribe 500m ap Ribe Bus Station

Attractions: ⌖ ⚲ 🚶 ∪2km ⚲1km ≈1km

Svendborg

Vestergade 45,
5700 Svendborg.
☎ 62216699
✆ 62202939
✉ danhostel.svendborg@get2net.dk

Open Dates:	03.01-17.12
Open Hours:	08.00-20.00hrs
Reservations:	**R** **⊂CC⊃**
Price Range:	DKK 100.00-400.00 🔟
Beds:	268 - 7x¹ 30x² 31x³ 16x⁴
Facilities:	♦♦♦ 84x ♦♦♦ ♨ (BD) ☎ ♨ 📺 🗄10 x ☍ ☐ 🖼 8 P ⓘ ⊠ ⋔ ▨ ❀ ⌂

Directions:

✈	42km
⛴	1km
🚌	800m
🚌	800m

Attractions: ⌖ ⚲2km ⚲ ≈ 2Km ⚲2km ≈2km

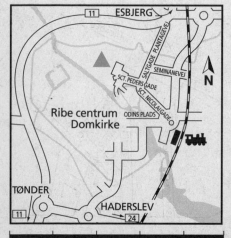

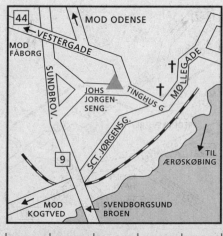

Sæby

Sæbygaardsvej 32,
9300 Sæby.
☎ 98463650
📠 98467630
📧 sabyfri@internord.dk

Open Dates: 🗓

Open Hours: 08.00-22.00hrs

Reservations: Ⓡ

Price Range: DKK 70.00-170.00 💷

Beds: 156 - 2x² 🚲 13x⁴ 🚲 3x⁵ 🚲 15x⁶ 🚲 2x⁶ 🚲

Facilities: 👬 32x 👬 ⏰ 📺 💺 📺 🧺 3 x 🍴 ▢ ⑧ P 🐾 ⛰ ⌗ ⚘ ⛲

Directions: 0.8 W from city centre

✈ Aalborg 50km

A🚌 500m

🚢 Frederikshavn 12km

🚂 Frederikshavn 12km

🚌 73 200m

Attractions: 🏌 🎈 1.3km ∪5km ⚲400m 🏊 12km

There is 1 hostel in Sæby. See following pages.

Sønderborg

Kærvej 70,
6400 Sønderborg.
☎ 74423112
📠 74425631
📧 gonzo.johannsen@
augustenborg.mail.telia.com

Open Dates: 01.02-30.11

Open Hours: 08.00-12.00; 16.00-20.00hrs

Reservations: Ⓡ

Price Range: DKK 100.00-350.00 💷

Beds: 200 - 38x⁴ 🚲 6x⁶ 🚲

Facilities: ♿ 👬 44x 👬 ⏰ 💺 🏩 📺 🧺 4 x 🍴 ▢ 📷 🏓 ⑧ 💺 P 🅹 🐾 🦮 ⛰ ⚘ ⚲ ⌗

Directions:

✈ Sønderborg 5km

🚢 Fynshav 14km

🚂 Sønderborg 1km

🚌 1km

Attractions: 🏌 🎈 🚴 ⚲1.5km 🏊500m

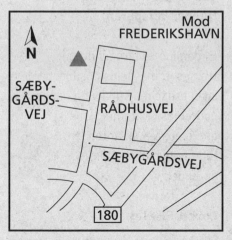

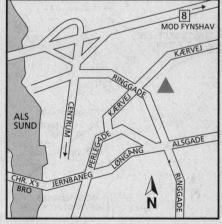

Tisvildeleje

St Helene Centeret,
Bygmarken 30,
3220 Tisvildeleje.
☎ 48709850
📠 48709897
✉ sch@helene.dk

Open Dates: 🗓

Open Hours: 08.00-21.00hrs

Price Range: DKK 100.00-450.00 💳

Beds: 160 - 40x 🛏

Facilities: ♿ 🚻 40x 🚻 🍽 ⛺ 🏨 📺 📱
5 x 🍴 🔒 🖼 🧺 🅿 ℹ 🧳 ♻
🛝 🍷 🏛 🏘

Directions:

✈ Copenhagen-Kastrup 60km

⛴ Elsinore (Helsingør) 28km

🚃 Tisvildeleje 500m

Attractions: 🎣 🔍 1km 🚴 🏃 ∪ 400m 🎿
⛵ 9km

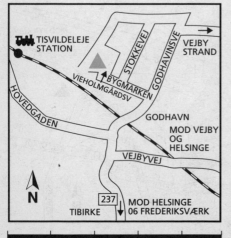

> The journey is difficult, immense. We will travel as far as we can, but we cannot in one lifetime see all that we would like to see or to learn all that we hunger to know.

Le voyage est difficile, immense. Nous voyagerons aussi loin que nous le pourrons, mais il ne nous sera pas possible, dans une vie, de voir tout ce que nous voudrions voir ni d'apprendre tout ce que nous avons soif de connaître.

Die Reise ist unheimlich kompliziert. Wir reisen so weit wie möglich, können aber in einem Leben nicht all das sehen, was wir gerne möchten oder das lernen, wonach wir Hunger verspüren.

El camino es largo y difícil. Iremos lo más lejos posible, pero en el espacio de una vida nunca podremos ver todo lo que queremos ver, ni aprender todo lo que ansiamos aprender.

Loren Eiseley

Location/Address	Telephone No. Fax No.	Beds	Opening Dates	Facilities
▲ **Aabenraa** Sønderskovvej 100, 6200 Aabenraa.	☎ 74622699 🖷 74622939	102	01.03–31.10	
▲ **Aalborg** - Aalborg Vandrerhjem 'Fjordparken', Skydebanevej 50, 9000 Aalborg.	☎ 98116044 🖷 98124711	140	20.01–15.12	
▲ **Århus** - Pavillonen **Marienlundsvej 10, 8240 Risskov.** ✉ danhostel.aarhus@get2net.dk	☎ 86167298 🖷 86105560	150	20.01-15.12	3N
▲ **Årup** Skolegade 3, 5560 Årup.	☎ 64431328 🖷 64432034	54	15.01–15.12	
▲ **Assens** - Ungdommens hus Adelgade 26, 5610 Assens.	☎ 64711357 🖷 64715657	54	01.03–31.10	
▲ **Billund** - Billund Vandrerhjem **Ellehammers Alle 2, 7190 Billund.** ✉ billund@danhostel.dk	☎ 75332777 🖷 75332877	228		CC
▲ **Blokhus-Hune** - Kirkevej 26 Kirkevej 26, 9492 Blokhus. ✉ blokvhj@post9.tele.dk	☎ 98249180 🖷 98209005	100	01.03–01.11 ( )	
▲ **Boderne** Bodernevej 28, 3720 Aakirkeby. ✉ danhostel@rosengaarden.dk	☎ 56974950 🖷 56974948	75		
▲ **Brande** Dr Arendsvej 2, 7330 Brande.	☎ 97182197 🖷 97182197	54	01.03–30.11 (01.01–20.12)	
▲ **Copenhagen** - Copenhagen Amager (IBN) **Vejlands Allé 200, 2300 København S.** ✉ copenhagen-amager@danhostel.dk	☎ 32522908 🖷 32522708	528	15.01–01.12	4SE
▲ **Copenhagen** - Copenhagen Bellahøj (IBN) **Herbergvejen 8, 2700 Brønshøj.** ✉ bellahoej@danhostel.dk	☎ 38289715 🖷 38890210	252	01.03–15.01	5NW
▲ **Ebeltoft** Søndergade 43, 8400 Ebeltoft.	☎ 86342053 🖷 86342077	72	01.02–31.12	
▲ **Enderupskov** Ribelandevej, 30, 6510 Gram.	☎ 74821711 🖷 74820782	50	01.03–31.10	
▲ **Esbjerg** Vardevej 80, 6700 Esbjerg. ✉ esbjerg@danhostel.dk	☎ 75124258 🖷 75136833	124	01.02–01.12	
▲ **Fåborg** Grønnegade 72, 5600 Fåborg.	☎ 62611203 🖷 62613508	75	01.04–01.10	
▲ **Fakse** Østervej 4, 4640 Fakse.	☎ 56714181 🖷 56715492	70	03.01–19.12	0.1S
▲ **Fjerritslev** **Brøndumvej 14-16, 9690 Fjerritslev.**	☎ 98211190 🖷 98212522	178		CC
▲ **Fredensborg** Østrupvej 3, 3480 Fredensborg. ✉ danhostel.fredensborg@post3.tele.dk	☎ 48480315 🖷 48481656	94	05.01–15.12	

Location/Address	Telephone No. Fax No.	Beds	Opening Dates	Facilities
▲ **Fredericia** Vestre Ringvej 98, 7000 Fredericia.	☎ 75921287 🖷 75932905	135	15.01–15.12	� ♙♙♙ ⑩ **R** 2SE ⌕ ☞ **P** ⌕
▲ **Frederikshavn** 'Fladstrand', Buhlsvej 6, 9900 Frederikshavn.	☎ 98421475 🖷 98426522	130	01.02–19.12	♙♙♙ ⑩ **R** 1NW ⌕ ☞ **P**
▲ **Frederiksværk** Strandgade 30, 3300 Frederiksværk. ✉ strandbo@image.dk	☎ 47770725 🖷 47720766	100	01.02–30.11	♙♙♙ ⑩ ⌕ ☞ **P** ⌕
▲ **Givskud** Løveparkvej 2, 7323 Givskud. ✉ danhostel@aof-rejser.dk	☎ 75730500 🖷 75730530	126	01.01–30.11	♙♙♙ ⑩ **R** ⌕ ⌁CC⌁ ☞ **P** ⌕
▲ **Gjerrild** 'Djursvold', Dyrehavevej 9, Gjerrild, 8500 Grenå. ✉ djursvold@post.tele.dk	☎ 86384199 🖷 86384302	92	01.04–30.09	♙♙♙ ⑩ ⌕ ☞ **P** ⌕
▲ **Grenå** Ydesvej 4, 8500 Grenå.	☎ 86326622 🖷 86321248	108	03.01–22.12	♙♙♙ ⑩ ⌕ ☞ **P** ⌕
▲ **Grindsted** Morsbøl Skolevej 24, Morsbøl 7200 Grindsted. ✉ gvh@image.dk	☎ 75322605 🖷 75310905	80	01.04–30.09 (♙♙♙ 01.02–30.11)	♙♙♙ ⑩ **R** 5SW ⌕ ☞ **P**
▲ **Gudhjem** Ejner Mikkelsens Vej 14, 3760 Gudhjem. ✉ danhostel-gudhjem@bornholm.net	☎ 56485035 🖷 56485635	220	🗓12	♙♙♙ ⑩ ☞ **P**
▲ **Haderslev** Erlevvej 34, 6100 Haderslev. ✉ bh-had@post12.tele.dk	☎ 74521347 🖷 74521364	102	01.02–30.11	♙♙♙ ⑩ ⌕ ☞ **P**
▲ **Hadsund** Stadionvej 33, 9560 Hadsund. ✉ hadsund@get2net.dk	☎ 98574345 🖷 98574356	48	01.04–30.09	♙♙♙ ⑩ **R** ⌁CC⌁ ☞ **P** ⌕ ☕
▲ **Hasle** Fælledvej 28, 3790 Hasle.	☎ 56964175 (01.11-01.04, 56966434) 🖷 56964175	100	01.05–30.10	♙♙♙ ⑩ ☞ **P**
▲ **Helsingør** - "Villa Moltke" **Ndr Strandvej 24, 3000 Helsingør.** ✉ helsingoer@danhostel.dk	☎ 49211640 🖷 49211399	180	01.02-30.11	♙♙♙ ⑩ **R** 1.5NW ⌕ ☞ **P**
▲ **Henne St** Strandvejen 458, 6854 Henne Strand.	☎ 75255075 🖷 75255075	44	🗓12	♙♙♙ ⑩ **R** ⌕ ☞ **P**
▲ **Herning** Holingknuden 2, Holing, 7400 Herning.	☎ 97123144 🖷 97216169	112	01.02–30.11	♙♙♙ ⑩ **R** 3NW ⌕ ☞ **P** ⌕
▲ **Hirtshals** Kystvejen 53, 9850 Hirtshals. ✉ danhostel.hirtshals@adr.dk	☎ 98941248 🖷 98945655	72	01.03–01.11	♙♙♙ ⑩ **R** ⌁CC⌁ ☞ **P**
▲ **Hjembæk** Tornbrinken 2, Hjembæk, 4450 Jyderup.	☎ 59268181 🖷 59268033	50	🗓12	♙♙♙ ⑩ **R** ☞ ⌕
▲ **Hjørring** Thomas Morildsvej, 9800 Hjørring.	☎ 98926700 🖷 98901550	140	01.03–01.10	♙♙♙ ⑩ ⌕ ☞ **P** ⌕

Location/Address	Telephone No. Fax No.	Beds	Opening Dates	Facilities
▲ **Hobro** Amerikavej 24, 9500 Hobro. ✉ danhostel.hobro@adr.dk	☏ 98521847 🖷 98511847	108	15.01–15.12	♦♦♦ �🍽 ⅋ ☞ 🅿 ▫
▲ **Holbæk** Ahlgade 1B, 4300 Holbæk. ✉ vandrehjem@vestnet.dk	☏ 59442919 🖷 59439485	90	04.01–20.12	♦♦♦ 🍽 ℝ ⅋ 🅿 ▫
▲ **Horsens** Flintebakken 150, 8700 Horsens. ✉ horsens@danhostel.dk	☏ 75616777 🖷 75610871	108	15.01–15.12	♦♦♦ 🍽 ⅋ ⅽⅽ 🅿 ▫
▲ **Hvide Sande** Numitvej 5, 6960 Hvide Sande. ✉ danhostel@hvidesande	☏ 97312105 🖷 97312196	88	🗓12	♦♦♦ 🍽 ☞ 🅿 ▫
▲ **Jels** Ørstedvej 10, Jels, 6630 Rødding. ✉ jelsdanh@post10.tele.dk	☏ 74552869 🖷 74553107	98	🗓12	♦♦♦ 🍽 ⅋ ⅽⅽ ☞ 🅿 ▫
▲ **Juelsminde** Rousthøj Alle 1, 7130 Juelsminde. ✉ turist@juelsmindekom.dk	☏ 75693313, 75693066 🖷 75693130, 75693957	68	01.05–30.10 (♦♦♦ 🗓12)	♦♦♦ 🍽 ⅋ ☞ 🅿 ▫
▲ **Jægerspris** Skovnæsvej 2, 3630 Jægerspris.	☏ 47311032 🖷 47312832	85	01.05–31.10	♦♦♦ 🍽 ⅽⅽ ☞ 🅿 ▫
▲ **Kalundborg** Stadion Alle 5, 4400 Kalundborg. ✉ welcome@post11.tele.dk	☏ 59561366 🖷 59564626	118	🗓12	♦♦♦ 🍽 ℝ 1 W ⅋ ⅽⅽ ☞ 🅿 ▫
▲ **Katrinedal** 'Rast', Vellingvej 53, 8654 Bryrup. ✉ katrinedal@silkeborg.bib.dk	☏ 75756146 🖷 75757810	64	01.05–01.09 (♦♦♦ 🗓12)	♦♦♦ 🍽 ☞ 🅿
▲ **Kerteminde** Skovvej 46, 5300 Kerteminde.	☏ 65323929 🖷 65323924	90	03.01–15.12	♦♦♦ 🍽 ⅋ ☞ 🅿 ▫
▲ **Kolding** Ørnsborgvej 10, 6000 Kolding. ✉ koldingv@post2.tele.dk	☏ 75509140 🖷 75509151	92	01.02–01.12	♦♦♦ 🍽 ☞ 🅿 ▫
▲ **Korsør** Tovesvej 30F, 4220 Korsør. ✉ korsoer@turisme.dk	☏ 58371022 🖷 58356870	80	07.01–15.12	♦♦♦ 🍽 ℝ 2.5 NE ⅋ ⅽⅽ ☞ 🅿 ▫
▲ **Køge** Lille Køgegaard, Vamdrupvej 1, 4600 Køge.	☏ 56651474 🖷 56660869	80	01.04–15.12	♦♦♦ 🍽 ℝ 2.5 W ☞ 🅿 ▫
▲ **Lyngby** Rådvad 1, 2800 Lyngby.	☏ 45803074 🖷 45803032	94	01.04–25.10 (♦♦♦ 10.01–15.12)	♦♦♦ 🍽 7 NE ☞ 🅿
▲ **Læsø** Lærkevej 6, 9950 Vesterø Havn, Læsø.	☏ 98499195 🖷 98499160	90	15.04–01.10	♦♦♦ 🍽 ☞ 🅿
▲ **Løgumkloster** Vænget 28, 6240 Løgumkloster.	☏ 74743618 🖷 74743619	42	06.04–13.12	♦♦♦ 🍽 ☞ 🅿
▲ **Maribo** Sdr Boulevard 82B, 4930 Maribo.	☏ 54783314 🖷 54783265	96	03.01–26.12	♦♦♦ 🍽 ℝ ⅽⅽ ☞ 🅿

Location/Address	Telephone No. Fax No.	Beds	Opening Dates	Facilities
▲ **Marstal** Færgestræde 29, 5960 Marstal. ✉ mav@adr.dk	☎ 62531064 🖷 62531057	82	01.05–31.08	♔ ⏻ ☞
▲ **Møn** Langebjergvej 1, 4791 Borre.	☎ 55812030 🖷 55812818	105	01.05–01.09	♔ ⏻ ☞ 🅿
▲ **Nakskov** Branderslevvej 11, 4900 Nakskov.	☎ 54922434 🖷 54923367	60	🖾	♔ ⏻ ♿ ☞ 🅿 ⎙
▲ **Næstved** Frejasvej 8, 4700 Næstved. ✉ nstvh@post4.tele.dk	☎ 55722091 🖷 55725645	87	15.03–15.11 (♔ 01.02–30.11)	♔ ⏻ 1SE ☞ 🅿
▲ **Nyborg** Havnegade 28, 5800 Nyborg.	☎ 65312704 🖷 65302604	88	11.01–10.12	♔ ⏻ ♿ ☞ 🅿 ⎙
▲ **Nykøbing Falster (Falster)** Østre Alle 10, 4800 Nykøbing Falster.	☎ 54856699 🖷 54823242	94	15.01–15.12	♔ ⏻ ♿ ☞ 🅿 ⎙
▲ **Nykøbing Mors (Jutland)** Østerstand, 7900 Nykøbing Mors. ✉ danhostel.nyk.mors@adr.dk	☎ 97720617 🖷 97720776	129	01.02–20.12	♔ ⏻ ♿ ☞ 🅿 ⎙
▲ **Nykøbing Sjælland (Sealand)** Egebjergvej 162, 4500 Nykøbing Sj. ✉ naturskole@mail.tele.dk	☎ 59930062 🖷 59930162	44	10.01–17.12	♔ ⏻ CC ☞ 🅿 ⎙
▲ **Odense** - The Hans Christian Andersen **Kragsbjerggården, Kragsbjergvej 121,** **5230 Odense M.** ✉ odensehostel@mailhost.net	☎ 66130425 🖷 65912863	170	15.02-01.12	♔ ⏻ ℝ 2SE ☞ 🅿 ⎙
▲ **Odense** - "The Ugly Duckling" Øtre Stationvej 31, 5000 Odense.	☎ 63110425 🖷 63113520	140	🖾	♔ ⏻ ℝ ☞ 🅿 ⎙ ☕
▲ **Oksbøl** Præstegårdsvej 21, 6840 Oksbøl. ✉ danhostel@post.tele.dk	☎ 75271877 🖷 75272544	100	15.01–15.12	♔ ⏻ ♿ ☞ 🅿 ⎙
▲ **Randers** Gethersvej 1, 8900 Randers. ✉ randers.danhostel@adr.dk	☎ 86425044 🖷 86419854	138	01.02–30.11	♔ ⏻ ℝ 0.5NW ♿ ☞ 🅿 ⎙
▲ **Rebild** Rebildvej 23, Rebild, 9520 Skørping. ✉ rebild@vandrerhjem.dk	☎ 98391340 🖷 98392740	100	20.01–20.12	♔ ⏻ ♿ ☞ 🅿 ⎙
▲ **Ribe** **Sct Pedersgade 16, 6760 Ribe.** ✉ ribehanh@post5.tele.dk	☎ 75420620 🖷 75424288	140	01.02-30.11	♔ ⏻ ℝ ♿ ☞ 🅿 ⎙
▲ **Ringe** Søvej 34, 5750 Ringe.	☎ 62622151 🖷 62622154	46	04.01–18.12	♔ ⏻ ♿ ☞ 🅿 ⎙
▲ **Ringkøbing** Kirkevej 26, 6950 Ringkøbing. ✉ rofi@rofi.dk	☎ 97322455 🖷 97324959	120	🖾	♔ ⏻ ℝ 1.5SW ♿ ☞ 🅿 ⎙
▲ **Ringsted** St Bendtsgade 18, 4100 Ringsted.	☎ 57611526 🖷 57613426	84	02.01–15.12	♔ ⏻ ☞ 🅿

Location/Address	Telephone No. Fax No.	Beds	Opening Dates	Facilities
▲ **Roskilde** Vindeboder 7, 4000 Roskilde. ℮ danhostel.roskilde@post.tele.dk	☏ 46352184 ✆ 46326690	152	🗓	♦♦♦ ⛶ 🅁 ⚫ ⟨CC⟩ ☞ 🅿 ⬚
▲ **Roslev** Viumvej 8, 7870 Roslev. ℮ roslevva@post11.tele.dk	☏ 97571385 ✆ 97572052	92	🗓	♦♦♦ ⛶ ☞ 🅿 ⬚
▲ **Rudbøl** Rudbølvej 19-21, Rudbøl, 6280 Højer. ℮ danhostelrudb@mail.tele.dk	☏ 74738298 ✆ 74738035	54	15.03–31.10	♦♦♦ ⛶ ☞ 🅿 ⬚
▲ **Rudkøbing** Engdraget 11, 5900 Rudkøbing.	☏ 62511830 ✆ 62511830	66	15.03–31.10 (♦♦♦ 🗓)	♦♦♦ ⛶ 🅁 ⚫ ☞ 🅿 ⬚
▲ **Ry** 'Knudhule', Randersvej 88, 8680 Ry. ℮ mail@danhostel-ry.dk	☏ 86891407 ✆ 86892870	117	15.01–15.12	♦♦♦ ⛶ ⚫ ⟨CC⟩ ☞ 🅿 ⬚
▲ **Rømø** Lyngvejen 7, 6792 Rømø ℮ romodanhostel@post.tele.dk	☏ 74755188 ✆ 74755187	91	15.03–15.10	♦♦♦ ⛶ ☞ 🅿
▲ **Rønde** Kaløvej 2, 8410 Rønde.	☏ 86371108 ✆ 86371128	70	🗓	♦♦♦ ⛶ ⚫ ☞ 🅿
▲ **Rønne** Arsenalvej 12, 3700 Rønne. ℮ rvh@post4.tele.dk	☏ 56951340 ✆ 56950132	140	01.03–01.11	♦♦♦ ⛶ ⟨CC⟩ ☞ 🅿 ⬚
▲ **Sakskøbing** Saxe's alle 10, 4990 Sakskøbing.	☏ 54706045 ✆ 54706041	82	03.01–19.12	♦♦♦ ⛶ ⚫ 🅿
▲ **Samsø** Klintevej 8, Ballen, 8305 Samsø.	☏ 86592044 ✆ 86592343	100	15.03–01.11	♦♦♦ ⛶ ☞ 🅿 ⬚
▲ **Sandvig** - Sjøljan Hammershusvej 94, 3770 Allinge. ℮ danhostel.sandvig@get2net.dk	☏ 56480362 ✆ 56481862	100	01.04–31.10	♦♦♦ ⛶ ☞ 🅿
△ *Sejerø* *Sejerbyvej 4, Sejerby, 4592 Sejerø.*	☏ *59590290,* *44980504* *(02.08-22.06)*	*35*	*19.06–01.08*	♦♦♦ ⛶ 🅁 ☞ 🅿
▲ **Silkeborg** Åhavevej 55, 8600 Silkeborg.	☏ 86823642 ✆ 86812777	93	01.03–30.11	♦♦♦ ⛶ ⚫ ☞ 🅿 ⬚
▲ **Skagen NY** Skagen NY Vandrerhjem, Rolighedsvej 2, 9990 Skagen. ℮ danhostel.skagen@adr.dk	☏ 98442200 ✆ 98442255	112	15.02–30.11	♦♦♦ ⛶ 🅁 ⚫ ☞ 🅿 ⬚
▲ **Skanderborg** Dyrehaven, 8660 Skanderborg. ℮ skanhostel@skanderborg-danhostel.dk	☏ 86511966 ✆ 86511334	138	01.05–01.10	♦♦♦ ⛶ 3N ☞ 🅿 ⬚
▲ **Skælskør** Lystskov, Slagelsevej 48, 4230 Skælskør.	☏ 58160980 ✆ 58160989	100	01.02–10.12	♦♦♦ ⛶ ⚫ ☞ 🅿 ⬚
▲ **Slagelse** Bjergbygade 78, 4200 Slagelse.	☏ 58522528 ✆ 58522540	125	15.01–10.12	♦♦♦ ⛶ ☞ 🅿
▲ **Sorø** Skælskørvej 34, 4180 Sorø	☏ 57849200 ✆ 57849201	77	01.04–30.09	♦♦♦ ⛶ ⚫ ⟨CC⟩ ☞ 🅿 ⬚

Location/Address	Telephone No. Fax No.	Beds	Opening Dates	Facilities
▲ **Store Heddinge** Ved Munkevænget 1, 4660 Store Heddinge.	☎ 56502022 🖷 56502022	63	30.03–30.09 (ⓘ 🗓)	ⅲ ⑩ ✆ 🅿
▲ **Struer** Fjordvejen 12, Bremdal, 7600 Struer.	☎ 97855313 🖷 97840950	90	01.02–30.11	ⅲ ⑩ Ⓡ 1.5SE 🅰 ✆ 🅿 ⓖ
▲ **Svaneke** Reberbanevej 9, 3740 Svaneke. 🅔 danhostel-svaneke@bornholm.net	☎ 56496242 🖷 56497383	152	27.03–01.10	ⅲ ⑩ Ⓡ ✆ 🅿 ⓖ
▲ **Svendborg** **Vestergade 45, 5700 Svendborg.** 🅔 danhostel.svendborg@get2net.dk	☎ 62216699 🖷 62202939	268	03.01-17.12	ⅲ ⑩ Ⓡ 🅲🅲 ✆ 🅿 ⓖ
▲ **Sæby** **Sæbygaardsvej 32, 9300 Sæby.** 🅔 sabyfri@internord.dk	☎ 98463650 🖷 98467630	156	🗓	ⅲ ⑩ Ⓡ 0.8W ✆ 🅿 ⓖ
▲ **Sønderborg-Vollerup** Mommarkvej, 17+22, 6400 Sønderborg 🅔 vollerup@post1.tele.dk	☎ 74423990 🖷 74425290	150	🗓	ⅲ ⑩ Ⓡ 🅰 🅲🅲 ✆ 🅿 ⓖ ☕
▲ **Sønderborg** **Kærvej 70, 6400 Sønderborg.** 🅔 gonzo.johannsen@augustenborg.mail.telia.com	☎ 74423112 🖷 74425631	200	01.02–30.11	ⅲ ⑩ Ⓡ 🅰 ✆ 🅿 ⓖ
▲ **Thisted** Skinnerup, Kongemøllevej 8, 7700 Thisted. 🅔 danhostel.thisted@adr.dk	☎ 97925042 🖷 97925150	88	01.03–31.10	ⅲ ⑩ 4N 🅲🅲 ✆ 🅿 ⓖ
▲ **Tisvildeleje** **St Helene Centeret, Bygmarken 30,** **3220 Tisvildeleje.** 🅔 sch@helene.dk	☎ 48709850 🖷 48709897	160	🗓	ⅲ ⑩ 🅰 ✆ 🅿 ⓖ
▲ **Tønder** 'Kogsgården', Sønderport 4, 6270 Tønder. 🅔 danhostel@tonder-net.dk	☎ 74723500 🖷 74722797	124	01.02–20.12	ⅲ ⑩ 🅰 ✆ 🅿 ⓖ
▲ **Varde** Ungdomsgården, Pramstedvej 10, 6800 Varde.	☎ 75221091 🖷 75223338	48	15.03–01.10	ⅲ ⑩ ✆ 🅿
▲ **Vejle** Gl Landevej 80, 7100 Vejle. 🅔 info@vejle-danhostel	☎ 75825188 🖷 75831783	120	02.01–30.11	ⅲ ⑩ 3SE ✆ 🅿 ⓖ
▲ **Viborg** 'Søndersø', Vinkelvej 36, 8800 Viborg. 🅔 vibhoste@post8.tele.dk	☎ 86671781 🖷 86671788	112	01.03–30.11	ⅲ ⑩ 2SE ✆ 🅿 ⓖ
▲ **Vordingborg** Præstegaardsvej 16, 4760 Vordingborg	☎ 45 55 360800 🖷 45 55 360801	112	04.01–20.12	ⅲ ⑩ 25S 🅰 🅲🅲 ✆ 🅿 ⓖ ☕
▲ **Ærøskøbing** Smedevejen 15, 5970 Ærøskøbing.	☎ 62521044 🖷 62521644	87	01.04–31.10	ⅲ ⑩ 🅰 ✆ 🅿 ⓖ

FAROE ISLANDS HOSTELS

All the hostels listed here are Simple Standard

Ferõamannaheimiõ Á - Gilijanes

FO-360 Sandavágur
- (298) 333465
- (298) 332901
- giljanes@post.olivant.fo

La Caretta

FO-350 Vestmanna
- (298) 424610
- (298) 424708
- carreta@post.olivant.fo

Gjáargarõur

FO-476 Gjógv
- (298) 423171
- (298) 423505
- trygvisivertsen@email.dk

Fjalsgarõur

FO-690 Oyndarfjøõur
- (298) 444522
- (298) 444570

Youth Hostel Íbúo
Garõavegur 31, FO-700 Klaksvik

- (298) 457555
- (298) 287965
- (298) 457555
- ibudkl@post.olivant.fo

Áargarõur

FO-827 Øravik
- (298) 371302
- (298) 372057

Bládýpi

Dr. Jakobsensgøta 14-16 FO-100 Tórshavn
- (298) 311951
- (298) 319451

Scout Centre Selatraõ

c/o Hoydalsvegur 6
Postboks 1080
FO-110 Tórshavn
- (298) 311075/288950
- (298) 448950
- (298) 310775
- kfumskfo@post.olivant.fo

Vallaraheimiõ Tórshavn

Viõ Oyggjarvegin
FO-100 Tórshavn
- (298) 318900
- (298) 315707
- booking@smyril-line.fo

Net Savings
@Hostelling
International

Don't leave your booking to chance

**HOSTELLING
INTERNATIONAL**

netsavings@hostellinginternational.org.uk

England & Wales

ANGLETERRE & PAYS DE GALLES
ENGLAND & WALES
INGLATERRA Y GALES

**YHA (England & Wales) Limited,
Trevelyan House, 8 St Stephen's Hill,
St Albans, Hertfordshire, AL1 2DY, England**

Customer Services
☎ (44) (1727) 845047
🖷 (44) (1727) 844126
🄴 customerservices@yha.org.uk
www.yha.org.uk

Office Hours: Monday-Friday, 09.00-18.30hrs

Central London Booking Service
☎ (44) (20) 73733400
🖷 (44) (20) 73733455
🄴 lonres@yha.org.uk

Opening Hours: Monday, 09.00-17.00hrs Tues-Fri, 09.00-19.00hrs Saturday, 09.00-17.00hrs

A copy of the Hostel Directory for this Country can be obtained from:
The National Office.

Capital:	London		**Population:**	52,211,175
Language:	English		**Size:**	151,207 sq km
Currency:	£ Sterling (Pound)		**Telephone Country Code:**	44

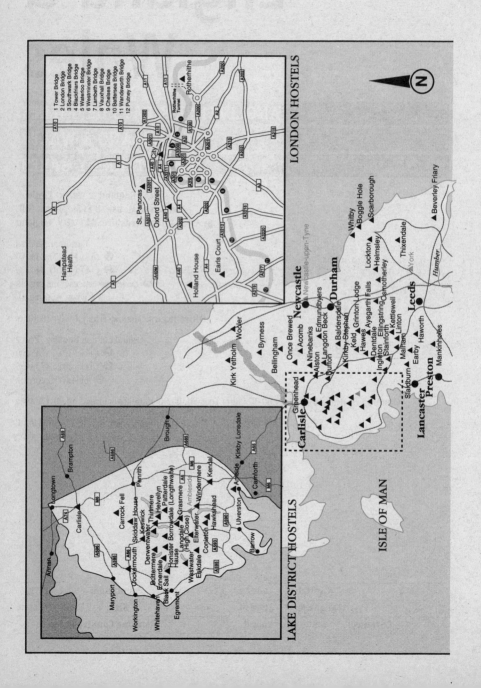

N

LONDON HOSTELS

1 Tower Bridge
2 London Bridge
3 Southwark Bridge
4 Blackfriars Bridge
5 Waterloo Bridge
6 Westminster Bridge
7 Lambeth Bridge
8 Vauxhall Bridge
9 Chelsea Bridge
10 Battersea Bridge
11 Wandsworth Bridge
12 Putney Bridge

Hampstead Heath
St. Pancras
Oxford Street
Holland House
Earls Court
Rotherhithe
Rotherhithe Tunnel

LAKE DISTRICT HOSTELS

Annas
Longtown
Brampton
Maryport
Carlisle
Penrith
Carrock Fell
Skiddaw House
Keswick
Helvellyn
Workington
Cockermouth
Derwentwater
Buttermere
Ennerdale
Hause
Patterdale (Longthwaite)
Longdale (High Close)
Grasmere
Windermere
Ambleside
Whitehaven
Black Sail
Honister Borrowdale
Westwater
Ellenwater
Hawkshead
Kendal
Egremont
Eskdale
Copledh
Ulverston
Kirkby Lonsdale
Barrow
Carnforth

Kirk Yetholm
Wooler
Byrness
Bellingham
Once Brewed
Greenhead
Carlisle
Acomb
Newcastle
Newcastle-upon-Tyne
Durham
Ninebanks
Edmundbyers
Alston
Dufton
Langdon Beck
Baldersdale
Kirkby Stephen
Keld
Grinton Lodge
Hawes
Dentdale
Aysgarth Falls
Ingleton
Ellingstring
Osmotherley
Stainforth
Kettlewell
Malham
Linton
Sladburn
Earby
Haworth
Preston
Lancaster
Mankinhotes
Lockton
Helmsley
Scarborough
Whitby
Boggle Hole
Thixendale
York
Humber
Beverley Friary
Leeds

ISLE OF MAN

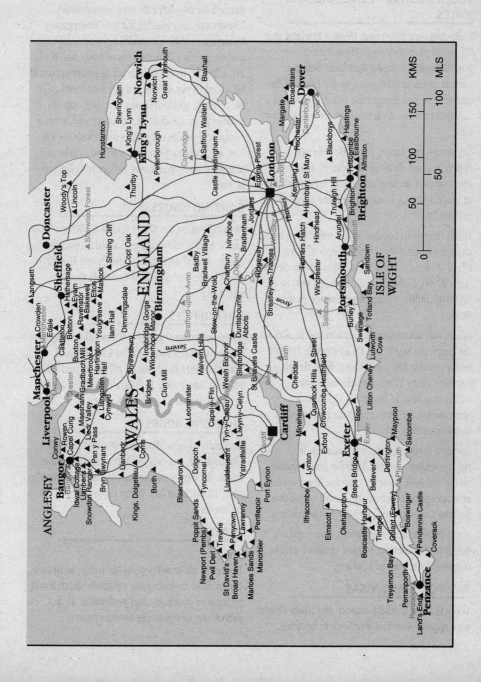

English

YOUTH HOSTELS IN ENGLAND AND WALES

There are over 230 Youth Hostels England and Wales, all participating in Hostelling International's Assured Standards Scheme. Hostels are in major towns, in the heart of the countryside and around the coast. Locations vary from medieval castles to remote mountain huts.

City centre and larger Youth Hostels are generally open through the season. However some smaller hostels are closed for one night or more a week - always telephone to check availability.

Youth Hostels in London and a number of large cities are open 24hrs, with reception open 07.30-23.00hrs. Most YHAs in the provinces are open 07.00-23.00hrs, with a closed period of 10.00-17.00hrs, except where stated in this Guide.

Prices vary according to location and facilities, ranging from £6.00 to £18.25 outside London - less for under 18s - including sheet sleeping bag hire. Many Youth Hostels serve meals, which may have to be booked in advance. Self-catering facilities and cycle storage are widely available.

Advance booking of accommodation is recommended - particularly for family rooms and in the busy summer months. Many hostels now accept reservations by e-mail – visit the website (www.yha.org.uk) for further details.

Some provincial hostels adopt a no smoking policy in the interests of your comfort. Please enquire at the time of booking.

PASSPORTS AND VISAS

You will need a valid passport. Not many visitors now require visas but do check in advance.

HEALTH

An international Certificate of Vaccination is not required to enter the UK, but check if one is needed for re-entry into your own country. Visitors are only eligible for free **emergency** treatment at National Health Service Accident and Emergency departments of hospitals. If you are admitted to hospital as an in-patient you will be asked to pay unless you are a national of an EC country, resident in any member country, or a national or resident of a country which has a reciprocal health care agreement with the UK. You are therefore strongly advised to take out adequate insurance cover before travelling to Britain.

BANKING HOURS

Generally open weekdays 09.30-17.00hrs. Most major banks also open on Saturday mornings. All are closed on Sundays and Public Holidays. Many large hostels offer bureau de change facilities.

POST OFFICES

Open weekdays 09.00-17.30hrs (although most sub post offices shut 13.00-14.00hrs) and Saturdays 09.00-12.30hrs. All are closed on Sundays and Public Holidays. Postage stamps are sold at hostels and many shops.

SHOPPING HOURS

Generally Monday-Saturday 09.00-17.30hrs, although this may vary in larger towns. Some shops do stay open late on Wednesday/Thursday until 20.00/21.00hrs. Many large shops open on Sundays.

TRAVEL

Air

Domestic air travel is possible within in Britain, but as most distances are relatively short, travel by train or coach is often preferable. Ticket prices vary dramatically between tour operators. Youth fares (under 25's) are available, although special offer fares are usually cheaper.

Rail

A comprehensive rail network links the country, and provides a reasonably inexpensive way to travel. Inter-Rail and Britrail cards are valid but are not available in Britain and must be bought in your country of origin.

Bus

Coach travel is cheaper than rail and there is a large network of services operated by 2/3 major companies. Most towns are served with good local services.

Ferry

Various routes available.

Driving

To drive in Britain you must be over the age of 17. Driving is on the left-hand side of the road. Seat belts must to be worn in both the front and back of cars, if fitted. The drink driving laws are very strict so don't do it! The AA and RAC and various other motoring organisations offer, amongst other things, breakdown and recovery services.

Français

AUBERGES DE JEUNESSE ANGLAISES ET GALLOISES

Vous pouvez choisir parmi plus de 230 auberges en Angleterre et au Pays de Galles et elles participent toutes au Plan Hostelling International pour la Garantie des Normes en Auberge. Elles sont implantées dans les villes principales, au coeur de la campagne, ainsi que le long de la côte et peuvent avoir pour cadre un château médiéval ou une cabane isolée dans la montagne.

Les auberges situées au coeur des villes, ainsi que les auberges les plus importantes, restent généralement ouvertes toute la saison. Mais il arrive que de plus petites auberges soient fermées une nuit ou plus par semaine. Il est conseillé de toujours vérifier les disponibilités par téléphone.

Les auberges de jeunesse de Londres et de certaines grandes villes sont ouvertes 24 heures sur 24 et la réception accueille les voyageurs de 7h30 à 23h. En province, la plupart des auberges sont ouvertes de 7h à 23h, et ferment entre 10h et 17h, sauf indication contraire mentionnée dans le guide.

Les prix varient selon les endroits et les services offerts et vont de 6,00 livres à 17,00 livres en dehors de Londres - moins pour les moins de 18 ans - location de draps comprise. Un grand nombre d'auberges servent des repas, qui doivent parfois être réservés à l'avance. Des cuisines pour individuels et des garages à vélos sont généralement mis à la disposition des visiteurs.

Il est conseillé de réserver des places à l'avance - surtout pour des chambres familiales et pendant l'été. De nombreux établissements acceptent maintenant des réservations par e-mail – Visitez notre site Web pour en savoir plus. (www.yha.org.uk)

Dans certaines auberges de province, il est interdit de fumer afin d'assurer le confort des voyageurs. Veuillez vous renseigner à la réservation.

PASSEPORTS ET VISAS

Les voyageurs doivent être munis d'un passeport valide. De nos jours, peu de visiteurs doivent être en possession d'un visa mais il est préférable de vérifier à l'avance.

SOINS MEDICAUX

Il n'est pas nécessaire d'être muni d'un certificat international de vaccination mais il vous est conseillé de vérifier qu'il ne vous en faudra pas un pour rentrer dans votre pays. Les visiteurs ne peuvent bénéficier que d'un traitement **d'urgence** gratuit dans les services d'accidents et d'urgence des hôpitaux de la Sécurité Sociale. Si vous êtes hospitalisé, il vous faudra payer à moins d'être un citoyen d'un pays de l'UE, de résider dans un pays membre ou d'être un citoyen ou de résider dans un pays ayant passé un accord médical réciproque avec le Royaume-Uni. Il vous est donc fortement conseillé de souscrire à une police d'assurance avant votre départ pour la Grande-Bretagne.

HEURES D'OUVERTURE DES BANQUES

Les banques sont en général ouvertes en semaine de 9h30 à 17h. La plupart des grandes banques sont aussi ouvertes le samedi matin. Elles ferment toutes le dimanche et les jours fériés. De nombreuses grandes auberges font bureau de change.

BUREAUX DE POSTE

Les bureaux de poste sont ouverts en semaine de 9h à 17h30 (bien que la plupart des bureaux de poste auxiliaires ferment entre 13h et 14h) et le samedi de 9h à 12h30. Ils sont tous fermés le dimanche et les jours fériés. Vous pourrez également vous procurer des timbres postes dans les auberges et dans de nombreux magasins.

HEURES D'OUVERTURE DES MAGASINS

Les magasins sont en général ouverts du lundi au samedi, de 9h à 17h30, bien que cela puisse varier dans les grandes villes. Certains magasins restent ouverts plus longtemps les mercredi/jeudi jusqu'à 20h/21h. De nombreux grands magasins sont ouverts le dimanche.

DEPLACEMENTS

Avions

Il est possible de se rendre par avion dans beaucoup de régions du pays, mais vu que la plupart des distances est relativement courte, il est préférable de se déplacer par le train ou en car. Les tarifs peuvent varier considérablement d'un tour operator à l'autre. Il existe des tarifs jeunes (pour les moins de 25 ans) encore que les offres spéciales soient généralement plus avantageuses.

Trains

Un réseau ferroviaire étendu dessert le pays. Le train est un bon moyen de voyager, et s'avère assez économique. Les cartes Inter-Rail et Britrail sont reconnues mais ne sont pas en vente en Grande-Bretagne. Il faudra donc vous les procurer dans votre pays d'origine.

Autobus

Les cars sont moins chers que le train et de nombreux services, assurés par 2/3 grandes compagnies, sont offerts. La plupart des villes sont desservies par de bons services locaux.

Ferry-boats

Diverses traversées possibles.

Automobiles

Si vous voulez conduire une voiture en Grande-Bretagne, vous devez être âgé de plus de 17 ans. La conduite est à gauche. Le port des ceintures de sécurité à l'avant et à l'arrière du véhicule, s'il en est équipé, est obligatoire. Les lois concernant l'alcool au volant sont très strictes; ne prenez pas de risques! Les organisations automobiles AA et RAC (et elles ne sont pas les seules) offrent, entre autres, des services de dépannage et de recouvrement de véhicule.

Deutsch

JUGENDHERBERGEN IN ENGLAND UND WALES

In England und Wales gibt es eine Auswahl von mehr als 230 Herbergen, die sich alle dem Konzept der "Zugesicherten Standards" des Hostelling Internationals angeschlossen haben. Herbergen befinden sich in bedeutenden Städten, auf dem Land und an der Küste. Sie sind in mittelalterlichen Burgen und entlegenen Berghütten untergebracht.

Große Jugendherbergen sowie im Stadtzentrum gelegene sind normalerweise ganzjährig geöffnet. Einige der kleineren Herbergen können ein oder mehrere Nächte in der Woche geschlossen sein. Fragen Sie nach, ob Zimmer zur Verfügung stehen.

Die Jugendherbergen in London und auch einige in großen Städten sind 24 Stunden geöffnet. Die Rezeption ist aber für Buchungen von 07.30-23.00 Uhr geöffnet. Die meisten ländlichen Herbergen sind von 07.00-23.00 Uhr geöffnet, schließen aber zwischendurch von 10.00-17.00 Uhr, wenn in diesem Führer nicht etwas anderes angegeben ist.

Die Preise hängen von der Lage und den Einrichtungen ab und liegen außerhalb Londons zwischen 6,00 £ -17,00 £. Es ist billiger für Jugendliche unter 18 Jahren. Die Gebühr für die Bettwäsche ist im Preis enthalten. Viele Jugendherbergen bieten Mahlzeiten, die aber oft im voraus bestellt werden müssen. In vielen Herbergen gibt es auch Einrichtungen für Selbstversorger und zur Fahrradaufbewahrung.

Es empfiehlt sich, die Unterkunft im voraus zu buchen - besonders für Familienzimmer und in den Sommermonaten, wenn viel Betrieb herrscht. Eine Vielzahl von Herbergen akzeptiert jetzt auch Buchungen per E-mail – für weitere Informationen besuchen Sie unsere Web-Site (www.yha.org.uk).

In manchen ländlichen Jugendherbergen herrscht im Interesse Ihres Komforts Rauchverbot. Bitte fragen Sie nach, wenn Sie die Buchung vornehmen.

PÄSSE UND VISA

Sie brauchen einen gültigen Reisepaß. Ein Visum wird nur noch von wenigen Reisenden benötigt. Sie sollten sich aber im voraus erkundigen.

GESUNDHEIT

Für die Einreise nach Großbritannien benötigt man kein Impfzeugnis. Erkundigen Sie sich aber, ob eines bei der Rückkehr in Ihr eigenes Land benötigt wird.

Eine Krankenversicherung ist erforderlich, da Besucher nur **in Notfällen** Anspruch auf kostenlose Behandlung durch die Unfall- oder Notfallabteilung des Nationalen Gesundheitsdienstes in Krankenhäusern haben. Wenn Sie zur stationären Behandlung in ein Krankenhaus eingewiesen oder an die ambulante Abteilung überwiesen werden (ob von der Unfall- oder Notfallabteilung eines Krankenhauses oder von einem anderen Arzt), müssen Sie selbst bezahlen. Ausnahmen: Sie besitzen die Staatsangehörigkeit eines EU-Landes, Sie sind in einem EU-Mitgliedsstaat wohnhaft, Sie besitzen die Staatsangehörigkeit eines Landes, mit dem Großbritannien ein gegenseitiges Abkommen über die Gesundheitspflege abgeschlossen hat bzw. Sie sind in einem solchen Land wohnhaft. Ehe Sie nach Großbritannien reisen, raten wir Ihnen deshalb dringend zum Abschluß einer ausreichenden Versicherung.

GESCHÄFTSSTUNDEN DER BANKEN

Im allgemeinen werktags von 09.30-17.00 Uhr. Die meisten größeren Banken sind auch am

Samstagvormittag geöffnet. An Sonn- und Feiertagen sind alle Banken geschlossen. Viele größere Herbergen bieten Geldwechselmöglichkeiten an.

POSTÄMTER

Öffnungszeiten: werktags von 09.00-17.30 Uhr (die meisten Poststellen machen jedoch eine Mittagspause von 13.00-14.00 Uhr) und samstags von 09.00-12.30 Uhr. An Sonn- und Feiertagen sind alle Postämter geschlossen. Briefmarken kann man in Herbergen und vielen Geschäften kaufen.

LADENÖFFNUNGSZEITEN

Im allgemeinen montags bis samstags von 09.00-17.30 Uhr, oft variierend in größeren Städten. Einige Geschäfte sind mittwochs/donnerstags bis 20.00/21.00 Uhr geöffnet. Viele größere Geschäfte sind auch sonntags geöffnet.

REISEN

Flugverkehr

Viele Orte in Großbritannien sind zwar mit dem Flugzeug erreichbar, aber da die Entfernungen im allgemeinen relativ kurz sind, ist das Reisen mit der Bahn oder dem Bus oft besser. Es gibt drastische Preisunterschiede bei Tickets der großen Reiseveranstalter. Fahrpreise für Jugendliche unter 25 werden ebenfalls angeboten, jedoch sind die Sonderangebote in der Regel billiger.

Eisenbahn

Über das ganze Land erstreckt sich ein umfangreiches Schienennetz. Es wird ein guter Eisenbahnverkehr angeboten, und das Reisen mit der Bahn ist auch verhältnismäßig preiswert. Es gelten sowohl Inter-Rail als auch Britrail-Karten, die allerdings im Herkunftsland gekauft werden müssen.

Busse

Reisebusse sind billiger als die Eisenbahn, und 2 oder 3 größere Unternehmen bieten in einem großen Netz gute Verbindungen an. Die meisten Städte haben einen guten Ortsverkehr.

Fähren

Auf verschiedenen Strecken wird ein Fährverkehr angeboten.

Autofahren

Wer in Großbritannien ein Kraftfahrzeug führen will, muß über 17 Jahre alt sein. Es herrscht Linksverkehr. Sowohl auf den Vorder- als auch auf den Rücksitzen müssen im Auto Sicherheitsgurte angelegt werden, sofern diese vorhanden sind. Die Gesetze zum Autofahren unter Alkoholeinfluß sind sehr streng - unterlassen Sie es daher! Der AA und der RAC sind nur zwei Kraftfahrzeugorganisationen, die u.a. einen Pannen- und Abschleppdienst anbieten.

Español

ALBERGUES JUVENILES INGLESES Y GALESES

Existen más de 230 albergues juveniles en Inglaterra y Gales que participan todos en el Plan Hostelling International de Normas Garantizadas. Se encuentran tanto en las grandes ciudades como en pleno campo y en la costa, en edificios tan variados como castillos medievales y remotas cabañas de montaña.

Los albergues situados en los centros de ciudad y los más grandes suelen estar abiertos todo el año, pero algunos más pequeños cierran una noche o más a la semana – asegúrese siempre por teléfono de que el albergue está abierto y tiene plazas libres antes de salir de viaje.

Los albergues juveniles de Londres y de algunas grandes ciudades están abiertos las 24 horas del día, con horario de recepción de 7.30 h. a 23 h. En las provincias, la mayoría abren de 7

h. a 23 h. y tienen un periodo de cierre entre las 10 h. y las 17 h., salvo que se indique otro horario en la guía.

Los precios dependen de la ubicación y de los servicios ofrecidos, y oscilan entre £6 y £17 fuera de Londres (menos para los menores de 18 años), saco de dormir de tela incluido. Muchos albergues sirven comidas, que posiblemente sea necesario encargar con antelación, y, además, es posible cocinar uno mismo en un gran número de ellos. Casi todos disponen de un cobertizo para las bicicletas.

Es recomendable reservar el alojamiento con antelación, sobre todo las habitaciones familiares y durante los meses de verano. Muchos albergues hoy día aceptan reservas por correo electrónico – consulte nuestra página Internet (www.yha.org.uk) para más información.

En algunos albergues provinciales no se permite fumar, a fin de cuidar del bienestar de los usuarios. Infórmese al hacer la reserva.

PASAPORTES Y VISADOS

Necesitará un pasaporte en regla. Actualmente, muy pocos visitantes requieren visado, pero es recomendable asegurarse de ello con antelación.

INFORMACIÓN SANITARIA

No es necesario un certificado internacional de vacunación para entrar en el Reino Unido, pero averigüe si necesita uno al regresar a su país. Los visitantes sólo tienen derecho a recibir asistencia médica gratuita **de urgencia** en la sección de Accidentes y Urgencias de los hospitales de la Seguridad Social. Si resulta necesario hospitalizarle, tendrá que pagar a menos que sea ciudadano de un país de la UE, residente en cualquier país miembro, o ciudadano o residente de un país que tenga un acuerdo mutuo de asistencia médica con el Reino Unido. Por lo tanto, es altamente recomendable hacerse un seguro con suficiente cobertura antes de salir de viaje para Gran Bretaña.

HORARIO DE LOS BANCOS

Generalmente, los bancos abren los días laborables de 9.30 h. a 17 h. La mayoría de los grandes bancos abren también los sábados por la mañana. Todos cierran los domingos y festivos. Es posible cambiar divisas en muchos de los grandes albergues.

OFICINAS DE CORREOS

Las oficinas de correos abren los días laborables de 9 h. a 17.30 h. (aunque casi todas las sucursales cierran de 13 h. a 14 h. para comer) y los sábados de 9 h. a 12.30 h. Todas cierran los domingos y festivos. Se venden sellos en los albergues y en muchas tiendas.

HORARIO COMERCIAL

Por regla general, las tiendas abren de lunes a sábado de 9 h. a 17.30 h., aunque es posible que este horario varíe en las poblaciones más grandes. Algunas tiendas abren hasta las 20 h./21 h. los miércoles/jueves y muchas de las más grandes abren los domingos.

DESPLAZAMIENTOS

Avión

Se puede viajar en avión dentro de Gran Bretaña, pero, como las distancias son relativamente cortas, suele ser preferible utilizar el tren o el autocar. Los principales operadores turísticos ofrecen billetes de avión a precios que varían enormemente de unos a otros. Existen también tarifas juveniles (para los menores de 25 años), pero las ofertas especiales suelen resultar más económicas.

Tren

Existe una amplia red ferroviaria que se extiende por todo el país. El tren es un medio de transporte relativamente económico. Se pueden utilizar las tarjetas Inter-Rail y Britrail, pero es necesario adquirirlas en el país de procedencia del viajero, ya que no es posible conseguirlas en Gran Bretaña.

Autobús

Viajar en autocar resulta más barato que viajar en tren y existe una amplia red de servicios ofrecidos por 2 ó 3 grandes compañías. La mayoría de las ciudades cuentan con un buen servicio local.

Ferry

Se pueden hacer diversas travesías.

Automóvil

Para conducir un automóvil en Gran Bretaña, es preciso ser mayor de 17 años. Se circula por la izquierda. Es obligatorio llevar el cinturón de seguridad abrochado tanto en los asientos delanteros como en los traseros, si el automóvil tiene estos últimos instalados. La legislación en materia de conducción bajo la influencia del alcohol es muy estricta. Por lo tanto, ¡no se arriesgue! La AA y el RAC son dos de las muchas organizaciones de automovilismo que ofrecen, entre otras prestaciones, servicios de asistencia en carretera y de grúa.

> **If you start now, you will know a lot next year that you don't know now, and that you will not know next year, if you wait.**

Si tu commences maintenant, tu sauras beaucoup de choses l'année prochaine que tu ne sais pas aujourd'hui et que tu ne sauras pas l'année prochaine, si tu attends.

Mach' Dich heute auf den Weg, dann wirst Du im nächsten Jahr eine Menge mehr als heute wissen, aber im nächsten Jahr dies nicht wissen, wenn Du wartest.

Si empiezas hoy, el año que viene sabrás muchas cosas que hoy no sabes y que no sabrás el año que viene si tardas en empezar.

The William Feather Magazine

Ambleside -
Waterhead

Ambleside,
Cumbria LA22 0EU.
- (15394) 32304
- (15394) 34408
- ambleside@yha.org.uk

Open Dates:	
Open Hours:	
Reservations:	IBN CC
Price Range:	£7.60-£11.15
Beds:	245 - 12x² 17x³ 9x⁴ 5x⁵ 4x⁶ 12x⁶
Facilities:	47x
Directions:	1.5 S from city centre

✈	Manchester 145km
⛴	Stranraer/Belfast 97km
🚂	Windermere 6.5km
🚌	555 500m ap Waterhead Pier

Attractions: 2km 1.5km 4km

Bath -
Bathwick Hill

Bath,
BA2 6JZ.
- (1225) 465674
- (1225) 482947
- bath@yha.org.uk

Open Dates:	
Open Hours:	
Reservations:	R IBN CC
Price Range:	£6.85-£10.15
Beds:	117 - 2x² 10x⁴ 1x⁵ 4x⁶ 4x⁶
Facilities:	
Directions:	1 E from city centre

🚂	Bath Spa 1.5km
🚌	18 1.5km ap Outside Hostel

Attractions: 1km 1km

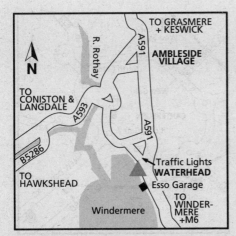

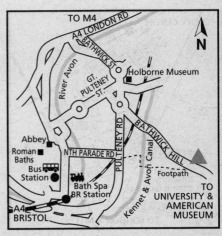

0   1.5km   0   750m

Cambridge

97 Tenison Rd,
Cambridge CB1 2DN.
☏ (1223) 354601
✆ (1223) 312780
✉ cambridge@yha.org.uk

Open Dates:	🗓
Open Hours:	🕐
Reservations:	[IBN] [CC]
Price Range:	£7.60-£11.15 💬
Beds:	100 - 7x² 1x³ 8x⁴ 1x⁵ 5x⁶ 2x⁶
Facilities:	�â▯ ⭕ ⌂ ⛺ 📺 ⭕ 📷 ⑧ 🐾 ♨

Directions:	[2 SE] from city centre	
✈	Stanstead 32km	
A🚌	Cambridge 1.6km	
🚂	Cambridge 400m	
🚌	No.1 400m ap Cambridge Railway Station	

Canterbury - Ellerslie

54 New Dover Rd,
Canterbury,
Kent CT1 3DT.
☏ (1227) 462911
✆ (1227) 470752
✉ canterbury@yha.org.uk

Open Dates:	01.03-01.01
Open Hours:	07.30-10.00 hrs; 13.00-23.00 hrs
Reservations:	[IBN] [CC]
Price Range:	£6.85-£10.15 💬
Beds:	86 - 1x² 6x⁶ 4x⁶
Facilities:	�â▯ ⭕ ⌂ ⛺ 📺 ⭕ 📷 ⭕ ⑧ 🅿 ✐ 🐾 ♨ ⛏ ♟ 🎴

Directions:	[1 SE] from city centre
✈	Gatwick 107.2km
⛴	Dover 22.4km
🚂	Canterbury East 1km; Canterbury West 2km

Attractions: 🚶 ∪5km ⚓3km ⛵2km

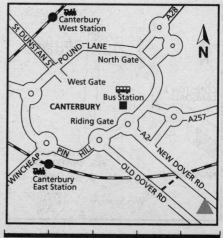

Dover

306 London Rd,
Dover,
Kent CT17 0SY.
☎ (1304) 201314
📠 (1304) 202236
✉ dover@yha.org.uk

Open Dates:	🗓
Open Hours:	07.30-10.00 hrs; 13.00-23.00 hrs
Reservations:	IBN CC
Price Range:	£6.85-£10.15 🔖
Beds:	132 - 6x🛏 1x🛏 2x🛏 12x🛏
Facilities:	👬 👬 🍴 🔒 🛋 📺 ♿ ℹ 🧺 🚲 🏠
Directions:	0.5 NW from city centre
⛴	Dover 2km
🚂	Dover Priory 1km
Attractions:	🔍1km 🏊1km

Liverpool

Wapping,
Liverpool,
L1 8EE.
☎ (151) 7098888
📠 (151) 7090417
✉ liverpool@yha.org.uk

Open Dates:	🗓
Open Hours:	🕐
Reservations:	IBN CC
Price Range:	£12.25-£16.40 BB inc 🔖
Beds:	110 - 2x🛏 17x🛏 6x🛏
Facilities:	♿ 👬 👬 👬 🍴 🔒 🛋 📺 3 x ⛽ 🍳 📦 8 P ℹ
Directions:	1 SW from city centre
✈	Liverpool 8km, Manchester 44km
⛴	Liverpool 1km
🚂	Lime Street 1.5km
U	James Street 600m
Attractions:	🚴

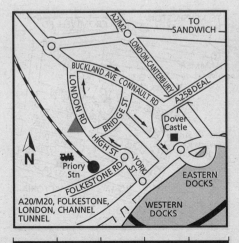

TO SANDWICH

A2/M20
LONDON-CANTERBURY
BUCKLAND AVE
CONNAULT RD
A258 DEAL
LONDON RD
BRIDGE ST
HIGH ST
YORK ST
N
Priory Stn
FOLKESTONE RD
Dover Castle
EASTERN DOCKS
A20/M20, FOLKESTONE, LONDON, CHANNEL TUNNEL
WESTERN DOCKS

0   3km

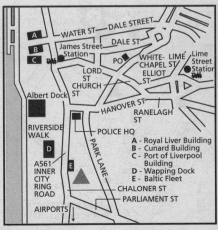

WATER ST   DALE STREET
A   James Street Station   DALE ST
B   PO
C   WHITE-CHAPEL ST   LIME ST   Lime Street Station
LORD ST   ELLIOT ST
CHURCH ST
Albert Dock
HANOVER ST
RANELAGH ST
RIVERSIDE WALK   POLICE HQ
D   PARK LANE
A561 INNER CITY RING ROAD   E
CHALONER ST
PARLIAMENT ST
AIRPORTS

A - Royal Liver Building
B - Cunard Building
C - Port of Liverpool Building
D - Wapping Dock
E - Baltic Fleet

0   2km

London -
City of London

36 Carter Lane,
London EC4V 5AB.
☎ (20) 72364965
📠 (20) 72367681
✉ city@yha.org.uk

Open Dates:	📅
Open Hours:	🕐
Reservations:	IBN CC
Price Range:	£18.65-£22.15 BB inc 🛏
Beds:	193 - 3x¹🛏 7x²🛏 7x³🛏 10x⁴🛏 5x⁵🛏 6x⁶🛏 6x⁶🛏
Facilities:	5x 👥 🍽 🛋 📺 🧺 1 x 🍷 📷 🖼 ♨ 🔒 ✒ 🧺 🎡
Directions:	2 NE from city centre
✈	Heathrow 12.8km; Gatwick 19.2km
🚂	Blackfriars 300m; St Pauls 500m
🚌	ap St. Pauls 500m
Ⓤ	Blackfriars 300m; St Pauls 274m
Attractions:	🚲

London - Earls Court

38 Bolton Gardens,
London,
SW5 0AQ.
☎ (20) 73737083
📠 (20) 78352034
✉ earlscourt@yha.org.uk

Open Dates:	📅
Open Hours:	🕐
Reservations:	IBN CC
Price Range:	£17.15-£19.45 BB inc 🛏
Beds:	154 - 3x³🛏 6x⁴🛏 2x⁶🛏 10x⁶🛏
Facilities:	🍽 (B) 🛀 🛋 📺 🧺 📷 🖼 ♨ 🔒 ✒ 🧺 🎡 🎡
Directions:	6 SW from city centre
✈	Heathrow 12km
🚂	Waterloo 3.5km
🚌	31; C1; C3; N31; N1; 6HT 100m
Ⓤ	Earl's Court 500m

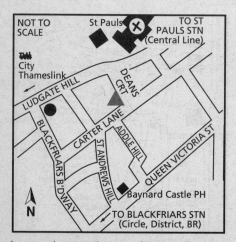

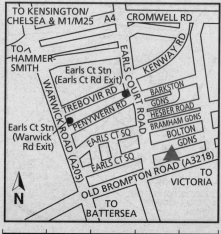

London -
Hampstead Heath

4 Wellgarth Rd,
Golders Green,
London NW11 7HR.
📞 **(20) 84589054**
📠 **(20) 82090546**
✉ **hampstead@yha.org.uk**

Open Dates:	📅
Open Hours:	🕐
Reservations:	IBN CC
Price Range:	£13.90-£16.25 📖
Beds:	200 - 14x² 9x³ 14x⁴ 9x⁵ 4x⁶ 2x⁶
Facilities:	🚹 10x 🚻 🍴 ⛱ 👥 📺 🔋 ♨ 🔥 🗄 ♿ 🔒 🅿 ℹ 🐾 🎡
Directions:	9NW from city centre
✈	Gatwick 76.8km; Heathrow 48km
🚂	Kings Cross/St. Pancras 4km
🚌	210 & 268 400m ap Golders Green Ⓤ
Ⓤ	Northern; Golder's Green 400m
Attractions:	🌳

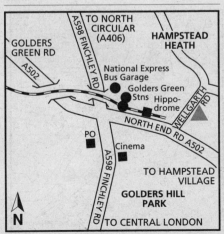

London -
Holland House

Holland House,
Holland Walk,
Kensington,
London W8 7QU.
📞 **(20) 79370748**
📠 **(20) 73760667**
✉ **hollandhouse@yha.org.uk**

Open Dates:	📅
Open Hours:	🕐
Reservations:	IBN CC
Price Range:	£17.15-£19.45 BB inc 📖
Beds:	201 - 1x¹ 1x² 1x³ 1x⁴ 1x⁶ 13x⁶
Facilities:	🚹 🚻 🍴 ⛱ 👥 📺 🔋 ♨ 1 x 🍴 🔒 🗄 ♿ 🔒 ℹ 🐾 🎡
Directions:	6SW from city centre
✈	Heathrow 48km; Gatwick 76.8km
A🚌	Airbus
🚂	Paddington 3.2km; Waterloo 14.4km
🚌	210 & 268 400m ap Golders Green Ⓤ
Ⓤ	Holland Park; Circle Line 400m; High Street, Kensington 400m
Attractions:	🌳 ⚲400km

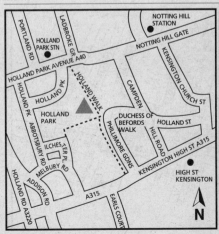

London - Oxford Street

14 Noel St,
London W1V 3PD.
☎ (20) 77341618
🗎 (20) 77341657
✉ oxfordst@yha.org.uk

Open Dates:	🗓
Open Hours:	◷
Reservations:	Ⓡ ⟮IBN⟯ ⟮CC⟯
Price Range:	£15.90-£19.45 🗐
Beds:	75 - 24x² 5x³ 4x⁴
Facilities:	⚿ 🛏 📺 🧺 ▣ ⑧ ⬍ 🛜

Directions:

✈	Heathrow 48km; Gatwick 76.8km
A🚌	A2 Kings Cross & Marblearch 1.5km
🚂	Victoria 3km; Waterloo 3km; Kings Cross 1.5km
🚌	10, 8, 73, 25, 55, 176 200m; 6, 12, 13, 15, 23, 94, 139, 113 400m ap Oxford Street; Regent Street
Ⓤ	Central, Bakerloo and Victoria Lines to Oxford Circus 400m, or Northern and Central Lines to Tottenham Court Road 500m

London - Rotherhithe

20 Salter Rd,
London SE16 1PP.
☎ (20) 72322114
🗎 (20) 72372919
✉ rotherhithe@yha.org.uk

Open Dates:	🗓
Open Hours:	◷
Reservations:	⟮IBN⟯ ⟮CC⟯
Price Range:	£18.65-£22.15 ⟮BB⟯ⁱⁿᶜ 🗐
Beds:	320 - 22x² 12x⁴ 33x⁶ 3x⁶
Facilities:	♿ 👨‍👩‍👧 👬 🍽 ⚿ 🛏 📺 🧺 ▣ 🛍 🎂 ⑧ ⬍ 🅿 ⓘ 🛜

Directions:

✈	Heathrow 40km; Gatwick 50km
⛴	Dover 125km
🚂	Waterloo 6km
🚌	P11; 225; N70 ap Outside Hostel
Ⓤ	Rotherhithe 400m

Attractions: 🛥 2km

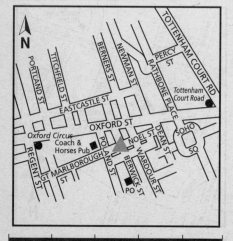

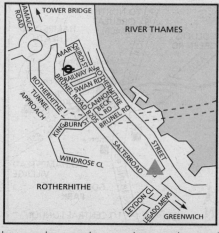

London - St Pancras

79-81 Euston Rd,
London NW1 2QS.
☎ **(20) 73889998**
📠 **(20) 73886766**
✉ **stpancras@yha.org.uk**

Open Dates:	🗓️
Open Hours:	🕐
Reservations:	**R** **IBN** **CC**
Price Range:	£18.65-£22.15 **BB** inc 🍽️
Beds:	152 - 10x² 1x³ 18x⁴ 3x⁵ 5x⁶
Facilities:	👫 🍽️ (BD) 🍴 🏠 📺 📷 ▢ 📷 ⑧ ◉ ⬆ ⅰ ♿

Directions:

✈	Heathrow 48km; Gatwick 76.8km
A🚌	Airbus 48km
🚉	St Pancras, Kings Cross 200m
🚌	73
Ⓤ	Kings Cross; St Pancras 200m

Attractions: 🚴

Manchester

Potato Wharf,
Castlefield,
Manchester M3 4NB
☎ **(161) 8399960**
📠 **(161) 8352054**
✉ **manchester@yha.org.uk**

Open Dates:	🗓️
Open Hours:	🕐
Reservations:	**IBN** **CC**
Price Range:	£9.40-£13.55 🍽️
Beds:	140 - 1x² 33x⁴ 4x⁶
Facilities:	♿ 👫 👫 🍽️ 🍴 🏠 📺 3 x ⍾ ▢ 🛗 ⑧ ⬆ **P** ⅰ ♿

Directions:

✈	Manchester 16km
⛴	Liverpool 44km
🚉	Manchester Piccadilly 1.5km
🚌	33 500m ap Liverpool Road
🚋	GMEX 500m ap G-Mex
Ⓤ	Metro Link GMEX 500m

Attractions: 🏊 100m

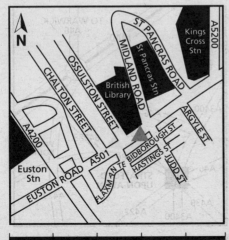

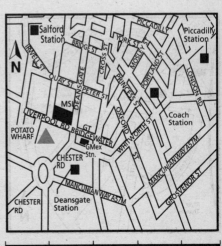

Oxford

**32 Jack Straw's Lane,
Oxford OX3 0DW.**
☎ (1865) 762997
🖶 (1865) 769402
✉ oxford@yha.org.uk

Open Dates:	🗓
Open Hours:	🕐
Reservations:	IBN CC
Price Range:	£6.20-£9.15 💷
Beds:	105 - 5x⁶🛏 10x⁶🛏
Facilities:	🚻 🍴 ☕ 🏫 📺 📷 🖼 ⛪ 8 P ✏ ♨

Directions: 3 NE from city centre

✈	Heathrow 80km; Gatwick 176km
⛴	Portsmouth 136km
🚃	Oxford 4km
🚌	13 700m ap Jack Straws Lane

Stratford-upon-Avon - Hemmingford House

**Alveston,
Stratford-upon-Avon,
Warwickshire CV37 7RG.**
☎ (1789) 297093
🖶 (1789) 205513
✉ stratford@yha.org.uk

Open Dates:	08.01-05.12; 29.12-28.02
Open Hours:	🕐
Reservations:	IBN CC
Price Range:	£10.50-£14.05 BB inc 💷
Beds:	130 - 8x²🛏 6x⁴🛏 1x⁵🛏 8x⁶🛏 5x⁶🛏
Facilities:	🚻 6x 🚻 🍴 ☕ 🏫 📺 🧺 2 x 🍷 📷 ⛪ P ✏ 🛝 ♨

Directions:

✈	Birmingham 32km
A🚌	National Express 3.5km
🚃	Stratford Upon Avon 4.5km
🚌	18 ap Youth Hostel Front Gate

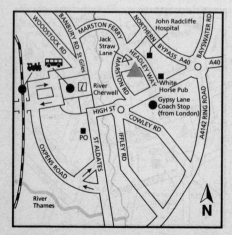

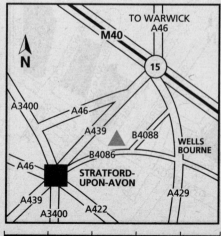

York

York International,
Water End,
Clifton,
York,
Yorkshire YO30 6LP.
☎ (1904) 653147
🖷 (1904) 651230
ⓔ york@yha.org.uk

Open Dates:	🔲12
Open Hours:	🕒
Reservations:	IBN CC
Price Range:	£11.25-£15.05 BB inc 🍴
Beds:	150 - 1x🛏 7x🛏 1x🛏 21x🛏 4x🛏 3x🛏
Facilities:	👪 21x 👪 🍽 ☕ 🛋 TV 🎱 ▢ 💼 🧺 P ℹ 🌿
Directions:	1.5NW from city centre
✈	Leeds-Bradford 40km
⛴	Hull 80km
🚃	York 2km
🚌	32-19 500m ap Clifton Green
Attractions:	⚓ 1.5km

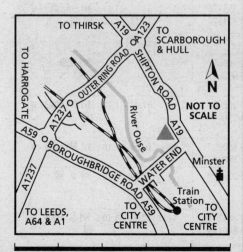

> **Travel, instead of broadening the mind, often merely lengthens the conversation.**
>
> Voyager, plutôt que d'élargir l'esprit a tendance simplement à rallonger la conversation.
>
> **Anstatt zu bilden, bietet Reisen oft lediglich mehr Stoff zur Unterhaltung.**
>
> A menudo, en vez de ampliar los horizontes de las personas, lo único que hacen los viajes es alargar la conversación.
>
> **Elizabeth Drew**

Location/Address	Telephone No. Fax No.	Beds	Opening Dates	Facilities
△ *Acomb* *Main St, Acomb, Hexham,* *Northumberland NE46 4PL.*	☎ *(1434) 602864*	*36*	▣	⊂cc⊃ ✂ Ⓟ
▲ **Alfriston** Frog Firle, Alfriston, Polegate, East Sussex BN26 5TT. ⓔ alfriston@yha.org.uk	☎ (1323) 870423 ⓕ (1323) 870615	68	12.02–25.11; 23.12–26.12	� ⊂cc⊃ ✂ Ⓟ
▲ **Alston** The Firs, Alston, Cumbria CA9 3RW.	☎ (1434) 381509 ⓕ (1434) 382401	30	17.04–31.10	⊣ ⊂cc⊃ ✂ Ⓟ
▲ **Ambleside** - Waterhead ⟨IBN⟩ **Ambleside, Cumbria LA22 0EU.** ⓔ ambleside@yha.org.uk	☎ (15394) 32304 ⓕ (15394) 34408	245	▣	⚇ ⊣ 1.5S ⊂cc⊃ ✂ Ⓟ ▣
▲ **Arnside** Oakfield Lodge, Redhills Rd, Arnside, Carnforth, Lancashire LA5 0AT. ⓔ arnside@yha.org.uk	☎ (1524) 761781 ⓕ (1524) 762589	72	11.02–25.11; 23.12–27.12	⚇ ⊣ ⊂cc⊃ ✂ Ⓟ ▣
▲ **Arundel** Warningcamp, Arundel, West Sussex BN18 9QY.	☎ (1903) 882204 ⓕ (1903) 882776	60	08.01–12.02; 14.02–28.10; 03.11–23.12; 29.12–01.01	⚇ ⊣ ⊂cc⊃ ✂ Ⓟ
▲ **Aysgarth Falls** Aysgarth, Leyburn, North Yorkshire DL8 3SR.	☎ (1969) 663260 ⓕ (1969) 663110	67	01.02–30.11; 29.12–01.01	⚇ ⊣ ⊂cc⊃ ✂ Ⓟ
▲ **Badby** Church Green, Badby, Daventry, Northamptonshire NN11 3AS.	☎ / ⓕ (1327) 703883	30	17.04–28.10	⊂cc⊃ ✂
▲ **Bakewell** Fly Hill, Bakewell, Derbyshire DE45 1DN.	☎ (1629) 812313 ⓕ (1629) 812313	32	01.01–21.12	⊣ ⊂cc⊃ ✂ Ⓟ
▲ **Baldersdale** Blackton, Baldersdale, Barnard Castle, Co Durham DL12 9UP.	☎ (1833) 650629 ⓕ (1833) 650629	39	17.04–30.09	⊣ ⊂cc⊃ ✂ Ⓟ
▲ **Bangor** ⟨IBN⟩ Tan-y-Bryn, Bangor, Gwynedd Wales LL57 1PZ. ⓔ bangor@yha.org.uk	☎ (1248) 353516 ⓕ (1248) 371176	84	01.01–25.11; 27.12–22.02	⚇ ⊣ ⊂cc⊃ ✂ Ⓟ ▣
▲ **Bath** - Bathwick Hill ⟨IBN⟩ **Bath, BA2 6JZ.** ⓔ bath@yha.org.uk	☎ (1225) 465674 ⓕ (1225) 482947	117	▣	⊣ Ⓡ 1E ⊂cc⊃ ✂ ▣
▲ **Beer** Bovey Combe, Townsend, Beer, Seaton, Devon EX12 3LL.	☎ (1297) 20296 ⓕ (1297) 23690	40	01.04–31.10	⚇ ⊣ ⊂cc⊃ ✂ Ⓟ
▲ **Bellever** Postbridge, Yelverton, Devon PL20 6TU.	☎ (1822) 880227 ⓕ (1822) 880302	38	10.04–31.10	⚇ ⊣ ⊂cc⊃ ✂ Ⓟ
△ *Bellingham* *Woodburn Rd, Bellingham, Hexham,* *Northumberland NE48 2ED.*	☎ *(1434) 220313*	*34*	*17.04–28.10*	⚇ ✂ Ⓟ
▲ **Beverley** The Friary, Friar's Lane, Beverley, East Yorkshire HU17 0DF.	☎ (1482) 881751 ⓕ (1482) 880118	34	17.04–28.10	⊣ ♿ ⊂cc⊃ ✂ Ⓟ

Location/Address	Telephone No. Fax No.	Beds	Opening Dates	Facilities
▲ **Blackboys** Uckfield, East Sussex TN22 5HU.	☏ (1825) 890607 ☏ (1825) 890104	30	19.04–04.09	☞ P ▣
△ *Black Sail* *Black Sail Hut, Ennerdale, Cleator, Cumbria CA23 3AY.*	☏ *(411) 108450* ☏ *(411) 159472*	*16*	*31.03–28.10*	⑩ Ⓡ ССС ☞
△ *Blaencaron* *Tregaron, Ceredigion, Wales SY25 6HL.*	☏ *(1974) 298441*	*16*	*01.04–23.09*	☞ P
▲ **Blaxhall** Heath Walk, Blaxhall, Woodbridge, Suffolk IP12 2EA.	☏ (1728) 688206 ☏ (1728) 689191	40	17.04–04.11	⑩ ССС ☞ P ▣
▲ **Boggle Hole** Mill Beck, Fylingthorpe, Whitby, North Yorkshire YO22 4UQ. ℮ bogglehole@yha.org.uk	☏ (1947) 880352 ☏ (1947) 880987	80	11.02–04.11	♯♯ ⑩ ССС ☞ P
▲ **Borrowdale (Longthwaite)** Longthwaite, Borrowdale, Keswick, Cumbria CA12 5XE. ℮ borrowdale@yha.org.uk	☏ (17687) 77257 ☏ (17687) 77393	88	01.02–21.12	♯♯ ⑩ ССС ☞ P ▣
▲ **Borth** Morlais, Borth, Ceredigion, Wales SY24 5JS. ℮ borth@yha.org.uk	☏ (1970) 871498 ☏ (1970) 871827	60	02.04–29.10	♯♯ ⑩ ССС ☞ P
▲ **Boscastle Harbour** Palace Stables, Boscastle, Cornwall PL35 0HD.	☏ (1840) 250287 ☏ (1840) 250615	25	01.04–31.10	⑩ ССС ☞
▲ **Boswinger** Gorran, St Austell, Cornwall PL26 6LL.	☏ (1726) 843234 ☏ (1726) 843234	38	10.04–31.10	♯♯ ⑩ ССС ☞ P ▣
▲ **Bradenham** Village Hall, Bradenham, High Wycombe, Buckinghamshire HP14 4HF. ℮ bradenham@yha.org.uk	☏ (1494) 562929 ☏ (1494) 564743	16	22.04–04.11	Ⓡ ССС ☞ P
▲ **Bradwell Village** Manor Farm, Vicarage Rd, Bradwell, Milton Keynes, Buckinghamshire MK13 9AJ.	☏ (1908) 310944 ☏ (1908) 310944	38	01.04–02.09	ССС ☞ P
△ *Bretton* *Nether Bretton, Derbyshire.*	☏ *(114) 2884541*	*18*	*17.04–24.06; 30.06–09.09; 15.09–30.12*	☞ P
△ *Bridges Long Mynd* *Ratlinghope, Shrewsbury SY5 0SP.*	☏ *(1588) 650656* ☏ *(1588) 650656*	*35*	▣	☞ P
▲ **Brighton** Patcham Place, London Rd, Brighton, Sussex BN1 8YD. ℮ brighton@yha.org.uk	☏ (1273) 556196 ☏ (1273) 509366	84	01.03–31.10; 01.11–23.12; 29.12–03.01	⑩ 6NW ССС ☞ P ▣
▲ **Bristol** ⒾⒷⓃ International YHA, Hayman House, 14 Narrow Quay, Bristol BS1 4QA. ℮ bristol@yha.org.uk	☏ (117) 9221659 ☏ (117) 9273789	88	▣	♯♯ ⑩ 1SW ССС ☞ ▣
▲ **Broad Haven** Broad Haven, Haverfordwest, Pembrokeshire, Wales SA62 3JH. ℮ broadhaven@yha.org.uk	☏ (1437) 781688 ☏ (1437) 781100	75	11.02–28.10	♯♯ ⑩ ♿ ССС ☞ P ▣

Location/Address	Telephone No. Fax No.	Beds	Opening Dates	Facilities
▲ **Broadstairs** Thistle Lodge, 3 Osborne Rd, Broadstairs, Isle-of-Thanet, Kent CT10 2AE. e broadstairs@yha.org.uk	☎ (1843) 604121 ✆ (1843) 604121	34	02.01–13.01; 26.03–28.10	ⅲ 0.5W ⊂CC⊃ ✔
▲ **Bryn Gwynant** Nantgwynant, Caernarfon, Gwynedd, Wales LL55 4NP. e bryngwynant@yha.org.uk	☎ (1766) 890251 ✆ (1766) 890479	67	07.01–26.02; 01.03–28.10	ⅲ ⅼⓄⅼ ⊂CC⊃ ✔ P
▲ **Burley** Cottesmore House, Cott Lane, Burley, Ringwood, Hampshire BH24 4BB.	☎ (1425) 403233 ✆ (1425) 403233	36	06.04–04.09; 08–30.09	ⅼⓄⅼ ⊂CC⊃ ✔ P
▲ **Buttermere** King George VI Memorial Hostel, Buttermere, Cockermouth, Cumbria CA13 9XA.	☎ (17687) 70245 ✆ (17687) 70231	70	03.01–21.12	ⅲ ⅼⓄⅼ ⊂CC⊃ ✔ P
▲ **Buxton** Sherbrook Lodge, Harpur Hill Rd, Buxton, Derbyshire SK17 9NB.	☎ (1298) 22287 ✆ (1298) 22287	56	11.02–20.12	ⅼⓄⅼ ⊂CC⊃ ✔ P
△ *Byrness* *7 Otterburn Green, Byrness, Newcastle-upon-Tyne, Northumberland NE19 1TS.*	☎ *(1830) 520425* ✆ *(1830) 520425*	*26*	*01.01–30.09*	⊂CC⊃ ✔ P ⏹
▲ **Cambridge** IBN **97 Tenison Rd, Cambridge CB1 2DN.** e cambridge@yha.org.uk	☎ (1223) 354601 ✆ (1223) 312780	100	🗓	ⅼⓄⅼ 2SE ⊂CC⊃ ✔ ⏹
▲ **Canterbury** - Ellerslie IBN **54 New Dover Rd, Canterbury, Kent CT1 3DT.** e canterbury@yha.org.uk	☎ (1227) 462911 ✆ (1227) 470752	86	01.03–31.12	ⅼⓄⅼ 1SE ⊂CC⊃ ✔ P ⏹
▲ **Capel Curig** Plas Curig, Capel Curig, Betws-y-Coed, Wales LL24 0EL.	☎ (1690) 720225 ✆ (1690) 720270	52	11.02–23.12	ⅲ ⅼⓄⅼ ⊂CC⊃ ✔ P
△ *Capel-y-Ffin* *Capel-y-Ffin, Llanthony, Nr. Abergavenny, Wales, NP7 7NP.*	☎ *(1873) 890650*	*40*	*05.02–11.07; 14.07–05.09; 08.09–28.10*	ⅼⓄⅼ ⊂CC⊃ ✔ P
▲ **Cardiff** IBN 2 Wedal Rd, Roath Park, Cardiff, Wales CF14 3QX. e cardiff@yha.org.uk	☎ (2920) 462303 ✆ (2920) 464571	68	02.01–20.12	ⅼⓄⅼ ♿ ⊂CC⊃ ✔ P ⏹
▲ **Carlisle** The University of Northumbria, The Old Brewery Residences, Bridge Lane, Caldewgate, Carlisle, Cumbria CA2 5SW.	☎ (1228) 597352 ✆ (1228) 597352	56	08.07–09.09	ⅲ Ⓡ ♿ ✔ P ⏹
▲ **Carrock Fell** High Row Cottage, Haltcliffe, Hesket Newmarket, Wigton, Cumbria CA7 8JT.	☎ (16974) 78325 ✆ (16974) 78325	20	17.04–28.10	ⅼⓄⅼ ⊂CC⊃ ✔ P
▲ **Castle Hedingham** 7 Falcon Square, Castle Hedingham, Halstead, Essex CO9 3BU. e castlehed@yha.org.uk	☎ (1787) 460799 ✆ (1787) 461302	50	12.02–29.10	ⅲ ⅼⓄⅼ ⊂CC⊃ ✔

Location/Address	Telephone No. Fax No.	Beds	Opening Dates	Facilities
▲ **Castleton** Castleton Hall, Castleton, Hope Valley S33 8WG. e castleton@yha.org.uk	t (1433) 620235 f (1433) 621767	150	04.02–23.12	CC P
▲ **Charlbury** The Laurels, The Slade, Charlbury, Oxfordshire OX7 3SJ. e charlbury@yha.org.uk	t (1608) 810202 f (1608) 810202	50	08.02–09.09; 12.09–11.11	P
▲ **Cheddar** Hillfield, Cheddar, Somerset BS27 3HN.	t (1934) 742494 f (1934) 744724	53	28.01–18.03; 21.03–23.12	CC P
▲ **Chester** IBN Hough Green House, 40 Hough Green, Chester CH4 8JD. e chester@yha.org.uk	t (1244) 680056 f (1244) 681204	117	14.01–16.12; 12.01.01–28.02	2SW CC P
▲ **Clun Mill** The Mill, Clun, Nr Craven Arms, Shropshire SY7 8NY.	t (1588) 640582 f (1588) 640582	24	17.04–31.08	CC P
▲ **Cockermouth** Double Mills, Cockermouth, Cumbria CA13 0DS.	t (1900) 822561 f (1900) 822561	28	17.04–28.10	CC P
▲ **Coniston (Holly How)** Holly How, Far End, Coniston, Cumbria LA21 8DD.	t (15394) 41323 f (15394) 41803	60	14.01–30.11	CC P
▲ **Coniston Coppermines** Coppermines House, Coniston, Cumbria LA21 8HP.	t (15394) 41261 f (15394) 41261	28	02.04–28.10	CC P
▲ **Conwy** Larkhill, Sychnant Pass Rd, Conwy, Wales, LL32 8AJ. e conwy@yha.org.uk	t (1492) 593571 f (1492) 593580	80	11.02–26.12	CC P
△ ***Copt Oak*** *Whitwick Rd, Markfield, Leicestershire LE67 9QB.*	t *(1530) 242661* f *(1530) 242661*	*18*	*17.04–16.09*	CC P
△ ***Corris*** *Old School, Old Rd, Corris, Machynlleth, Powys SY20 9QT.*	t *(1654) 761686* f *(1654) 761686*	*46*	*04.01–12.02; 17.02–16.12; 27–31.12*	P
▲ **Coverack** Parc Behan, School Hill, Coverack, Helston, Cornwall TR12 6SA.	t (1326) 280687 f (1326) 280119	38	03.04–31.10	CC P
▲ **Crowcombe Heathfield** Denzel House, Crowcombe Heathfield, Taunton, Somerset TA4 4BT.	t (1984) 667249 f (1984) 667249	50	10.04–07.09	CC P
△ ***Crowden-in-Longdendale*** *Peak National Park Hostel, Crowden, Glossop, SK13 1HZ.*	t *(1457) 852135* f *(1457) 852135*	*50*	*03.04–18.11*	CC P
△ ***Cynwyd*** *The Old Mill, Cynwyd, Corwen, Denbighshire, Wales LL21 0LW.*	t *(1490) 412814* f *(1490) 412814*	*30*	*20.04–30.09*	CC P
▲ **Dartington** Lownard, Dartington, Totnes, Devon TQ9 6JJ.	t (1803) 862303 f (1803) 865171	30	19.04–04.09	CC P

Location/Address	Telephone No. Fax No.	Beds	Opening Dates	Facilities
▲ **Dentdale** Cowgill, Dent, Sedbergh, Cumbria LA10 5RN.	☎ (15396) 25251 ✆ (15396) 25068	38	01.01–03.01; 28.01–09.12; 24–26.12	ⓘⓞⓛ ⒸⒸ ☞ Ⓟ
▲ **Derwentwater** Barrow House, Borrowdale, Keswick, Cumbria CA12 5UR. ⊜ derwentwater@yha.org.uk	☎ (17687) 77246 ✆ (17687) 77396	88	04.01–16.12; 28–31.12	ⅲ ⓘⓞⓛ ⒸⒸ ☞ Ⓟ ⓞ
▲ **Dimmingsdale** Little Ranger, Dimmingsdale, Oakamoor, Stoke-on-Trent, Staffordshire ST10 3AS.	☎ (1538) 702304	20	17.04–21.09	ⒸⒸ ☞ Ⓟ
△ *Dolgoch* *Tregaron, Ceredigion SY25 6NR.*	☎ *(1550) 740225* *Llanddeusant YH*	*22*	*14.04–23.09*	☞ Ⓟ
▲ **Dover** ⒾⒷⓃ **306 London Rd, Dover, Kent CT17 0SY.** ⊜ dover@yha.org.uk	☎ (1304) 201314 ✆ (1304) 202236	132	🖾	ⅲ ⓘⓞⓛ ⓞⓝ₅ₙw ⒸⒸ ☞
▲ **Dufton** 'Redstones', Dufton, Appleby, Cumbria CA16 6DB.	☎ (17863) 51236 ✆ (17683) 53798	36	17.04–31.10	ⓘⓞⓛ ⒸⒸ ☞ Ⓟ ⓞ
△ *Earby* *Katherine Bruce Glasier Memorial Hostel, Glen Cottage, Birch Hall Lane, Earby,Barnoldswick, Lancashire BB18 6JX.*	☎ *(1282) 842349* ✆ *(1282) 842349*	*22*	*17.04–28.10*	ⒸⒸ ☞ Ⓟ
▲ **Eastbourne** East Dean Rd, Eastbourne, East Sussex BN20 8ES.	☎ (1323) 721081 ✆ (1323) 721081	31	19.04–30.09	ⅲ ⒸⒸ ☞ Ⓟ
▲ **Edale** Hostel and Activity Centre, Rowland Cote, Edale, Hope Valley S33 7ZH. ⊜ edale@yha.org.uk	☎ (1433) 670302 ✆ (1433) 670243	141	03.01–31.12	ⓘⓞⓛ ⒸⒸ ☞ Ⓟ ⓞ
▲ **Edmundbyers** Low House, Edmundbyers, Consett, Co Durham DH8 9NL.	☎ (1207) 255651 ✆ (1207) 255651	40	17.04–28.10	♿ ⒸⒸ ☞ Ⓟ
▲ **Ellingstring** Lilac Cottage, Ellingstring, Masham, Ripon, North Yorks HG4 4PW.	☎ (1677) 460216	18	21.04–03.09	☞ Ⓟ
▲ **Elmscott** Hartland, Bideford, Devon EX39 6ES.	☎ (1237) 441367 ✆ (1237) 441910	32	19.04–04.09	ⒸⒸ ☞ Ⓟ
▲ **Elterwater** Ambleside, Cumbria LA22 9HX.	☎ (15394) 37245 ✆ (15394) 37120	46	04.02–27.12	ⓘⓞⓛ Ⓡ ⒸⒸ ☞ Ⓟ
▲ **Elton** Elton Old Hall, Main St, Elton, Matlock, Derbyshire DE4 2BW.	☎ (1629) 650394	32	🖾	ⒸⒸ ☞ Ⓟ
▲ **Ennerdale (Gillerthwaite)** Cat Crag, Ennerdale, Cleator, Cumbria CA23 3AX.	☎ (1946) 861237	24	02.04–28.10	ⓘⓞⓛ ⒸⒸ ☞ Ⓟ
▲ **Epping Forest** Wellington Hill, High Beach, Loughton, Essex IG10 4AG. ⊜ epping@yha.org.uk	☎ (20) 85085161 ✆ (20) 85085161	36	19.04–31.10	ⅲ ⒸⒸ ☞ Ⓟ

Location/Address	Telephone No. Fax No.	Beds	Opening Dates	Facilities
▲ **Eskdale** Boot, Holmrook, Cumbria CA19 1TH.	☎ (19467) 23219 🖷 (19467) 23163	54	11.02–31.10	⁙⁙ ⦿ ⊟ ⸰ P ⊡
▲ **Exeter** [IBN] 47 Countess Wear Rd, Exeter, Devon EX2 6LR. ✉ exeter@yha.org.uk	☎ (1392) 873329 🖷 (1392) 876939	88	15.01–30.12; 13.01–28.02	⁙⁙ ⦿ 3SE ⊟ ⸰ P ⊡
▲ **Exford** Exe Mead, Exford, Minehead, Somerset TA24 7PU.	☎ (1643) 831288 🖷 (1643) 831650	51	14.02–31.10	⁙⁙ ⦿ ⊟ ⸰ P ⊡
▲ **Eyam** Hawkhill Rd, Eyam, Hope Valley S32 5QP. ✉ eyam@yha.org.uk	☎ (1433) 630335 🖷 (1433) 639202	60	11.02–02.12; 23.12–27.12	⦿ ⊟ ⸰ P
▲ **Golant** Penquite House, Golant, Fowey, Cornwall PL23 1LA. ✉ golant@yha.org.uk	☎ (1726) 833507 🖷 (1726) 832947	94	01.02–31.10	⁙⁙ ⦿ ⊟ ⸰ P ⊡
▲ **Gradbach Mill** Gradbach, Quarnford, Buxton, Derbyshire SK17 0SU. ✉ gradbach@yha.org.uk	☎ (1260) 227625 🖷 (1260) 227334	87	11.02–26.11; 28.12–31.12	⁙⁙ ⦿ ♿ ⊟ ⸰ P ⊡
▲ **Grasmere** - Butterlip How Butterlip How, Easedale Rd, Grasmere, Cumbria LA22 9QG. ✉ grasmerebh@yha.org.uk	☎ (15394) 35316 🖷 (15394) 35798	128	04.01–16.12; 23.12–31.12	⁙⁙ ⦿ ⊟ ⸰ P ⊡
▲ **Great Yarmouth** 2 Sandown Rd, Great Yarmouth, Norfolk NR30 1EY.	☎ (1493) 843991 🖷 (1493) 843991	40	19.04–02.05; 26.05–29.05; 01.07–04.09	⊟ ⸰
▲ **Greenhead** Carlisle, Cumbria CA6 7HG.	☎ (16977) 47401 🖷 (16977) 47401	40	03.04–31.10	⦿ ⊟ ⸰
▲ **Grinton Lodge** Grinton Lodge, Grinton, Richmond, North Yorkshire DL11 6HS. ✉ grinton@yha.org.uk	☎ (1748) 884206 🖷 (1748) 884876	66	11.02–25.11; 28.12–31.12	⦿ ⊟ ⸰ P ⊡
▲ **Hartington** Hartington Hall, Hartington, Buxton, Derbyshire SK17 0AT. ✉ hartington@yha.org.uk	☎ (1298) 84223 🖷 (1298) 84415	140	11.02–23.12	⁙⁙ ⦿ ♿ ⊟ ⸰ P ⊡
▲ **Hastings** Guestling Hall, Rye Rd, Guestling, Hastings, East Sussex TN35 4LP.	☎ (1424) 812373 🖷 (1424) 814273	51	27.01–02.09; 19.09–17.12	⁙⁙ ⦿ Ⓡ ⊟ ⸰ P
▲ **Hathersage** Castleton Rd, Hathersage, Hope Valley S32 1EH.	☎ (1433) 650493 🖷 (1433) 650493	42	02.01–25.11	⦿ ⊟ ⸰ P
▲ **Hawes** Lancaster Terrace, Hawes, North Yorkshire DL8 3LQ.	☎ (1969) 667368 🖷 (1969) 667723	58	11.02–26.12	⦿ ⊟ ⸰ ⊡
▲ **Hawkshead** Esthwaite Lodge, Hawkshead, Ambleside, Cumbria LA22 0QD. ✉ hawkshead@yha.org.uk	☎ (15394) 36293 🖷 (15394) 36720	106	11.02–16.12; 28–31.12	⁙⁙ ⦿ ⊟ ⸰ P ⊡

Location/Address	Telephone No. Fax No.	Beds	Opening Dates	Facilities
▲ **Haworth** Longlands Hall, Longlands Drive, Lees Lane, Haworth, Keighley, West Yorkshire BD22 8RT. ✉ haworth@yha.org.uk	☎ (1535) 642234 🖷 (1535) 643023	100	11.02–16.12; 28–31.12	¶◎| ▣ ✿ 🅿 ▣
▲ **Helmsley** Carlton Lane, Helmsley, York YO62 5HB.	☎ (1439) 770433 🖷 (1439) 770433	40	03.04–31.10	¶◎| ▣ ✿
▲ **Helvellyn** Greenside, Glenridding, Penrith, Cumbria CA11 0QR.	☎ (17684) 82269 🖷 (17684) 82009	64	01.01–30.11	¶◎| ▣ ✿ 🅿
High Close ☞ **Langdale**				
Holford ☞ **Quantock Hills**				
▲ **Holmbury St Mary** Radnor Lane, Holmbury St Mary, Dorking, Surrey RH5 6NW. ✉ holmbury@yha.org.uk	☎ (1306) 730777 🖷 (1306) 730933	52	11.02–28.10	¶◎| ▣ ✿ 🅿
▲ **Honister Hause** Seatoller, Keswick, Cumbria CA12 5XN.	☎ (17687) 77267 🖷 (17687) 77267	26	31.03–11.11	¶◎| ▣ ✿ 🅿
▲ **Hunstanton** 15 Ave Rd, Hunstanton, Norfolk PE36 5BW.	☎ (1485) 532061 🖷 (1485) 532632	46	01.04–30.10	¶¶¶ ¶◎| ▣ ✿ 🅿 ▣
▲ **Idwal Cottage** Nant Ffrancon, Bethesda, Bangor, Gwynedd, Wales LL57 3LZ.	☎ (1248) 600225 🖷 (1248) 602952	43	07.01–02.09; 08.09–16.12; 29–31.12	▣ ✿ 🅿
▲ **Ilam** Ilam Hall, Ashbourne, Derbyshire DE6 2AZ. ✉ ilam@yha.org.uk	☎ (1335) 350212 🖷 (1335) 350350	135	11.02–28.10; 28–31.12	¶¶¶ ¶◎| ♿ ▣ ✿ 🅿 ▣
▲ **Ilfracombe** Ashmour House, 1 Hillsborough Terrace, Ilfracombe, Devon EX34 9NR.	☎ (1271) 865337 🖷 (1271) 862652	50	01.03–31.10	¶¶¶ ¶◎| ▣ ✿ 🅿
▲ **Ingleton** Greta Tower, Sammy Lane, Ingleton, Carnforth, Lancashire LA6 3EG.	☎ (15242) 41444 🖷 (15242) 41854	58	11.02–17.12; 22.12–02.01	¶¶¶ ¶◎| ▣ ✿ 🅿
▲ **Ironbridge Gorge** John Rose Building, High St, Coalport, Telford, Shropshire TF8 7HT. ✉ ironbridge@yha.org.uk	☎ (1952) 588755 🖷 (1952) 588722	165	01.02–31.10	¶¶¶ ¶◎| ♿ ▣ ✿ 🅿
▲ **Ivinghoe** The Old Brewery House, Ivinghoe, Leighton Buzzard, Bedfordshire LU7 9EP.	☎ (1296) 668251 🖷 (1296) 662903	50	27.01–02.09; 19.09–17.12	¶◎| ▣ ✿ 🅿
▲ **Jordans** Welders Lane, Jordans, Beaconsfield, Buckinghamshire HP9 2SN.	☎ (1494) 873135 🖷 (1494) 875907	20	04.03–31.10	▣ ✿ 🅿
▲ **Keld** Keld Lodge, Upper Swaledale, Keld, Richmond, North Yorkshire DL11 6LL.	☎ (1748) 886259 🖷 (1748) 886013	40	07.01–30.11; 30.12–02.01	¶◎| ▣ ✿
▲ **Kemsing** Church Lane, Kemsing, Sevenoaks, Kent TN15 6LU.	☎ (1732) 761341 🖷 (1732) 763044	50	29.01–18.12	¶¶¶ ¶◎| ▣ ✿ 🅿

Location/Address	Telephone No. Fax No.	Beds	Opening Dates	Facilities
▲ **Kendal** 118 Highgate, Kendal, Cumbria LA9 4HE.	☎ (1539) 724066 ✆ (1539) 724906	54	04.02–02.01	⊙ CC ✓ P
▲ **Keswick** Station Rd, Keswick, Cumbria CA12 5LH. ● keswick@yha.org.uk	☎ (17687) 72484 ✆ (17687) 74129	91	12.02–31.12	⊙ CC ✓ P ▣
▲ **Kettlewell** Whernside House, Kettlewell, Skipton, North Yorkshire BD23 5QU.	☎ (1756) 760232 ✆ (1756) 760402	54	11.02–19.12	⋔ ⊙ CC ✓ P
▲ **Kings, Dolgellau** Kings, Penmaenpool, Dolgellau, Gwynedd, Wales LL40 1TB.	☎ (1341) 422392 ✆ (1341) 422477	56	11.02–15.04; 21.04–02.09	⋔ ⊙ 6SW CC ✓ P
▲ **King's Lynn** Thoresby College, College Lane, King's Lynn, Norfolk PE30 1JB.	☎ (1553) 772461 ✆ (1553) 772461	35	01.04–05.09 ⋔	⋔ CC ✓
Kirk Yetholm ☞ **Scotland**				
▲ **Kirkby Stephen** Fletcher Hill, Market St, Kirkby Stephen, Cumbria CA17 4QQ.	☎ (17683) 71793 ✆ (17683) 71793	44	17.04–31.10	⋔ ⊙ CC ✓ P ▣
▲ **Land's End** Letcha Vean, St Just in Penwith, Penzance, Cornwall TR19 7NT. (7km N of Land's End)	☎ (1736) 788437 ✆ (1736) 787337	43	01.03–31.10	⋔ ⊙ CC ✓ P
▲ **Langdale** - High Close High Close, Loughrigg, Ambleside, Cumbria LA22 9HJ. ● langdale@yha.org.uk	☎ (15394) 37313 ✆ (15394) 37101	80	03.03–28.10	⊙ CC ✓ P
▲ **Langdon Beck** Forest-in-Teesdale, Barnard Castle, Co Durham DL12 0XN. ● langdonbeck@yha.org.uk	☎ (1833) 622228 ✆ (1833) 622372	34	11.02–30.11	⋔ ⊙ CC ✓ P ▣
△ *Langsett* *Nr Penistone, Sheffield S30 5GY.*	☎ *(114) 2884541*	*30*	*01.01–24.06; 30.06–02.09; 08–30.09*	✓ P
△ *Lawrenny* *Millenium YH, Lawrenny, Kilgetty, Pembrokeshire, Wales SA68 0PN.*	☎ *(1646) 651270*	*24*	*01.04–30.10*	✓ P
▲ **Leominster** - Leominster Priory The Old Priory, Leominster, Herefordshire.	☎ (1727) 855215 for information		16.07–02.09; 03.09–19.10	0.2NE
▲ **Lincoln** 77 South Park, Lincoln LN5 8ES. ● lincoln@yha.org.uk	☎ (1522) 522076 ✆ (1522) 567424	45	02.02–05.11	⋔ ⊙ 2SE CC ✓ P ▣
▲ **Linton** The Old Rectory, Linton-in-Craven, Skipton, North Yorkshire BD23 5HH.	☎ (1756) 752400 ✆ (1756) 753159	38	31.03–29.10	⊙ CC ✓ P
▲ **Litton Cheney** Dorchester, Dorset DT2 9AT.	☎ (1308) 482340 ✆ (1308) 482636	24	19.04–04.09	⋔ CC ✓ ▣
▲ **Liverpool** IBN **Wapping, Liverpool, L1 8EE.** ● liverpool@yha.org.uk	☎ (151) 7098888 ✆ (151) 7090417	110	▣	⋔ ⊙ 1SW ♿ CC ✓ P ▣

Location/Address	Telephone No. Fax No.	Beds	Opening Dates	Facilities
▲ **Llanbedr** Plas Newydd, Llanbedr, Barmouth, Gwynedd, Wales LL45 2LE.	☎ (1341) 241287 🖷 (1341) 241389	46	21.04–28.10	ᛮᛮᛮ ᠯᠥᠯ ⊂CC⊃ ☞ 🅿
▲ **Llanberis** Llwyn Celyn, Llanberis, Caernarfon, Gwynedd, Wales LL55 4SR.	☎ (1286) 870280 🖷 (1286) 870936	60	01.01–26.02; 03.03–15.04; 18.04–28.10; 03.11–16.12; 29.12–31.12	ᠯᠥᠯ ⊂CC⊃ ☞ 🅿
△ *Llanddeusant* *The Old Red Lion, Llanddeusant, Llangadog, Carmarthenshire, Wales SA19 6UL.*	☎ *(1550) 740619*	*28*	*21.04–07.09*	ᠯᠥᠯ ☞ 🅿
▲ **Llangollen** Tyndwr Hall, Tyndwr Rd, Llangollen, Denbighshire, Wales LL20 8AR. ✉ llangollen@yha.org.uk	☎ (1978) 860330 🖷 (1978) 861709	134	🗓12	ᛮᛮᛮ ᠯᠥᠯ ⊂CC⊃ ☞ 🅿 🖸
▲ **Lledr Valley Betws-y-Coed** Lledr House, Pont-y-Pant, Dolwyddelan, Wales LL25 0DQ.	☎ (1690) 750202 🖷 (1690) 750410	60	11.02–15.04; 20.04–06.05; 26.05–03.06; 09.06–15.07; 21.07–16.12	ᠯᠥᠯ 7SW ⊂CC⊃ ☞ 🅿
▲ **Llwyn y Celyn** Libanus, Brecon, Powys, Wales LD3 8NH.	☎ (1874) 624261 🖷 (1874) 625916	42	12.02–10.04; 13.04–04.09; 07.09–25.11	ᠯᠥᠯ ⊂CC⊃ ☞ 🅿
△ *Lockton* *The Old School, Lockton, Pickering, North Yorkshire YO18 7PY.*	☎ *(1751) 460376* 🖷 *(1751) 460376*	*22*	*17.04–21.09*	⊂CC⊃ ☞ 🅿
▲ **London** - City of London IBN **36 Carter Lane, London EC4V 5AB.** ✉ city@yha.org.uk	☎ (20) 72364965 🖷 (20) 72367681	193	🗓12	ᛮᛮᛮ ᠯᠥᠯ 2NE ⊂CC⊃ 🖸
▲ **London** - Earls Court IBN **38 Bolton Gardens, London, SW5 0AQ.** ✉ earlscourt@yha.org.uk	☎ (20) 73737083 🖷 (20) 78352034	154	🗓12	ᠯᠥᠯ 6SW ⊂CC⊃ ☞ 🖸
▲ **London** - Hampstead Heath IBN **4 Wellgarth Rd, Golders Green, London NW11 7HR.** ✉ hampstead@yha.org.uk	☎ (20) 84589054 🖷 (20) 82090546	200	🗓12	ᛮᛮᛮ ᠯᠥᠯ 9NW ⊂CC⊃ ☞ 🅿 🖸
▲ **London** - Holland House IBN **Holland House, Holland Walk, Kensington, London W8 7QU.** ✉ hollandhouse@yha.org.uk	☎ (20) 79370748 🖷 (20) 73760667	201	🗓12	ᠯᠥᠯ 6SW ⊂CC⊃ ☞ 🖸
▲ **London** - Oxford Street IBN **14 Noel St, London W1V 3PD.** ✉ oxfordst@yha.org.uk	☎ (20) 77341618 🖷 (20) 77341657	75	🗓12	Ⓡ ⊂CC⊃ ☞ 🖸
▲ **London** - Rotherhithe IBN **20 Salter Rd, London SE16 1PP.** ✉ rotherhithe@yha.org.uk	☎ (20) 72322114 🖷 (20) 72372919	320	🗓12	ᛮᛮᛮ ᠯᠥᠯ ♿ ⊂CC⊃ ☞ 🅿 🖸
▲ **London** - St Pancras IBN **79-81 Euston Rd, London NW1 2QS.** ✉ stpancras@yha.org.uk	☎ (20) 73889998 🖷 (20) 73886766	152	🗓12	ᛮᛮᛮ ᠯᠥᠯ Ⓡ ⊂CC⊃ ☞ 🖸

Location/Address	Telephone No. Fax No.	Beds	Opening Dates	Facilities
Longthwaite ☞ Borrowdale				
▲ **Lulworth Cove** School Lane, West Lulworth, Wareham, Dorset BH20 5SA.	☎ (1929) 400564 ☏ (1929) 400640	34	03.03–28.10	�037 ⦿ 𝄞 ℄₌ ⬟ P
▲ **Lynton** Lynbridge, Lynton, Devon EX35 6AZ.	☎ (1598) 753237 ☏ (1598) 753305	34	01.04–31.10	�037 ⦿ ℄₌ ⬟ P ▣
△ *Maeshafn* *Holt Hostel, Maeshafn, Mold, Denbighshire,* *Wales CH7 5LR.*	☎ *(1352) 810320* ☏ *(1352) 810320*	*31*	*20.04–28.05;* *07.07–31.08*	⬟ P
▲ **Malham** John Dower Memorial Hostel, Malham, Skipton, North Yorkshire BD23 4DE. ⓔ malham@yha.org.uk	☎ (1729) 830321 ☏ (1729) 830551	82	01.01–16.12; 28–31.12	�037 ⦿ ℄₌ ⬟ P ▣
▲ **Malvern Hills** 18 Peachfield Rd, Malvern Wells, Malvern, Worcestershire WR14 4AP. ⓔ malvern@yha.org.uk	☎ (1684) 569131 ☏ (1684) 565205	59	07.01–31.10; 03.11–23.12	�037 ⦿ ® ℄₌ ⬟ P
▲ **Manchester** ⟦IBN⟧ **Potato Wharf, Castlefield,** **Manchester M3 4NB** ⓔ manchester@yha.org.uk	☎ (161) 8399960 ☏ (161) 8352054	140	▤	�037 ⦿ ♿ ℄₌ ⬟ P ▣
▲ **Mankinholes** Todmorden, Lancashire OL14 6HR.	☎ (1706) 812340 ☏ (1706) 812340	40	07.04–09.11	℄₌ ⬟ P ▣
▲ **Manorbier** Nr Tenby, Pembrokeshire, Wales SA70 7TT. ⓔ manorbier@yha.org.uk	☎ (1834) 871803 ☏ (1834) 871101	68	01.03–28.10	�037 ⦿ ♿ ℄₌ ⬟ P ▣
▲ **Margate** The Beachcomber, 3-4 Royal Esplanade, Westbrook Bay, Margate, Kent CT9 5DL. ⓔ margate@yha.org.uk	☎ (1843) 221616 ☏ (1843) 221616	50	26.03–24.04; 26.05–30.09 �037	�037 ⟦0.7W⟧ ℄₌ ⬟
▲ **Marloes Sands** Runwayskiln, Marloes, Haverfordwest, Pembrokeshire, Wales SA62 3BH.	☎ (1646) 636667 ☏ (1646) 636667	30	20.04–28.10	⬟ P
▲ **Matlock** 40 Bank Rd, Matlock, Derbyshire DE4 3NF. ⓔ matlock@yha.org.uk	☎ (1629) 582983 ☏ (1629) 583484	49	03.01–16.12	�037 ⦿ ♿ ℄₌ ⬟ P ▣
▲ **Maypool** Maypool House, Galmpton, Brixham, Devon TQ5 0ET.	☎ (1803) 842444 ☏ (1803) 845939	70	14.02–31.10	⦿ ℄₌ ⬟ P
▲ **Meerbrook** Old School, Meerbrook, Leek, Staffordshire ST13 8SJ.	☎ (1538) 300244	22	17.04–24.06; 30.06–09.09; 15.09–28.10	⬟ P
Milton Keynes ☞ Bradwell Village				
▲ **Minehead** Alcombe Combe, Minehead, Somerset TA24 6EW.	☎ (1643) 702595 ☏ (1643) 703016	36	10.04–03.09	�037 ⦿ ℄₌ ⬟ P

Location/Address	Telephone No. Fax No.	Beds	Opening Dates	Facilities
▲ **Newport** Lower St Mary St, Newport, Pembrokeshire, Wales SA42 0TS.	☏ (1239) 820080 🖷 (1239) 820080	28	14.04–11.07; 14.07–30.09	♦♦♦ ♿ ☞ 🅿
▲ **Newcastle upon Tyne** [IBN] 107 Jesmond Rd, Newcastle upon Tyne NE2 1NJ. ✉ newcastle@yha.org.uk	☏ (191) 2812570 🖷 (191) 2818779	60	31.01–19.12; 22.12–28.01	¶◎¶ €€€ ☞ 🅿
△ *Ninebanks* *Orchard House, Mohope, Ninebanks,* *Hexham, Northumberland NE47 8DO.*	☏ *(1434) 345288* 🖷 *(1434) 345288*	*26*	*05.01–31.12*	€€€ ☞ 🅿
▲ **Norwich** 112 Turner Rd, Norwich NR2 4HB. ✉ norwich@yha.org.uk	☏ (1603) 627647 🖷 (1603) 629075	63	01.03–31.10; 01.11–21.12	♦♦♦ ¶◎¶ 2W €€€ ☞ 🅿
▲ **Okehampton** Klondyke Rd, Okehampton, Devon EX20 1EW. ✉ okehampton@yha.org.uk	☏ (1837) 53916 🖷 (1837) 53965	74	29.01–30.11	♦♦♦ ¶◎¶ 0.5SW €€€ ☞ 🅿 ◙
▲ **Once Brewed** Military Rd, Bardon Mill, Hexham, Northumberland NE47 7AN. ✉ oncebrewed@yha.org.uk	☏ (1434) 344360 🖷 (1434) 344045	90	11.02–25.11	♦♦♦ ¶◎¶ €€€ ☞ 🅿 ◙
▲ **Osmotherley** Cote Ghyll, Osmotherley, Northallerton, North Yorkshire DL6 3AH. ✉ osmotherley@yha.org.uk	☏ (1609) 883575 🖷 (1609) 883715	72	30.01–04.11; 29.12–02.01	♦♦♦ ¶◎¶ €€€ ☞ 🅿
▲ **Oxford** [IBN] **32 Jack Straw's Lane, Oxford OX3 0DW.** ✉ oxford@yha.org.uk	☏ (1865) 762997 🖷 (1865) 769402	105	🔟	¶◎¶ 3NE €€€ ☞ 🅿 ◙
▲ **Patterdale** Goldrill House, Patterdale, Penrith, Cumbria CA11 0NW. ✉ patterdale@yha.org.uk	☏ (17684) 82394 🖷 (17684) 82034	82	01.02–27.12	¶◎¶ €€€ ☞ 🅿 ◙
▲ **Pendennis Castle** Falmouth, Cornwall TR11 4LP. ✉ pendennis@yha.org.uk	☏ (1326) 311435 🖷 (1326) 315473	76	13.02–31.10	♦♦♦ ¶◎¶ €€€ ☞ 🅿 ◙
△ *Pentlepoir* *The Old School, Pentlepoir, Saundersfoot,* *Pembrokeshire, Wales SA9 9BJ.*	☏ *(1834) 812333*	*34*	*20.04–01.07;* *04.07–02.09;* *05.09–28.10*	€€€ ☞ 🅿
▲ **Penycwm (Solva)** Solva, Whitehouse, Penycwm, Nr Solva, Haverfordwest, Pembrokeshire, Wales SA61 6LA. ✉ penycwm@yha.org.uk	☏ (1437) 721940 🖷 (1437) 720959	26	🔟	♦♦♦ ¶◎¶ 4SE ☞ 🅿
▲ **Pen-y-Pass** Nantgwynant, Caernarfon, Gwynedd, Wales LL55 4NY. ✉ penypass@yha.org.uk	☏ (1286) 870428 🖷 (1286) 872434	84	01.01–08.01; 12.02–27.02; 20.04–06.05; 26.05–04.06; 21.07–30.09; 13.10–29.10; 29.12–03.01	♦♦♦ ¶◎¶ ♿ €€€ ☞ 🅿

Location/Address	Telephone No. Fax No.	Beds	Opening Dates	Facilities
▲ **Penzance** [IBN] Castle Horneck, Alverton, Penzance, Cornwall TR20 8TF. e penzance@yha.org.uk	t (1736) 362666 f (1736) 362663	80	29.02–29.12;	❍ [1.5 N] [CC] ☞ P ⬚
▲ **Perranporth** Droskyn Point, Perranporth, Cornwall TR6 0DS.	t (1872) 573812 f (1872) 573319	26	19.04–04.09	[CC] ☞
▲ **Peterborough** - Nene Park Millennium Youth Hostel Thorpe Meadows, Peterborough, PE3 6GA e peterborough@yha.org.uk	t (1629) 825850 for information f (1629) 824571	40	01.08–04.11	[1.5 W]
▲ **Plymouth** [IBN] Belmont House, Belmont Place, Stoke, Plymouth PL3 4DW. e plymouth@yha.org.uk	t (1752) 562189 f (1752) 605360	68	01.01–23.12; 29.12–28.02	♦♦♦ ❍ [3 W] [CC] ☞ P ⬚
▲ **Poppit Sands** 'Sea View', Poppit, Cardigan, Cardiganshire, Wales SA43 3LP.	t (1239) 612936 f (1239) 612936	36	11.02–15.04; 18.04–08.07; 11.07–02.09; 05.09–28.10	♦♦♦ [CC] ☞ P
▲ **Port Eynon** The Old Lifeboat House, Port Eynon, Swansea, Wales SA3 1NN.	t (1792) 390706 f (1792) 390706	30	14.04–01.07; 03.07–02.09; 05.09–28.10	[CC] ☞
▲ **Portsmouth** [IBN] Wymering Manor, Old Wymering Lane, Cosham, Portsmouth, Hampshire PO6 3NL. e portsmouth@yha.org.uk	t (23) 92375661 f (23) 92214177	64	01.02–30.09; 01.10–21.12	❍ [6 NE] [CC] ☞ P
▲ **Pwll Deri** Castell Mawr, Tref Asser, Goodwick, Pembrokeshire, Wales SA64 0LR.	t (1348) 891233 f (1348) 891385	30	14.04–28.10	[CC] ☞ P
▲ **Quantock Hills** Sevenacres, Holford, Bridgwater, Somerset TA5 1SQ.	t (1278) 741224 f (1278) 741224	34	20.04–02.05; 09.07–04.09	[CC] ☞ P
▲ **Ravenstor** Millers Dale, Buxton, Derbyshire SK17 8SS. e ravenstor@yha.org.uk	t (1298) 871826 f (1298) 871275	79	11.02–28.10; 28–31.12	♦♦♦ ❍ [CC] ☞ P
▲ **Ridgeway** Ridgeway Centre, Courthill, Wantage, Oxfordshire OX12 9NE.	t (12357) 60253 f (12357) 68865	59	08.01–25.03; 28.03–03.09; 06.09–25.11; 01–16.12	♦♦♦ ❍ ♿ [CC] ☞ P ⬚
▲ **Rochester** Capstone Farm (Rochester) YH, Capstone Rd, Gillingham, Kent ME7 3JE.	t (1634) 400788 f (1634) 400794	40	15.02–17.12	♦♦♦ ❍ ♿ [CC] ☞ P ⬚
△ *Rowen* *Rhiw Farm, Rowen, Conwy, Wales LL32 8YW.*	t (1492) 650089	24	20.04–02.09	☞ P
▲ **Saffron Walden** 1 Myddylton Place, Saffron Walden, Essex CB10 1BB.	t (1799) 523117 f (1799) 520840	40	26.02–04.09; 21.09–30.10	❍ [CC] ☞ P

Location/Address	Telephone No. Fax No.	Beds	Opening Dates	Facilities
▲ **St Briavels Castle** The Castle, St Briavels, Lydney, Gloucestershire GL15 6RG. ℮ stbriavels@yha.org.uk	☎ (1594) 530272 ✆ (1594) 530849	70	11.02–28.10	⑩ ⒸⒸ ✔ Ⓟ
△ *St David's* *Llaethdy, St David's, Haverfordwest, Pembrokeshire, Wales SA62 6PR.*	☎ *(1437) 720345* ✆ *(1437) 721831*	*44*	*14.04–11.07; 14.07–05.09; 08.09–28.10*	ⒸⒸ ✔ Ⓟ
▲ **Salcombe** 'Overbecks', Sharpitor, Salcombe, Devon TQ8 8LW.	☎ (1548) 842856 ✆ (1548) 843865	51	10.04–31.10	⑪ ⑩ ⒸⒸ ✔ Ⓟ
▲ **Salisbury** ⒾⒷⓃ Milford Hill House, Milford Hill, Salisbury, Wiltshire SP1 2QW. ℮ salisbury@yha.org.uk	☎ (1722) 327572 ✆ (1722) 330446	70	🖷	⑩ ⒸⒸ ✔ Ⓟ 🗇
▲ **Sandown** The Firs, Fitzroy St, Sandown, Isle of Wight PO36 8JH.	☎ (1983) 402651 ✆ (1983) 403565	47	15.02–02.09; 06–30.09	⑪ ⑩ ⒸⒸ ✔ Ⓟ
▲ **Scarborough** The White House, Burniston Rd, Scarborough, North Yorkshire YO13 0DA.	☎ (1723) 361176 ✆ (1723) 500054	64	17.04–31.10	⑪ ⑩ ⒸⒸ ✔ Ⓟ 🗇
▲ **Sheringham** 1 Cremer's Drift, Sheringham, Norfolk NR26 8HX. ℮ sheringham@yha.org.uk	☎ (1263) 823215 ✆ (1263) 824679	109	11.02–28.10	⑪ ⑩ ♿ ⒸⒸ ✔ Ⓟ
▲ **Sherwood Forest** ⒾⒷⓃ Forest Corner, Edwinstowe, Nottinghamshire, NG21 9RN. ℮ sherwood@yha.org.uk	☎ (1623) 825794 ✆ (1623) 825796	39	04.02–26.12	⑪ ⑩ ♿ ⒸⒸ ✔ Ⓟ
△ *Shining Cliff* *Shining Cliff Woods, near Ambergate, Derbyshire.*	☎ *(1629) 760827* ✆ *(1629) 760827*	*22*	*17.04–02.05; 26.05–28.05; 30.06–01.07; 22.07–09.09*	✔ Ⓟ
▲ **Shrewsbury** The Woodlands, Abbey Foregate, Shrewsbury, Shropshire SY2 6LZ. ℮ shrewsbury@yha.org.uk	☎ (1743) 360179 ✆ (1743) 357423	54	01.02–28.10	⑩ ⒸⒸ ✔ Ⓟ 🗇
△ *Skiddaw House* *Skiddaw Forest, Bassenthwaite, Keswick, Cumbria, CA12 4QX.*	☎ *(16974) 78325* ✆ *(16974) 78325*	*20*	*31.03–28.10*	✔
▲ **Slaidburn** King's House, Slaidburn, Clitheroe, Lancashire BB7 3ER.	☎ (15242) 41567	21	17.04–30.10	ⒸⒸ ✔ Ⓟ
▲ **Slimbridge** Shepherd's Patch, Slimbridge, Gloucestershire GL2 7BP. ℮ slimbridge@yha.org.uk	☎ (1453) 890275 ✆ (1453) 890625	56	11.02–28.10; 29–31.12	⑪ ⑩ ⒸⒸ ✔ Ⓟ 🗇
▲ **Snowdon Ranger** Rhyd Ddu, Caernarfon, Gwynedd, Wales LL54 7YS.	☎ (1286) 650391 ✆ (1286) 650093	66	11.02–17.12	⑩ ⒸⒸ ✔ Ⓟ

Location/Address	Telephone No. Fax No.	Beds	Opening Dates	Facilities
Solva ☞ Penycwm				
▲ Stainforth Taitlands, Stainforth, Settle, North Yorkshire BD24 9PA. ⓔ stainforth@yha.org.uk	ⓣ (1729) 823577 ⓕ (1729) 825404	47	11.02–28.10; 28–31.12	CC P
△ Steps Bridge *Dunsford, Exeter, Devon EX6 7EQ.*	ⓣ *(1647) 252435* ⓕ *(1647) 252948*	*24*	*19.04–04.09*	CC P
▲ Stow-on-the-Wold The Square, Stow on the Wold, Cheltenham, Gloucestershire GL54 1AF.	ⓣ (1451) 830497 ⓕ (1451) 870102	50	29.01–16.12; 28.12–01.01	CC P
▲ Stratford-upon-Avon - Hemmingford House IBN **Alveston, Stratford-upon-Avon, Warwickshire CV37 7RG.** ⓔ stratford@yha.org.uk	ⓣ (1789) 297093 ⓕ (1789) 205513	130	08.01–05.12; 29.12–28.02	CC P
▲ Streatley-on-Thames Hill House, Reading Rd, Streatley, Reading, Berks RG8 9JJ.	ⓣ (1491) 872278 ⓕ (1491) 873056	51	04.02–30.10; 03.11–16.12; 29.12–02.01	CC P
▲ Street The Chalet, Ivythorn Hill, St, Somerset BA16 0TZ.	ⓣ (1458) 442961 ⓕ (1458) 442738	28	19.04–04.09	CC P
▲ Swanage Cluny, Cluny Crescent, Swanage, Dorset BH19 2BS. ⓔ swanage@yha.org.uk	ⓣ (1929) 422113 ⓕ (1929) 426327	105	02.02–29.10; 24–26.12	CC P
△ Tanners Hatch *Polesden Lacey, Dorking, Surrey RH5 6BE.* ⓔ *tanners@yha.org.uk*	ⓣ *(1306) 877964* ⓕ *(1306) 877964*	*25*	*03.01–16.12; 24–27.12*	CC
△ Telscombe *Bank Cottages, Telscombe, Lewes, East Sussex BN7 3HZ.*	ⓣ *(1273) 301357* ⓕ *(1273) 301357*	*22*	*19.04–04.09*	CC
△ Thirlmere *The Old School, Stanah Cross, Keswick, Cumbria CA12 4TH.*	ⓣ *(17687) 73224* ⓕ *(17687) 73224*	*28*	*31.03–30.10*	CC P
△ Thixendale *The Village Hall, Thixendale, Malton, North Yorkshire YO17 9TG.*	ⓣ *(1377) 288238*	*18*	*17.04–02.09*	CC P
△ Thurlby *16 High St, Thurlby, Bourne, Lincolnshire PE10 0EE.*	ⓣ *(1778) 425588* ⓕ *(1778) 425588*	*24*	*17.04–21.09*	♿ CC P
▲ Tintagel Dunderhole Point, Tintagel, Cornwall PL34 0DW.	ⓣ (1840) 770334 ⓕ (1840) 770733	26	19.04–30.09	CC P
▲ Totland Bay Hurst Hill, Totland Bay, Isle of Wight PO39 0HD.	ⓣ (1983) 752165 ⓕ (1983) 756443	72	01.01–28.02; 01.03–30.06	CC P

Location/Address	Telephone No. Fax No.	Beds	Opening Dates	Facilities
▲ **Trevine** Fford-yr-Afon Trevine, Haverfordwest, Pembrokeshire, Wales SA62 5AU.	☎ (1348) 831414 ✆ (1348) 831414	26	14.04–08.07; 11.07–02.09; 05.09–30.09	♦♦♦ CC ☞ P
▲ **Treyarnon Bay** Tregonnan, Treyarnon, Padstow, Cornwall PL28 8JR.	☎ (1841) 520322 ✆ (1841) 520322	41	10.04–31.10	♦♦♦ ۝ CC ☞ P
▲ **Truleigh Hill** Tottington Barn, Truleigh Hill, Shoreham-by-Sea, West Sussex BN43 5FB.	☎ (1903) 813419 ✆ (1903) 812016	56	03.04–30.09	♦♦♦ ۝ CC ☞ P
△ *Tyncornel* *Llanddewi-Brefi, Tregaron, Ceredigion, Wales SY25 6PH.*	☎ *(1550) 740225* *Llanddeusant YH*	16	*14.04–21.10*	R ☞ P
▲ **Ty'n-y-Caeau** Groesffordd, Brecon, Powys, Wales LD3 7SW. ✉ tynycaeau@yha.org.uk	☎ (1874) 665270 ✆ (1874) 665278	54	04.02–01.07; 03.07–02.09; 04.09–28.10; 30.10–09.12	♦♦♦ ۝ CC ☞ P
▲ **Wastwater** Wasdale Hall, Wasdale, Seascale, Cumbria CA20 1ET.	☎ (19467) 26222 ✆ (19467) 26056	50	02.01–16.12; 28–31.12	♦♦♦ ۝ CC ☞ P
▲ **Welsh Bicknor** The Rectory, Welsh Bicknor, Nr Goodrich, Ross-on-Wye, Herefordshire HR9 6JJ. ✉ welshbicknor@yha.org.uk	☎ (1594) 860300 ✆ (1594) 861276	78	10.02–25.03; 31.03–28.10; 03.11–16.12	♦♦♦ ۝ CC ☞ P ▯
▲ **Whitby** East Cliff, Whitby, North Yorkshire YO22 4JT.	☎ (1947) 602878 ✆ (1947) 825146	66	01.02–11.12; 30.12–02.01	♦♦♦ ۝ CC ☞ P
Wight, Isle of ☞ **Sandown and Totland Bay**				
▲ **Wilderhope Manor** The John Cadbury Memorial Hostel, Longville in the Dale, Much Wenlock, Shropshire TF13 6EG. ✉ wilderhope@yha.org.uk	☎ (1694) 771363 ✆ (1694) 771520	70	11.02–28.10	۝ CC ☞ P
▲ **Winchester** The City Mill, 1 Water Lane, Winchester, Hampshire SO23 8EJ.	☎ (1962) 853723 ✆ (1962) 855524	31	10.03–29.04; 02.05–28.10	۝ CC ☞
▲ **Windermere** High Cross, Bridge Lane, Troutbeck, Windermere, Cumbria LA23 1LA. ✉ windermere@yha.org.uk	☎ (15394) 43543 ✆ (15394) 47165	73	01.02–16.12; 28–31.12	♦♦♦ ۝ CC ☞ P ▯
▲ **Windsor** IBN Edgeworth House, Mill Lane, Windsor, Berkshire SL4 5JE. ✉ windsor@yha.org.uk	☎ (1753) 861710 ✆ (1753) 832100	74	01.03–23.12	♦♦♦ ۝ CC ☞ P ▯
▲ **Woody's Top** Ruckland, near Louth, Lincs LN11 8RQ.	☎ (1529) 413421 ✆ (1529) 413421	22	17.04–16.09	♦♦♦ CC ☞ P
▲ **Wooler** 30 Cheviot St, Wooler, Northumberland NE71 6LW.	☎ (1668) 281365 ✆ (1668) 282368	52	01.03–31.10	۝ & CC ☞ P ▯

Location/Address	Telephone No. Fax No.	Beds	Opening Dates	Facilities
▲ **York** `IBN` **York International, Water End, Clifton,** **York, Yorkshire YO30 6LP.** ✉ york@yha.org.uk	☎ (1904) 653147 ✆ (1904) 651230	150	🏠	♀♂ ⭤ 1.5NW ⅊CC⅊ ☂ P ◙
▲ **Youlgreave** Fountain Square, Youlgreave, Bakewell, Derbyshire DE45 1UR.	☎ (1629) 636518 ✆ (1629) 636518	42	11.02–16.12	♀♂ ⭤ ⅊CC⅊ ☂
△ *Ystradfellte* *Tai'r Heol, Ystradfellte, Aberdare,* *Wales CF44 9JF.*	☎ *(1639) 720301* ✆ *(1639) 720301*	*28*	*07.04–11.07;* *14.07–28.10*	☂ P

YOUTH HOSTEL ACCOMMODATION
OUTSIDE THE ASSURED STANDARDS SCHEME

Duntisbourne Abbots Cirencester, Gloucestershire GL7 7JN.	☎ (1285) 821682 ✆ (1285) 821697	37	20.04–28.10	⭤ ⅊CC⅊ ☂ P ◙
Hindhead Devils Punchbowl, off Portsmouth Rd, Thursley, Nr Godalming, Surrey GU8 6NS.	☎ (1428) 604285 ✆ (1428) 604285	16	19.04–02.05; 21.07–04.09	⅊CC⅊ ☂ P ◙

The only aspect of our travels that is interesting to others is disaster.

Le seul aspect de nos voyages qui intéresse les autres sont les désastres qui nous sont arrivés.

Das Einzige, was andere an unseren Reisen interessiert, sind Katastrophen.

Lo único que les interesa a los demás de nuestros viajes son las catástrofes.

Martha Gellman

HOSTELLING INTERNATIONAL

Make your credit card bookings at these centres

Réservez par carte de crédit auprès des centres suivants

Reservieren Sie per Kreditkarte bei diesen Zentren

Reserve con tarjeta de crédito en los siguientes centros

English

Australia	☎ (2) 9261 1111
Canada	☎ (1) (800) 663 5777
England & Wales	☎ (1629) 581 418
France	☎ (1) 44 89 87 27
Northern Ireland	☎ (1232) 324 733
Republic of Ireland	☎ (1) 830 1766
New Zealand	☎ (9) 303 9524
Scotland	☎ (541) 553 255
Switzerland	☎ (1) 360 1414
USA	☎ (202) 783 6161

Français

Angleterre & Pays de Galles	☎ (1692) 581 418
Australie	☎ (2) 9261 1111
Canada	☎ (1) (800) 663 5777
Écosse	☎ (541) 553 255
États-Unis	☎ (202) 783 6161
France	☎ (1) 44 89 87 27
Irlande du Nord	☎ (1232) 324 733
Nouvelle-Zélande	☎ (9) 303 9524
République d'Irlande	☎ (1) 830 1766
Suisse	☎ (1) 360 1414

Deutsch

Australien	☎ (2) 9261 1111
England & Wales	☎ (1629) 581 418
Frankreich	☎ (1) 44 89 87 27
Irland	☎ (1) 830 1766
Kanada	☎ (1) (800) 663 5777
Neuseeland	☎ (9) 303 9524
Nordirland	☎ (1232) 324 733
Schottland	☎ (541) 553 255
Schweiz	☎ (1) 360 1414
USA	☎ (202) 783 6161

Español

Australia	☎ (2) 9261 1111
Canadá	☎ (1) (800) 663 5777
Escocia	☎ (541) 553 255
Estados Unidos	☎ (202) 783 6161
Francia	☎ (1) 44 89 87 27
Inglaterra y Gales	☎ (1629) 581 418
Irlanda del Norte	☎ (1232) 324 733
Nueva Zelanda	☎ (9) 303 9524
República de Irlanda	☎ (1) 830 1766
Suiza	☎ (1) 360 1414

IBN INTERNATIONAL BOOKING NETWORK

Finland

FINLANDE
FINNLAND
FINLANDIA

Suomen Retkeilymajajärjestö-SRM ry,
Yrjönkatu 38 B 15, FIN-00100 Helsinki,
Finland.

t (358) (9) 6940377, 6931347
f (358) (9) 6931349
e info@srm.inet.fi
www.srmnet.org

Office Hours: Monday-Friday, 09.00-16.00hrs

A copy of the Hostel Directory for this Country can be obtained from:
The National Office.

Capital:	Helsinki	**Population:**	5,200,000
Language:	Finnish and Swedish	**Size:**	338,145 sq km
Currency:	FIM (markka)	**Telephone Country Code:**	358

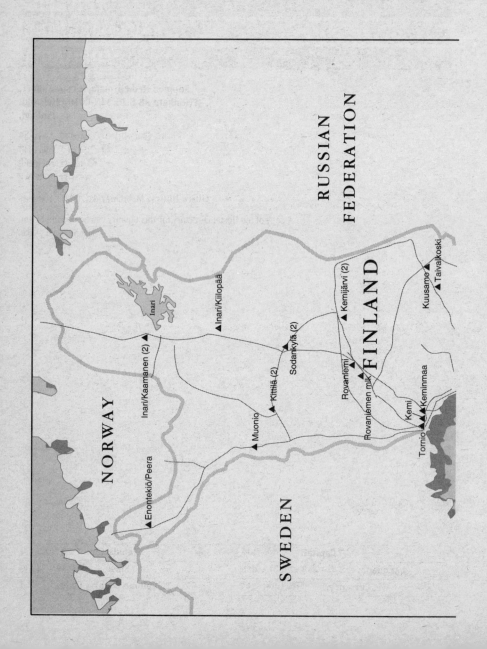

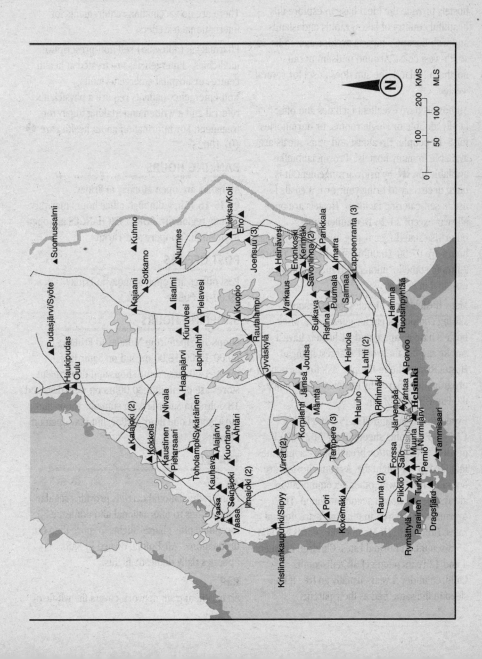

English

FINNISH HOSTELS

With more than 115 locations, youth and family hostels provide the ideal base to explore this beautiful country of lakes, rapids and islands and with Europe's biggest archipelago off its south-west coast. Around midsummer in northern Finland, the sun doesn't set for several weeks.

All hostels have excellent facilities and offer family, double or single rooms, or dormitories for 5-10 people. Breakfast and other meals are available in many hostels. Provincial buffets available for ♙♙♙ by prior arrangement. It is often necessary to bring your own utensils for use in self-catering facilities. Hostels are open all year except 24-26 December unless otherwise stated (see listing for details). Open hours are 07.00-10.00hrs and 17.00-22.00hrs, 24hrs in some locations. Advance booking is essential in winter.

Many hostels have bicycles, boats, canoes, ski-ing equipment etc for guests' use. Most hostels have a sauna, and 11 hostels have a smoke sauna - the world's largest being at Hostel Rauhalahti in Kuopio. Ask for the activity programmes offered by hostels to experience the Finnish ways of life.

Expect to pay around FIM 45-240 FIM (7.5-40 ECU) plus sheet hire (FIM 25-30) if needed. Sheets and/or breakfast are sometimes included in overnight fee. As some hostels are operated jointly with other accommodation, always specify Hostel accommodation. The overnight rates given in this Guide are normal rates. Holders of HI Membership Cards get FIM 15 discount on normal rates. Children between 4 and 12 years often get 50% discount. Children under 4 years usually go free if they sleep in the same bed as their parents.

PASSPORTS AND VISAS

Please contact Finnish Embassy or Consulate in your country of residence.

HEALTH

There are no vaccination requirements for international travellers.

Pharmacies (apteekki) sell non-prescriptive medicines. Emergencies are treated at health centres or hospital emergency units. Non-emergency patients require a physician's referral and a written undertaking to pay for treatment. For information about health care ☏ (9) 10023.

BANKING HOURS

All banks are open Monday to Friday, 09.15-16.15hrs although office hours may vary slightly regionally. FOREX EXCHANGES are open in Helsinki, Tampere and Turku.

POST OFFICES

Post offices are open Monday to Friday 09.00-17.00hrs.

SHOPPING HOURS

Shops are open from Monday to Friday, 09.00-17.00/18.00hrs and on Saturdays 09.00-15.00hrs. Some shops and department stores are open until 20.00hrs on weekdays and 18.00hrs on Saturdays. In summer shops may close about one hour earlier, but may open on Sundays.

TRAVEL

Air

Finnair, the national carrier, provides regular connections to international and domestic locations, plus charter flights to more than 60 destinations. Air Botnia, owned by SAS, operates daily domestic flights.

Rail

An excellent train network covers the whole of

Finland, including transportation for cars. Ask for economical Finnrailpass.

There are two daily connections to St Petersburg in Russia and one night train to Moscow.

Bus

An excellent coach network covers the whole of Finland. Oy Matkahuolto Ab's 150 customer service points throughout Finland give additional information and sell tickets. Coach Holiday Tickets are available.

Ferry

The main passenger ports are Helsinki and Turku. There are excellent services to Sweden, Tallinn in Estonia and during the summer season to Rostock in Germany. Explore the coasts and lakes on local boats. Some Finnish hostels can be reached by boat.

Driving

Traffic drives on the right. Winter weather can be hazardous. Motorists can hire snow tyres at ISKO shops. Beware of elk and reindeer, and report any collision with these animals to local police immediately. A red warning triangle must be carried to display in case of breakdown. Use headlights at all times. Seat belts must be worn by all occupants. Driving under the influence of alcohol or drugs carries heavy penalties. All drivers of foreign vehicles should carry a green card or arrange insurance immediately on arrival in Finland. The nationality of foreign vehicles must be clearly marked.

Français

AUBERGES DE JEUNESSE FINLANDAISES

Plus de 115 auberges pour jeunes et familles vous offrent un point de départ idéal pour vous permettre d'explorer ce si beau pays de lacs, de rapides et d'îles – le plus grand archipel d'Europe se trouvant au large de la côte sud-ouest. Au nord du pays, aux environs de la Saint-Jean, le soleil ne se couche pas pendant plusieurs semaines.

Toutes les auberges offrent d'excellentes prestations et sont équipées de chambres familiales, de chambres à un ou deux lits ou bien, dans certains cas, de dortoirs pour 5 à 10 personnes. Le petit-déjeuner et d'autres repas vous sont proposés dans de nombreuses auberges. Des buffets campagnards sont proposés aux groupes, par accord préalable. Il est souvent nécessaire d'apporter votre propre matériel de cuisine si vous souhaitez cuisiner à l'auberge vous-même. Les auberges sont ouvertes toute l'année, sauf du 24 au 26 décembre, à moins qu'il en soit indiqué autrement (voir liste), de 7h à 10h et de 17h à 22h, et jusqu'à 24h dans certains endroits. En hiver, il est nécessaire de réserver.

De nombreuses auberges offrent aux voyageurs la possibilité d'utiliser des vélos, des bateaux, des canoës, du matériel de ski etc. La plupart sont équipées d'un sauna et 11 d'entre elles disposent d'un sauna à fumée, le plus grand du monde se trouvant à l'auberge de Rauhalahti à Kuopio. Renseignez-vous sur les programmes d'activités que vous proposent nos auberges pour vous faire goûter les différents modes de vie finlandais.

Une nuit vous coûtera entre 45 et 240 FIM (7.5-40 ECU), plus location de draps (25-30 FIM) le cas échéant. Il arrive que les draps et/ou le petit-déjeuner soient compris dans le tarif de la nuitée. Du fait que certaines auberges sont gérées conjointement avec d'autres types d'hébergement, n'oubliez pas de préciser à la réservation que vous souhaitez séjourner dans une auberge de jeunesse. Le tarif par nuit indiqué dans ce guide est le tarif normal. Le titulaire d'une carte d'adhérent des auberges de jeunesse (Hostelling International) profite d'un rabais de 15 MF sur le tarif normal. Les enfants âgés entre 4 et 12 ans bénéficient souvent d'une remise de 50%. En général, les moins de 4 ans ne paient pas à condition qu'ils partagent le lit d'un de leurs parents.

PASSEPORTS ET VISAS

Veuillez contacter l'ambassade ou le consulat finlandais de votre pays de résidence.

SOINS MEDICAUX

Aucune vaccination n'est requise pour les voyageurs internationaux.

Les médicaments sont vendus en pharmacie (apteekki). Les cas urgents sont traités dans les centres médicaux ou dans les services d'urgences des hôpitaux. Les personnes requérant des soins non urgents doivent y être envoyées par un docteur et s'engager par écrit à payer le traitement. Des renseignements sur les soins médicaux offerts sont disponibles nuit et jour, ☎ (9) 10023.

HEURES D'OUVERTURE DES BANQUES

Toutes les banques sont ouvertes du lundi au vendredi, de 9h15 à 16h15, bien que les horaires puissent varier légèrement selon les régions. FOREX EXCHANGES sont en service à Helsinki, Tampere et Turku.

BUREAUX DE POSTE

Les bureaux de poste sont ouverts du lundi au vendredi de 9h à 17h.

HEURES D'OUVERTURE DES MAGASINS

Les magasins sont ouverts du lundi au vendredi, de 9h à 17h/18h et le samedi de 9h à 15h. Certains magasins et grands magasins sont ouverts jusqu'à 20h en semaine et jusqu'à 18h le samedi. En été, il est possible que les magasins ferment une heure plus tôt. En revanche, ils pourront ouvrir le dimanche.

DEPLACEMENTS

Air
Finnair, la compagnie aérienne nationale, assure un service régulier vers de nombreuses villes à l'intérieur ou à l'extérieur du pays et propose également des vols charters vers plus de 60 destinations. Air Botnia, qui appartient à SAS, assure également des vols intérieurs quotidiens.

Trains
La Finlande possède un excellent réseau ferroviaire qui dessert tout le pays et qui offre également la possibilité d'embarquer votre voiture. Demandez votre Finnrailpass pour profiter de réductions!

Il existe également deux trains par jour pour St Petersbourg (Russie) et un train de nuit pour Moscou.

Autobus
Toute la Finlande est également bien desservie par un excellent réseau d'autobus. Vous pourrez vous procurer des billets et obtenir de plus amples renseignements auprès des 150 bureaux d'information d'Oy Matkahuolto Ab, répartis dans toute la Finlande. Des billets 'Vacances en Car' sont en vente.

Ferry-boats
Les ports d'Helsinki et de Turku sont les ports principaux d'accueil des voyageurs. Il existe d'excellents services entre la Suède et la Finlande, ainsi que de bonnes liaisons à destination de Tallinn en Estonie et pendant la

saison estivale, à destination de Rostock, en Allemagne.

Des entreprises locales vous permettront également d'explorer le littoral et les lacs en bateau. L'accès à certaines auberges finlandaises peut aussi se faire par voie maritime.

Automobiles

La conduite est à droite. Les conditions climatiques en hiver peuvent rendre la conduite dangereuse et les automobilistes peuvent louer des pneus-neige dans les magasins Isko. Les conducteurs doivent faire attention aux élans et aux rennes. En cas de collision avec l'un de ces animaux, il convient d'en informer la police locale sans tarder. Vous devez avoir dans votre véhicule un triangle rouge de présignalisation et le placer sur la route en cas de panne. Les phares doivent être allumés en tout temps. Le port des ceintures de sécurité à l'avant et à l'arrière est obligatoire. Les conducteurs ayant testé positif lors d'un contrôle anti-alcool ou anti-drogue seront fortement pénalisés. Tous les conducteurs de véhicules étrangers doivent être munis d'une carte verte ou prendre des dispositions pour s'assurer dès qu'ils arrivent en Finlande. La nationalité des véhicules étrangers doit être clairement indiquée.

Deutsch

FINNISCHE JUGENDHERBERGEN

Die mehr als 115 Jugend- und Familienherbergen, die es in Finnland gibt, sind ein idealer Ausgangspunkt zum Kennenlernen dieses schönen Landes mit Seen, Stromschnellen, Inseln und Europas größtem Archipel vor der Südwestküste Finnlands. Um die Sommersonnenwende geht die Sonne in Nordfinnland mehrere Wochen lang nicht unter.

Alle Herbergen haben ausgezeichnete Einrichtungen und bieten Familienräume, Doppel- und Einzelzimmer oder Schlafsäle für 5 bis 10 Personen. Frühstück und andere Mahlzeiten sind in vielen Jugendherbergen erhältlich. Buffets für ♦♦♦ auf Vorbestellung. Oft müssen Selbstversorger ihre eigenen Utensilien mitbringen. Die Herbergen sind, außer vom 24.-26. Dezember, ganzjährig von 07.00-10.00 Uhr und von 17.00-22.00 Uhr geöffnet, sofern nichts anderes angegeben ist (siehe nähere Informationen). An einigen Orten sind sie sogar 24 Stunden geöffnet. Im Winter ist Voranmeldung unerläßlich.

Viele Herbergen stellen den Gästen Fahrräder, Boote, Kanus, Skiausrüstungen usw. zur Verfügung. Die meisten Jugendherbergen haben eine Sauna. Es gibt 11 Jugendherbergen, die eine Rauchsauna haben. Die größte der Welt ist in der Jugendherberge Rauhalahti in Kuopio. Erkundigen Sie sich nach Aktivprogrammen in Jugendherbergen, wo Sie die finnischen Lebensweisen kennenlernen können.

Es ist mit einem Preis von ca. 45-240 FIM (7.5-40 ECU) zu rechnen, zuzüglich einer Leihgebühr für Bettlaken (25-30 FIM), wenn Bedarf besteht. Bettlaken und/oder Frühstück sind manchmal im Übernachtungspreis inklusive. Da einige Herbergen gemeinsam mit anderen Unterkünften verwaltet werden, sollte immer 'Jugendherbergsunterkunft' angegeben werden. Die in diesem Handbuch angegebenen Übernachtungspreise sind die normalen Preise. Besitzer einer Hostelling International-Mitgliedskarte erhalten 15 FIM Rabatt auf die normalen Preise. Kinder im Alter von 4 bis 12 Jahren erhalten oft einen Preisnachlaß von 50%. Für Kinder unter 4 Jahren ist die Übernachtung im allgemeinen kostenlos, wenn sie das Bett mit den Eltern teilen.

PÄSSE UND VISA

Bitte erkundigen Sie sich vor der Abreise bei der finnischen Botschaft oder dem finnischen Konsulat in Ihrem Land.

GESUNDHEIT

Für international Reisende gibt es keine Impfvorschriften.

Nichtverschreibungspflichtige Arzneimittel werden in Apotheken (apteekki) verkauft. Notfälle werden in Gesundheitszentren oder im Krankenhaus in der Abteilung für Notfälle behandelt. In nicht dringenden Fällen sind eine ärztliche Überweisung sowie eine schriftliche Verpflichtung zur Bezahlung für die Behandlung erforderlich. Informationen über die Gesundheitspflege sind unter ✆ (9) 10023 erhältlich.

GESCHÄFTSSTUNDEN DER BANKEN

Alle Banken sind montags bis freitags von 09.15-16.15 Uhr geöffnet. Die Geschäftsstunden können sich aber von Region zu Region etwas unterscheiden. FOREX-Wechselstuben gibt es in Helsinki, Tampere und Turku.

POSTÄMTER

Postämter sind montags bis freitags von 09.00-17.00 Uhr geöffnet.

LADENÖFFNUNGSZEITEN

Die Geschäfte sind montags bis freitags von 09.00-17.00/18.00 Uhr und samstags von 09.00-15.00 Uhr geöffnet. Einige Geschäfte und Warenhäuser sind werktags bis 20.00 Uhr und samstags bis 18.00 Uhr geöffnet. Im Sommer schließen viele Geschäfte etwa eine Stunde früher, können aber sonntags öffnen.

REISEN

Flugverkehr

Mit Finnair kann man 60 internationale Zielorte anfliegen und 21 Ziele innerhalb Finnlands. Es gibt auch gute Flugverbindungen von Helsinki zu den Ostseeländern und nach Rußland. Finnair bietet außer den regulären Linienflügen auch Charterflüge zu mehr als 60 Zielorten. Air Botnia, die zu SAS gehört, bietet täglich Flüge zu 12 Zielen innerhalb Finnlands an.

Eisenbahn

Ein ausgezeichnetes Eisenbahnnetz erstreckt sich über ganz Finnland, das auch den Transport von Autos einschließt. Fragen Sie nach dem preisgünstigen Finnrail-Paß! Es gibt täglich zwei Verbindungen nach St. Petersburg in Rußland und einen Nachtzug nach Moskau.

Busse

Es gibt auch ein ausgezeichnetes Busnetz, das sich über ganz Finnland erstreckt. Es gibt 150 Servicestellen von Oy Matkahuolto Ab, die weitere Auskunft erteilen und Fahrkarten verkaufen. Fahrkarten für Ferienreisen mit dem Bus sind auch erhältlich.

Fähren

Die Haupthäfen für den Passagierverkehr befinden sich in Helsinki und Turku. Es wird ein ausgezeichneter Service nach Schweden und Tallinn in Estland geboten sowie in der Sommersaison nach Rostock in Deutschland. Entdecken Sie Küsten und Seen auf Schiffsreisen in die nähere Umgebung. Einige finnische Herbergen können mit dem Schiff erreicht werden.

Autofahren

Es herrscht Rechtsverkehr. Im Winter kann das Autofahren wegen des Wetters gefährlich sein. Autofahrer können jedoch in ISKO-Läden Schneereifen mieten. Die Fahrer müssen auf Elche und Rentiere achten. Wenn ein solches Tier angefahren wird, ist der Unfall unverzüglich der örtlichen Polizei zu melden. Für den Fall einer Panne, muß ein rotes Dreieck auf die Straße gestellt werden. Scheinwerfer müssen jederzeit genutzt werden. Sicherheitsgurte müssen von allen Insassen getragen werden. Fahren unter Alkohol- oder Drogeneinfluß wird schwer bestraft. Alle Fahrer eines ausländischen Fahrzeugs sollten eine grüne Karte mit sich führen oder sofort nach der Ankunft in Finnland eine Versicherung abschließen. Die Herkunft ausländischer Fahrzeuge muß deutlich angegeben sein.

Español

ALBERGUES JUVENILES FINLANDESES

Más de 115 albergues juveniles y familiares representan una base ideal para explorar este hermoso país lleno de lagos, rápidos e islas, y cerca de cuya costa suroeste se encuentra el archipiélago más grande de Europa. En el norte de Finlandia, en verano, alrededor del día de San Juan, el sol no se pone durante varias semanas.

Todos los albergues están dotados de excelentes instalaciones y ofrecen habitaciones familiares, dobles e individuales, así como dormitorios para 5-10 personas. Muchos de ellos sirven desayunos y otras comidas. Si se solicita con antelación, también preparan buffets campestres para los ♦♦♦. Suele ser necesario disponer de utensilios de cocina propios para cocinar uno mismo. Los albergues están abiertos todo el año excepto del 24 al 26 de diciembre, a no ser que se indiquen otros periodos de apertura (consulte la lista de albergues). El horario es de 7 h. a 10 h. y de 17 h. a 22 h., y las 24 horas del día en algunos lugares. En invierno, es imprescindible reservar con antelación.

La mayoría de los albergues ponen bicicletas, barcas, canoas, equipos de esquí, etc. a disposición de los huéspedes y también suelen tener sauna. 11 de ellos están dotados con una sauna de estufa de humo y la más grande del mundo se encuentra en el albergue Rauhalahti,

en Kuopio. Infórmese sobre los programas de actividades que ofrecen los albergues para descubrir las costumbres y forma de vida de los finlandeses.

El precio por noche oscila entre 45 y 240 mk (marcos finlandeses) (7,5-40 Euros). Las sábanas, si las necesita, se cobran aparte (25-30 mk), aunque en algunos casos estas últimas y el desayuno están incluidos en el precio. Especifique siempre que desea alojarse en el albergue juvenil, ya que algunos establecimientos ofrecen también otros tipos de alojamiento. Las tarifas indicadas en esta guía son las normales, pero a los titulares del carnet de socio de Hostelling International se les concede 15 mk de descuento. Los niños de 4 a 12 años suelen pagar mitad de precio y, en general, los menores de 4 años que compartan la cama con sus padres son alojados gratuitamente.

PASAPORTES Y VISADOS

Infórmese en la embajada o consulado finlandeses de su país.

INFORMACIÓN SANITARIA

No se exigen vacunas a los viajeros procedentes del extranjero.

Los medicamentos sin receta se venden en las farmacias (apteekki). En caso de urgencia, le atenderán en los centros de asistencia médica y en las salas de guardia de los hospitales. Para casos menos urgentes, le tratarán sólo si le deriva un médico de cabecera y deberá garantizar el pago por escrito. Información sobre asistencia médica: ☎ (9) 10023.

HORARIO DE LOS BANCOS

Todos los bancos abren de lunes a viernes de 9.15 h. a 16.15 h., aunque este horario puede variar algo de una región a otra. FOREX EXCHANGE tiene sucursales en Helsinki, Tampere y Turku.

OFICINAS DE CORREOS

Las oficinas de correos abren de lunes a viernes de 9 h. a 17 h.

HORARIO COMERCIAL

Las tiendas abren de lunes a viernes de 9 h. a 17 h. ó 18 h. y los sábados de 9 h. a 15 h. Algunas tiendas y grandes almacenes están abiertos hasta las 20 h. entre semana y hasta las 18 h. los sábados. En verano, algunas tiendas cierran una hora antes, pero abren los domingos.

DESPLAZAMIENTOS

Avión

Finnair, la red aérea nacional, tiene vuelos regulares internacionales y nacionales, así como vuelos chárter con destino a más de 60 poblaciones. Air Botnia, línea aérea perteneciente a SAS, ofrece vuelos nacionales diarios.

Tren

Existe una excelente red ferroviaria que recorre toda Finlandia y que transporta también automóviles. Solicite el económico Finnrailpass. Existen dos enlaces diarios con San Petersburgo (Rusia) y un tren nocturno a Moscú.

Autobús

También es excelente la red de autocares que cubre toda Finlandia. Oy Matkahuolto Ab tiene 150 oficinas de información y venta de billetes repartidas por toda Finlandia. Es posible adquirir unos billetes especiales denominados "Vacaciones en Autocar".

Ferry

Helsinki y Turku son los principales puertos de pasajeros. Los servicios desde Finlandia a Suecia, a Tallinn (Estonia) y, en verano, a Rostock (Alemania) son excelentes. Explore la costa y los lagos en los barcos locales. Se puede ir en barco a algunos de los albergues.

Automóvil

Se circula por la derecha. En invierno puede ser peligroso conducir. Es posible alquilar neumáticos para la nieve en las tiendas ISKO. Los conductores deben estar atentos a la aparición de alces y renos en las carreteras y avisar inmediatamente a la policía si atropellan a alguno de estos animales. Es obligatorio transportar un triángulo rojo de advertencia en caso de avería en carretera. Circule con los faros siempre encendidos. Todos los pasajeros deben abrocharse el cinturón de seguridad. Conducir bajo la influencia del alcohol o de drogas es un delito severamente castigado. Los conductores de vehículos extranjeros deben ser titulares de una carta verde o hacerse un seguro en cuanto lleguen a Finlandia y su vehículo debe llevar su nacionalidad claramente indicada.

Helsinki -
Eurohostel

Linnankatu 9,
00160 Helsinki.
☏ (9) 6220470
✆ (9) 655044
✉ eurohostel@eurohostel.fi

Open Dates: 🔲

Open Hours: ◷

Reservations: ⓡ IBN CC

Price Range: FIM 120-195 € 20.18-32.80 ▣

Beds: 305 - 25x¹ 100x² 10x³

Facilities: ⭍ 135x ⭍ ⏏ ⌁ ⬛ 📺 ▢ ▢ 🔲 8 ⬆ ♒

Directions: 2 SE from city centre

✈ Helsinki-Vantaa 20km

A🚌 2km

⛴ Viking Line & Finnjet Terminal 500m

🚂 2km

🚌 #4 ap 100m

Ⓤ Railway Station 2km

There are 5 hostels in Helsinki. See following pages.

Rovaniemi -
Hostel Tervashonka

Hallituskatu 16,
96100 Rovaniemi.
☏ (16) 344644
✆ (16) 344644

Open Dates: 🔲

Open Hours: 06.00-10.00hrs; 17.00-22.00hrs

Price Range: FIM 90-100 € 15.14-16.82 ▣

Beds: 62 - 11x² 4x³ 5x⁴ 1x⁶

Facilities: ⭍ 20x ⭍ ⏏ (B) ⌁ ⛴ 🅿

Directions:

✈ Rovaniemi 10km

🚂 Rovaniemi 800m

🚌 ap 🚌 station 500m

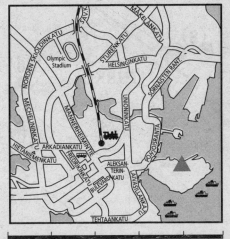

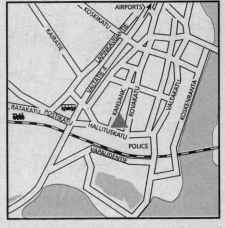

Tampere -
Hostel Uimahallin Maja

Pirkank 10-12,
33230 Tampere.
☏ (3) 2229460
🖷 (3) 2229940
🖃 aris@sci.fi

Open Dates:	🗓12
Open Hours:	06.00 (07.30)-11.00, 14.00-22.00 (22.30)
Reservations:	**Ⓡ**
Price Range:	FIM 105-210 € 17.66-35.32 💳
Beds:	103 - 35x¹🛏 10x²🛏 3x⁴🛏 2x⁶🛏
Facilities:	♦♦♦ 15x ♦♦♦ 🍽 ☂ 📺 ⬆ 🅿

Directions:

✈	Tampere 17km
🚂	Tampere 1.5km
🚌	50m ap Pyynikintori

Attractions: ⌖1.5km ⛷1.5km

There are 3 hostels in Tampere. See following pages.

Turku -
Hostel Turku

Linnankatu 39,
20100 Turku.
☏ (2) 2316578
🖷 (2) 2311708

Open Dates:	🗓12
Open Hours:	06.00-10.00hrs; 15.00-24.00hrs
Price Range:	FIM 60-120 € 10.09-20.18 💳
Beds:	120 - 2x²🛏 10x⁴🛏 2x⁶🛏 7x⁶🛏
Facilities:	♿ ♦♦♦ 12x ♦♦♦ 🍽 (B) ☂ 🛏 📺 1 x🍽 🔲 🖼 🅿
Directions:	2S from city centre
✈	Turku 10km
⛴	Turku 2km
🚌	ap Boren Puisto 100m

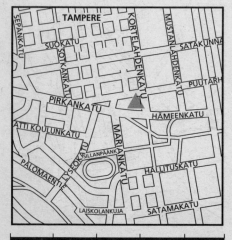

0   1km   0   1.8km

Location/Address	Telephone No. Fax No.	Beds	Opening Dates	Facilities
▲ **Ähtäri** - Hostel Ouluvesi Ähtärintie, 63700 Ähtäri. Postal address: Koulutie 16, 63700 Ähtäri.	☏ (6) 5337482 ❶ (6) 5337479	60	01–31.07	⑉ ⑩ ⓡ ☞ P
▲ **Alajärvi** - Kuusiniemi Camp and Course Centre Heikinkankaantie 44, 62900 Alajärvi ❷ kuusiniemi@japo.fi	☏ (6) 5574542, (6) 55777242	50	01.06–31.08	⑉ ⑩ 6W ⴲ ☞ P ☕
▲ **Dragsfjärd** - Dragsfjärds vandrarhotell Kulla, 25870 Dragsfjärd.	☏ (2) 424553 ❶ (2) 424553	41	03.04–31.10	⑉ ⑩ ⓡ ☞ P
▲ **Eno** - Jokipirtin Majatalo Uimaharjuntie 751, 81270 Paukkaja.	☏ (13) 774607 ❶ (13) 774607	44	🗓	⑉ ⑩ 8N ⴲ ☞ P ☕
▲ **Enonkoski** - Kievari Enonhovi Urheilukentäntie 1, 58175 Enonkoski.	☏ (15) 479431 ❶ (15) 479435	30	🗓	⑉ ⑩ CC ☞ P ☕
△ *Enontekiö / Peera -* *Peeran Retkeilykeskus* *99490 Kilpisjärvi.*	☏ *(16) 532659* ❶ *(16) 532659*	*53*	*20.02–31.10*	⑉ ⑩ 90NW CC ☞ P 🅾
▲ **Forssa** - Summer Hostel Forssa Saksankatu 25, 30100 Forssa ❷ hostel@fai.fi	☏ (3) 414 0270 ❶ (3) 414 0270	52	01.06–31.07	⑉ ⑩ ☞ P 🅾
▲ **Haapajärvi** - Haapajärven retkeilymaja Erkkiläntie 1, 85800 Haapajärvi.	☏ (8) 7699223 ❶ (8) 7699200	24	05.06–07.08	⑉ ⑩ 1SE ☞ P 🅾
▲ **Hamina** - Kesähotelli Anna Annankatu 1, 49400 Hamina.	☏ (400) 433561 ❶ (5) 3541600	80	01.06–15.08	⑩ 1S ☕
▲ **Hauho** - Hostel Miekka Häränvattantie 67, 14700 Hauho.	☏ (3) 6545112 ❶ (3) 6545321	35	15.05–31.08	⑉ ⑩ 6W ☞ P ☕
▲ **Haukipudas** - Hostel Virpiniemi Hiihtomajantie 27, 90820 Kello. ❷ virpiniemi@mail.suomi.net	☏ (8) 5614200 ❶ (8) 5614224	101	🗓	⑉ ⑩ 12SW ⴲ ☞ P ☕
△ *Heinävesi - Pohjataipaleen kartano* *Pyylintie 8, 79700 Heinävesi.*	☏ *(17) 566419*	*20*	*01.05–30.09*	⑉ 18S ☞ P
▲ **Heinola** - Finnhostel Heinola Opintie 3, 18200 Heinola. ❷ gasthaus@sci.fi	☏ (3) 7141655 ❶ (3) 7188103	76	03.06–06.08	⑉ ⑩ 1.2N ☞ P ☕
▲ **Helsinki** - Eurohostel ⒾⒷⓃ **Linnankatu 9, 00160 Helsinki.** ❷ eurohostel@eurohostel.fi	☏ (9) 6220470 ❶ (9) 655044	305	🗓	⑉ ⑩ ⓡ 2SE CC ☞ 🅾 ☕
▲ **Helsinki** - Stadion Hostel ⒾⒷⓃ Pohj Stadiontie 3 B, 00250 Helsinki.	☏ (9) 496071 ❶ (9) 496466	162	01.01–23.12; 25–31.12	⑉ ⑩ ⓡ 2N CC ☞ P 🅾
▲ **Helsinki** - Hostel Academica Hietaniemenkatu 14, 00100 Helsinki. ❷ hostel.academica@hyy.fi	☏ (9) 13114334 ❶ (9) 441201	66	01.06–01.09	⑉ ⑩ 1W CC ☞ P 🅾
▲ **Helsinki** - Summer Hostel Satakunta Lapinrinne 1A, 00180 Helsinki.	☏ (9) 69585231 ❶ (9) 6854245	147	01.06–31.08	⑉ ⑩ 1SW CC 🅾
▲ **Helsinki** - Hostel Erottanpuisto Uudenmaankatu 9, 00120 Helsinki.	☏ (9) 642169 ❶ (9) 6802757	54	🗓	⑉ ⑩ 0.3S CC ☞
▲ **Iisalmi** - Iisalmen NMKY:n hostel (YMCA) Sarvikatu 4C, 74120 Iisalmi.	☏ (17) 823940 ❶ (17) 823940	46	01.06–31.07	⑉ ⑩ ☞ P 🅾

Location/Address	Telephone No. Fax No.	Beds	Opening Dates	Facilities
▲ **Ilmajoki** - Hostel Viitala Ristimäentie 207, 61350 Huissi.	☎ (6) 4227657	20	01.06–31.08	††† ⁑ 10W ⚲ P ▣
▲ **Ilmajoki** - Hostel Palonkortteeri Kauppatie 26, 60800 Ilmajoki. ✉ artrockcafe@artrockcafe.fi	☎ (6) 4240000 ✆ (6) 4240057	120	🛏12	††† ⁑ CC ⚲ P ▣ ☕
▲ **Imatra** - Ukonlinna Leiritie 8, 55420 Imatra.	☎ (5) 4321270 ✆ (5) 4321270	22	🛏12	††† ⁑ 3SE ⚲ P
▲ **Inari/Kaamanen** - Kaamasen Kievari 99910 Kaamanen ✉ kaamanen@na.netppl.fi	☎ (16) 672713 ✆ (16) 672786	97	🛏12	††† ⁑ 28N CC ⚲ P ▣ ☕
▲ **Inari/Kaamanen** - Hostel Jokitörmä 99910 Kaamanen. ✉ lomakyla@jokitorma.inet.fi	☎ (16) 672725 ✆ (16) 672745	50	🛏12	††† ⁑ 27N CC ⚲
▲ **Inari/Kiilopää** - Hostel Ahopää Fell Resort Kiilopää, 99830 Saariselkä. ✉ kiilopaa@suomenlatu.fi	☎ (16) 6700700 ✆ (16) 667121	36	🛏12	††† ⁑ ℝ 45S CC ⚲ P ▣ ☕
▲ **Jämsä** - Ratsastuskievari (Riding-hostel) Lopeistontie 75, 42100 Jämsä.	☎ (14) 762388 ✆ (14) 762389	30	🛏12	††† ⁑ 7S P
▲ **Järvenpää** - Järvenpään Matkailukeskus Stålhanentie, 04400 Järvenpää.	☎ (9) 287775 ✆ (9) 2911441	21	🛏12	††† ⁑ 2.5S CC ⚲ P ▣ ☕
▲ **Joensuu** - Finnhostel Joensuu The Eastern Finland Sport College, Kalevankatu 8, 80110 Joensuu ✉ finnhostel@islo.jns.fi	☎ (13) 2675076 ✆ (13) 2675075	84	🛏12	††† ⁑ 0.5W ⚲ P ▣
▲ **Joensuu** - Joensuun Elli Länsikatu 18, 80110 Joensuu. ✉ hotel.elli@kolumbus.fi	☎ (13) 225927 ✆ (13) 225763	53	01.06–20.08	††† ⁑ CC ⚲ P ☕
△ *Joensuu - Partiotalo Vanamokatu 25, 80130 Joensuu.*	☎ *(13) 123381*	*44*	*01.06–31.08*	††† ℝ 1S ♿ ⚲ P
▲ **Joutsa** - Vaihelan tila Vaihelantie 24, 19920 Pappinen. ✉ vaihelan.tila@co.inet.fi	☎ (14) 889107 ✆ (14) 889197	14	🛏12	††† ⁑ 16NW ⚲ P
▲ **Jyväskylä** - Finnhostel Laajari Laajavuorentie 15, 40740 Jyväskylä. ✉ kristiina.enkenberg@jkl.fi	☎ (14) 624885 ✆ (14) 624888	89	01.01–22.12; 27–31.12	††† ⁑ 4W CC ⚲ P ▣ ☕
▲ **Kajaani** - Hostel Huone ja Aamiainen Pohjolankatu 4, 87100 Kajaani.	☎ (8) 622254 ✆ (8) 622254	46	🛏12	††† ⁑ 0.6SE CC
▲ **Kalajoki/Hiekkasärkät** - Tapion Tupa Hiekkasärkät, 85100 Kalajoki.	☎ (8) 466622 ✆ (8) 466699	36	🛏12	††† ⁑ 4S ♿ ⚲ P ☕
▲ **Kalajoki** - Hostel Kaju Opintie 1, 85100 Kalajoki.	☎ (8) 462933 ✆ (8) 462319	72	15.06–31.07	††† ⁑ ⚲ P
▲ **Kauhava** - Tuppiroska Yrittäjäopisto, Kauppatie 109, 62200 Kauhava.	☎ (6) 4315350 ✆ (6) 4315352	200	01.06–15.08	††† ⁑ CC ⚲ P ▣ ☕
▲ **Kaustinen** - Koskelan Lomatalo Känsäläntie 123, 69600 Kaustinen. ✉ koskelan.lomatalo@kaustinen.fi	☎ (6) 8611338	31	🛏12	††† ⁑ 5W ⚲ P ▣

Location/Address	Telephone No. Fax No.	Beds	Opening Dates	Facilities
▲ **Kemi** - Hostel Turisti Valtakatu 39, 94100 Kemi.	☎ (16) 258294	36		♀♂ ☞ Ⓟ ▣
△ *Kemijärvi - Matkatupa* *A725 Ulkuniemi PL, 98100 Kemijärvi.*	☎ *(16) 888517*	74	*01.05–31.10*	♀♂ ⊠ 26S ☞ Ⓟ ▣ ☕
▲ **Kemijärvi** - Hostel Kemijärvi Lohelankatu 1, 98100 Kemijärvi.	☎ (16) 813253, 813341 ☏ (16) 813342	100		♀♂ ⊠ 0.3W ⊞ ☞ Ⓟ ☕
▲ **Keminmaa** - Kapernaumin Lomakylä Heimarintie 90, 94500 Lautiosaari.	☎ (16) 288166 ☏ (16) 288166	33		♀♂ 15N ☞ Ⓟ
▲ **Kerimäki** - Korkeamäen Majatalo Ruokolahdentie 545, 58200 Kerimäki.	☎ (15) 442186	49	20.06–20.08	♀♂ ⊠ 6S ☞ Ⓟ ▣ ☕
▲ **Kittilä** - Hostel Kittilä Valtatie 82, 99100 Kittilä.	☎ (16) 642002 ☏ (16) 642016	48	01.06–05.08	♀♂ ⊠ Ⓡ ⊞ ☞ Ⓟ ▣
▲ **Kittilä** - Hostel Majari Valtatie 5, 99100 Kittilä.	☎ (16) 648508, (400) 410592 ☏ (16) 642259	59	10.06–05.08	♀♂ ⊠ ☞ Ⓟ
▲ **Kiuruvesi** - Matkamaja Kiurusoppi Museokatu 17, 74700 Kiuruvesi.	☎ (17) 754444 ☏ (17) 753286	32	01.06–10.08	♀♂ ⊠ ☞ Ⓟ ▣
▲ **Kokemäki** - Kesähotelli Tyrni Kauvatsantie 189, 32800 Kokemäki 📧 hannu.pihkala@huittinen.fi	☎ (50) 3366996, (2) 5604711 ☏ (2) 5604703	96	01.06–31.07	♀♂ ⊠ 1.9N ♿ ☞ Ⓟ ▣
▲ **Kokkola** - Hostel Tankkari Vanhansatamanlahti, 67100 Kokkola.	☎ (6) 8314006 ☏ (6) 8310306	23	01.06–31.08	♀♂ ⊠ 2.5N ☞ Ⓟ ☕
▲ **Korpilahti** - Matkailutila Surkeenjärvi Surkeejärventie, 41800 Korpilahti.	☎ (14) 827437 ☏ (14) 827437	38		♀♂ ⊠ 20W ☞ Ⓟ
▲ **Kristiinankaupunki** - Hostel Kilstrand/Kiilinranta Kiilintie 90, 64490 Siipyy.	☎ (6) 2225611 ☏ (6) 2225615	38	01.06–16.08	♀♂ ⊠ Ⓡ 30S ☞ Ⓟ ▣ ☕
▲ **Kuhmo** - Kuhmon retkeilymaja Piilolan koulu, 88900 Kuhmo.	☎ (8) 6556245 ☏ (8) 6556384	33	01–31.07	♀♂ ☞ Ⓟ
▲ **Kuopio** - Hostel Rauhalahti Katiskaniementie 8, 70700 Kuopio. 📧 myynti@rauhalahti.com	☎ (17) 473111 ☏ (17) 473470	63		♀♂ ⊠ 5S ⊞ Ⓟ ▣ ☕
▲ **Kuortane** - Finnhostel VirtaniemenLomatila Virtala (Virtaniementie 35) 63100 Kuortane. 📧 pirjo.virtaniemi@virtaniemen-lomatila.inet.fi	☎ (6) 5256689 ☏ (6) 5256694	70		♀♂ ⊠ 14SE ⊞ ☞ Ⓟ ☕
▲ **Kuusamo** - Kuusamon Kansanopisto Kitkantie 35, 93600 Kuusamo.	☎ (8) 8522132 ☏ (8) 8521134	110	26.06–31.08	♀♂ ⊠ ☞ Ⓟ ▣
▲ **Lahti** - Lahden Kansanopisto Harjukatu 46, 15100 Lahti. 📧 lahden.kansanopisto@lahdenko.sci.fi	☎ (3) 8781181 ☏ (3) 8781234	72	05.06–13.08	♀♂ ⊠ ⊞ Ⓟ
▲ **Lahti** - Mukkulan kesähotelli Ritaniemenkatu 10, 15240 Lahti.	☎ (3) 874140 ☏ (3) 8741444	120		⊠ 4N ⊞ ☞ Ⓟ
▲ **Lapinlahti** - Hostel Portaanpää 73100 Lapinlahti. 📧 toimisto@portaanpaa.fi	☎ (17) 768860 ☏ (17) 731998	72	01.06–15.08	♀♂ ⊠ 2S ♿ Ⓟ ▣

Location/Address	Telephone No. Fax No.	Beds	Opening Dates	Facilities
▲ **Lappeenranta** - Finnhostel Lappeenranta Kuusimäenkatu 18, 53810 Lappeenranta. e huhtiniemi@loma-oksa.inet.fi	☎ (5) 4515555 🖷 (5) 4515558	80	15.01–15.12	♦♦♦ �🍴 2W ♿ ⌷CC⌷ P ☕
▲ **Lappeenranta** - Huhtiniemi Kuusimäenkatu 18, 53810 Lappeenranta. e huhtiniemi@loma-oksa.inet.fi	☎ (5) 4515555 🖷 (5) 4515558	24	01.06–15.08	🍴 2W ⌷CC⌷ ☞ P ⌷ ☕
▲ **Lappeenranta** - Karelia Park Korpraalinkuja 1, 53810 Lappeenranta. e kari.nalli@armpa.inet.fi	☎ (5) 675211, 4530405, 🖷 (5) 4528454	50	01.06–31.08	♦♦♦ 🍴 2W ⌷CC⌷ P ⌷ ☕
▲ **Lieksa/Koli** - Kolin retkeilymaja Niinilahdentie 47, 83960 Koli.	☎ (13) 673131 🖷 (13) 673131	47	⌷12⌷	♦♦♦ 🍴 96W ☞ P ☕
▲ **Mänttä** - Mäntän retkeilymaja Koulukatu 6, 35800 Mänttä.	☎ (3) 4888641 🖷 (3) 4888500	30	01.06–13.08	♦♦♦ 🍴 ♿ ☞ P ⌷
▲ **Muonio** - Lomamaja Pekonen Lahenrannantie 10, 99300 Muonio. e loma.maja@pekonen.inet.fi	☎ (16) 532237 🖷 (16) 532236	30	01.04–30.09	♦♦♦ 0.5W ☞ P
▲ **Muurla** - Kesähostelli MuurlanEvankelinen Opisto Muurlantie 365, 25130 Muurla.	☎ (2) 7320511 🖷 (2) 7320533	58	01.06–31.08	♦♦♦ 🍴 ♿ ☞ P ☕
▲ **Nivala** - Hostel Nivala Maliskyläntie 2, 85500 Nivala.	☎ (8) 443171 🖷 (8) 442555	112	01–31.07	♦♦♦ 🍴 Ⓡ ☞ P ⌷
▲ **Nurmes** - Hyvärilän Matkailukeskus Lomatie 75500 Nurmes. e hyvarila@oyk.pkky.fi	☎ (13) 481770 🖷 (13) 481775	70	⌷12⌷	♦♦♦ 🍴 4E ⌷CC⌷ ☞ P ⌷ ☕
▲ **Nurmijärvi** - Lomakoti Kotoranta Kotorannantie 74, 05250 Kiljava.	☎ (9) 2765879, 2765255 🖷 (9) 2765928	34	⌷12⌷	♦♦♦ 🍴 15N ♿ ☞ P ☕
▲ **Oulu** - Summer Uni Hostel Välkkylä Kajaanintie 36, 90100 Oulu.	☎ (8) 8803311 🖷 (8) 8803754	160	02.06–29.08	♦♦♦ 🍴 Ⓡ 1.5E ⌷CC⌷ ☞ P ⌷
▲ **Parainen** - Hostel Norrdal Solliden Camping, Norrby, 21600 Parainen.	☎ (2) 4585955 🖷 (2) 4585955	14	⌷12⌷	🍴 1.5N ⌷CC⌷
▲ **Parikkala** - Karjalan Lomahovi 59100 Parikkala. e lomahovi@lomayhtyma.fi	☎ (5) 430851 🖷 (5) 470597	20	01.06–31.08	♦♦♦ 🍴 4S ⌷CC⌷ ☞ P ⌷ ☕
▲ **Perniö** - Matildedalin ruukki Matildan Puistotie 11, 25660 Matildedal e post@teijo.com	☎ (2) 7366811 🖷 (2) 7366810	100	⌷12⌷	♦♦♦ 🍴 Ⓡ 15W ☞ P ☕
▲ **Pielavesi** - Pielavesi Hostelli Laurinpurontie 23, 72400 Pielavesi.	☎ (17) 862970 🖷 (17) 861327	28	01.06–10.08	♦♦♦ 🍴 0.5E P ⌷ ☕
▲ **Pietarsaari** - Svanen/Joutsen Luodontie 50, 68660 Pietarsaari. e svanen@multi.fi	☎ (6) 7230660 🖷 (6) 7810008	24	15.05–31.08	♦♦♦ 🍴 4N ♿ ⌷CC⌷ ☞ P ⌷ ☕
▲ **Piikkiö** - Hostel Tuorla Country College of South Western Finland, Tuorlantie 1, 21500 Piikkiö. e toimisto.tuorla@tuorla.com	☎ (2) 2731672, (50) 3039803 🖷 (2) 2731672	84	⌷12⌷	♦♦♦ 🍴 Ⓡ 4W ☞ P ⌷ ☕

Location/Address	Telephone No. Fax No.	Beds	Opening Dates	Facilities
▲ **Pori** - Hostel Tekunkorpi Tekniikantie 4, 28600 Pori.	☎ (2) 6378400 🖷 (2) 6378125	160	15.05–15.08	♦♦♦ ⑩ 5W ⌐cc⌐ ⚲ P ⌼
▲ **Porvoo** - Porvoon retkeilymaja Linnankoskenkatu 1-3, 06100 Porvoo.	☎ (19) 5230012 🖷 (19) 5230012	41	02.01–20.12	♦♦♦ ⑩ ⚲ P
▲ **Pudasjärvi/Syöte** - Hostel Syöte Pikku-Syöte tunturi, 93280 Syöte.	☎ (8) 838172 🖷 (8) 838173	52	🗓12	♦♦♦ ⑩ 55NE ⌐cc⌐ ⚲ P ⌼ ☕
▲ **Puumala** - Hostel Reissumaja Koskenseläntie 98, 52200 Puumala. ✉ koskenselka@lomavinkki-oy.inet.fi	☎ (15) 4681119 🖷 (15) 4681809	21	🗓12	♦♦♦ 2NW ⌐cc⌐ ⚲ P ⌼ ☕
▲ **Rauma** - Hostel Poroholma Camping Site, 26100 Rauma.	☎ (2) 83882500 🖷 (2) 83882502	38	15.05–31.08	♦♦♦ ⑩ 2N ⌐cc⌐ ⚲ P ⌼ ☕
▲ **Rauma** - Summer Hostel Rauma Satamakatu 20, 26100 Rauma	☎ (2) 8240130	195	01.06–31.08	♦♦♦ ⑩ ⌐cc⌐ ⚲ P ☕
▲ **Rautalampi** - Korholan Kartano Korholantie 111, 77700 Rautalampi.	☎ (17) 530320	50	01.01–21.12	♦♦♦ ⑩ Ⓡ 2N ♿ ⚲ P ⌼
▲ **Riihimäki** - Riihimäen Retkeilyhotelli Merkuriuksenkatu 7, 11130 Riihimäki.	☎ (400) 876169	139	01.06–31.07	♦♦♦ ⑩ ⚲ P ⌼
▲ **Ristiina** - Löydön Kartano Kartanontie 151, 52300 Ristiina.	☎ (15) 664101 🖷 (15) 664109	58	🗓12	♦♦♦ ⑩ 6N ⚲ P ⌼
▲ **Rovaniemen maalaiskunta** - TH-Kievari Gasthaus Kemintie 1956, 97130 Hirvas.	☎ (16) 382017 🖷 (16) 382191	45	🗓12	♦♦♦ ⑩ 3N ♿ ⌐cc⌐ P ⌼
▲ **Rovaniemi** - Hostel Tervashonka **Hallituskatu 16, 96100 Rovaniemi.**	☎ (16) 344644 🖷 (16) 344644	62	🗓12	♦♦♦ ⑩ ⚲ P
▲ **Rymättylä** - Hostel Päiväkulma Kuristentie 225, 21140 Rymättylä. ✉ hostelp@saunalahti.fi	☎ (2) 2521894 🖷 (2) 2521794	50	01.05–30.09	♦♦♦ ⑩ 3SE ⌐cc⌐ ⚲ P ⌼
▲ **Ruotsinpyhtää** - Finnhostel Krouvinmäki Ruotsinpyhtään Ruukkialue Oy, 07970 Ruotsinpyhtää. ✉ ruotsinpyhtaan.ruukkialue@co.inet.fi	☎ (19) 618474 🖷 (19) 618475	18	🗓12	♦♦♦ ⑩ Ⓡ ♿ ⚲ P ⌼ ☕
▲ **Salo** - Laurin koulu Venemestarinkatu 37, 24240 Salo. ✉ helja.karjalainen@salo.fi	☎ (2) 7784409 🖷 (2) 7784810	60	07.06–10.08	♦♦♦ Ⓡ ⚲ P
▲ **Savonlinna** - Malakias Pihlajavedenkuja 6, 57170 Savonlinna. ✉ casino.myynti@svlkylpylaitos.fi	☎ (15) 533283 🖷 (15) 533283	30	30.06–06.08	♦♦♦ ⑩ 2W ⌐cc⌐ ⚲ P ⌼
▲ **Savonlinna** - Vuorilinna Kylpylaitoksentie, 57130 Savonlinna. ✉ casino.myynti@svlkylpylaitos.fi	☎ (15) 7395495 🖷 (15) 272524	30	02.06–27.08	♦♦♦ ⑩ ♿ ⌐cc⌐ ⚲ P ⌼ ☕
▲ **Seinäjoki** - Marttilan Kortteeri Puskantie 38, 60100 Seinäjoki.	☎ (6) 4204800 🖷 (6) 4234226	157	01.06–09.08	♦♦♦ ⑩ 1N ⌐cc⌐ ⚲ P ⌼
▲ **Sodankylä** - Lapin opisto Kansanopistontie 5, 99600 Sodankylä. ✉ kanslia@lapinopisto.fi	☎ (16) 612181 🖷 (16) 611503	27	01.06–14.08	♦♦♦ ⑩ 2E ⌐cc⌐ ⚲ P ☕

Location/Address	Telephone No. Fax No.	Beds	Opening Dates	Facilities
▲ **Sodankylä/Raudanjoki** - Hostel Visatupa Seipäjärventie 409, 99510 Raudanjoki. 🄴 skangas@iki.fi	☎ (16) 634133 🛆 (16) 634101	45	🄲12	👪 🍴 56S ♿ 🚲 P 🅿
▲ **Sotkamo** - Hostel Tikkanen Kainuuntie 31, 88600 Sotkamo.	☎ (8) 6660541	38	🄲12	👪 🍴 🚲 P 🅿
▲ **Sulkava/Kaartilankoski** - Partalansaaren Lomakoti Hirviniementie 5, 58720 Kaartilankoski.	☎ (15) 478850 🛆 (15) 478850	47	🄲12	👪 🍴 Ⓡ 16S 🚲 P 🅿 ☕
▲ **Suomussalmi/Kuivajärvi** - Domnan Pirtti Kuivajärventie 195, 89840 Ylivuokki.	☎ (8) 723179 🛆 (8) 711189	31	01.04–30.09	👪 🍴 75SE P ☕
▲ **Taivalkoski** - Jokimutka Parviaisentie 64, 93420 Jurmu.	☎ (8) 845762	34	12.06–31.07	👪 🍴 Ⓡ 25SE 🚲 P 🅿 ☕
▲ **Tammisaari** - Ekenäs Vandrarhem/TammisaarenRetkeilymaja Höijerintie 10, 10600 Tammisaari.	☎ (19) 2416393 🛆 (19) 2413917	88	16.05–20.08	👪 🍴 🚲 P 🅿
▲ **Tampere** - Hostel Uimahallin Maja **Pirkank 10-12, 33230 Tampere.** 🄴 aris@sci.fi	☎ (3) 2229460 🛆 (3) 2229940	103	🄲12	👪 🍴 Ⓡ 🚲 P
▲ **Tampere** - Hostel Tampere YWCA Tuomiokirkonkatu 12 A, 33100 Tampere.	☎ (3) 2544020 🛆 (3) 2544022	70	01.06–25.08	👪 🍴 🚲 P
▲ **Tampere** - Summer Hotel Härmälä Nuolialantie 50, 33900 Tampere. 🄴 myyntipalvelu@lomaliitto.fi	☎ (3) 2651355 🛆 (3) 2660365	35	01.06–31.08	👪 🍴 4S ⌐CC 🚲 P 🅿
▲ **Toholampi** - Hirvikosken kurssikeskus Tornikoskentie 50, 69410 Sykäräinen.	☎ (6) 8623086 🛆 (6) 8623080	84	🄲12	👪 🍴 24W ♿ ⌐CC 🚲 P 🅿 ☕
▲ **Tornio** - Hostel Tornio Kivirannantie 13-15, 95410 Kiviranta. 🄴 pptoimisto@ppopisto.fi	☎ (16) 2119244 🛆 (16) 2119222	90	29.05–18.08	👪 🍴 25N ♿ 🚲 P 🅿
▲ **Turku** - Hostel Turku **Linnankatu 39, 20100 Turku.**	☎ (2) 2316578 🛆 (2) 2311708	120	🄲12	👪 🍴 2S ♿ 🚲 P 🅿
▲ **Vaasa** - Hostel Tekla Palosaarentie 58, 65200 Vaasa.	☎ (6) 3276411 🛆 (6) 3213989	220	🄲12	👪 🍴 Ⓡ 3N ⌐CC 🚲 P 🅿 ☕
▲ **Vantaa/Tikkurila** - Vantaan Retkeilyhotelli Valkoisenlähteentie 52, 01300 Vantaa.	☎ (9) 8720067 🛆 (9) 8720068	100	🄲12	👪 🍴 ♿ ⌐CC 🚲 P 🅿 ☕
▲ **Varkaus** - Varkauden Retkeilymaja Kuparisepänkatu 5, 78870 Varkaus. 🄴 tyopajat.kv&perhe@edu.varkaus.fi	☎ (17) 5795700 🛆 (17) 5795700	73	01.06–08.08	👪 2W 🚲 P 🅿 ☕
▲ **Virrat** - Domus Virrat Sipiläntie 3, 34800 Virrat.	☎ (3) 4755600 🛆 (3) 4755605	78	01.06–15.08	👪 🍴 ♿ 🚲 P 🅿 ☕
▲ **Virrat/Vaskivesi** - Finnhostel Haapamäki 34710 Vaskivesi.	☎ (3) 4758845; (400) 627854 🛆 (3) 4758811	100	01.05–30.09	👪 🍴 Ⓡ 20S ♿ 🚲 P 🅿

France

FRANCE	
FRANKREICH	
FRANCIA	

Fédération Unie des Auberges de Jeunesse (FUAJ),
27 rue Pajol, 75018 Paris, France.

☎ (33) (0) 1 44898727
❶ (33) (0) 836 688698 (2,23 Francs per min)
📠 (33) (0) 1 44898710
www.fuaj.org

Office Hours: Monday-Friday, 09.30-18.00hrs
Saturday, 10.00-17.00hrs

Travel Section: Groups and individuals, Fédération Unie des Auberges de Jeunesse,
27 rue Pajol, 75018 Paris, France.

☎ (33) (0) 1 44898727
📠 (33) (0) 1 44898749

A copy of the Hostel Directory for this Country can be obtained from:
The National Office.

Capital:	Paris	**Population:**		58,256,000
Language:	French	**Size (includes Corsica):**		550,000 sq km
Currency:	F (franc)	**Telephone Country Code:**		33

France

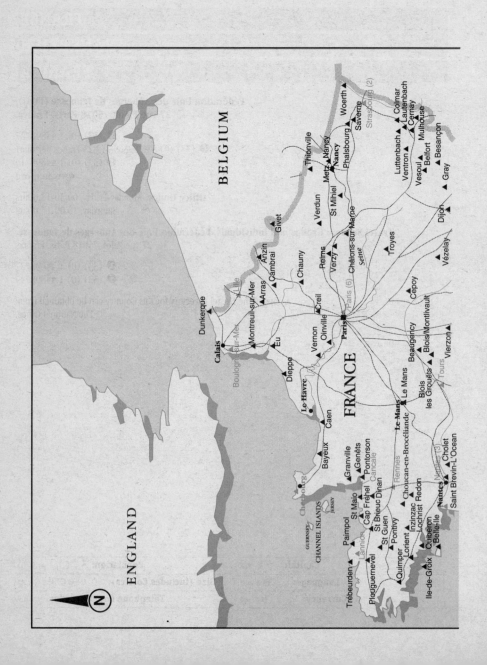

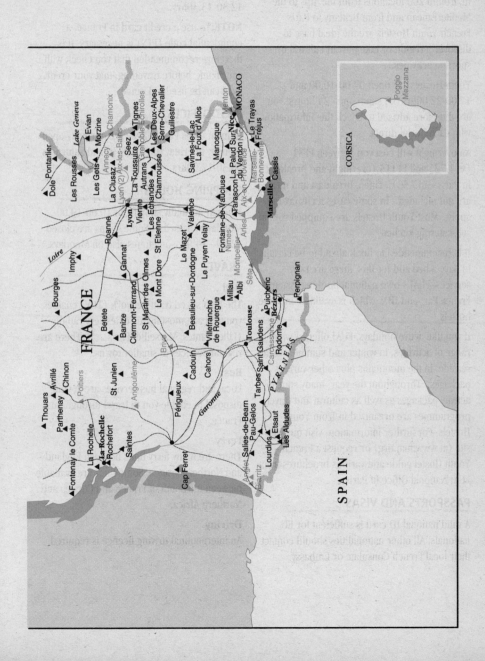

FRANCE

CORSICA

Poggio Mezzana

SPAIN

Cap Ferret

Fontenay le Comte
La Rochelle
Rochefort
Saintes
Thouars
Parthenay
Arvillé
Chinon
Poitiers
St Junien
Angoulême
Périgueux
Brive
Cadouin
Cahors
Bourges
Imphy
Banize
Betete
Gannat
Clermont-Ferrand
St Martin des Olmes
Le Mont Dore
Roanne
Lyon
Vienne
Les Echandes
St Etienne
Le Mazet
Le Puy en Velay
Beaulieu-sur-Dordogne
Villefranche de Rouergue
Toulouse
Albi
Millau
Rodome
Carcassonne
Béziers
Puichéric
Perpignan
Sète
Montpellier
Nîmes
Arles
Fontaine-de-Vaucluse
Valence
Tarascon
La Palud Sur Nice
Aix-en-Provence
Marseille
Cassis
Marseille
Bonneveine
Manosque
Savines-le-Lac
La Foux d'Allos
Guillestre
Serre-Chevalier
Les Deux-Alpes
Chamrousse
Autrans
Grenoble
Chirolles
La Toussuire
Seez
Tignes
Aix-les-Bains
Aix
Lyon (2)
Annecy
La Clusaz
Les Gets
Morzine
Les Rousses
Lake Geneva
Evian
Chamonix
Pontarlier
Dole
Menton
MONACO
Le Trayas
Fréjus
Loire
Garonne
Tarbes
Saint Gaudens
Pau-Gelos
Salies-de-Bearn
Arçat
Lourdes
Esaut
Les Aldudes
Biarritz
PYRENEES

English

FRENCH YOUTH HOSTELS

In around 200 locations from the Alps to the Mediterranean and from Brittany to Paris, French Youth Hostels are the ideal base to discover a region or take part in cultural or sporting activities.

Youth Hostels are open 07.00-10.00 and 17.00-22.00hrs but some open 24 hours: you are therefore advised to check this information with each hostel direct.

An overnight will cost you between FF31 (€4.73) and FF115 (overnight and breakfast in Paris - £17.53). Linen, breakfast and meals are not included. In some cases a city tax may apply. Most Youth Hostels are equipped with a self-catering kitchen.

It is recommended to book ahead to be certain to have a bed and for this, there are two services: FUAJ's own national booking system, France Fax, and IBN, which is available in some hostels.

If you like active holidays, FUAJ offers a wide range of activities, in winter and summer, at the seaside, in the mountains plus other various packages. Throughout the year, many sporting activity packages as well as cultural and travel programmes are organized in/from Youth Hostels. For further information, visit our web site (at www.fuaj.org) or request a French Youth Hostel guide and various brochures from FUAJ National Office in Paris.

PASSPORTS AND VISAS

A valid national ID card is sufficient for EU nationals. All other nationalities should contact their local French Consulate or Embassy.

BANKING HOURS

Banks in Paris are normally open 09.00-17.00hrs (or 16.00hrs) Monday to Friday. In other cities they are normally closed 12.30-13.30hrs.

NOTE: To use a credit card in France, a confidential code (PIN) is necessary. It is therefore recommended that you check with your bank, before travelling, that your credit card can be used in France.

POST OFFICES

In main cities Post Offices are normally open Monday to Friday 08.30-18.30 and Saturdays 08.30-12.00hrs.

SHOPPING HOURS

You can normally shop from 10.00-19.00 Monday to Saturday. Some shops are closed 12.30 - 14.00, sometimes also on Mondays.

TRAVEL

Rail

The high speed train network (TGV) enables you to reach most major cities very rapidly (Lille, Nantes, Marseille, Paris…). There are regular services to smaller towns.

Bus

Local and regional bus services are at your disposal to enable you to travel throughout France.

Ferry

There are many ferry links between England and Northern France. Some lines are available between the South of France and Corsica and Northern Africa.

Driving

An international driving licence is required.

Français

AUBERGES DE JEUNESSE FRANÇAISES

Avec près de 200 Auberges de Jeunesse, des Alpes à la Méditerranée en passant par Paris, les Auberges de Jeunesse françaises constituent un excellent moyen de découvrir une région ou de participer à des activités culturelles et sportives.

Les Auberges de Jeunesse sont ouvertes au minimum de 7h à 10h et de 17h à 22h, certaines vous accueillent 24h sur 24, il est donc conseillé de vérifier cette information auprès de l'Auberge concernée.

Une nuit vous coûtera entre 31FF (4,73 Euros) et 115FF (nuit et petit-déjeuner à Paris – 17,53 Euros). Les draps, le petit-déjeuner et les déjeuners/dîners sont en supplément. Une taxe de séjour pourra également vous être demandée. La plupart des AJ mettent une cuisine à la disposition des individuels.

Il est conseillé de réserver à l'avance pour être sûr de disposer d'un lit. Pour cela, la FUAJ vous propose son système de réservation national, France Fax, ainsi qu'IBN dans certaines auberges.

Si vous aimez les vacances actives, la FUAJ vous propose un vaste choix d'activités en hiver comme en été, à la mer comme à la montagne et diverses formules pour en profiter. Tout au long de l'année, de nombreux stages sportifs et programmes culturels et touristiques sont organisés dans les auberges de jeunesse. Pour en savoir plus, connectez-vous sur notre Web (www.fuaj.org) ou demandez notre guide des AJ et nos brochures au Centre National de la FUAJ, à Paris.

PASSEPORTS ET VISAS

Une carte nationale d'identité en cours de validité suffit pour les ressortissants de l'Union Européenne. Dans les autres cas, il est nécessaire de contacter le consulat français ou l'ambassade de votre pays.

HEURES D'OUVERTURE DES BANQUES

A Paris, les banques sont normalement ouvertes de 9h à 17h (ou 16h), du lundi au vendredi. Dans les autres villes, elles ferment en principe entre 12h30 et 13h30.

REMARQUE: Pour utiliser une carte de crédit en France, un code confidentiel (Pincode) est nécessaire. Avant votre départ, assurez-vous auprès de votre banque que votre carte de crédit peut être utilisée en France.

BUREAUX DE POSTE

Dans les grandes villes, les bureaux de poste sont ouverts de 8h30 à 18h30 en semaine et de 8h30 à 12h le samedi.

HEURES D'OUVERTURE DES MAGASINS

Vous pourrez faire vos achats ou vous promener dans les boutiques de 10h à 19h du lundi au samedi. Certains magasins ferment entre 12h30 et 14h, parfois aussi le lundi.

DEPLACEMENTS

Trains

Un réseau de TGV (trains à grande vitesse) vous permet d'accéder très rapidement à la majorité des grandes villes (Lille, Nantes, Marseille, Paris…). Les villes plus modestes sont desservies régulièrement.

Autobus

Des services d'autobus locaux ou nationaux sont à votre disposition pour voyager à travers toute la France.

Ferry-boats

De nombreux ferry-boats relient l'Angleterre au nord de la France. Certaines lignes relient également la France à la Corse et à l'Afrique du Nord.

Automobiles
Un permis de conduire international est
nécessaire.

Deutsch

FRANZÖSISCHE JUGENDHERBERGEN

Ungefähr 200 französische Jugendherbergen -
von den Alpen bis zum Mittelmeer von der
Britannie bis nach Paris – stellen die ideale
Grundlage dar, um die Gegenden zu erkunden
oder an Kultur- und Sportveranstaltungen
teilzunehmen.

Jugendherbergen sind von 07.00-10.00 Uhr und
17.00-22.00 Uhr geöffnet. Einige sind 24
Stunden geöffnet, daher raten wir Ihnen, diese
Information mit jeder Herberge direkt zu
überprüfen.

Übernachtungspreise liegen zwischen 31 F
(4.73 €) und 115 F (Übernachtung und
Frühstück in Paris - 17.53 €), Bettwäsche und
Mahlzeiten ausgeschlossen. In einigen Fällen
kann eine tägliche Besuchersteuer erhoben
werden. Die meisten Herbergen sind mit
Küchen zur Selbstversorgung ausgestattet.

Vorausbuchung wird empfohlen, um auch
wirklich sicherzugehen, daß man ein Bett für
die Nacht hat. Es kann auf zwei Wegen erfolgen:
FUAJ's Nationaler Buchungsservice (France
Fax) und IBN, das in einigen Herbergen zur
Verfügung steht.

Wenn Sie ein Liebhaber von Aktivurlauben sind
- FUAJ bietet eine Vielzahl an Aktivitäten im
Winter und Sommer, an der Küste und in den
Bergen sowie verschiedene andere Pakete.
Während des ganzen Jahres werden von den
Herbergen viele Sport- und
Kulturveranstaltungen sowie Reiseprogramme
organisiert.

Für mehr Informationen schauen Sie in unsere
Web-Site unter www.fuaj.org, oder fordern Sie
einen französischen Jugendherbergsführer und
verschiedene Broschüren vom Nationalen Büro
der FUAJ in Paris an.

PÄSSE UND VISA

Für EU-Staatsbürger ist ein gültiger Paß
ausreichend. Staatsangehörige anderer Länder
sollten sich mit ihrem Französischen Konsulat
oder Botschaft in ihrem Land in Verbindung
setzen.

GESCHÄFTSSTUNDEN DER BANKEN

In Paris sind die Banken im allgemeinen von
09.00-17.00 Uhr (oder 16.00 Uhr) geöffnet. In
anderen Städten schließen sie gewöhnlich
zwischen 12.30 und 13.30 Uhr.

Bitte beachten: Wenn man eine Kreditkarte in
Frankreich benutzt, braucht man in vielen
Einrichtungen eine Geheimnummer.
Erkundigen Sie sich daher bei Ihrer Bank im
voraus, ob Sie Ihre Karte in Frankreich nutzen
können.

POSTÄMTER

In größeren Städten sind die Postämter im
allgemeinen montags bis freitags von
08.30-18.30 Uhr und samstags von
08.30-12.00 Uhr geöffnet.

LADENÖFFNUNGSZEITEN

Die Geschäfte sind im allgemeinen montags bis
samstags von 10.00-19.00 Uhr geöffnet. Einige
Geschäfte sind von 12.30-14.00 Uhr
geschlossen, manche auch montags.

REISEN

Eisenbahn

Die Hochgeschwindigkeitszüge (TGVs)
ermöglichen Reisenden, sehr schnell die
meisten der größeren Städten (wie Lille, Nantes,
Marseille, Paris …) zu erreichen. Es gibt
regelmäßige Verbindungen in kleinere Städte.

Busse

Es steht lokaler und regionaler Busverkehr zu Ihrer Verfügung, der es Ihnen ermöglicht, durch ganz Frankreich zu reisen.

Fähren

Es gibt viele Fähren von England nach Nordfrankreich und auch einige Fährverbindungen zwischen Südfrankreich, Korsika und Nordafrika.

Autofahren

Es wird ein internationaler Führerschein verlangt.

Español

ALBERGUES JUVENILES FRANCESES

Con casi 200 Albergues Juveniles repartidos de los Alpes al Mediterráneo pasando por París, los Albergues Juveniles franceses constituyen una excelente forma de descubrir una región o de participar en actividades culturales y deportivas.

Los albergues abren como mínimo de 7 h. a 10 h. y de 17 h. a 22 h. y algunos están abiertos las 24 horas del día, por lo que es aconsejable comprobar el horario de cada albergue en particular contactando con el mismo.

Una noche le costará entre 31 FF (4,73 Euros) y 115 FF (desayuno incluido en París - 17,53 Euros), más impuesto de visitante en algunos casos. Las sábanas, el desayuno y las comidas/cenas se cobran aparte. Es posible cocinar uno mismo en casi todos los albergues.

Se recomienda reservar con antelación para garantizar las plazas. Con este fin, la FUAJ le ofrece su sistema nacional de reservas France Fax, así como la red internacional de reservas IBN en algunos albergues.

Si le gustan las vacaciones deportivas, la FUAJ le propone una amplia gama de actividades tanto en invierno como en verano, desde el mar hasta la montaña, y varias fórmulas para disfrutar de ellas. A lo largo de todo el año, se organizan numerosos cursos deportivos y programas culturales y turísticos en los albergues juveniles. Si desea más información, consulte nuestra página Internet (www.fuaj.org) o solicite nuestra guía de albergues juveniles y nuestros folletos informativos dirigiéndose a la sede de la FUAJ en París.

PASAPORTES Y VISADOS

Los ciudadanos de la Unión Europea sólo necesitan un carnet de identidad nacional en regla. En los demás casos, infórmese en la embajada o en el consulado franceses de su país.

HORARIO DE LOS BANCOS

En París, los bancos abren normalmente de 9 h. a 17 h. (ó 16 h.) de lunes a viernes. En las demás ciudades, suelen cerrar de 12.30 h. a 13.30 h.

IMPORTANTE: Para utilizar una tarjeta de crédito en Francia, es necesaria una clave confidencial (Pincode). Antes de salir de viaje, pregunte en su banco si su tarjeta de crédito puede ser utilizada en Francia.

OFICINAS DE CORREOS

En las grandes ciudades, las oficinas de correos abren de 8.30 h. a 18.30 h. entre semana y de 8.30 h. a 12.00 h. los sábados.

HORARIO COMERCIAL

Usted podrá realizar sus compras o pasearse por las tiendas de 10 h. a 19 h. de lunes a sábado. Algunos comercios cierran de 12.30 h. a 14 h. y también a veces los lunes.

DESPLAZAMIENTOS

Tren

Una red de TGVs (trenes de gran velocidad) le permite acceder muy rápidamente a la mayoría de las grandes ciudades (Lille, Nantes, Marsella, París…). Las ciudades más pequeñas disfrutan de un servicio regular de trenes.

Autobús
Existen servicios de autobuses locales y nacionales a su disposición para viajar por toda Francia.

Ferry
Numerosas líneas de ferry enlazan Inglaterra con el norte de Francia. También existen algunas líneas entre Francia y Córcega y el norte de Africa.

Automóvil
Es necesario un permiso de conducir internacional.

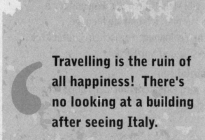

Travelling is the ruin of all happiness! There's no looking at a building after seeing Italy.

Le voyage tue le bonheur! Il est impossible d'admirer un bâtiment après voir vu l'Italie.

Reisen ist der Ruin allen Glückes! Nach Italien hat man kein Auge mehr für ein anderes Bauwerk.

Los viajes destruyen nuestra felicidad para siempre. ¿Quién es capaz de admirar un edificio cualquiera después de haber visitado Italia?

Fanny Burney

Aix-en-Provence

Le Jas de Bouffan,
3 Ave Marcel-Pagnol,
13090 Aix-en-Provence.
☎ 0442201599
📠 0442593612

Open Dates:	01.02-20.12
Open Hours:	07.00-24.00hrs (Sundays & Bank Holidays. 07.00-12.00hrs; 17.00-24.00hrs)
Reservations:	**R** **IBN** **CC**
Price Range:	68 FF € 10.37 BB inc 🏠
Beds:	101 - 1x🛏 2x🛏 1x🛏 1x🛏 1x🛏 9x🛏
Facilities:	♿ ♦♦♦ 2x ♦♦♦ 🍴 ☕ 🏢 📺 ▤ 2 x🍽 🔒 🖼 🅿 🛈 🌐 ♻ 🏔 🔍 ▦ ⛺
Directions:	2W from city centre
✈	Marseille-Provence 20km
A🚌	To Bus Station, then #4 2km
⛴	Marseille Prado 20km
🚂	Aix-en-Provence 2km
🚌	4 20m ap Vasarely-Auberge de Jeunesse
Attractions:	♨ 🚲 🚶 ∪2km ♀ ⚓500m

Aix-les-Bains

Promenade du Sierroz,
73100 Aix-les-Bains (Savoie).
☎ 0479883288
📠 0479611405
📧 aix-les-bains@fuaj.org

Open Dates:	05.02-05.11; 23.12-07.01 (🏠 ♦♦♦)
Open Hours:	07.00-23.00hrs
Reservations:	**R** **IBN** **CC**
Price Range:	51 FF € 7.77 🏠
Beds:	92 - 2x🛏 18x🛏 1x🛏 1x🛏
Facilities:	♿ ♦♦♦ 23x ♦♦♦ 🍴 ☕ 🏢 📺 ▤ 4 x🍽 🔒 🖼 ♿ ⬆ 🅿 ♻ 🏔 🔍 ▦ ⛺
Directions:	3NW from city centre
✈	Geneve 70km
🚂	Aix-les Bains TGV 3km
🚌	2 Plage Aix 200m ap Camping
Attractions:	♨ 🏔 ♨ 🏊 1600m 🎿 🚶 ∪10km ♀4km ⚓200m

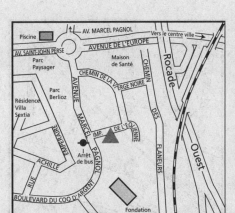

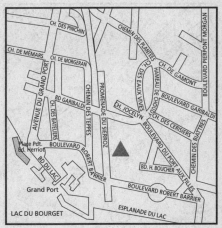

Annecy

4 Route du Semnoz,
74000 Annecy (Haute-Savoie).
☎ 0450453319
🖷 0450527752

Open Dates:	01.01-14.12; 26-31.12
Open Hours:	◷
Reservations:	IBN CC
Price Range:	72 FF € 10.98 BBinc 🍴
Beds:	117 - 1x¹🛏 2x²🛏 2x³🛏 19x⁴🛏 6x⁵🛏
Facilities:	♿ 🚻 30x 🚻 🍴 🚪 🍺 🛋 📺 🧺 2 x🍷 🔲 📷 🔲 🅿 🛈 ♨ 🏛 🔍
Directions:	1S from city centre
✈	Genève 40km
🚆	Annecy 2km
🚌	#1 1km ap Hôtel de Police
Attractions:	⛳ ⛰ 🎣 800m 🎿 1700m 🤸 🚶 🏊 1km

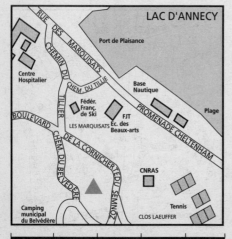

Arles

20 Ave Foch,
13200 Arles (Bouches-du-Rhône).
☎ 0490961825
🖷 0490963126

Open Dates:	05.02-20.12
Open Hours:	07.00-10.00hrs; 17.00-24.00hrs (Su), 07.00-10.00; 17.00-23.00hrs (Wi)
Reservations:	IBN CC
Price Range:	48 FF € 7.32 BBinc 🍴
Beds:	108 - 12x⁶🛏
Facilities:	🚻 🍴 🍺 🛋 📺 📷 1 x🍷 📷 🔲 🛈 ♨
Directions:	1S from city centre
✈	Nîmes 20km
⛴	Marseille 90km
🚆	Arles 2km
🚌	#3
Attractions:	🚴 🚶 ⚲ 🏊

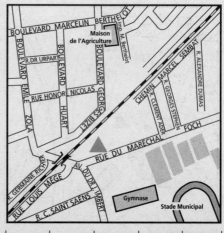

Biarritz -
Aintziko Gazte Etxea

8 Rue Chiquito de Cambo,
64200 Biarritz
☎ 0559417600
🖷 0559417607
📧 biarritz@fuaj.org

Open Dates:	20.01-20.12
Open Hours:	🕐
Reservations:	**R** (IBN) ⊂CC⊐
Price Range:	72 FF € 10.98 BB inc 🍴
Beds:	96 - 8x²🛏 4x³🛏 17x⁴🛏
Facilities:	♿ 👬 🍽 🍷 🖥 📺 🔥 🧺 3 x🍴 🖼 8 P 🚲 🛝 ⛰
Directions:	1.5 SW from city centre
✈	Biarritz Parme 1.5km
🚂	La Négresse 500m
🚌	#2 ap Gare la Négresse 500m
Attractions:	⛳ 🔍 1.5km 🚴 🏃 ∪1km 🤿 500m 🏊 500m

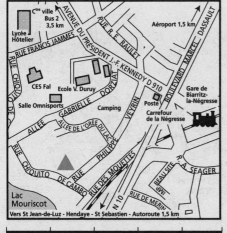

Boulogne-sur-Mer

Place Rouget de Lisle,
62200 Boulogne-sur-Mer (Pas-de-Calais).
☎ 0321991530
🖷 0321991539
📧 boulogne-sur-mer@fuaj.org

Open Dates:	31.01-22.12
Open Hours:	07.30-01.00hrs
Reservations:	**R** (IBN) ⊂CC⊐
Price Range:	72 FF € 10.98 BB inc 🍴
Beds:	132 - 1x²🛏 29x³🛏 11x⁴🛏
Facilities:	♿ 👬16x 👫 🍽 🍷 🍷 🖥 🛗 📺 🧺 1 x🍴 🖼 🏠 🔼 P 🚲 🛝 ⛰ 🎾
Directions:	0.5 S from city centre
✈	Lille Lesquin 110km
⛴	Seacat Boulogne 1.5km
🚂	Boulogne City
🚌	6, 7, 10, 11, 15, 19, 20 ap Gare SNCF
Attractions:	⛳ 🔍 1km 🏃 ∪5km 🏊 1.5km

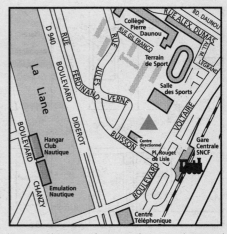

Cadouin

Place de l'Abbaye,
24480 Cadouin.
☎ 0553732878
✆ 0553732879

Open Dates:	01.02-15.12

Open Hours:	08.00-13.00hrs; 17.00-23.00hrs; 08.00-23.00hrs (01.06-31.08)

Reservations:	**R**

Price Range:	68 FF € 10.37 [BB] inc [SH]

Beds:	73 - 6x² 1x³ 10x⁴ 1x⁶ 1x⁶⁺

Facilities:	♿ �"' 10x �" ⑩ ☞ ☕ 🛏 📺 2 x ⛷ ⬛ P i 👫 ❄ ⚠ 🔍 📶 ⛩

Directions:

✈	Bergerac 35km
⛴	Bordeaux 120km
🚆	Le Buisson 5km

Attractions:	⛵ 🚴 🚶 ⋃5km ⚓300m ⛷15km

Cancale

Port Picain,
35260 Cancale
☎ 0299896262
✆ 0299897879
✉ cancale@fuaj.org

Open Dates:	01.02-02.01

Open Hours:	08.00-13.00hrs; (17.00-22.00hrs 01.05-30.09), (09.00-13.00; 18.00-20.00hrs - 01.10-30.04)

Reservations:	**R** IBN CC

Price Range:	51 FF € 7.77 [SH]

Beds:	82 - 2x¹ 13x² 1x³ 7x⁴ 2x⁵ 1x⁶⁺

Facilities:	♿ �"' 5x �" ⑩ ☞ ☕ 🛏 📺 📺 2 x ⛷ ⬛ 📷 📶 8 P i ❄ ⚠ 📶 🏠

Directions:

2N	from city centre
✈	Rennes/Dinard 70km
⛴	Port Picain
🚆	St. Malo 15km
🚌	500m ap Cancale - Port Picain

Attractions:	⛵ 🔍50m 🚶 ⋃2km ⚓2km ⛷

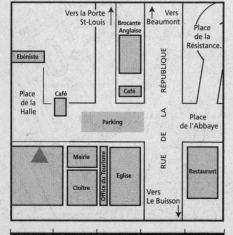

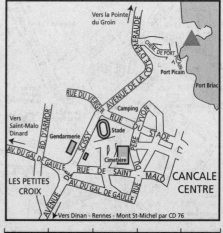

0   300m

0   1.4km

Carcassonne

Rue Vicomte de Trencavel,
Cité Médiévale,
11000 Carcassonne (Aude).
☎ 0468252316
✆ 0468711484
✉ carcassonne@fuaj.org

Open Dates:	01.02-15.12
Open Hours:	⊘
Reservations:	IBN CC
Price Range:	72 FF € 10.98 BB inc ⊠
Beds:	120 - 2x² 8x⁴ 14x⁶
Facilities:	♦♦♦ 4x ♦♦♦ ⏱ ⊠ ⛄ ⊡ 🖥 📺 📹 1 x✗ ☷ 🗄 ℹ ⛲ ⚲ 🏠 🏫
Directions:	2SE from city centre
✈	Toulouse 100km
🚂	Carcassonne 2km
🚌	#2 150m
Attractions:	⚲ ☀ ∪3km ⚲1km ≈2km

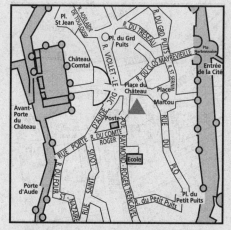

Chamonix Mont Blanc

127 Montée J Balmat,
Les Pélerins d'en Haut,
74400 Chamonix Mont Blanc
(Haute-Savoie).
☎ 0450531452
✆ 0450559234
✉ chamonix@fuaj.org

Open Dates:	10.12-10.05; 18.05-01.10 (R2 ♦♦♦)
Open Hours:	⊘
Reservations:	IBN CC
Price Range:	72 FF € 10.98 BB inc ⊠
Beds:	120 - 12x² 15x⁴ 6x⁶
Facilities:	♿ ♦♦♦ 10x ♦♦ ⏱ ⊠ ⛄ 🖥 📺 📖 📹 3 x✗ ☷ 🗄 ⚒ 8 P ℹ ⛲ ⚟ ⊘ ⚲ 🖩
Directions:	
✈	Genève 80km
A🚌	S.A.T. (Société Alpes Transport) 2.5km
🚂	Les Pelerins 700m
🚌	ap Pelerins Ecole 400m
Attractions:	⚲ ⛰ 🚴 🏊 1000m ☀ ∪200m ⚲2.5km ≈2.5km

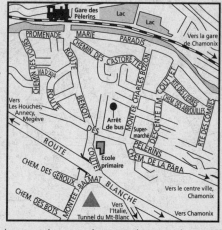

Lille

12 Rue Malpart,
59000 Lille.
☎ 0320570894
✆ 0320639893
✉ lille@fuaj.org

Open Dates:	01.02-20.12
Open Hours:	07.00-12.00hrs; 14.00-01.00hrs (02.00hrs Su)
Reservations:	ℝ IBN
Price Range:	72 FF € 10.98 BB inc 🏠
Beds:	168 - 5x² 13x³ 6x⁴ 7x⁵ 6x⁶ 1x⁶
Facilities:	♿ ♦♦♦ 20x ♦♦♦ 🍽 🔒 ☕ 🛏 📺 2 x 🍷 📷 ⚡ 🅿 ℹ 🎱

Directions:

✈	Lille-Lesquin 12km
⛴	Dunkerque 80km
🚂	Lille-Flandres 600m
🚌	#13 200m ap Hôtel de Ville
Ⓤ	Mairie de Lille #1 & 2 300m

Attractions: ↻2km ⚲2km ⛵1km

Lyon - AJ du Vieux Lyon

41-45 Montée du Chemin Neuf,
69005 Lyon
☎ 0478150550
✆ 0478150551
✉ lyon@fuaj.org

Open Dates:	🗓
Open Hours:	🕐
Reservations:	IBN CC
Price Range:	70 FF € 10.67 BB inc 🏠
Beds:	180 - 2x² 9x⁴ 3x⁵ 17x⁶ 2x⁶
Facilities:	♿ ♦♦♦ 5x ♦♦♦ 🍽 (BD) 🔒 ☕ 🛏 📺 🐕 1 x 🍷 📷 ⚡ ℹ 🎱 ✴

Directions:

✈	Satolas 30km
A🚌	Satobus 2km
🚂	Part-Dieu, Perrache 2km
🚌	From Part-Dieu, #28; From Perrache, #31 ap Funiculaire, Minimes Station 100m
Ⓤ	St. Jean, Line D 100m

Attractions: ⚲ ⛰

There are 2 hostels in Lyon. See following pages.

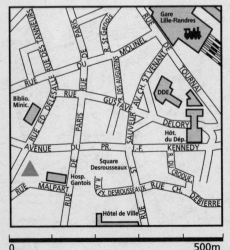

Paris - Le d'Artagnan

80 rue Vitruve,
75020 Paris.
☎ 0140323456
✆ 0140323455
✉ paris.le-dartagnan@fuaj.org

Open Dates:	🗓️₁₂
Open Hours:	🕐
Reservations:	R IBN CC
Price Range:	115 FF € 17.53 BB inc 🍽️
Beds:	439 - 20x² 77x³ 28x⁴ 7x⁶
Facilities:	♿ ♂♀ ♂♀ 🍽️ ☕ 🛏️ 📺 📇 🎒 3 x 🍴 📻 🖼️ 🏧 🔒 ➆ 📶 📋 🧺
Directions:	3E from city centre
✈	Roissy 20km
A🚌	Porte de Bagnolet #351
🚂	Gare de Lyon 1km
🚌	PC & #57 ap Vitruve
Ⓤ	Porte de Bagnolet - Line 3 800m

Poggio Mezzana

"L'Avillanella",
20230 Poggio Mezzana (Corse).
☎ 0495385010
✆ 0495385011

Open Dates:	01.04-30.10
Open Hours:	08.00-02.00hrs
Reservations:	R IBN
Price Range:	68 FF € 10.37 BB inc 🍽️
Beds:	100 - 6x¹ 8x² 15x⁴ 3x⁶
Facilities:	♂♀ 12x ♂♀ 🍽️ ☕ 🛏️ 📺 2 x 🍴 🏧 🅿️ 📇 🎿 ⛰️ 🌳 🔍 🎯 📶 🏡
Directions:	2E from city centre
✈	Bastia Poretta 20km
⛴	Bastia 40km
🚂	Casamozza 20km
🚌	ap "Lotissement" St Michel 100m
Attractions:	🔍100m 🚴 🚶 ∪1km 🏊

There are 4 hostels in Paris. See following pages.

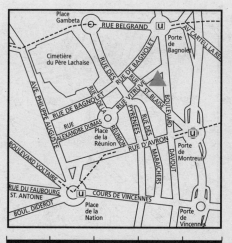

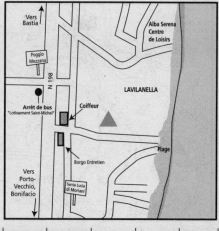

Poitiers

1 Allée Roger Tagault,
86000 Poitiers (Vienne).
☎ 0549300970
🖷 0549300979
📧 poitiers@fuaj.org

Open Dates:	03.01-31.12
Open Hours:	16.00-03.00hrs; 07.00-12.00hrs
Reservations:	[IBN] [CC]
Price Range:	51 FF € 7.77 🏠
Beds:	132 - 2x²🛏 26x⁴🛏 2x⁶🛏 1x⁶🛏
Facilities:	♿ ♦♦♦ 29x ♦♦♦ ⵑⵁⵏ ♂ 🍽 🏢 📺 🛏 2 x 🍷 🎞 🔢 🅿 ✏ 🚲 ⚠ 🅾 🍴 ▦ 🏠
Directions:	3SW from city centre
✈	Biard 5km
🚂	Poitiers 3km
🚌	#3, Pierre Loti ap Cap Sud 100m
Attractions:	🏊 10m 🚴

Rennes

10-12 Canal Saint-Martin,
35700 Rennes (Ille-et-Vilaine).
☎ 0299332233
🖷 0299590621

Open Dates:	03.01-24.12
Open Hours:	07.00-01.00hrs
Reservations:	[R] [IBN] [CC]
Price Range:	51 FF € 7.77 [BB]inc 🏠
Beds:	96 - 7x¹🛏 18x²🛏 7x³🛏 8x⁴🛏
Facilities:	♿ ♦♦♦ 15x ♦♦♦ 🍽 ♂ 🍵 🛏 📺 2 x 🍷 🎞 🔢 🅿 ✏ 🚲 ⚠ 🍴 ▦
Directions:	1.5N from city centre
✈	Rennes St. Jacques 12km
A🚌	57, 58 1.2km
🚂	Rennes 2km
🚌	18, 1 ap (Su 🚌 2) 100m ap Port St Martin
Attractions:	🚶 🎿1km 🏊1km

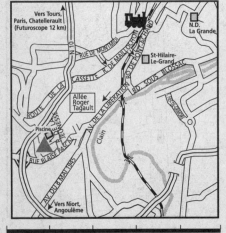

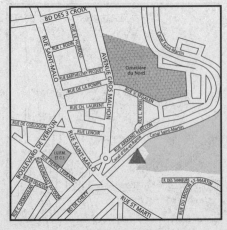

Saint-Brieuc

Manoir de la Ville Guyomard,
Les Villages,
22000 St-Brieuc (Côtes-d'Armor).
☎ 0296787070
✆ 0296782747
✉ saint-brieuc@fuaj.org

Open Dates:	🗓12
Open Hours:	⏰
Reservations:	Ⓡ ⊂CC⊃
Price Range:	72 FF € 10.98 BB inc 🏠
Beds:	127 - 20x³🛏 16x⁴🛏
Facilities:	♿ 👬 36x 👬 🍽 ☕ 🍷 🛄 📺 📖 🧺 6 x🍴 🔲 💼 🚪 8 🅿 ℹ ⚡ 🔋 🚡 🔨 🎪
Directions:	3NW from city centre
🚢	St Malo, Roskof 110km
🚂	St Brieuc 3km
🚌	#1, #3 500m
Attractions:	🔍 🚴 🚶 ∪4km ⚓ 🏊2km

Strasbourg -
René Cassin

9 rue de l'Auberge de Jeunesse,
67200 Strasbourg (Bas-Rhin).
☎ 0388302646
✆ 0388303516

Open Dates:	01.02-31.12 △
Open Hours:	⏰
Reservations:	[IBN]
Price Range:	72 FF € 10.98 BB inc 🏠
Beds:	280 - 12x¹🛏 16x²🛏 11x³🛏 16x⁴🛏 23x⁶🛏
Facilities:	♿ 👬 43x 👬 🍽 ☕ 🍷 🛄 📺 🧺 2 x🍴 💼 🅿 ℹ 🔋 ⚡ 🚡 🔍
Directions:	2SW from city centre
✈	Entzheim 7km
A🚌	2km
🚢	Port du Rhin 5km
🚂	Strasbourg 2km
🚌	3, 23 200m ap Auberge de Jeunesse
Attractions:	∪6km ⚓1km 🏊4km

There are 2 hostels in Strasbourg. See following pages.

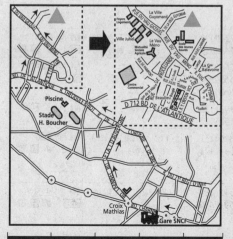

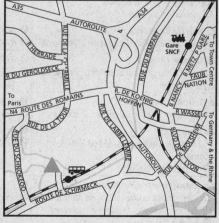

0	2km

0	2.2km

Location/Address	Telephone No. Fax No.	Beds	Opening Dates	Facilities
▲ **Aix-en-Provence** ⟨IBN⟩ **Le Jas de Bouffan, 3 Ave Marcel-Pagnol,** **13090 Aix-en-Provence.**	☎ 0442201599 ✆ 0442593612	101	01.02–20.12	⁝⁝⁝ ⊺◎⊺ ⓇR ⸤2W⸥ ⅇ ⸤CC⸥ P ⸤◎⸥ ☕
▲ **Aix-les-Bains** ⟨IBN⟩ **Promenade du Sierroz,** **73100 Aix-les-Bains (Savoie).** ⓔ aix-les-bains@fuaj.org	☎ 0479883288 ✆ 0479611405	92	05.02–05.11; 23.12–07.01 (⸤12⸥ ⁝⁝⁝)	⁝⁝⁝ ⊺◎⊺ ⓇR ⸤3NW⸥ ⅇ ⸤CC⸥ ⸋ P ⸤◎⸥
△ *Albi (Assoc)* *AJ MJC, 13 Rue de la Republique,* *81000 Albi (Tarn).*	☎ *0563545365* ✆ *0563546155*	*36*	⸤12⸥	⊺◎⊺ ⸤0.5NE⸥ ⸋ P ⸤◎⸥
▲ **Anglet** ⟨IBN⟩ **"Gazte Etxea", 19 Route des Vignes,** **64600 Anglet (Pyrénées Atlantiques).** ⓔ biarritz@fuaj.org	☎ 0559587000 ✆ 0559587007	96	20.01–20.12	⊺◎⊺ ⓇR ⸤0.5W⸥ ⸤CC⸥ ⸋ P ☕
▲ **Angoulême** ⟨IBN⟩ Parc de Bourgines, 16000 Angoulême (Charente). ⓔ angouleme@fuaj.org	☎ 0545924580 ✆ 0545959071	84	04.01–18.12	⊺◎⊺ ⸤2N⸥ ⸤CC⸥ P ⸤◎⸥ ☕
▲ **Annecy** ⟨IBN⟩ **4 Route du Semnoz,** **74000 Annecy (Haute-Savoie).**	☎ 0450453319 ✆ 0450527752	117	01.01–14.12; 26–31.12	⁝⁝⁝ ⊺◎⊺ ⸤1S⸥ ⅇ ⸤CC⸥ ⸋ P ⸤◎⸥ ☕
△ *Anzin (Assoc)* *Auberge du Parc Mathieu,* *43 rue des Martyrs, 59410 Anzin (Nord).*	☎ *0327282100* ✆ *0327282101*	*40*	⸤12⸥	⁝⁝⁝ ⓇR ⸋ P
▲ **Arles** ⟨IBN⟩ **20 Ave Foch,** **13200 Arles (Bouches-du-Rhône).**	☎ 0490961825 ✆ 0490963126	108	05.02–20.12	⊺◎⊺ ⸤1S⸥ ⸤CC⸥ ☕
△ *Arras* *59 Grand-Place, 62000 Arras (Pas-de-Calais).*	☎ *0321227002* ✆ *0321074615*	*54*	*01.02–30.11*	⊺◎⊺ ⸋ P
△ *Autrans* *Auberge de Jeunesse "Les Hirondelles",* *Les Gaillards, 38880 Autrans* ⓔ *autrans@fuaj.org*	☎ *0476947715* ✆ *0476947789*	*55*	⸤12⸥	⁝⁝⁝ ⊺◎⊺ ⓇR ⸤1S⸥ P ☕
△ *Avrillé-Langeais (Assoc)* *"Pause-Gâtines", Rue des Tilleuls, 37340 Avrillé.*	☎ *0247249600* ✆ *0247482659*	*35*	*01.07–31.08* *(⸤12⸥ ⁝⁝⁝)*	⁝⁝⁝ ⊺◎⊺ ⓇR ⅇ ⸤CC⸥ ⸋ P ⸤◎⸥
△ *Banize (Assoc)* *Centre d'Hebergement Lou-Pélélé, Puy-Joint,* *23120 Banize*	☎ *0555660063* ✆ *0555660207* *(Mairie)*	*29*	⸤12⸥	⁝⁝⁝ ⊺◎⊺ ⓇR ⸋ P
▲ **Bayeux (Assoc)** "Family Home", 39 Rue Gal de Dais, 14400 Bayeux.	☎ 0231921522 ✆ 0231925572	140	⸤12⸥	⁝⁝⁝ ⊺◎⊺ ⅇ ⸤CC⸥ ⸋ P ⸤◎⸥
▲ **Beaugency** 152 route de Châteaudun, 45190 Beaugency (Loiret). ⓔ beaugency@fuaj.org	☎ 0238446131 ✆ 0238441473	110	01.03–31.12	⁝⁝⁝ ⊺◎⊺ ⓇR ⸤2N⸥ ⅇ ⸋ P ☕
△ *Beaulieu-sur-Dordogne* *'La Riviera Limousine', Place du Monturu,* *19120 Beaulieu-sur-Dordogne (Corrèze).* ⓔ *bealieu@fuaj.org*	☎ *0555911382* ✆ *0555912606*	*28*	*01.04–30.09*	⁝⁝⁝ ⊺◎⊺ ⸤0.5N⸥ ⸤CC⸥ ⸋ P ⸤◎⸥

Location/Address	Telephone No. Fax No.	Beds	Opening Dates	Facilities
▲ **Belfort (Assoc)** Résidence Madrid, FJT, 6 rue de Madrid, 90000 Belfort.	☎ 0384213916 🖷 0384285895	20	🔒12	ᵻᵻᵻ ﾛ 1S ⊂CC⊃ P ☑
▲ **Belle-Ile en Mer** Haute Boulogne, Belle Ile, 56360 Le Palais (Morbihan).	☎ 0297318133 🖷 0297315838	93	03.01–30.09; 01.10–24.12	ﾛ 1.5N ⅍ ⊂CC⊃ ⚲ P ☕
▲ **Besançon (Assoc)** FJT/AJ "Les Oiseaux", 48 rue des Cras, 25000 Besançon.	☎ 0381403200 🖷 0381403201	20	🔒12	ﾛ 2NE ⅍ ⊂CC⊃ P ☕
△ *Betete* *AJ Verte/Country Hostel,* *AJ-Centre d'Animation de l'Abbaye de* *Prebenoit, 23270 Betete (Creuse).*	☎ *0555807891* 🖷 *0555808680*	*50*	*01.04–01.11*	ᵻᵻᵻ ﾛ R 4.5SW ⚲ P ☑
▲ **Biarritz** - Aintziko Gazte Etxea IBN **8 Rue Chiquito de Cambo, 64200 Biarritz** ✉ biarritz@fuaj.org	☎ 0559417600 🖷 0559417607	96	20.01–20.12	ﾛ R 1.5SW ⅍ ⊂CC⊃ P ☕
▲ **Boulogne-sur-Mer** IBN **Place Rouget de Lisle, 62200 Boulogne-** **sur-Mer (Pas-de-Calais).** ✉ boulogne-sur-mer@fuaj.org	☎ 0321991530 🖷 0321991539	132	31.01–22.12	ᵻᵻᵻ ﾛ R 0.5S ⅍ ⊂CC⊃ ⚲ P ☕
▲ **Bourges** "Jacques Coeur", 22 rue Henri Sellier, 18000 Bourges (Cher). ✉ bourges@fuaj.org	☎ 0248245809 🖷 0248655146	86	17.01–17.12	ᵻᵻᵻ ﾛ R 0.8SW ⚲ P ☑ ☕
▲ **Brive La Gaillarde** IBN 56 Av Maréchal Bugeaud, Parc Monjauze, 19100 Brive La Gaillarde (Corrèze). ✉ brive@fuaj.org	☎ 0555243400 🖷 0555848280	100	🔒12	ᵻᵻᵻ ﾛ R 0.5E ⊂CC⊃ ⚲ P
▲ **Cadouin** **Place de l'Abbaye, 24480 Cadouin.**	☎ 0553732878 🖷 0553732879	73	01.02–15.12	ᵻᵻᵻ ﾛ R ⅍ ⚲ P ☑
▲ **Caen (Assoc)** FJT "Robert Rême", 68 rue Eustache Restout, 14000 Caen (Calvados).	☎ 0231521996 🖷 0231842949	58	01.06–30.09	ᵻᵻᵻ R 2S ⅍ ⚲ P ☑ ☕
△ *Cahors (Assoc)* *Espace Frédéric Suisse, 20 Rue F Suisse,* *46000 Cahors.*	☎ *0565356471,* *0565539702* 🖷 *0565359592*	*36*	🔒12	ﾛ R ⚲ ☑
▲ **Cambrai (Assoc)** "Etape", 22 Rue de Crevecoeur, 59400 Cambrai. ✉ aubergejeunesseetape@minitel.net	☎ 0327749803 🖷 0327749803	73	🔒12	ᵻᵻᵻ ﾛ 1.5S ⚲ P
▲ **Cancale** IBN **Port Picain, 35260 Cancale** ✉ cancale@fuaj.org	☎ 0299896262 🖷 0299897879	82	01.02–02.01	ᵻᵻᵻ ﾛ R 2N ⅍ ⊂CC⊃ ⚲ P ☑ ☕
Cannes ☞ **Le Trayas**				
△ *Cap Frébel* *AJ Verte/Country Hostel, Kérivet-la ville* *Hardrieux-Plevenon,* *22240 Cap Frébel (Côtes-d'Armor).*	☎ *0296414898* 🖷 *0296414898*	*46*	*01.04–15.09*	ᵻᵻᵻ ﾛ 2N ⅍ ⚲ P ☑

Location/Address	Telephone No. Fax No.	Beds	Opening Dates	Facilities
▲ Carcassonne IBN Rue Vicomte de Trencavel, Cité Médiévale, 11000 Carcassonne (Aude). ⓔ carcassonne@fuaj.org	☎ 0468252316 ❺ 0468711484	120	01.02-15.12	♦♦♦ ⑩ 2SE ⒼⒸⒸ ☞ ⓞ ☕
△ Cassis La Fontasse, 13260 Cassis (Bouches-du-Rhône).	☎ 0442010272	65	02.03–09.01	4W ☞ Ⓟ ⓞ
▲ Cepoy-Montargis 25 Quai du Port, 45120 Cepoy (Loiret): (Montargis 6km N).	☎ 0238932545 ❺ 0238931925	100	01.02–19.12	♦♦♦ ⑩ Ⓡ 0.2N ⒼⒸⒸ ☞ Ⓟ ⓞ ☕
▲ Cernay (Assoc) MJC/Auberge Internationale de la Jeunesse 16a, Faubourg deColmar, 68700 Cernay (Haut-Rhin).	☎ 0389754459 ❺ 0389758748	55	02.01–24.12	♦♦♦ ⑩ 0.5NE ☞ Ⓟ ☕
Chambord ☞ Blois-Montlivault				
▲ Chamonix Mont Blanc IBN 127 Montée J Balmat, Les Pélerins d'en Haut,74400 Chamonix Mont Blanc (Haute-Savoie). ⓔ chamonix@fuaj.org	☎ 0450531452 ❺ 0450559234	120	10.12-10.05; 18.05-01.10 (🔋 ♦♦♦)	♦♦♦ ⑩ ♿ ⒼⒸⒸ Ⓟ ⓞ ☕
▲ Chamrousse Le St. Christophe, 38410 Chamrousse. ⓔ chamrousse@fuaj.org	☎ 0476899131 ❺ 0476899666	84	01.01–01.05; 01.06–15.09	♦♦♦ ⑩ 0.3S ⒼⒸⒸ Ⓟ
▲ Chaumont (Assoc) FJT/AJ, 1 rue de Carcassonne, 52000 Chaumont.	☎ 0325032277	23	🔋	♦♦♦ ⑩ 1SW ☞ Ⓟ ⓞ ☕
▲ Chauny Bd Bad-Kostritz, 02300 Chauny (Aisne).	☎ 0323520996 ❺ 0323399092	40	🔋	♦♦♦ ⑩ Ⓡ 1N ♿ ☞ Ⓟ ⓞ
▲ Cherbourg IBN 57 Rue de L'Abbaye, 50100 Cherbourg	☎ 0233781515 ❺ 0233781516	99	04.01–23.12	♦♦♦ ⑩ Ⓡ 0.5W ♿ ⒼⒸⒸ ☞ Ⓟ ☕
▲ Chinon (Assoc) Centre Animation Accueil/AJ, Rue Descartes BP 233, 37500 Chinon.	☎ 0247931048 ❺ 0247984498	40	🔋 (call before arrival)	♦♦♦ ⑩ Ⓡ ☞ ⓞ
▲ Cholet - Les Pâquerettes (Assoc) FJT, 5 rue de la Casse, BP 316, 49303 Cholet Cedex (Maine et Loire).	☎ 0241713636 ❺ 0241626222	20	15.06–15.09	♦♦♦ ⑩ 0.5E ♿ Ⓟ ⓞ ☕
△ Clermont-Ferrand "Auberge du Cheval Blanc", 55 Ave de l'URSS, 63000 Clermont-Ferrand (Puy-de-Dôme).	☎ 0473922639 ❺ 0473929996	58	01.03–31.10	♦♦♦ ⑩ 1NW ☞
△ Colmar (Assoc) AJ "Mittelbart", 2 Rue Pasteur, 68000 Colmar (Haut-Rhin).	☎ 03 89805739 ❺ 0389807616	110	15.01–15.12	♦♦♦ ⑩ Ⓡ 1W ⒼⒸⒸ Ⓟ
▲ Creil (Assoc) Centre des Cadres Sportifs, 1 rue du Général Leclerc, 60100 Creil (Oise).	☎ 0344646220 ❺ 0344646229	144	🔋	⑩ Ⓡ 1S ⒼⒸⒸ ☞ Ⓟ ⓞ

Location/Address	Telephone No. Fax No.	Beds	Opening Dates	Facilities
△ *Dieppe* 48 Rue Louis Fromager, Quartier Janval de Dieppe, 76550 Saint Aubin/Scie (the YH is in Dieppe). ❸ dieppe@fuaj.org	❶ 0235848573 ❺ 0235848962	*41*	*15.03–15.10*	⊕⊕ 3.5S ⚲ P ▣
▲ Dijon (Assoc) CRISD,1 bd Champollion, 21000 Dijon (Côte d'Or). ❸ crisd@planetb.fr	❶ 0380729520 ❺ 0380700061	100	02.01–24.12; 26–31.12	⊕⊕ ⍾⍾ 3NE ♿ ⴹCC P ▣
▲ Dinan Moulin de Méen,Vallée de la Fontaine des Eaux, 22100 Dinan (Côtes d'Armor). ❸ dinan@fuaj.org	❶ 0296391083 ❺ 0296391062	72	▣12	⊕⊕ ⍾⍾ 2NE ⚲ P ▣
▲ Dole (Assoc) "Le St Jean", Place Jean XXIII, BP 164, 39101 Dole Cedex (Jura).	❶ 0384823674 ❺ 0384791769	60	▣12	⍾⍾ R 1S ⚲ P ▣
▲ Dunkerque Place Paul Asseman, 59140 Dunkerque (Nord)	❶ 0328633634 ❺ 0328632454	70	02.01–20.12	⍾⍾ R 3NW P
▲ Etsaut (Assoc) Centre International de Séjour, Auberge de Jeunesse, Vallée d'Aspe, 64490 Etsaut (Pyrénées Atlantiques).	❶ 0559348898 ❺ 0559348691	70	▣12	⊕⊕ ⍾⍾ R ⚲ ▣
▲ Eu (Assoc) Centre des Fontaines, rue des Fontaines, BP 123, 76260 Eu (Seine Maritime).	❶ 0235860503 ❺ 0235864512	55	05.01–19.12	⊕⊕ ⍾⍾ ⴹCC P ☕
▲ Evian (Assoc) Centre International de Séjour, ave de Neuvecelle, BP 31, 74500 Evian les Bains Cedex (Haute Savoie). ❸ jptreil@cur-archamps.fr	❶ 0450753587 ❺ 0450754567	50	▣12	⊕⊕ ⍾⍾ R 1E ♿ ⴹCC ⚲ P ▣ ☕
△ *Fontaine-de-Vaucluse* Chemin de la Vignasse, 84800 Fontaine-de-Vaucluse (Vaucluse).	❶ 0490203165 ❺ 0490202620	*50*	*15.02–15.11*	⊕⊕ ⍾⍾ 0.7S ⚲ P ▣
▲ Fontenay-le-Comte (Assoc) "Les Trois Portes", Foyer Sud Vendée/AJ, 16 Rue des Gravants,BP 347, 85206 Fontenay le Comte Cedex.	❶ 0251691344 ❺ 0251690423	50	15.06–15.09	⊕⊕ ⍾⍾ R 0.5E ♿ ⴹCC ⚲ P ▣ ☕
▲ Fréjus Chemin du Counillier, 83600 Fréjus (Var).	❶ 0494531875 ❺ 0494532586	147	01.02–20.12	⊕⊕ ⍾⍾ 1.7NE ⚲ P ☕
▲ Gannat (Assoc) Maison des cultures et Traditions, Route de St Priest, 03800 Gannat. ❸ jeanroche@compuserve.com	❶ 0470901267 ❺ 0470901922	66	01.04–31.10	⍾⍾ R P ☕
△ *Givet* AJ Verte/Country Hostel, Château 'Mon Bijou', Route des Chaumières, 08600 Givet (Ardennes).	❶ 0324420960 ❺ 0324420244	*13*	▣12 *(Closed for restoration)*	⊕⊕ ⍾⍾ R 3N ⚲ P ▣

Location/Address	Telephone No. Fax No.	Beds	Opening Dates	Facilities
▲ Granville (Assoc) Centre Régional de Nautisme, Bd des Amiraux, 50400 Granville (Manche). ❸ crng@dial.oleane.com	☎ 0233912262 📠 0233505199	165	03.01–21.12	††† ⑩ 0.2SW ⊞CC P ⬤
▲ Gray (Assoc) "Le Foyer", 2 Rue André Maginot, 70100 Gray. ❸ lefoyer@wanadoo.fr	☎ 0384649920 📠 0384649929	100	🗓12	††† ⑩ 0.2E ⊞CC ☛ P ◙ ⬤
▲ Grenoble-Echirolles (IBN) 10 Ave du Grésivaudan, 38130 Echirolles (Isère). ❸ grenoble-echirolles@fuaj.org	☎ 0476093352 📠 0476093899	120	🗓12	††† ⑩ ℝ 5S ♿ ⊞CC ☛ P ◙ ⬤
▲ Guillestre (Assoc) les Quatre Vents, "La Rochette", BP22, 05600 Guillestre (Hautes Alpes).	☎ 0492450432 📠 0492450432	56	01.12–30.09	††† ⑩ ℝ 1.5SW ☛ P ◙ ⬤
△ Ile-de-Groix Fort du Méné, 56590 Ile de Groix (Morbihan).	☎ 0297868138 📠 0297865243	50	01.04–15.10	††† 1.2NE ☛ P ◙
▲ Imphy (Assoc) Résidence Gerorges Bouqueau, 8 Rue Jean Sounié, 58160 Imphy.	☎ 0386909520 📠 0386383187	20	🗓12	⑩ 1SE ☛ P ◙ ⬤
▲ Inzinzac-Lochrist AJ Verte/Country Hostel, Ferme du Gorée, 56650 Inzinzac-Lochrist (Morbihan).	☎ 0297360808 📠 0297369083	35	01.03–15.10; (ℝ 01.11–28.02)	††† ⑩ 1N ♿ ☛ P
▲ La Clusaz Route du Col de Croix Fry, "Les Etages", BP47, 74220 La Clusaz Cedex (Haute-Savoie). ❸ laclusaz@fuaj.org	☎ 0450024173 📠 0450026585	85	17.12–26.09 (ℝ ††† 26.09–17.12)	⑩ ℝ 3SE ♿ ⊞CC P ⬤
▲ La Foux d'Allos Neige et soleil, "Les Chauvets" 04260 La Foux Allos (Alpes-de-Haute-Provence).	☎ 0492838108 📠 0492838370	72	01.12–25.04; 10.06–15.09	††† ⑩ ℝ 0.2N P ⬤
△ La Palud-sur-Verdon "L'immense Botte de Paille", Départementale 23,04120 La Palud-sur-Verdon (Alpes-de-Haute-Provence).	☎ 0492773872 📠 0492773872	67	01.03–31.10	††† ⑩ 0.5S ☛ P ◙
▲ La Rochelle Ave des Minimes, BP 305, 17013 La Rochelle Cedex (Charente-Maritime).	☎ 0546444311 📠 0546454148	224	01.01–18.12	††† ⑩ ℝ 1.5SW ♿ P ◙ ⬤
▲ La Toussuire La Toussuire, 73300 Fontcouverte (Savoie).	☎ 0479567204 📠 0479830093	72	30.11–30.04; 01.07–14.09	††† ⑩ 1SE P ⬤
△ Lannion - Beg Leguer AJ Verte/Country Hostel, Plage de Goalagorn, Beg Leguer, 22300 Lannion.	☎ 0296472486 📠 0296370206	14	15.04–15.09 (ℝ ††† 🗓12)	⑩ 6W ☛ P ⬤
▲ Lannion - Les Korrigans (IBN) Rive Gauche - 6, Rue du 73e Territorial, 22300 Lannion (Cotes D'Armor). ❸ lannion@fuaj.org	☎ 0296379128 📠 0296370206	68	🗓12	††† ⑩ 0.3SW ♿ ☛ P ◙ ⬤

Location/Address	Telephone No. Fax No.	Beds	Opening Dates	Facilities
▲ **Le Mans (Assoc)** AJ-FJT le Flore, 23 rue Maupertuis, 72000 le Mans (Sarthe). @ florefjt@cybercable.tm.fr	☎ 0243812755 ✆ 0243810610	28	⬚12	♯♯♯ ⏏◎⏏ ⟨R⟩ [0.2N] ⬚ ⬚ ⬚
△ *Le Mazet St Voy (Assoc)* *"Ferme du Besset", La Bataille,* *43520 Le Mazet St Voy (Haute Loire).*	☎ 0471650035 ✆ 0471650544	*30*	⬚12	♯♯♯ ◎ ⟨R⟩ [4SW] ⬚ P ⬚
▲ **Le Mont-Dore** "Le Grand Volcan", 63240 Le Mont-Dore (Puy-de-Dome). @ le-mont-dore@fuaj.org	☎ 0473650353 ✆ 0473652639	90	⬚12	♯♯♯ ◎ ⟨R⟩ [3.5S] ⊂CC⊃ ⬚ P ⬚ ⬚
△ *Le Puy en Velay (Assoc)* *Centre Pierre Cardinal, 9 Rue Jules Vallès,* *43000 Le Puy en Velay.*	☎ 0471055240 ✆ 0471056124	70	01.10–31.03 (except weekends & holidays); 01.04–30.09	♯♯♯ ◎ ⟨R⟩ [0.2NE] ⬚ P
▲ **Le Trayas/Théoule-sur-Mer** 9 Av de la Véronèse, Le Trayas, 06590 Théoule-sur-Mer (Alpes-Maritimes).	☎ 0493754023 ✆ 0493754345	100	15.02–02.01	♯♯♯ ◎ [8W] ⬚ P ⬚
△ *Les Aldudes (Assoc)* *Association École des Buissons, Urtxintxenea,* *Route d'Urepel, 64430 Les Aldudes* @ *urtintx@ad.com*	☎ 0559375658 ✆ 0559375658	*60*	15.02–15.12	♯♯♯ ◎ ♿ P ⬚
▲ **Les Deux Alpes** "Les Brûleurs de Loups", 38860 Les Deux Alpes (Isère). @ les-deux-alpes@fuaj.org	☎ 0476792280 ✆ 0476792615	57	05.12–02.05; 20.06–05.09 (⟨R⟩ ♯♯♯ ⬚12)	♯♯♯ ◎ ⊂CC⊃ P ⬚
▲ **Les Gets** "Les Farfadets", Le Poncet, Les Gets, 74160 Les Gets.	☎ 0450791486 (Morzine)	60	⬚12 ♯♯♯	⟨R⟩ [2.5W] ⊂CC⊃ P ⬚ ⬚
▲ **Les Rousses** 2400 Le Bief de la Chaille,39220 Les Rousses (Jura).	☎ 0384600280 ✆ 0384600967	50	20.12–24.04; 11.05–25.09 (♯♯♯ ⬚12)	♯♯♯ ◎ ⟨R⟩ [3SW] ⬚ P ⬚ ⬚
▲ **Lille** IBN **12 Rue Malpart, 59000 Lille.** @ lille@fuaj.org	☎ 0320570894 ✆ 0320639893	168	01.02–20.12	♯♯♯ ◎ ⟨R⟩ ♿ ⬚ P ⬚
▲ **Lorient** 41 rue Victor Schoelcher, 56100 Lorient (Morbihan).	☎ 0297371165 ✆ 0297879549	104	01.02–22.12	♯♯♯ ◎ [3SW] ♿ ⬚ P ⬚ ⬚
▲ **Lourdios/Ichère (Assoc)** AJ, Estivade d'Aspe Pyrénées, "Maison Pelou", 64570 Lourdios Ichère (Pyrénées Atlantique).	☎ 0559344639 ✆ 0559344804	25	⬚12	♯♯♯ ◎ [3N] ⬚ P ⬚
△ *Luttenbach Près Munster* *13 Rue de la Gare, 68140 Luttenbach Près* *Munster.*	☎ 0389773420	*30*	⬚12	♯♯♯ ◎ ⬚ P
▲ **Lyon** - AJ du Vieux Lyon IBN **41-45 Montée du Chemin Neuf,** **69005 Lyon** @ lyon@fuaj.org	☎ 0478150550 ✆ 0478150551	180	⬚12	♯♯♯ ◎ ♿ ⊂CC⊃ ⬚ ⬚ ⬚

Location/Address	Telephone No. Fax No.	Beds	Opening Dates	Facilities
▲ **Lyon-II** IBN 51 rue Roger Salengro, 69200 Vénissieux (Rhône).	☎ 0478763923 🛈 0478775111	118	17.01–23.12 before 12.00hrs	⁖⁖ ⑩ R 5SW ♿ ☛ P ⓞ
△ *Manosque* *Parc de la Rochette, 04100 Manosque (Alpes de Haute-Provence).*	☎ 0492875744 🛈 0492724391	60	🗓	⁖⁖ ⑩ 1N ☛ P
▲ **Marseille** - Bonneveine IBN (Impasse du Dr Bonfils) Av J Vidal, 13008 Marseille (Bouches-du-Rhône). 📧 marseille@fuaj.org	☎ 0491732181 🛈 0491739723	150	01.02–21.12	⑩ 5S CC P ⓞ ☕
▲ **Marseille** - Château de Bois-Luzy Allée des Primevères, 13012 Marseille (Bouches-du-Rhône).	☎ 0491490618 🛈 0491490618	90	🗓	⁖⁖ ⑩ R 4NE ☛ P ⓞ
△ *Martinique* - Morne Rouge *Av Jean Jaurés, Hauts du Bourg, 97260 Morne Rouge.*	☎ 0596523981 🛈 0596523981	43	🗓	⁖⁖ ⑩ R 0.5N ♿ ☛ P ⓞ ☕
▲ **Menton** IBN Plateau St-Michel, 06500 Menton (Alpes-Maritimes).	☎ 0493359314 🛈 0493359307	80	01.02–15.11	⑩ 1.5N ⓞ
▲ **Metz (Assoc)** - Carrefour 6 rue Marchant, 57000 Metz (Moselle). 📧 ascarrefour@wanadoo.fr	☎ 0387750726 🛈 0387367144	60	🗓	⁖⁖ ⑩ CC P ⓞ
△ *Metz (Assoc)* - Plage *1 Allée de Metz Plage, 57000 Metz 📧 aubjeumetz@ad.com*	☎ 0387304402 🛈 0387331980	62	🗓	⁖⁖ ⑩ 0.5N CC ☛ P ⓞ ☕
▲ **Millau (Assoc)** FJT Sud Aveyron Accueil, 26 rue Lucien Costes, 12100 Millau (Aveyron).	☎ 0565612774 🛈 0565619058	60	🗓	⁖⁖ ⑩ R 0.8NW ☛ P ⓞ
Montargis ☞ **Cepoy**				
△ *Montpellier* IBN *Rue des Ecoles Laïques (Impasse Petite Corraterie), 34000 Montpellier (Hérault).*	☎ 0467603222 🛈 0467603230	89	10.01–17.12	⁖⁖ ⑩ R CC ☕
▲ **Morzine/Avoriaz** Holiday Campus, La Coutettaz, 74110 Morzine (Haute-Savoie).	☎ 0450791486	76	24.12–22.04; 14.06–12.09	⁖⁖ ⑩ R 0.4E CC P ☕
▲ **Mulhouse** 37 Rue de l'Illberg, 68200 Mulhouse (Haut-Rhin).	☎ 0389426328 🛈 0389597495	70	11.01–18.12	⁖⁖ ⑩ R 2SW ♿ CC ☛ P
Munster ☞ **Luttenbach**				
▲ **Nancy (Assoc)** "Chateau de Remicourt", 149, Rue de Vandoeuvre, 54600 Villers les Nancy.	☎ 0383277367 🛈 0383414135	60	02.01–23.12	⁖⁖ ⑩ 4SW ♿ CC P ☕
▲ **Nantes** - La Manu IBN 2 Place de la Manu, 44000 Nantes (Loire-Atlantique).	☎ 0240292920 🛈 0240292920	73	01.07–12.09	⑩ ♿ ☛ ☕
▲ **Nantes** - Porte Neuve (Assoc) 1 place Ste Elisabeth, 44042 Nantes Cedex 01 (Loire Atlantique).	☎ 0240206363 🛈 0240206379	50	🗓	⁖⁖ ⑩ CC ☛ P ⓞ ☕

Location/Address	Telephone No. Fax No.	Beds	Opening Dates	Facilities
▲ **Nantes** - Port Beaùlieu (Assoc) FJT, 9 Bd Vincent Gâche, 44200 Nantes (Loire Atlantique).	☎ 0240122400 🖷 0251820005	66	01.06–31.08	� ⓧ [3S] ⓓ [CC] ⛶ P ⓪ ☕
▲ **Nice** [IBN] Route Forestière du Mont Alban, 06300 Nice (Alpes-Maritimes).	☎ 0493892364 🖷 0492040310	56	[12]	[2E] ⛶ P ⓪
▲ **Nîmes** [IBN] Chemin de la Cigale, 30900 Nîmes (Gard). ℮ nimes@fuaj.org	☎ 0466232504 🖷 0466238427	75	01.04–31.12	� ⓧ [3NW] ⓓ [CC] ⛶ P ⓪ ☕
▲ **Nouméa** City Hostel, 51 bis rue Olry, BP 767, 98845 Nouméa Cedex (New Caledonia).	☎ 0687275879 🖷 0687254817	94	[12]	(R) [CC] ⛶ P ⓪
▲ **Paimpol** Château de Kerraoul, 22500 Paimpol (Côtes-d'Armor).	☎ 0296208360 🖷 0296209646	80	[12]	� ⓧ (R) [2W] [CC] ⛶ P
▲ **Paris** - Cité des Sciences [IBN] 24, Rue des Sept Arpents, 93310 Le Pré St Gervais. ℮ paris.cite-des-sciences@fuaj.org	☎ 0148432411 🖷 0148432682	184	[12]	� ⓧ [5NE] ⓓ [CC] ⛶ P ⓪
▲ **Paris** - Le d'Artagnan [IBN] **80 rue Vitruve, 75020 Paris.** ℮ paris.le-dartagnan@fuaj.org	☎ 0140323456 🖷 0140323455	439	[12]	� ⓧ (R) [3E] ⓓ [CC] ⓪ ☕
▲ **Paris** - Jules Ferry 8 Boulevard Jules Ferry, 75011 Paris. ℮ paris.jules-ferry@fuaj.org	☎ 0143575560 🖷 0143148209	99	[12]	ⓧ (R) [CC] ⛶ ⓪
▲ **Paris** - Clichy [IBN] "Léo Lagrange", 107 Rue Martre, 92110 Clichy. ℮ paris.clichy@fuaj.org	☎ 0141272690 🖷 0142705263	340	[12]	ⓧ (R) [CC] ⛶ P ⓪ ☕
▲ **Parthenay** Periscope, 16, Rue Blaise Pascal, 79200 Parthenay. ℮ periscope@district-parthenay.fr	☎ 0549954689 🖷 0549946485	105	[12]	� ⓧ (R) [0.8S] ⓓ ⛶ P ⓪ ☕
▲ **Pau-Gelos** (Assoc) FJT, Logis des Jeunes, Base de Plein Air, 64110 Gelos. ℮ logis.des.jeunes.pau@wanadoo.fr	☎ 0559065302 🖷 0559110520	40	[12]	[3SE] ⛶ P ⓪ ☕
▲ **Périgueux** (Assoc) FJT Rue des Thermes Prolongés, 24000 Périgueux (Dordogne). ℮ fjtdordogne@wanadoo.fr	☎ 0553068140 🖷 0553068149	16	[12]	ⓧ (R) [0.5S] P ⓪ ☕
△ *Perpignan* *Parc de la Pépinière, Av de Grande-Bretagne, 66000 Perpignan (Pyrénées-Orientales).*	☎ *0468346332* 🖷 *0468511602*	*49*	*20.01–20.12*	⛶
△ *Plouguernevel (Assoc)* *AJ Verte/Country Hostel, Village Vacances de Kermarc'h, 22110 Plouguernevel.*	☎ *0296291095*	*25*	[12]	[4W] ⛶ P ⓪
▲ **Poggio Mezzana** [IBN] **"L'Avillanella", 20230 Poggio Mezzana (Corse).**	☎ 0495385010 🖷 0495385011	100	01.04–30.10	� ⓧ (R) [2E] P ☕

Location/Address	Telephone No. Fax No.	Beds	Opening Dates	Facilities
▲ **Poitiers** `IBN` **1 Allée Roger Tagault, 86000 Poitiers (Vienne).** ℮ poitiers@fuaj.org	☎ 0549300970 🖷 0549300979	132	03.01–31.12	⁑ �ⓄⓁ 3SW ⅊ CC ⌁ P ☕
△ *Pontarlier* *2 rue Jouffroy, 25300 Pontarlier (Doubs).*	☎ 0381390657 🖷 0381390657	72	*20.12–11.11*	⁑ ⓄⓁ Ⓡ 0.1N ⌁ P ☕
▲ **Pontivy** Ile des Récollets, 56300 Pontivy (Morbihan).	☎ 0297255827 🖷 0297257648	65	04.01–22.12	⁑ ⓄⓁ 0.2N ⌁ P ⊡
△ *Pontorson (Assoc)* *Centre Duguesclin, 21 rue Patton,* *50170 Pontorson (Manche).*	☎ 0233601865 🖷 0233601865	57	🔲12	⁑ Ⓡ 0.5NW ⅊ ⌁ P
△ *Quimper (Assoc)* *Auberge de Jeunesse, 6 ave des Oiseaux,* *29000 Quimper (Finistère).*	☎ 0298649797 🖷 0298553837	54	*05.01–23.12*	ⓄⓁ Ⓡ 1W ⌁ P
▲ **Redon (Assoc)** Mapar, 2, Rue Chantebel, BP 101, 35603 Redon Cedex (Ille et Vilaine). ℮ mapar@wanadoo.fr	☎ 0299721439 🖷 0299721653	20	01.06–31.08	ⓄⓁ Ⓡ 0.5N ⌁ P ⊡ ☕
▲ **Reims (Assoc)** Centre International de Séjour, Chaussée Bocquaire, Allée Polonceau, 51100 Reims (Marne).	☎ 0326405260 🖷 0326473570	150	02.01–24.12	⁑ ⓄⓁ Ⓡ 0.5W ⅊ CC ⌁ P ⊡
Reims ☞ **Verzy**				
▲ **Rennes** `IBN` **10-12 Canal Saint-Martin,** **35700 Rennes (Ille-et-Vilaine).**	☎ 0299332233 🖷 0299590621	96	03.01–24.12	⁑ ⓄⓁ Ⓡ 1.5N ⅊ CC ⌁ P ⊡ ☕
▲ **Roanne** AJ "Centre Jeunesse Pierre Bérégovoy", 4 Rue Fontenille, 42300 Roanne (Loire).	☎ 0477725211 🖷 0477706628	60	🔲12	ⓄⓁ ⅊ ⌁ ⊡ ☕
△ *Rochefort-sur-Mer (Assoc)* *Logis Etape/AJ, 20 rue de la République,* *17300 Rochefort-sur-Mer.* ℮ *jeunesserochefort@neotech.fr*	☎ 0546997462 (in July & August), 0546821040 🖷 0546992125, 0546997462	50	*01.07–31.08*	⁑ ⓄⓁ Ⓡ ⌁ ⊡
▲ **Rodez (Assoc)** AJ/FJT, "Les Quatre Saisons", 26 Bd des Capucines, 12034 Rodez Cedex 9 (Aveyron). ℮ assoc.fjt.gd.rodez@wanadoo.fr	☎ 0565775105 🖷 0565673797	60	🔲12	⁑ ⓄⓁ 3N ⅊ CC P ⊡ ☕
▲ **Rodome (Assoc)** AJ Verte/Country Hostel, Ferme Équestre H'Val, 11140 Rodome. ℮ h-val@club-internet.fr	☎ 0468203222 🖷 0468207610	19	15.02–15.11	⁑ ⓄⓁ ⌁
▲ **Saintes** 2 Place Geoffroy Martel, 17100 Saintes (Charente-Maritime). ℮ saintes@fuaj.org	☎ 0546921492 🖷 0546929782	70	🔲12	⁑ ⓄⓁ ⅊ ⌁ P

Location/Address	Telephone No. Fax No.	Beds	Opening Dates	Facilities
▲ **St Brevin** - Les Pins "La Pinède", 1 Allée de la Jeunesse, 44250 St-Brévin Les Pins (Loire Atlantique).	☎ 0240272527 ✆ 0240644877	59	08.02–09.10; 01.11–02.01	♦♦♦ ⑩ ⓡ ⓪.⑤W ⚲ P ☕
▲ **Saint-Brieuc** **Manoir de la Ville Guyomard,** **Les Villages, 22000** **St-Brieuc (Côtes-d'Armor).** 📧 saint-brieuc@fuaj.org	☎ 0296787070 ✆ 0296782747	127	⑫	♦♦♦ ⑩ ⓡ ③NW ♿ ⌫CC⌫ ⚲ P ⓞ
△ *Saint Etienne* - *Les Echandes* *AJ Verte/Country Hostel,* *"Les Echandes" Lieudit "Le Pertuiset",* *42240 Unieux (Loire): St Etienne 10km.*	☎ *0477357294* ✆ *0477357294*	*49*	*01.05–01.11;* *(♦♦♦* *01.03–15.12)*	♦♦♦ ⓡ ②S ⚲ P
Les Echandes ☞ **Saint-Etienne**				
▲ **Saint-Gaudens** (Assoc) "Le Venasque", 3 Rue de la Résidence, 31804 Saint-Gaudens Cedex.	☎ 0561947273 ✆ 0561947274	20	02.01–30.12	♦♦♦ ⑩ ⓪.⑤W P ⓞ ☕
△ *Saint-Guen* *AJ Verte/Country Hostel, 10, Rue du Sénéchal,* *22530 St Guen (Côtes d'Armor).*	☎ *0296285434* ✆ *0296260156*	*40*	*01.04–01.11*	♦♦♦ ⑩ ⓡ ⑤W ♿ ⚲ P ⓞ
▲ **Saint-Junien** Auberge de St. Amand, 13 rue de St. Amand, 87200 St. Junien (Haute-Vienne).	☎ 0555022279 ✆ 0555022279	50	⑫	♦♦♦ ①SW ⚲ P
▲ **Saint-Malo** CRI Patrick Varangeot, 37 Av du RP Umbricht, BP 108, 35407 St-Malo Cedex (Bretagne).	☎ 0299402980 ✆ 0299402902	150	⑫	♦♦♦ ⑩ ①NE ♿ ⌫CC⌫ ⚲ P ⓞ ☕
△ *Saint-Martin des Olmes* (Assoc) *"Auberge de Saint Martin" Le Bourg,* *St Martin des Olmes 63600* *Ambert (Puy de Dome).*	☎ *0473820138* ✆ *0473820138*	*49*	*15.02–15.11* *(♦♦♦ ⑫)*	♦♦♦ ⑩ ⓡ ⑥E ⚲ P ⓞ
△ *Saint-Mihiel* *12 rue sur Meuse, 55300 St-Mihiel (Meuse).*	☎ *0329891506* ✆ *0329891506*	*60*	*03.04–30.11* *(♦♦♦ ⑫)*	♦♦♦ ⑩ ⚲
Saint-Raphaël ☞ **Fréjus**				
△ *Saverne* *Château des Rohan, 67700 Saverne* *(Bas-Rhin).* 📧 *saverne@fuaj.org*	☎ *0388911484* ✆ *0388711597*	*86*	*15.01–15.12*	♦♦♦ ⑩ P
△ *Savines-le-Lac* *"Les Chaumettes", 05160 Savines-le-Lac* *(Hautes-Alpes).*	☎ *0492442016* ✆ *0492442454*	*50*	*01.04–30.11*	♦♦♦ ⑩ ⓪.⑧SW ♿ ⚲ P ☕
▲ **Seez Les Arcs** "La Verdache", 73700 Seez (Savoie). 📧 seez-les-arcs@fuaj.org	☎ 0479410193 ✆ 0479410336	80	19.12–30.09; (♦♦♦ ⑫)	♦♦♦ ⑩ ⓡ ♿ ⌫CC⌫ P ☕
▲ **Serre-Chevalier** Le Bez, BP2, 05240 Serre-Chevalier (Hautes-Alpes). 📧 serre-chevalier@fuaj.org	☎ 0492247454 ✆ 0492248339	130	⑫	♦♦♦ ⑩ ⓡ ⓪.⑤SW ⌫CC⌫ ⚲ P ☕

Location/Address	Telephone No. Fax No.	Beds	Opening Dates	Facilities
▲ **Sète** [IBN] "Villa Salis", rue du Général Revest, 34200 Sète (Hérault)	☎ 0467534668 🛈 0467513401	80	15.01–15.12	♦♦♦ ⑩ (R) [CC] P 🍴
▲ **Strasbourg** - Parc du Rhin [IBN] Rue des Cavaliers, BP 58, 67017 Strasbourg Cedex (Bas-Rhin) ✉ strasbourg.parc-du.rhin@fuaj.org	☎ 0388455420 🛈 0388455421	221	01.01–20.12	⑩ (R) [4E] ♿ [CC] ☞ P 🔲 🍴
▲ **Strasbourg** - René Cassin [IBN] **9 rue de l'Auberge de Jeunesse,** **67200 Strasbourg (Bas-Rhin).**	☎ 0388302646 🛈 0388303516	280	01.02–31.12	♦♦♦ ⑩ [2SW] ♿ ☞ P 🍴
△ *Tarascon* *31 Boulevard Gambetta,* *13150 Tarascon (Bouches-du-Rhône).* ✉ *tarascon@fuaj.org*	☎ 0490910408 🛈 0490915417	65	01.03–15.12	♦♦♦ ⑩ [0.5SE] ☞ P
▲ **Tarbes** (Assoc) 88 Rue Alsace Lorraine, 65000 Tarbes.	☎ 0562389120 🛈 0562376981	58	🔲12	♦♦♦ ⑩ [2N] ♿ ☞ P 🔲 🍴
Théoule-sur-Mer ☞ **Le Trayas**				
▲ **Thionville** (Assoc) Centre Européen de Séjour/AJ, 3 Place de la Gare, 57100 Thionville.	☎ 0382563214, 0382561606	60	🔲12	♦♦♦ ⑩ [0.5E] ☞ P
△ *Thouars (Assoc)* *F.J.T./AJ "Hector Etoubleau",* *5 Boulevard du 8 Mai, BP 77, 79102* *Thouars Cedex*	☎ 0549662240 🛈 0549661074	19	🔲12	⑩ [1N] ♿ P 🔲
▲ **Tignes** "Les Clarines", 73320 Tignes. ✉ tignes@fuaj.org	☎ 0479063507; 0479410193 (R) 🛈 0479410336	66	28.06–02.05; (♦♦♦ 🔲12)	⑩ (R) [6SW] [CC] P 🍴
△ *Tours* [IBN] *Ave D'Arsonval, Parc de Grandmont,* *37200 Tours (Indre-et-Loire).*	☎ 0247251445 🛈 0247482659	170	🔲12	♦♦♦ ⑩ (R) [4S] ♿ [CC] ☞ P 🔲
△ *Trébeurden* *Le Toëno, Route de la Corniche,* *22560 Trébeurden (Côtes-d'Armor).*	☎ 0296235222 🛈 0296154434	56	20.01–20.11	⑩ [1N] ☞
▲ **Troyes-Rosières** Chemin Ste Scholastique 10430, Rosières (Aube). ✉ troyes-rosieres@fuaj.org	☎ 0325820065 🛈 0325729378	104	🔲12	♦♦♦ ⑩ (R) [5SW] ♿ ☞ P
Unieux ☞ **Saint-Etienne**				
▲ **Valence** (Assoc) Vacanciel l'Epervière, Chemin de l'Epervière, 26000 Valence (Drome).	☎ 0475423200 🛈 0475562067	60	🔲12	♦♦♦ ⑩ [25S] ♿ [CC] P 🔲 🍴
▲ **Val Cenis Lanslebourg** Hameau des Champs, 73480 Lanslebourg/Mont-Cenis (Savoie). ✉ valcenis@fuaj.org	☎ 0479059096 🛈 0479058252	75	01.12–30.04; 15.06–20.09; 15.05–15.06 (♦♦♦ (R))	⑩ [1E] [CC] ☞ P

Location/Address	Telephone No. Fax No.	Beds	Opening Dates	Facilities
▲ **Vesolil** Ave des Rives du Lac, 70000 Vaivre Montoille.	☎ 0384764855, 0384762286 ✉ 0384757493	72	🗓	R 3W P
Vénissieux ☞ **Lyon-Vénissieux**				
△ *Ventron* *AJ Verte/Country Hostel, "Les Roches",* *8 Chemin de Fondronfaing,* *88310 Ventron (Vosges).*	☎ *0329241956*	*35*	🗓	ⅲ R 2S CC ⛄ P 🅾
▲ **Verdun** AJ Centre Mondial de la Paix, Place Monseigneur Ginisty, 55100 Verdun.	☎ 0329862828 ✉ 0329862882	69	01.02–31.12	ⅲ 🍽 R 0.2SW ♿ P ☕
△ *Vernon (Assoc)* *Centre d'Hebergement Ile de France,* *28 Av de l'Ile-de-France,* *27200 Vernon (Eure).*	☎ *0232516648* ✉ *0232212341*	*24*	*01.04–30.09*	ⅲ R 3W ⛄
△ *Verzy* *16 Rue du Bassin, 51380 Verzy (Marne).*	☎ *0326979010*	*48*	*01.03–30.11*	ⅲ 🍽 0.2W ♿ ⛄ P
Vesoul ☞ **Vaivre**				
▲ **Vienne (Assoc)** 11 Quai Riondet, 38200 Vienne.	☎ 0474532197 ✉ 0474319893	56	Closed Sun 16.09–15.05	ⅲ 🍽 0.2S ⛄ P
△ *Vierzon* *1 rue François Mitterrand,* *18100 Vierzon (Cher).* ✉ *vierzon@fuaj.org*	☎ *0248753062* ✉ *0248711903*	*83*	*02.01–24.12*	ⅲ 🍽 0.3W ⛄ P 🅾 ☕
△ *Villefranche de Rouergue (Assoc)* *FJT du Rouergue, Rue Lapeyrade,* *Place de La Gare, 12200* *Villefranche de Rouergue (Aveyron).*	☎ *0565450968* ✉ *0565456226*	*6*	🗓	🍽 0.5W ♿ ⛄ P 🅾 ☕
△ *Woerth* *10 rue du Moulin, 67360 Woerth (Bas-Rhin).* ✉ *woerth@fuaj.org*	☎ *0388540330* ✉ *0388095832*	*60*	*01.03–01.11*	ⅲ 🍽 0.5E ⛄ P 🅾

YOUTH HOSTEL ACCOMMODATION
OUTSIDE THE ASSURED STANDARDS SCHEME

Blois - Les Grouëts 18 rue de l'Hôtel Pasquier, Les Grouëts, 41000 Blois (Loir-et-Cher). ✉ blois@fuaj.org	☎ 0254782721 ✉ 0254782721	48	01.03–15.11	R 5W ⛄ P
Blois - Montlivault AJ Verte/Country Hostel, Levée de la Loire, Cedex 181, Montlivault, 41350 Vineuil (Loir-et-Cher).	☎ 0254782721 ✉ 0254782721	28	01.07–31.08	ⅲ R 1N ⛄ P
Cap Ferret AJ Verte/Country Hostel, 87 Ave de Bordeaux, 33970 Cap Ferret (Gironde).	☎ 0556606462	60	01.07–31.08	🍽 R 0.5E ⛄

Location/Address	Telephone No. Fax No.	Beds	Opening Dates	Facilities
Châlons en Champagne "L'Embellie""Square Antral", 6 rue Kellermann, 51000 Châlons-en-Champagne (Marne).	☎ 0326681356	40	🛏12	1 NE 🛡 P ⊡
Choucan Paimpont AJ Verte/Country Hostel, Choucan, Paimpont, 35380 Plélan-le-Grand (Ille-et-Vilaine).	☎ 0297227675	24	01.05–30.09	4 NW 🛡 P ⊡
Lautenbach AJ Verte/Country Hostel, "Dynamo", La Schellimatt, 68610 Lautenbach (Haut-Rhin)	☎ 0389742681	30	Weekends + School holidays	R 8 NW 🛡 ⊡
Maël-Pestivien (Assoc) "Ferme -Manoir de Kérauffret", 22160 Maël Pestivien.	☎ 0296457528	15	01.04–31.10	�🍴 3 E 🛡 P ⊡
Montreuil-Sur-Mer (Assoc) AJ Verte/Country Hostel, "La Hulotte", Citadelle, rue Carnot, 62170 Montreuil-Sur-Mer (Pas de Calais).	☎ 0321061083 📠 0321061083	43	01.03–30.10	⭥⭥ 0.2 W 🛡
Oinville AJ Verte/Country Hostel "Relais Randonnée", Impasse 10 bis de la rue de Gournay, Oinville-sur-Montcient, 78250 Meulan (Yvelines).	☎ 0134753391 📠 0134753391	19	🛏12	⭥⭥ 🍴 0.5 NW 🛡 ⊡
Phalsbourg (Assoc) Centre Européen de Rencontres, 6 Rue de Général Rottembourg, 57370 Phalsbourg.	☎ 0387243737 📠 0387241356	76	🛏12	🍴 0.4 S ♿ CC P ☕
Puicheric 2 rue Marcellin Albert, 11700 Puicheric.	☎ 0468437381 📠 0468437184	10	🛏12	⭥⭥ 🍴 R 🛡 ⊡
Quiberon "Les Filets Bleus", 45 rue du Roch Priol, 56170 Quiberon (Morbihan).	☎ 0297501554	28	01.05–30.09	1 S ♿ 🛡 P
Salies-de-Béarn AJ Verte/Country Hostel, Route du Padu, 64270 Salies-de-Béarn (Pyrénées-Atlantiques).	☎ 0559650696 📠 0559650696	16	🛏12	0.4 W 🛡 P
Vézelay (Assoc) AJ Verte/Country Hostel, Route de l'Etang, 89450 Vézelay (Yonne).	☎ 0386332418 📠 0386332418	40	01.02–31.12 (R 01.02–30.06; 01.09–31.12)	⭥⭥ R 0.6 SE 🛡 P
Yvetot AJ Verte/Country Hostel, 4 rue de la Briqueterie, 76190 Yvetot (Seine Maritime).	☎ 0235953701	8	01.04–31.10	⭥⭥ 🍴 0.8 NE 🛡 P

Germany

ALLEMAGNE

DEUTSCHLAND

ALEMANIA

Deutsches Jugendherbergswerk,
Hauptverband für Jugendwandern,
und Jugendherbergen e.V.,
im GILDE Zentrum, Bad Meinberger Str. 1,
D-32760 Detmold, Germany.

☎ (49) (5231) 9936-0
⊕ (49) (5231) 9936-66,(49) (5231) 9995-90
℮ info@djh.org
www.djh.de

Office Hours: Monday-Thursday 08.00-16.30hrs; Fri 08.00-14.30hrs.

Travel Section:
DJH Service GmbH
Postfach 1462
32704 Detmold, Germany.

☎ (49) (5231) 7401-0
⊕ (49) (5231) 7401-49
℮ service@djh.de
www.djh.de

Office Hours: Monday-Thursday 08.00-16.30hrs; Fri 08.00-14.30hrs.

Capital:	Berlin		**Population:**	81,817,499
Language:	German		**Size:**	356,978 sq km
Currency:	DM (Deutsche Mark)		**Telephone Country Code:**	49

GERMANY

This area appears on the page following the next

DENMARK

NETHERLANDS

HAMBURG

BREMEN

HANNOVER

BRAUN-SCHWEIG

KASSEL

0   50   100   KMS
   25   50   MLS

N

List-Mövenbeg
Hörnum
Niebüll
Flensburg
Wyk
Kappeln
Wittdün
Schleswig
Eckern-förde
Husum
Borgwedel
Aschberg
Tönning
Friedrich-stadt
Kiel
Helgoland
Heide
Rends-burg
Westen-see
Büsum
Albersdorf
Neu-münster
St. Michaelis-donn
Cuxhaven
Itzehoe
Bad Segeberg
Lange-Spieker-oog
Wanger-ooge
Ottern-dorf
Norderney
Schillig-hörn
Glückstadt
Juist
Esens
Carolin-ensiel
Bad Bederkesa
Wingst
Borkum
Nordeich
Ben-sersiel
Jever
Wüste-wohlde
Stade
Greetsiel
Wilhelms-haven
Tossens
Norden-ham
Bremer-haven
HAMBURG
Hamburg (2)
Emden
Aurich
Bremervörde
Geest-hacht
Rutteler feld
Leer
Wester-stede
Zeven-Bademühlen
Lüneburg
Olden-burg
Worpswede
Inzmühlen
Papenburg
Zwischenahn
Sand-hatten
Hude
BREMEN
Bremen JGH
Rotenbug
Bispingen
Börger
Syke
Verden
Haren
Thülsfelder Talsperre
Müden
Fallingbostel
Uelsen
Lingen
Damme
Nienburg
Celle
Mardorfa
Bad Bentheim
Osnabrück
Bad Essen
Röding-hausen
Porta Westfalica
Graf-horn
Rheine
Tecklen-burg
Rohden
Springe
Hildes-heim
Bad Iburg
Melle
Löhne
Gohfeld
Vlotho
Rinteln
Bielefeld
Oerling-hausen
Hameln
Lauen-stein
Goslar
Detmold
Blomberg
Boden-werder
Bad Gan-dersheim
Hahnenklee Altenau
Horn-BadMeinberg
Holzminden
Silber-born
Clausthal-Zellerfeld
Paderborn
Bad Dribug
Höxter
Uslar
Northeim
Wewels-burg
Helmars-hausen
Bad Karls-hafen
Göttingen
Bad Lauter-berg
Brilon
Hann. Münden
Willingen
Korbach
Steinber-haus
Burg Ludwigstein
Martinfeld
Mühl-hausen
Hohe Fahrt
Waldeck
Melsungen
Eschwege
Burg Hessenstein
Mosenberg

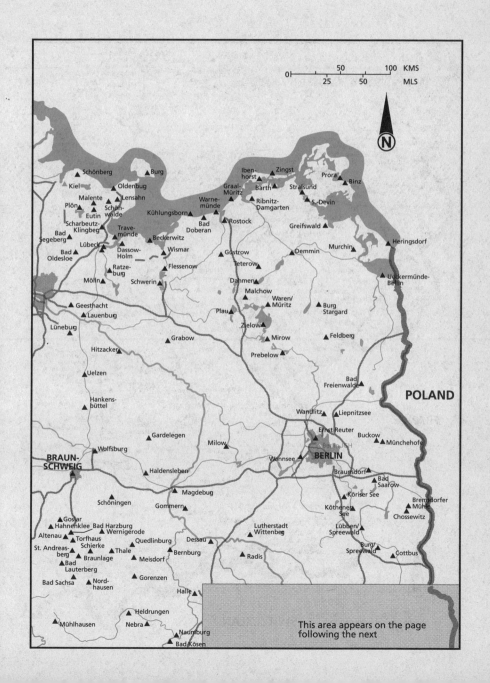

0 | 50 | 100 KMS
25 | 50 MLS

N

Schönberg
Burg
Kiel
Oldenbug
Malente
Lensahn
Eutin
Plön
Schön-
walde
Scharbeutz-
Klingbeg
Bad
Segeberg
Lübeck
Travemünde
Bad
Oldesloe
Dassow-
Holm
Mölln
Ratzeburg
Geesthacht
Lauenburg
Lüneburg
Hitzacker
Uelzen
Hankensbüttel
BRAUN-
SCHWEIG
Wolfsburg
Haldensleben
Gardelegen
Schöningen
Gosiar
Hahnenklee Bad Harzburg
Altenau
Torfhaus
St. Andreas-
berg
Schierke
Braunlage
Bad
Lauterberg
Bad Sachsa
Nordhausen
Mühlhausen
Heldrungen
Nebra

Iben-
horst
Zingst
Prora
Binz
Barth
Stralsund
Graal-
Müritz
Ribnitz-
Damgarten
S-Devin
Warnemünde
Kühlungsborn
Bad
Doberan
Rostock
Greifswald
Heringsdorf
Beckerwitz
Wismar
Güstrow
Demmin
Murchin
Flessenow
Teterow
Dahmen
Uckermünde-
Berlin
Schwerin
Malchow
Waren/
Müritz
Burg
Stargard
Plau
Zielow
Mirow
Feldberg
Grabow
Prebelow
Bad
Freienwalde

POLAND

Wandlitz
Liepnitzsee
Ernst Reuter
Buckow
Milow
Münchehofe
Wannsee
BERLIN
Braunsdorf
Bad
Saarow
Magdebug
Köriser See
Bremsdorfer
Mühle
Gommern
Köthener
See
Chossewitz
Lutherstadt
Wittenbeg
Lübben/
Spreewald
Quedlinburg
Dessau
Bernburg
Burg/
Spreewald
Meisdorf
Radis
Cottbus
Gorenzen
Halle
Naumburg
Bad Kösen

This area appears on the page
following the next

This area appears on the page following the next

KASSEL

Willingen
Korbach
Steinberghaus
Hohe Fahrt
Waldeck
Burg Ludwigstein
Martinfeld
Mühlhausen
Burg Hessenstein
Melsungen
Eschwege
Mosenberg
Rotenburg a.d. Fulda
Eisenach
Inselsberg
Brotterode

Marbug
Lauterbach
Bad Salzungen

Rutberg
Nideggen
Bad Münster-eifel
Bad Honnef
Bad Neuenahr-Ahrweiler
Wetzlar
Gießen
Hilders
Monschau
Gemünd
Hellenthal
Blankenheim
Altenahr
Koblenz
Weilbug
Laubach
Hoherodskopf
Fulda
Oberbernhards

Prüm
Gerolstein
Mayen
Dietz
Limbug a.d.
Grävenwiesbach
Bad Homburg
Büdingen
Gersfeld
Bischofsheim
Daun
Brodenbach
Bad Ems
Oberreifenbeg

Manderscheid
Cochem
St. Goar
Linsengericht
Königsberg

Traben-Trabach
Oberwesel
Bacharach
Wiesbaden
FRANKFURT
Aschaffenbug
Löhr
Schweinfurt

Bollendorf
Bingen
Rüdesheim
Maing
Würzburg

Bernkastel-Kues
Sargenroth
Bad Kreuznach
Darmstadt
Rothenfels

Trier
Hermeskeil
Idar-Oberstein
Steinbach
Worms
Breubeg
Zwingenbeg
Wertheim
Würzburg

Saarburg
Weiskirchen
Burg Lichtenberg
Tholey
Wolfstein
Altleiningen
Heppenheim
Erbach
Amorbach
Tauberbischofsheim
Ochsenfurt

Dreisbach
Hochspeyer
Weinheim
Walldürn
Weikersheim
Creglingen

Saarbrücken
Homburg
Mannheim
Heidelberg
Eberbach
Igersheim

Merzalben
Neustadt
Dilsberg
Mosbach
Rothenburg

Dahn
Speyer
Kirchberg
Feuchtwangen

Bad Bergzabern
Heilbronn
Schwäbisch Hall
Rechenberg
Gunzenhausen
Dinkelsbühl

Karlsruhe
Murrhardt
Ellwangen

Pforzheim
Ludwigsburg
STUTTGART
Aalen
Nördlingen

Baden-Baden
Bad Herrenalb
Hohenstaufen
Königsbronn
Donauwörth

FRANCE
Herrenwies
Forbach
Esslingen
Heidenheim

Kehl
Sohlberg
Tübingen
Bad Urach

Zuflucht
Freudenstadt
Dornstetten-Halfwangen
Ulm
Günzburg

Alpirsbach
Erpfingen
Blaubeuren

Balingen
Rottweil
Lochen

Breisach
Freiburg
Villingen
Sigmaringen
Biberach

Todtnauberg
Titisee-Neustadt
Burg Wildenstein
Memmingen

Wieden
Feldberg
Bonndorf
Ottobeuren

Platzhof
Menzenschwand
Schluchsee
Seebrugg
Singen
Überlingen
Ravensburg

Lörrach
Konstanz
Friedrichshafen
Isny
Kempten

Lindau
Füssen

Oberstdorf-Kornau

N

0   50   100 KMS
  25   50   MLS

SWITZERLAND

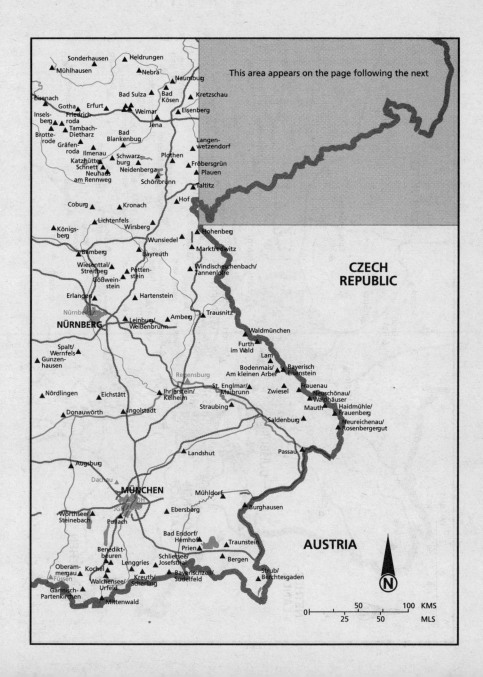

This area appears on the page following the next

Sonderhausen
Mühlhausen
Heldrungen
Nebra
Naumbug
Bad Sulza
Bad Kösen
Kretzschau
Eisenach
Gotha
Inselsberg
Friedrichroda
Erfurt
Weimar
Eisenberg
Brotterode
Tambach-Dietharz
Jena
Gräfenroda
Bad Blankenbug
Ilmenau
Langenwetzendorf
Katzhütte
Schwarzburg
Plothen
Schnett
Neidenberga
Fröbersgrün
Neuhaus am Rennweg
Schönbrunn
Plauen
Taltitz
Coburg
Kronach
Hof
Königsberg
Lichtenfels
Wirsberg
Hohenberg
Bamberg
Wunsiedel
Marktredwitz
Wiesenttal/Streitberg
Bayreuth
Pottenstein
Windischeschenbach/Tannenlohe
Gößweinstein
Erlangen
Hartenstein

CZECH REPUBLIC

Nürnberg
Leinburg/Weißenbrunn
Amberg
Trausnitz
NÜRNBERG
Waldmünchen
Spalt/Wernfels
Furth im Wald
Lam
Gunzenhausen
Bodenmais/Am kleinen Arber
Bayerisch Eisenstein
Nördlingen
Eichstätt
Ihrlerstein/Kelheim
St. Englmar/Maibrunn
Zwiesel
Frauenau
Neuschönau/Waldhäuser
Regensburg
Mauth
Haidmühle/Frauenberg
Donauwörth
Ingolstadt
Straubing
Saldenburg
Neureichenau/Rosenbergergut

Augsburg
Landshut
Passau
Dachau
MÜNCHEN
Mühldorf
Wörthsee/Steinebach
Ebersberg
Burghausen
Putlach
Bad Endorf/Hemhof
Prien
Traunstein
AUSTRIA
Benediktbeuren
Schliersee/Josefsthal
Bergen
Oberammergau
Kochel
Lenggries
Bayerischzell/Sudelfeld
Strub/Berchtesgaden
Füssen
Walchensee/Urfeld
Kreuth/Scharling
Garmisch-Partenkirchen
Mittenwald

0 1   25   50   100 KMS

0 25 50 MLS

N

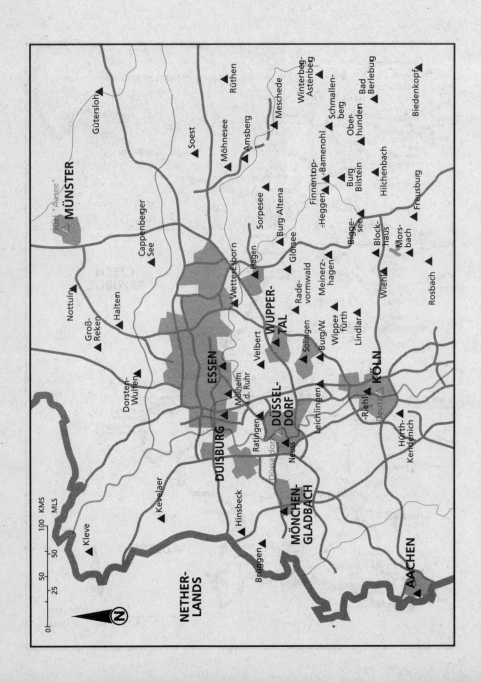

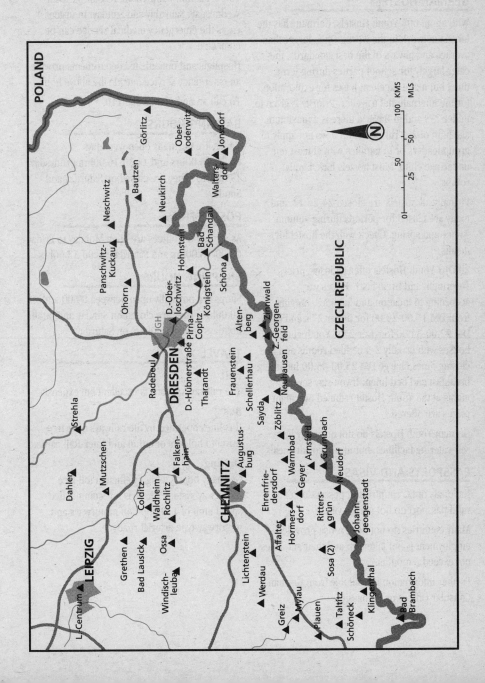

POLAND

Görlitz
Ober-
oderwitz
Jonsdorf
Neschwitz
Bautzen
Walters-
dorf
Neukirch
Panschwitz-
Kuckau
Bad
Schandau
Ohorn
Hohnstein
Schöna
D.-Ober-
loschwitz
Copitz
Königstein
Zinnwald
Pirna
Altenberg
Z.-Georgen-
feld
Radebeul
DRESDEN
D.-Hübnerstraße
Tharandt
Frauenstein
Schellerhau
Neuhausen
Strehla
Sayda
Zöblitz
Dahlen
Mutzschen
Falken-
hain
Augustus-
burg
Warmbad
Geyer
Arnsfeld
Grumbach
Colditz
Waldheim
Rochlitz
CHEMNITZ
Ehrenfrie-
dersdorf
Neudorf
Grethen
Bad Lausick
Ossa
Lichtenstein
Affalter
Hormers-
dorf
Ritters-
grün
Johann-
georgenstadt
LEIPZIG
L. Centrum
Windisch-
leuba
Werdau
Mylau
Sosa (2)
Greiz
Plauen
Talttz
Schöneck
Klingenthal
Bad
Brambach

CZECH REPUBLIC

N

100 KMS
50   MLS

50   50
0   25

English

GERMAN HOSTELS

With about 605 Youth Hostels, Germany has the largest network in the world. Often larger than average and always of the best standards, they cater largely for school parties during term time, but make excellent bases for exploration for the international traveller. Priority is given to under 27s and in Bavaria there is a maximum age limit of 26. This age limit does not apply to group leaders or to families with at least one under-age child. Most hostels have family rooms.

Virtually all hostels are closed 24-26.12, and many are closed for periods during autumn, winter and spring. Check with the hostel for details.

All DJH Youth Hostels offer inclusive prices (overnight and breakfast). Prices vary according to location and facilities, ranging from DM 17.00-29.00 for under 27's and from DM 22.00-34.00 for over 27's. Youth guest houses with usually 2-4 bedded rooms and late closing times charge DM 25.00-45.00 including breakfast and bed linen. If you stay several nights at the Youth Hostel reduced overnight prices are offered.

German Youth Hostels do not normally have self-catering facilities, but most provide meals.

PASSPORTS AND VISAS

Nationals of EC countries in possession of a valid passport do not need a visa.

Many countries do not need a visa provided employment is not taken up and their stay does not exceed 3 months.

Further information is available from German Consular Offices or Embassies.

HEALTH

Doctors' consulting hours are normally 10.00-12.00hrs and 16.00-18.00hrs except Wednesday, Saturday and Sunday. In urgent cases the emergency medical service can be contacted.

Hospitals and outpatients' departments provide an emergency service outside the above hours.

To call an ambulance dial 110.

BANKING HOURS

Banks are normally open weekdays 08.30-13.00hrs and 14.30-16.00hrs (Thursday 17.30hrs). They are closed on Saturday and Sunday.

POST OFFICES

As a rule post offices are open Monday to Friday 08.00-18.00hrs and Saturday 08.00-12.00hrs.

SHOPPING HOURS

Shops are normally open between 09.00 and 20.00hrs. They are closed on Sunday and public holidays and at 16.00hrs on Saturday.

TRAVEL

Rail
The railway network is excellent but expensive.

Bus
Bus lines operated by the railways offer free travel to holders of Eurail and Inter-Rail cards.

Driving
Germany boasts a highly efficient toll-free motorway system. There is a recommended speed limit of 130kmph on motorways and motorway-type arterial roads.

Français

AUBERGES DE JEUNESSE ALLEMANDES

Avec environ 605 auberges de jeunesse, l'Allemagne a le réseau le plus vaste du monde. Souvent plus grandes que la normale, et toujours de très haute qualité, elles reçoivent fréquemment des groupes d'écoliers pendant l'année scolaire, mais constituent une base excellente pour le voyageur international. Priorité est donnée aux moins de 27 ans et, en Bavière, l'âge limite supérieur est 26 ans. Cette limite d'âge ne s'applique ni aux chefs de groupe ni aux familles avec au moins un enfant mineur. La plupart des auberges offrent des chambres familiales.

Pratiquement toutes les auberges sont fermées du 24 au 26 décembre et beaucoup d'entre elles ferment pendant certaines périodes en automne, en hiver et au printemps. Vérifiez auprès de l'auberge en question.

Toutes les auberges de jeunesse de DJH offrent un prix tout compris (nuitée et petit déjeuner). Les prix varient selon les endroits et les services offerts et vont de DM 17,00-29,00 pour les moins de 27 ans et de DM 22,00-34,00 pour les plus de 27 ans. Une nuit dans un centre d'hébergement vous coûtera DM 25,00-45,00 petit déjeuner et linge compris. Si vous restez plusieurs jours à l'auberge de jeunesse, des réductions vous seront offertes.

Les auberges de jeunesse allemandes n'ont en principe pas de cuisine pour les voyageurs mais la plupart servent des repas.

PASSEPORTS ET VISAS

Les citoyens des pays de la CE munis d'un passeport valide n'ont pas besoin de visa.

Les ressortissants de nombreux pays n'ont pas besoin de visa s'ils s'engagent à ne pas prendre d'emploi et à ne pas séjourner plus de 3 mois.

De plus amples renseignements peuvent être obtenus auprès des bureaux du Consulat allemand ou des Ambassades.

SOINS MEDICAUX

Les médecins consultent normalement entre 10h et 12h et 16h et 18h sauf le mercredi, le samedi et le dimanche. En cas d'urgence, contacter le service des urgences.

Les hôpitaux et les services de consultations externes assurent un service d'urgences en dehors des heures mentionnées ci-dessus.

Pour appeler une ambulance, faites le 110.

HEURES D'OUVERTURE DES BANQUES

Les banques sont normalement ouvertes en semaine de 8h30 à 13h et de 14h30 à 16h (17h30 le jeudi). Elles sont fermées le samedi et le dimanche.

BUREAUX DE POSTE

Les bureaux de poste sont en principe ouverts du lundi au vendredi de 8h à 18h, et le samedi de 8h à 12h.

HEURES D'OUVERTURE DES MAGASINS

Les magasins sont en général ouverts entre 9h et 20h. Ils sont fermés le dimanche et les jours fériés et ferment à 16h le samedi.

DEPLACEMENTS

Trains
Le réseau ferroviaire est excellent mais cher.

Autobus
Les services d'autobus gérés par les chemins de fer offrent des voyages gratuits aux personnes munies de cartes Eurail et Inter-Rail.

Automobiles
L'Allemagne est fière de son excellent réseau autoroutier sans péage. La limite de vitesse conseillée est de 130 km/h sur les autoroutes et les grandes artères du genre autoroute.

Deutsch

DEUTSCHE JUGENDHERBERGEN

Mit etwa 605 Jugendherbergen hat Deutschland das größte Herbergsnetz der Welt. Die Herbergen sind oft überdurchschnittlich groß und immer von allerbestem Niveau. Während der Schulzeit werden sie hauptsächlich von Schulgruppen benutzt. Sie sind aber auch für Reisende aus der ganzen Welt ein hervorragendes Quartier zum näheren Kennenlernen der Umgebung. Junge Leute unter 27 Jahren werden bevorzugt aufgenommen. In Bayern beträgt die obere Altersgrenze 26 Jahre. Diese Altersbeschränkung gilt nicht für Gruppenleiter sowie für Familien mit mindestens einem minderjährigen Kind. Die meisten Herbergen haben Familienzimmer.

Fast alle Herbergen sind vom 24. bis 26.12. geschlossen und viele auch zu bestimmten Zeiten im Herbst, Winter und Frühling. Erkundigen Sie sich bei der betreffenden Herberge.

Alle Jugendherbergen des DJH bieten Übernachtung und Frühstück zu Inklusivpreisen an. Die Preise hängen von der Lage der Jugendherberge und der Ausstattung ab und liegen zwischen 17,00 DM und 29,00 DM für Junioren unter 27 Jahren und zwischen 22,00 DM und 34,00 DM für Senioren ab 27 Jahre. In Jugendgästehäusern (in der Regel 2-4-Bettzimmer und späte Schließzeiten) kostet die Übernachtung einschließlich Frühstück und Bettwäsche zwischen 25,00 DM und 45,00 DM. Bei mehrtägigen Aufenthalten in Jugendherbergen besteht die Möglichkeit von Preisnachlässen.

In deutschen Jugendherbergen gibt es gewöhnlich keine Einrichtungen zur Selbstversorgung. In den meisten werden aber Mahlzeiten angeboten.

PÄSSE UND VISA

Staatsangehörige aus EU-Ländern, die im Besitz eines gültigen Reisepasses sind, brauchen kein Visum.

Reisende aus vielen Ländern brauchen kein Visum, sofern sie in Deutschland keine Arbeit aufnehmen und sich nicht länger als 3 Monate im Land aufhalten.

Weitere Auskunft erteilen die deutschen Konsulate oder Botschaften.

GESUNDHEIT

Normale Sprechstundenzeit der Ärzte: 10.00-12.00 Uhr und 16.00-18.00 Uhr, außer mittwochs, samstags und sonntags. In dringenden Fällen kann man sich an den Notarzt wenden.

Krankenhäuser und ambulante Abteilungen bieten außerhalb der obigen Zeiten einen Notdienst.

Ein Krankenwagen wird über die Nr.110 gerufen.

GESCHÄFTSSTUNDEN DER BANKEN

Die Banken sind gewöhnlich werktags von 08.30-13.00 Uhr und von 14.30-16.00 Uhr (donnerstags bis 17.30 Uhr) geöffnet. Samstags und sonntags sind sie geschlossen.

POSTÄMTER

Postämter sind in der Regel montags bis freitags von 08.00-18.00 Uhr und samstags von 08.00-12.00 Uhr geöffnet.

LADENÖFFNUNGSZEITEN

Die Geschäfte sind im allgemeinen von 09.00-20.00 Uhr geöffnet. An Sonn- und Feiertagen sind sie geschlossen, und samstags schließen sie um 16.00 Uhr.

REISEN

Eisenbahn

Das Eisenbahnnetz ist ausgezeichnet, aber Fahrkarten sind teuer.

Busse

Wer im Besitz einer Eurail- oder Inter-Rail-Karte ist, kann die von der Eisenbahn betriebenen Busse kostenlos benutzen.

Autofahren

Deutschland ist stolz auf sein überaus leistungsfähiges, gebührenfreies Autobahnnetz. Für Autobahnen und autobahnartige Bundesstraßen wird ein Tempolimit von 130 km/h empfohlen.

Español

ALBERGUES JUVENILES ALEMANES

Alemania disfruta de la red de albergues juveniles más extensa del mundo, con un total de aprox. 605 establecimientos. Los albergues suelen ser más grandes de lo normal y son siempre de primera calidad. Están ocupados principalmente por grupos escolares durante el curso lectivo, pero representan una excelente base para los turistas de todo el mundo que deseen explorar el país. Se da prioridad a los menores de 27 años y, en Bavaria, el límite máximo de edad es de 26 años, aunque éste no se aplica a los jefes de grupo ni a las familias con por lo menos un niño menor de edad. La mayoría de los albergues disponen de habitaciones familiares.

Prácticamente todos los albergues cierran del 24 al 26 de diciembre y muchos de ellos también cierran durante determinados períodos del otoño, invierno y primavera. Diríjase al albergue deseado para más información.

Los precios de todos los albergues de la DJH son con todo incluido (alojamiento y desayuno). Dependen de la ubicación y de los servicios ofrecidos, y oscilan entre 17 y 29 DM para menores de 27 años y entre 22 y 34 DM para los demás. En las pensiones para jóvenes que, por regla general, están dotadas de habitaciones de 2 a 4 camas y cierran más tarde, los precios oscilan entre 25 y 45 DM, desayuno y sábanas incluidos. Se pueden conseguir precios especiales alojándose varios días en el mismo albergue.

Generalmente, no es posible cocinar uno mismo en los albergues juveniles alemanes, pero la mayoría sirven comidas.

PASAPORTES Y VISADOS

Los ciudadanos de los países pertenecientes a la UE que sean titulares de un pasaporte en regla no necesitan visado.

Tampoco requieren visado los visitantes procedentes de un buen número de países, siempre y cuando no busquen empleo y su estancia no supere los 3 meses.

Para más información, infórmese en la embajada o consulado alemanes.

INFORMACIÓN SANITARIA

El horario de consulta de los médicos de cabecera suele ser de 10 h. a 12 h. y de 16 a 18 h. excepto los miércoles, sábados y domingos. En caso de urgencia, llame al servicio médico de urgencias.

Los hospitales y las consultas para pacientes externos ofrecen un servicio de urgencias fuera del horario de consulta.

Para llamar a una ambulancia, marque el 110.

HORARIO DE LOS BANCOS

Los bancos suelen abrir los días laborables de 8.30 h. a 13 h. y de 14.30 h. a 16 h. (hasta las 17.30 h. los jueves), y cierran los sábados y domingos.

OFICINAS DE CORREOS

Por lo general, las oficinas de correos abren de lunes a viernes de 8 h. a 18 h. y los sábados de 8 h. a 12 h.

HORARIO COMERCIAL

Las tiendas abren normalmente de 9 h. a 20 h. Cierran los domingos y festivos y a las 16 h. los sábados.

DESPLAZAMIENTOS

Tren

La red ferroviaria es excelente, pero cara.

Autobús

Las líneas de autobuses de la compañía ferroviaria ofrecen transporte gratuito a los titulares de las tarjetas Eurail e Inter-Rail.

Automóvil

Alemania disfruta de una excelente red de autopistas gratuitas. El límite de velocidad recomendado para autopistas y carreteras principales tipo autopista es de 130 km/h.

**John Galt,
in Ayn Rand's Atlas Shrugged:**

‘ **Do not lose your knowledge that man's proper estate is an upright posture, an intransigent mind, and a step that travels unlimited roads.**

Ne perdez pas de vue que l'état propre de l'homme est une posture droite, un esprit intransigeant et un pas qui voyage sur une multitude de routes.

Man sollte nie vergessen, daß der Reichtum eines Menschen in folgendem besteht: einer aufrechten Haltung, einem festen Willen und einem festen Schritt, der unzählige Straßen beschreitet.

Nunca olvides que el verdadero ser del hombre es una postura erguida, una mente intransigente y un paso que camina por infinitos senderos. ’

Bad Homburg

Mühlweg 17,
61348 Bad Homburg.
❶ (6172) 23950
❷ (6172) 22132
❸ bad-homburg@djh-hessen.de

Open Dates: 01.01-23.12; 27-31.12

Open Hours: 07.00-24.00hrs

Price Range: 29.50-34.50 DM [BB] inc 📖

Beds: 5x² 14x³ 37x⁴ 1x⁶

Facilities: ♿ 👫 56x 👫 🍽️ 💺 📺
8 x 🍴 💶 ♨ ⚗ 🔍

Directions: [0.5 SW] from city centre

✈ Frankfurt Rhein-Main 20km

🚇 Bad Homburg 2km

Attractions: ⚓ 2km

Berlin -
JH Ernst Reuter

Hermsdorfer Damm 48-50,
13467 Berlin.
❶ (30) 4041610
❷ (30) 4045972
❸ jh-ernst-reuter@jugendherberge.de

Open Dates: 07.01-05.12

Open Hours: 🕐

Reservations: **Ⓡ**

Price Range: 28.00-35.00 DM € 14.32-17.90
[BB] inc 📖

Beds: 111 - 16x⁶

Facilities: 👫 🍽️ 💺 📺 🖥️ 📷 8️⃣ ℹ️ 🔍

Directions: [15 N] from city centre

✈ Tegel (TXL) 5km

🚇 Berlin-Zoo 15km

🚌 125 5m ap Jugendherberge

🚈 (S-Bahn) S 25 Tegel 2km

Ⓤ U 6 ALT-Tegel 2km

Attractions: 🎠 🚶 ⚓

Ⓡ > 2 weeks   **❶** (30) 2623024
❷ (30) 2629529

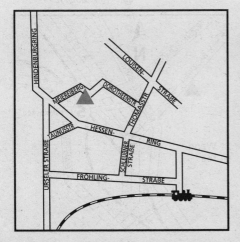

Berlin - JGH Berlin

Kluckstr. 3,
10785 Berlin.
🕿 (30) 2611097
📠 (30) 2650383
📧 jh-berlin@jugendherberge.de

Open Dates:	🗓12
Open Hours:	🕐
Reservations:	R IBN
Price Range:	34.00-50.00 DM € 17.38-25.56 BB inc 🍴
Beds:	350
Facilities:	👭 👬 🍴 ☕ 👥 📺 🧺 3 x 🍴 💺 P 🛈 👶 ♿ 🍴
Directions:	3W from city centre
✈	Berlin Tegel 10km
A🚌	X09 500m
🚃	Zoologischer Garten 2km
🚌	129 ap Gedenkstätte
🚋	Potsdamer Platz 1km
U	U 1 Kurfürstenstrasse 0.8km, U 2 Bülowstrasse 1.2km
Attractions:	🚴 ⚓5km

R > 2 weeks   🕿 (30) 2623024
                📠 (30) 2629529

Berlin - JGH am Wannsee

Badeweg 1,
Ecke Kronprinzessinnenweg,
14129 Berlin.
🕿 (30) 8032035
📠 (30) 8035908
📧 jh-wannsee@jugendherberge.de

Open Dates:	🗓12
Open Hours:	🕐
Reservations:	R
Price Range:	34.00-42.00 DM € 17.38-21.47 BB inc 🍴
Beds:	288 - 72x 🛏
Facilities:	♿ 👭 👬 🍴 👥 📺 🗄 💺 P 👶 ♿ 🍴
Directions:	20SW from city centre
✈	Tegel
🚃	Berlin-Wannsee 1.5km
🚌	118 Badeweg 30m
🚋	(S-Bahn) S1, S3, S7, Nikolassee 500m
Attractions:	🎣 ⚓ ⚓1km

R > 2 weeks   🕿 (30) 2623024
                📠 (30) 2629529

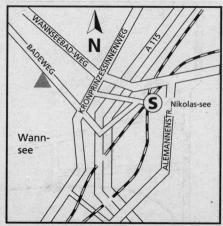

Bremen

YGH,
Kalkstr 6,
28195 Bremen.
☎ (421) 171369
✆ (421) 171102

Open Dates:	02.01-23.12
Open Hours:	⏰
Reservations:	IBN CC
Price Range:	29.90-34.90 DM BB inc 🖥
Beds:	172 - 11x² 32x⁴ 5x⁶
Facilities:	♿ ⅲ 6x ⅲ 🍽 🖼 📺 📖 2 x🍷 🖼 🚿 🅿 ⊗ 🔍

Directions: 1 NW from city centre

✈	Bremen 5km
🚉	Bremen Central 3km
🚌	26 200m ap Brill
🚃	1, 8 200m ap Brill

Attractions: 🚶 ⚓1km

Dresden - JGH

Maternistraße 22,
01067 Dresden
☎ (351) 492620
✆ (351) 4926299
✉ servicecenter@djh-sachsen.de

Open Dates:	🗓
Open Hours:	⏰
Reservations:	R IBN
Price Range:	33.00-45.00 DM BB inc 🖥
Beds:	450 - 149x² 38x⁴
Facilities:	ⅲ 38x ⅲ 🍽 (BD) 🖼 📺 2 x🍷 🖼 ⬍ 🔍

Directions:

✈	Dresden 10km
A🚌	Airport-Cityliner & S-Bahn 12km
⛴	Dresden-City 2km
🚉	Dresden Central 1km
🚃	7, 9, 10, 26 200m

Attractions: 🚵 ⚓50m

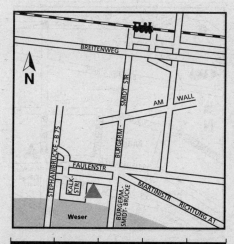

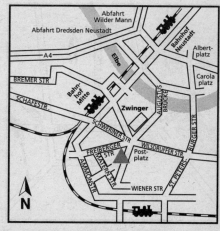

Düsseldorf

Düsseldorfer Str 1,
40545 Düsseldorf.
☎ (211) 557310
✆ (211) 572513

Open Dates: 03.01-21.12

Open Hours: 06.00-01.00hrs

Reservations: [IBN]

Price Range: 38.00 DM € 19.43 [BB] inc 🍴

Beds: 272 - 9x¹🛏 27x²🛏 10x³🛏
37x⁴🛏 1x⁵🛏 4x⁶🛏 3x⁶🛏

Facilities: ♿ 👥 37x 👥 🍽 (BD) 🛏 📺
8 x 🍴 📷 🔧 Ⓟ 🔍

Directions: 3W from city centre

✈ Düsseldorf 12km

🚉 Düsseldorf Central 6km

Ⓤ 70, 74, 75, 76, 77, Luegplatz 1km

Attractions: ⚓ 3km

Frankfurt

"Haus der Jugend" Deutschherrnufer 12,
60594 Frankfurt.
☎ (69) 6100150
✆ (69) 61001599
✉ jugendherberge_frankfurt@t-online.de

Open Dates: 03.01-22.12

Open Hours: 06.30-02.00hrs

Reservations: Ⓡ [IBN]

Price Range: 27.00-44.00 DM € 13.80-22.50
[BB] inc 🍴

Beds: 470 - 15x²🛏 2x³🛏 36x⁴🛏 4x⁶🛏
32x⁶🛏

Facilities: ♿ 👥 👥 🍽 ☕ 🛏 📺 📖
1 x 🍴 📷 ♨ 🔧 🔍

Directions: 1SE from city centre

✈ Frankfurt 12km

A🚌 61 South, then tram 14 to
Bornheim, stop "Frankensteiner
Platz"

🚉 Frankfurt 3km

🚋 16 or S-Bahn 2-6 ap Lokalbahnhof

Ⓤ S-Bahn 2-6 to Lokalbahnhof

Attractions: ⚓ 800m

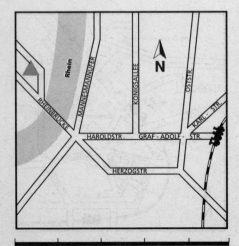

Freiburg

Kartäuserstr 151,
79104 Freiburg.
☎ (761) 67656
✆ (761) 60367

Open Dates: 27.12-22.12

Open Hours: 07.00-23.30hrs

Reservations: **R**

Price Range: 26.00-31.00 DM BB inc ⌂

Beds: 405 - 8x² 🛏 30x⁴ 🛏 30x⁶ 🛏

Facilities: ⚐ ♦♦♦ 4x ♦♦♦ �🍴 🏠 📺 11 x ⬭
🔒 🅿 ✎ ⚒ 🎣 ⊗ ⚲ ⊞ ♠

Directions: 6E from city centre

✈ Strassburg 70km

🚊 L1 500m ap Römerhof

Attractions: ⚑ ⛰ 🏊 ⛷ 🚶 ∪5km ⚲3km
🏊2km

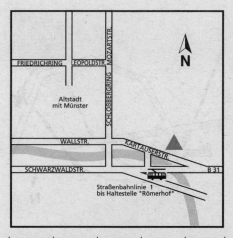

Güstrow-Schabernack

Jugendherberge Güstrow-Schabernack,
Heidberg 33,
18273 Güstrow
☎ (3843) 840044
✆ (3843) 840045
@ jh-guestrow@t-online.de

Open Dates: 10.01-20.12; 28-31.12

Open Hours: 07.00-22.00

Reservations: **R**

Price Range: 27.00-30.00 DM BB inc

Beds: 72 - 4x¹ 🛏 9x² 🛏 4x³ 🛏 8x⁴ 🛏 4x⁵ 🛏
4x⁶ 🛏

Facilities: ♦♦♦ ♦♦♦ �🍴 ⊞ 🏠 📺 📓 2 x ⬭ 🔒
🖼 🅿 ✎ ⚒ ⚲ ⊞

Directions: 6SE from city centre

🚂 Güstrow Central 6km

🚌 1km ap in front of hostel

Attractions: ⚑ ⚲1.5km ⚴ 🚶 ∪1.5km
⚲1.5km 🏊2km

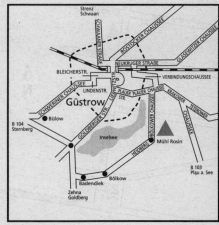

Halle

August-Bebel-Str 48a,
06108 Halle.
☎ (345) 2024716
ℹ (345) 2025172

Open Dates:	01.01-23.12; 28-31.12
Open Hours:	07.00-10.00hrs; 17.00-23.00hrs
Price Range:	24.00-29.00 DM € 11.25-13.80 BB inc
Beds:	72 - 1x² 3x⁴ 4x⁶ 4x⁶
Facilities:	ⅲ 3x ⅲ ⅶⅠ ⅱ ⅰ2 x⅏ 回 P 🏕

Directions:	
✈	Halle-Schkeuditz 25km
🚃	Halle 1.5km
🚋	5, 7, 9
Attractions:	🚴 🚶 ∪6km ⚲1km ⚓1.5km

Hamburg -
Auf dem Stintfang

Alfred-Wegener-Weg 5,
20459 Hamburg.
☎ (40) 313488, ⅲ Ⓡ (40) 3191037
ℹ (40) 315407
✉ jh-stintfang@t-online.de

Open Dates:	01.02-23.12; 27.12-31.01
Open Hours:	06.30-09.30hrs; 11.30-01.00hrs
Reservations:	Ⓡ ⒾⒷⓃ
Price Range:	from 27.00 DM BB inc
Beds:	320 - 9x² 14x⁴ 21x⁶ 15x⁶
Facilities:	♿ ⅲ ⅶⅠ ⚲ ⅱ TV 1 x⅏ 回 ▣ 🏕

Directions:	2SW from city centre
✈	Hamburg-Fuhlsbüttel 10km
A🚌	to Main Station 10km
⛴	Hamburger Hafen 200m
🚃	Hauptbahnhof 2km
🚌	112 200m
Ⓤ	S1, S3, U3 Landungsbrücken 200m
Attractions:	⚓1km

There are 2 hostels in Hamburg. See following
pages.

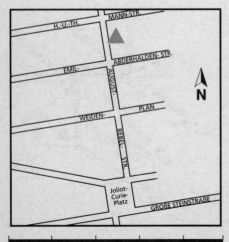

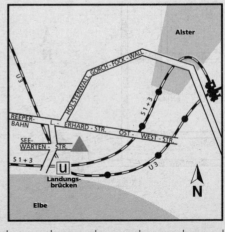

Hannover

Ferdinand-Wilhelm-Fricke-Weg 1,
30169 Hannover.
☎ (511) 1317674
🖷 (511) 18555
📧 djh-lub-hannover@t-online.de

Open Dates:	01.01-23.12; 27-31.12
Open Hours:	🕐
Price Range:	27.00-34.00 DM € 13.80-17.38 BB inc 🍴
Beds:	317 - 1x¹ 39x² 22x⁴ 24x⁶ 1x⁶
Facilities:	♿ ♦♦♦ 26x ♦♦♦ ¶O¶ (BD) ☕ 🛏 📺 6 x🍴 🖼 ⑧ ♦ P ✿ ✦ ▦
Directions:	2S from city centre
✈	Hannover
🚂	Hannover Hauptbahnhof 5km
🚃	3, 7 1km ap Fischerhof
Attractions:	🧍 ✎ 🏊

Heidelberg

Tiergartenstr 5,
69120 Heidelberg.
☎ (6221) 412066
🖷 (6221) 402559

Open Dates:	01.01-23.12; 27-31.12
Open Hours:	07.00-23.30hrs
Reservations:	Ⓡ
Price Range:	26.00-31.00 DM BB inc 🍴
Beds:	440 - 1x¹ 3x² 19x⁴ 34x⁶ 17x⁶
Facilities:	♦♦♦ ♦♦♦ ¶O¶ 🛏 📺 📱 5 x🍴 🗄 🖼 ⑧ P ⅰ ✿ ⚠ 🕐 ✦ ▦
Directions:	4NW from city centre
✈	Frankfurt 80km
A🚌	bis Heidelberg
🚂	Heidelberg 15km
🚌	33 10m ap YH
Attractions:	🧍 🚲 🧍 ✎1km ⚓500m

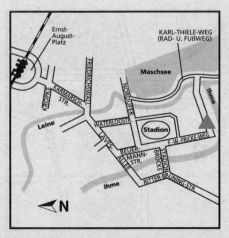

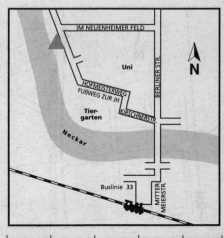

Koblenz

**Festung Ehrenbreitstein,
56077 Koblenz.**
☎ (261) 97287-0
🖷 (261) 97287-30

Open Dates:	01.01-23.12; 27-31.12
Open Hours:	07.00-23.30hrs
Reservations:	⌐CC⌐
Price Range:	25.20-31.20 DM € 12.88-15.95 BB inc 🔌
Beds:	183 - 8x²🛏 2x³🛏 11x⁴🛏 9x⁶🛏 9x⁶🛏
Facilities:	♿ ♟♟♟ 8x ♟♟♟ ⧉🍽 ⚏ 📺 5 x 🍴 💼 ⒤ 🖿 ♨ ⚠ 🔍 🎏
Directions:	6NE from city centre
✈	Frankfurt 120km
🚄	Koblenz Central 5km
🚌	7, 8, 9 800m ap Ehrenbreitstein Berg Str
Attractions:	🏞 🚴 🏃 ∪3km ⚓500m 🏊3km

Köln - Deutz

**Siegesstr 5a,
50679 Köln.**
☎ (221) 814711
🖷 (221) 884425
🖃 jh-deutz@t-online.de

Open Dates:	01.01-23.12; 27-31.12
Open Hours:	🕐
Reservations:	⌐IBN⌐
Price Range:	33.00 DM € 16.87 BB inc 🔌
Beds:	374 - 4x¹🛏 4x²🛏 20x³🛏 3x⁴🛏 39x⁶🛏 8x⁶🛏
Facilities:	♿ ♟♟♟ 10x ♟♟♟ ⧉🍽 (BD) ⚏ 📺 5 x 🍴 ⓢ ⓢ P 🔍
Directions:	3E from city centre
✈	Köln-Bonn 12km
🚄	Köln Central 600m
Attractions:	🏊5km

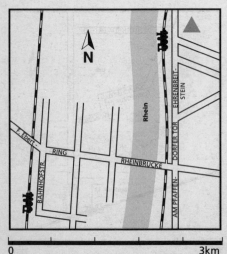

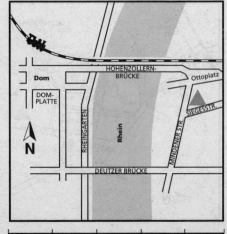

Köln - Riehl

JGH,
An der Schanz 14,
50735 Köln.
☏ (221) 767081
ⓕ (221) 761555

Open Dates:	01.01-23.12; 27-31.12
Open Hours:	◔
Price Range:	39.00 DM € 19.94 [BB]inc 🛏
Beds:	366 - 15x^1🛏 21x^2🛏 6x^3🛏 52x^4🛏 12x^6🛏
Facilities:	♿ 🚻 52x 🚻 🍽 (BD) 🍺 🛏 📺 🧺 1 x🍴 🔒 ⬆ 🅿 🔆 🔍
Directions:	6 NE from city centre
✈	14km
🚂	Köln 3km
Ⓤ	16,18

Lübeck

Am Gertrudenkirchhof 4,
23568 Lübeck.
☏ (451) 33433
ⓕ (451) 34540

Open Dates:	01.01-23.12; 27-31.12
Open Hours:	07.30-24.00hrs
Price Range:	from 27.00 DM [BB]inc 🛏
Beds:	218 - 3x^1🛏 16x^2🛏 8x^4🛏 4x^5🛏 22x^6🛏
Facilities:	♿ 🚻 🍽 🛏 1 x🍴 🔒 🖼 ⬆ 🅿 🔆 🔍 🔍
Directions:	2 NE from city centre
🚂	Hauptbahnhof 2km
🚌	1,3,11,12 200m ap Gustav-Radbruch-Platz

Attractions: 🚴 ⛵

There are 2 hostels in Lübeck. See following
pages.

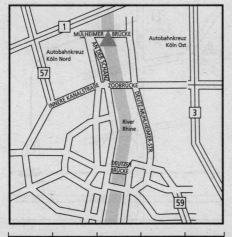

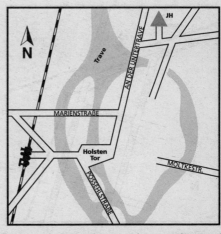

Mainz -
Rhein-Main-Jugendherberge

Jugendgästehaus Mainz,
Otto-Brunfels-Schneise 4,
55130 Mainz.
📞 (6131) 85332
📠 (6131) 82422

Open Dates:	01.01-23.12; 27-31.12
Open Hours:	06.30-00.00hrs
Reservations:	® ⌐CC⌐
Price Range:	29.10-38.60 DM € 14.88-19.74 BB inc 🍴
Beds:	166 - 22x² 🛏 27x⁴ 🛏
Facilities:	👫 👫 🍴 � 📺 🛍 5 x 🍷 ♨ ⚠ 🔍 🏢

Directions: 5SE from city centre

🚃 Mainz Central 3.5km

🚌 22; 1 ap Jugendgästehaus
Weisenau 400m

Attractions: 🚶 🏊 3km

München -
Neuhausen

Wendl-Dietrich Str 20,
80634 München (Bavaria).
📞 (89) 131156
📠 (89) 1678745
📧 jhmuenchen@djh-bayern.de

Open Dates:	01.01-30.11
Open Hours:	🕐
Reservations:	® ⌐IBN⌐ ⌐CC⌐
Price Range:	30.00 DM € 15.34 BB inc 🍴
Beds:	388 - 5x¹ 🛏 17x² 🛏 24x⁴ 🛏 36x⁶ 🛏 1x⁶ 🛏
Facilities:	👫 🍴 🍷 🛏 📺 2 x 🍷 🔲 🏢 ♨ 🔒 🛈 ⚓

Directions:

✈ München 30km

🚃 Hauptbahnhof 3km

🚋 12, 17 5 minutes

Ⓤ 1 Rotkreuzplatz

Attractions: 🚴 🚶 🏊 5km

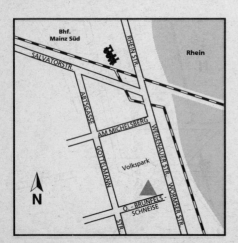

0 ━━━━━━━━━━━━━━ 2km

München -
JGH Thalkirchen

Miesingstr 4,
81379 München (Bavaria).
☏ (89) 7236550, 7236560
✆ (89) 7242567
✉ jghmuenchen@djh-bayern.de

Open Dates:	🗓
Open Hours:	🕐
Reservations:	Ⓡ IBN
Price Range:	32.50 DM € 16.62 BBinc 🍴
Beds:	352 - 58x² 11x³ 42x⁴ 6x⁶
Facilities:	👪 👪 🍽 🛏 📺 2 x 🍷 🔒 📷 8 P 🚲 ♿ ⛰ 🔍

Directions:

✈	München, 40 minutes by public transport
🚂	10km
Ⓤ	3 Thalkirchen 350m

Attractions: 🚴 🏃 🏊

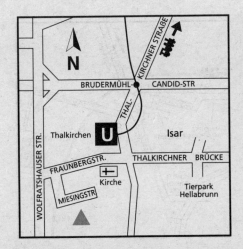

Münster -
Aasee

"JGH",
Bismarckallee 31,
48151 Münster.
☏ (251) 532470, 532477
✆ (251) 521271

Open Dates:	01.01-23.12; 27-31.12
Open Hours:	07.00-01.00hrs
Reservations:	Ⓡ IBN
Price Range:	40.50-50.50 DM
Beds:	208 - 22x² 41x⁴
Facilities:	♿ 👪 41x 👪 🍽 🍷 🛏 📺 8 x 🍷 🔒 📷 ♨ 8 ⬆ P 🚲 ♿ 🔍

Directions: 2W from city centre

🚂	Münster 2km
🚌	10, 34 500m Hoppendamm

Attractions: 🚴 🏊 3km

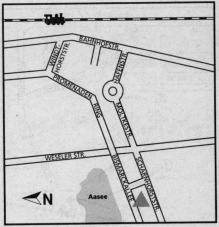

Nürnberg -
JGH

Burg 2,
90403 Nürnberg (Bavaria).
☎ (911) 2309360
✆ (911) 23093611

Open Dates: 01.01-24.12; 27-31.12

Open Hours: 07.00-01.00hrs

Reservations: **R** IBN

Price Range: 30.00 DM € 15.34 BB inc 🗄

Beds: 320 - 10x² 2x³ 33x⁴
13x⁵ 15x⁶

Facilities: ♿ ♙♙♙ ♙♙ 🍽 🛏 📺 4 x 🍷 🖼
8 ⬆ i 🔍 🏠

Directions:

✈ Nürnberg 6km

🚆 Nürnberg Central 1.5km

🚃 9 to Krelingstraße

Ⓤ 1, 2 1km

Attractions: 🏊 3km

Saarbrücken -
Europa JH JGH

Meerwiesertalweg 31,
66123 Saarbrücken.
☎ (681) 33040
✆ (681) 374911

Open Dates: 01.01-23.12; 27-31.12

Open Hours: 02.00-01.00hrs

Price Range: 29.10-38.60 DM € 14.88-19.74
BB inc 🔟

Beds: 192 - 37x² 32x⁴

Facilities: ♿ ♙♙♙ ♙♙ 🍽 🛏 📺 5 x 🍷 ⛰
🔍

Directions: 4 NE from city centre

✈ Ensheim 20km

🚆 Saarbrücken Central

🚌 49, 69 ap Prinzenweiher

Attractions: 🏇 🔍500m 🏊500m

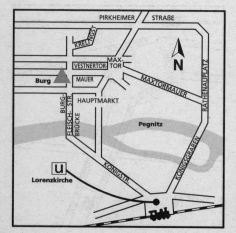

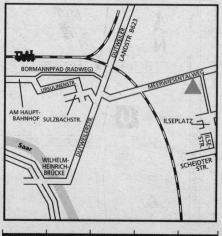

0   3km

Stuttgart

**Haußmannstr 27,
70188 Stuttgart (enter via Werastr,
corner Kernerstr).**
☎ (711) 241583
✆ (711) 2361041

Open Dates:	🗓12
Open Hours:	07.00-24.00hrs
Price Range:	26.00-31.00 DM BB inc 🍴
Beds:	245 - 1x¹🛏 7x²🛏 42x⁴🛏 15x⁶🛏
Facilities:	👪 42x 🏃 🍽 🏫 📺 📖 3 x 🍷 ♨
Directions:	1 SE from city centre
🚆	Stuttgart 500m
🚌	42 200m ap Eugensplatz
🚋	15 200m ap Eugensplatz
Attractions:	🏃 ⛷ 🚣 3km

Weimar -
JGH "Maxim Gorki"

**Zum Wilden Graben 12,
99425 Weimar.**
☎ (3643) 850750
✆ (3643) 850749

Open Dates:	01.01-21.12; 28-31.12
Open Hours:	🕐
Reservations:	R
Price Range:	26.00-31.00 DM € 13.50-16.00 BB inc 🍴
Beds:	60 - 2x¹🛏 3x²🛏 4x⁴🛏 4x⁵🛏 3x⁶🛏
Facilities:	👪 10x 🏃 🍽 🏫 📺 📖 1 x 🍷 📷 🅿 ♿ ⊙ ♨
Directions:	
🚆	Weimar Central 4km
🚌	8 ap Rainer-Maria-Rilke Str
Attractions:	⛷ 2km 🚣 2km

There are 4 hostels in Weimar. See following pages.

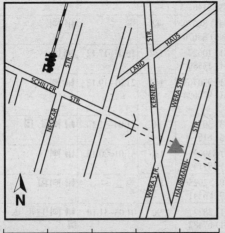

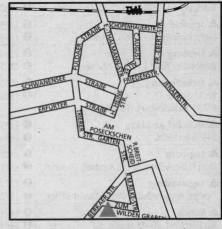

Location/Address	Telephone No. Fax No.	Beds	Opening Dates	Facilities
▲ **Aachen** - Euregionales JGH Aachen Maria-Theresia-Allee 260, 52074 Aachen.	☎ (241) 711010 🖷 (241) 7110120	180	01.01–23.12; 27–31.12	♦♦♦ ⦿⧉ 5SW ♿ P ☕
▲ **Aalen** "Schubart- Jugendherberge", Stadionweg 8, 73430 Aalen.	☎ (7361) 49203 🖷 (7361) 44682	127	01.01–19.11; 27–31.12	♦♦♦ ⦿⧉
▲ **Affalter** Weg zur Jugendherberge 4, 08294 Affalter.	☎ (3771) 33940 🖷 (3771) 33951	35	⓬	⦿⧉ P
▲ **Albersdorf** Bahnhofstraße 19, 25767 Albersdorf.	☎ (4835) 642 🖷 (4835) 8462	114	06.01–22.12	♦♦♦ ⦿⧉ ♿ P ⬛
▲ **Alpirsbach** Reinerzauer Steige 80, 72275 Alpirsbach.	☎ (7444) 2477 🖷 (7444) 1304	122	03.01–22.12	⦿⧉
▲ **Altena** "Burg Altena", Fritz-Thomee-Straße 80, 58762 Altena.	☎ (2352) 23522 🖷 (2352) 26330	59	27.12–23.12	⦿⧉ Ⓡ P
▲ **Altenahr** - Naturschutz-Jugendherberge Langfigtal 8, 53505 Altenahr.	☎ (2643) 1880 🖷 (2643) 8136	98	01.01–23.12; 27–31.12	⦿⧉
▲ **Altenau** Auf der Rose 11, 38707 Altenau.	☎ (5328) 361 🖷 (5328) 8276	164	27.12–23.12	♦♦♦ ⦿⧉ 0.5SE P
▲ **Altenberg** Dresdener Str 70, 01773 Altenberg.	☎ (35056) 32318 🖷 (35056) 32707	115	⓬	♦♦♦ ⦿⧉ P
▲ **Altglashütten** "Turnerheim", Am Sommerberg 26, 79868 Feldberg.	☎ (7655) 90010 🖷 (7655) 900199	91	27.12–22.12	⦿⧉ P
▲ **Altleiningen** - Burg-Jugendherberge, Jugendgästehaus 67317 Altleiningen.	☎ (6356) 1580 🖷 (6356) 6364	160	01.01–23.12; 27–31.12	♦♦♦ ⦿⧉ ♿ ☕
Am Kleinen Arber ☞ **Bodenmais**				
▲ **Amberg** Fronfestgasse 22, 92224 Amberg (Bavaria).	☎ (9621) 10369 🖷 (9621) 10369	36	04.01–23.12	♦♦♦ ⦿⧉
▲ **Amorbach** Kniebreche 4, 63916 Amorbach (Bavaria).	☎ (9373) 1366 🖷 (9373) 7140	92	16.01–30.11	♦♦♦ ⦿⧉
▲ **Arnsfeld** Jugendherbergsstr. 1, 09477 Arnsfeld	☎ (37343) 88670 🖷 (37343) 88670	42	⓬	♦♦♦ ⦿⧉
▲ **Arnsberg** Rumbecker Höhe 1, 59821 Arnsberg.	☎ (2931) 10627 🖷 (2931) 13589	132	16.01–17.12	⦿⧉ P
▲ **Aschaffenburg** Beckerstraße 47, 63739 Aschaffenburg (Bavaria).	☎ (6021) 930763 🖷 (6021) 970694	114	21.01–19.12	♦♦♦ ⦿⧉
▲ **Ascheffel-Aschberg** 24358 Ascheffel.	☎ (4353) 307 🖷 (4353) 815	36	21.04–31.10	♦♦♦ ⦿⧉ 🧺 P
▲ **Augsburg** Beim Pfaffenkeller 3, 86152 Augsburg (Bavaria).	☎ (821) 33909 🖷 (821) 151149	136	31.01–20.12	♦♦♦ ⦿⧉
▲ **Augustusburg** 'Schloss Augustusburg', 09573 Augustusburg.	☎ (37291) 20256 🖷 (37291) 6341	114	⓬	♦♦♦ ⦿⧉ P
▲ **Aurich** Am Ellernfeld, 26603 Aurich.	☎ (4941) 2827 🖷 (4941) 67482	90	01.03–31.10	♦♦♦ ⦿⧉ 1SW ♿ P

Location/Address	Telephone No. Fax No.	Beds	Opening Dates	Facilities
▲ **Bacharach** "Burg Stahleck", 55422 Bacharach.	☎ (6743) 1266 ❺ (6743) 2684	166	01.01–23.12; 27–31.12	ᴪᴪ ⵚ
▲ **Bad Bederkesa** Margaretenweg 2, 27624 Bad Bederkesa. ✉ jugendherberge-badbederkesa@t-online.de	☎ (4745) 406 ❺ (4745) 8058	70	01.03–31.10	ᴪᴪ ⵚ [1W]
▲ **Bad Bentheim** Am Wasserturm 34, 48455 Bad Bentheim.	☎ (5922) 2480 ❺ (5922) 6043	122	🗓12	ᴪᴪ ⵚ [1E] ♿ P
▲ **Bad Bergzabern** Altenbergweg, 76887 Bad Bergzabern.	☎ (6343) 8383 ❺ (6343) 5184	141	01.01–23.12; 27–31.12	ᴪᴪ ⵚ
▲ **Bad Berleburg** Goetheplatz 1, 57319 Bad Berleburg	☎ (2751) 7340 ❺ (2751) 2076	61	02.01–30.11	ᴪᴪ ⵚ P
▲ **Bad Blankenburg** Am Kesselberg 1, 07422 Bad Blankenburg.	☎ (36741) 2528 ❺ (36741) 47625	141	28.12–22.12	ⵚ ⓡ P
▲ **Bad Brambach** Röthenbach 4, 08648 Bad Brambach.	☎ (37438) 20541	42	🗓12	ᴪᴪ ⵚ P
▲ **Bad Doberan** Tempelberg, 18209 Bad Doberan.	☎ (38203) 62439 ❺ (38203) 62229	124	01.01–20.12; 29–31.12	ⵚ ⓡ
▲ **Bad Driburg** "Kulturstudienplatz", Schirrmannweg 1, 33014 Bad Driburg.	☎ (5253) 2570 ❺ (5253) 3882	124	16.01–14.12	ᴪᴪ ⵚ P
▲ **Bad Ems** Alte Kemmenauer Str 41, 56130 Bad Ems.	☎ (2603) 2680 ❺ (2603) 50384	120	01.01–23.12; 27–31.12	ᴪᴪ ⵚ
▲ **Bad Endorf** - JH Hemhof Rankhamer Weg ll, 83093 Bad Endorf (Bavaria).	☎ (8053) 509 ❺ (8053) 3292	40	01.01–30.11	ᴪᴪ ⵚ
▲ **Bad Essen** Schledehauser Str 81, 49152 Bad Essen.	☎ (5472) 2123 ❺ (5472) 6233	140	🗓12	ᴪᴪ ⵚ P
▲ **Bad Freienwalde** Hammerthal 3, 16259 Bad Freienwalde ✉ jh-bad-freienwalde@jugendherberge.de	☎ (3344) 3875 ❺ (3344) 31598	48	01.03–31.10	ᴪᴪ ⵚ ⓡ [2W]
▲ **Bad Gandersheim** Am Kantorberge 17, 37581 Bad Gandersheim.	☎ (5382) 2967 ❺ (5382) 8368	91	27.12–23.12	ᴪᴪ ⵚ P
▲ **Bad Harzburg** Waldstr. 5, 38667 Bad Harzburg	☎ (5322) 4582 ❺ (5322) 1867	84	27.12–23.12	ⵚ
▲ **Bad Herrenalb** "Ev Ferienheim", Aschenhüttenweg 44, 76332 Bad Herrenalb.	☎ (7083) 2430 ❺ (7083) 51031	87	27.12–22.12	ᴪᴪ ⵚ ♿ P
▲ **Bad Homburg** **Mühlweg 17, 61348 Bad Homburg.** ✉ bad-homburg@djh-hessen.de	☎ (6172) 23950 ❺ (6172) 22132		01.01–23.12; 27–31.12	ᴪᴪ ⵚ [0.5SW] ♿
▲ **Bad Honnef** Selhoferstr 106, 53604 Bad Honnef.	☎ (2224) 71300 ❺ (2224) 79226	210	02.01–01.12	ᴪᴪ ⵚ ☛ P
▲ **Bad Iburg** Offenes Holz, 49186 Bad Iburg.	☎ (5403) 74220 ❺ (5403) 9770	142	🗓12	ᴪᴪ ⵚ [1.5N] P
▲ **Bad Karlshafen** Winnefelder Str 7, 34385 Bad Karlshafen.	☎ (5672) 338 ❺ (5672) 8361	99	27.12–23.12	ᴪᴪ ⵚ [0.5N] P

Location/Address	Telephone No. Fax No.	Beds	Opening Dates	Facilities
▲ **Bad Kösen** Bergstr 3, 06628 Bad Kösen.	☎ (34463) 27597	119	01.01–23.12 28–31.12	♦♦ ⵌ P ▣
▲ **Bad Kreuznach** Auf dem Kuhberg, 55543 Bad Kreuznach.	☎ (671) 62855 ✆ (671) 75351	136	01.01–23.12; 27–31.12	♦♦ ⵌ ⵣ CC
▲ **Bad Lausick** Herbergsweg 2, 04651/ Bad Lausick/OT Buchheim.	☎ (34345) 7270 ✆ (34345) 72723	146	01.01–19.12; 30–31.12	♦♦ ⵌ ⵣ P ▣
▲ **Bad Lauterberg** Flösswehrtal 25, 37431 Bad Lauterberg.	☎ (5524) 3738 ✆ (5524) 5708	131	27.12–23.12	♦♦ ⵌ P
Bad Mergentheim ☞ **Igersheim**				
▲ **Bad Münstereifel-Rodert** Herbergsweg 1-5, 53902 Bad Münstereifel-Rodert.	☎ (2253) 7438 ✆ (2253) 7483	164	01.01–23.12	♦♦ ⵌ ⵣ ⛗ P
▲ **Bad Neuenahr-Ahrweiler** "Jugendgästehaus" St Pius-Str 7, 53474 Bad Neuenahr-Ahrweiler.	☎ (2641) 34924 ✆ (2641) 31574	140	01.01–23.12; 27–31.12	♦♦ ⵌ ⵣ CC
▲ **Bad Oldesloe** Konrad- Adenauer-Ring 2, 23843 Bad Oldesloe.	☎ (4531) 5945 ✆ (4531) 67574	125	06.01–04.12	♦♦ ⵌ ⵣ P
▲ **Bad Sachsa** Jugendherbergsstr 9-11, 37441 Bad Sachsa.	☎ (5523) 8800 ✆ (5523) 7163	121	27.12–23.12	♦♦ ⵌ P
▲ **Bad Salzungen** Kaltenborner-Str-70, 36433 Bad Salzungen.	☎ (3695) 622208 ✆ (3695) 628833	63	28.12–23.12	♦♦ ⵌ R P
▲ **Bad Saarow-Pieskow** Dorfstr. 20, 15526 Bad Saarow ✉ jh-bad-saarow@jugendherberge.de	☎ (33631) 2664 ✆ (33631) 59023	92	▣ (R 01.11–28.02)	♦♦ ⵌ
▲ **Bad Schandau-Ostrau** Dorfstr 14, 01814 Bad Schandau-Ostrau.	☎ (35022) 42408 ✆ (35022) 42409	101	▣	♦♦ ⵌ
▲ **Bad Segeberg** Kastanienweg 1, 23795 Bad Segeberg.	☎ (4551) 2531 ✆ (4551) 4518	152	06.01–22.12	♦♦ ⵌ ⵣ P ▣
▲ **Bad Sulza** August-Bebel-Str 27, 99518 Bad Sulza.	☎ (36461) 20567 ✆ (36461) 20963	74	28.12–23.12	♦♦ ⵌ R P ▣
▲ **Bad Urach** Burgstr 45, 72574 Bad Urach.	☎ (7125) 8025 ✆ (7125) 40358	123	17.01–18.12	♦♦ ⵌ P ▣
▲ **Bad Zwischenahn** Schirrmannweg 14, 26160 Bad Zwischenahn.	☎ (4403) 2393 ✆ (4403) 64588	115	01.12–31.10	ⵌ P
▲ **Baden-Baden** Werner-Dietz JH, Hardbergstr 34, 76532 Baden-Baden.	☎ (7221) 52223 ✆ (7221) 60012	151	01–09.01; 12.01–23.12; 27–31.12	♦♦ ⵌ 2NW P
▲ **Balingen** Schloßstr 5, 72336 Balingen.	☎ (7433) 20805 ✆ (7433) 5911	44	01.01–10.12; 28–31.12	♦♦ ⵌ
Balingen ☞ **Lochen**				
▲ **Bamberg** - JH "Wolfsschlucht" Oberer Leinritt 70, 96049 Bamberg (Bavaria).	☎ (951) 56002 ✆ (951) 55211	84	01.02–14.12	♦♦ ⵌ
▲ **Barth** Donnerberg, 18356 Barth.	☎ (38231) 2843 ✆ (38231) 2090	155	01.01–20.12; 29–31.12	♦♦ ⵌ R ⵣ P
▲ **Bautzen** Am Zwinger 1, 02625 Bautzen.	☎ (3591) 40347 ✆ (3591) 40348	50	▣	♦♦ ⵌ

Location/Address	Telephone No. Fax No.	Beds	Opening Dates	Facilities
▲ **Bayerisch-Eisenstein** Brennesstr 23, 94252 Bayerisch-Eisenstein (Bavaria).	☏ (9925) 337 ℻ (9925) 730	166	01.01–14.11; 27.12–31.12	ⅲ ⅱ◉ ⌑
▲ **Bayreuth** Universitätsstr 28, 95447 Bayreuth (Bavaria).	☏ (921) 251262 ℻ (921) 512805	150	01.02–14.12	ⅲ ⅱ◉ ⌑
▲ **Bayrischzell** - JH Sudelfeld Unteres Sudelfeld 9, 83735 Bayrischzell (Bavaria).	☏ (8023) 675 ℻ (8023) 274	94	01.01–14.11; 28–31.12	ⅲ ⅱ◉
▲ **Beckerwitz** Haus Nr 21, 23968 Gramkow OT. Beckerwitz.	☏ (38428) 60362 ℻ (38428) 60362	106	01.01–20.12; 29–31.12	ⅲ ⅱ◉ ® P
▲ **Benediktbeuern** - "Don-Bosco-JH" Don-Bosco-Str 3, 83671 Benediktbeuern (Bavaria). ✉ lichtenstern@don-bosco-jh.de	☏ (8857) 88350 ℻ (8857) 88351	170	11.01–14.12	ⅲ ⅱ◉ ® ♿
▲ **Benediktbeuern** - "JH für Mädchen" Bahnhofstr 58, 83671 Benediktbeuern (Bavaria).	☏ (8857) 9050	130	16.01–14.12	ⅲ ⅱ◉ ® P
Berchtesgaden ☞ **Strub**				
▲ **Bergen** Hochfellnstr 18, 83346 Bergen (Bavaria).	☏ (8662) 48830 ℻ (8662) 48838	62	01.01.–14.11; 26–31.12	◉ P
▲ **Berlin** - JH Ernst Reuter **Hermsdorfer Damm 48-50, 13467 Berlin.** ✉ jh-ernst-reuter@jugendherberge.de	☏ (30) 4041610 ℻ (30) 4045972	111	07.01–05.12	◉ ® 15N ⌑
▲ **Berlin** - JGH Berlin ⒤ⒷⓃ **Kluckstr. 3, 10785 Berlin.** ✉ jh-berlin@jugendherberge.de	☏ (30) 2611097 ℻ (30) 2650383	350	▣₁₂	ⅲ ⅱ◉ ® 3W P ♨
▲ **Berlin** - JGH am Wannsee **Badeweg 1, Ecke Kronprinzessinnenweg, 14129 Berlin.** ✉ jh-wannsee@jugendherberge.de	☏ (30) 8032035 ℻ (30) 8035908	288	▣₁₂	ⅲ ⅱ◉ ® 20SW ♿ P ⌑
▲ **Bernburg** Krumbholzallee 2, 06406 Bernburg. ✉ jh-bbg@t-online.de	☏ (3471) 352027 ℻ (3471) 352027	65	01.01–23.12; 27–30.12	ⅲ ⅱ◉ ♿ P ⌑
▲ **Bernkastel-Kues** Jugendherbergsstr 1, 54470 Bernkastel-Kues.	☏ (6531) 2395 ℻ (6531) 1529	96	01.01–23.12; 27–31.12	ⅲ ⅱ◉
▲ **Biberach** Heusteige 40, 88400 Biberach.	☏ (7351) 21885 ℻ (7351) 21315	147	01.01–09.01; 07.02–31.12	ⅲ ⅱ◉ P
▲ **Biedenkopf** "Haus der Jugend", Am Freibad 15, 35216 Biedenkopf.	☏ (6461) 5100; 6569 ℻ (6461) 2425	207	27.12–23.12	ⅲ ⅱ◉ 0.5W P
▲ **Bielefeld** Oetzer Weg 25, 33605 Bielefeld-Sieker.	☏ (521) 22227 ℻ (521) 25196	164	17.01–17.12	ⅲ ⅱ◉ P
▲ **Biggesee** Auf dem Mühlenberg, 57462 Olpe-Stade.	☏ (2761) 6775 ℻ (2761) 64714	240	27.12–23.12	ⅲ ⅱ◉ P
▲ **Bilstein** "Burg Bilstein", Von-Gevore-Weg 10, 57368 Lennestadt.	☏ (2721) 81217 ℻ (2721) 83016	227	03.01–01.12	◉ P
▲ **Bingen-Bingerbrück** Herterstr 51, 55411 Bingen.	☏ (6721) 32163 ℻ (6721) 34012	176	01.01–23.12; 27–31.12	ⅲ ⅱ◉

Location/Address	Telephone No. / Fax No.	Beds	Opening Dates	Facilities
▲ **Binz** Strandpromenade 35, 18609 Ostseebad Binz/Rügen. ☻ jugendherberge_binz@t-online.de	☏ (38393) 32597 ✆ (38393) 32596	143	01.01–20.12; 29–31.12	♟ ⑩ ℝ
▲ **Bispingen** Töpinger Str 42, 29646 Bispingen.	☏ (5194) 2375 ✆ (5194) 7743	108	27.12–23.12	⑩ ℙ
▲ **Blankenheim** - JH Burg-Blankenheim Burg 1, 53945 Blankenheim ☻ jh-burgblankenheim@t-online.de	☏ (2449) 95090 ✆ (2449) 950910	164	03.01–22.12; 27–31.12	♟ ⑩ ℙ ☕
▲ **Blaubeuren** Auf dem Rucken 69, 89143 Blaubeuren.	☏ (7344) 6444 ✆ (7344) 21416	125	01–09.01; 24.01–05.11; 27.11–31.12	♟ ⑩ ▣
▲ **Blockhaus** 51580 Reichshof-Eckenhagen.	☏ (2265) 8628 ✆ (2265) 9042	58	28.12–30.11	⑩ ℙ
▲ **Blomberg** Ulmenallee 15, 32825 Blomberg.	☏ (5235) 7255 ✆ (5235) 2130	163	27.12–23.12	⑩ ℙ
Bockswiese ☞ **Hahnenklee**				
▲ **Bodenmais** - JH Am Kleinen Arber 94249 Bodenmais (Bavaria).	☏ (9924) 281 ✆ (9924) 850	71	01.01–19.04; 21.05–14.11; 27.12–31.12	♟ ⑩
▲ **Bodenwerder** Richard-Schirrmann-Weg, 37619 Bodenwerder.	☏ (5533) 2685 ✆ (5533) 6203	124	27.12–23.12	♟ ⑩ ♿ ℙ
▲ **Bollendorf** Zur Ritschlay 1, 54669 Bollendorf.	☏ (6526) 200 ✆ (6526) 1204	156	01.01–23.12; 27–31.12	♟ ⑩
▲ **Bonn** - JGH Bonn-Venusberg,Kulturstudienplatz (IBN) Haager Weg 42, 53127 Bonn. ☻ jgh-bonn@t-online.de	☏ (228) 289970 ✆ (228) 2899714	249	01.01–23.12; 27–31.12	⑩ 4SW ♿ ⒸⒸ ℙ ▣ ☕
▲ **Bonndorf/Schw** Waldallee 27, 79848 Bonndorf.	☏ (7703) 359 ✆ (7703) 1686	215	27.12–23.12	♟ ⑩ 1W ℙ ▣
▲ **Börger** Herbergsweg 2, 26904 Börger.	☏ (5953) 228	62	01.04–31.10	♟ ⑩ 1NW
▲ **Borgwedel** Kreisstr 17, 24857 Borgwedel.	☏ (4354) 219 ✆ (4354) 1305	261	06.01–22.12	♟ ⑩ ♿ ℙ ▣
▲ **Borkum** Reedestr.231, 26757 Borkum, (North Sea).	☏ (4922) 579 ✆ (4922) 7124	530	�foto12	⑩ ℝ 7SE ℙ
▲ **Born-Ibenhorst** Im Darßer Wald, 18375 Born-Ibenhorst.	☏ (38234) 229 ✆ (38234) 231	180	01.01–20.12; 29–31.12	♟ ⑩ ℝ ♿ ℙ ▣
▲ **Braunlage** Von-Langen-Str 28, 38700 Braunlage.	☏ (5520) 2238 ✆ (5520) 1569	130	27.12–23.12	♟ ⑩ ℙ
▲ **Braunschweig** Salzdahlumer Str. 170, 38126 Braunschweig	☏ (531) 264320 ✆ (531) 2643270	160	27.12–23.12	♟ ⑩ ♿ ℙ
▲ **Braunsdorf** Dorfstr 17, 15518 Braunsdorf.	☏ (33633) 635 ✆ (33633) 65630	54	�foto12 (ℝ)	♟ ⑩
▲ **Breisach** Rheinuferstr 12, 79206 Breisach.	☏ (7667) 7665 ✆ (7667) 1847	156	27.12–22.12	⑩ ℙ ▣

Location/Address	Telephone No. Fax No.	Beds	Opening Dates	Facilities*
▲ Bremen (IBN) YGH, Kalkstr 6, 28195 Bremen.	☎ (421) 171369 ✆ (421) 171102	172	02.01-23.12	ⅲ ⅷ 1 NW ♿ ⅽⅽ P
▲ Bremerhaven YH + YGH Gaußstr 54-56, 27580 Bremerhaven.	☎ (471) 982080 ✆ (471) 87426	170	🔲12	ⅷ
▲ Bremervörde Feldstr 9, 27432 Bremervörde.	☎ (4761) 1275 ✆ (4761) 70701	122	🔲12	ⅲ ⅷ P
▲ Bremsdorfer Mühle 15890 Bremsdorf. 🅔 jh-bremsdorfer-muehle@jugendherberge.de	☎ (33654) 272 ✆ (33654) 49044	140	🔲12 (ⓡ 01.11–28.02)	ⅲ ⅷ
▲ Breuberg, Burg 64747 Breuberg.	☎ (6165) 3403 ✆ (6165) 6469	129	03.01–23.12	3E P
▲ Brilon "EURO-Umweltstudienplatz", Hölsterloh 3, 59929 Brilon.	☎ (2961) 2281 ✆ (2961) 51731	165	16.01–14.12	ⅷ P
▲ Brodenbach Moorkamp 7, 56332 Brodenbach.	☎ (2605) 3389 ✆ (2605) 4244	105	01.01–23.12; 27–31.12	ⅲ ⅷ
▲ Brotterode Am Zainhammer 4, 98599 Brotterode.	☎ (36840) 32125 ✆ (36840) 32125	65	28.12–23.12	ⅲ ⅷ ⓡ P
▲ Brüggen Auf dem Eggenberg 1, 41379 Brüggen.	☎ (2163) 5161 ✆ (2163) 59967	134	01.01–31.01; 01.03–23.12; 27–31.12	ⅲ ⅷ 👟 P
Buchheim ☞ **Bad Lausick**				
▲ Buckow Berliner Str 36, 15377 Buckow. 🅔 jh-buckow@jugendherberge.de	☎ (33433) 286 ✆ (33433) 56274	106	🔲12	ⅲ ⅷ ⓡ 1.5 S
▲ Büdingen Jugendherberge 1, 63654 Büdingen.	☎ (6042) 3697 ✆ (6042) 68178	121	27.12–23.12	ⅲ ⅷ 2NE P
▲ Burg auf Fehmarn Mathildenstr 34, 23769 Burg auf Fehmarn.	☎ (4371) 2150 ✆ (4371) 6680	188	06.01–22.12	ⅷ ♿ P 🔲
▲ Burg an der Wupper An der Jugendherberge 11, 42659 Solingen.	☎ (212) 41025 ✆ (212) 49449	118	01.01–23.12; 27–31.12	ⅲ ⅷ P
▲ Burg/Spreewald JH 'Friedrich-Ludwig-Jahn', Jugendherbergsweg 8, 03096 Burg/Spreewald. 🅔 jh-burg@jugendherberge.de	☎ (35603) 225 ✆ (35603) 13248	182	🔲12 (ⓡ ⅲ 01.11–28.02)	ⅲ ⅷ ⓡ
▲ Burg Stargard Dewitzer Chausse 07, 17094 Burg Stargard.	☎ (39603) 20207 ✆ (39603) 20207	126	01.01–20.12; 29–31.12	ⅲ ⅷ ⓡ P
Burg Wildenstein ☞ **Wildenstein**				
▲ Burghausen Kapuzinergasse 235, 84489 Burghausen (Bavaria)	☎ (8677) 4187 ✆ (8677) 911318	110	01.01–30.11	ⅲ ⅷ 0.5 S ♿ 👟 P 🔲
▲ Büsum Dr Martin-Bahr-Str 1, 25761 Büsum.	☎ (4834) 93371 ✆ (4834) 93376	206	19.01–22.12	ⅲ ⅷ ♿ P
▲ Cappenberger See Richard-Schirrmann-Weg 7, 44534 Lünen.	☎ (2306) 53546 ✆ (2306) 73000	122	09.01–22.12	ⅲ ⅷ P
▲ Carolinensiel Herbergsmense 13, 26409 Wittmund.	☎ (4464) 252 ✆ (4464) 655	123	01.01–30.11	ⅷ ⓡ 0.5 W P

Location/Address	Telephone No. Fax No.	Beds	Opening Dates	Facilities
▲ **Celle** Weghausstr 2, 29223 Celle.	☎ (5141) 53208 ☎ (5141) 53005	128	27.12–23.12	⑩ Ⓟ
▲ **Chemnitz** Augustusburger Str 369, 09127 Chemnitz.	☎ (371) 71331 ☎ (371) 73331	88	01.01–19.12; 28–31.12	⋔ ⑩ Ⓟ
▲ **Chossewitz** Weichensdorfer Str 3, 15848 Chossewitz. ✉ jh-chossewitz@jugendherberge.de	☎ (33673) 5757 ☎ (33673) 55100	58	📅 (Ⓡ 01.11–28.02)	⋔ ⑩ Ⓡ
▲ **Clausthal-Zellerfeld** Altenauer Str 55, 38678 Clausthal-Zellerfeld.	☎ (5323) 84293 ☎ (5323) 83827	122	27.12–23.12	⑩ Ⓟ
▲ **Coburg** Parkstr 2, 96450 Coburg (Bavaria).	☎ (9561) 15330 ☎ (9561) 28653	145	16.01–14.12	⋔ ⑩
▲ **Cochem** Klottener Str 9, 56812 Cochem.	☎ (2671) 8633 ☎ (2671) 8568	146	01.01–23.12; 27–31.12	⑩
▲ **Colditz** Haingasse 42, 04680 Colditz.	☎ (34381) 43335	40	📅	⋔ ⑩ Ⓟ
Cologne ☞ **Köln**				
▲ **Cottbus** Klosterplatz 2/3, 03046 Cottbus.	☎ (355) 22558 ☎ (355) 23798	40	📅	⋔ ⑩ ☞
▲ **Creglingen** Erdbacher Str 30, 97993 Creglingen.	☎ (7933) 336 ☎ (7933) 1326	144	01.01–23.01; 03.02–31.12	⋔ ⑩ ♿
▲ **Cuxhaven-Duhnen** Schlensenweg 2, 27476 Cuxhaven.	☎ (4721) 48552 ☎ (4721) 45794	277	01.02–14.12	⋔ ⑩ ♿ Ⓟ
▲ **Dachau** - JGH ⒾⒷⓃ Rosswachtstrasse 15, 85221 Dachau (Bavaria).	☎ (8131) 322950 ☎ (8131) 3229550	110	📅	⋔ ⑩ ♿ Ⓟ ☕
▲ **Dahlen** Belgernsche Str 25, 04774 Dahlen.	☎ (34361) 55002 ☎ (34361) 55003	125	📅	⋔ ⑩ Ⓟ
▲ **Dahmen** Dorfstr 14, 17166 Dahmen.	☎ (39933) 70552 ☎ (39933) 70650	130	01.01–20.12; 29–31.12	⋔ ⑩ Ⓡ Ⓟ ⓪
▲ **Dahn** Am Wachtfelsen 1, 66994 Dahn.	☎ (6391) 1769 ☎ (6391) 5122	108	01.01–23.12; 27–31.12	⋔ ⑩
▲ **Damme** Steinfelder Str 57, 49401 Damme.	☎ (5491) 96720 ☎ (5491) 967229	164	📅	⋔ ⑩ 1.5NW ♿ Ⓟ ☞
▲ **Darmstadt** "Am grossen Woog", Landgraf-Georg-Str 119, 64287 Darmstadt.	☎ (6151) 45293 ☎ (6151) 422535	122	27.12–23.12	⑩ 0.8E Ⓟ
▲ **Dassow-Holm** An der B 105, 23942 Dassow.	☎ (38826) 80614 ☎ (38826) 80614	122	01.01–20.12; 29–31.12	⋔ ⑩ Ⓡ ♿ Ⓟ
▲ **Daun** Maria-Hilf Str. 21, 54550 Daun.	☎ (6592) 2884 ☎ (6592) 1506	147	01.01–23.12; 27–31.12	⋔ ⑩
▲ **Damme/Dümmer** Steinfelder Str. 57, 49401 Damme	☎ (421) 598300 ☎ (421) 5983055	150	📅	⑩
▲ **Demmin** R-Breitscheid-Str, Postfach 1201, 17102 Demmin.	☎ (3998) 223388 ☎ (3998) 223388	32	01.01–20.12; 29–31.12	⑩ Ⓡ
▲ **Dessau** Waldkaterweg 11, 06846 Dessau.	☎ (340) 619452 ☎ (340) 619452	63	01.01–23.12 28–31.12	⋔ ⑩ Ⓟ

Location/Address	Telephone No. Fax No.	Beds	Opening Dates	Facilities
▲ **Detmold** Schirrmannstr 49, 32756 Detmold.	☎ (5231) 24739 ✆ (5231) 28927	126	16.01–13.12	⁉ ⦁ ℗
▲ **Diez** Schloss, 65582 Diez.	☎ (6432) 2481 ✆ (6432) 4504	91	01.01–23.12; 27–31.12	⁉ ⦁
▲ **Dilsberg** Untere Strasse 1, 69151 Neckargmünd-Dilsberg	☎ (6223) 2133 ✆ (6223) 74871	77	27.12–22.12	⦁
▲ **Dinkelsbühl** Koppengasse 10, 91550 Dinkelsbühl (Bavaria).	☎ (9851) 9509 ✆ (9851) 4874	148	01.03–30.09	⁉ ⦁
▲ **Donauwörth** Goethestr 10, 86609 Donauwörth (Bavaria).	☎ (906) 5158 ✆ (906) 243817	95	07.01–05.12	⁉ ⦁
▲ **Dornstetten** "Pfahlberg", Auf dem Pfahlberg 39, 72280 Dornstetten-Hallwangen.	☎ (7443) 6469 ✆ (7443) 20212	125	01.01–10.12; 27.12–31.12	⁉ ⦁ ♿ ℗
▲ **Dorsten-Wulfen** Im Schöning 83, 46286 Dorsten-Wulfen.	☎ (2369) 8722 ✆ (2369) 23867	104	10.01–20.12	⁉ ⦁ ℗
▲ **Dreisbach** "Zur Saarschleife", Herbergstr 1, 66693 Mettlach.	☎ (6868) 270 ✆ (6868) 556	133	until 28.02.01	⦁
▲ **Dresden** - "Rudi Arnolt" Hübnerstr 11, 01069 Dresden.	☎ (351) 4710667 ✆ (351) 4728959	81	🄵₁₂	⦁ 🄶
▲ **Dresden** - Oberloschwitz Sierksstr 33, 01326 Dresden.	☎ (351) 2683672 ✆ (351) 2683672	51	🄵₁₂	⦁ 🅁 ℗ 🄶
▲ **Dresden** - Radebeul Weintraubenstr 12, 01445 Radebeul.	☎ (351) 8382880 ✆ (351) 8382881	82	🄵₁₂	⦁ ℗
▲ **Dresden** - JGH IBN **Maternistraße 22, 01067 Dresden** ℮ servicecenter@djh-sachsen.de	☎ (351) 492620 ✆ (351) 4926299	450	🄵₁₂	⁉ ⦁ 🅁
▲ **Duisburg** Kalkweg 148E, 47279 Duisburg.	☎ (203) 724164 ✆ (203) 720834	134	11.01–23.12; 27–31.12	⁉ ⦁ 4.5W ℗ 🄶
▲ **Düsseldorf** IBN **Düsseldorfer Str 1, 40545 Düsseldorf.**	☎ (211) 557310 ✆ (211) 572513	272	03.01–21.12	⁉ ⦁ 3W ♿ ℗ 🄶
▲ **Eberbach/N** "Neckartal", Richard-Schirrmann-Str 6, 69412 Eberbach.	☎ (6271) 2593 ✆ (6271) 71395	127	27.12–22.12	⁉ ⦁ 2SW ℗
▲ **Ebersberg** Attenberger- Schillinger Str 1, 85560 Ebersberg (Bavaria).	☎ (8092) 22523 ✆ (8092) 87623	56	02.01–30.11	⦁
▲ **Eckernförde** Sehestedter Str 27, 24340 Eckernförde.	☎ (4351) 2154 ✆ (4351) 3604	164	06.01–22.12	⁉ ⦁ ℗ 🄶
▲ **Ehrenfriedersdorf** Greifensteinstr 46, 09427 Ehrenfriedersdorf.	☎ (37346) 1253	46	01.01–31.10 (⁉01.11–30. 11) 01–31.12	⁉ ⦁ ℗
▲ **Eichstätt** Reichenaustr 15, 85072 Eichstätt (Bavaria). ℮ jheichstaett@djh-bayern.de	☎ (8421) 98040 ✆ (8421) 980415	112	16.01–30.11	⁉ ⦁ 🄶
▲ **Eisenach** - Artur Becker "Artur Becker", Mariental 24, 99817 Eisenach.	☎ (3691) 743259 ✆ (3691) 743260	102	28.12–23.12	⁉ ⦁ 🅁 ℗

Location/Address	Telephone No. Fax No.	Beds	Opening Dates	Facilities
▲ Eisenberg - "Froschmühle" JH "Froschmühle", Mühltal 5, 07607 Eisenberg	☎ (36691) 43462 ✆ (36691) 60034	105	28.12–23.12	♔♔ Ⓡ P
▲ Ellwangen Schloß ob Ellwangen, 73479 Ellwangen.	☎ (7961) 53880 ✆ (7961) 55331	65	27.12–22.12	♔♔ ⑽
▲ Emden An der Kesselschleuse 5, 26725 Emden.	☎ (4921) 23797 ✆ (4921) 32161	90	01.02–30.11	♔♔ ⑽ P
▲ Erbach Eulbacher Str 33, 64711 Erbach.	☎ (6062) 3515 ✆ (6062) 62848	156	01.01–23.12; 27–31.12	♔♔ ⑽ 1.5NE P
▲ Erfurt Hochheimerstr 12, 99094 Erfurt. ℮ jugendherberge-erfurt@t-online.de	☎ (361) 5626705 ✆ (361) 5626706	201	28.12–23.12	♔♔ ⑽ Ⓡ ♿ ☞ P ⮑
▲ Erlangen - JH Frankenhof Südliche Stadtmauerstr 35, 91054 Erlangen (Bavaria).	☎ (9131) 862274; 862555 ✆ (9131) 862119	66	03.01–22.12	⑽
▲ Erpfingen Auf der Reute 1, 72820 Sonnenbühl.	☎ (7128) 1652 ✆ (7128) 3370	150	01.01–03.12; 27.12–31.12	♔♔ ⑽ P ⊡
▲ Esborn Wacholderstr 11, 58300 Wetter.	☎ (2335) 7718 ✆ (2335) 73519	60	15.01–17.12	⑽ P
▲ Eschwege "Haus der Jugend", Fritz-Neuenroth-Weg 1, 37269 Eschwege.	☎ (5651) 60099 ✆ (5651) 70916	182	27.12–23.12	♔♔ ⑽ 0.3NE ♿
▲ Esens-Bensersiel - "Ewald-Neemann - JH" Grashauser Flage 2, 26427 Esens.	☎ (4971) 3717 ✆ (4971) 659	146	01.01–31.01; 01.03–31.12	♔♔ ⑽ Ⓡ 1N ♿ P
▲ Essen-Werden Pastoratsberg 2, 45239 Essen-Werden.	☎ (201) 491163 ✆ (201) 492505	130	07.01–22.12	♔♔ ⑽ 10N P
▲ Esslingen Neuffenstr 65, 73734 Esslingen.	☎ (711) 381848 ✆ (711) 388886	96	03.01–03.12	♔♔ ⑽ P
▲ Eutin Jahnhöhe 6, 23701 Eutin.	☎ (4521) 2109 ✆ (4521) 74602	172	06.01–22.12	♔♔ ⑽ P ⊡
▲ Falkenhain An der Talsperre Kriebstein, 09648 Mittweida.	☎ (3727) 2952 ✆ (3727) 600050	220	01.05–30.09	♔♔ ⑽ P ⊡
▲ Fallingbostel Liethweg 1, 29683 Fallingbostel.	☎ (5162) 2274 ✆ (5162) 5704	92	27.12–23.12	♔♔ ⑽ P
▲ Feldberg Klinkecken 6, 17258 Feldberg.	☎ (39831) 20520 ✆ (39831) 20520	75	01.01–20.12; 29–31.12	♔♔ ⑽ Ⓡ P
▲ Feldberg/Schw "Hebelhof", Passhöhe 14, 79868 Feldberg.	☎ (7676) 221 ✆ (7676) 1232	270	27.12–22.12	♔♔ ⑽ Ⓡ P
▲ Feuchtwangen Dr.-Hans-Güthlein-Weg 1, 91555 Feuchtwangen (Bavaria)	☎ (9852) 670990 ✆ (9852) 6709920	76	⑫	♔♔ ⑽ P
▲ Finnentrop-Bamenohl "Jupp- Schöttler-Jugendherberge", Herbergsweg 1, 57413 Finnentrop-Bamenohl.	☎ (2721) 7293 ✆ (2721) 5486	30	27.12–23.12	⑽ P
▲ Finnentrop-Heggen Ahauser Str 22-24, 57405 Finnentrop-Heggen.	☎ (2721) 50345 ✆ (2721) 79460	223	27.12–23.12	♔♔ ⑽ ♿ P

Location/Address	Telephone No. Fax No.	Beds	Opening Dates	Facilities
▲ **Flensburg** Fichtestr 16, 24943 Flensburg.	☎ (461) 37742 ☎ (461) 312952	198	31.01–22.12	ⅲ ⑩ 4NE P
▲ **Flessenow** Am Schweriner See 1B, 19067 Rubow OT. Flessenow.	☎ (3866) 82400 ☎ (3866) 82401	123	01.01–20.12; 29–31.12	ⅲ ⑩ R P
▲ **Forbach** - "Heinrich-Kastner-YH" Birket 1, Postfach 1175, 76594 Forbach.	☎ (7228) 2427 ☎ (7228) 1551	84	27.12–23.12	ⅲ ⑩ 2E P
▲ **Forbach** Environmental Study Centre, "Franz-Köbele-JH", OT Herrenwies, Haus Nr 33, 76596 Forbach.	☎ (7226) 257 ☎ (7226) 1318	143	27.12–22.12	ⅲ ⑩ P
▲ **Frankfurt** [IBN] **"Haus der Jugend" Deutschherrnufer 12, 60594 Frankfurt.** ✉ jugendherberge_frankfurt@t-online.de	☎ (69) 6100150 ☎ (69) 61001599	470	03.01–22.12	ⅲ ⑩ R 1SE ♿ ☕
▲ **Frauenau** Hauptstr 29a, 94258 Frauenau (Bavaria).	☎ (9926) 735 ☎ (9926) 735	24	01.01–30.11	⑩
Frauenberg ☞ **Haidmühle**				
▲ **Frauenstein** Walkmühlenstr 13, 09623 Frauenstein.	☎ (37326) 1307 ☎ (37326) 84400	86	12	ⅲ ⑩ P
▲ **Freiburg** **Kartäuserstr 151, 79104 Freiburg.**	☎ (761) 67656 ☎ (761) 60367	405	27.12-22.12	ⅲ ⑩ R 6E ♿ P
▲ **Freudenstadt** Eugen-Nägele-Str 69, 72250 Freudenstadt.	☎ (7441) 7720 ☎ (7441) 85788	130	01–10.11; 27.12–31.12	ⅲ ⑩
▲ **Freusburg** Burgstrasse 46, 57548 Kirchen-Freusburg.	☎ (2741) 61094 ☎ (2741) 63135	219	27.12–23.12	ⅲ ⑩ P
▲ **Friedrichroda** - "Rudolf Breitscheid" Waldstrasse 25, 99894 Friedrichroda. ✉ jugendherberge_friedrichroda@t-online.de	☎ (3623) 304410 ☎ (3623) 305003	125	28.12–23.12	⑩ R P
▲ **Friedrichshafen** "Graf- Zeppelin-JH", Lindauer Str 3, 88046 Friedrichshafen.	☎ (7541) 72404 ☎ (7541) 74986	220	01.01–10.12; 27.12–31.12	⑩ R 2E P
▲ **Friedrichstadt** Ostdeutsche Str 1, 25840 Friedrichstadt.	☎ (4881) 7984 ☎ (4881) 7984	65	16.01–14.12	ⅲ ⑩ P
▲ **Fröbersgrün** - Umweltstudienplatz Umweltstudienplatz, Ortsstr 17, 08548 Syrau, Ortsteil Fröbersgrün.	☎ (37431) 3256 ☎ (37431) 88963	98	01.02–31.10 (ⅲ01.11–30.01)	ⅲ ⑩ P
▲ **Fulda** Schirrmannstr 31, 36041 Fulda.	☎ (661) 73389 ☎ (661) 74811	122	27.12–23.12	ⅲ ⑩ 2SW P
▲ **Furth im Wald** Daberger Str 50, 93437 Furth im Wald (Bavaria).	☎ (9973) 9254 ☎ (9973) 2447	128	01.01–14.11; 27.12–31.12	ⅲ ⑩
▲ **Füssen** [IBN] Mariahilferstr 5, 87629 Füssen (Bavaria).	☎ (8362) 7754 ☎ (8362) 2770	138	01.01–14.11; 27–31.12	ⅲ ⑩
▲ **Gardelegen** - Otto-Reutter-Haus Waldschnibbe, 39638 Gardelegen.	☎ (3907) 712629 ☎ (3907) 712629	90	01.01–23.12 28–31.12	ⅲ ⑩ P

Location/Address	Telephone No. Fax No.	Beds	Opening Dates	Facilities
▲ **Garmisch-Partenkirchen** Jochstr 10, 82467 Garmisch-Partenkirchen (Bavaria).	☎ (8821) 2980 ✆ (8821) 58536	210	01.01–14.11; 27–31.12	♦♦ ⑩ ☞ ▣
▲ **Geesthacht** Berliner Str 117, 21502 Geesthacht.	☎ (4152) 2356 ✆ (4152) 77918	123	06.01–22.12	♦♦ ⑩ ♿ ▣
Gehringswalde ☞ **Warmbad**				
▲ **Gerolstein** Zur Büschkapelle 1, 54568 Gerolstein.	☎ (6591) 4745 ✆ (6591) 7243	184	01.01–23.12; 27–31.12	♦♦ ⑩ ♿
▲ **Gersfeld** Jahnstr 6, 36129 Gersfeld.	☎ (6654) 340 ✆ (6654) 7788	107	27.12–23.12	♦♦ ⑩ 0.5 SE ▣
▲ **Geyer** Anton-Günther-Weg 3, 09468 Geyer.	☎ (37346) 1364 ✆ (37346) 1770	93	🅛	♦♦ ⑩ ®️ ▣
▲ **Gießen** Richard-Schirrmann-Weg 53, 35398 Giessen.	☎ (641) 65879 ✆ (641) 9605502	91	27.12–23.12	♦♦ ⑩ 3W ▣
▲ **Glörsee** 58339 Breckerfeld.	☎ (2338) 434 ✆ (2338) 3674	124	27.12–17.12	⑩ ▣
▲ **Glückstadt** Pentzstr 12, 25348 Glückstadt.	☎ (4124) 2259 ✆ (4124) 2259	45	01.05–30.09	♦♦ ⑩ ®️ ▣
▲ **Gommern** Manheimerstr 12, 39245 Gommern.	☎ (39200) 40080 ✆ (39200) 40082	102	01.01–23.12; 28–31.12	⑩ ▣ ▣
Göppingen ☞ **Hohenstaufen**				
▲ **Gorenzen** Hagen 2-4, 06343 Gorenzen.	☎ (34782) 20384; 21356 ✆ (34782) 21357	125	01.01–23.12; 28–31.12	♦♦ ⑩ ♿ ▣
▲ **Görlitz** - "Friedensgrenze" "Friedensgrenze", Goethestr 17, 02826 Görlitz.	☎ (3581) 406510 ✆ (3581) 406510	100	🅛	♦♦ ⑩ ▣
▲ **Goslar** Rammelsberger Str 25, 38644 Goslar.	☎ (5321) 22240 ✆ (5321) 41376	168	27.12–23.12	♦♦ ⑩ ♿ ▣
▲ **Gößweinstein** Etzdorferstr 6, 91327 Gößweinstein (Bavaria).	☎ (9242) 259 ✆ (9242) 7135	129	16.01–30.11	♦♦ ⑩
▲ **Göttingen** Habichtsweg 2, 37075 Göttingen.	☎ (551) 57622 ✆ (551) 43887	161	27.12–23.12	♦♦ ⑩ ♿ ▣
▲ **Gotha** Mozartstr. 1, Postfach 100246, 99852 Gotha	☎ (3621) 854008 ✆ (3621) 854008	120	28.12–23.12	♦♦ ⑩ ®️ ▣
▲ **Graal-Müritz** An der Jugendherberge 32, 18181 Seeheilbad Graal-Müritz.	☎ (38206) 77520 ✆ (38206) 77204	80	01.01–20.12; 29–31.12	♦♦ ⑩ ®️ ▣
▲ **Grabow** Jugendherberge 01, 19300 Grabow.	☎ (38756) 27954 ✆ (38756) 27954	46	01.01–20.12; 29–31.12	♦♦ ⑩ ®️
▲ **Gräfenroda** - "Olga Benario" Waldstr 134, 99330 Gräfenroda.	☎ (36205) 76290 ✆ (36205) 76421	60	27.12–23.12	♦♦ ⑩ ®️ ▣
▲ **Grafhorn-Lehrte** Grafenhornstr. 30, 31275 Grafhorn-Lehrte	☎ (5175) 2790 ✆ (5175) 93151	28	27.12–23.12	⑩
▲ **Grävenwiesbach** "Richard- Schirrmann-JH", Hasselborner Str. 20, 61279 Grävenwiesbach.	☎ (6086) 520 ✆ (6086) 970352	150	27.12–23.12	♦♦ ⑩ 2.5 NE ▣

Location/Address	Telephone No. Fax No.	Beds	Opening Dates	Facilities
▲ Greetsiel Kleinbahnstr 15, 26736 Krummhörn.	☎ (4926) 550 ✆ (4926) 1473	64	01.03–31.10	⑩ 🅿
▲ Greifswald Pestalozzistr. 11/12, D-17489 Greifswald.		132	opening 01.07.00	♦♦♦ ⑩ Ⓡ 1SE ♿ 🅿 ☕
▲ Greiz - "Juri Gagarin" Amselstieg 12, O7973 Greiz.	☎ (3661) 2176 ✆ (3661) 687808	92	28.12–23.12	♦♦♦ ⑩ Ⓡ 🅿 ▣ ☕
▲ Grethen Herbergsweg 5, 04668 Parthenstein.	☎ (3437) 763449 ✆ (3437) 763449	105	🈵	♦♦♦ ⑩ ♿ 🅿
▲ Groß Reken Coesfelder Str 18, 48734 Reken.	☎ (2864) 1023 ✆ (2864) 2044	126	27.12–23.12	♦♦♦ ⑩ 🅿
▲ Grumbach Jöhstädter Str 19, 09477 Jöhstadt.	☎ (37343) 2288 ✆ (37343) 88003	62	🈵	♦♦♦ ⑩ 🅿 ▣
▲ Günzburg Schillerstr 12, 89312 Günzburg (Bavaria).	☎ (8221) 34487 ✆ (8221) 31390	34	16.01–14.11	♦♦♦ ⑩
▲ Güstrow-Schabernack Jugendherberge Güstrow-Schabernack, Heidberg 33, 18273 Güstrow 🄴 jh-guestrow@t-online.de	☎ (3843) 840044 ✆ (3843) 840045	72	10.01–20.12; 28–31.12	♦♦♦ ⑩ Ⓡ 6SE 🅿 ▣ ☕
▲ Gunzenhausen Spitalstr. 3, 91710 Gunzenhausen (Bavaria)	☎ (9831) 67020 ✆ (9831) 670211	132	🈵	♦♦♦ ⑩ Ⓡ 0.5N ♿ 🐕 🅿 ▣
▲ Gütersloh "Haus der Jugend und des Sports", Wiesenstr 40, 33330 Gütersloh.	☎ (5241) 822181 ✆ (5241) 822184	67	27.12–23.12	♦♦♦ ⑩ ♿ 🅿
▲ Hagen Eppenhauser Str 65a, 58093 Hagen.	☎ (2331) 50254 ✆ (2331) 588576	138	27.12–23.12	♦♦♦ ⑩ 🅿
▲ Hahnenklee Hahnenkleer Str 11, 38644 Goslar - OT Hahnenklee- Bockswiese.	☎ (5325) 2256 ✆ (5325) 3524	122	27.12–23.12	⑩ 🅿
▲ Haidmühle - JH Frauenberg Frauenberg 45, 94145 Haidmühle (Bavaria).	☎ (8556) 467 ✆ (8556) 1021	157	01.01–14.11; 27–31.12	♦♦♦ ⑩ ▣
▲ Haldensleben Bornsche Str 94, 39340 Haldensleben.	☎ (3904) 40386 ✆ (3904) 40386	40	01.01–23.12; 28–31.12	♦♦♦ ⑩ 🐕 🅿 ▣
▲ Halle August-Bebel-Str 48a, 06108 Halle.	☎ (345) 2024716 ✆ (345) 2025172	72	01.01-23.12; 28-31.12	♦♦♦ ⑩ 🅿 ▣
Hallwangen ☞ Dornstetten				
▲ Haltern Stockwieser Damm 255, 45721 Haltern/Stausee.	☎ (2364) 2258 ✆ (2364) 169604	138	27.12–23.12	♦♦♦ ⑩ 🅿
▲ Hamburg - Auf dem Stintfang ⒾⒷ⒩ Alfred-Wegener-Weg 5, 20459 Hamburg. 🄴 jh-stintfang@t-online.de	☎ (40) 313488, ♦♦♦ Ⓡ (40) 3191037 ✆ (40) 315407	320	01.02–23.12; 27.12–31.01	⑩ Ⓡ 2SW ♿ 🐕 ▣
▲ Hamburg ⒾⒷ⒩ JGH "Horner-Rennbahn", Rennbahnstr 100, 22111 Hamburg. 🄴 jgh-hamburg@t-online.de	☎ (40) 6511671 ✆ (40) 6556516	267	01.01–31.01; 01.03–22.12	♦♦♦ ⑩ 5E ♿ 🐕 🅿

Location/Address	Telephone No. Fax No.	Beds	Opening Dates	Facilities
▲ **Hameln** Fischbecker Str 33, 31785 Hameln.	☏ (5151) 3425 🖷 (5151) 42316	106	27.12–23.12	⦿ ♿ P
▲ **Hamm** Jugendgästehaus "Sylverberg", Ostenallee 101, 59071 Hamm.	☏ (2381) 83837 🖷 (2381) 83844	60	27.12–23.12	⦿ P
▲ **Hankensbüttel** Helmrichsweg 24, 29386 Hankensbüttel.	☏ (5832) 2500 🖷 (5832) 6596	142	27.12–23.12	ⅲ ⦿ ♿ P
▲ **Hannover** **Ferdinand-Wilhelm-Fricke-Weg 1, 30169 Hannover.** ✉ djh-lub-hannover@t-online.de	☏ (511) 1317674 🖷 (511) 18555	317	01.01–23.12; 27–31.12	ⅲ ⦿ [2S] ♿ P ⬤
▲ **Hannover -** Naturfreundehaus in der Eilenriede Hermann-Bahlsen-Allee 8, 30665 Hannover.	☏ (511) 691493 🖷 (511) 690652	82	27.12–23.12	⦿ [4N] P
▲ **Hannover-Misburg** Am. Fahrhorstfelde 5, 30629 Hannover	☏ (511) 580537 🖷 (511) 9585836	32	27.12–23.12	ⅲ ⦿
▲ **Hann.Münden** Prof-Oelkers-Str 10, 34346 Hann.Münden.	☏ (5541) 8853 🖷 (5541) 73439	135	27.12–23.12	ⅲ ⦿ P
Hardter Wald ☞ **Mönchengladbach**				
▲ **Haren/EMS** "St Nikolaus- JH", Nikolausweg 17, 49733 Haren (EMS).	☏ (5932) 2726	85	01.03–31.10	ⅲ ⦿ P
▲ **Hartenstein** Salzlecke 10, 91235 Hartenstein (Bavaria).	☏ (9152) 1296 🖷 (9152) 1328	68	16.01–30.11	⦿
▲ **Hattingen** Jugendbildungsstätte Welper, Falken- Freizeitwerk, Hüttenbauvereinigung Welper eV, Rathenaustrasse 59a, 45527 Hattingen- Welper.	☏ (2324) 94640 🖷 (2324) 946494	104	27.12–23.12	⦿ P
▲ **Heide** Poststr 4, 25746 Heide.	☏ (481) 71575 🖷 (481) 72901	82	01.02–22.12	ⅲ ⦿ ♿ P
▲ **Heidelberg** **Tiergartenstr 5, 69120 Heidelberg.**	☏ (6221) 412066 🖷 (6221) 402559	440	01.01–23.12; 27–31.12	ⅲ ⦿ ⓡ [4NW] P 🖥
▲ **Heidenheim** Liststr 15, 89518 Heidenheim.	☏ (7321) 42045 🖷 (7321) 949045	128	03.01–19.11	ⅲ ⦿ ♿
▲ **Heilbronn** "JH Reinhardt", Schirrmannstr 9, 74074 Heilbronn.	☏ (7131) 172961 🖷 (7131) 164345	130	10.01–11.12	⦿ P 🖥
▲ **Heldrungen** - "Wasserburg" Schloßstr. 13, 06577 Heldrungen	☏ (34673) 91224 🖷 (34673) 98136	52	28.12–23.12	ⅲ ⦿ ⓡ P
▲ **Helgoland** "Haus der Jugend", Postfach 580, 27487 Helgoland.	☏ (4725) 341 🖷 (4725) 7467	146	01.04–31.10	ⅲ ⦿
▲ **Hellenthal** Platis 3, 53940 Hellenthal.	☏ (2482) 2238 🖷 (2482) 2557	161	01.01–23.12	ⅲ ⦿ ♿ ⬚ P 🖥

Location/Address	Telephone No. Fax No.	Beds	Opening Dates	Facilities
▲ **Helmarshausen** Gottsbürener Str. 15, 34385 Bad Karlshafen-Helmarshausen.	☎ (5672) 1027 ❶ (5672) 2976	178	27.12–23.12	�037 ⑩ 1SE P
Hemhof ☞ **Bad Endorf**				
▲ **Heppenheim** JH "Starkenburg", 64646 Heppenheim.	☎ (6252) 77323 ❶ (6252) 78185	121	25.12–21.12	�037 ⑩ 1.5NE P
▲ **Heringsdorf** Puschkinstr 7/9, 17424 Seebad Heringsdorf. ❷ jh_heringsdorf@t-online.de	☎ (38378) 22325 ❶ (38378) 32301	167	01.01–20.12; 29–31.12	�037 ⑩ R 🚹 P
▲ **Hermeskeil** Adolf-Kolping-Str 4, 54411 Hermeskeil.	☎ (6503) 3097 ❶ (6503) 6146	111	01.01–23.12; 27–31.12	�037 ⑩
Herrenwies ☞ **Forbach**				
▲ **Hessenstein, Burg** 34516 Vöhl Ederbringhausen.	☎ (6455) 300 ❶ (6455) 8771	126	27.12–23.12	�037 ⑩ 12S P
▲ **Hilchenbach** Wilhelm-Münker-Str 9, 57271 Hilchenbach.	☎ (2733) 4396 ❶ (2733) 8085	86	01.02–23.12	⑩ P
▲ **Hilders** "Haus der Jugend", 36115 Hilders.	☎ (6681) 365 ❶ (6681) 8429	148	27.12–23.12	�037 ⑩ 1.5E P
▲ **Hildesheim** Schirrmannweg 4, 31139 Hildesheim.	☎ (5121) 42717 ❶ (5121) 47847	104	27.12–23.12	�037 ⑩ 🚹 P
▲ **Hitzacker** Wolfsschlucht 2 (An der Elbuferstrasse), 29456 Hitzacker.	☎ (5862) 244 ❶ (5862) 7767	165	27.12–23.12	�037 ⑩ 🚹 P 🗔
▲ **Hochspeyer -** Naturpark-undWaldjugendherberge Trippstadter Strasse 150, 67691 Hochspeyer.	☎ (6305) 336 ❶ (6305) 5152	149	27.12–23.12	�037 ⑩
▲ **Hof** Beethovenstr 44, 95032 Hof (Bavaria).	☎ (9281) 93277 ❶ (9281) 92016	91	01.01–30.11; 29–31.12	�037 ⑩ 🗔
▲ **Hohe Fahrt** Am Edersee, 34516 Vöhl.	☎ (5635) 251 ❶ (5635) 8142	230	27.12–23.12	�037 ⑩ 4SW P
▲ **Hohenberg** Auf der Burg, 95691 Hohenberg (Bavaria).	☎ (9233) 77260 ❶ (9233) 772611	137	01.01–20.12; 27–31.12	�037 ⑩ 🗔
▲ **Hohenstaufen** Schottengasse 45, 73037 Göppingen, Hohenstaufen.	☎ (7165) 438 ❶ (7165) 1418	128	03.01–27.11	⑩ P
▲ **Hoherodskopf** Haus der Jugend, 63679 Schotten.	☎ (6044) 2760 ❶ (6044) 784	125	01.01–23.12; 27–31.12	�037 8NE P
▲ **Hohnstein** - Burg Hohnstein Am. Markt. 1, 01848 Hohnstein	☎ (35975) 81202 ❶ (35975) 81203	250	🗓	�037 ⑩
▲ **Holzminden** Am Steinhof, 37603 Holzminden.	☎ (5531) 4411 ❶ (5531) 120630	123	27.12–23.12	�037 ⑩ P
▲ **Homburg** Sickinger Str 12, 66424 Homburg.	☎ (6841) 3679 ❶ (6841) 120220	76	01.01–23.12; 27–31.12	�037 ⑩
▲ **Hormersdorf** Am Greifenbachstauweiher, 09468 Geyer	☎ (37346) 1396 ❶ (37346) 1645	205	🗓	�037 ⑩ 🚹 P ☕

Location/Address	Telephone No. Fax No.	Beds	Opening Dates	Facilities
▲ **Horn-Bad Meinberg** Jahnstr 36, 32805 Horn-Bad Meinberg.	☎ (5234) 2534 🖷 (5234) 69199	123	22.01–23.12	⏸️🅿️
▲ **Hörnum** Friesenplatz 2, 25997 Hörnum/Sylt.	☎ (4651) 880294 🖷 (4651) 881392	168	16.01–30.11	👫 ⏸️🅿️
▲ **Höxter** "EURO-Umweltstudienplatz", An der Wilhelmshöhe 59, 37671 Höxter.	☎ (5271) 2233 🖷 (5271) 1237	130	03.01–22.12	⏸️🅿️
▲ **Hude** Linteler Str 3, 27798 Hude.	☎ (4408) 414 🖷 (4408) 970322	90	01.03–31.10	⏸️🅿️
▲ **Hürth** "Villehaus" Adolf- Dasbach-Weg 5, 50354 Hürth.	☎ (2233) 42463 🖷 (2233) 16351	72	01.01–23.12; 27–31.12	👫 ⏸️🅿️
▲ **Husum** Schobüller Str 34, 25813 Husum.	☎ (4841) 2714 🖷 (4841) 81568	181	06.01–30.11	👫 ⏸️ ♿ ☂ 🅿️ 🅾️
▲ **Idar-Oberstein** Alte Treibe 23, 55743 Idar-Oberstein.	☎ (6781) 24366 🖷 (6781) 26712	128	01.01–23.12; 27–31.12	👫 ⏸️
▲ **Igersheim** Erlenbachtalstr 44, 97999 Igersheim	☎ (7931) 6373 🖷 (7931) 52795	162	10.01–11.12	👫 ⏸️🅿️
▲ **Ihrlerstein** - JH Kelheim Kornblumenweg 1, 93346 Ihrlerstein (Bavaria).	☎ (9441) 3309 🖷 (9441) 21792	122	01.01–30.11	👫 ⏸️🅾️
▲ **Ilmenau** Am Stollen 49, 98693 Ilmenau. 📧 jh-ilmenau@t-online.de	☎ (3677) 884681 🖷 (3677) 884682	130	29.12–22.12	👫 ⏸️ Ⓡ ♿ 🅿️
▲ **Ingolstadt** Friedhofstr 4 1/2, 85049 Ingolstadt (Bavaria).	☎ (841) 34177 🖷 (841) 910178	84	01.02–14.12	👫 ⏸️♿
▲ **Inselsberg** - "Großer Inselsberg" 98599 Brotterode.	☎ (36259) 62329 🖷 (36259) 62329	63	28.12–22.12	⏸️ Ⓡ
▲ **Inzmühlen** Wehlener Weg 10, 21256 Handeloh.	☎ (4188) 342 🖷 (4188) 7858	164	01.02–22.12	👫 ⏸️♿ 🅿️
▲ **Isny** "Georg-Sulzberger-JH", Dekan-Marquardt-Str 18, 88316 Isny.	☎ (7562) 2550 🖷 (7562) 55547	130	10.01–27.11	⏸️🅿️
▲ **Itzehoe** Juliengardeweg 13, 25524 Itzehoe.	☎ (4821) 62270 🖷 (4821) 5710	75	16.01–14.12	👫 ⏸️🅿️
▲ **Jena** - InternationalesJugendgästehaus des Ib "Am Herrenberge", Am Herrenberge 3, 07745 Jena.	☎ (3641) 687230 🖷 (3641) 687202	140	06.01–19.12	👫 ⏸️ Ⓡ 3.5W ⊞CC⊟ 🅿️
▲ **Jever** Mooshütter Weg 12,26441 Jever.	☎ (4461) 3590 🖷 (4461) 3565	50	01.04–31.10	👫 ⏸️
▲ **Johanngeorgenstadt** Hospitalstr 5, 08349 Johanngeorgenstadt.	☎ (3773) 882194 🖷 (3773) 889150	60	🔒₁₂	👫 ⏸️🅿️🅾️
▲ **Jonsdorf** - "Dreiländereck" Hainstr 14, 02796 Jonsdorf.	☎ (35844) 72130 🖷 (35844) 72131	72	🔒₁₂	👫 ⏸️🅿️
Josefsthal ☞ **Schliersee**				
▲ **Juist** Loogster Pad 20, 26571 Juist, (North Sea).	☎ (4935) 92910 🖷 (4935) 8294	294	01.01–31.10	👫 ⏸️ Ⓡ 1.5W

Location/Address	Telephone No. Fax No.	Beds	Opening Dates	Facilities
▲ **Kandern** "Platzhof", Auf der Scheideck, 79400 Kandern.	☎ (7626) 484 ☏ (7626) 6809	69	01.03–31.10	♦♦♦ ⛌ 🅿
▲ **Kappeln** Eckernförder Str 2, 24376 Kappeln.	☎ (4642) 8550 ☏ (4642) 81086	170	06.01–22.12	♦♦♦ ⛌ ♿ 🅿 🗗
▲ **Karlsruhe** Moltkestr 24, 76133 Karlsruhe.	☎ (721) 28248 ☏ (721) 27647	164	27.12–22.12	♦♦♦ ⛌ 4NW 🅿
▲ **Kassel** Schenkendorfstr 18, 34119 Kassel. @ kassel@djh-hessen.de	☎ (561) 776455; 776933 ☏ (561) 776832	209	02.01–23.12; 27–30.12	♦♦♦ ⛌ 1.5NW ♿
▲ **Katzhütte** Bahnhofstr 82, 98746 Katzhütte.	☎ (36781) 37785 ☏ (36781) 33806	70	28.12–22.12	⛌ ⓡ
▲ **Kehl** Altrheinweg 11, 77694 Kehl.	☎ (7851) 2330 ☏ (7851) 76608	122	27.12–22.12	♦♦♦ ⛌ 1SW 🅿
Kelheim ☞ **Ihrlerstein**				
▲ **Kempten** Saarlandstr 1, 87437 Kempten (Bavaria).	☎ (831) 73663 ☏ (831) 770381	90	01.01–14.11; 28.12–31.12	⛌
▲ **Kevelaer** Am Michelsweg 11, 47626 Kevelaer.	☎ (2832) 8267 ☏ (2832) 899432	130	01.01–23.12; 27–31.12	♦♦♦ ⛌ 🖮 🅿
▲ **Kiel** (IBN) Johannesstr 1, 24143 Kiel.	☎ (431) 731488 ☏ (431) 735723	265	04.01–19.12	♦♦♦ ⛌ 2SE ♿ 🅿
▲ **Kirchberg** Gaggstatter Str 35, 74592 Kirchberg.	☎ (7954) 230 ☏ (7954) 1319	90	24.01–23.12	⛌ 🅿
▲ **Kleve** St Annaberg 2, 47533 Kleve Materborn.	☎ (2821) 23671 ☏ (2821) 24778	106	01.01–23.12; 27–31.12	♦♦♦ ⛌ 🅿
▲ **Klingenthal** - "Aschberg" Grenzweg 22, 08248 Klingenthal.	☎ (37467) 22094 ☏ (37467) 22099	122	🄵₁₂	♦♦♦ ⛌ ⓡ 🅿
▲ **Koblenz** **Festung Ehrenbreitstein, 56077 Koblenz.**	☎ (261) 97287-0 ☏ (261) 97287-30	183	01.01-23.12; 27-31.12	♦♦♦ ⛌ 6NE ♿ ⊂CC⊃
▲ **Kochel** Badstr 2, 82431 Kochel (Bavaria).	☎ (8851) 5296 ☏ (8851) 7019	31	01.01–14.11; 27–31.12	⛌
▲ **Köln** - Deutz (IBN) **Siegesstr 5a, 50679 Köln.** @ jh-deutz@t-online.de	☎ (221) 814711 ☏ (221) 884425	374	01.01–23.12; 27–31.12	♦♦♦ ⛌ 3E ♿ 🅿 🗗
▲ **Köln** - Riehl **JGH, An der Schanz 14, 50735 Köln.**	☎ (221) 767081 ☏ (221) 761555	366	01.01–23.12; 27–31.12	♦♦♦ ⛌ 6NE ♿ 🅿 🗗 ☕
▲ **Königsberg** Schlossberg 10, 97486 Königsberg (Bavaria).	☎ (9525) 237 ☏ (9525) 8114	89	08.01–14.12	♦♦♦ ⛌
▲ **Königsbronn** Weilerweg 12, 89551 Königsbronn-Ochsenberg.	☎ (7328) 6600 ☏ (7328) 7451	112	01.02–23.12	♦♦♦ ⛌ ♿ 🅿
▲ **Königstein** Halbestadt 13, 01824 Königstein	☎ (35022) 42432 ☏ (35022) 42432	104	🄵₁₂	♦♦♦ ⛌ ♿
▲ **Konstanz** "Otto-Möricke-Turm", Zur Allmannshöhe 18, 78464 Konstanz.	☎ (7531) 32260 ☏ (7531) 31163	163	🄵₁₂	♦♦♦ ⛌ 5NE 🅿

Location/Address	Telephone No. Fax No.	Beds	Opening Dates	Facilities
▲ **Korbach** Enser Str 9, 34497 Korbach.	☎ (5631) 8360 🖷 (5631) 4835	98	27.12–23.12	ⅲ ⏹ 0.5W ♿
▲ **Köriser See** Am See 5, 15746 Groß Köris 📧 jh-koeriser-see@jugendherberge.de	☎ (33766) 62730 🖷 (33766) 62734	78	🗓12 (Ⓡ 01.11–28.02)	ⅲ ⏹ Ⓡ
▲ **Köthener See** Dorfstr 20, 15748 Märkisch-Bucholz 📧 jh-koethener-see@jugendherberge.de	☎ (33765) 80555 🖷 (33765) 84870	110	🗓12 (Ⓡ 01.11–28.02)	ⅲ ⏹ Ⓡ ☐
▲ **Kretzschau** 06712 Kretzschau.	☎ (3441) 212678; 210173 🖷 (3441) 210174	204	01.01–23.12; 28–31.12	ⅲ ⏹ ♿ 🅿
▲ **Kreuth** - JH Scharling Nördliche Hauptstr 91, 83708 Kreuth (Bavaria).	☎ (8029) 99560 🖷 (8029) 995629	103	01.01–14.11; 27–31.12	ⅲ ⏹ Ⓡ ☐
▲ **Kronach** Festung 1, 96317 Kronach (Bavaria).	☎ (9261) 94412	106	01.03–30.11	⏹ ☐
▲ **Kühlungsborn** Dünenstr 4, 18225 Ostseebad Kühlungsborn.	☎ (38293) 17270 🖷 (38293) 17279	124	01.01–20.12; 29–31.12	ⅲ ⏹ Ⓡ ♿ 🅿
▲ **Lam** Jugendherbergsweg 1, 93462 Lam (Bavaria).	☎ (9943) 1068 🖷 (9943) 2936	130	01.01–14.11; 27–31.12	ⅲ ⏹
▲ **Landshut** Richard-Schirrmann-Weg 6, 84028 Landshut (Bavaria).	☎ (871) 23449 🖷 (871) 274947	100	08.01–22.12	ⅲ ⏹ ♿ ☞
▲ **Langenwetzendorf** Greizerstr. (Am Schwimmbad), 07957 Langenwetzendorf	☎ (36625) 20305	72	28.12–22.12	⏹ Ⓡ 🅿
▲ **Langeoog** Domäne Melkhörn, 26465 Langeoog, (North Sea).	☎ (4972) 276 🖷 (4972) 6694	126	01.04–31.10	⏹ Ⓡ 5E
▲ **Laubach** Felix-Klipstein-Weg 35, 35321 Laubach.	☎ (6405) 1376 🖷 (6405) 7046	122	27.12–23.12	⏹ 2N 🅿
▲ **Lauenburg** Am Sportplatz 7, 21481 Lauenburg.	☎ (4153) 2598 🖷 (4153) 2310	130	06.01–22.12	ⅲ ⏹ 🅿
▲ **Lauenstein** Vogelsang 53, 31020 Lauenstein-Salzhemmendorf	☎ (5153) 6474 🖷 (5153) 5029	73	27.12–23.12	ⅲ ⏹
▲ **Lauterbach** Fritz-Ebel-Allee 50, 36341 Lauterbach.	☎ (6641) 2181 🖷 (6641) 61200	172	27.12–23.12	ⅲ ⏹ 4NE 🅿
▲ **Leer** Süderkreuzstr 7, 26789 Leer.	☎ (491) 2126 🖷 (491) 61576	94	01.03–31.10	ⅲ ⏹
▲ **Leichlingen** "Naturfreundehaus", Am Block 4, 42799 Leichlingen.	☎ (2175) 2917	43	🗓12	⏹ 🅿
▲ **Leinburg** - JH Weissenbrunn Badstr 15, 91227 Leinburg (Bavaria).	☎ (9187) 1529 🖷 (9187) 5920	60	16.01–30.11	⏹
▲ **Leipzig** - Leipzig-Centrum Volksgartenstrasse 24, 04347 Leipzig.	☎ (341) 2457011 🖷 (341) 2457012	176	01.01–22.12; 28–31.12	ⅲ ⏹ Ⓡ 4NE 🅿
▲ **Lenggries** Jugendherbergsstr 10, 83661 Lenggries (Bavaria).	☎ (8042) 2424 🖷 (8042) 4532	93	01.01–30.11; 27–31.12	⏹ 🅿

Location/Address	Telephone No. Fax No.	Beds	Opening Dates	Facilities
▲ **Lichtenfels** Alte Coburger Str 43, 96215 Lichtenfels (Bavaria).	☎ (9571) 71039 🖷 (9571) 71877	87	01.02–14.12	††† ⑩ P
▲ **Lichtenstein** An der Jugendherberge 3, 09350 Lichtenstein.	☎ (37204) 2718 🖷 (37204) 87387	80	🛏12	††† ⑩ P
▲ **Liepnitzsee** Wandlitzer Str 6, 16359 Lanke/Ützdorf. ✉ jh-liepnitzsee@jugendherberge.de	☎ (33397) 21659 🖷 (33397) 62750	39	🛏12 (R) 01.11–28.02)	††† ⑩ R
▲ **Limburg** Auf dem Guckucksberg, 65549 Limburg.	☎ (6431) 41493 🖷 (6431) 43873	162	27.12–23.12	††† ⑩ 1.5S P
▲ **Lindau** Herbergsweg 11, 88131 Lindau (Bavaria). ✉ jhlindau@djh-bayern.de	☎ (8382) 96710 🖷 (8382) 967150	240	🛏12	††† ⑩ 5NW ♿ P 🅾 ☕ ⑫
▲ **Lindlar** Umweltstudienplatz, Jugendherberge 30, 51789 Lindlar. ✉ jugendherberge@lindlar.de	☎ (2266) 5264 🖷 (2266) 45517	170	01.01–23.12; 27–31.12	††† ⑩ P
▲ **Lingen** Lengericher Str 62, 49811 Lingen.	☎ (591) 973060 🖷 (591) 76954	152	01.01–14.12	††† ⑩ ♿ P
▲ **Linsengericht** "Haus der Jugend Geislitz", 63589 Linsengericht.	☎ (6051) 72029 🖷 (6051) 75694	124	27.12–23.12	††† ⑩ 6S P
▲ **List** JH Mövenberg, 25992 List/Sylt.	☎ (4651) 870397 🖷 (4651) 871039	384	01.04–04.11; 27–31.12	††† ⑩ P 🅾
▲ **Lochen** Auf der Lochen 1, 72336 Balingen-Lochen,	☎ (7433) 37383 🖷 (7433) 382296	100	01.01–10.12; 27.12–31.12	††† ⑩ P
▲ **Löhne-Gohfeld** TV Die Naturfreunde e.V., In den Tannen 63, 32584 Löhne.	☎ (5731) 81012 🖷 (5731) 81031	84	27.12–23.12	††† ⑩ ♿ P
▲ **Lohr** Brunnenwiesenweg 13, 97816 Lohr (Bavaria).	☎ (9352) 2444 🖷 (9352) 70873	94	16.01–30.11	††† ⑩
▲ **Lörrach** Steinenweg 40, 79540 Lörrach.	☎ (7621) 47040 🖷 (7621) 18156	168	27.12–22.12	††† ⑩ 3SE ♿ P
▲ **Lübben** Zum Wendenfürsten 8, 15907 Lübben. ✉ jh-luebben@jugendherberge.de	☎ (3546) 3046 🖷 (3546) 3046	127	🛏12 (R ††† 01.11–28.02)	††† ⑩ R 2.5SE 🅾
▲ **Lübeck** **Am Gertrudenkirchhof 4, 23568 Lübeck.**	☎ (451) 33433 🖷 (451) 34540	218	01.01–23.12; 27–31.12	⑩ 2NE ♿ P 🅾
▲ **Lübeck - JGH** Mengstr 33, 23552 Lübeck.	☎ (451) 7020399 🖷 (451) 77012	73	06.01–22.12	††† ⑩ 1W
▲ **Ludwigsburg JH + YGH** Gemsenbergstr 21, 71640 Ludwigsburg.	☎ (7141) 51564 🖷 (7141) 59440	121	10.01–17.12	⑩ P
▲ **Ludwigstein** "Jugendburg", 37214 Witzenhausen.	☎ (5542) 1812 🖷 (5542) 3649	175	🛏12	††† ⑩ R P
▲ **Lüneburg** Soltauer Str 133, 21335 Lüneburg.	☎ (4131) 41864 🖷 (4131) 45747	105	27.12–23.12	⑩ P
▲ **Magdeburg, Magdeburger Hof** Leiterstrasse 10, 39104 Magdeburg	☎ (391) 532101 🖷 (391) 532102	240	01.01–23.12; 28–31.12	††† ⑩ R ♿

Location/Address	Telephone No. Fax No.	Beds	Opening Dates	Facilities
Maibrunn ☞ **St Englmar**				
▲ **Mainz** - Rhein-Main-Jugendherberge **Jugendgästehaus Mainz,** **Otto-Brunfels-Schneise 4, 55130 Mainz.**	☎ (6131) 85332 🖷 (6131) 82422	166	01.01–23.12; 27–31.12	ⅲ ⦿ Ⓡ 5SE CC
▲ **Malente** Kellerseestr 48, 23714 Malente.	☎ (4523) 1723 🖷 (4523) 2539	206	24.01–04.12	ⅲ ⦿ � P
▲ **Malchow** Platz der Freiheit 3, 17213 Malchow	☎ (39932) 14590 🖷 (39932) 14579	88	01.01–20.12; 29–31.12	P
▲ **Manderscheid** Vulkaneifel Jugendherberge Jugendgästehaus, Mosenbergstr 17, 54531 Manderscheid.	☎ (6572) 557 🖷 (6572) 4759	105	01.01–23.12; 27–31.12	ⅲ ⦿
▲ **Mannheim** "Lindenhof", Rheinpromenade 21, 68163 Mannheim.	☎ (621) 822718 🖷 (621) 824073	115	27.12–22.12	ⅲ ⦿ 2W P
▲ **Marburg** "Emil-von-Behring-JH", Jahnstr 1, 35037 Marburg.	☎ (6421) 23461 🖷 (6421) 12191	164	27.12–23.12	ⅲ ⦿ 0.5SE Ⅹ
▲ **Mardorf** Warteweg 2, 31535 Neustadt-Mardorf.	☎ (5036) 457 🖷 (5036) 1554	164	27.12–23.12	ⅲ ⦿ Ⅹ P
▲ **Marktredwitz** Wunsiedlerstr 29, 95615 Marktredwitz (Bavaria).	☎ (9231) 81082 🖷 (9231) 87346	40	🔒12	⦿
▲ **Martinfeld** Bernteröderstr. 141, 37308 Schimberg/ OT Martinfeld.	☎ (36082) 89339 🖷 (36082) 89339	100	28.12–23.12	ⅲ ⦿ P
▲ **Mauth** Jugendherbergsstr 11, 94151 Mauth (Bavaria).	☎ (8557) 289 🖷 (8557) 1581	96	01.01–14.11; 27–31.12	ⅲ ⦿ 🗆
▲ **Mayen**⁕ Am Knüppchen 5, 56727 Mayen.	☎ (2651) 2355 🖷 (2651) 78378	130	01.01–23.12; 27–31.12	ⅲ ⦿
▲ **Meinerzhagen** Bergstr. 1, 58540 Meinerzhagen.	☎ (2354) 2280 🖷 (2354) 14341	150	02.01–01.11; 01.12–23.12	⦿ Ⅹ P
▲ **Meisdorf** Falkensteiner Weg 2B, 06463 Meisdorf.	☎ (34743) 8257 🖷 (34743) 92540	108	01.01–23.12; 28–31.12	ⅲ ⦿ P 🗆
▲ **Melle** Fr-Ludwig-Jahn-Str 1, 49324 Melle.	☎ (5422) 2434 🖷 (5422) 3988	67	🔒12	ⅲ ⦿ P
▲ **Melsungen** Lindenbergstr 23, 34212 Melsungen.	☎ (5661) 2650 🖷 (5661) 51928	132	27.12–23.12	ⅲ ⦿ 1W Ⅹ
▲ **Memmingen** Kempterstr 42, 87700 Memmingen (Bavaria).	☎ (8331) 494087 🖷 (8331) 494087	67	01.03–30.11	ⅲ ⦿
▲ **Menzenschwand** OT Menzenschwand, Vorderdorfstr 10, 79837 St Blasien.	☎ (7675) 326 🖷 (7675) 1435	102	27.12–22.12	ⅲ ⦿ P
▲ **Merzalben** Tannenstr 20, 66978 Merzalben.	☎ (6395) 6271 🖷 (6395) 7089	103	01.01–23.12; 27–31.12	⦿
▲ **Meschede** "Haus Dortmund", Warsteiner Straße, 59872 Meschede.	☎ (291) 6666 🖷 (291) 1589	100	27.12–23.12	ⅲ ⦿ P

Location/Address	Telephone No. Fax No.	Beds	Opening Dates	Facilities
▲ **Milow** Friedensstr 21, 14715 Milow. ❷ jh-milow@jugendherberge.de	❶ (3386) 280361 ❸ (3386) 280369	96	🈂 (ⓡ ♦♦♦ 15.12–15.02)	♦♦♦ ⑩ ⓡ
▲ **Mirow** Retzower Str, 17252 Mirow.	❶ (39833) 20726 ❸ (39833) 22057	60	Partly closed in 2000	♦♦♦ ⑩ ⓡ 🚹 P
▲ **Mittenwald** Buckelwiesen 7, 82481 Mittenwald (Bavaria).	❶ (8823) 1701 ❸ (8823) 2907	121	01.01–14.11; 28–31.12	♦♦♦ ⑩
▲ **Möhnesee** Südufer 20, 59519 Möhnesee-Körbecke.	❶ (2924) 305 ❸ (2924) 2788	203	27.12–23.12	♦♦♦ ⑩ P
▲ **Mölln** Am Ziegelsee 2, 23879 Mölln.	❶ (4542) 2601 ❸ (4542) 86718	162	27.01–14.12	♦♦♦ ⑩ P
▲ **Mönchengladbach** - JH "Hardter Wald" Umweltstudienplatz, Brahmsstr 156, 41169 Mönchengladbach.	❶ (2161) 560900 ❸ (2161) 556464	131	01.01–23.12; 27–31.12	⑩ ⓡ
▲ **Monschau** - JH Burg-Monschau Auf dem Schloss 4, 52156 Monschau.	❶ (2472) 2314 ❸ (2472) 4391	96	03.01–23.12; 27–31.12	⑩
▲ **Monschau** - JH Monschau-Hagard Hargardsgasse 5, 52156 Monschau.	❶ (2472) 2180 ❸ (2472) 4527	148	10.01–03.12	⑩ P
▲ **Montabaur** Richard-Schirrmann-Str, 56410 Montabaur.	❶ (2602) 5121 ❸ (2602) 180176	136	01.01–23.12; 27–31.12	♦♦♦ ⑩
▲ **Morbach** Jugendherberge und Kreisjugendzentrum Bischofsdron, Jugendherbergsstr 16, 54497 Morbach.	❶ (6533) 3389 ❸ (6533) 2787	137	01.01–23.12; 27–31.12	♦♦♦ ⑩
▲ **Morsbach** Obere Kirchstr 21, 51597 Morsbach.	❶ (2294) 8662 ❸ (2294) 7807	166	01.01–23.12; 27–31.12	♦♦♦ ⑩ P
▲ **Mosbach** "Mutschlers Mühle", Beim Elzstadion (OT Neckarelz), 74821 Mosbach.	❶ (6261) 7191 ❸ (6261) 61812	147	27.12–22.12	♦♦♦ ⑩ 3SW P 🔲
▲ **Mosenberg** 34590 Wabern.	❶ (5681) 2691 ❸ (5681) 60208	130	27.12–23.12	♦♦♦ ⑩ 7S P
▲ **Müden** Wiesenweg 32, 29328 Müden.	❶ (5053) 225 ❸ (5053) 1021	156	27.12–23.12	♦♦♦ ⑩ 🚹 P 🔲
▲ **Mühldorf** Friedr-Ludwig-Jahn-Str 19, 84453 Mühldorf (Bavaria).	❶ (8631) 7370 ❸ (8631) 7437	58	01.01–31.10; 01–31.12	⑩ ☞
▲ **Mühlhausen** Auf dem Tonberg 1, 99974 Mühlhausen.	❶ (3601) 813318 ❸ (3601) 813320	80	28.12–21.12	♦♦♦ ⑩ ⓡ 🚹 P
▲ **Mülheim** - "JH Kahlenberg" Mendener Str 3, 45470 Mülheim.	❶ (208) 382191 ❸ (208) 382196	70	06.01–20.12 every second weekend in the month	♦♦♦ ⑩ P
▲ **Münchehofe** Strasse der Jugend 2, 15374 Münchehofe.	❶ (33432) 8734 ❸ (33432) 8734	96	🈂	♦♦♦ ⑩

Location/Address	Telephone No. Fax No.	Beds	Opening Dates	Facilities
▲ München - Neuhausen (IBN) Wendl-Dietrich Str 20, 80634 München (Bavaria). @ jhmuenchen@djh-bayern.de	☎ (89) 131156 ✆ (89) 1678745	388	01.01–30.11	⊕ R CC □ ⊕
▲ München - JGH Thalkirchen (IBN) Miesingstr 4, 81379 München (Bavaria). @ jghmuenchen@djh-bayern.de	☎ (89) 7236550, 7236560 ✆ (89) 7242567	352	[12]	♦♦♦ ⊕ R P □
▲ Münster - Aasee (IBN) "JGH", Bismarckallee 31, 48151 Münster.	☎ (251) 532470, 532477 ✆ (251) 521271	208	01.01–23.12; 27–31.12	♦♦♦ ⊕ R 2W ⅋ P □ ⊕
▲ Murchin Jugendherberge Nr 1, 17390 Murchin.	☎ (3971) 210732 ✆ (3971) 210732	50	01.01–20.12; 29–31.12	R P
▲ Murrhardt "Eugen-Nägele-JH", Karnsberger Str 1, 71540 Murrhardt.	☎ (7192) 7501 ✆ (7192) 29058	141	[12]	♦♦♦ ⊕ P □
▲ Mutzschen - Schloß Mutzschen Str. der Jugend 7, 04688 Mutzschen.	☎ (34385) 51241 ✆ (34385) 51502	100	[12]	♦♦♦ ⊕
▲ Mylau - "Walderholung" 08468 Schneidenbach.	☎ (3765) 34584 ✆ (3765) 69537	43	[12]	⊕
▲ Naumburg JGH, Am Tennisplatz 9, 06618 Naumburg.	☎ (3445) 703422 ✆ (3445) 703422	204	01.01–23.12; 28–31.12	♦♦♦ ⊕ R P
▲ Nebra Altenburgstrasse 29, 06642 Nebra	☎ (34461) 25454 ✆ (34461) 25456	140	01.01–23.12; 28–31.12	♦♦♦ ⊕ P □
▲ Neckargemünd-Dilsberg OT Dilsberg, Untere Str 1, 69151 Neckargemünd.	☎ (6223) 2133 ✆ (6223) 74871	77	[12]	♦♦♦ ⊕ P
▲ Neidenberga - "Schloss" Ortsstr 1, 07338 Neidenberga.	☎ (36737) 22262 ✆ (36737) 32503	80	28.12–22.12	⊕ R P
▲ Neschwitz - Scloß Neschwitz Kastanienallee 1, 02699 Neschwitz.	☎ (35933) 30040 ✆ (35933) 38611	61	[12]	♦♦♦ ⊕ P
▲ Nettetal-Hinsbeck - JH Hinsbeck Heide 1, 41334 Nettetal.	☎ (2153) 6492 ✆ (2153) 89598	161	01.01–23.12; 27–31.12	♦♦♦ ⊕ P
▲ Neudorf Vierenstr 26, 09465 Sehmatal, OT Neudorf.	☎ (37342) 8282 ✆ (37342) 8220	128	[12]	♦♦♦ ⊕ P □
▲ Neuhaus am Rennweg - "Am Rennweg" Apelsbergstr 54, 98724 Neuhaus.	☎ (3679) 722862 ✆ (3679) 700384	80	29.12–20.12	♦♦♦ ⊕ R P
▲ Neuhausen - Am Schwartenberg Bergstr 12, 09544 Neuhausen	☎ (37361) 45634 ✆ (37361) 45626	68	[12]	♦♦♦ ⊕
▲ Neukirch - "Valtenberghaus" Karl-Berger-Str. 16, 01904 Neukirch/Lausitz	☎ (35951) 31484 ✆ (35951) 37108	112	[12]	⊕
▲ Neumünster Gartenstr. 32, 24534 Neumünster	☎ (4321) 419960 ✆ (4321) 4199699	208	[12]	♦♦♦ ⊕ ⅋ P
▲ Neureichenau - JH Rosenbergergut Ortsteil Lackenhäuser 146, 94089 Neureichenau (Bavaria).	☎ (8583) 1239 ✆ (8583) 1566	109	01.01–14.12; 27–31.12	♦♦♦ ⊕
▲ Neuschönau - JH Waldhäuser Herbergsweg 2, 94556 Neuschönau (Bavaria).	☎ (8553) 6000 ✆ (8553) 829	121	01.01–14.11; 27–31.12	♦♦♦ ⊕ ☛ □

Location/Address	Telephone No. Fax No.	Beds	Opening Dates	Facilities
▲ **Neuss-Uedesheim** Macherscheiderstr 113, 41468 Neuss-Uedesheim.	☎ (0211) 5770349 ✆ (0211) 5770350	77	Re–opening May 2000	¶⊙ ⚏ ℙ
▲ **Neustadt/Weinstr.** Pfalz-JH JGH Neustadt, Hans-Geiger-Str. 27, 67434 Neustadt/Weinstr.	☎ (6321) 2289 ✆ (6321) 82947	122	01.01–23.12; 27–31.12	♦♦ ¶⊙
Neustadt/Schw ☞ **Titisee-Neustadt**				
▲ **Nideggen** Rather Str 27, 52385 Nideggen.	☎ (2427) 1226 ✆ (2427) 8453	122	03.01–31.10	¶⊙ ℙ
▲ **Niebüll** Deezbülldeich 2, 25899 Niebüll-Deezbüll.	☎ (4661) 8762 ✆ (4661) 20457	38	21.04–31.10	♦♦ ¶⊙ ⓡ ℙ
▲ **Nienburg** - Naturfreundehaus Nienburg Luise-Wyneken Str.4, 31582 Nienburg-Weser	☎ (5021) 2812 ✆ (5021) 2812	41	27.12–23.12	♦♦ ¶⊙
▲ **Norddeich** Strandstr 1, 26506 Norden.	☎ (4931) 8064 ✆ (4931) 81828	96	▣₁₂	¶⊙ ℙ
▲ **Nordenham** Strandallee 12, 26954 Nordenham.	☎ (4731) 88262 ✆ (4731) 88034	158	▣₁₂	♦♦ ¶⊙ ⚼ ℙ
▲ **Norderney** - Südstr Südstr 1, 26535 Norderney, (North Sea).	☎ (4932) 2451 ✆ (4921) 83600	121	01.02–31.10	♦♦ ¶⊙ ⓡ 1E
▲ **Norderney** - Dünensender Am Dünensender 3, 26548 Norderney, (North Sea).	☎ (4932) 2574 ✆ (4921) 83266	144	01.03–31.10	¶⊙ ⓡ 4E
▲ **Nördlingen** Kaiserwiese 1, 86720 Nördlingen (Bavaria).	☎ (9081) 271816 ✆ (9081) 271816	104	01.03–31.10	♦♦ ¶⊙
▲ **Nordhausen** - JGH "Rothleimmühle" Parkallee 2, 99734 Nordhausen.	☎ (3631) 902391 ✆ (3631) 902393	128	01.12–30.01	♦♦ ¶⊙ ⓡ ℙ
▲ **Northeim** "Adolf-Galland-Jugendheim", Brauereistr 1, 37154 Northeim.	☎ (5551) 8672 ✆ (5551) 911108	103	27.12–23.12	♦♦ ¶⊙ ℙ
▲ **Nottuln** St Amand-Montrond-Str 6, 48301 Nottuln.	☎ (2502) 7878 ✆ (2502) 9619	132	08.01–20.12	♦♦ ¶⊙ ℙ
▲ **Nürnberg** - JGH ⓘⒷⓃ **Burg 2, 90403 Nürnberg (Bavaria).**	☎ (911) 2309360 ✆ (911) 23093611	320	01.01–24.12; 27–31.12	♦♦ ¶⊙ ⓡ ⚼
▲ **Oberammergau** Malensteinweg 10, 82487 Oberammergau (Bavaria).	☎ (8822) 4114 ✆ (8822) 1695	130	01.01–14.11; 27–31.12	♦♦ ¶⊙
▲ **Oberbernhards** Hauptstr 5, 36115 Hilders-Oberbernhards.	☎ (6657) 240 ✆ (6657) 8896	257	01.01–23.12; 27–31.12	♦♦ ¶⊙ 8NW ℙ
▲ **Oberhundem** Wilhelm-Münker-Weg 1, 57399 Kirchhundem.	☎ (2723) 72640 ✆ (2723) 73597	106	16.01–14.12	¶⊙ ℙ
▲ **Oberoderwitz** Zur Lindenallee 5, 02791 Oderwitz.	☎ (35842) 26544 ✆ (35842) 27726	138	▣₁₂	♦♦ ¶⊙ ℙ
▲ **Oberreifenberg** Limesstr 14, 61389 Schmitten.	☎ (6082) 2440 ✆ (6082) 3305	226	01.01–23.12; 27–31.12	¶⊙ 3SW ℙ
▲ **Oberstdorf-Kornau** Kornau 8, 87561 Oberstdorf-Kornau (Bavaria).	☎ (8322) 2225; 2510 ✆ (8322) 80446	188	01.01–14.11; 28–31.12	♦♦ ¶⊙ ℙ ⬚

Location/Address	Telephone No. Fax No.	Beds	Opening Dates	Facilities
▲ **Oberwesel** "Jugendgästehaus", Auf dem Schönberg, 55430 Oberwesel.	☎ (6744) 93330 ✆ (6744) 7446	179	01.01–23.12; 27–31.12	♦♦♦ ⦿ ♿ ⊂CC⊃
▲ **Ochsenfurt** Hauptstr 1, 97199 Ochsenfurt (Bavaria).	☎ (9331) 2666 ✆ (9331) 2696	30	01.04–31.10	♦♦♦ ⦿
Oelsnitz ☞ **Taltitz**				
▲ **Oerlinghausen** Auf dem Berge 11, 33813 Oerlinghausen.	☎ (5202) 2053 ✆ (5202) 15456	127	03.01–20.12	♦♦♦ ⦿ P
▲ **Ohorn** Schleißbergstr 39, 01896 Ohorn.	☎ (35955) 72762 ✆ (35955) 72762	46	⓬	♦♦♦ ⦿ P
▲ **Oldenburg/Holstein** Göhlerstr 58a, 23758 Oldenburg.	☎ (4361) 7670 ✆ (4361) 60731	84	06.01–22.12	♦♦♦ ⦿ P ▤
▲ **Oldenburg/Oldenburg** Alexander Str 65, 26121 Oldenburg.	☎ (441) 87135 ✆ (441) 8852493	104	⓬	♦♦♦ ⦿ 1 NE P
▲ **Ortenberg** Burgweg 21/Schloss, 77799 Ortenberg.	☎ (781) 31749 ✆ (781) 9481031	146	27.12–22.12	♦♦♦ ⦿ P
▲ **Osnabrück** YGH, Iburger Str 183A, 49082 Osnabrück.	☎ (541) 54284 ✆ (541) 54294	145	⓬	♦♦♦ ⦿ 2 S ♿ P
▲ **Ossa** Dorfstr 69, 04643 Ossa.	☎ (34346) 60587 ✆ (34346) 60587	52	⓬	♦♦♦ ⦿ P
▲ **Ottenhöfen-Sohlberg** Sohlberg 5, 77883 Ottenhöfen.	☎ (7842) 2629 ✆ (7842) 30008	73	27.12–22.12	♦♦♦ ⦿ 5 S P
▲ **Otterndorf** Schleusenstr 147, 21762 Otterndorf.	☎ (4751) 3165 ✆ (4751) 4577	212	06.01–22.12	♦♦♦ ⦿ ♿ P ▤
▲ **Ottobeuren** Kaltenbrunnweg 11, 87724 Ottobeuren (Bavaria).	☎ (8332) 368 ✆ (8332) 7219	101	01.03–31.10	⦿
▲ **Paderborn** Meinwerkstr 16, 33098 Paderborn.	☎ (5251) 22055 ✆ (5251) 280017	108	03.01–03.12	♦♦♦ ⦿ P
▲ **Panschwitz-Kuckau** Cisinskistr 1, 01920 Panschwitz-Kuckau.	☎ (35796) 96963 ✆ (35796) 96964	60	⓬	♦♦♦ ⦿ P ▤
▲ **Papenburg** Kirchstr 38-40, 26871 Papenburg.	☎ (4961) 2793 ✆ (4961) 916554	75	01.03–31.10	♦♦♦ ⦿ P
▲ **Passau** Veste Oberhaus 125, 94034 Passau (Bavaria).	☎ (851) 41351 ✆ (851) 43709	72	⓬	♦♦♦ ⦿ P
▲ **Pforzheim** "Burg Rabeneck", OT Dillweissenstein, Kräheneckstr 4, 75180 Pforzheim.	☎ (7231) 972660 ✆ (7231) 972661	96	27.12–22.12	♦♦♦ ⦿ 3 SW P
▲ **Pirna-Copitz -** "Tor zur sächsischen Schweiz" Birkwitzer Str 51, 01796 Pirna-Copitz.	☎ (3501) 445601 ✆ (3501) 445602	166	⓬	♦♦♦ ⦿ P
▲ **Plau am See** Meyenburger Chaussee 1a, 19395 Plau am See.	☎ (38735) 44345 ✆ (38735) 44345	128	01.01–20.12; 29–31.12	♦♦♦ ⦿ Ⓡ P
▲ **Plauen** Reusaer Waldhaus 1, 08529 Plauen	☎ (3741) 472811 ✆ (3741) 472812	74	⓬	♦♦♦ ⦿ P
▲ **Plön** Ascheberger Str 67, 24306 Plön.	☎ (4522) 2576 ✆ (4522) 2166	221	06.01–22.12	♦♦♦ ⦿ P

Location/Address	Telephone No. Fax No.	Beds	Opening Dates	Facilities
▲ Plothen - "Am Hausteich" 07907 Plothen.	☎ (36648) 22329 ✆ (36648) 26013	193	28.12–22.12	ᵻᵻᵻ �|◯| ⓡ P
▲ Porta Westfalica Kirchsiek 30, 32457 Porta Westfalica-Hausberge.	☎ (571) 70250 ✆ (571) 7100047	95	27.12–23.12	⍾◯⍾ P
▲ Pottenstein Jugendherbergsstr 20, 91278 Pottenstein (Bavaria).	☎ (9243) 92910 ✆ (9243) 929111	163	🛏	ᵻᵻᵻ ⍾◯⍾ ♿
▲ Prebelow Prebelow 02, 16831 Zechlinerhütte ❸ jh-prebelow@jugendherberge.de	☎ (33921) 70222 ✆ (33921) 70362	98	🛏 (ⓡ 01.11–28.02)	ᵻᵻᵻ ⍾◯⍾ ⓡ
▲ Prien Carl-Braun-Str. 66, 83209 Prien (Bavaria).	☎ (8051) 68770 ✆ (8051) 687715	130	16.01–30.11	ᵻᵻᵻ ⍾◯⍾
▲ Prora 18609 Ostseebad Binz OT-Prora, Strandstr. 12 ❸ jh-prora@t-online.de	☎ (38393) 32844 ✆ (38393) 32845	401	01.01–20.12; 29–31.12	ᵻᵻᵻ ⍾◯⍾ ⓡ P
▲ Prüm Pferdemarkt, 54595 Prüm.	☎ (6551) 2500 ✆ (6551) 70030	74	01.01–23.12; 27.12–31.12	ᵻᵻᵻ ⍾◯⍾
▲ Pullach - JH "Burg Schwaneck" Burgweg 4-6, 82049 Pullach (Bavaria).	☎ (89) 7930643, 7930644 ✆ (89) 7937922	128	06.01–21.12	⍾◯⍾
▲ Quedlinburg Neuendorf 28, 06484 Quedlinburg.	☎ (3947) 2881 ✆ (3947) 91653	54	01.01–23.12; 27–31.12	ᵻᵻᵻ ⍾◯⍾ P ♥
Radebeul ☞ Dresden				
▲ Radevormwald Telegrafenstr 50, 42477 Radevormwald.	☎ (2195) 1063 ✆ (2195) 6323	97	01.01–23.12; 27–31.12	ᵻᵻᵻ ⍾◯⍾ P
▲ Radis Bahnhofstr 18, 06773 Radis.	☎ (34953) 39288 ✆ (34953) 21429	121	01.01–23.12; 28–31.12	ᵻᵻᵻ ⍾◯⍾ P 🔋
▲ Ratingen Götschenbeck 8, 40882 Ratingen.	☎ (2102) 20400 ✆ (2102) 204010	160	01.01–23.12; 27–31.12	ᵻᵻᵻ ⍾◯⍾ ♿ P
▲ Ratzeburg Fischerstr 20, 23909 Ratzeburg.	☎ (4541) 3707 ✆ (4541) 84780	135	06.01–22.12	ᵻᵻᵻ ⍾◯⍾ P 🔋
▲ Ravensburg "Veitsburg", Veitsburgstr 1, 88212 Ravensburg.	☎ (751) 25363 ✆ (751) 13769	103	24.01–18.12; 27–31.12	ᵻᵻᵻ ⍾◯⍾ ♿ P 🔋
▲ Rechenberg Zum Schloß 7, 74597 Stimpfach	☎ (7967) 372 ✆ (7967) 8985	100	17.01–11.12	ᵻᵻᵻ ⍾◯⍾ P
▲ Regensburg (IBN) Wöhrdstr 60, 93059 Regensburg (Bavaria).	☎ (941) 57402 ✆ (941) 52411	203	🛏	ᵻᵻᵻ ⍾◯⍾ ⓡ 🔋
▲ Rendsburg Rotenhöfer Weg 48, 24768 Rendsburg.	☎ (4331) 71205 ✆ (4331) 75521	138	06.01–23.12	ᵻᵻᵻ ⍾◯⍾ ♿ P 🔋
▲ Rheine Mühlenstr 75, 48431 Rheine.	☎ (5971) 2407 ✆ (5971) 13526	53	27.12–23.12	⍾◯⍾ ♿ P
▲ Ribnitz Damgarten Am Wasserwerk, 18311 Ribnitz-Damgarten	☎ (3821) 812311 ✆ (3821) 812311	24	01.01–20.12; 29–31.12	⍾◯⍾
▲ Rinteln Am Bären 1, 31737 Rinteln.	☎ (5751) 2405 ✆ (5751) 44630	96	27.12–23.12	ᵻᵻᵻ ⍾◯⍾ ♿ P

Location/Address	Telephone No. Fax No.	Beds	Opening Dates	Facilities
▲ **Rittersgrün** Zur Jugendherberg 2, 08355 Rittersgrün.	☎ (37757) 7260 ❶ (37757) 7260	52	🔟	⑪ P 🔟
▲ **Rochlitz** - "Schweizerhaus" Zaßnitzer Str 1, 09306 Rochlitz.	☎ (3737) 42131 ❶ (3737) 149053	49	🔟	⫼ ⑪ P 🔟
▲ **Rödinghausen** Jugendheim des Kreises Herford, Zum Nonnenstein 21, 32289 Rödinghausen.	☎ (5746) 8173 ❶ (5746) 920425	80	27.12–23.12	⫼ ⑪ P
▲ **Rohden/Hess Oldendorf** - Naturfreundehaus SchneegrundRohden 31840 Rohden/Hess Oldendorf	☎ (5152) 2607	42	27.12–23.12	⑪
Rosenbergergut ☞ **Neureichenau**				
▲ **Rostock** JGS 'Traditionsschiff', PF 48, 18106 Rostock, Schmarl-Dorf.	☎ (381) 716224 ❶ (381) 714014	85	01.01–20.12; 29–31.12	⫼ ⑪ ℝ P
▲ **Rostock-Warnemünde** Parkstraße 46, 18119 Rostock OT. Warnemünde. ✉ jh.warne@t-online.de	☎ (381) 548170 ❶ (381) 5481723	184	01.01–18.12	⫼ ⑪ ℝ P
▲ **Rotenburg/Fulda** Obertor 17, 36199 Rotenburg.	☎ (6623) 2792 ❶ (6623) 43177	125	27.12–23.12	⫼ ⑪ 0.5N
▲ **Rotenburg/Wümme** Verdener Str 104, 27356 Rotenburg. ✉ jhrow@t-online.de	☎ (4261) 83041 ❶ (4261) 84233	224	🔟	⫼ ⑪ ℝ 1 SW P 🔟
▲ **Rothenburg-Tauber** [IBN] Mühlacker 1, 91541 Rothenburg (Bavaria). ✉ jhrothen@aol.com.de	☎ (9861) 94160 ❶ (9861) 941620	180	🔟	⫼ ⑪ P 🔟
▲ **Rothenfels** 97851 Rothenfels (Bavaria).	☎ (9393) 99999 ❶ (9393) 99997	168	06.01–14.12	⑪
▲ **Rottweil** Lorenzgasse 8, 78628 Rottweil.	☎ (741) 7664 ❶ (741) 7604	62	🔟	⑪
Rudenberg ☞ **Titisee-Neustadt**				
▲ **Rüdesheim** Am Kreuzberg, 65385 Rüdesheim.	☎ (6722) 2711 ❶ (6722) 48284	205	27.12–23.12	⫼ ⑪ 1.5E P
▲ **Rurberg** 52152 Simmerath-Rurberg.	☎ (2473) 2200 ❶ (2473) 4911	174	01.01–23.12; 27–31.12	⫼ ⑪ ☞ P
▲ **Rüthen** Am Rabenknapp 4, 59602 Rüthen.	☎ (2952) 483 ❶ (2952) 2717	121	15.01–14.12	⑪ P
▲ **Ruttelerfeld** Zollweg 27, 26340 Zetel.	☎ (4452) 416 ❶ (4452) 8230	111	🔟	⫼ ⑪ P
▲ **Saarbrücken** - Europa JH JGH **Meerwiesertalweg 31, 66123 Saarbrücken.**	☎ (681) 33040 ❶ (681) 374911	192	01.01–23.12; 27-31.12	⫼ ⑪ 4NE ♿
▲ **Saarburg** Bottelter 8, 54439 Saarburg.	☎ (6581) 2555 ❶ (6581) 1082	102	01.01–23.12; 27–31.12	⫼ ⑪
▲ **Saldenburg** Ritter-Tuschl-Str 20, 94163 Saldenburg (Bavaria).	☎ (8504) 1655 ❶ (8504) 4449	140	01–09.01; 01.02–30.11; 27–31.12	⫼ ⑪

Location/Address	Telephone No. Fax No.	Beds	Opening Dates	Facilities
▲ **Sandhatten** Wöschenweg 28, 26209 Hatten.	☏ (4482) 330 🖷 (4482) 8498	122	🛏️	ⅲ ⑩ 1.5 NW P
▲ **Sargenroth** - Waldjugendherberge Kirchweg 1, 55471 Sargenroth.	☏ (6761) 2500 🖷 (6761) 6378	134	01.01–23.12; 27–31.12	ⅲ ⑩ ⅋
▲ **Sayda** Mortelgrund 8, 09619 Sayda.	☏ (37365) 1277 🖷 (37365) 1337	140	🛏️	ⅲ ⑩ P 🖻
▲ **Scharbeutz-Klingberg** Uhlenflucht 30, 23684 Scharbeutz.	☏ (4524) 428 🖷 (4524) 1637	262	21.01–14.12	ⅲ ⑩ P
Scharling ☞ **Kreuth**				
▲ **Schellerhau** - "Rotwasserhütte" Hauptstr 115, 01776 Schellerhau.	☏ (35052) 64227 🖷 (35052) 64227	46	🛏️	ⅲ ⑩ P
▲ **Schierke** - JGH Brockenstrasse 48, 38879 Schierke.	☏ (39455) 51066 🖷 (39455) 51067	260	1.1–23.12; 28–31.12	ⅲ ⑩ ⅋ P 🖻
▲ **Schillighörn** Inselstr 6, 26434 Wangerland.	☏ (4426) 371 🖷 (4426) 506	132	01–31.01; 01.03–31.12	⑩ 0.5 N P
▲ **Schleiden-Gemünd** - JH Gemünd Im Wingertchen 9, 53937 Schleiden-Gemünd. ℮ jugendherberge-gemuend@t-online.de	☏ (2444) 2241 🖷 (2444) 3386	163	01.01–23.12; 27–31.12	ⅲ ⑩ 🖙 P
▲ **Schleswig** Spielkoppel 1, 24837 Schleswig.	☏ (4621) 23893 🖷 (4621) 20796	122	01.04–14.12	ⅲ ⑩ P
▲ **Schliersee** - JH Josefsthal Josefsthaler Str. 19, 83727 Schliersee (Bavaria). ℮ jhjosefsthal@djh-bayern.de	☏ (8026) 97380 🖷 (8026) 71610	93	01.01–14.11; 27–31.12	ⅲ ⑩ 🖻
▲ **Schluchsee** - Im Wolfsgrund Im Wolfsgrund 28, 79859 Schluchsee.	☏ (7656) 329 🖷 (7656) 9237	133	27.12–22.12	ⅲ ⑩ 1 NE P 🖻
▲ **Schluchsee** - Seebrugg Haus 9, 79859 Schluchsee, (OT Seebrugg).	☏ (7656) 494 🖷 (7656) 1889	134	27.12–22.12	ⅲ ⑩ 3 SW P
▲ **Schmallenberg** Im Lenninghof 20, 57392 Schmallenberg.	☏ (2972) 6098 🖷 (2972) 4918	134	27.12–01.11; 01.12–23.12	ⅲ ⑩ P
▲ **Schnett** "Auf dem Simmersberg", Kirchberg 25, 98666 Schnett	☏ (36874) 39532 🖷 (36874) 39532	61	28.12–22.12	ⅲ ⑩ ℞ P
▲ **Schöna** - "Zirkelsteinhaus" Am Zirkelstein Nr. 109 B, 01814 Schöna.	☏ (35028) 80425 🖷 (35028) 81424	154	🛏️	
▲ **Schönberg** Stakendorfer Weg 1, 24217 Schönberg.	☏ (4344) 2974 🖷 (4344) 4484	233	06.01–22.12	ⅲ ⑩ ⅋ P 🖻
▲ **Schönbrunn/Ebersdorf** - Bellevue Nr 102 (Bellevue), 07368 Schönbrunn/Ebersdorf	☏ (36651) 87064 🖷 (36651) 55413	72	28.12–21.12	⑩ ℞ P ☕
▲ **Schöneck** Am Stadtpark 52, 08261 Schöneck.	☏ (37464) 8106 🖷 (37464) 8107	67	🛏️	ⅲ ⑩ P 🖻
▲ **Schöningen am Elm** Richard-Schirrmann-Str 6a, 38364 Schöningen am Elm.	☏ (5352) 3898 🖷 (5352) 3752	92	27.12–23.12	ⅲ ⑩ P
▲ **Schönwalde** Am Ruhsal 1, 23744 Schönwalde am Bungsberg.	☏ (4528) 206 🖷 (4528) 9732	61	21.04–31.10	ⅲ ⑩

Location/Address	Telephone No. Fax No.	Beds	Opening Dates	Facilities
▲ **Schwäbisch Hall** Langenfelderweg 5, 74523 Schwäbisch Hall.	☎ (791) 41050 🖷 (791) 47998	120	03–16.01; 07.02–11.12	♦♦ ⑂ 🅿 ▣
▲ **Schwarzburg** "Hans Breuer" Am Buschbach 2, 07427 Schwarzburg. 📧 jugendherberge_hans_breuer_@t-online.de	☎ (36730) 22223 🖷 (36730) 33555	163	28.12–22.12	♦♦ ⑂ ⓡ 🅿
▲ **Schweinfurt** Niederwerrnerstr 17 1/2, 97421 Schweinfurt (Bavaria).	☎ (9721) 21404 🖷 (9721) 23581	110	09.01–21.12	♦♦ ⑂
▲ **Schwerin** Waldschulweg 3, 19061 Schwerin.	☎ (385) 3260006 🖷 (385) 3260303	91	01.01–20.12; 29–31.12	♦♦ ⑂ 🅿
Seebrugg ☞ **Schluchsee**				
▲ **Sigmaringen** "Hohenzollern-JH", Hohenzollernstr 31, 72488 Sigmaringen.	☎ (7571) 13277 🖷 (7571) 61159	129	03–27.01; 07.02–11.12	♦♦ ⑂ 🅿
▲ **Silberborn** Schießhäuser Str 4, 37603 Holzminden.	☎ (5536) 568 🖷 (5536) 1533	161	27.12–23.12	♦♦ ⑂ 🅿
▲ **Singen** Friedingerstr 28, 78224 Singen.	☎ (7731) 42590 🖷 (7731) 48842	109	🔟₁₂	♦♦ ⑂ 1 NE 🅿
▲ **Soest** Kaiser-Friedrich-Platz 2, 59494 Soest.	☎ (2921) 16283 🖷 (2921) 14623	70	27.12–23.12	♦♦ ⑂ 🅿
Sohlberg ☞ **Ottenhöfen**				
▲ **Solingen-Gräfrath** Flockertsholzerweg 10, 42653 Solingen.	☎ (212) 591198 🖷 (212) 594179	120	01.01–23.12; 27–31.12	⑂ 🅿
Sonnenbühl ☞ **Erpfingen**				
▲ **Sondershausen** - JH "Juventas" Güntherstr 26/27 99706 Sondershausen	☎ (3632) 601193 🖷 (3632) 782259	50	🔟₁₂	⑂ 🅿 ▣
▲ **Sorpesee** Am Sorpesee 7, 59846 Sundern-Langscheid.	☎ (2935) 1776 🖷 (2935) 7254	166	21.01–17.12	♦♦ ⑂ 🅿
▲ **Sosa** - "Skihütte" Am Fröhlichwald 9, 08326 Sosa.	☎ (37752) 8268 🖷 (37752) 8268	28	🔟₁₂	♦♦ ⑂ 🅿
▲ **Sosa** - "Rote Grube" Rote Grube 1, 08326 Sosa	☎ (3773) 58019 🖷 (3773) 882540	60	🔟₁₂	♦♦ ⑂ 🅿
▲ **Spalt** - JH Wernfels Burgweg 7-9, 91174 Spalt (Bavaria).	☎ (9873) 515 🖷 (9873) 244	150	01.01–19.12; 28–31.12	♦♦ ⑂ 🖬 ▣
▲ **Speyer** Kurpfalz-JH JGH, Geibstr 5, 67346 Speyer.	☎ (6232) 61597 🖷 (6232) 61596	160	01.01–23.12; 27–31.12	⑂ ♿
▲ **Spiekeroog** Bid' Utkiek 1, 26474 Spiekeroog, (North Sea).	☎ (4976) 329	54	15.3–30.10	♦♦ ⓡ
▲ **Springe** In der Worth 25, 31832 Springe.	☎ (5041) 1455 🖷 (5041) 2963	92	27.12–23.12	⑂ 🅿
▲ **St Andreasberg** - Naturfreunde Haus Am Gesehr 37, 37444 St. Andreasberg/Oberharz	☎ (5582) 269 🖷 (5582) 517	53	27.12–23.12	♦♦ ⑂
St Blasien ☞ **Menzenschwand**				

Location/Address	Telephone No. Fax No.	Beds	Opening Dates	Facilities
▲ **St Englmar** - JH Maibrunn Haus Nr 5, 94379 St Englmar (Bavaria).	☎ (9965) 271 🖷 (9965) 1342	59	01.01–31.10; 16–31.12	¶⊙¶
▲ **St Goar** Bismarckweg 17, 56329 St Goar.	☎ (6741) 388 🖷 (6741) 2869	130	01.01–23.12; 27.12–31.12	♦♦♦ ¶⊙¶
▲ **St Michaelisdonn** Am Sportplatz 1, 25693 St Michaelisdonn.	☎ (4853) 923 🖷 (4853) 8576	70	11.01–09.12	♦♦♦ ¶⊙¶ 🚭 🖥
▲ **Stade** Kehdinger Mühren 11, 21682 Stade.	☎ (4141) 46368 🖷 (4141) 2817	84	15.04–22.12	♦♦♦ ¶⊙¶
▲ **Steinbach/Donnersberg** Brühlstraße, 67808 Steinbach.	☎ (6357) 360 🖷 (6357) 1583	104	01.01–23.12; 27–31.12	♦♦♦ ¶⊙¶
▲ **Steinberghaus** - Naturfreundehaus Staufenberg, 34346 Hann-Münden	☎ (5543) 1609 🖷 (5543) 2854	50	27.12–23.12	♦♦♦ ¶⊙¶
Steinebach ☞ **Wörthsee**				
▲ **Stralsund** Am Kütertor 1, 18439 Stralsund.	☎ (3831) 292160 🖷 (3831) 297676	180	01.01–20.12; 29–31.12	♦♦♦ ¶⊙¶ R
▲ **Stralsund-Devin** Strandstr 21, 18439 Stralsund OT. Devin.	☎ (3831) 490289 🖷 (3831) 490291	204	01.01–20.12; 29–31.12	♦♦♦ ¶⊙¶ R 🚭 P
▲ **Straubing** Friedhofstr 12, 94315 Straubing (Bavaria).	☎ (9421) 80436 🖷 (9421) 12094	57	01.04–31.10	¶⊙¶
▲ **Strehla** Torgauer Str 33, 01616 Strehla.	☎ (35264) 92030 🖷 (35264) 92031	72	🚃	♦♦♦ ¶⊙¶ P
Streitberg ☞ **Wiesenttal**				
▲ **Strub** - JH Berchtesgaden Gebirgsjägerstr 52, 83489 Strub (Bavaria).	☎ (8652) 94370 🖷 (8652) 943737	320	01.01–14.11; 27–31.12	♦♦♦ ¶⊙¶ ✍ 🖥
▲ **Stuttgart** **Haußmannstr 27, 70188 Stuttgart** **(enter via Werastr, corner Kernerstr).**	☎ (711) 241583 🖷 (711) 2361041	245	🚃	♦♦♦ ¶⊙¶ 1 SE 🛬
Sudelfeld ☞ **Bayrischzell**				
▲ **Syke** - "Oscar-Heidrich-JH" Nordwohlder Str 59, 28857 Syke.	☎ (4242) 50314 🖷 (4242) 66346	128	🚃	♦♦♦ ¶⊙¶ 3 W 🚭 P
▲ **Taltitz** - "Talsperre Pirk" Dobenecker Weg 27, 08606 Oelsnitz, OT Taltitz.	☎ (37421) 23019 🖷 (37421) 20202	82	🚃	♦♦♦ ¶⊙¶ P
▲ **Tambach-Dietharz** Oberhoferstr 3, 99897 Tambach-Dietharz.	☎ (36252) 36149 🖷 (36252) 36564	120	28.12–22.12	♦♦♦ ¶⊙¶ R 🚭 P ☕
Tannenlohe ☞ **Windischeschenbach**				
▲ **Tauberbischofsheim** Schirrmannweg 2, 97941 Tauberbischofsheim.	☎ (9341) 3152 🖷 (9341) 95052	103	27.12–22.12	♦♦♦ ¶⊙¶ 2 NW P
▲ **Tecklenburg** Am Herrengarten 5, 49545 Tecklenburg.	☎ (5482) 360 🖷 (5482) 7937	128	27.12–23.12	♦♦♦ ¶⊙¶ P
▲ **Teterow** Am Seebahnhof 7, 17166 Teterow.	☎ (3996) 172668 🖷 (3996) 172668	100	01.01–20.12; 29–31.12	♦♦♦ ¶⊙¶ R P
▲ **Thale** Waldkater-Bodetal 1, 06502 Thale.	☎ (3947) 2881 🖷 (3947) 91653	204	1.1–23.12; 28–31.12	♦♦♦ ¶⊙¶ P 🖥

Location/Address	Telephone No. Fax No.	Beds	Opening Dates	Facilities
▲ **Thallichtenberg** "Burg Lichtenberg", Burgstr 12, 66871 Thallichtenberg.	☎ (6381) 2632 ✆ (6381) 80933	106	01.01–23.12; 27–31.12	♦♦♦ ⦿ ⮃
▲ **Tharandt** - "Am Tharandter Wald" Pienner Str 55, 01737 Tharandt.	☎ (35203) 37272 ✆ (35203) 37738	69	🔒12	♦♦♦ ⦿ Ⓟ ⬛
▲ **Tholey** - Jugendgästehaus Schaumberg-JH, Am Schaumberg 2, 66636 Tholey.	☎ (6853) 2271 ✆ (6853) 5534	142	01.01–23.12; 27–31.12	♦♦♦ ⦿ ⮃
▲ **Thülsfelder Talsperre** Am Campingplatz 7, 49681 Garrel-Petersfeld.	☎ (4495) 475 ✆ (4495) 365	130	🔒12	⦿ ⮃ Ⓟ
▲ **Titisee-Neustadt** - OT Neustadt "JH Rudenberg", Ortsteil Neustadt, Rudenberg 6, 79822 Titisee-Neustadt.	☎ (7651) 7360 ✆ (7651) 4299	146	27.12–22.12	♦♦♦ ⦿ 2NE Ⓟ
▲ **Titisee-Neustadt** - OT Titisee "JH Veltishof", Ortsteil Titisee, Bruderhalde 27, 79822 Titisee-Neustadt.	☎ (7652) 238 ✆ (7652) 756	128	27.12–22.12	♦♦♦ ⦿ 2NW Ⓟ
▲ **Todtnauberg** "Fleinerhaus", OT Todtnauberg, Radschertstr 12, 79674 Todtnau.	☎ (7671) 275 ✆ (7671) 721	146	27.12–22.12	♦♦♦ ⦿ 1N Ⓟ
▲ **Tönning** Badallee 28, 25832 Tönning.	☎ (4861) 1280 ✆ (4861) 5956	133	23.01–14.12	♦♦♦ ⦿ ⮃ Ⓟ ⬛
▲ **Torfhaus** Nr 3, 38667 Torfhaus.	☎ (5320) 242 ✆ (5320) 254	174	27.12–23.12	♦♦♦ ⦿ ⮃ Ⓟ
▲ **Tossens** Meidgrodenweg 1, 26969 Butjadingen.	☎ (4736) 716 ✆ (4736) 817	123	01.04–31.10	⦿ Ⓡ Ⓟ
▲ **Traben-Trarbach** Hirtenpfad 6, 56841 Traben-Trarbach.	☎ (6541) 9278 ✆ (6541) 3759	176	01.01–23.12; 27–31.12	♦♦♦ ⦿ ⮃ ⒸⒸ 🛏
▲ **Traunstein** Traunerstr 22, 83278 Traunstein (Bavaria).	☎ (861) 4742 ✆ (861) 12382	57	16.01–30.11	⦿
▲ **Trausnitz** Burggasse 2, 92555 Trausnitz (Bavaria)	☎ (9655) 9215-0 ✆ (9655) 921531	131	🔒12	♦♦♦ ⦿ Ⓟ
▲ **Travemünde** "Jugendfreizeitstätte Priwall", Mecklenburger Landstr 69, 23570 Travemünde.	☎ (4502) 2576 ✆ (4502) 4620	80	01.04–14.10	♦♦♦ ⦿ Ⓟ
▲ **Triberg/Schw** Rohrbacher Str 35, 78098 Triberg.	☎ (7722) 4110 ✆ (7722) 6662	125	27.12–22.12	♦♦♦ ⦿ 2SE Ⓟ ⬛
▲ **Trier** Jugendgästehaus, An der Jugendherberge 4, 54292 Trier.	☎ (651) 146620 ✆ (651) 1466230	248	01.01–23.12; 27–31.12	♦♦♦ ⦿ 3SW ⮃ ⒸⒸ ⬛
▲ **Tübingen** Gartenstr 22/2, 72074 Tübingen.	☎ (7071) 23002 ✆ (7071) 25061	161	🔒12	♦♦♦ ⦿ Ⓟ
▲ **Überlingen** "Martin-Buber- Jugendbegegnungsstätte", Alte Nussdorfer Str 26, 88662 Überlingen.	☎ (7551) 4204 ✆ (7551) 1277	247	27.12–22.12	♦♦♦ ⦿ 2SE Ⓟ ⬛
▲ **Ueckermünde-Bellin** Altwarper Straße, 17375 Bellin.	☎ (39771) 22411 ✆ (39771) 22554	80	01.01–20.12; 29–31.12	♦♦♦ ⦿ Ⓡ 7W ⮃ Ⓟ

Location/Address	Telephone No. Fax No.	Beds	Opening Dates	Facilities
▲ **Uelsen/ Grafschaft Bentheim** Linnenbachweg 12, 49843 Uelsen.	☎ (5942) 718 ✆ (5942) 20960	104	01.03–31.10	¶Ⓞ❙ 2S
▲ **Uelzen** Fischerhof 1, 29525 Uelzen.	☎ (581) 5312 ✆ (581) 14210	166	27.12–23.12	♦♦ ¶Ⓞ❙ P ▣
▲ **Ulm** "Geschwister-Scholl-JH", Grimmelfinger Weg 45, 89077 Ulm.	☎ (731) 384455 ✆ (731) 384511	144	10.01–11.12	¶Ⓞ❙ P ▣
Urach ☞ **Bad Urach**				
Urfeld ☞ **Walchensee**				
▲ **Uslar** Kupferhammer 13, 37170 Uslar.	☎ (5571) 2298 ✆ (5571) 1288	104	27.12–23.12	♦♦ ¶Ⓞ❙ ⅋ P
▲ **Velbert** Am Buschberg 17, 42549 Velbert (YH + YGH).	☎ (2051) 84317 ✆ (2051) 81202	120	01.02–30.11	♦♦ ¶Ⓞ❙ ⅋ P
▲ **Verden** Saumurplatz 1, 27283 Verden.	☎ (4231) 61163 ✆ (4231) 68121	124	🅷12	♦♦ ¶Ⓞ❙ ⅋ P
▲ **Villingen** OT Villingen, St-Georgener-Str 36, 78048 Villingen-Schwenningen.	☎ (7721) 54149 ✆ (7721) 52616	133	🅷12	♦♦ ¶Ⓞ❙ 2NW P ▣
▲ **Vlotho** Oeynhauser Str 15, 32602 Vlotho.	☎ (5733) 4063 ✆ (5733) 18139	108	27.12–23.12	♦♦ ¶Ⓞ❙ P
Vöhl ☞ **Hessenstein**				
Wabern ☞ **Mosenberg**				
▲ **Walchensee** - JH Urfeld Mittenwalder Str 17, 82432 Walchensee (Bavaria).	☎ (8851) 230 ✆ (8851) 1022	97	01.01–14.11; 27–31.12	♦♦ ¶Ⓞ❙
▲ **Waldeck** Klippenberg 3, 34513 Waldeck.	☎ (5623) 5313 ✆ (5623) 6254	161	27.12–23.12	♦♦ ¶Ⓞ❙ 2.5NW P
▲ **Waldheim** Breitenbergstr. 21, 04736 Waldheim	☎ (34327) 92116 ✆ (34327) 92116	39	🅷12	♦♦ ¶Ⓞ❙
Waldhäuser ☞ **Neuschönau**				
▲ **Waldmünchen** Schlosshof 1, 93449 Waldmünchen (Bavaria).	☎ (9972) 94140 ✆ (9972) 941433	120	🅷12	♦♦ ¶Ⓞ❙ Ⓡ ⅋ P ▣
▲ **Walldürn** Auf der Heide 37, 74731 Walldürn.	☎ (6282) 283 ✆ (6282) 40194	102	27.12–22.12	♦♦ ¶Ⓞ❙ 3N P
▲ **Waltersdorf** - "Gut Drauf-JH" Am Jägerwäldchen 2, 02763 Bertsdorf-Hörnitz. ✉ stbpers@-t-online.de	☎ (35841) 35099 ✆ (35841) 37773	166	🅷12	♦♦ ¶Ⓞ❙ ⅋ P
▲ **Wandlitz** Prenzlauer Chaussee 146, 16348 Wandlitz. ✉ jh-wandlitz@jugendherberge.de	☎ (33397) 22109 ✆ (33397) 62735	176	01.05-31.12 (Ⓡ 01.11–28.02)	♦♦ ¶Ⓞ❙
▲ **Wangerooge** "Westturm", 26486 Wangerooge, (North Sea)	☎ (4469) 439 ✆ (4469) 8578	136	01.05–30.9	¶Ⓞ❙ Ⓡ 4W
▲ **Waren** Auf dem Nesselberg 2, 17192 Waren.	☎ (3991) 667606 ✆ (3991) 667606	58	01.01–20.12; 29–31.12	♦♦ ¶Ⓞ❙ Ⓡ ✆ P
▲ **Warmbad** 09429 Gehringswalde, Ortsteil Warmbad.	☎ (37369) 9437 ✆ (37369) 5665	62	01.01–23.12; 27–31.12	♦♦ ¶Ⓞ❙ P

Location/Address	Telephone No. Fax No.	Beds	Opening Dates	Facilities
▲ **Weikersheim** YGH "Haus der Musik", Im Heiligen Wöhr 1, 97990 Weikersheim.	☎ (7934) 7025, 7026 🖷 (7934) 7709	143	01.01–19.11; 27–31.12	ⅲ ⅰ◎ⅼ ♿ Ⓟ ◌
▲ **Weilburg** Am Steinbühl, 35781 Weilburg-Odersbach.	☎ (6471) 7116 🖷 (6471) 1542	135	27.12–23.12	ⅲ ⅰ◎ⅼ 2E Ⓟ
▲ **Weimar** - JGH "Maxim Gorki" **Zum Wilden Graben 12, 99425 Weimar.**	☎ (3643) 850750 🖷 (3643) 850749	60	01.01–21.12; 28-31.12	ⅲ ⅰ◎ⅼ R Ⓟ
▲ **Weimar** - "Germania" Carl-August Allee 13, 99423 Weimar.	☎ (3643) 850490 🖷 (3643) 850491	121	28.12–22.12	ⅲ ⅰ◎ⅼ R ⫟CC⫠ ☕
▲ **Weimar** - "Am Poseckschen Garten" Humboldtstr 17, 99423 Weimar.	☎ (3643) 850792 🖷 (3643) 850793	104	28.12–20.12	ⅲ ⅰ◎ⅼ ⫟CC⫠ ☕
▲ **Weimar** - JGH "Am Ettersberg" Ettersberg-Siedlung, 99427 Weimar	☎ (3643) 421111 🖷 (3643) 421112	66	01.01-21.12; 28-31.12	ⅲ ⅰ◎ⅼ R Ⓟ ◌
▲ **Weinheim/Bgstr** Breslauer Str 46, 69469 Weinheim.	☎ (6201) 68484 🖷 (6201) 182730	143	27.12–22.12	ⅲ ⅰ◎ⅼ 2W Ⓟ ◌
▲ **Weiskirchen** Jugendherbergsstr 12, 66709 Weiskirchen.	☎ (6876) 231 🖷 (6876) 1444	126	01.01–23.12; 27–31.12	ⅲ ⅰ◎ⅼ ♿
Weißenbrunn ☞ **Leinburg**				
▲ **Werdau** Jugendheimweg 1, 08412 Werdau.	☎ (3761) 3514 🖷 (3761) 3514	40	🔲12	ⅲ ⅰ◎ⅼ Ⓟ ◌
Wernfels ☞ **Spalt**				
▲ **Wernigerode** Am Eichberg 5, 38855 Wernigerode.	☎ (3943) 606176 🖷 (3943) 606177	150	01.01–23.12; 28–31.12	ⅲ ⅰ◎ⅼ 1.5NW ♿ Ⓟ ☕
▲ **Wertheim** "Frankenland", Alte-Steige 16, 97877 Wertheim.	☎ (9342) 6451 🖷 (9342) 7354	105	27.12–22.12	ⅲ ⅰ◎ⅼ 2W Ⓟ
▲ **Westensee** Am See 24, 24259 Westensee.	☎ (4305) 542 🖷 (4305) 1360	138	06.01–22.12	ⅲ ⅰ◎ⅼ ♿ Ⓟ ◌
▲ **Westerstede** "Hössensportanlage", Jahnallee 1, 26655 Westerstede; Postfach 1129, 26641 Westerstede.	☎ (4488) 84690 🖷 (4488) 78317	68	3.1–21.12	ⅲ ⅰ◎ⅼ 2SW ♿ Ⓟ
▲ **Wetzlar** Richard-Schirrmann-Str 3, 35578 Wetzlar.	☎ (6441) 71068 🖷 (6441) 75826	190	27.12–23.12	ⅲ ⅰ◎ⅼ 2SW ♿
▲ **Wewelsburg** Burgwall 17, 33142 Büren-Wewelsburg.	☎ (2955) 6155 🖷 (2955) 6946	210	27.12–09.01; 11.02–23.12	ⅲ ⅰ◎ⅼ Ⓟ
▲ **Wieden** "JH Belchen", Oberwieden 16, 79695 Wieden.	☎ (7673) 538 🖷 (7673) 504	157	27.12–22.12	ⅲ ⅰ◎ⅼ 2W Ⓟ
▲ **Wiehl** An der Krähenhardt 6, 51674 Wiehl.	☎ (2262) 93410 🖷 (2262) 91598	175	01.01–23.12; 27–31.12	ⅲ ⅰ◎ⅼ Ⓟ
▲ **Wiesbaden** Blücherstr 66, 65195 Wiesbaden. ✉ wiesbaden@djh-hessen.de	☎ (611) 48657, 449081 🖷 (611) 441119	161	02.01–23.12	ⅲ ⅰ◎ⅼ 2W Ⓟ
▲ **Wiesenttal-Streitberg** - JH Streitberg Am Gailing 6, 91346 Wiesenttal (Bavaria).	☎ (9196) 288 🖷 (9196) 1543	122	🔲12	ⅲ ⅰ◎ⅼ ◌
▲ **Wildenstein, Burg** 88637 Leibertingen.	☎ (7466) 411 🖷 (7466) 417	161	01.01–26.11; 27–31.12	ⅲ ⅰ◎ⅼ Ⓟ ◌

Location/Address	Telephone No. Fax No.	Beds	Opening Dates	Facilities
▲ **Wilhelmshaven** Freiligrathstr 131, 26386 Wilhelmshaven.	☎ (4421) 60048 ⊕ (4421) 64716	126	01.12–31.10	¶⊙ 3E P
▲ **Willingen** Am Lukasheim 9-12, 34508 Willingen.	☎ (5632) 6347 ⊕ (5632) 4343	124	27.12–23.12	♦♦♦ ¶⊙ 4NE P
▲ **Windeck-Rosbach** - "Waldjugendherberge" Herbergsstr 19, 51570 Windeck-Rosbach. ✉ jh-windeck@t-online.de	☎ (2292) 5042 ⊕ (2292) 6569	142	01.01–23.12; 27–31.12	♦♦♦ ¶⊙ ♿ ✎ P
▲ **Windischeschenbach** - JH Tannenlohe Tannenlohe 1, 92670 Windischeschenbach (Bavaria).	☎ (9637) 267, 1067 ⊕ (9637) 276	162	16.01–14.12	♦♦♦ ¶⊙ ♿ ⊡
▲ **Windischleuba** - JH Schloß Windischleuba Pestalozziplatz 1, 04603 Windischleuba.	☎ (3447) 834471 ⊕ (3447) 832702	149	🅵12	♦♦♦ ¶⊙ P
▲ **Wingst** Molkereistr 11, 21789 Wingst.	☎ (4778) 262 ⊕ (4778) 7594	202	06.01–31.01; 01.03–22.12	♦♦♦ ¶⊙ ♿ P ⊡
▲ **Winterberg** Astenberg 1, 59955 Winterberg.	☎ (2981) 2289 ⊕ (2981) 569	170	27.12–31.10; 01.12–23.12	¶⊙ P
▲ **Wipperfürth** Ostlandstr 34, 51688 Wipperfürth.	☎ (2267) 1228 ⊕ (2267) 80977	144	01.01–23.12; 27–31.12	¶⊙ ♿ P
▲ **Wirsberg** Sessenreuther Str. 31, 95339 Wirsberg	☎ (9227) 6432 ⊕ (9227) 902767	50	🅵12	♦♦♦ ¶⊙ P
▲ **Wismar** Gagarin-Ring 30A, D-23966 Wismar.	☎ (3841) 32680		Opens December 1999	♦♦♦ ¶⊙ R 2W ♿ P
▲ **Wittdün** Mittelstr 1, 25946 Wittdün/Amrum.	☎ (4682) 2010 ⊕ (4682) 1747	218	03.01–30.11	♦♦♦ ¶⊙ ♿ ⊡
▲ **Wittenberg-Lutherstadt** JH Schloss Wittenberg, 06886 Lutherstadt-Wittenberg.	☎ (3491) 403255 ⊕ (3491) 403255	104	01.01–23.12; 28–31.12	¶⊙ P ⊡
▲ **Wolfsburg** Lessingstr 60, 38440 Wolfsburg	☎ (5361) 13337 ⊕ (5361) 16630	68	27.12–23.12	¶⊙ ♿ P
▲ **Wolfstein** Rötherweg 24, 67752 Wolfstein.	☎ (6304) 1408 ⊕ (6304) 683	160	01.01–23.12; 27–31.12	♦♦♦ ¶⊙ ♿ ⊡
▲ **Worms** Jugendgästehaus, Dechaneigasse 1, 67547 Worms.	☎ (6241) 25780 ⊕ (6241) 27394	114	01.01–23.12; 27–31.12	♦♦♦ ¶⊙ CC
▲ **Worpswede** Hammeweg 2, 27726 Worpswede.	☎ (4792) 1360 ⊕ (4792) 4381	164	🅵12	♦♦♦ ¶⊙ ♿ P
▲ **Wörthsee** - JH Steinebach Herbergsstr 10, 82237 Wörthsee (Bavaria).	☎ (8153) 7206 ⊕ (8153) 89214	30	16.01–30.11	¶⊙
▲ **Wunsiedel** Am Katharinenberg 4, 95632 Wunsiedel (Bavaria).	☎ (9232) 1851 ⊕ (9232) 70629	112	11.01–30.11	♦♦♦ ¶⊙ R ♿ ✎ ⊡
▲ **Wuppertal-Barmen** Obere Lichtenplatzerstr 70, 42287 Wuppertal.	☎ (202) 552372 ⊕ (202) 557354	140	🅵12	¶⊙ ✎
▲ **Würzburg** - JGH IBN Burkarderstr 44, 97082 Würzburg (Bavaria).	☎ (931) 42590 ⊕ (931) 416862	254	🅵12	♦♦♦ ¶⊙ ♿

Location/Address	Telephone No. Fax No.	Beds	Opening Dates	Facilities
▲ **Wüstewohlde** Wüstewohlde Nr 20, 27624 Ringstedt.	☎ (4708) 234 🖷 (4708) 234	72	🕿12	⑩ 🅿
▲ **Wyk auf Föhr** Fehrstieg 41, 25938 Wyk auf Föhr.	☎ (4681) 2355 🖷 (4681) 5527	168	01.02–22.12	ⅲ ⑩ 🅿 🖸
▲ **Zeven-Bademühlen** Haus Nr 1, 27404 Zeven.	☎ (4281) 2550 🖷 (4281) 80293	130	🕿12	ⅲ ⑩ 4W ♿ 🅿
▲ **Zielow** 17207 Ludorf, OT. Zielow.	☎ (39923) 2547 🖷 (39923) 2547	92	01.01–20.12; 29–31.12	ⅲ ⑩ ℝ 🅿
▲ **Zingst** Glebbe 14, 18374 Ostseebad Zingst.	☎ (38232) 15465 🖷 (38232) 15465	170	01.01–20.12; 29–31.12	ⅲ ⑩ ℝ 🅿
▲ **Zinnwald** - "Jägerhütte" Bergmannsweg 8, 01773 Altenberg.	☎ (35056) 32361 🖷 (35056) 32458	70	🕿12	ⅲ ⑩ 🅿
▲ **Zinnwald** - "Klügelhütte" Hochmoorweg 12, 01773 Altenberg.	☎ (35056) 35882 🖷 (35056) 32458	47	🕿12	ⅲ ⑩ 🖸
▲ **Zöblitz** Freiberger Str. 37, 09517 Zöblitz	☎ (37363) 14871 🖷 (37363) 14871	55	🕿12	ⅲ ⑩
▲ **Zuflucht** Schwarzwaldhochstrasse, 72250 Zuflucht.	☎ (7804) 611 🖷 (7804) 1323	228	01.01–10.11; 27–31.12	ⅲ ⑩ 🅿 🖸
▲ **Zwiesel** Hindenburgstr 26, 94227 Zwiesel (Bavaria).	☎ (9922) 1061 🖷 (9922) 60191	53	01.01–14.11; 27–31.12	ⅲ ⑩ 🅿
▲ **Zwingenberg** "Carl-Ulrich-JH" Die Lange Schneise 11, 64673 Zwingenberg.	☎ (6251) 75938 🖷 (6251) 788113	125	27.12–23.12	⑩ 1 NE

Greece

GRECE

GRIECHENLAND

GRECIA

IYHF Athens International Hostel,
16 Victor Hugo Street,
Athens, Greece.

☎ (30) (1) 5234170
✆ (30) (1) 5234015

Capital:	Athens	**Population:**	10,257,000
Language:	Greek (Hellenic)	**Size:**	131,044 sq km
Currency:	GDR (drachma)	**Telephone Country Code:**	30

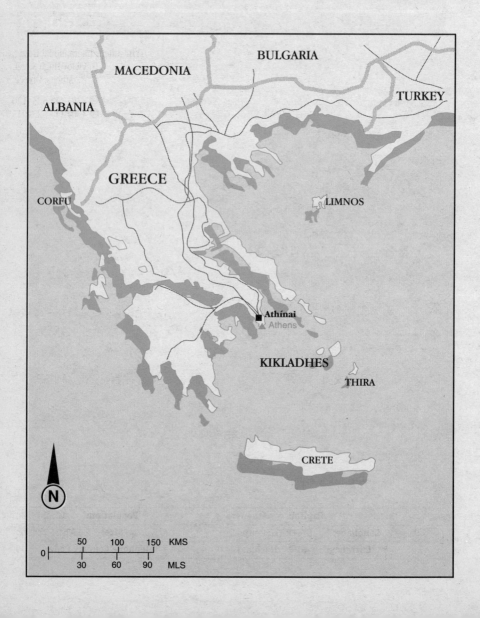

ALBANIA

MACEDONIA

BULGARIA

TURKEY

GREECE

CORFU

LIMNOS

Athínai
Athens

KIKLADHES

THIRA

CRETE

N

50   100   150   KMS

0

30   60   90   MLS

English

GREEK HOSTELS

Due to the change of circumstances in Greece, there is no YHA recognised by the IYHF. For the time being we are including only limited hostel information, but we hope to add futher hostels in the future. For further and latest information please contact the Athens International Youth Hostel.

PASSPORTS AND VISAS

EC citizens can enter Greece with their identity card. Other Europeans need a valid passport. All non-Europeans should contact their local Greek Consulate for visa requirements.

HEALTH

No vaccinations are required. Some medical services are provided to EC citizens, but in general medical insurance is advisable.

BANKING HOURS

All major tourist centres have at least one bank open 08.00-18.00hrs. Otherwise hours are 08.00-14.00hrs Monday to Thursday and 08.00-13.30hrs on Friday.

POST OFFICES

Monday to Friday 08.00-14.00hrs. Post offices in Athens and major tourist centres operate extended hours of 08.00-19.00hrs.

SHOPPING HOURS

In general, Monday, Wednesday and Saturday 08.00-14.00hrs; Tuesday, Thursday and Friday 08.00-13.30hrs and 17.00-20.00hrs.

TRAVEL

Air

There is a good airline network to Europe and all major Greek cities and islands.

Rail

The main lines run from north to south, with limited branch lines at Central and Northern Greece and Peloponese. Eurail and Inter-Rail cards are accepted.

Bus

An extensive bus network runs between all cities and villages, with frequent departures from Athens.

Ferry

There is an extensive ferry and boat network to all the Greek islands and Italy, Cyprus and Israel. Eurail and Inter-Rail card holders can have free ferry transportation between Brindisi and Patras.

Driving

Driving is on the right. An emergency triangle, fire extinguisher, first aid kit and use of safety belts are mandatory. For EC citizens, their national (pink) driving licence is valid. Other motorists should obtain an international driving licence. International motor insurance (green card) is compulsory.

Français

AUBERGES DE JEUNESSE GRECQUES

Du fait de changements survenus dans la situation des auberges grecques, il n'y a pas d'Association d'Auberges de Jeunesse reconnue par l'IYHF en Grèce. Pour le moment, nous n'avons introduit que les coordonnées d'un nombre limité d'auberges mais nous espérons pouvoir être en mesure d'en ajouter davantage à l'avenir. Pour obtenir un complément d'informations, veuillez contacter l'Auberge Internationale d'Athènes.

PASSEPORTS ET VISAS

Les citoyens de la CE peuvent entrer en Grèce avec leur carte d'identité. Les autres Européens doivent être munis d'un passeport valide. Tous les non-Européens doivent s'adresser à leur consulat grec local en ce qui concerne un visa.

SOINS MEDICAUX

Aucune vaccination n'est requise. Les citoyens de la CE ont droit à certains soins médicaux, mais en général, il est préférable de souscrire à une police d'assurance maladie.

HEURES D'OUVERTURE DES BANQUES

Tous les grands centres touristiques ont au moins une banque ouverte de 8h à 18h. Sinon, les banques sont ouvertes de 8h à 14h du lundi au jeudi et de 8h à 13h30 le vendredi.

BUREAUX DE POSTE

Les bureaux de poste sont ouverts du lundi au vendredi de 8h à 14h. Les bureaux d'Athènes et ceux des grands centres touristiques ouvrent plus longtemps, de 8h à 19h.

HEURES D'OUVERTURE DES MAGASINS

Les magasins sont en général ouverts le lundi, le mercredi et le samedi, de 8h à 14h et le mardi, le jeudi et le vendredi, de 8h à 13h30 et de 17h à 20h.

DEPLACEMENTS

Avions
Il y a un bon réseau aérien à destination de l'Europe et de toutes les grandes villes et îles grecques.

Trains
Les grandes lignes vont du nord au sud, avec un nombre limité de lignes secondaires au centre et au nord du pays et dans le Péloponnèse. Les cartes Eurail et Inter-Rail sont acceptées.

Autobus
Toutes les grandes villes et tous les villages sont reliés par un vaste réseau d'autobus; les départs depuis Athènes sont fréquents.

Ferry-boats
Tout un service de ferry-boats et de bateaux dessert la totalité des îles grecques, ainsi que l'Italie, Chypre et Israël. Les voyageurs munis de cartes Eurail et Inter-Rail peuvent bénéficier de transport gratuit par ferry entre Brindisi et Patras.

Automobiles
La conduite est à droite. Les conducteurs doivent transporter un triangle de présignalisation, un extincteur et une trousse de premiers secours, et le port des ceintures de sécurité est obligatoire. Pour les citoyens de la CE, leur permis de conduire national (rose) suffira. Les autres automobilistes devront obtenir un permis de conduire international. Il est obligatoire d'avoir une assurance automobile internationale (carte verte).

Deutsch

GRIECHISCHE JUGENDHERBERGEN

Aufgrund einer veränderten Situation in Griechenland wird von der Internationalen Föderation für Jugendherbergen kein griechischer Jugendherbergsverband anerkannt.

PÄSSE UND VISA

Staatsbürger eines EU-Landes können mit ihrem Personalausweis in Griechenland einreisen. Andere Europäer brauchen einen gültigen Reisepaß. Alle Nichteuropäer sollten sich beim nächsten griechischen Konsulat nach den Visumsvorschriften erkundigen.

GESUNDHEIT

Impfungen sind nicht erforderlich. Gewisse ärztliche Leistungen werden auch Staatsbürgern eines EG-Landes geboten, aber im allgemeinen empfiehlt sich der Abschluß einer Krankenversicherung.

GESCHÄFTSSTUNDEN DER BANKEN

Alle bekannten Fremdenverkehrsorte haben mindestens eine Bank, die von 08.00-18.00 Uhr geöffnet ist. Sonst sind Banken montags bis donnerstags von 08.00-14.00 Uhr und freitags von 08.00-13.30 Uhr geöffnet.

POSTÄMTER

Montags bis freitags von 08.00-14.00 Uhr geöffnet. In Athen und größeren Fremdenverkehrsorten sind Postämter jedoch von 08.00-19.00 Uhr geöffnet.

LADENÖFFNUNGSZEITEN

Im allgemeinen montags, mittwochs und samstags von 08.00-14.00 Uhr und dienstags, donnerstags und freitags von 08.00-13.30 Uhr und von 17.00-20.00 Uhr.

REISEN

Flugverkehr

Es gibt gute Flugverbindungen in andere Länder Europas und in alle größeren Städte in Griechenland sowie auf die bekannteren Inseln.

Eisenbahn

Die Haupteisenbahnlinien verlaufen von Norden nach Süden. In Zentral- und Nordgriechenland sowie auf den Peloponnes gibt es ein beschränktes Netz von Nebenstrecken. Es werden auch Eurail- und Inter-Rail-Karten akzeptiert.

Busse

Zwischen allen Städten und Dörfern gibt es einen umfangreichen Busverkehr. Besonders von Athen aus verkehren die Busse sehr häufig.

Fähren

Auf alle griechischen Inseln und nach Italien, Zypern und Israel verkehren zahlreiche Fähren und Schiffe. Wer im Besitz einer Eurail- oder Inter-Rail-Karte ist, kann die Fähre zwischen Brindisi und Patras kostenlos benutzen.

Autofahren

In Griechenland herrscht Rechtsverkehr. Man muß ein Warndreieck, ein Feuerlöschgerät und einen Erste-Hilfe-Kasten mit sich führen, und das Tragen von Sicherheitsgurten ist Pflicht. Der von einem EU-Land ausgestellte (rosarote) Führerschein gilt auch in Griechenland. Andere Autofahrer sollten sich einen internationalen Führerschein beschaffen. Eine internationale Kraftfahrzeugversicherung (grüne Karte) ist Pflicht.

Español

ALBERGUES JUVENILES GRIEGOS

En Grecia no existe una Asociación de Albergues Juveniles reconocida por la IYHF por haber cambiado la situación. Por el momento, sólo incluimos información limitada sobre albergues, pero esperamos poder añadir más albergues en el futuro. Rogamos contactar con el Albergue de Juventud Internacional de Atenas para más información.

PASAPORTES Y VISADOS

Los ciudadanos de la UE pueden entrar en Grecia con su carnet de identidad. Los demás ciudadanos europeos necesitan un pasaporte en regla. Todos los ciudadanos no europeos deben ponerse en contacto con el Consulado de Grecia de su país para informarse sobre los requisitos en materia de visados.

INFORMACIÓN SANITARIA

No hacen falta vacunas. Se facilitan algunos servicios médicos a los ciudadanos de la UE, pero en general se recomienda hacerse un seguro médico.

HORARIO DE LOS BANCOS

Todos los grandes centros turísticos tienen al menos un banco abierto desde las 08.00 hasta las 18.00 horas. Si no, las horas de apertura al público son de 08.00 a 14.00 de lunes a jueves y de 08.00 a 13.30 los viernes.

OFICINAS DE CORREOS

De lunes a viernes, de 08.00 a 14.00 horas. Las oficinas de correos de los principales centros turísticos y de Atenas abren hasta más tarde, de 08.00 a 19.00 horas.

HORARIO COMERCIAL

En general los lunes, miércoles y sábados de 08.00 a 14.00 horas. Los martes, jueves y viernes de 08.00 a 13.30 horas y de 17.00 a 20.00 horas.

DESPLAZAMIENTOS

Avión

Hay una buena red de líneas aéreas que vuelan a Europa y a las principales ciudades e islas griegas.

Tren

Las líneas principales van de norte a sur, con líneas secundarias limitadas en el centro y norte de Grecia y en el Peloponeso. Se aceptan las tarjetas Eurail e Inter-Rail.

Autobús

Una extensa red de autocares comunica todas las ciudades y pueblos, con salidas frecuentes desde Atenas.

Ferry

Hay una extensa red de ferrys y barcos a todas las islas griegas y a Italia, Chipre e Israel. Los titulares de las tarjetas Eurail e Inter-Rail pueden viajar gratis en ferry desde Brindisi hasta Patras.

Automóvil

Se conduce por la derecha. Es obligatorio llevar un triángulo de emergencia, un extintor de incendios, un botiquín de primeros auxilios y los cinturones de seguridad abrochados. Para los ciudadanos de la UE el permiso de conducir nacional (rosa) es suficiente. Los conductores de otros países deben tener un permiso internacional. Es obligatorio ser titular de un seguro automovilístico internacional (carta verde).

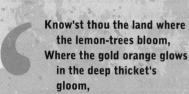

Know'st thou the land where
the lemon-trees bloom,
Where the gold orange glows
in the deep thicket's
gloom,
Where a wind ever soft from the blue
heaven blows,
And the groves are of laurel and myrtle
and rose?

Connais-tu le pays où fleurissent les
citronniers,
Où les oranges d'or flamboyent sur leur
feuillage foncé,
Où souffle un vent toujours doux venu des
cieux azurés,
Et où les vergers sentent la myrte, la rose
et le laurier?

**Kennst Du das Land, wo die Zitronen
blühen,
In dunklem Laub die Goldorangen
glühen,
Ein sanfter Wind vom blauen Himmel
weht,
Die Myrte still und hoch der Lorbeer
steht?**

¿Conoces la tierra donde los limoneros
florecen,
Donde la naranja dorada en el oscuro
follaje resplandece,
Donde del cielo azul una brisa siempre
tenue sopla
Y en cuyos vergeles crece el
laurel y el mirto y la rosa?

Goethe (1749-1832)

Athens - IYHF Athens International Hostel "Victor Hugo"

16 Victor Hugo St,
10438 Athens.
📞 (1) 5234170
📠 (1) 5234015

Open Dates:	🗓️
Open Hours:	⏱️
Reservations:	**R** (IBN) (CC)
Price Range:	GDR 1750-1900 € 5.38-6.15 💳
Beds:	140 - 1x¹ 🛏️ 20x² 🛏️ 29x⁴ 🛏️
Facilities:	👪 4x 👪 🍽️ (BL) ☕ 🍺 🏛️ 🧺 🔒 💼 🔞 ⚡ ℹ️ ♿

Directions:	1.2 NW from city centre
✈️	Helliniko 15km
A🚌	#91 Omonia Bus Stop 600m
⛴️	Piraeus 8km
🚃	Central 500m
🚌	A7, B7 400m ap Kanigos Square
🚊	#1, #12 300m ap Agiou Konstantinou str
U	Omonia Sq. 500m

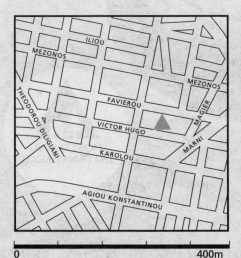

Net Savings @Hostelling International

Simply ring us ...

HOSTELLING INTERNATIONAL

netsavings@hostellinginternational.org.uk

Hungary

HONGRIE

UNGARN

HUNGRIA

**Magyarországi Ifjusági Szállások Szövetsége
H-1077 Budapest VII., Almàssy tèr 6. IV/404, Hungary**

Postal address: H-1410 Budapest, PO Box 119, Hungary

❶ (36) (1) 3435167
❸ (36) (1) 3435167

Travel Section: Express Travel Centre,
Szabadság tér 16, 1054 Budapest V.
❶ (36) (1) 3123849, 3324108
❸ (36) (1) 3533172

A copy of the Hostel Directory for this country can be obtained from:
30 Express Travel Offices, eg,
Keleti Rail Station,
Budapest.

Capital:	Budapest		**Population:**	10,750,000
Language:	Hungarian		**Size:**	93,030, sq km
Currency:	Ft (forints)		**Telephone Country Code:**	36

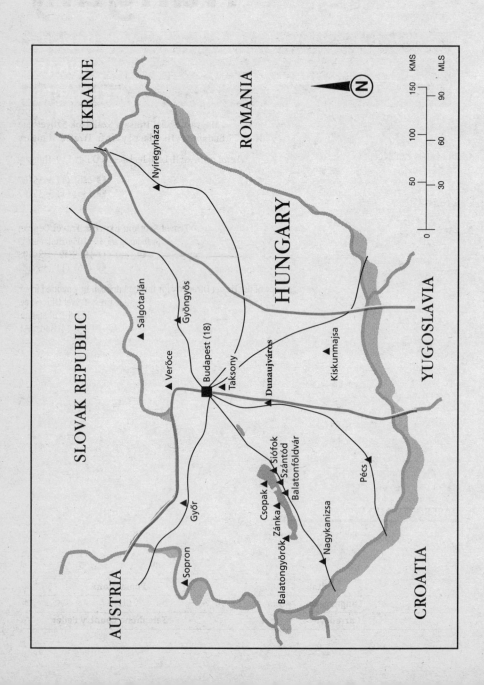

English

HUNGARIAN HOSTELS

Hostels are open 24hrs. Expect to pay US$ 3.00-29.00 (700-7000 Ft) per night including sheets. All hostels serve meals or use restaurants near by, a few have self-catering facilities.

Express as Travel Section offers central booking for groups and concessions for youth and student travel.

All hostels can accept families - advance booking recommended!

Advance booking for individuals to hostels or hostel booking centres if seasonal hostels are closed:
Travellers Hostels: 1134 Budapest XIII, Dózsa Gy ut 152.
❶ (1) 3408585
❸ (1) 3208425
❷ travellers@mail.matav.hu
Hungarohostels: H - 1077 Budapest VII, Almàssy tèr 6.
❶ (1) 3435167
❸ (1) 3435167

General Services: On-the-spot booking on arrival for individuals in Budapest in Express offices during working hours:
e.g. Express Main Office, 1052 Budapest V, Semmelweis u 4.
❶ (1) 3178600
❸ (1) 3176823

PASSPORTS AND VISAS

Hungary is visa-free for citizens of most European countries, Canada and the USA.

HEALTH

There are no vaccination requirements for visitors entering Hungary.

BANKING HOURS

Banks are open weekdays between 09.00 and 13.00hrs.

POST OFFICES

Generally open 08.00-18.00hrs. In Budapest Keleti and Nyugati Railway Stations the post offices are open 0800-21.00hrs.

SHOPPING HOURS

Shops are normally open between 10.00 and 18.00hrs, however they are open later on Thursday until 19.00hrs but on Saturday close early at 14.00hrs.

TRAVEL

Travel in Hungary is very centralized, when entering or leaving the country it is easiest to go via Budapest.

Air
EXPRESS ticketing office can arrange flights and youth discount air tickets.

Rail
There is a reliable train service. Train tickets and youth discount tickets are available from EXPRESS ticket offices. In Budapest there is a good underground/subway system.

Bus
There is a reliable bus service. Central information in Central Bus Station, Erzsébet tér. In Budapest and main cities there are good bus, tram and trolley bus services.

Ferry
There is a good ferry service on Lake Balaton and the Danube from May to October.

Driving
Drinking alcohol and driving is strictly forbidden in Hungary.

Français

AUBERGES DE JEUNESSE HONGROISES

Les auberges sont ouvertes jour et nuit. Une nuit, draps compris, vous coûtera aux environs de 3 à 29 $US (700-7000 Ft). Toutes les auberges servent des repas ou utilisent les restaurants locaux. Quelques-unes ont une cuisine à la disposition des touristes.

Express, la section voyage, offre un service de réservation central aux groupes, ainsi que des tarifs voyage spéciaux aux jeunes et aux étudiants.

Toutes les auberges peuvent recevoir des familles - il est conseillé de réserver à l'avance!

Réservations à l'avance pour les individuels dans les auberges ou aux centres de réservation si les auberges saisonnières sont fermées:

Travellers Auberges: 1134 Budapest XIII, Dózsa Gy ut 152,
☎ (1) 3408585
✆ (1) 3208425
✉ travellers@mail.matav.hu
Hungaro Auberges: H - 1077 Budapest VII, Almàssy tèr 6.
☎ (1) 3435167
✆ (1) 3435167

Services Généraux: Réservation sur place à l'arrivée à Budapest pour les individuels dans les bureaux Express, pendant les heures de travail: Bureau Principal d'Express, 1052 Budapest V, Semmelweis u 4,
☎ (1) 3178600
✆ (1) 3176823

PASSEPORTS ET VISAS

Les visas ne sont pas requis pour les citoyens de la plupart des pays européens, du Canada et des Etats-Unis.

SOINS MEDICAUX

Aucune vaccination n'est requise pour les étrangers se rendant en Hongrie.

HEURES D'OUVERTURE DES BANQUES

Les banques sont ouvertes en semaine de 9h à 13h.

BUREAUX DE POSTE

En général, ils sont ouverts de 8h à 18h. Dans les gares Keleti et Nyugati de Budapest, les bureaux de poste sont ouverts de 8h à 21h.

HEURES D'OUVERTURE DES MAGASINS

Les magasins sont normalement ouverts entre 10h et 18h; ils sont ouverts plus longtemps le jeudi, jusqu'à 19h, mais ferment tôt le samedi, à 14h.

DEPLACEMENTS

Les transports en Hongrie sont très centralisés. Il est plus facile de passer par Budapest pour entrer ou sortir du pays.

Avions
Les bureaux EXPRESS peuvent organiser des vols et des billets à prix réduit pour les jeunes.

Trains
Les trains sont fiables. Les billets normaux et les billets à tarif spécial pour les jeunes sont vendus aux guichets EXPRESS. Budapest possède un bon réseau de métro.

Autobus
Les autobus sont fiables. Pour tous renseignements, s'adresser à la station d'autobus centrale d'Erzsébet ter. A Budapest et dans les grandes villes, les services d'autobus, de trams et de trolleybus sont fiables.

Ferry-boats
Il y a un bon service de ferry-boats sur le lac Balaton et le Danube de mai à octobre.

Automobiles
Il est formellement interdit en Hongrie de conduire après avoir consommé de l'alcool.

Deutsch

UNGARISCHE JUGENDHERBERGEN

Die Herbergen sind 24 Stunden geöffnet. Es ist mit einem Preis von 3,00-29,00 US$ (700-7.000 Ft) pro Nacht, einschließlich Bettlaken, zu rechnen. Alle Herbergen bieten Mahlzeiten, manchmal in einem nahegelegenen Restaurant, einige haben Einrichtungen für Selbstversorger.

Express bietet als Reisedienst die Möglichkeit zentraler Buchungen für Gruppen sowie Ermäßigungen für junge Leute und Studenten.

Alle Herbergen können auch Familien aufnehmen - Vorausbuchung ist ratsam!

Vorausbuchungen für Einzelreisende können in den Jugendherbergen oder Reservierungszentralen vorgenommen werden, wenn Sommerherbergen geschlossen sind.
Travellers Herbergen: 1134 Budapest XIII, Dózsa Gy ut 152.
☎ (1) 3408585
📠 (1) 3208425
✉ travellers@mail.matav.hu
Hungaro Herbergen: H - 1077 Budapest VII, Almàssy tèr 6.
☎ (1) 3435167
📠 (1) 3435167

Allgemeine Dienste: Bei Ankunft in Budapest können Einzelreisende während der Öffnungszeiten in den Express-Geschäftsstellen buchen: z.B. Hauptbüro Express, 1052 Budapest V, Semmelweis u 4.
☎ (1) 3178600
📠 (1) 3176823

PÄSSE UND VISA

Staatsangehörige der meisten europäischen Länder, Kanadas und der USA brauchen für Ungarn kein Visum.

GESUNDHEIT

Es gibt keine Impfvorschriften für nach Ungarn reisende Besucher.

GESCHÄFTSSTUNDEN DER BANKEN

Die Banken sind werktags zwischen 09.00 und 13.00 Uhr geöffnet.

POSTÄMTER

Im allgemeinen von 08.00-18.00 Uhr geöffnet. Auf den Bahnhöfen Budapest Keleti und Nyugati sind die Postämter zwischen 08.00 und 21.00 Uhr geöffnet.

LADENÖFFNUNGSZEITEN

Die Geschäfte sind im allgemeinen zwischen 10.00 und 18.00 Uhr geöffnet. Donnerstags wird jedoch erst um 19.00 Uhr und samstags schon um 14.00 Uhr geschlossen.

REISEN

Das Reisen ist in Ungarn sehr zentralisiert. Bei der Ein- und Ausreise des Landes fährt man am besten über Budapest.

Flugverkehr
EXPRESS-Flugbüros können Flüge buchen und für junge Leute ermäßigte Flugtickets beschaffen.

Eisenbahn
Es gibt einen zuverlässigen Zugverkehr. Fahrkarten mit Ermäßigung für junge Leute sind in den EXPRESS-Verkaufsstellen erhältlich. In Budapest gibt es ein gutes U-Bahn-Netz.

Busse
Es gibt einen zuverlässigen Busverkehr. Auskunftszentrale auf dem Zentralen Busbahnhof, Erzsébet tér. In Budapest und anderen größeren Städten gibt es einen guten Bus-, Straßenbahn- und Omnibusservice.

Fähren
Auf dem Balaton und der Donau gibt es von Mai bis Oktober einen guten Fährverkehr.

Autofahren
Das Autofahren nach Alkoholgenuß ist in
Ungarn strengstens verboten.

Español

ALBERGUES JUVENILES HÚNGAROS

Los albergues están abiertos las 24 horas del
día y una noche le costará entre 3 y 29 $USA
(700-7000 Ft), sábanas incluidas. Todos los
albergues sirven comidas o utilizan restaurantes
próximos, y en algunos es posible cocinar uno
mismo.

Express, la Sección de Viajes, ofrece un servicio
centralizado de reservas para grupos y precios
especiales para jóvenes y estudiantes.

Todos los albergues disponen de alojamiento
para las familias, pero ¡reserve con antelación!

Para hacer reservas individuales con antelación,
diríjase directamente a los albergues o a un
centro de reservas si se trata de albergues
estacionales que estén cerrados:

Albergues Travellers: 1134 Budapest XIII,
Dózsa Gy ut 152
📞 (1) 3408585
📠 (1) 3208425

📧 travellers@mail.matav.hu
Albergues Hungaro: H - 1077 Budapest VII,
Almàssy tèr 6.
📞 (1) 3435167
📠 (1) 3435167

Servicios Generales: Al llegar a Budapest, las
reservas se pueden hacer en el acto en las
oficinas de Express en horas de oficina: Oficina
Central de Express, 1052 Budapest V,
Semmelweis u 4,
📞 (1) 3178600
📠 (1) 3176823

PASAPORTES Y VISADOS

Los ciudadanos procedentes de la mayoría de
los países europeos, del Canadá y de los
Estados Unidos no necesitan visado de entrada
a Hungría.

INFORMACIÓN SANITARIA

Los visitantes a Hungría no necesitan vacunas.

HORARIO DE LOS BANCOS

Los bancos abren los días laborables de 9 h. a
13 h.

OFICINAS DE CORREOS

Por lo general, abren de 8 h. a 18 h. En las
estaciones de tren de Keleti y Nyugati en
Budapest, las oficinas de correos abren de 8 h.
a 21 h.

HORARIO COMERCIAL

Las tiendas suelen abrir de 10 h. a 18 h. y hasta
las 19 h. los jueves, pero los sábados cierran
más temprano, a las 14 h.

DESPLAZAMIENTOS

Las comunicaciones en Hungría están muy
centralizadas. Es más fácil entrar y salir del país
a través de Budapest.

Avión
Se pueden conseguir billetes de avión y
descuentos para jóvenes en las oficinas de
vuelos de EXPRESS.

Tren
El servicio ferroviario es fiable. Se pueden
conseguir billetes de tren y descuentos para
jóvenes en las taquillas de EXPRESS. Budapest
cuenta con una buena red de metro.

Autobús
El servicio de autobuses es fiable. La oficina de
información central se encuentra en la Estación
Central de Autobuses, Erzsébet ter. En Budapest
y en las ciudades principales, hay buenos
servicios de autobús, tranvía y trolebús.

Ferry

Existe un buen servicio de ferrys en el Balatón y el Danubio de mayo a octubre.

Automóvil

En Hungría está estrictamente prohibido conducir bajo la influencia del alcohol.

Adventure is worthwhile in itself.

L'aventure elle-même en vaut la peine.

Abenteuer allein lohnt sich.

La aventura merece la pena por la experiencia en sí.

Amelia Earhart

Balaton -
Zánkai Gyermek és Ifjúsági Centrum

8250 Zánka/Balaton Nord.
☎ (87) 568500
📠 (87) 568588
✉ zankaedu@sednet.hu

Open Dates:	🗓12
Open Hours:	🕐
Reservations:	R
Price Range:	US$ 6.00-26.00 📖
Beds:	2600 - 5x¹ 🛏 222x² 🛏 82x³ 🛏 60x⁴ 🛏 146x⁶ 🛏 85x⁶ 🛏
Facilities:	♿ 🚻 300x 🚻 🍽 ☞ 🍺 🛏 📺 📷 5 x🍴 🔲 🧺 ⬆ P ℹ ✂ 🏔 🌐 🍴 🏫 🏠

Directions:

🚢	Zánka
🚂	Zánkafürdö
🚌	Zánka

Attractions: 🎣 ⛰ 📷 🏃 ∪3km 🏊 🚣

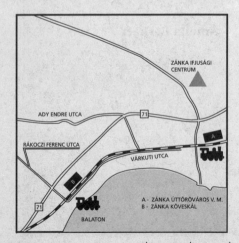

Budapest -
Csillebérci Szabadidö és Ifjúsági Központ

Konkoly Thege Miklós u. 21,
1121 Budapest XII.
☎ (1) 2754033 or (1) 3956537
📠 (1) 3957327
✉ csill@mail.datanet.hu

Open Dates:	🗓12
Open Hours:	🕐
Reservations:	R ⊂CC⊃
Price Range:	US$ 6.00-22.00 📖
Beds:	200 - 30x² 🛏 40x³ 🛏 4x⁴ 🛏
Facilities:	♿ 🚻 4x 🚻 🍽 ☞ 🍺 🛏 📺 📷 5 x🍴 🔲 🖼 🧺 8 P ℹ 🔌 ✂ 🏔 🌐 🍴 🔍 🏫 🏠

Directions:

🚂	Déli 5km
🚌	No. 90
Ⓤ	U2 Déli 5km

Attractions: 🎣 ⛰ 📷 🚴 🏃 🏊 🚣

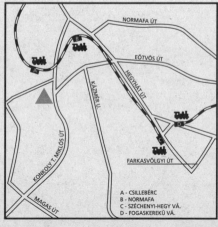

Budapest - Travellers' Hostel Diáksport

Dózsa György út 152,
1134 Budapest XIII.
📞 (1) 3298644, 3408585
📠 (1) 3208425
📧 travellers@mail.matav.hu

Open Dates:	🗓
Open Hours:	🕐
Reservations:	**R** ⊂CC⊃
Price Range:	US$ 8.00-15.00 💶
Beds:	140 - 11x¹🛏 27x²🛏 1x³🛏 2x⁴🛏 2x⁶🛏 5x⁶⁺🛏
Facilities:	👫 3x 👫 🍽 (B) 👕 🛋 📺 🧺 📠 🖼 🎱 ☎ 🅿 ℹ 🧑‍🦽

Directions:

🚂	Nyugati 1km
Ⓤ	U3, Dòzsa Gy ut 300m

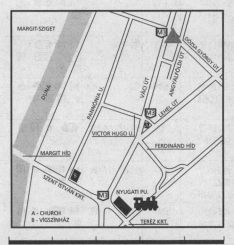

Location/Address	Telephone No. Fax No.	Beds	Opening Dates	Facilities
△ *Balaton Csopak* - *Ifjúsági Üdülő* *Sport u 9, 8229 Csopak*	☎ *(87) 446505* 🖷 *(87) 446515*	*292*	*01.05–30.09*	ⅲ ⅱⅹⅼ Ⓡ ♿ Ⓟ ☕
▲ Balaton Balatonföldvár - Hotel Juventus József Attila u 6, 8623 Balatonföldvár. ✉ hotjuve@matavnet.hu	☎ (84) 340313 🖷 (84) 340303	200	01.05–30.09	ⅲ ⅱⅹⅼ 1 NE Ⓟ ☕
△ *Balatongyörök* - *Ifjùsàgi Üdülö* *Szépkilàtó, 8313 Balatongyörök.*	☎ *(83) 346018* 🖷 *(92) 312770*	*264*	*15.05–15.09*	ⅱⅹⅼ Ⓡ Ⓟ ☕
△ *Balaton Siófok* - *Benjamin Panzió* *Siófoki út 9, 8600 Balatonszéplak-Felsö*	☎ *(84) 350704*	*35*	🅓	ⅲ
△ *Balaton Szántód* - *Hotel Rév* *Szt. István u. 162, 8622 Szántód.* ✉ *revhotel@elender.hu*	☎ *(84) 348245* 🖷 *(1) 3945926*	*132*	*01.04–31.10*	ⅲ ⅱⅹⅼ Ⓡ Ⓟ ☕
▲ Balaton - Zánka **Zánkai Gyermek és Ifjúsági Centrum, 8250 Zánka/Balaton Nord.** ✉ zankaedu@sednet.hu	☎ (87) 568500 🖷 (87) 568588	2600	🅓	ⅲ ⅱⅹⅼ Ⓡ ♿ ✂ Ⓟ 🗑
▲ Budapest - Hostel Apáczai Papnövelde u 4-6, 1053 Budapest V. Universum ✉ universumhostels@mail.matav.hu	☎ (1) 2670311 🖷 (1) 2757046	160	23.06–25.08	ⅲ Ⓡ ✂ 🗑
△ *Budapest* - *Caterina Hostel* *Andrássy ut 47. III/18, 1061 Budapest VI.*	☎ *(1) 3420804, 2919538* 🖷 *(1)3526147*	*32*	🅓	ⅲ ✂ Ⓟ 🗑
▲ Budapest - Csillebérci Szabadidö és Ifjúsági Központ **Konkoly Thege Miklós u. 21, 1121 Budapest XII.** ✉ csill@mail.datanet.hu	☎ (1) 2754033 or (1) 3956537 🖷 (1) 3957327	200	🅓	ⅲ ⅱⅹⅼ Ⓡ ♿ ⌐CC⌐ ✂ Ⓟ 🗑 ☕
▲ Budapest - Travellers' Hostel Diáksport **Dózsa György út 152, 1134 Budapest XIII.** ✉ travellers@mail.matav.hu	☎ (1) 3298644, 3408585 🖷 (1) 3208425	140	🅓	ⅲ ⅱⅹⅼ Ⓡ ⌐CC⌐ ✂ Ⓟ 🗑
▲ Budapest - Hotel Flandria Szegedi ut 27, 1135 Budapest XIII. ✉ flandria@eravishotels.hu	☎ (1) 3503181 🖷 (1) 3208853	120	🅓	ⅲ ⅱⅹⅼ Ⓡ ♿ Ⓟ
▲ Budapest - Hotel Góliat Kerekes u. 12-20, 1135 Budapest XIII. ✉ goliat@eravishotels.hu	☎ (1) 3501456 🖷 (1) 3494985	363	🅓	ⅲ ⅱⅹⅼ Ⓡ 5 NE ⌐CC⌐ Ⓟ 🗑 ☕
▲ Budapest - Hotel Griff Junior Bartók B ut 152, 1113 Budapest XI. ✉ griffjunior@eravishotels.hu	☎ (1) 2032398 🖷 (1) 2040062	625	🅓	ⅲ ⅱⅹⅼ Ⓡ ♿ ✂ Ⓟ 🗑 ☕
▲ Budapest - Hostel Szt Ignácz Hunyadi u.2-4, 1191 Budapest XIX. ✉ hostels@elender.hu	☎ (1) 3521572 🖷 (1) 3435167	48	05.07–05.09	Ⓡ ✂ Ⓟ 🗑
△ *Budapest* - *Hostel Landler* *Bartók B 17, 1114 Budapest XI, Universum* ✉ *universumhostels@mail.matav.hu*	☎ *(1) 4633621, 4633622* 🖷 *(1) 2757046*	*250*	*01.07–31.08*	ⅲ Ⓡ ✂ Ⓟ 🗑 ☕
△ *Budapest* - *Hostel Rózsa* *Bercsényi u 28, 1117 Budapest XI, Universum* ✉ *universumhostels@mail.matav.hu*	☎ *(1) 4634250* 🖷 *(1) 2757046*	*200*	*01.07–31.08*	ⅲ Ⓡ ✂ Ⓟ 🗑

Location/Address	Telephone No. Fax No.	Beds	Opening Dates	Facilities
▲ **Budapest** - Hotel Touring Pünkösdfürdő u 38, 1039 Budapest III. 🄴 touring@eravishotels.hu	🅣 (1) 2503184 🅕 (1) 2431595	365	🄼	††† 🍽 Ⓡ ♿ ⬛CC⬛ ·P· ▣ ☕
△ *Budapest* - *Hostel Vásárhelyi* *Kruspér u 2, 1111 Budapest XI, Universum.* 🄴 *universumhostels@mail.matav.hu*	🅣 *(1) 4634326,* *(1) 4634356* 🅕 *(1) 2757046*	*600*	*01.07–03.09*	††† 🍽 Ⓡ ⬝ ▣ ☕
△ *Budapest* - *Travellers' Hostel Bánki* *Podmaniczky u 8, 1067 Budapest VI.* 🄴 *travellers@mail.matav.hu*	🅣 *(1) 3408585* 🅕 *(1) 3208425*	*80*	*01.07–31.08*	††† 1N ⬝ ▣
△ *Budapest* - *Best Hostel* *Podmaniczky u. 27, I/13., 1067 Budapest VI.* 🄴 *bestyh@mail.datanet.hu*	🅣 *(1) 3324934* 🅕 *(1) 2692926*	*30*	🄼	††† 1N ⬝ ▣ ☕
△ *Budapest* - *Central Park Hostel* *Ajtósi Dürer sor 23, 1146 Budapest XIV.*	🅣 *(1) 3517393* 🅕 *(1) 3517393*	*210*	*05.07–31.08*	††† 🍽 1.5SW ⬛CC⬛ ⬝ ▣ ☕
△ *Budapest* - *Happy Days Hostel* *Vezér ut 112., 1144 Budapest XIV.*	🅣 *(1) 3517393* 🅕 *(1) 3517393*	*300*	*05.07–31.08*	††† 🍽 2NE ⬛CC⬛ ⬝ P ▣ ☕
▲ **Budapest** - Travellers' Hostel Hill Ménesi ut 5., 1118 Budapest XI. 🄴 travellers@mail.matav.hu	🅣 (1) 3408585 🅕 (1) 3208425	120	01.07–05.09	††† 🍽 0.5E ♿ ⬛CC⬛ ⬝ P ▣ ☕
△ *Budapest* - *Travellers Hostel Universitas* *Irinyi u. 9-11, 1111 Budapest XI.* 🄴 *travellers@mail.matav.hu*	🅣 *(1) 3408585* 🅕 *(1) 3208425*	*400*	*01.07–31.08*	††† 🍽 1W ♿ ⬝ P ▣ ☕
△ *Dunaujváros* - *Kerpely Antal Kollégium* *Dózsa Gy. ut 33-37, 2400 Dunaujváros* 🄴 *kerpely@makacs.poliod.hu*	🅣 *(25) 410434* 🅕 *(25) 410434*	*110*	🄼	††† 🍽 ⬝ P ▣ ☕
△ *Gyöngyös* - *Energia Szálló* *Róbert Károly út 19, 3200 Gyöngyös*	🅣 *(37) 311363* 🅕 *(37) 328027*	*100*	🄼	††† 🍽 Ⓡ ⬝ P ▣ ☕
△ *Kecskemét* - *GAMF Kollégium Hostel* *Izsáki u 10, 6000 Kecskemét* 🄴 *koll@gamf.hu*	🅣 *(76) 321916* 🅕 *(76) 516399*	*230*	*01.07–31.08*	††† 🍽 Ⓡ ⬝ P ▣ ☕
▲ **Kiskunmajsa** - Jonathermál Rt. Motel, Kemping Kökút 26, 6120 Kiskunmajsa 🄴 jonathermal@mail.datanet.hu	🅣 (77) 481245 🅕 (77) 481013	100	🄼	Ⓡ ♿ ⬛CC⬛ ⬝ P ▣ ☕
△ *Nagykanizsa* - *Touring Hotel* *Attila u.4, 8800 Nagykanizsa* 🄴 *touring@mail.matav.hu*	🅣 *(93) 318800,* *313015* 🅕 *(93) 320194*	*64*	🄼	††† 🍽
▲ **Nyiregyháza** - Paradise Hotel and Youth Center Sóstófürdő, Sóstói u 76, 4431 Nyiregyháza	🅣 (42) 402011, 402038 🅕 (42) 402011, 402038	200	15.04–15.10	††† 🍽 Ⓡ ♿ ⬛CC⬛ P ▣ ☕
△ *Pécs* - *Hotel Laterum* *Hajnóczy J.u. 37-39., 7633 Pécs*	🅣 *(72) 252108,* *(72) 252113* 🅕 *(72) 252131*	*60*	🄼	††† 🍽 Ⓡ ⬛CC⬛ P ☕
△ *Pécs* - *JPTE Kollégium* *Szántó Kovács János u. 1, 7633 Pécs* 🄴 *sebestye@btkstud.jpte.hu*	🅣 *(72) 251203* 🅕 *(72) 251203*	*255*	🄼	††† 🍽 Ⓡ ⬝ P ▣

Location/Address	Telephone No. Fax No.	Beds	Opening Dates	Facilities
▲ **Salgótarjàn** - Strand Hotel Tóstrand 1. Pf. 83, 3100 Salgótarjàn ❷ hostels@elender.hu	❶ (32) 430277, 430085 ❸ (32) 430837	80	🔲12	👬 🍴 🅡 3N ♿ 🅿
△ *Siófok - Hotel Ezüstpart* *Liszt Ferenc sétány 2-4, 8609 Siófok,* *Balatonszéplak Felsö* ❷ *reserve@balaton.hunguest.hu*	❶ *(84) 350622* ❸ *(84) 350358*	*2398*	🔲12	🍴 🅡 ♿ ⒸⒸ 🅿 ☕
△ *Sopron - Ciklámen Bungalows* *Brennbergi-völgy, 9400 Sopron* ❷ *pannonia_med_hotel@sopron.hu*	❶ *(99) 312180* ❸ *(99) 340766*	*52*	*01.05–31.10*	👬 🅡 ⒸⒸ ⚲ 🅿
▲ **Taksony** - Sziget Panzió Sziget sétány, Pf.9., 2335 Taksony ❷ sziget@mail.interware.hu	❶ (24) 477477 ❸ (24) 477774	64	🔲12	👬 🍴 🅡 ♿ ⒸⒸ ⚲ 🅿 ☕
△ *Verőce - Danube Bend* *Express International Youth Center,* *Motel and Touring Hotel* *2623 Kismaros*	❶ *(27) 350166* ❸ *(27) 350166*	*200*	*15.04–15.10*	👬 🍴 🅡 ♿ ⚲ 🅿 ☕

YOUTH HOSTEL ACCOMMODATION
OUTSIDE THE ASSURED STANDARDS SCHEME

Location/Address	Telephone No. Fax No.	Beds	Opening Dates	Facilities
Budapest - Travellers' Hostel Schönherz Irinyi J. u. 42, 1114 Budapest XI. ❷ travellers@mail.matav.hu	❶ (1) 3408585 ❸ (1) 3208425	600	01.07–31.08	👬 🍴 🅡 2SW ♿ ⒸⒸ ⚲ 🅿 🚿 ☕
Budapest - Station Guesthouse . Mexikói ut 36/B, 1145 Budapest XIV. ❷ station@mail.matav.hu	❶ (1) 2218864 ❸ (1) 3834034	48	🔲12	👬 🅡 3.5NE ⚲ 🅿 🚿 ☕

Iceland

ISLANDE

ISLAND

ISLANDIA

Bandalag Íslenskra Farfugla,
(Icelandic Youth Hostel Association) Sundlaugavegur 34,
105 Reykjavík, Iceland.

t (354) 553 8110
f (354) 588 9201
e info@hostel.is
www.hostel.is

Office Hours: Monday-Friday, 09.00-17.00hrs

A copy of the Hostel Directory for this Country can be obtained from:
The National Office.

Capital:	Reykjavík	Population:	265,000
Language:	Icelandic	Size:	103,000 sq km
Currency:	Kr (kronúr)	Telephone Country Code:	354

Iceland

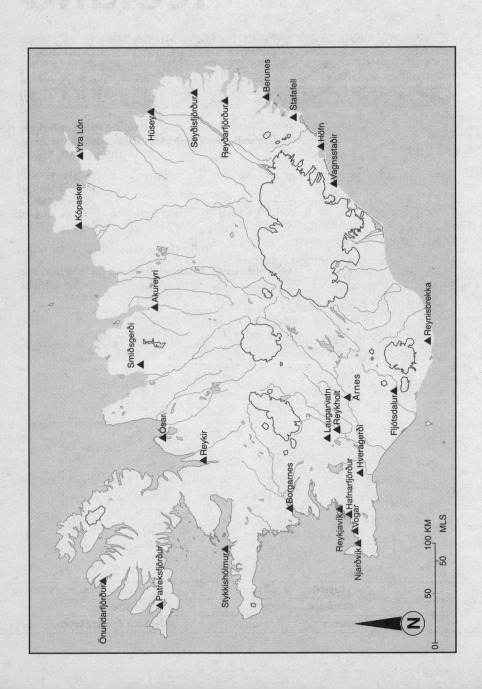

Berunes
Stafafell
Húsey
Seyðisfjörður
Reyðarfjörður
Hófn
Vagnsstaðir
Ytra Lón
Kópasker
Akureyri
Reynisbrekka
Smiðsgerði
Ósar
Laugarvatn
Reykholt
Árnes
Reykir
Fljótsdalur
Borgarnes
Hafnarfjörður
Hveragerði
Reykjavík
Vogar
Njarðvík
Stykkishólmur
Önundarfjörður
Patreksfjörður

100 KM
MLS
50
50
0

N

English

ICELAND HOSTELS

Get beyond Reykjavík and sample the wild and remote side of Iceland. 28 hostels encircle the country, all have family rooms except Fljötsdalur.

Hostels are normally open between 08.00 and 01.00hrs, Reykjavík, Akureyri and Höfn are open until 24.00hrs but have limited access between 11.00 and 16.00hrs. Expect to pay in the region of Kr 1,100-1,300 plus linen hire if needed. Self-catering is available at all hostels. Some hostels provide meals, but they must be booked on arrival.

Late arrivals are accepted in all hostels, but they must be booked in advance.

PASSPORTS AND VISA

A valid passport is always needed to enter Iceland, except for nationals of Norway, Sweden, Finland, Denmark, the Faroe Islands and Greenland.

BANKING HOURS

Banks are open Monday to Friday between 09.15 and 16.00hrs.

POST OFFICES

Post Offices are open Monday to Friday between 09.00 and 16.30hrs.

SHOPPING HOURS

Shops are open Monday to Friday 09.00-18.00hrs and Saturday 10.00-14.00hrs. Shops are usually closed on Sunday.

TRAVEL

Rail
There is no rail network in Iceland.

Bus
In summer buses run daily to most places in Iceland and in July and August into the highland. It is possible to buy a circlebus or omnibus pass from June to August and this is one of the best ways to travel in Iceland. It is possible to combine these passes with youth hostel overnight vouchers. These passes are available at our Travel Section office.

Ferry
During June, July and August there is a ferry, once a week, from Denmark and Norway.

Driving
In summer it is possible to drive all around Iceland and in bigger vehicles into the highland. In winter you must get information about the road conditions before you start to travel, due to weather and snow conditions. The Travel Section provides hired cars at reasonable prices. It is also possible to combine hired cars with youth hostel overnight vouchers.

Français

AUBERGES DE JEUNESSE ISLANDAISES

Au-delà de Reykjavík, vous ferez l'expérience du côté sauvage et reculé de l'Islande. 28 auberges font le tour du pays et toutes ont des chambres familiales sauf celle de Fljötsdalur.

Les auberges sont normalement ouvertes de 8h à 1h; celles de Reykjavík, Akureyri et Höfn sont ouvertes jusqu'à minuit mais sont d'accès limité entre 11h et 16h. Une nuit vous coûtera entre 1 100 et 1 300 KIS, plus location de draps le cas échéant. Il est possible de faire sa propre cuisine dans toutes les auberges. Certaines auberges servent des repas, mais ils doivent être réservés à l'arrivée.

Les arrivées tardives sont acceptées, mais doivent avoir été réservées à l'avance.

PASSEPORTS ET VISAS

Un passeport valide est toujours requis pour entrer en Islande, sauf pour les citoyens de Norvège, de Suède, de Finlande, du Danemark, des Iles Féroé et du Groenland.

HEURES D'OUVERTURE DES BANQUES

Les banques sont ouvertes du lundi au vendredi, de 9h15 à 16h.

BUREAUX DE POSTE

Les bureaux de poste sont ouverts du lundi au vendredi, de 9h à 16h30.

HEURES D'OUVERTURE DES MAGASINS

Les magasins sont ouverts du lundi au vendredi de 9h à 18h, et le samedi de 10h à 14h. Ils sont en général fermés le dimanche.

DEPLACEMENTS

Trains
Il n'y a pas de réseau ferroviaire en Islande.

Autobus
En été, les autobus assurent un service journalier vers la plupart des régions d'Islande, et en juillet et août vers les hautes terres. Il est possible de se procurer une carte circlebus ou omnibus de juin à août et cela représente la meilleure façon de se déplacer dans le pays. Il est également possible d'acheter des forfaits comprenant carte bus + hébergement en auberge. Ces cartes sont en vente au bureau de notre Service Voyages.

Ferry-boats
En juin, juillet et août, il y a un ferry, une fois par semaine, en provenance du Danemark et de la Norvège.

Automobiles
En été, il est possible de conduire dans tout le pays et, avec des véhicules plus lourds, dans les hautes terres. En hiver, il est essentiel d'obtenir des renseignements sur l'état des routes avant d'entreprendre un voyage, les conditions atmosphériques pouvant rendre la conduite très dangereuse. Notre section voyages met à la disposition des voyageurs un service de location de véhicules à tarifs très concurrentiels. Il est également possible d'acheter des forfaits comprenant location de voiture + hébergement en auberge.

Deutsch

ISLÄNDISCHE JUGENDHERBERGEN

Sie sollten versuchen, Reykjavík hinter sich zu lassen und die abgelegene Seite Islands, die von wilder Schönheit geprägt ist, näher kennenzulernen. Im ganzen Land gibt es 28 Herbergen, alle mit Familienzimmern, außer der Herberge in Fljótsdalur.

Die Herbergen sind normalerweise von 08.00 bis 01.00 Uhr geöffnet. Die in Reykjavík, Akureyri und Höfn sind bis 24.00 Uhr geöffnet, aber zwischen 11.00 und 16.00 Uhr nur beschränkt zugänglich. Es ist mit einem Preis von ca. 1.100-1.300 Kr zu rechnen, plus einer Mietgebühr für Bettwäsche, wenn Bedarf besteht. Es gibt auch Einrichtungen zur Selbstversorgung in allen Herbergen. In einigen Herbergen gibt es Mahlzeiten, die bei der Ankunft bestellt werden müssen.

In allen Herbergen werden auch Spätankömmlinge aufgenommen, sofern sie sich im voraus angemeldet haben.

PÄSSE UND VISA

Wer nicht aus Norwegen, Schweden, Finnland, Dänemark, von den Faröer Inseln oder aus Grönland stammt, braucht für die Einreise nach Island immer einen gültigen Reisepaß.

GESCHÄFTSSTUNDEN DER BANKEN

Banken sind montags bis freitags zwischen 09.15 und 16.00 Uhr geöffnet.

POSTÄMTER

Postämter sind montags bis freitags zwischen 09.00 und 16.30 Uhr geöffnet.

LADENÖFFNUNGSZEITEN

Die Geschäfte sind montags bis freitags von 09.00-18.00 Uhr und samstags von 10.00-14.00 Uhr geöffnet. Sonntags sind sie normalerweise geschlossen.

REISEN

Eisenbahn

In Island gibt es keine Eisenbahn.

Busse

Im Sommer gibt es einen täglichen Busverkehr zu den meisten Orten in Island und im Juli und August auch ins Hochland. Von Juni bis August kann man einen Rundreisebus- oder Omnibus-Paß kaufen. Das ist eine der besten Möglichkeiten, durch Island zu reisen. Man kann diese Pässe mit Übernachtungsgutscheinen für Jugendherbergen kombinieren. Diese Pässe gibt es in der Geschäftsstelle der Reiseabteilung des isländischen JH-Verbandes.

Fähren

Im Juni, Juli und August kommt einmal in der Woche eine Fähre aus Dänemark und Norwegen.

Autofahren

Im Sommer kann man quer durch Island und mit größeren Fahrzeugen auch ins Hochland fahren. Im Winter muß man sich wegen des Wetters und der Schneefälle nach den Straßenverhältnissen erkundigen. Die Reiseabteilung bietet preiswert Mietwagen an. Es besteht die Möglichkeit, den Ausleih von Mietwagen mit Übernachtungsgutscheinen für Jugendherbergen zu kombinieren.

Español

ALBERGUES JUVENILES ISLANDESES

Si viaja más allá de Reykjavík, descubrirá el lado salvaje y remoto de Islandia. 28 albergues rodean el país, todos ellos provistos de habitaciones familiares, salvo el de Fljótsdalur.

Los albergues suelen abrir de 8 h. a 1 h. Los de Reykjavík, Akureyri y Höfn están abiertos hasta las 24 h., pero tienen acceso limitado entre las 11 h. y las 16 h. Los precios oscilan entre 1.100 y 1.300 Kr más sábanas, si las necesita. Es posible cocinar uno mismo en todos los albergues y algunos sirven comidas, aunque hay que encargarlas al llegar.

Todos los albergues aceptan llegadas tarde por la noche con previo aviso.

PASAPORTES Y VISADOS

Se requiere siempre un pasaporte en regla para entrar en Islandia, excepto para los ciudadanos de Noruega, Suecia, Finlandia, Dinamarca, Islas Faroe y Groenlandia.

HORARIO DE LOS BANCOS

Los bancos abren de lunes a viernes de 9.15 h. a 16 h.

OFICINAS DE CORREOS

Las oficinas de correos abren de lunes a viernes de 9 h. a 16.30 h.

HORARIO COMERCIAL

El horario de las tiendas es de lunes a viernes de 9 h. a 18 h. y los sábados de 10 h. a 14 h. Normalmente cierran los domingos.

DESPLAZAMIENTOS

Tren

Islandia no tiene red ferroviaria.

Autobús

En verano existen servicios de autocar diarios

que recorren casi toda Islandia. En julio y
agosto, llegan hasta las tierras altas. De junio a
agosto es posible adquirir un abono para el
autocar circular o el omnibús, lo que
representa una de las mejores maneras de
viajar por Islandia. Este abono puede
combinarse con vales que permiten alojarse en
los albergues juveniles y es posible conseguirlo
en la Sección de Viajes de nuestra oficina.

Ferry
En junio, julio y agosto sale un ferry de
Dinamarca y Noruega una vez por semana.

Automóvil
En verano se puede conducir por toda Islandia,
incluso hasta las tierras altas en los vehículos
más pesados. En invierno es imprescindible
informarse sobre el estado de las carreteras
antes de salir de viaje, ya que las condiciones
meteorológicas y la nieve pueden resultar muy
peligrosas. En nuestra Sección de Viajes se
alquilan coches a precios asequibles y es
también posible combinar el alquiler con vales
para los albergues.

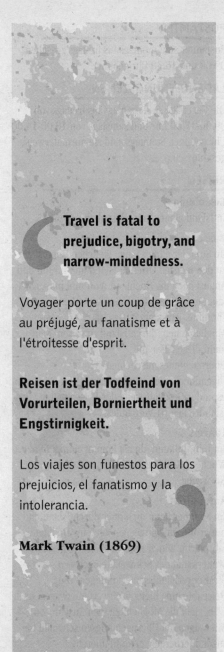

Travel is fatal to prejudice, bigotry, and narrow-mindedness.

Voyager porte un coup de grâce au préjugé, au fanatisme et à l'étroitesse d'esprit.

Reisen ist der Todfeind von Vorurteilen, Borniertheit und Engstirnigkeit.

Los viajes son funestos para los prejuicios, el fanatismo y la intolerancia.

Mark Twain (1869)

Location/Address	Telephone No. Fax No.	Beds	Opening Dates	Facilities
▲ **Akureyri** Stórholt 1, 600 Akureyri.	☎ 4623657, 8944299 🖷 4612549	49	🛏12	⋔ CC ☞ P 🖶
▲ **Árnes** Gnúpverjahreppur, 801 Selfoss. ⊜ bergleif@centrum.is	☎ 4866048/ 8612645 🖷 4866091	17	🛏12	⋔ ❄ Ⓡ CC ☞ P
▲ **Berunes** Berufjörd, 765 Djúpivogur. ⊜ berunes@simnet.is	☎ 4788988 🖷 4788988	30	15.05–15.09	⋔ ❄ CC ☞ P
△ *Fljótsdalur* *Fljótshlíð, 861 Hvolsvollur.*	☎ *4878498,* *4878497*	*15*	*15.04–15.10*	☞ P
▲ **Hafnarfjörður** - Arahús Strandgata 21, 220 Hafnarfjörður. ⊜ arah@mmedia.is	☎ 5550795 🖷 5553658	34	🛏12	⋔ ☞ P
▲ **Hafnarfjörður** - Hraunbyrgi Hjallabraut 51, Box 190, 220 Hafnarfjörður. ⊜ tourist.hfj@scout.is	☎ 5650900 🖷 5551211	50	🛏12	⋔ ❄ CC ☞ P 🖶
▲ **Hamar** Golfskálinn Hamri, 310 Borgarnes. ⊜ gb@aknet.is	☎ 4371663/ 8621363 🖷 4372063	14	15.05–15.09	⋔ ❄ ☞ P
▲ **Höfn** - Nýibær Hafnarbraut 8, 780 Höfn. ⊜ nyibaer@simnet.is	☎ 4781736, 4781559, 8412159 🖷 4781965	33	15.05–30.09	⋔ ❄ CC ☞ P 🖶
▲ **Húsey** Hróarstungu, 701 Egilsstadir.	☎ 4713010 🖷 4713009	21	20.05–30.09	⋔ ☞ P 🖶
▲ **Hveragerði** Ból, Hveramörk 14, 810 Hveragerði.	☎ 4834198, 4834588 🖷 4834088	33	01.05–01.09	⋔ ❄ CC ☞ P
▲ **Kópasker** Bakkagata 8, 670 Icòpasker	☎ 4652121 🖷 4652102	14	🛏12	⋔ ❄ ☞ P 🖶
▲ **Langanes** - Ytra Lón Langanes, 681 Pórshöfn.	☎ 4681242 🖷 4681242	8	🛏12	⋔ ❄ ☞
▲ **Laugarvatn** - Dalsel 840 Laugarvatn.	☎ 4861215 🖷 4861215	21	🛏12	⋔ ❄ CC ☞ P 🖶
▲ **Njarðvík-Strönd** Njarðvíkurbraut 52-54, 260 Innri Njarðvík. ⊜ strond@centrum.is	☎ 4216211 🖷 4216211	50	🛏12	⋔ ❄ CC ☞ P 🖶
▲ **Önundarfjördur** Korpudalur Kirkjubol, 425 Flateyri. ⊜ korpudalur@centrum.is	☎ 4567808/ 8922030 🖷 4567808	24	01.06–01.09	⋔ ❄ ☞ P 🖶
▲ **Ósar** Pverárhreppi, V-Hún, 531 Hvammstangi. ⊜ osar@simnet.is	☎ 4512678, 8939828 🖷 4512678	20	🛏12	⋔ CC ☞ P 🖶
▲ **Patreksfjörður** Stekkar 21, 450 Patreksfjörður.	☎ 4561675 🖷 4561547	12	🛏12	⋔ ❄ ☞ P

Location/Address	Telephone No. Fax No.	Beds	Opening Dates	Facilities
▲ **Reydarfjördur** - Tærgesenshùsinu Búdargata 4, 730 Reydarfjördur. ✉ gistirey@mmedia	☎ 4741447 📠 4741447	22	🔒12	ⅱ 🍽 ᴄᴄ ☞ Ⓟ ⊡
▲ **Reykholt** Biskupstungum, 801 Selfoss.	☎ 4868830, 4868810 📠 4868709	70	05.06–20.08	ⅱ ᴄᴄ ☞ Ⓟ
▲ **Reykjavík** Sundlaugavegur 34, 105 Reykjavík. ✉ info@hostel.is	☎ 5538110 📠 5889201	104	05.01–20.12	ⅱ 🍽 3W ᴄᴄ ☞ Ⓟ
▲ **Reynisbrekka** Mýrdalur, 870 Vík.	☎ 4871106, 4871243 📠 4871303	28	01.06–15.09	ⅱ 🍽 ᴄᴄ ☞ Ⓟ ⊡
▲ **Seyðisfjörður** - Hafaldan Ránargata 9, 710 Seyðisfjörður. ✉ thorag@simnet.is	☎ 4721410/ 8917010 📠 4721610	28	🔒12	ⅱ ᴄᴄ ☞ Ⓟ ⊡
▲ **Sæberg** Reykir, Hrútafjörður, 500 Brú. ✉ saeberg@isholf.is	☎ 4510015 📠 4510034	32	🔒12	ⅱ 🍽 ☞ Ⓟ
▲ **Smiðsgerði** Hólahreppur, 550 Sauðárkrókur. ✉ jaf@ismennt.is	☎ 4537483/ 4311050 📠 4537483	11	15.06–20.08	ⅱ ☞ Ⓟ
▲ **Stafafell** Lóni, 781 Höfn. ✉ stafafel@eldhorn.is	☎ 4781717 📠 4781785	50	🔒12	ⅱ 🍽 ☞ Ⓟ ⊡
▲ **Stykkishólmur** Höfðagata 1, 340 Stykkishólmur.	☎ 4381095/ 8612517 📠 4381417	50	01.05–15.09	ⅱ ☞ Ⓟ
▲ **Vagnsstadir** Sudursveit, A-Skaftafellssysla, 781 Höfn. ✉ glacierjeeps@simnet.is	☎ 4781048, 4781567 📠 4782167	28	01.06–10.09	ⅱ ᴄᴄ ☞ Ⓟ
▲ **Vogar** - Stóru-Vogaskóli Vogar, 190 Vogar. ✉ postmaster@kristina.is	☎ 4215662 📠 4215648	50	05.06–25.08	ⅱ 🍽 ♿ ☞ Ⓟ

The more we travel and know one another, the more we are likely to build a peaceful world.

Plus nous voyagerons et apprendrons à nous connaître, plus nous aurons de chance de bâtir un monde de paix.

Je mehr wir reisen und einander kennenlernen, desto wahrscheinlicher ist es, eine friedliche Welt zu schaffen.

Cuanto más viajemos y nos conozcamos los unos a los otros, más posibilidades tendremos de crear un mundo en el que reine la paz.

Margaret Thatcher (1993)

Ireland (Northern)

IRLANDE DU NORD
NORDIRLAND
IRLANDA DEL NORTE

Hostelling International - Northern Ireland,
22 Donegall Road, Belfast,
BT12 5JN, Northern Ireland.

☎ (44) (28) 90315435
✆ (44) (28) 90439699
@ info@hini.org.uk
www.hini.org.uk

Office Hours: Monday-Friday, 09.00-17.00hrs

A copy of the Hostel Directory for this Country can be obtained from:
The National Office.

Capital:	Belfast	**Population:**	1,578,100
Language:	English	**Size:**	14,120 sq km
Currency:	£ (Sterling)	**Telephone Country Code:**	44

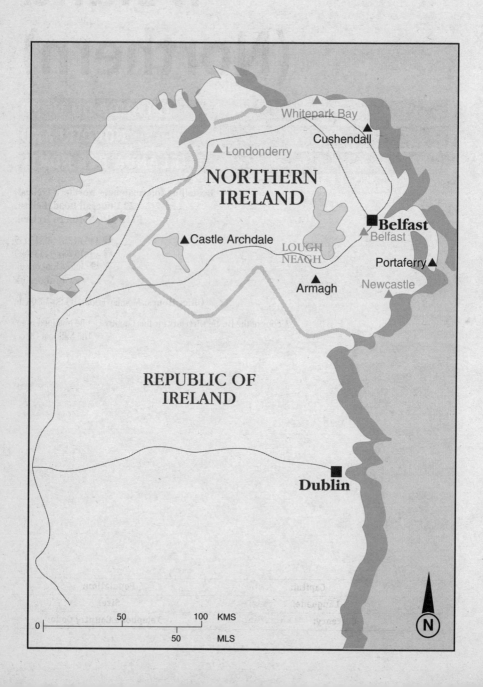

Whitepark Bay

Cushendall

Londonderry

NORTHERN
IRELAND

Castle Archdale

Belfast

Belfast

LOUGH
NEAGH

Portaferry

Armagh

Newcastle

REPUBLIC OF
IRELAND

Dublin

| 0 | 50 | 100 | KMS |

50   MLS

N

English

NORTHERN IRELAND HOSTELS

Less travelled than the neighbouring Republic, Northern Ireland, with its 8 Youth Hostels, has many attractions of its own. Dramatic lakeland scenery in the west contrasts with the wild and rugged Antrim coast and the unique Giant's Causeway.

Hostels are normally open 07.30-11.00hrs and 17.00-23.30hrs, with longer hours at some hostels. Expect to pay in the region of £8.00-£13.00 per night including bedlinen. All hostels have self catering facilities, except Belfast.

Most hostels are closed 22.12-2.1, and many close for other periods between November and February. Check with the hostel or HINI. All hostels take advance bookings made with a credit card except Barholm.

PASSPORTS AND VISAS

You will need a valid passport. Not many visitors now require visas but do check in advance.

HEALTH

An international Certificate of Vaccination is not required to enter the UK, but you should check if one is needed on your re-entry into your own country.

Medical Insurance is essential because visitors are only eligible for free **emergency** treatment at National Health Service Accident and Emergency departments of hospitals. If you are admitted to hospital as an in-patient, even from an accident and emergency department, or referred to an out-patient clinic, you will be asked to pay unless you are a national of an EC country, resident in any member country, or a national or resident of a country which has a reciprocal health care agreement with the UK.

You are strongly advised to take out adequate insurance cover before travelling.

BANKING HOURS

Generally open weekdays 09.30-15.30hrs, but many stay open for an extra hour. All are closed on Sundays and Public Holidays.

POST OFFICES

Open weekdays 09.00-17.30hrs and Saturdays 09.00-12.30hrs. They are closed on Sundays and Public Holidays.

SHOPPING HOURS

Generally Monday-Saturday 09.00-17.30hrs, although this may vary in larger towns. Some shops do stay open late on Wednesday/Thursday/Friday until 20.00/21.00hrs.

TRAVEL

Rail
Main routes are served by rail. An Emerald Card is available which gives unlimited travel throughout the whole of Ireland using bus and rail networks.

Bus
There is an excellent network of regular bus services and in particular good bus links between those towns which are not served by train. Freedom of Northern Ireland Tickets provide 7 days' unlimited travel throughout Northern Ireland and are available from bus stations. The Emerald Card gives unlimited travel throughout the whole of Ireland using bus and rail networks.

Driving
If you want to drive a motor vehicle you must be over the age of 17. Driving is on the left-hand side of the road. Seat belts are required to be worn in both the front and back of cars, if seat belts are fitted. The drink driving laws are very strict so don't do it! The AA and RAC are just

two of the motoring organizations offering, amongst other things, breakdown and recovery services.

Français

AUBERGES DE JEUNESSE NORD-IRLANDAISES

Moins visitée que sa voisine, la République d'Irlande, l'Irlande du Nord, avec ses 8 auberges de jeunesse, ne manque cependant pas d'attractions touristiques. Les régions de lacs spectaculaires à l'ouest contrastent avec la côte sauvage et déchiquetée d'Antrim et avec l'unique Giant's Causeway (Chaussée des Géants).

Les auberges sont en principe ouvertes de 7h30 à 11h et de 17h à 23h30, et certaines ouvrent plus longtemps. Une nuit vous coûtera entre £8,00 et £13,00, draps compris. Toutes les auberges offrent la possibilité de cuisiner, sauf celle de Belfast.

La plupart des auberges sont fermées du 22 décembre au 2 janvier, et beaucoup ferment pendant certaines périodes entre novembre et février. Vérifiez avec l'auberge ou auprès de l'Association (HINI). Toutes les auberges, sauf celle de Barholm, acceptent les réservations a l'avance faites par carte de crédit.

PASSEPORTS ET VISAS

Les voyageurs doivent être munis d'un passeport valide. De nos jours, peu de visiteurs doivent avoir un visa mais vérifiez à l'avance.

SOINS MEDICAUX

Il n'est pas nécessaire d'être muni d'un certificat international de vaccination mais il vous est conseillé de vérifier qu'il ne vous en faudra pas un pour rentrer dans votre pays.

Il est essentiel d'être couvert par une assurance maladie car les visiteurs ne peuvent bénéficier que d'un traitement **d'urgence** gratuit dans les services d'accidents et d'urgence des hôpitaux de la Sécurité sociale. Si vous êtes hospitalisé, même à la demande d'un service d'accidents et d'urgence, ou si vous êtes envoyé dans un service de consultations externes, il vous faudra payer, à moins d'être un citoyen d'un pays de l'Union Européenne, de résider dans un pays membre ou d'être un citoyen ou de résider dans un pays ayant passé un accord médical réciproque avec le Royaume-Uni. Il vous est fortement conseillé de souscrire à une police d'assurance avant votre départ.

HEURES D'OUVERTURE DES BANQUES

En général, les banques sont ouvertes en semaine de 9h30 à 15h30, mais beaucoup restent ouvertes une heure de plus. Elles sont toutes fermées le dimanche et les jours fériés.

BUREAUX DE POSTE

Les bureaux de poste sont ouverts en semaine de 9h à 17h30, et le samedi de 9h à 12h30. Ils sont fermés le dimanche et les jours fériés.

HEURES D'OUVERTURE DES MAGASINS

En général, les magasins sont ouverts du lundi au samedi de 9h à 17h30, bien que cela puisse varier dans les grandes villes. Certains magasins restent ouverts tard le mercredi/jeudi/vendredi jusqu'à 20h/21h.

DEPLACEMENTS

Trains

Les itinéraires principaux sont desservis par le train. La carte Emeraude donne droit à des déplacements illimités dans toute l'Irlande, sur les réseaux d'autobus et ferroviaires.

Autobus

Un excellent réseau d'autobus assure des services réguliers et les villes qui ne sont pas sur les lignes de chemin de fer sont particulièrement bien desservies par les autobus. Les billets 'Freedom of Northern Ireland' donnent droit à des déplacements illimités pendant 7 jours à travers l'Irlande du Nord et sont en vente dans les gares d'autobus. La carte Emeraude donne droit à des déplacements illimités dans toute l'Irlande,sur les réseaux d'autobus et ferroviaires.

Automobiles

Vous devez avoir plus de 17 ans si vous voulez conduire une voiture. La conduite est à gauche. Le port des ceintures de sécurité est obligatoire à l'avant et à l'arrière des véhicules, s'ils en sont équipés. Les lois sur l'alcool au volant sont très strictes; ne prenez pas de risques! Les organisations automobiles, dont AA et RAC, offrent, entre autres, des services de dépannage et de recouvrement de véhicule.

Deutsch

JUGENDHERBERGEN IN NORDIRLAND

Nordirland wird nicht so viel bereist wie die benachbarte Republik, bietet aber ebenfalls viele Sehenswürdigkeiten und 8 Jugendherbergen. Von der wild zerklüfteten Küste von Antrim und dem einmaligen Giant's Causeway hebt sich im Westen eine phantastische Seenlandschaft ab.

Die Herbergen sind gewöhnlich von 07.30-11.00 Uhr und von 17.00-23.30 Uhr, einige auch etwas länger, geöffnet. Es ist mit einem Preis von ca. 8,00 - 13,00£ pro Nacht, einschließlich Bettwäsche, zu rechnen. Alle Herbergen haben Einrichtungen für Selbstversorger, außer Belfast.

Die meisten Herbergen sind vom 22.12.-2.1. geschlossen, und viele schließen zwischen November und Februar auch zu anderen Zeiten. Erkundigen Sie sich in der jeweiligen Herberge oder bei der HINI. Alle Herbergen, außer der in

Barholm, nehmen bei Bezahlung mit einer Kreditkarte Voranmeldungen entgegen.

PÄSSE UND VISA

Sie brauchen einen gültigen Reisepaß. Ein Visum wird nur noch von wenigen Reisenden benötigt. Sie sollten sich aber im voraus erkundigen.

GESUNDHEIT

Wer ins Vereinigte Königreich einreist, braucht kein internationales Impfzeugnis, sollte sich aber erkundigen, ob bei der Rückkehr in sein Heimatland eines verlangt wird.

Eine Krankenversicherung ist erforderlich, da Besucher nur **in Notfällen** Anspruch auf kostenlose Behandlung durch die Unfall- oder Notfallabteilung eines Krankenhauses des National Health Service haben. Wenn Sie (ob von der Unfall- oder Notfallabteilung eines Krankenhauses oder von einem anderen Arzt) zur stationären Behandlung in ein Krankenhaus eingewiesen oder an die ambulante Abteilung überwiesen werden, müssen Sie selbst bezahlen, es sei denn, Sie besitzen die Staatsangehörigkeit eines EU-Landes oder Sie sind in einem Mitgliedsstaat wohnhaft oder Sie besitzen die Staatsangehörigkeit eines Landes, mit dem das Vereinigte Königreich einen gegenseitigen Vertrag über die Gesundheitspflege abgeschlossen hat, bzw. Sie sind in einem solchen Land wohnhaft. Wir raten Ihnen dringend zum Abschluß einer ausreichenden Versicherung vor Antritt Ihrer Reise.

GESCHÄFTSSTUNDEN DER BANKEN

Im allgemeinen werktags von 09.30-15.30 Uhr geöffnet, aber viele schließen erst eine Stunde später. An Sonn- und Feiertagen sind alle Banken geschlossen.

POSTÄMTER

Öffnungszeiten: werktags von 09.00-17.30 Uhr und samstags von 09.00-12.30 Uhr. An Sonn- und Feiertagen sind alle Postämter geschlossen.

LADENÖFFNUNGSZEITEN

Im allgemeinen montags bis samstags von 09.00-17.30 Uhr, in größeren Städten oft anders. Einige Geschäfte sind mittwochs/donnerstags/ freitags bis 20.00/21.00 Uhr geöffnet.

REISEN

Eisenbahn

Die wichtigsten Orte sind an das Eisenbahnnetz angeschlossen. Es gibt eine 'Emerald Card', die in ganz Irland zu unbeschränkter Benutzung des Bus- und Schienennetzes berechtigt.

Busse

Es gibt ein ausgezeichnetes Linienbusnetz, und zwischen Städten, die nicht mit der Bahn erreicht werden können, gibt es besonders gute Busverbindungen. 'Freedom of Northern Ireland Tickets', die auf Busbahnhöfen erhältlich sind, berechtigen zu siebentägigem unbegrenztem Reisen in ganz Nordirland. Die 'Emerald Card' berechtigt in ganz Irland zu unbeschränkter Benutzung des Bus- und Schienennetzes.

Autofahren

Wer ein Kraftfahrzeug führen will, muß über 17 Jahre alt sein. Es herrscht Linksverkehr. Sowohl auf den Vorder- als auch auf den Rücksitzen müssen im Auto, sofern vorhanden, Sicherheitsgurte angelegt werden. Die Gesetze über das Autofahren nach dem Genuß von Alkohol sind sehr streng - unterlassen Sie es daher! Die AA und der RAC sind nur zwei Kraftfahrzeugorganisationen, die u.a. einen Pannen- und Rückführdienst bieten.

Español

ALBERGUES JUVENILES DE IRLANDA DEL NORTE

Menos concurrida por los turistas que la vecina República de Irlanda, Irlanda del Norte, con sus 8 albergues juveniles, tiene un gran atractivo propio. Los espectaculares paisajes de lagos del oeste del país contrastan con la agreste y rocosa costa de Antrim y el singular Giant's Causeway (Paso del Gigante).

Los albergues suelen abrir de 07.30 a 11.00 horas y de 17.00 a 23.30 horas, ofreciendo algunos un horario más amplio. Los precios oscilan entre £8,00 y £13,00 por noche incluyendo las sábanas. Todos los albergues tienen cocina para huéspedes, salvo el de Belfast.

La mayor parte de los albergues cierran entre el 22 de diciembre y el 2 de enero y algunos cierran durante determinados períodos de noviembre y febrero. Confírmelo con el albergue deseado o con HINI. Todos los albergues aceptan reservas anticipadas con tarjeta de crédito, salvo el de Barholm.

PASAPORTES Y VISADOS

Se necesita un pasaporte válido. En la actualidad, muy pocos visitantes requieren visado, pero se recomienda confirmarlo con antelación.

INFORMACIÓN SANITARIA

Para entrar en el Reino Unido no se precisa un Certificado Internacional de Vacunación, pero se aconseja verificar la necesidad de presentar uno al regresar a su país de origen.

Un seguro médico es fundamental porque los visitantes sólo tienen derecho a tratamiento gratuito de **urgencia** en el departamento de Accidentes y Urgencias de los hospitales de la Seguridad Social. Si se le ingresa en un hospital como paciente interno, aunque venga del departamento de urgencias, o se le manda a una consulta para pacientes externos, se le pedirá que pague el coste del servicio a menos que sea ciudadano de un país de la UE, residente en cualquier país miembro, o ciudadano o residente en un país que tenga un acuerdo de asistencia sanitaria mutua con el Reino Unido. Se recomienda encarecidamente hacerse un seguro adecuado antes de viajar al Reino Unido.

HORARIO DE LOS BANCOS

Por lo general, abren los días laborables de 09.30 a 15.30 horas, aunque muchos están abiertos una hora más. Todos los bancos cierran los domingos y festivos.

OFICINAS DE CORREOS

Abren los días laborables de 09.00 a 17.30 horas y los sábados de 09.00 a 12.30 horas. Todas cierran los domingos y festivos.

HORARIO COMERCIAL

Por lo general, las tiendas abren de lunes a sábado de 09.00 a 17.30 horas, aunque el horario puede variar en las poblaciones más importantes. Algunas tiendas permanecen abiertas hasta las 20.00/21.00 horas los miércoles/jueves/viernes.

DESPLAZAMIENTOS

Tren

Las principales rutas están cubiertas por servicios de tren. Se puede comprar una Emerald Card que permite viajar de forma ilimitada por toda Irlanda en tren y en autobús.

Autobús

Existe una excelente red de servicios regulares de autobús que es especialmente buena entre las poblaciones a las que no se llega en tren. Los billetes Freedom of Northern Ireland permiten viajar de forma ilimitada durante 7 días por toda Irlanda del Norte y se pueden comprar en las estaciones de autobús. La tarjeta Emerald Card permite viajar de forma ilimitada por toda Irlanda en tren y en autobús.

Automóvil

Para conducir un automóvil hay que ser mayor de 17 años. Se conduce por la izquierda. Es obligatorio llevar puestos los cinturones de seguridad en los asientos delanteros y en los traseros si los hay. La legislación sobre la conducción bajo la influencia del alcohol es muy estricta ¡No se arriesgue! La AA y la RAC son dos de las organizaciones de automovilismo que ofrecen, entre otros, servicios de asistencia en carretera y de grúa.

Belfast -
International YH

22 Donegall Rd,
Belfast BT12 5JN.
t (2890) 315435
f (2890) 439699
e info@hini.org.uk

Open Dates:	📅12
Open Hours:	🕐
Reservations:	R IBN CC
Price Range:	£12.00-13.00 🍽
Beds:	120
Facilities:	♿ 👬 👫 🍽 ☕ 🖼 📺 🔒 💼 🧺 8️⃣ 🧳 🅿 ℹ 🚲 ⛪
Directions:	1 SW from city centre
✈	Belfast International 30.6km
⛴	Larne 35.7km, Donegall Quay 3.2km
🚂	Central 5km
🚌	89, 90 from City centre ap YH
Attractions:	🚲

Whitepark Bay

157 Whitepark Bay Rd,
Ballintoy,
Ballycastle,
Co Antrim BT54 6NH.
t (28207) 31745
f (28207) 32034
e info@hini.org.uk

Open Dates:	📅12
Reservations:	R IBN CC
Price Range:	£8.50-12.50
Beds:	54
Facilities:	♿ 👬 👫 🍽 (BD) 🔒 🖼 📺 🔒 💼 🅿 ℹ
Directions:	9 W of Ballycastle
✈	Belfast International 80km
🚂	Portrush 19km
🚌	200m
Attractions:	🔍200m 🚲 🚶

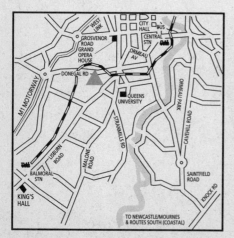

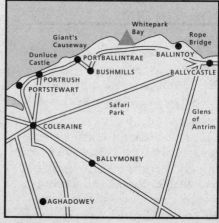

0   6km

Location/Address	Telephone No. Fax No.	Beds	Opening Dates	Facilities
▲ **Armagh City** 39 Abbey St, Armagh, BT61 7EB ⓔ info@hini.org.uk	ⓣ (2837) 511800 ⓕ (2837) 511801	62	▣	⁉ ⁑ 0.2SW ♿ ECC ☞ P ⊡ ☕
▲ **Belfast** - International YH IBN **22 Donegall Rd, Belfast BT12 5JN.** ⓔ info@hini.org.uk	ⓣ (2890) 315435 ⓕ (2890) 439699	120	▣	⁉ ⁑ R 1SW ♿ ECC P ⊡ ☕
△ *Castle Archdale* *Irvinestown, Co Fermanagh BT94 1PP.* ⓔ *info@hini.org.uk*	ⓣ *(28686) 28118* ⓕ *(28686) 28118*	*52*	*01.03–31.10*	⁉ ⁑ R ECC ☞ P ⊡
▲ **Cushendall** Layde Rd, Cushendall, Co Antrim BT44 0NQ. ⓔ info@hini.org.uk	ⓣ (28217) 71344 ⓕ (28217) 72042	54	01.03–23.12	⁉ ⁑ R ECC ☞ P
▲ **Londonderry** IBN The Oakgrove Manor, Derry YH, 4-6 Magazine St, Londonderry BT48 6HJ.	ⓣ (2871) 284100 ⓕ (2871) 284101	120	▣	⁉ ⁑ R ♿ ECC ☞ ⊡ ☕
▲ **Newcastle** 30 Downs Rd, Newcastle, Co Down BT33 0AG. ⓔ info@hini.org.uk	ⓣ (28437) 22133 ⓕ (28437) 22133	40	01.03–23.12	⁉ ⁑ ECC ☞ ⊡
▲ **Portaferry** Barholm, 11 The Strand, Portaferry, Co Down BT22 1PS. ⓔ info@hini.org.uk	ⓣ (28427) 29598 ⓕ (28427) 29598	42	▣	⁉ ⁑ R ♿ P ⊡
▲ **Whitepark Bay** IBN **157 Whitepark Bay Rd, Ballintoy,** **Ballycastle, Co Antrim BT54 6NH.** ⓔ info@hini.org.uk	ⓣ (28207) 31745 ⓕ (28207) 32034	54	▣	⁉ ⁑ R ♿ ECC ☞ P ⊡

International Booking Network

The advantages are clear

HOSTELLING
INTERNATIONAL

IBN INTERNATIONAL
BOOKING
NETWORK

netsavings@hostellinginternational.org.uk

Ireland (Republic of)

IRLANDE (REPUBLIQUE D')

IRLAND

IRLANDA (REPUBLICA DE)

An Óige, Irish Youth Hostel Association,
61 Mountjoy Street, Dublin 7, Republic of Ireland.

t (353) (1) 8304555
f (353) (1) 8305808
e anoige@iol.ie
www.irelandyha.org

Office Hours: Monday-Friday, 09.00-17.30hrs.
Also Saturday (1.4-30.9) 10.00-12.30hrs.

A copy of the Hostel Directory for this Country can be obtained from:
The National Office.

Capital: Dublin	**Population:** 3,626,087
Language: English/Irish	**Size:** 70,283 sq km
Currency: IR£ (Irish punt)	**Country Code:** 353

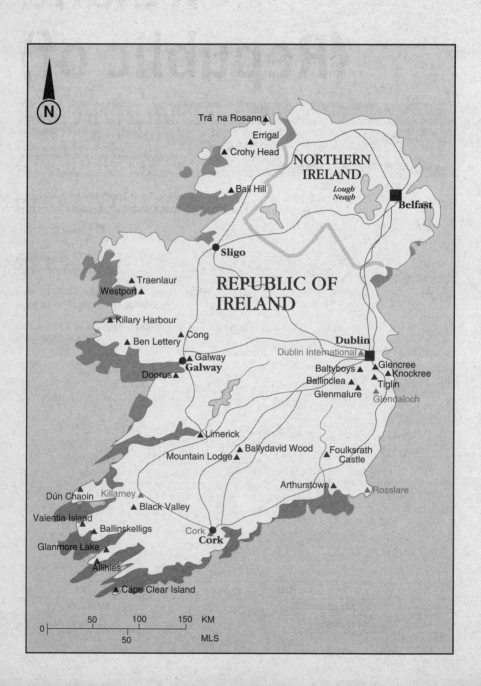

English

REPUBLIC OF IRELAND HOSTELS

The hospitality of the Irish is world renowned, and hostels are no exception. There are Youth Hostels in all major tourist areas.

There is access to some hostels all day. Hostels with "*" next to their opening dates are also open weekends throughout the year. Dublin International Hostel, Glendaloch International Hostel and Cork International Hostel are open 24 hours and Rosslare operates special opening times to coincide with ferry schedules. All hostels have self-catering facilities and most provide meals if advance notice is given. On average expect to pay in the region of IR£ 5.00-8.00, however the overnight fee including breakfast and sheets is from IR£ 9.50 in Dublin and IR£ 9.50 (breakfast only) in Galway.

PASSPORTS AND VISAS

With the exception of nationals of the United Kingdom a valid passport or National Identity card is required.

EU nationals and those from the following countries do not require a visa: Andorra, Austria, Cyprus, Czech & Slovak Republics, Finland, Hungary, Iceland, Liechtenstein, Malta, Norway, San Marino, Sweden, Switzerland and Vatican City.

HEALTH

Visitors from the United Kingdom are entitled to urgent medical treatment without charge, when it is obtained at a public hospital or from a doctor participating in the General Medical Service Scheme. Evidence of residence in the UK is required - for example, Social Security documentation, driving licence.

Visitors from other EU member states are entitled to urgent medical treatment without charge, provided that they present the EU form E111 which should be obtained from the health authorities of their own country before travelling.

Visitors from countries outside the EU may be charged for any treatment.

BANKING HOURS

Monday, Tuesday, Wednesday and Friday 10.00-16.00hrs. Thursday only, 10.00-17.00hrs.

POST OFFICES

Post offices are open Monday to Friday, 09.00-17.30hrs, however some are closed between 13.00 and 14.15hrs for lunch.

SHOPPING HOURS

Normally 09.00/09.30-17.30/18.00hrs. There is late night shopping usually on Thursday or Friday until 20.00hrs. Some provincial towns may have an early closing day but this will vary.

TRAVEL

Air
Good internal network operated by AER Lingus and Ryan Air.

Rail
Irish Rail operates services to all main cities and towns.

Bus
Good bus services: Irish Bus (Bus Éireann) provides a nationwide network service. Irish Bus and/or Rambler tickets, Dublin Explorer tickets are available, as well as the Overlander ticket for travel to Northern Ireland. There is also a large number of independent carriers.

Ferry
There are ferry services from various ports in Great Britain and France to Dublin, Dun Laoghaire, Rosslare and Cork.

Driving
Driving is on the left. Seat belts must be worn in the front and back.

Français

AUBERGES DE JEUNESSE EN REPUBLIQUE IRLANDAISE

Les Irlandais sont connus dans le monde entier pour leur hospitalité, et les auberges ne font pas exception à la règle. Il y a des auberges dans toutes les principales régions touristiques.

Dans certaines auberges, l'accès est possible toute la journée. Les auberges dont les dates d'ouverture sont accompagnées de "*" sont aussi ouvertes pendant le weekend toute l'année. Les auberges internationales de Dublin, Gendaloch et Cork sont ouvertes 24 heures sur 24 tandis que celle de Rosslare a des heures d'ouverture spéciales pour coïncider avec les horaires des bateaux. Toutes les auberges ont des cuisines pour les voyageurs et la plupart servent des repas s'ils sont commandés à l'avance. En principe, une nuit vous coûtera entre 5,00 et 8,00 £IR. En revanche, le prix de la nuitée, petit déjeuner et location de draps compris, est à 9.50 £IR à l'auberge de Dublin et à 9.50 £IR également à l'auberge de Galway (avec petit-déjeuner seulement).

PASSEPORTS ET VISAS

A l'exception des citoyens du Royaume-Uni, les voyageurs doivent être munis d'un passeport ou d'une carte d'identité nationale en cours de validité.

Les citoyens de l'UE et ceux des pays suivants n'ont pas besoin de visa: Andorre, Autriche, Chypre, les Républiques tchèque et slovaque, Finlande, Hongrie, Islande, Liechtenstein, Malte, Norvège, Saint-Marin, Suède, Suisse et Cité du Vatican.

SOINS MEDICAUX

Les visiteurs du Royaume-Uni ont droit à un traitement médical d'urgence gratuit quand celui-ci a été administré dans un hôpital public ou par un médecin participant au Plan Général de Service Médical (General Medical Service Scheme). Il vous faudra fournir la preuve que vous résidez au Royaume-Uni en présentant, par exemple, des papiers de Sécurité Sociale ou un permis de conduire britannique.

Les visiteurs provenant d'autres pays de l'UE ont droit au traitement médical d'urgence gratuit, à condition de présenter le formulaire E111 de l'UE, qui doit être obtenu auprès des autorités médicales de leurs pays respectifs, avant leur départ.

Les visiteurs provenant de pays en dehors de l'UE devront peut-être payer pour tout traitement médical reçu.

HEURES D'OUVERTURE DES BANQUES

Les banques sont ouvertes les lundi, mardi, mercredi et vendredi de 10h à 16h. Le jeudi, elles ouvrent de 10h à 17h.

BUREAUX DE POSTE

Les bureaux de poste sont ouverts du lundi au vendredi, de 9h à 17h30, mais ferment entre 13h et 14h15.

HEURES D'OUVERTURE DES MAGASINS

Les magasins sont normalement ouverts de 9h/9h30 à 17h30/18h. Ils sont en général ouverts plus tard le jeudi ou le vendredi, jusqu'à 20h. Dans certaines villes de province, il se peut que les magasins ferment tôt un jour par semaine, mais cela varie.

DEPLACEMENTS

Avions
Bonnes liaisons intérieures assurées par AER Lingus et Ryan Air.

Trains
Irish Rail assure des services à destination de toutes les grandes villes.

Autobus
Les services d'autobus sont bons: Irish Bus

(Bus Éireann) assure un service sur l'ensemble du territoire national. Vous pourrez vous procurer des billets Irish Bus et/ou Rambler, des billets Dublin Explorer de même que des billets Overlander, pour vous rendre en Irlande du Nord. Il existe également un certain nombre de compagnies indépendantes.

Ferry-boats
Des lignes maritimes, en partance de plusieurs ports britanniques et français, assurent des services à destination de Dublin, Dun Laoghaire, Rosslare et Cork.

Automobiles
Les véhicules roulent à gauche. Le port des ceintures de sécurité est obligatoire à l'avant comme à l'arrière.

Deutsch

JUGENDHERBERGEN IN DER REPUBLIK IRLAND

Die Gastfreundschaft der Iren ist weltbekannt, und Jugendherbergen sind da keine Ausnahme. In allen bekannten Fremdenverkehrsgebieten gibt es Herbergen.

Manche Herbergen sind den ganzen Tag über zugänglich. Wenn neben den Öffnungszeiten ein "*" steht, ist die betreffende Herberge ganzjährig, auch am Wochenende, geöffnet. Dublin International Hostel, Glendaloch und Cork International Hostel sind 24 Stunden geöffnet, und die Herberge in Rosslare hat besondere Öffnungszeiten, die den Fahrplänen der Fähren angepaßt sind. Alle Herbergen haben Einrichtungen zur Selbstversorgung, und in den meisten sind bei Vorbestellung auch Mahlzeiten erhältlich. Durchschnittlich ist mit einem Preis von ca. 5,00-8,00 IR£ zu rechnen. In Dublin liegt der Übernachtungspreis, einschließlich Frühstück und einer Mietgebühr

für Bettwäsche, ab 9,50 IR£ und in Galway 9,50 IR£ (nur Frühstück).

PÄSSE UND VISA

Mit Ausnahme von Staatsbürgern des Vereinigten Königreichs, brauchen alle Reisenden einen gültigen Reisepaß oder einen Personalausweis.

Staatsangehörige eines EU-Landes oder folgender Länder brauchen kein Visum: Andorra, Finnland, Island, Liechtenstein, Malta, Norwegen, Österreich, San Marino, Schweden, Schweiz, Tschechische und Slowakische Republik, Ungarn, Vatikanstadt und Zypern.

GESUNDHEIT

Besucher vom Vereinigten Königreich haben in Notfällen Anspruch auf kostenlose Behandlung, wenn sie in einem öffentlichen Krankenhaus oder von einem Arzt, der am "General Medical Service Scheme" beteiligt ist, behandelt werden. Sie müssen beweisen, daß sie im Vereinigten Königreich wohnhaft sind, zum Beispiel durch Sozialhilfepapier, Führerschein.

Besucher aus anderen EU-Ländern haben in Notfällen Anspruch auf kostenlose Behandlung, wenn sie das EU-Formular E111, das sie im eigenen Land vor der Reise erwerben sollten, vorlegen.

Besuchern aus Ländern außerhalb der EU kann die Behandlung in Rechnung gestellt werden.

GESCHÄFTSSTUNDEN DER BANKEN

Montags, dienstags, mittwochs und freitags von 10.00-16.00 Uhr. Donnerstags nur von 10.00-17.00 Uhr.

POSTÄMTER

Postämter sind montags bis freitags von 09.00-17.30 Uhr geöffnet, jedoch schließen einige über Mittag zwischen 13.00 und 14.15 Uhr.

LADENÖFFNUNGSZEITEN

Gewöhnlich von 09.00/09.30-17.30/18.00 Uhr.
Die Geschäfte sind gewöhnlich donnerstags
oder freitags bis 20.00 Uhr geöffnet. In einigen
Provinzstädten sind die Geschäfte an einem Tag
der Woche (nicht überall am gleichen Tag)
nachmittags geschlossen.

REISEN

Flugverkehr
AER Lingus und Ryan Air bieten gute nationale
Flugverbindungen.

Eisenbahn
Irish Rail bietet Eisenbahnverbindungen in alle
größeren Städte.

Busse
Gute Busverbindungen: Irish Bus (Bus Eireann)
bietet einen landesweiten Busverkehr. Es
werden Irish Bus und/oder Rambler Tickets,
Dublin Explorer Tickets und für Reisen nach
Nordirland Overlander Tickets angeboten. Es
gibt ebenso eine Vielzahl von unabhängigen
Transportunternehmen.

Fähren
Es verkehren Fähren von verschiedenen Häfen
in Großbritannien und Frankreich nach Dublin,
Dun Laoghaire, Rosslare und Cork.

Autofahren
Es herrscht Linksverkehr. Sowohl auf den
Vorder- als auch auf den Rücksitzen müssen
Sicherheitsgurte angelegt werden.

Español

ALBERGUES JUVENILES DE LA REPÚBLICA DE IRLANDA

La hospitalidad de los irlandeses es famosa en
todo el mundo y los albergues no son
excepción. Existen albergues juveniles en todos
los principales puntos turísticos del país.

Algunos albergues abren todo el día. Los que
lleven un asterisco "*" junto a sus fechas de
apertura también están abiertos todos los fines
de semana del año. Los albergues
internacionales de Dublín, Glendaloch y Cork
están abiertos las 24 horas del día y el de
Rosslare tiene un horario especial de apertura
que coincide con el de los ferrys. Es posible
cocinar uno mismo en todos los albergues y la
mayoría sirven comidas si se avisa con
suficiente antelación. Los precios oscilan entre
5 y 8 libras irlandesas, aunque una noche en
Dublín le costará a partir de IR£9,50
incluyendo el desayuno y las sábanas, y el
mismo precio en Galway incluyendo sólo el
desayuno.

PASAPORTES Y VISADOS

Con excepción de los ciudadanos del Reino
Unido, se requiere un pasaporte o documento
nacional de identidad válido.

Los ciudadanos de los países pertenecientes a la
UE y de los siguientes países no requieren
visado: Andorra, Austria, Chipre, Repúblicas
Checa y Eslovaca, Finlandia, Hungría, Islandia,
Liechtenstein, Malta, Noruega, San Marino,
Suecia, Suiza y Ciudad del Vaticano.

INFORMACIÓN SANITARIA

Los visitantes residentes en el Reino Unido
tienen derecho a asistencia médica de urgencia
gratuita en los hospitales del estado o a través
de un médico que pertenezca al Plan de
Servicio Médico General (General Medical
Service Scheme). Se requiere prueba de su
residencia en el Reino Unido, por ejemplo,
documentos expedidos por la seguridad social
o el permiso de conducir.

Los visitantes de los demás países miembros de
la UE tienen derecho a cuidados médicos de
urgencia gratuitos siempre y cuando tengan en
su poder un impreso E111 de la UE, que

deberán solicitar a la Seguridad Social de su país antes de salir de viaje.

A los visitantes de los países que no pertenezcan a la UE se les cobrará todo tratamiento médico.

HORARIO DE LOS BANCOS

Lunes, martes, miércoles y viernes de 10 h. a 16 h. Jueves de 10 h. a 17 h.

OFICINAS DE CORREOS

Las oficinas de correos abren de lunes a viernes de 9 h. a 17.30 h., pero algunas cierran de 13 h. a 14.15 h. para almorzar.

HORARIO COMERCIAL

El horario normal es de 9 h./9.30 h. a 17.30 h./18 h., pero normalmente los jueves o los viernes las tiendas abren hasta las 20 h. En algunas poblaciones provinciales, cierran temprano un día a la semana, pero esto varía de un sitio a otro.

DESPLAZAMIENTOS

Avión

Existe una buena red aérea nacional operada por AER Lingus y Ryan Air.

Tren

La compañía ferroviaria irlandesa (Irish Rail) ofrece servicios a todas las ciudades y poblaciones importantes.

Autobús

Los servicios de autobús son buenos: la compañía Irish Bus (Bus Éireann) opera una red nacional. Es posible adquirir un billete de Irish Bus y/o un billete Rambler, el billete Dublin Explorer y el Overlander para viajar a Irlanda del Norte. Existen también muchas compañías de autobuses independientes.

Ferry

Hay servicios de ferry desde varios puertos de Gran Bretaña y Francia a Dublín, Dun Laoghaire, Rosslare y Cork.

Automóvil

Se conduce por la izquierda. Es obligatorio llevar los cinturones de seguridad abrochados tanto en los asientos delanteros como en los traseros.

Cork

1-2 Redclyffe,
Western Rd,
Cork.
☎ (21) 543289
❺ (21) 343715
e anoige@iol.ie

Open Dates:	🗓️
Open Hours:	🕐
Reservations:	(IBN) (CC)
Price Range:	IRP7.50-14.50 € 9.52-18.41 💳
Beds:	102 - 2x²🛏 5x⁴🛏 11x⁶🛏 1x⁶🛏
Facilities:	♿ ♦♦♦ 18x ♦♦♦ 🍴 👕 🏠 📺 ♨️ 🅿️ ℹ️ 🎒 ♻️
Directions:	2W from city centre
✈	Cork 5km
A🚌	Airport bus to Central Bus Station 2km
⛴	Cork (Seasonal) 16km
🚃	Cork 2km
🚌	No 8 from City 1km ap Outside Hostel
Attractions:	⚓ ⛵

Dublin -
International YH

61 Mountjoy St.,
Dublin 7.
☎ (1) 8301766
❺ (1) 8301600
e anoige@iol.ie

Open Dates:	🗓️
Open Hours:	🕐
Reservations:	(R) (IBN) (CC)
Price Range:	IRP9.50-15.00 € 12.06-19.05 BB inc 💳
Beds:	369 - 3x²🛏 3x³🛏 3x⁴🛏 11x⁶🛏 26x⁶🛏
Facilities:	♦♦♦ 14x ♦♦♦ 🍴 👕 🏠 📺 ♨️ 🔒 💼 ♨️ 🔢 🅿️ ℹ️ 🎒 ♻️
Directions:	1NW from city centre
✈	Dublin 16km
A🚌	41/41a/41b/41c 500m
⛴	Dublin 4km; Dun Laoghaire 10km
🚃	Connolly 2km; Heuston 3km
🚌	10/16/19/120 ap Outside Hostel
U	Connolly 2km
Attractions:	🚴 ⚓ ⛵ 1.5km

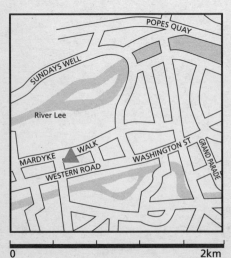

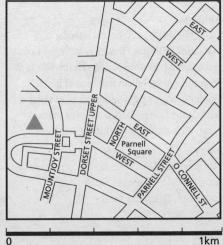

Dún Chaoin

Ballyferriter,
Tralee,
Co Kerry.
☎ (66) 9156121
🖷 (66) 9156355
📧 anoige@iol.ie

Open Dates:	🗓
Open Hours:	07.00-10.30 hrs; 17.00-00.00 hrs
Price Range:	IRP5.00-9.50 € 6.35-12.07
Beds:	52 - 1x² 2x⁴ 4x⁶ 2x⁶
Facilities:	††† 7x ††† 🍽 🚿 🖥 📺 1 x 🍷 🏠 🅿 ℹ ♻

Directions:

✈	Kerry International 90km
🚂	Tralee 64km
🚌	Killarney/Tralee-Dun Chaoin 90km ap Outside Hostel

Attractions: ⛰ 🔍5km 🚶 ⋃5km ⛵5km

Glendaloch

The Lodge,
Glendalough,
Co Wicklow.
☎ (404) 45342
🖷 (404) 45690
📧 anoige@iol.ie

Open Dates:	🗓
Open Hours:	🕐
Reservations:	Ⓡ IBN CC
Price Range:	IRP9.00-15.00 € 11.43-19.05
Beds:	120 - 2x² 6x⁴ 10x⁶ 4x⁶
Facilities:	♿ ††† 18x ††† 🍽 🚿 🖥 📺 🧺 1 x 🍷 🅾 🖼 🏠 🅿 ℹ ⛽ ♻

Directions:

✈	Dublin 60km
⛴	Dublin 50km; Dun Laoghaire 40km
🚂	Rathdrum 13km
🚌	St Kevins bus from Dublin City 50km ap Glendalough

Attractions: 🐟 ⛰ 🔍40km 🚶 ⋃

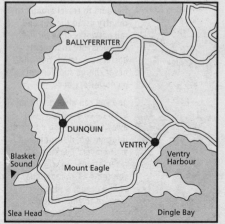

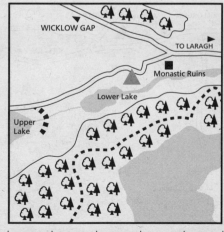

Killarney

Aghadoe House,
Killarney,
Co Kerry.
☎ (64) 31240
🖷 (64) 34300
✉ anoige@killarney.iol.ie

Open Dates:	🗓
Open Hours:	🕐
Reservations:	(IBN) (CC)
Price Range:	IRP7.00-12.00 € 8.89-15.24 💶
Beds:	200 - 3x² 6x⁴ 17x⁶
Facilities:	♟ 7x ♟ ⑪ ⛶ ⛺ 📺 ⛺1 x ⛳ 🔲 🖼 ♨ Ⓟ ⓘ 🍴 ♿ 🎱

Directions:

✈	Kerry International 10km; Cork 92km; Shannon 120km
⛴	Cork (Seasonal) 92km
🚎	Killarney 5km
🚌	Free transfer from station by Youth Hostel bus ap At Hostel

Attractions: ⚕ ⛰ 🚴 🚶 ∪5km ⚲5km

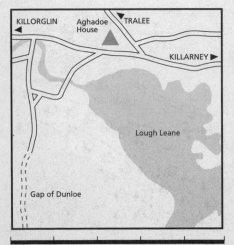

KILLORGLIN ◀
Aghadoe House
▼ TRALEE
KILLARNEY ▶
Lough Leane
Gap of Dunloe

0   5km

Location/Address	Telephone No. Fax No.	Beds	Opening Dates	Facilities
△ *Allihies* Cahermeelabo Allihies, Beara, Co Cork. e anoige@iol.ie	☎ (27) 73014	34	01.06–30.09	✄ P 🔒
△ *Arthurstown* Coastguard Station, Arthurstown, Co Wexford. e anoige@iol.ie	☎ (51) 389411	32	01.06–30.09	♦♦♦ ✄ P
△ *Ball Hill* Donegal Town, Donegal. e anoige@iol.ie	☎ (73) 21174 ✆ (73) 21174	66	01.04–30.09	♦♦♦ ✄ P
▲ Ballinclea Donard, Co Wicklow. e anoige@iol.ie	☎ (45) 404657 ✆ (45) 404657	40	* 01.03–30.11	♦♦♦ ⬤R ✄ P
△ *Ballinskelligs* Prior House, Ballinskelligs, Co Kerry. e anoige@iol.ie	☎ (66) 9479229 ✆ (66) 9479229	22	01.04–30.09	♦♦♦ ✄ P
△ *Ballydavid Wood House* Glen of Aherlow, Bansha, Co Tipperary. e anoige@iol.ie	☎ (62) 54148	40	* 01.03–30.11	♦♦♦ ✄ P
△ *Baltyboys* Blessington, Co Wicklow. e anoige@iol.ie	☎ (45) 867266 ✆ (45) 867032	36	* 01.03–30.11	⬤R ✄ P
△ *Ben Lettery* Clifden, Co Galway. e anoige@iol.ie	☎ (95) 51136 ✆ (95) 51136	50	01.04–30.09	✄ P
△ *Black Valley* Beaufort, Killarney, Co Kerry. e anoige@iol.ie	☎ (64) 34712	50	01.03–30.11	♦♦♦ ✄ P
△ *Cape Clear Island* South Harbour, Cape Clear Island, Skibbereen, Co Cork. e anoige@iol.ie	☎ / ✆ (28) 39198 ✆ (28) 39198	40	01.03–30.11	✄
▲ Cong Lisloughrey, Quay Rd, Cong, Co Mayo. e anoige@iol.ie	☎ (92) 46089 ✆ (92) 46448	102	🗓12	♦♦♦ ⊏CC⊐ ✄ P 🔒
▲ Cork (IBN) **1-2 Redclyffe, Western Rd, Cork.** e anoige@iol.ie	☎ (21) 543289 ✆ (21) 343715	102	🗓12	♦♦♦ 🍴 2W ♿ ⊏CC⊐ ✄ P
△ *Croby Head* Dungloe, Co Donegal. e anoige@iol.ie	☎ (75) 21950	38	01.04–30.09	♦♦♦ ✄ P
△ *Doorus House* Kinvara, Co Galway. e anoige@iol.ie	☎ (91) 637512 ✆ (91) 637512	56	🗓12	✄ P
▲ Dublin - International YH (IBN) **61 Mountjoy St., Dublin 7.** e anoige@iol.ie	☎ (1) 8301766 ✆ (1) 8301600	369	🗓12	♦♦♦ 🍴 ⬤R 1 NW ⊏CC⊐ ✄ P 🔒

Location/Address	Telephone No. Fax No.	Beds	Opening Dates	Facilities
▲ Dún Chaoin Ballyferriter, Tralee, Co Kerry. e anoige@iol.ie	☏ (66) 9156121 ✆ (66) 9156355	52	🗓12	††† ⏹ ⚲ P
△ Errigal Dunlewy, Gweedore, Letterkenny, Co Donegal. e anoige@iol.ie	☏ (75) 31180	46	🗓12	††† ⚲ P
△ Foulksrath Castle Jenkinstown, Co Kilkenny. e anoige@iol.ie	☏ (56) 67144 ✆ (56) 67144	52	🗓12	⚲ P
△ Galway St Mary's College, St Mary's Rd, Galway. e anoige@iol.ie	☏ (91) 527411 ✆ (91) 528710	120	01.07–25.08	††† ⏹ R 1 W CC ⚲ P 🔒
△ Glanmore Lake Lauragh, Killarney, Co Kerry. e anoige@iol.ie	☏ (64) 83181	36	01.04–30.09	⚲ P
△ Glencree Stone House, Glencree, Enniskerry, Co Wicklow. e anoige@iol.ie	☏ (1) 2864037 ✆ (1) 2766142	40	🗓12	††† R ⚲
▲ Glendaloch [IBN] The Lodge, Glendalough, Co Wicklow. e anoige@iol.ie	☏ (404) 45342 ✆ (404) 45690	120	🗓12	††† ⏹ R ♿ CC ⚲ P 🔒
△ Glenmalure Greenane, Co Wicklow. e anoige@iol.ie		16	* 01.07–31.08	R ⚲ P
▲ Killarney [IBN] Aghadoe House, Killarney, Co Kerry. e anoige@killarney.iol.ie	☏ (64) 31240 ✆ (64) 34300	200	🗓12	††† ⏹ CC ⚲ P 🔒
△ Killary Harbour Rosroe, Renvyle, Co Galway. e anoige@iol.ie	☏ (95) 43417	44	* 01.03–30.09	⚲ P
△ Knockree Lacken House, Knockree, Enniskerry, Co Wicklow. e anoige@iol.ie	☏ (1) 2864036	58	🗓12	R ⚲ P
▲ Limerick 1 Pery Square, Limerick. e anoige@iol.ie	☏ (61) 314672 ✆ (61) 314672	66	🗓12	CC ⚲ P
△ Mountain Lodge Burncourt, Co Tipperary. e anoige@iol.ie	☏ (52) 67277	30	01.03–30.09	††† ⚲ P
△ Rosslare Harbour [IBN] Goulding St, Rosslare Harbour, Co Wexford. e rosslareyh@oceanfree.net	☏ (53) 33399 ✆ (53) 33624	82	🗓12	††† CC ⚲ P
△ Tiglin Ashford, Co Wicklow. e anoige@iol.ie	☏ (404) 49049 ✆ (404) 49049	50	🗓12	††† R ⚲ P

Location/Address	Telephone No. Fax No.	Beds	Opening Dates	Facilities
△ *Trá na Rosann* *Downings, Co Donegal.* e *anoige@iol.ie*	☎ *(74) 55374*	*34*	*01.04–30.09*	♂ 🅿
△ *Traenlaur Lodge* *Lough Feeagh, Newport, Co Mayo.* e *anoige@iol.ie*	☎ *(98) 41358*	*32*	*01.04–30.09*	� ♂ 🅿
△ *Valentia Island* *Knightstown, Valentia Island, Co Kerry.* e *anoige@iol.ie*	☎ *(66) 76154*	*40*	*01.06–30.09*	� ♂ 🅿
▲ Westport Club Atlantic Hostel, Altamont St, Westport, Co Mayo. e anoige@iol.ie	☎ (98) 26644 📠 (98) 26241	140	01.03–31.10	♙ 🍽 ♿ ♂ 🅿 📷

> **The man who goes alone can start today; but he who travels with another must wait till that other is ready.**
>
> Celui qui va seul peut partir aujourd'hui, mais celui qui voyage avec un autre doit attendre que l'autre soit prêt.
>
> **Wer alleine reist, braucht auf andere nicht zu warten.**
>
> El que viaja solo puede partir hoy mismo, pero el que viaja acompañado tiene que esperar a que esté listo su compañero.
>
> **Henry David Thoreau, Walden (1854)**

HOSTELLING INTERNATIONAL

Make your credit card bookings at these centres
Réservez par carte de crédit auprès des centres suivants
Reservieren Sie per Kreditkarte bei diesen Zentren
Reserve con tarjeta de crédito en los siguientes centros

English

Australia	☎ (2) 9261 1111
Canada	☎ (1) (800) 663 5777
England & Wales	☎ (1629) 581 418
France	☎ (1) 44 89 87 27
Northern Ireland	☎ (1232) 324 733
Republic of Ireland	☎ (1) 830 1766
New Zealand	☎ (9) 303 9524
Scotland	☎ (541) 553 255
Switzerland	☎ (1) 360 1414
USA	☎ (202) 783 6161

Français

Angleterre & Pays de Galles	☎ (1692) 581 418
Australie	☎ (2) 9261 1111
Canada	☎ (1) (800) 663 5777
Écosse	☎ (541) 553 255
États-Unis	☎ (202) 783 6161
France	☎ (1) 44 89 87 27
Irlande du Nord	☎ (1232) 324 733
Nouvelle-Zélande	☎ (9) 303 9524
République d'Irlande	☎ (1) 830 1766
Suisse	☎ (1) 360 1414

Deutsch

Australien	☎ (2) 9261 1111
England & Wales	☎ (1629) 581 418
Frankreich	☎ (1) 44 89 87 27
Irland	☎ (1) 830 1766
Kanada	☎ (1) (800) 663 5777
Neuseeland	☎ (9) 303 9524
Nordirland	☎ (1232) 324 733
Schottland	☎ (541) 553 255
Schweiz	☎ (1) 360 1414
USA	☎ (202) 783 6161

Español

Australia	☎ (2) 9261 1111
Canadá	☎ (1) (800) 663 5777
Escocia	☎ (541) 553 255
Estados Unidos	☎ (202) 783 6161
Francia	☎ (1) 44 89 87 27
Inglaterra y Gales	☎ (1629) 581 418
Irlanda del Norte	☎ (1232) 324 733
Nueva Zelanda	☎ (9) 303 9524
República de Irlanda	☎ (1) 830 1766
Suiza	☎ (1) 360 1414

IBN INTERNATIONAL BOOKING NETWORK

Israel

ISRAEL

ISRAEL

ISRAEL

**Israel Youth Hostels Association,
Binyanei Hauma, 1 Shazar Street, PO Box 6001
Jerusalem 91060, Israel**

☎ (972) (2) 655 8400
🖷 (972) (2) 655 8430
🖷 (972) (2) 655 8432 (Travel)

✉ iyha@iyha.org.il
www.youth-hostels.org.il

Office Hours: Sunday-Thursday, 08.00-16.00hrs

A copy of the Hostel Directory for this country can be obtained from:
All I.Y.H.A. Hostels

Capital:	Jerusalem	**Population:**	6,000,000
Language:	Hebrew/Arabic	**Size:**	20,770 sq km
Currency:	New shequel	**Country Code:**	972

ISRAEL

English

ISRAEL HOSTELS

The IYHA offers 30 high quality Youth Hostels throughout the country. Expect to pay about US$16.50 for one overnight including breakfast. Groups should order meals in advance.

PASSPORTS AND VISAS

Every visitor to Israel must hold a valid passport. Visitors may remain in Israel for up to three months from date of arrival, subject to the terms of the visa issued. Whilst nationals of many countries can obtain a visitor's visa free of charge at the point of entry, others should apply prior to their departure at any Israel diplomatic or consular mission.

BANKING HOURS

Most banks are open 08.30-12.30hrs Sunday to Thursday; afternoons on Sundays, Tuesdays and Thursdays; 08.30-12.00hrs on Fridays and eves of major holidays.

POST OFFICES

Post offices are generally open 08.00-13.00hrs, 16.00-18.30hrs Sunday to Thursday; Fridays 08.00-12.00hrs. Post offices are closed on the Sabbath and major holidays.

SHOPPING HOURS

Most shops are open Sunday to Thursday. On Fridays and the eves of major Jewish Holidays shops close early in the afternoon.

TRAVEL

Air
Several airlines offer domestic flights.

Rail
Israel Railways provides regular services between Tel Aviv and Herzliya, Netanya, Hadera, Haifa, Acre and Nahariya, as well as a daily scenic train between Tel Aviv and Jerusalem.

There is no train service on Sabbaths and major holidays.

Bus
The Egged Bus Cooperative operates nearly all inter-city bus routes and urban services in most cities and towns. Most bus lines do not operate on the Sabbath and on major Jewish Holidays.

Driving
Most major international car rental companies have offices in Israel's major cities and at Ben-Gurion Airport. Vehicles may be reserved abroad. To rent a car you must be over 21 years of age and in possession of a valid national or international driving licence and an international credit card. The IYHA offers special prices for car rentals.

Français

AUBERGES DE JEUNESSE ISRAELIENNES

L'Association Israélienne (la IYHA) vous accueille dans 30 auberges de jeunesse de haute catégorie, disséminées dans tout le pays. Une nuit, petit déjeuner compris, vous coûtera à partir de 16,50 $US. Il est conseillé aux groupes de commander leurs repas à l'avance.

PASSEPORTS ET VISAS

Tous les visiteurs doivent être en possession d'un passeport valide. Il leur sera permis de rester en Israël un maximum de 3 mois à partir de leur date d'arrivée, conformément aux termes du visa émis. Les citoyens de nombreux pays peuvent obtenir un visa de visiteur gratuitement à leur entrée dans le pays, mais certains devront en faire la demande avant leur départ auprès d'une mission israélienne diplomatique ou consulaire.

HEURES D'OUVERTURE DES BANQUES

La plupart des banques ouvrent de 8h30 à 12h30, du dimanche au jeudi, l'après midi les dimanche, mardi et jeudi et de 8h30 à 12h le vendredi et la veille des fêtes israéliennes les plus importantes.

BUREAUX DE POSTE

Les bureaux de poste sont en général ouverts de 8h à 13h et de 16h à 18h30, du dimanche au jeudi; ils sont ouverts de 8h à 12h le vendredi. Les bureaux de poste sont fermés le jour du Sabbat et les jours fériés les plus importants.

HEURES D'OUVERTURE DES MAGASINS

La plupart des magasins sont ouverts du dimanche au jeudi. Le vendredi et la veille des fêtes juives les plus importantes, les magasins ferment tôt l'après-midi.

DEPLACEMENTS

Avions
Plusieurs lignes aériennes offrent des vols intérieurs (3 à 10 passagers).

Trains
Israel Railways assurent des services réguliers entre Tel-Aviv et Herzliya, Netanya, Hadera, Haïfa, Acre et Nahariya, ainsi qu'un train journalier entre Tel-Aviv et Jérusalem. Il n'y a pas de trains le jour du Sabbat et pendant les fêtes importantes.

Autobus
La coopérative Egged Bus gère presque tous les services interurbains et assure également des services urbains dans la plupart des villes et grandes villes. La plupart des services ne fonctionnent pas le jour du Sabbat et pendant les fêtes juives principales.

Automobiles
La plupart des grandes agences internationales de location de voitures ont des bureaux dans les grandes villes du pays et à l'aéroport

Ben-Gurion. Il est possible de réserver un véhicule de l'étranger. Pour avoir le droit de louer une voiture, vous devez avoir plus de 21 ans et détenir un permis de conduire national ou international en cours de validité, ainsi qu'une carte de crédit internationale. La IYHA offre des tarifs spéciaux pour la location de voitures.

Deutsch

ISRAELISCHE JUGENDHERBERGEN

Der Israelische Jugendherbergsverband (IYHA) bietet 30 qualitativ hochwertige Jugendherbergen. Es ist mit einem Preis von 16,50 US\$ pro Übernachtung mit Frühstück zu rechnen. Gruppen sollten ihr Mittag und Abendessen im voraus bestellen.

PÄSSE UND VISA

Alle Israel-Besucher müssen im Besitz eines gültigen Reisepasses sein. Vorbehaltlich der Bedingungen des ausgestellten Visums, können Besucher vom Tag der Ankunft an bis zu 3 Monate im Land bleiben. Staatsangehörige vieler Länder können bei der Einreise kostenlos ein Besuchervisum erhalten, andere wiederum müssen vor ihrer Abreise bei einer diplomatischen Mission Israels oder einem israelischen Konsulat ein Visum beantragen.

GESCHÄFTSSTUNDEN DER BANKEN

Die meisten Banken sind sonntags bis donnerstags von 08.30-12.30 Uhr; sonntags, dienstags und donnerstags am Nachmittag; und freitags von 08.30-12.00 Uhr sowie an Nachmittagen hoher jüdischer Feiertage geöffnet.

POSTÄMTER

Postämter sind im allgemeinen sonntags bis donnerstags von 08.00-13.00 Uhr,

16.00-18.30 Uhr und freitags von
08.00-12.00 Uhr geöffnet. Am Sabbat und an
hohen Feiertagen sind sie geschlossen.

LADENÖFFNUNGSZEITEN

Die meisten Geschäfte sind von Sonntag bis
Donnerstag geöffnet. Freitags und am Vortag
hoher jüdischer Feiertage schließen die
Geschäfte am frühen Nachmittag.

REISEN

Flugverkehr
Mehrere Fluggesellschaften bieten Inlandsflüge
an.

Eisenbahn
Zwischen Tel Aviv und Herzliya, Netanya,
Hadera, Haifa, Acre und Naharya gibt es einen
regelmäßigen Eisenbahnverkehr, und auch
zwischen Tel Aviv und Jerusalem verkehrt
täglich ein Zug, der durch eine besonders
schöne Landschaft führt. Am Sabbat und an
hohen Feiertagen verkehren keine Züge.

Busse
Die Autobusgenossenschaft Egged betreibt fast
alle Inter-City-Buslinien und bietet in den
meisten Städten auch einen regelmäßigen
städtischen Verkehr. Am Sabbat und an hohen
jüdischen Feiertagen liegt der Busverkehr
größtenteils still.

Autofahren
Die meisten großen internationalen
Mietwagen-Unternehmen haben in größeren
Städten Israels und auf dem Flughafen Ben
Gurion eine Niederlassung. Fahrzeuge können
auch im Ausland vorbestellt werden. Wer einen
Wagen mieten will, muß über 21 Jahre alt und
im Besitz eines gültigen nationalen oder
internationalen Führerscheines sowie einer
internationalen Kreditkarte sein. Die IYHA bietet
spezielle Preise für Mietwagen an.

Español

ALBERGUES JUVENILES ISRAELÍES

La Asociación israelí (la IYHA) dispone de 30
albergues juveniles de primera categoría
repartidos por todo el país. Una noche le
costará aprox. 16,50 $USA, desayuno incluido.
Los grupos deberán encargar las comidas con
antelación.

PASAPORTES Y VISADOS

Toda persona que desee entrar en Israel deberá
ser titular de un pasaporte vigente. Los
visitantes pueden permanecer en Israel un
máximo de tres meses a partir de su fecha de
llegada, sujeto a las condiciones de su visado. Si
bien los ciudadanos de muchos países pueden
obtener un visado de visitante gratuitamente en
el punto de entrada al país, algunos deberán
solicitarlo antes de salir de viaje en cualquier
misión diplomática o consular israelí.

HORARIO DE LOS BANCOS

La mayoría de los bancos abren de 8.30 h. a
12.30 h. de domingo a jueves, los domingos,
martes y jueves por la tarde, y de 8.30 h. a 12
h. los viernes y vísperas de las principales
fiestas.

OFICINAS DE CORREOS

Por lo general, las oficinas de correos abren de
8 h. a 13 h. y de 16 h. a 18.30 h. de domingo a
jueves, y los viernes de 8 h. a 12 h. Cierran los
sábados y principales días festivos.

HORARIO COMERCIAL

La mayoría de las tiendas abren de domingo a
jueves. Los viernes y vísperas de las principales
festividades judías, cierran a primera hora de la
tarde.

DESPLAZAMIENTOS

Avión

Varias compañías aéreas ofrecen vuelos nacionales.

Tren

La red de ferrocarriles israelíes dispone de servicios regulares de Tel Aviv a Herzliya, Netanya, Hadera, Haifa, Acre y Nahariya, así como un tren diario que realiza un recorrido pintoresco de Tel Aviv a Jerusalén. No hay trenes los sábados ni los principales días festivos.

Autobús

La Cooperativa Egged Bus opera casi todas las líneas de autobús interurbanas y los servicios urbanos de la mayoría de las ciudades y poblaciones. No suele haber autobuses los sábados ni los principales días de fiesta judíos.

Automóvil

Casi todas las principales compañías internacionales de alquiler de coches tienen sucursales en las grandes ciudades de Israel y en el aeropuerto de Ben-Gurion. También es posible alquilar automóviles desde el extranjero. Para alquilar un coche es preciso tener más de 21 años y ser titular de un permiso de conducir nacional o internacional vigente, así como de una tarjeta de crédito internacional. La Asociación israelí ofrece tarifas especiales para el alquiler de coches.

> **Two roads diverged in a wood, and I, I took the one less travelled by, and that has made all the difference.**
>
> Deux routes divergeaient dans le bois, et moi... moi, j'ai pris la moins utilisée et c'est ce qui a tout changé.
>
> **Im Wald traf ich auf eine Weggabelung, und ich - ich nahm den weniger betretenen Pfad, und seitdem ist alles anders.**
>
> De un camino, en el bosque, salían dos senderos, y yo... yo tomé el menos usado. Y esto lo ha cambiado todo.
>
> **Robert Frost, The Road Not Taken**

Eilat

**Arava Rd,
Eilat.**
☎ (7) 6370088
✆ (7) 6375835
e eilat@iyha.org.il

Open Dates:	🗓
Open Hours:	🕐
Reservations:	IBN CC
Price Range:	$16.50-26.00 BB inc 🍽
Beds:	502 - 50x⁴ 25x⁵ 27x⁶
Facilities:	♿ ††† 102x ††† 🍴 ☕ 🏛 📺 🧺 1 x 🍽 📷 🏠 8 ⊜ ⬍ P ℹ ⛽ ♨ ⊘ 🔍

Directions:	2S from city centre
✈	Ben Gurion 354km
A🚌	475 354km
⛴	Eilat 1km
🚌	394 from Tel Aviv Central Bus Station to Eilat

Attractions: ⛰ ⊕ 🚶 🏊

Ein Gedi - Beit Sarah

**Ein Gedi,
Mobile Post,
Dead Sea 86980.**
☎ (7) 6584165
✆ (7) 6584445
e eingedi@iyha.org.il

Open Dates:	🗓
Open Hours:	07.00-21.00 hrs (Sun-Fri); 07.00-11.00 hrs; 16.00-19.00 hrs (Sat)
Reservations:	IBN CC
Price Range:	$16.50-26.00 BB inc 🍽
Beds:	249 - 1x² 24x⁴ 25x⁶
Facilities:	††† 52x ††† 🍴 ☕ 📺 🧺 2 x 🍽 📷 8 ⊜ P ℹ ♨

Directions:	
✈	Ben Gurion 175km
🚌	475 from Tel Aviv Bus Station to Eilat

Attractions: ⛰ ⊕ 100m 🚶 🏊

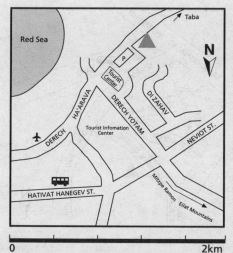

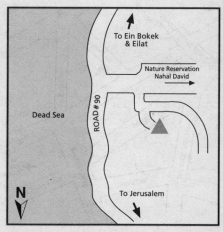

Jerusalem -
Hadavidka

67 Ha Nevi'im St,
Jerusalem.
☏ (2) 5384555
f (2) 5388790
e davidka@iyha.org.il

Open Dates:	📅
Open Hours:	🕐
Reservations:	IBN CC
Price Range:	$16.50-26.00 BB inc 📖
Beds:	333 - 1x² 5x³ 58x⁴ 16x⁶
Facilities:	♿ �203 58x �203 🍴 ☕ 🛄 📺 🧺 4 x 🍽 🖼 ♨ 8 🅱 🛗 🅿 ℹ ⚃

Directions:	0.5 W from city centre
✈	Ben Gurion 65km
A🚌	Jerusalem Central Bus Station
🚌	13, 18, 20, 21, 23 ap Davidka

Jerusalem -
Yitzhak Rabin

Hamuseonim Blvd,
PO Box 39100,
Jerusalem 91390
☏ (2) 6780101
f (2) 6796566
e rabin@iyha.org.il

Open Dates:	📅
Open Hours:	🕐
Reservations:	CC
Price Range:	$16.50-26.00 BB inc 📖
Beds:	308
Facilities:	♿ �203 77x �203 🍴 ☕ 🛄 📺 🧺 9 x 🍽 ♨ 8 🅱 🛗 🅿 ℹ ⚃

Directions:	4 SE from city centre
✈	Ben Gurion 65km
A🚌	Jerusalem Central Bus Station
🚌	17, 28, 9 from Central Bus Station

Attractions: Museums

There are 8 hostels in Jerusalem. See following pages.

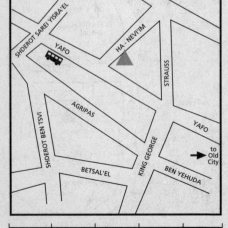

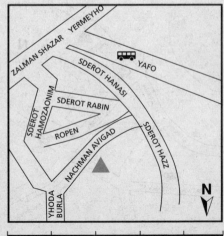

Karei Deshe -
Yoram Walter Katz

Yoram,
Karei Deshe,
Mobile Post,
Korazim 12365.
☎ (6) 6720601
✆ (6) 6724818

Open Dates:	🗓
Open Hours:	07.00-22.00 (Su Sun-Fri); 07.00-19.00 (Wi Sun-Fri)
Reservations:	CC
Price Range:	$16.50-26.00 BB inc 🍽
Beds:	288 - 10x² 28x⁴ 26x⁶
Facilities:	♿ ††† 64x ††† 🍴 ⛲ 📺 7 x 🍷 💼 🔋 ⊜ 🅿 ℹ ♻ ⛰

Directions:

✈	Ben Gurion 150km
A🚌	830/835 from Tel Aviv Bus Station - Tiberias 140km
🚌	459, 841 from Tiberias Central Bus Station Tiberias 10km
Attractions:	🎣 ⛰ 🔍100m 🚶 🏊

Metzada -
Massada

Isaac H Taylor Hostel,
Metzada,
Mobile Post,
Dead Sea 86935.
☎ (7) 6584349
✆ (7) 6584650
✉ massada@iyha.org.il

Open Dates:	🗓
Open Hours:	08.00-13.00 hrs; 16.00-19.00 hrs (Sun-Fri); 16.00-19.00 hrs (Sat)
Reservations:	CC
Price Range:	$16.50-26.00 BB inc 🍽
Beds:	150 - 3x³ 4x⁴ 13x⁶ 3x⁶
Facilities:	♿ ††† 23x ††† 🍴 📺 🧺 1 x 🍷 💼 🔋 ⊜ ℹ ♻

Directions:

✈	Ben Gurion 195km
🚌	421 (1 morning only) Tel Aviv Central Bus Station ap Massada YH
Attractions:	⛰ 🔍 🚶 🏊2km 🏊5km

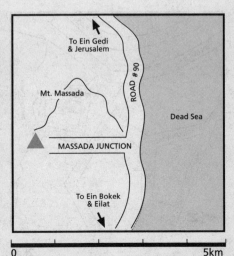

Mitzpe Ramon -
Beit Noam

PO Box 2,
Mitzpe Ramon 80600.
☎ (7) 6588443
📠 (7) 6588074
✉ mitzpe@iyha.org.il

Open Dates:	🗓
Open Hours:	07.00-23.00 hrs (Sun-Thu); 08.00-13.00 hrs (Fri)
Reservations:	CC
Price Range:	BB inc 🛏
Beds:	242 - 4x² 7x³ 3x⁴ 34x⁶
Facilities:	♿ ♦♦ 37x ♦♦♦ 🍴 🛋 📺 3 x🍷 🧳 ♨ 🔒 ⊜ P 📋 ♻ ⊙
Directions:	0.1 E from city centre
✈	Ben Gurion 250km
A🚌	Tel Aviv Central Bus Station 370 113km
🚌	060 from Beersheba Central Bus Station ap Mitzpe Ramon YH
Attractions:	🔺 🚶

Tel Aviv

36 Bnei Dan St,
Tel Aviv 62260
☎ (3) 5441748, 5460719
📠 (3) 5441030
✉ telaviv@iyha.org.il

Open Dates:	🗓
Open Hours:	🕐
Reservations:	IBN CC
Price Range:	$16.50-26.00 BB inc 🛏
Beds:	305 - 3x² 50x⁴ 24x⁵
Facilities:	♿ ♦♦ 77x ♦♦♦ 🍴 🛋 📺 ⛾ 10 x🍷 🧳 ♨ 🔒 ⊜ 📋 ♻ ✿
Directions:	3N from city centre
✈	Ben Gurion 20km
A🚌	222
🚂	Northern Railway 3km
🚌	5, 24, 25 from Tel Aviv Central Bus Station 3km ap Yehuda Macabi St
Attractions:	🔍 🏊 2km

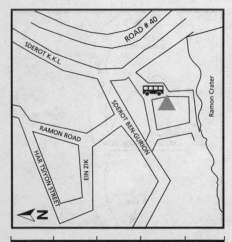

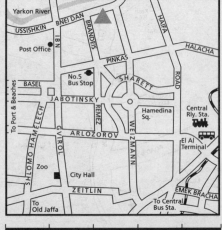

Tel Hai -
Posluns Family

Mobile Post,
Upper Galilee 12210.
- ☎ (6) 6940043
- ☏ (6) 6941743
- ✉ telhai@iyha.org.il

Open Dates:	🗓
Open Hours:	🕐
Reservations:	CC
Price Range:	BB inc 🛏
Beds:	256 - 10x^2⏦ 47x⏦
Facilities:	♿ ♟ 57x ♟ 🍽 ♨ 📺 5 x 🍸 💼 🔌 🍴 P 🛈 🔧 🀄
Directions:	3N from city centre
✈	Ben Gurion 200km
🚌	842/845 from Tel Aviv Central Bus Station 19.4km ap 20, 23 Kiriat Shmone to Tel Hai 2Km
Attractions:	🎿 ⛰ 🏊 🚶 ⛳40km ⚓ 🏊10km

Tiberias -
Yosef Meyouhas

PO Box 81,
Tiberias 14100.
- ☎ (6) 6721775, 6790350
- ☏ (6) 6720372
- ✉ tiberias@iyha.org.il

Open Dates:	🗓
Open Hours:	🕐
Reservations:	IBN CC
Price Range:	$16.50-26.00 BB inc 🛏
Beds:	248 - 8x^2⏦ 3x^3⏦ 25x⏦ 7x^5⏦ 13x^6⏦
Facilities:	♟ 56x ♟ 🍽 ♨ 📺 1 x 🍸 💼 🔌 🍴 🛈 🛎 🔧 🔍 🏛
Directions:	0.1NW from city centre
✈	Ben Gurion 132km
🚌	830/835 Tel Aviv Bus Station - Tiberas Central Bus Station
Attractions:	🎿 ⛰ 🔍1km 🚶 🏊

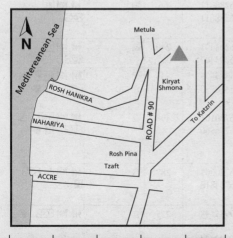

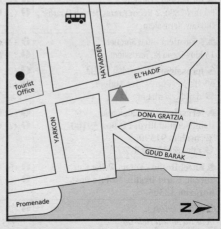

Location/Address	Telephone No. Fax No.	Beds	Opening Dates	Facilities
▲ **Arad** - Blau-Weiss Blau-Weiss Hostel, 4 Ha'atad St, Arad. ✉ arad@iyha.org.il	☎ (7) 9957150 ✆ (7) 9955078	203	🗓12	♟ ⚭ ♿ ⌐CC⌐ P
▲ **Beersheba/Be'er Sheva** - Beit Yatziv Beit Yatziv, PO Box 7, 79 Rehov Ha' Atzmaut, Beersheba.	☎ (7) 6277444, 6271490 ✆ (7) 6275735	220	🗓12	♟ ⚭ 1N ♿ ⌐CC⌐ P
▲ **Beit Meir** - Ramot Shapita Ramot Shapira, Beit Meir, PO Box 7216, Jerusalem. (20km W Jerusalem)	☎ (2) 5342691, 5343793 ✆ (2) 5342098	300	🗓12	♟ ⚭ ⌐CC⌐ P
▲ **Eilat** IBN **Arava Rd, Eilat.** ✉ eilat@iyha.org.il	☎ (7) 6370088 ✆ (7) 6375835	502	🗓12	♟ ⚭ 2S ♿ ⌐CC⌐ P ☕
▲ **Ein Gedi** - Beit Sarah IBN **Ein Gedi, Mobile Post, Dead Sea 86980.** ✉ eingedi@iyha.org.il	☎ (7) 6584165 ✆ (7) 6584445	249	🗓12	♟ ⚭ ⌐CC⌐ P ☕
△ *Gush Katif* *Hadarom, Hevel Katif, Hof Gaza,* *Mobile Post 79779.*	☎ *(7) 6847596* ✆ *(7) 6847680*	*220*	🗓12	♟ ⚭ R
▲ **Haifa** 'Carmel', Haifa, Mobile Post, Hof Hacarmel.	☎ (4) 8531944 ✆ (4) 8532516	188	🗓12	♟ ⚭ 8S ⌐CC⌐ P
▲ **Jerusalem** - Waterman Wise 8 Hapisga St, PO Box 16350, Jerusalem, Bayit Vegan.	☎ (2) 6420990, 6423366 ✆ (2) 6423362	300	🗓12	♟ ⚭ 3SW ⌐CC⌐
△ *Jerusalem* - *Ein Karem* *PO Box 16091, Jerusalem.*	☎ *(2) 6416282*	*32*	🗓12	⚭ 6SW ⌐CC⌐
△ *Jerusalem* - *Beit-Bernstein* *Town Centre, 1 Keren Hayessod St,* *Jerusalem.*	☎ *(2) 6258286* ✆ *(2) 6245875*	*55*	🗓12	♟ ⚭ 1W ⌐CC⌐
▲ **Jerusalem** - Forest PO Box 3353, Jerusalem 91032.	☎ (2) 6752911 ✆ (2) 6413522	140	🗓12	♟ ⚭ 6SW ⌐CC⌐ P
▲ **Jerusalem** - Old City PO Box 7880, 2 Rehov Ararat, Jewish Quarter, Old City, Jerusalem.	☎ (2) 6288611 ✆ (2) 6288611	66	🗓12	♟ ⚭ 2E ⌐CC⌐
▲ **Jerusalem** - Beit Shmuel 13 King David St, Jerusalem.	☎ (2) 6203491 ✆ (2) 6203467	240	🗓12	♟ ⚭ 1E ⌐CC⌐
▲ **Jerusalem** - Hadavidka IBN **67 Ha Nevi'im St, Jerusalem.** ✉ davidka@iyha.org.il	☎ (2) 5384555 ✆ (2) 5388790	333	🗓12	♟ ⚭ 0.5W ♿ ⌐CC⌐ P ☕
▲ **Jerusalem** - Yitzhak Rabin **Hamuseonim Blvd, PO Box 39100,** **Jerusalem 91390** ✉ rabin@iyha.org.il	☎ (2) 6780101 ✆ (2) 6796566	308	🗓12	♟ ⚭ 4SE ♿ ⌐CC⌐ P ☕
▲ **Karei Deshe** - Yoram Walter Katz **Yoram, Karei Deshe, Mobile Post,** **Korazim 12365.**	☎ (6) 6720601 ✆ (6) 6724818	288	🗓12	♟ ⚭ ♿ ⌐CC⌐ P
△ *Kfar Etzion* *Doar Na Mount Hebron*	☎ *(2) 9935133,* *9935233* ✆ *(2) 9932433*	*225*	🗓12	♟ ⚭ ⌐CC⌐ ♂

Location/Address	Telephone No. Fax No.	Beds	Opening Dates	Facilities
▲ **Ma'ayan Harod** Hankin, Maayan Harod, Mobile Post, Gilboa. 🅔 mayan@iyha.org.il	☎ (6) 6531669 🖷 (6) 6531660 .	140	🖻	ⅲ 🍽 ⅭⅭ 🅿
▲ **Metzada** - Massada **Isaac H Taylor Hostel, Metzada, Mobile Post, Dead Sea 86935.** 🅔 massada@iyha.org.il	☎ (7) 6584349 🖷 (7) 6584650	150	🖻	ⅲ 🍽 ⅋ ⅭⅭ
▲ **Mitzpe Ramon** - Beit Noam **PO Box 2, Mitzpe Ramon 80600.** 🅔 mitzpe@iyha.org.il	☎ (7) 6588443 🖷 (7) 6588074	242	🖻	ⅲ 🍽 0.1E ⅋ ⅭⅭ 🅿
▲ **Nordia** PO Box 90, Moshau Nordia	☎ (9) 8620089 🖷 (9) 8610130	208	🖻	ⅲ 🍽 ⅭⅭ 🅿
▲ **Peki'in** PO Box 910, Peki'in 24914 🅔 pekin@iyha.org.il	☎ (4) 9574111 🖷 (4) 9574116	250	🖻	ⅲ 🍽 ⅋ ⅭⅭ 🅿
▲ **Petah Tikva** Yad Labanim, Petah Tiqva 49404, Yahalom St.	☎ (3) 9226666 🖷 (3) 9226666	204	🖻	ⅲ 🍽 ⅭⅭ
▲ **Poria** Taiber, Poria, PO Box 232, Tiberias 14104. 🅔 poria@iyha.org.il	☎ (6) 6750050 🖷 (6) 6751628	180	🖻	ⅲ 🍽 ⅭⅭ 🅿
▲ **Rosh Pina** Nature Friends, Rehov HaHalutzim, Rosh Pina 1200	☎ (6) 6937086 🖷 (6) 6934312	100	🖻	ⅲ 🍽 ⅭⅭ 🅿
▲ **Safed** Beit Binyamin, PO Box 1139, Zfat 13401. 🅔 tzfat@iyha.org.il	☎ (6) 6921086 🖷 (6) 6973514	120	🖻	ⅲ 🍽 ⅋ ⅭⅭ 🅿
▲ **Shlomi** PO Box 2120, Shlomi. (5km E of Rosh Haniqra) 🅔 shlomi@iyha.org.il	☎ (4) 9808975 🖷 (4) 9809163	400	🖻	ⅲ 🍽 ⅋ ⅭⅭ 🅿
▲ **Tel Aviv** [IBN] **36 Bnei Dan St, Tel Aviv 62260** 🅔 telaviv@iyha.org.il	☎ (3) 5441748, 5460719 🖷 (3) 5441030	305	🖻	ⅲ 🍽 3N ⅋ ⅭⅭ
▲ **Tel Hai** - Posluns Family **Mobile Post, Upper Galilee 12210.** 🅔 telhai@iyha.org.il	☎ (6) 6940043 🖷 (6) 6941743	256	🖻	ⅲ 🍽 3N ⅋ ⅭⅭ 🅿
▲ **Tiberias** - Yosef Meyouhas [IBN] **PO Box 81, Tiberias 14100.** 🅔 tiberias@iyha.org.il	☎ (6) 6721775, 6790350 🖷 (6) 6720372	248	🖻	ⅲ 🍽 0.1NW ⅭⅭ

Net Savings @Hostelling International

The advantages are clear

HOSTELLING INTERNATIONAL

netsavings@hostellinginternational.org.uk

Italy

ITALIE
ITALIEN
ITALIA

Associazione Italiana Alberghi per la Gioventù, Via Cavour 44, 00184 Roma, Italy.

☏ (39) (06) 4871152
📠 (39) (06) 4880492
e aig@uni.net
www.hostels-aig.org

Office Hours: Monday-Thursday, 07.30-17.00hrs, Friday 07.30-15.00hrs

A copy of the Hostel Directory for this Country can be obtained from: The National Office.

Capital:	Rome	**Population:**	57,000,000
Language:	Italian	**Size:**	301,225 sq km
Currency:	L (lire)	**Telephone Country Code:**	39

GERMANY

AUSTRIA

HUNGARY

SWITZERLAND

SLOVENIA

CROATIA

BOSNIA
HERZ.

Rivamonte Agordino

Verbania
Arpy Morgex
Como
Menaggio
Trento
Rovereto
Asiago
Riva del Garda
Vicenza
Venice
Bergamo
Verona
Venezia
Trieste-Grignano
Milano
Milano
Padova
Torino
Turin
Guastalla
Parma
San Salvaro
Reggio Emilia
Ferrara
Bergolo
Bologna
Argenta-Campotto
Ravenna
Savona
Bologna
Genoa
San Lazzaro di Savena
Bagnacavallo
Finale-marina
Abetone
Santa Sofia
Marina di Massa
Prato
Florence
Ancona
Lucca
Firenze
Gran
Paradiso
National
Park
Montagnana

Isola Polvese
Cortona
Loreto
Trasimeno Lake
Assisi
Foligno
Ascoli Piceno
Acquasparta
Terni
Tevere
Rieti-Terminillo
Bomba Lake
CORSE
Roma
Rome
Villetta Barrea
Castel del Giudice
ITALY
Naples
Castelsardo
Napoli
Salerno
Bari
Ischia Isle
Agerola
Alghero-Fertilia
Bosa
Agropoli-Paestum
Taranto
SARDEGNA
Soveria Mannelli
Cagliari

Palermo
Messina
Erice-Trapani
Castroreale
Reggio di Calabria
Nicolosi
SICILA
Catania

N

| 100 | 200 | KMS |
0
| 50 | 100 | MLS |

English

ITALIAN HOSTELS

Italy has about 70 hostels in cities and in the countryside, some of which are 'green hostels' situated in or near areas of environmental interest.

Expect to pay in the region of 14,000-30,000 lire (7,23-15,49 ECU) including sheets and in most cases breakfast otherwise where available 2500 lire. Other meals when available up to 14,000 lire and packed lunches 10,000 lire.

A free fax booking service exists, connecting the "art" cities of Florence, Naples, Rome and Venice.

PASSPORTS AND VISAS

A valid passport or visitors card is required.

HEALTH

Health Service is available to nationals of EC countries. Other nationals should obtain private health insurance before travelling.

BANKING HOURS

Banks are open 08.30-13.20hrs and for one hour in the afternoon, generally 15.00-16.00hrs but check locally as times of opening in the afternoon vary from bank to bank.

Banks are not open on Saturdays, Sundays or National Holidays. Tourists can change money at main railway stations and airports.

POST OFFICES

Post Offices are open Monday to Friday 08.30-13.30hrs, Saturday 08.30-12.30hrs. In the main cities the main post offices are open 08.30-18.30hrs.

SHOPPING HOURS

Shops are generally open 08.30/09.00-13.00hrs and 15.30/16.00-19.30/20.00hrs.

TRAVEL

Rail

Rail is the cheapest way to travel in Italy. 'Ferrovie dello Stato' (FS) offers an extensive network of railways. High speed trains operate between the main cities. A supplement is payable. FS offer discounts to members – see Concessions.

Bus

Every city has its own bus system. A bus service operates between smaller cities that cannot be reached by train.

Ferry

There are several ferry companies which link the mainland to the islands.

Driving

Visitors must carry their Vehicle Registration Book which must either be in their name or include the owner's written permission to drive the vehicle. The highway network is one of the largest in Europe.

Français

AUBERGES DE JEUNESSE ITALIENNES

Environ 70 auberges sont disséminées dans les villes et la campagne italiennes. Certaines d'entre elles sont en fait des "auberges vertes", situées dans des régions d'intérêt écologique ou à proximité.

Une nuit vous coûtera environ de 14,000 à 30,000 lires (7,23-15,49 ECU), draps et, dans la plupart des cas, petit déjeuner compris. Lorsqu'il n'est pas compris dans le prix de la nuitée et dans les établissements où il est servi, un petit déjeuner vous coûtera 2 500 lires. Les autres repas, quand ils sont proposés, coûtent jusqu'à 14 000 lires et les paniers-repas, 10 000 lires.

Un service gratuit de réservation par téléfax est proposé et relie les villes d'art de Florence, Naples, Rome et Venise.

PASSEPORTS ET VISAS

Un passeport valide ou une carte de visiteur est nécessaire.

SOINS MEDICAUX

Les citoyens des pays du Marché commun peuvent bénéficier du système de Sécurité sociale italien. Il est conseillé aux citoyens d'autres pays de souscrire à une assurance maladie privée avant leur départ.

HEURES D'OUVERTURE DES BANQUES

Les banques sont ouvertes de 8h30 à 13h20 et pendant une heure au cours de l'après-midi, en général de 15h à 16h, mais il est prudent de vérifier les horaires locaux car les heures d'ouverture l'après-midi varient selon les banques.

Les banques n'ouvrent pas le samedi, le dimanche et les jours fériés. Les touristes peuvent changer de l'argent dans les gares principales et dans les aéroports.

BUREAUX DE POSTE

Les bureaux de poste sont ouverts du lundi au vendredi de 8h30 à 13h30 et le samedi de 8h30 à 12h30. Dans les grandes villes, les bureaux principaux sont ouverts de 8h30 à 18h30.

HEURES D'OUVERTURE DES MAGASINS

Les magasins sont généralement ouverts de 8h30/9h à 13h et de 15h30/16h à 19h30/20h.

DEPLACEMENTS

Trains

Le train est le moyen le moins cher de voyager en Italie. Les "Ferrovie dello Stato" (FS) gèrent un vaste réseau ferroviaire. Des trains à grande vitesse relient les grandes villes pour lesquels il faut payer un supplément. FS offre des réductions aux adhérents (voir la section sur les remises).

Autobus

Chaque grande ville gère son propre système d'autobus. Les villes moins importantes auxquelles on ne peut pas se rendre par le train sont desservies par un service d'autobus.

Ferry-boats

Plusieurs compagnies maritimes relient le pays aux îles.

Automobiles

Les visiteurs doivent être munis des papiers de leur voiture, qui doivent être à leur nom. Si le véhicule ne leur appartient pas, les papiers devront être accompagnés de l'autorisation écrite du propriétaire du véhicule. Le réseau autoroutier est l'un des plus développés d'Europe.

Deutsch

ITALIENISCHE JUGENDHERBERGEN

Italien hat in Städten und auf dem Land ungefähr 70 Jugendherbergen von denen einige "grüne Jugendherbergen" sind und in der Nähe von interessantem Umweltmilieu liegen.

Es ist mit einem Preis von etwa 14.000-30.000 Lire (7.23-15.49 ECU) zu rechnen, einschließlich Bettlaken und in den meisten Fällen Frühstück. Wenn nicht im Preis enthalten, kostet das Frühstück 2.500 lire. Weitere Mahlzeiten (wenn verfügbar) kosten bis zu 14.000 lire. Eingepacktes Mittagessen kostet 10.000 lire.

Unter den Kunststädten Florenz, Neapel, Rom und Venedig gibt es einen kostenlosen Telefax-Buchungsservice.

PÄSSE UND VISA

Es wird ein gültiger Reisepaß oder gültiger Personalausweis verlangt.

GESUNDHEIT

Der Gesundheitsdienst steht Staatsangehörigen der EU-Länder zur Verfügung. Staatsangehörige anderer Länder sollten vor Antritt ihrer Reise eine private Krankenversicherung abschließen.

GESCHÄFTSSTUNDEN DER BANKEN

Die Banken sind von 08.30-13.20 Uhr und eine Stunde am Nachmittag, gewöhnlich zwischen 15.00 und 16.00 Uhr, geöffnet. Erkundigen Sie sich am Ort, da sich die Öffnungszeiten am Nachmittag von Bank zu Bank unterscheiden.

Samstags, sonn- und feiertags sind die Banken nicht geöffnet. Touristen können auf großen Bahnhöfen und Flugplätzen Geld wechseln.

POSTÄMTER

Postämter sind montags bis freitags von 08.30-13.30 Uhr und samstags von 08.30-12.30 Uhr geöffnet. In größeren Städten sind die Hauptpostämter von 08.30-18.30 Uhr geöffnet.

LADENÖFFNUNGSZEITEN

Geschäfte sind in der Regel von 08.30/09.00 Uhr bis 13.00 Uhr sowie zwischen 15.30/16.00 Uhr und 19.30/20.00 Uhr geöffnet.

REISEN

Eisenbahn

Die Eisenbahn ist das billigste Verkehrsmittel in Italien. 'Ferrovie dello Stato' (FS) verfügt über ein umfangreiches Schienennetz. Zwischen größeren Städten sind Hochgeschwindigkeitszüge eingesetzt, für die ein Zuschlag erhoben wird. FS bietet Mitgliedern Rabatte an (siehe "Rabatte & Ermäßigungen").

Busse

Jede Stadt hat ihr eigenes Bussystem. Zwischen kleineren Städten, die nicht mit der Bahn erreicht werden können, verkehren Busse.

Fähren

Es gibt mehrere Fähren, die das Festland mit den Inseln verbinden.

Autofahren

Besucher müssen ihren Kraftfahrzeugbrief mit sich führen, der entweder auf ihren eigenen Namen ausgestellt oder von einer schriftlichen Fahrerlaubnis des Fahrzeughalters begleitet sein muß. Italien verfügt über eines der umfangreichsten Straßennetze Europas.

Español

ALBERGUES JUVENILES ITALIANOS

En Italia existen unos 70 albergues repartidos por las ciudades y el campo, algunos de los que son albergues "medioambientales", situados en zonas de interés ecológico o en su proximidad.

Los precios oscilan entre 14.000 y 30.000 liras (7.23-15.49 Euros), incluyendo las sábanas y, en la mayoría de los casos, el desayuno. Donde se sirva desayuno y no esté incluido en el precio, éste le costará 2.500 liras. Las demás comidas, donde se puedan obtener, ascenderán a un máximo de 14.000 liras y las meriendas 10.000 liras.

Existe un servicio gratuito de reservas por fax que une las "ciudades del arte": Florencia, Nápoles, Roma y Venecia.

PASAPORTES Y VISADOS

Es necesario un pasaporte en regla o un carnet de visitante.

INFORMACIÓN SANITARIA

Los ciudadanos de los países pertenecientes a la U.E. tienen derecho a recibir la asistencia médica de la Seguridad Social. Se recomienda a los ciudadanos de otros países hacerse un seguro médico privado antes de salir de viaje.

HORARIO DE LOS BANCOS

Los bancos abren de 8.30 a 13.20 h. y durante una hora por la tarde, por lo general de 15 h. a 16 h., pero es recomendable confirmarlo a nivel local, ya que el horario de la tarde varía de un banco a otro.

Los bancos están cerrados los sábados, domingos y días festivos. Los turistas pueden cambiar monèda en las principales estaciones ferroviarias y aeropuertos.

OFICINAS DE CORREOS

Las oficinas de correos abren de lunes a viernes de 8.30 h. a 13.30 h. y los sábados de 8.30 h. a 12.30 h. En las grandes ciudades, las principales oficinas de correos abren de 8.30 h. a 18.30 h.

HORARIO COMERCIAL

Generalmente, las tiendas abren de 8.30/9 h. a 13 h. y de 15.30/16 h. a 19.30/20 h.

DESPLAZAMIENTOS

Tren
El tren es el medio de transporte más económico de Italia. "Ferrovie dello Stato" (FS) posee una extensa red ferroviaria. Las principales ciudades están enlazadas por trenes de alta velocidad, para los que es preciso abonar un suplemento. FS ofrece descuentos a los socios (véase la sección sobre descuentos).

Autobús
Cada ciudad tiene su propia red de autobuses. Las poblaciones más pequeñas, a las que no llega el tren, pueden alcanzarse en autobús.

Ferry
Existen varias compañías de ferry que enlazan la Italia peninsular con las islas.

Automóvil
Los visitantes deben llevar la documentación de su automóvil que deberá estar a su nombre. Si el vehículo no les pertenece, deberán tener además una autorización escrita del propietario. La red de carreteras de Italia es una de las más extensas de Europa.

Ancona -
Ostello Ancona

Via Lamaticci 7,
60126 Ancona AN
☎ (071) 42257
🛈 (071) 42257

Open Dates:	🗓
Open Hours:	🕐
Price Range:	23000 Lire € 11.88 💶
Beds:	56 - 4x² 3x⁴ 6x⁶
Facilities:	♿ 👬 🚼 ⛺ 📺 🧺 🅿
Directions:	2SE from city centre
✈	Raffaello Sanzio 15km
🚆	Ancona Centrale 200m
🚌	Atma 200m ap Piazza Rosselli

Assisi -
Ostello della Pace

Via Valecchie 177,
06081 Assisi PG.
☎ (075) 816767
🛈 (075) 816767

Open Dates:	01-09.01; 01.03-31.12
Open Hours:	07.00-10.00; 15.30-23.30hrs
Reservations:	R CC
Price Range:	22000 Lire (👫 28000 Lire) € 11.36 (👫 14.46) BB|inc 💶
Beds:	70 - 2x² 3x⁴ 6x⁶ 2x⁶
Facilities:	👬 3x 👬 🍴 🍷 ⛺ 📦 🔘 📷 🅿 ℹ 🚼 ♨ 🏪 🏨

Directions:

✈	Sant'egidio-Francesco D'Assisi 11km
🚆	Assisi 1.7km
🚌	S.ta Maria Degli Angeli-Assisi 800m ap Porta San Pietro 800m

Attractions: 🏞 ⛰ 🚴 ∪400m ⚲2.5km ⚓2.5km

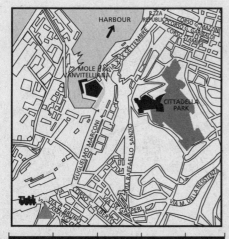

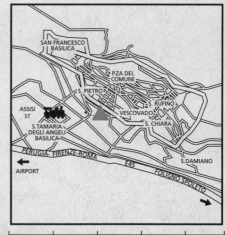

Bergamo - Nuovo Ostello di Bergamo

Via Galileo Ferraris 1,
24123 Bergamo BG.
☏ (035) 361724, 343038
🖷 (035) 361724
✉ hostelbg@spm.it

Open Dates: 🗓️

Open Hours: 07.00-24.00hrs

Reservations: **R** **IBN** **CC**

Price Range: 23000-25000 Lire
(👫 30000-35000 Lire)
€ 11.88-12.91 (👫 15.49-18.08)
BB inc 🍽️

Beds: 84 - 2x¹🛏️ 11x²🛏️ 5x⁴🛏️ 2x⁵🛏️
6x⁶🛏️

Facilities: ♿ 👫 9x 👫 🍽️ 🍺 📺 🧺
1 x🍴 🔘 🖼️ 🔢 ⬇️ 🅿️ ℹ️ 🎱 🌿
🏠

Directions: 2S from city centre

✈ Orio al Serio 7km

🚂 Bergamo 2km

🚌 14 100m ap Via Quintino Basso

Attractions: 🌳 ⛰️ ⚡4km 🚴 🚶 ✆2km
🏊4km

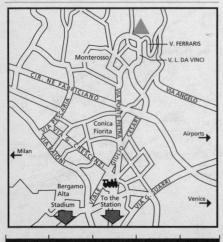

Bologna - Due Torri-San Sisto 2

Via Viadagola 5,
40127 Bologna BO.
☏ (051) 501810
🖷 (051) 501810

Open Dates: 20.01-19.12

Open Hours: 07.00-12.00hrs; 15.30-24.00hrs

Price Range: 21000 Lire (👫 22000-24000
Lire) € 10.85 (👫 11.36-12.39)
BB inc 🍽️

Beds: 75 - 7x²🛏️ 2x³🛏️ 12x⁴🛏️ 2x⁵🛏️

Facilities: ♿ 👫 3x 👫 🍽️ 🍺 🛏️ 📺
1 x🍴 🔘 🔢 🅿️ ℹ️ 🎱 🌿 🗄️ 🐾
🏠 🏠

Directions: 6 NE from city centre

✈ Marconi 10km

🚂 Centrale 5km

🚌 93-301 100m ap San Sisto 100m

Attractions: 🌳 ⛰️ 🚴 ∪5km ✆2km 🏊2km

There are 2 hostels in Bologna. See following pages.

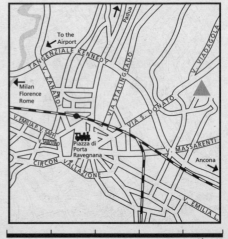

Florence - Villa Camerata

**Viale Augusto Righi 2-4,
50137, Firenze, FI.**
☏ (055) 601451
⊕ (055) 610300

Open Dates: 🗓️

Open Hours: 07.00-24.00hrs
(Rooms open from 14.00hrs)

Reservations: **R** **IBN**

Price Range: 25000 Lire (👫 26000-32000 Lire)
€ 12.91 (👫 13.43-16.53) BBinc 🍵

Beds: 322 - 6x³🛏️ 34x⁴🛏️ 9x⁵🛏️ 3x⁶🛏️
12x⁶⁺🛏️

Facilities: ♿ 👫👫 7x 👫👫 🍴 (BD) ☕ 🛏️ 📺
🖥️ 1 x🍽️ 🔲 ♨ P 🛈 🧺 ❀ 🎡

Directions: 3NE from city centre

✈ Vespucci 10km

⛴ Livorno 99km

🚂 Santa Maria Novella 5km

🚌 17 400m ap Salviatino 400m

Attractions: ⛰ 🚶

Foligno - Ostello Pierantoni

**Via Pierantoni 23,
06034 Foligno PG**
☏ (0742) 342566
⊕ (0742) 343559
⊜ falcinelli@edisons.it

Open Dates: 🗓️

Open Hours: 07.00-24.00hrs
(Rooms from 15.00hrs)

Reservations: **R**

Price Range: 25000 Lire (👫 30000 Lire)
€ 12.91 (👫 15.49) BBinc 🍵

Beds: 207 - 4x²🛏️ 8x⁴🛏️ 1x⁵🛏️ 21x⁶🛏️
4x⁶⁺🛏️

Facilities: ♿ 👫👫 👫👫 🍴 ☕ 🛏️ 📺 🖥️
1 x🍽️ 🔲 🖼️ 8 ⬆ P 🛈 🧺 ❀
🎡

Directions: 0.4E from city centre

✈ Sant'Egidio-Francesco D'assisi.
26km

🚂 Foligno 500m

🚌 Navetta B 100m

Attractions: 🐎 ⛰ 🚴 ⚲2.5km 🏊1km

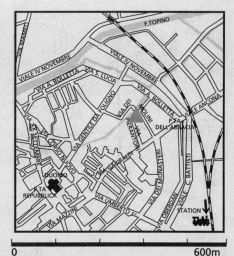

Genoa - Genova

Via Costanzi 120N-16136,
Genova GE.
☎ (010) 2422457
✆ (010) 2422457
✉ hostelge@iol.it

Open Dates:	01.02-19.12
Open Hours:	07.00-11.30; 15.30-24.00hrs
Reservations:	**R** **IBN**
Price Range:	23000 Lire (👫 25000-30000 Lire) € 11.88 (👫 12.91-15.49) BB inc 🍽
Beds:	213 - 13x⁴ 19x⁶
Facilities:	♿ 👪 9x 👫 🍽 (BD) 🍺 🏨 📺 📖 1 x 🍷 🔘 🖼 ♨ 🔟 ⬆ 🅿 ℹ 🎣
Directions:	**3N** from city centre
✈	Cristoforo Colombo 10km
⛴	Genova 3km
🚇	Principe 3km
🚌	40 50m ap Via Costanzi

Loreto - Loreto

Via Aldo Moro 46,
60025 Loreto AN.
☎ (071) 7501026
✆ (071) 7501026

Open Dates:	🗓
Open Hours:	🕐
Reservations:	**R**
Price Range:	25000 Lire (👫 27000-35000 Lire) € 12.91 (👫 13.94-18.08) 🍽
Beds:	250 - 5x¹ 11x² 11x³ 11x⁴ 16x⁵ 11x⁶
Facilities:	♿ 👪 👫 🍽 🍺 🏨 📺 🧺 1 x 🍷 🔘 🖼 🔟 ⬆ 🅿 ℹ 🎣 ⛺
Directions:	
✈	Ancona-Falconara 30km
⛴	Ancona 25km
🚇	Loreto 2km
🚌	Cotran (Line) 50m ap Via Marconi

Attractions: 🔺 🚶 ⛳4km 📷400m 🏊400m

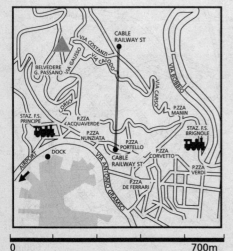

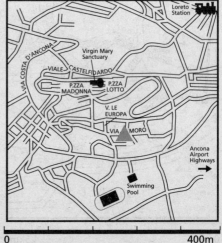

Marina di Massa e Carrara-Partaccia -
Ostello Apuano

Viale delle Pinete 237,
54037 Marina di Massa e Carrara
Partaccia MS.
☎ (0585) 780034
✆ (0585) 774266; (0585) 74858

Open Dates:	16.03-30.09
Open Hours:	07.00-23.30hrs
Reservations:	**R** **CC**
Price Range:	14000-15000 Lire € 7.23-7.75 ▨
Beds:	200 - 1x² 2x⁴ 21x⁶
Facilities:	♦♦♦ 2x♦♦♦ (except July & Aug) ⵙ ♂ ▤ ♨ 📺 🗄 🖨 P ⓘ 🚿 ⚘ ⚲ ▦

Directions:

✈	Galilei 60km
⛴	Livorno 70km
🚆	Carrara 4km
🚌	N. Via Avenza Mare ap Viale Delle Pinete 500m

Attractions: ⛰ ⵙ 10m 🚴 🚶 ∪ 30km ⚲ 1km ⚊ 10m

Naples -
Mergellina

Salita della Grotta a Piedigrotta 23,
80122 Napoli NA.
☎ (081) 7612346, 7611215
✆ (081) 7612391

Open Dates:	🗓
Open Hours:	06.30-00.30hrs
Reservations:	**R** **IBN**
Price Range:	24000 Lire (♦♦♦ 30000 Lire) € 12.39 (♦♦♦ 15.40) **BB** inc ▨
Beds:	200 - 36x² 16x⁴ 11x⁶
Facilities:	♦♦♦ 16x ♦♦♦ ⵙ (BD) ♨ ▤ 📺 🗄 🖨 8 ♨ P ⓘ 🚿 ⚘ ♠

Directions: 1N from city centre

✈	Capodichino 8km
⛴	Napoli 2km
🚆	Mergellina 300m
🚌	150-152 400m ap Via G. Bruno 400m
Ⓤ	Mergellina 300m

Attractions: ⛰ ⵙ 5km ⚊ 5km

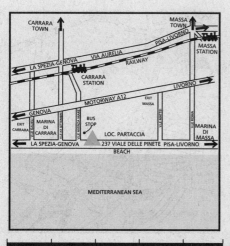

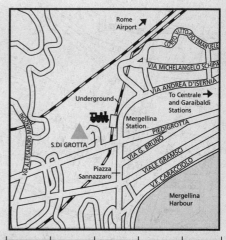

Ravenna - Dante

Via Aurelio Nicolodi 12
(quartiere Trieste),
48100 Ravenna RA.
t (0544) 421164
f (0544) 421164
e hostelravenna@hotmail.com

Open Dates:	🗓
Open Hours:	07.00-12.00; 14.00-23.30hrs
Reservations:	**R** **CC**
Price Range:	23000 Lire (👪 25000 Lire) € 11.88 (👪 12.91) BBinc 🍴
Beds:	140 - 4x👟 2x👟 12x👟 8x👟
Facilities:	♿ 👪 5x 👪 🍴 🍷 🖥 📺 📖 🧺 1 x 🍷 🧳 8 ⬆ 🅿 ♻ 🏕

Directions:

✈	Bologna "Marconi" 85km
🚉	Ravenna 800m
🚌	1, 11, 70 100m

Attractions: ⛳ ⛺ ♨1.2km ⚲1km ⛵2km

Rome - Foro Italico - A F Pessina YH

Viale delle Olimpiadi 61,
00194 Roma RM.
t (06) 3236267
f (06) 3242613

Open Dates:	🗓
Open Hours:	07.00-24.00hrs (Rooms open from 14.00hrs)
Reservations:	**R** **IBN**
Price Range:	25000-26000 Lire € 12.91-13.40 BBinc 🍴
Beds:	334 - 14x👟 35x👟
Facilities:	♿ 👪 🍴 🍷 🖥 📺 1 x 🍷 🧳 🏧 8 ⬆ 🅿 📷 ♻ 🏕 🏕

Directions: 5 NW from city centre

✈	Fiumicino 28km
🚉	Termini 6km
🚌	32, 280, 628 ap Lungotevere Maresciallo Cadorna
Ⓤ	Line A Ottaviano 2km

Attractions: 🚵

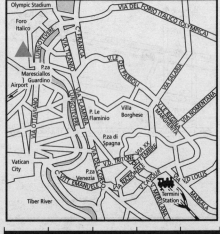

Trieste-Grignano - Tergeste

Viale Miramare 331,
34136 Trieste,
TS.
☎ (040) 224102
✆ (040) 224102

Open Dates:	01.03-31.12 (👪 🔟)
Open Hours:	07.00-10.00; 12.00-24.00hrs
Reservations:	Ⓡ
Price Range:	20000-21000 Lire (👪 22000-23000) € 10.33-10.85 (👪 11.36-11.88) BBinc 🔲
Beds:	74 - 1x³🛏 1x⁴🛏 1x⁶🛏 5x⁶🛏
Facilities:	👪 2x 👪 🍽 ☕ 📺 🍷1 x 🍺 💼 🅿 ℹ ♿ ⚠ ☉ 🏠
Directions:	8NW from city centre
✈	Ronchi dei-Legionari 30km
A🚌	Miramare 500m
⛴	Trieste 6km
🚂	Trieste 6km
🚌	36 200m ap Miramare 200m

Attractions: ⛳ ⊕ 🚴

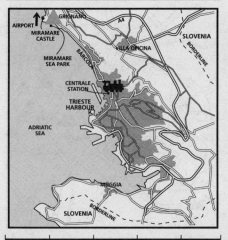

Turin - Torino

Via Alby 1,
10131 Torino TO.
☎ (011) 6602939
✆ (011) 6604445
✉ hostelto@tin.it

Open Dates:	01.02-17.12
Open Hours:	07.00-10.00; 15.30-23.30hrs
Reservations:	Ⓡ
Price Range:	20000-22000 Lire (👪 22000-24000 Lire) € 10.33-11.36 (👪 11.36-12.39) BBinc 🔲
Beds:	76 - 1x🛏 2x²🛏 2x³🛏 10x⁴🛏 4x⁶🛏
Facilities:	4x 👪 🍽 (BD) 📺 🔘 💼 🔢 🅿 ♿ 🔍 🏧
Directions:	2E from city centre
✈	Caselle 16km
🚂	Porta Nuova 1.8km
🚌	52 (64 on Sunday) 200m

Attractions: ∪6km ⚲500m ⛵2km

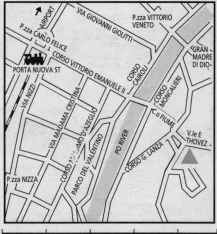

Venice - Venezia

Fondamenta Zitelle 86,
Isola della Giudecca,
30123 Venezia VE.
☎ (041) 5238211
🖷 (041) 5235689
✉ vehostel@tin.it

Open Dates:	01-15.01; 01.02-31.12
Open Hours:	07.00-24.00hrs (Rooms open from 14.00hrs)
Reservations:	Ⓡ ⒾⒷⓃ ⒸⒸ
Price Range:	27000 Lire € 13.94 ᴮᴮⁱⁿᶜ 🗐
Beds:	260 - 20x⁶🛏
Facilities:	👬 🍽 🍵 🛏 🖼 🔟 ℹ️ 🏠 🏤
Directions:	1S from city centre
✈	Marco Polo 10km
🚆	Santa Lucia 2km
🚌	42 Boat, 82 200m ap Zitelle

Vicenza - Olimpico

Viale Giuriolo 9,
36100,
Vicenza
☎ (0444) 540222
🖷 (0444) 547762

Open Dates:	🔟₂
Open Hours:	07.30-09.30; 15.30-23.30hrs
Price Range:	25000 Lire (👬 27000-30000 Lire) € 12.91 (👬 13.94-15.49) 🗐
Beds:	85
Facilities:	♿ 👬 🛏 📺 🅿 🏤
Directions:	
✈	"Marco Polo" Venezia 75km
🚆	1.5km
🚌	1, 2, 4, 5, 7 50m
Attractions:	🚲

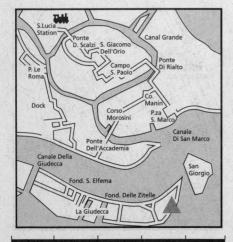

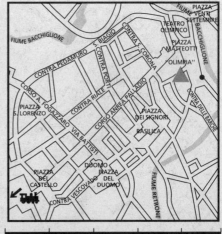

Location/Address	Telephone No. Fax No.	Beds	Opening Dates	Facilities
▲ **Abetone** - 'Renzo Bizzarri' Strada Statale dell'Abetone, 51021 Abetone PT.	☎ (0573) 60117	64	01.01–30.04; 15.06–30.09; 01–31.12	⁂ ⑩ ℝ ℙ ▤ ☕
▲ **Acquasparta** - San Francesco Via San Francesco 1, 05021 Acquasparta, TR.	☎ (0744) 943167 ☏ (0744) 944168	120	🔒	⁂ ⑩ ℝ ♿ ▤ ℙ
△ *Agerola-San Lazzaro* - *'Beata Solitudo'* *Piazza Generale Avitabile,* *80051 Agerola-San Lazzaro NA.* ✉ *paolog@ptn.pandora.it*	☎ *(081) 8025048* ☏ *(081) 8025048*	*16*	*01.01–14.09;* *01.10–31.12*	⑩ ☞ ℙ ▤
▲ **Agropoli-Paestum** - La Lanterna Via Lanterna 8, Loc.tà San Marco, 84043 Agropoli SA.	☎ (0974) 838364 ☏ (0974) 838364	56	15.03–30.10	⁂ ⑩ ♿ ☕ ☕
△ *Alghero-Fertilia* - *'Ostello dei Giuliani'* *Via Zara 1, 07040 Alghero-Fertilia SS.*	☎ *(079) 930353;* *930015* ☏ *(079) 930353*	*50*	🔒	⑩ ℙ
▲ **Ancona** - Ostello Ancona **Via Lamaticci 7, 60126 Ancona AN**	☎ (071) 42257 ☏ (071) 42257	56	🔒	⁑ ②SE ♿ ☞ ℙ
▲ **Argenta** - Campotto Via Cardinala 27, 44010 Campotto di Argenta FE.	☎ (0532) 808035 ☏ (0532) 808035	52	01.03; 31.10 (⁂ 🔒)	⁂ ♿ ℙ ▤
△ *Arpy Morgex* - *'Valdigne. M. Blanc'* *Loc.Arpy, 11017 Morgex AO.*	☎ *(0165) 841684;* *(010) 2471826* ☏ *(0165)* *841684;(010)* *2471828*	*130*	*01.01–03.05;* *24.06–03.09* *(⁂* *07.12–31.12)*	⁂ ⑩ ♿ ℙ ▤ ☕
▲ **Ascoli Piceno** - 'Ostello de Longobardi' Via Soderini 26, Palazzetto Longobardo, 63100 Ascoli Piceno AP.	☎ (0736) 259007 ☏ (0736) 259191	30	🔒	⑩ ☞ ℙ
△ *Asiago* - *Ekar* *Costalunga Ekar 1, 36012 Asiago VI.*	☎ / ☏: *(0424)* *455138*	*130*	*01.01–28.02;* *20.05–10.09;* *01–31.12* *(⁂ 🔒)*	⁂ ⑩ ℝ ℙ ☕
▲ **Assisi** - Ostello della Pace **Via Valecchie 177, 06081 Assisi PG.**	☎ (075) 816767 ☏ (075) 816767	70	01–09.01; 01.03–31.12	⁂ ⑩ ℝ ЄCC ℙ ▤ ☕
▲ **Bagnacavallo** - Antico Convento Di San Francesco Via Cadorna, 48012 Bagnacavallo (RA).	☎ (051) 224913 ☏ (051) 224913	73	🔒	⑩ ⁂ ♿ ℙ ▤ ☕
▲ **Bergamo** - Nuovo Ostello di Bergamo ⟦IBN⟧ **Via Galileo Ferraris 1, 24123 Bergamo BG.** ✉ hostelbg@spm.it	☎ (035) 361724, 343038 ☏ (035) 361724	84	🔒	⁂ ⑩ ℝ ②S ♿ ЄCC ℙ ▤
△ *Bergolo* - *Le Langhe* *Via Roma 22, 12070 Bergolo CN.*	☎ *(0173) 87222* ☏ *(0173) 87222*	*34*	*01.03–31.10* *(⁂ 🔒)*	⁂ ⑩ ЄCC ℙ ☕
▲ **Bologna** - Due Torri-San Sisto 2 **Via Viadagola 5, 40127 Bologna BO.**	☎ (051) 501810 ☏ (051) 501810	75	20.01–19.12	⁂ ⑩ ⑥NE ♿ ℙ ▤
▲ **Bologna** - San Sisto Via Viadagola 14, 40127 Bologna.	☎ (051) 501810 ☏ (051) 501810		🔒	ℝ ⑥NE ℙ

Location/Address	Telephone No. Fax No.	Beds	Opening Dates	Facilities
▲ **Bomba Lake** - Isola Verde Via Lago, 66042 Bomba CH.	☎ (0872) 860475, 860568 🖷 (0872) 860450	28	🔟	⊪† 🍴 ⊂⊂⊐ ▯ ⊡ ☕
△ *Bosa* - *Malaspina* *Via Sardegna 1-08013, Bosa Marina NU.*	☎ *(0785) 375009* 🖷 *(0785) 375009*	*63*	🔟	🍴 ▯ ☕
▲ **Castelsardo** - Golfo Dell' Asinara Via Sardegna 1, Loc-Ta' Lu Bagnu (SS).	☎ (079) 474031, 587008 🖷 (079) 587142	110	01.04–30.09	🍴 2E 🦽 ⊂⊂⊐ ▯ ⊡
▲ **Castel del Giudice** - "La Castellana" Via Fontana Vecchia 1, 86080 Castel del Giudice IS.	☎ (0865) 946222 🖷 (0865) 946222	60	🔟	⊪† 🍴 ⊂⊓ ▯ ☕
△ *Castroreale* - *'Ostello Delle Aquile'* *Salita Federico II d'Aragona,* *98053 Castroreale Centro ME.*	☎ *(090) 9746398* 🖷 *(090) 9746446*	*24*	*01.04–31.10*	🍴 ☞
▲ **Como** - 'Villa Olmo' Via Bellinzona 2, 22100 Como CO.	☎ (031) 573800 🖷 (031) 573800	76	01.03–30.11	⊪† 🍴 ▯ ⊡ ☕
▲ **Cortona** - 'San Marco' Via Maffei 57, 52044 Cortona AR.	☎ (0575) 601392-601765 🖷 (0575) 601392	80	15.03–15.10 (⊪† 🔟)	⊪† 🍴 ⊡ ▯ ☕
▲ **Erice-Trapani** - G.Amodeo Strada Provinciale Trapani-Erice, Km 2°, 91100 Raganzili Erice TP.	☎ (0923) 552964 🖷 (0923) 552964	52	01.01–03.11; 04–31.12	🍴 ▯ ☕
▲ **Ferrara** - Estense Corso Biagio Rossetti 67, 44100 Ferrara.	☎ (051) 224913 🖷 (051) 224913	84	🔟	⊪† ⊂⊓ 0.5N 🦽 ▯ ⊡ ☕
▲ **Finale-Ligure** - 'Vuillermin Castle' Via Generale Caviglia 46, 17024 Finale-Marina SV. ✉ ostellof@ivg.it	☎ (019) 690515; (0347) 2414683 🖷 (019) 690515	69	15.03–15.10	⊪† 🍴 ⊂⊓ ⊂⊂⊐ ⊡ ☕
▲ **Florence** - Villa Camerata ⟨IBN⟩ **Viale Augusto Righi 2-4, 50137, Firenze, FI.**	☎ (055) 601451 🖷 (055) 610300	322	🔟	⊪† 🍴 ⊂⊓ 3NE 🦽 ▯ ⊡ ☕
▲ **Foligno** - Ostello Pierantoni **Via Pierantoni 23, 06034 Foligno PG** ✉ falcinelli@edisons.it	☎ (0742) 342566 🖷 (0742) 343559	207	🔟	⊪† 🍴 ⊂⊓ 04E 🦽 ▯ ⊡ ☕
▲ **Genoa** - Genova ⟨IBN⟩ **Via Costanzi 120N-16136, Genova GE.** ✉ hostelge@iol.it	☎ (010) 2422457 🖷 (010) 2422457	213	01.02–19.12	⊪† 🍴 ⊂⊓ 3N 🦽 ▯ ⊡ ☕
▲ **Gran Paradiso National Park-Noasca** - "Parco Nazionale" frazione Gere Sopra, 10080 Noasca TO.	☎ (0124) 901107 🖷 (0124) 901107	68	01.03–15.10 (⊪† ⊂⊓ 01.01–10.01; 01.03–31.12)	⊪† 🍴 🦽 ☕
△ *Guastalla* - *'Quadrio Michelotti"* *Via Lido Po 11-13, 42016 Guastalla, RE.* ✉ *lunetia@tin.it*	☎ *(0522) 219287* 🖷 *(0522) 839228*	*25*	*01.04–15.10*	⊪† ⊂⊓ 🦽 ☞ ▯ ☕
▲ **Ischia** - Il Gabbiano ⟨IBN⟩ SS. Forio-Panza N.162, 80075 Forio D'Ischia (NA).	☎ (081) 909422 🖷 (081) 909422	100	01.04–30.09	⊪† ⊂⊓ 🦽

Location/Address	Telephone No. Fax No.	Beds	Opening Dates	Facilities
▲ Isola Polvese-Trasimeno Lake - Il Poggio Isola Polvese, 06060 San Feliciano, PG.	☎ (075) 843508 🖷 (075) 843508	76	01.03–31.10 (🚹🚺 🗓)	🚻 🍴 2NE ♿ 🗐 🍷
▲ Loreto - Loreto **Via Aldo Moro 46, 60025 Loreto AN.**	☎ (071) 7501026 🖷 (071) 7501026	250	🗓	🚻 🍴 ℝ ♿ P 🗐 🍷
▲ Lucca - 'Il Serchio' Via del Brennero 673, 55100 Lucca LU.	☎ (0583) 341811; (0586) 862517 🖷 (0583) 341811	90	🗓	🚻 🍴 P 🍷
▲ Marina di Massa e Carrara-Partaccia - Ostello Apuano **Viale delle Pinete 237, 54037 Marina di Massa e Carrara Partaccia MS.**	☎ (0585) 780034 🖷 (0585) 774266; (0585) 74858	200	16.03–30.09	🚻 🍴 ℝ ⅽⅽ 🗝 P 🗐 🍷
▲ Menaggio - La Primula Via Quattro Novembre 86, 22017 Menaggio CO. ✉ menaggiohostel@mclink.it	☎ (0344) 32356 🖷 (0344) 31677	50	15.03–05.11	🚻 🍴 ℝ 🗝 P 🗐 🍷
▲ Milano - "Piero Rotta" Via Martino Bassi 2 (access from via Salmoiraghi 1) (QT8-San Siro), 20148 Milano MI.	☎ (02) 39267095 🖷 (02) 33000191	380	13.01–23.12	🚻 🍴 ℝ ♿ 3NW P 🗐 🍷
▲ Montagnana - 'Rocca degli Alberi' Castello degli Alberi (Porta Legnago), 35044 Montagnana PD.	☎ (0429) 81076; (049) 8070266 🖷 (0429) 81076;(049) 8070266	48	01.04–15.10	🚻 ℝ P
▲ Naples - Mergellina IBN **Salita della Grotta a Piedigrotta 23, 80122 Napoli NA.**	☎ (081) 7612346, 7611215 🖷 (081) 7612391	200	🗓	🚻 🍴 ℝ 1N P 🗐 🍷
▲ Nicolosi - Etna Via della Quercia 7, 95030 Nicolosi CT.	☎ (095) 7914686 🖷 (095) 7914701	78	🗓	🚻 🍴 🗐 🍷
▲ Padova - Centro Ospitalita' Città di Padova, Via A. Aleardi 30, 35122 Padova PD.	☎ (049) 8752219 🖷 (049) 654210	112	07.01–24.12	🚻 🍴 ♿ ⅽⅽ P 🗐 🍷
△ *Parma - 'Cittadella' Parco Cittadella 5, 43100 Parma PR.*	☎ *(0521) 961434*	50	*01.04–31.10*	🍴 P
▲ Prato - Villa Fiorelli Parco Di Galceti, 59100 Prato.	☎ (0574) 697611	52	🗓	🚻 🍴 ℝ 3N ♿ 🗐 🍷
▲ Ravenna - Dante **Via Aurelio Nicolodi 12 (quartiere Trieste), 48100 Ravenna RA.** ✉ hostelravenna@hotmail.com	☎ (0544) 421164 🖷 (0544) 421164	140	🗓	🚻 🍴 ℝ ♿ ⅽⅽ P 🍷
△ *Reggio Emilia - Reggio Emilia Via dell'Abbadessa 8, 42100 Reggio Emilia RE.*	☎ *(0522) 454795*	36	*03.01–31.03; 07.04–22.12* (🚹🚺 🗓)	🍴 🗝 P
▲ Rieti-Terminillo - 'Ostello della Neve' IBN Anello Panoramico (Campoforogna), 02017 Rieti-Terminillo RI.	☎ (0746) 261169 🖷 (0746) 261169	120	01.01–15.05; 15.06–31.08; 01–31.12	🚻 🍴 ℝ P 🍷

Location/Address	Telephone No. Fax No.	Beds	Opening Dates	Facilities
▲ **Riva del Garda** - 'Benacus' Piazza Cavour 10, 38066 Riva del Garda TN. **e** ostelloriva@anthesi.com	☎ (0464) 554911 🖷 (0464) 559966	100	01.04–31.10	⫶◯ R P
△ *Rivamonte Agordino - Imperina Localita le Miniere, 32020 Rivamonte Agordino BL*	☎ *(0437) 62451*	*44*	☎ *for information*	P ☕
▲ **Rome** - Foro Italico - A F Pessina YH [IBN] **Viale delle Olimpiadi 61, 00194 Roma RM.**	☎ (06) 3236267 🖷 (06) 3242613	334	🖷	⫶◯ R [5NW] ♿ ☕
▲ **Rovereto** - Città di Rovereto Via delle Scuole 16/18, 38068 Rovereto TN.	☎ (0464) 433707 🖷 (0464) 424137	90	01.01–02.02; 25.02–31.12	⫶⫶ ⫶◯ ♿ CC P 🗗 ☕
△ *Salerno - Irno Via Luigi Guercio 112, 84100 Salerno SA.*	☎ *(089) 790251* 🖷 *(089) 405792*	*100*	🖷	⫶◯ ☕
▲ **San Lazzaro di Savena** - Village Centro Europa Uno Localita' Cicogna, Via Emilia 297, 40068 San Lazzaro di Savena - BO.	☎ (051) 6258352; 6255239 🖷 (051) 6258352	42	🖷	⫶⫶ ⫶◯ R ♿ ☞ P 🗗 ☕
△ *San Salvaro - Monastero Di San Salvaro Loc. San Salvaro, 35044 Urbana (PD).*	☎ *(0429) 81076,* *(049) 8070266* 🖷 *(049) 8070266*	*24*	🖷	R
▲ **Santa Sofia** Piazza Matteotti, 47018 Santa Sofia FO.	☎ (0543) 974511	26	🖷	⫶⫶ ♿ P ☕
▲ **Savona** - 'Villa De Franceschini' Via alla Stra 29 (Conca Verde), 17100 Savona SV. **e** concaverd@hotmail.com	☎ (019) 263222 🖷 (019) 263222	244	15.03–15.10	⫶⫶ ⫶◯ ♿ P 🗗 ☕
▲ **Savona** - "Priamar Fortress" Corso Giuseppe Mazzini, Fortezza Priamar, 17100 Savona SV. **e** priamarhostel@iol.it	☎ (019) 812653 🖷 (019) 812653	60	15.01–14.12	⫶⫶ ⫶◯ R CC P 🗗 ☕
▲ **Soveria Mannelli** - 'La Pineta' Localita' Bivio Bonacci, 88049 Soveria Mannelli-CZ.	☎ (0968) 666079; 662115 🖷 (0968) 666079	52	🖷	⫶◯ R CC P ☕
▲ **Terni** - Ostello Dei Garibaldini Corso Dei Garibaldini 61, 05033 Collescipoli Terni.	☎ (0744) 800467 🖷 (0744) 800467	37	🖷	⫶⫶ [4.5SW]
▲ **Trasimeno Lake** - Torricella Via Del Lavoro 10, 06060 Torricella di San Feliciano PG.	☎ (075) 843508 🖷 (075) 843508	88	01.03–31.10	⫶⫶ ⫶◯ P 🗗 ☕
▲ **Trento** - Giovane Europa Via Manzoni 17, 38100 Trento TN.	☎ (0461) 234567 🖷 (0461) 268434	68	01–06.01; 01.02–31.12	⫶⫶ ⫶◯ CC ☕
▲ **Trieste-Grignano** - Tergeste **Viale Miramare 331, 34136 Trieste, TS.**	☎ (040) 224102 🖷 (040) 224102	74	01.03–31.12 (⫶⫶ 🖷)	⫶⫶ ⫶◯ R [8NW] P ☕
▲ **Turin** - Torino **Via Alby 1, 10131 Torino TO.** **e** hostelto@tin.it	☎ (011) 6602939 🖷 (011) 6604445	76	01.02–17.12	⫶⫶ ⫶◯ R [2E] P 🗗

Location/Address	Telephone No. Fax No.	Beds	Opening Dates	Facilities
▲ **Venice** - Venezia (IBN) **Fondamenta Zitelle 86, Isola della Giudecca, 30123 Venezia VE.** ⊖ vehostel@tin.it	❶ (041) 5238211 ❶ (041) 5235689	260	01–15.01; 01.02–31.12	❍❍ R 1 S ⊂CC⊃ ☕
▲ **Verbania** - Verbania Via Alle Rose 7 - 28048 Verbania VB.	❶ (0323) 501648 ❶ (0323) 507877	72	01.01–06.01; 01.03–31.10; 05.12–31.12 (♦♦♦ R 06–29.02)	♦♦♦ ❍❍ ♿ P ▣ ☕
▲ **Verona** - 'Villa Francescatti' Salita Fontana del Ferro 15 (Veronetta), 37129 Verona VR.	❶ (045) 590360 ❶ (045) 8009127	120	🗓12	♦♦♦ ❍❍ 3 NW ▣
▲ **Vicenza** - Olimpico **Viale Giuriolo 9, 36100, Vicenza**	❶ (0444) 540222 ❶ (0444) 547762	85	🗓12	♦♦♦ ♿ P
▲ **Villetta Barrea** - Ostello Dell' Orso Via Roma, 67030 Villetta Barrea AQ	❶ (06) 4871152 ❶ (06) 4880492	35	❶ for information	♦♦♦ ♿ P

NEW HOSTELS: the following new hostels open in 2000.

For more details contact the National Office.

Location	Opening Dates
▲ **Bari** - Apulia region	01.01-31.08; 01.10-31.12
▲ **Castellaneta Marina (TA)** - Apuilia regiona	🗓12
▲ **Correggio (RE)** - Emilia Romagna region	01.04-31.10
▲ **Domaso (CO)** - Lombardy region	01.04-31.10
▲ **Modena** - Emilia Romagna region	🗓12
▲ **Reggio Emilia** - Emilia Romagna region	🗓12

Net Savings @Hostelling International

Don't leave your booking to chance

HOSTELLING INTERNATIONAL

netsavings@hostellinginternational.org.uk

Luxembourg

LUXEMBOURG

LUXEMBURG

LUXEMBURGO

**Centrale des Auberges de Jeunesse Luxembourgeoises,
2 rue du Fort Olisy, L-2261 Luxembourg.**

☎ (352) 225588
✆ (352) 463987
e information@youthhostels.lu
www.youthhostels.lu

Office Hours: Monday-Friday, 08.30-12.00hrs; 13.30-18.00hrs

A copy of the Hostel Directory for this Country can be obtained from:
The National Office.

Capital:	Luxembourg	**Population:**	400,000
Language:	Lëtzebuergesch	**Size:**	2,586 sq km
Currency:	LUF (franc) and BEF	**Telephone Country Code:**	352

English

LUXEMBOURG YOUTH HOSTELS

With 12 hostels, this tiny country is well served by excellent facilities. Most hostels are open 07.30-10.00hrs and 17.00-22.00hrs. It is recommended that you check in between 17.00 and 21.00hrs (Luxembourg City hostel 13.00-02.00hrs). Between 14.00 and 17.00hrs there is only access to the common room.

Expect to pay in the region of 375-670 LUF (9-16 ECU) for one night's bed and breakfast, plus linen hire if needed (125 LUF per stay). Most hostels have self-catering facilities only for individuals, for which there is no charge. Meals are also available. We recommend that you book in advance.

PASSPORTS AND VISAS

Visitors from most East European, African, Asian and South American countries require a visa for entry to Luxembourg. For nationals of Australia, Canada and the USA, a valid passport is sufficient.

HEALTH

There are no special entry requirements, but you are advised to take out medical insurance.

BANKING HOURS

Hours of business are 08.30-12.00hrs and 13.00-16.30hrs Monday-Friday. There are also banking facilities in Luxembourg Station which operate 09.00-21.00hrs 7 days a week.

POST OFFICES

08.00-12.00hrs and 14.00-17.00hrs Monday-Friday.

SHOPPING HOURS

Shops are open 09.00-12.00hrs and 13.00-18.00hrs Monday-Saturday, but are closed on Monday morning.

TRAVEL

Rail
Rail travel is good.

Bus
Bus travel is good on weekdays, but there are many restrictions on Sundays.

Driving
Driving is on the right-hand side. A valid driving licence and motor insurance are needed. Safety belts must be worn in the front and back, and cars must carry a warning triangle.

Français

AUBERGES DE JEUNESSE LUXEMBOURGEOISES

Ce tout petit pays, avec 12 auberges, offre d'excellents services. La plupart des auberges sont ouvertes de 7h30 à 10h00 et de 17h00 à 22h00. Il est recommandé d'arriver entre 17h00 et 21h00 (entre 13h00 et 02h00 pour l'auberge située à Luxembourg). Entre 14h00 et 17h00, seule la salle commune est ouverte.

Une nuit vous coûte entre 375 et 670 LUF (9-16 ECU), petit déjeuner compris, plus éventuellement la location de draps (125 LUF par séjour). La plupart des auberges ont une cuisine qu'elles mettent à la disposition des individuels seulement, et ce, à titre gratuit. Les auberges servent aussi des repas. Nous vous conseillons de réserver à l'avance.

PASSEPORTS ET VISAS

Les visiteurs venant de la plupart des pays d'Europe de l'Est, d'Afrique, d'Asie et d'Amérique du Sud doivent être en possession d'un visa pour entrer au Luxembourg; un passeport en cours de validité suffit pour les citoyens australiens, canadiens et Nord-américains.

SOINS MEDICAUX

Il n'y a pas d'exigences spéciales pour entrer au Luxembourg mais il vous est conseillé de souscrire à une police d'assurance maladie.

HEURES D'OUVERTURE DES BANQUES

Les banques sont ouvertes du lundi au vendredi de 8h30 à 12h et de 13h à 16h30. Il y a aussi un guichet de banque à la gare de Luxembourg ouvert de 9h à 21h, sept jours sur sept.

BUREAUX DE POSTES

Les bureaux de postes sont ouverts du lundi au vendredi de 8h à 12h et de 14h à 17h.

HEURES D'OUVERTURE DES MAGASINS

Les magasins sont ouverts du lundi au samedi de 9h à 12h et de 13h à 18h; fermés le lundi matin.

DEPLACEMENTS

Trains
Le réseau ferroviaire est bien développé.

Autobus
Les services d'autobus sont bons en semaine, mais sont soumis à de nombreuses restrictions le dimanche.

Automobiles
Conduite à droite. Il est nécessaire d'être en possession d'un permis de conduire valable et d'une assurance-voiture. Le port des ceintures de sécurité à l'avant et à l'arrière est obligatoire. Les voitures doivent être munies d'un triangle de présignalisation.

Deutsch

LUXEMBURGISCHE JUGENDHERBERGEN

Mit 12 Herbergen verfügt dieses kleine Land über eine große Zahl ausgezeichneter Einrichtungen. Die meisten Herbergen sind von 07.30-10.00 Uhr und von 17.00-22.00 Uhr geöffnet. Wir empfehlen jedoch, zwischen 17.00 und 21.00 Uhr anzukommen (in der Jugendherberge der Stadt Luxemburg zwischen 13.00 und 02.00 Uhr). Zwischen 14.00 und 17.00 Uhr ist nur der Gemeinschaftsraum zugänglich.

Es ist mit einem Preis von ungefähr 375-670 LUF (9-16 ECU) für eine Übernachtung mit Frühstück zu rechnen. Dazu kommt bei Bedarf noch die Gebühr für die Miete von Bettwäsche (125 LUF pro Aufenthalt). Für Einzelreisende haben die meisten Herbergen Möglichkeiten zur Selbstversorgung, für die keine Gebühr erhoben wird. Es sind auch Mahlzeiten erhältlich. Wir empfehlen Voranmeldung.

PÄSSE UND VISA

Besucher aus den meisten osteuropäischen, afrikanischen, asiatischen und südamerikanischen Ländern brauchen für die Einreise nach Luxemburg ein Visum. Für Staatsbürger Australiens, Kanadas und der USA genügt ein gültiger Reisepaß.

GESUNDHEIT

Es gibt keine besonderen Vorschriften für die Einreise. Wir raten jedoch zum Abschluß einer Krankenversicherung.

GESCHÄFTSSTUNDEN DER BANKEN

Banken sind montags-freitags von 08.30-12.00 Uhr und von 13.00-16.30 Uhr geöffnet. Auf dem Bahnhof von Luxemburg gibt es ebenfalls eine Bank, die an 7 Tagen der Woche von 09.00-21.00 Uhr geöffnet ist.

POSTÄMTER

Montags-freitags von 08.00-12.00 Uhr und von 14.00-17.00 Uhr.

LADENÖFFNUNGSZEITEN

Die Geschäfte sind montags von 13.00-18.00 Uhr und dienstags-samstags von 09.00-12.00 Uhr und von 13.00-18.00 Uhr geöffnet.

REISEN

Eisenbahn
Die Eisenbahnverbindungen sind gut.

Busse
Werktags sind die Busverbindungen gut, aber sonntags sind sie sehr beschränkt.

Autofahren
Es herrscht Rechtsverkehr. Man braucht einen gültigen Führerschein und eine Kraftfahrzeugversicherung. Sowohl auf den Vorder- als auch auf den Rücksitzen müssen Sicherheitsgurte getragen werden, und das Auto muß ein Warndreieck mitführen.

Español

ALBERGUES JUVENILES LUXEMBURGUESES

Con sus 12 excelentes albergues, este diminuto país está bien dotado de establecimientos de calidad. La mayoría de los albergues abren de 7.30 h. a 10 h. y de 17 h. a 22 h. Se recomienda registrarse entre las 17 h. y las 21 h. (entre las 13 h. y las 2 h. en el albergue de Luxemburgo). De 14 h. a 17 h. sólo hay acceso a la sala común.

Los precios oscilan entre 375 y 670 FLU (9-16 Euros) por noche, desayuno incluido. Las sábanas, si las necesita, se cobran aparte (125 FLU por estancia). Es posible cocinar uno mismo gratuitamente en casi todos los albergues, pero este servicio es sólo para viajeros independientes. También se sirven comidas. Recomendamos reservar con antelación.

PASAPORTES Y VISADOS

Los ciudadanos de la mayoría de los países de Europa del Este, Africa, Asia y Sudamérica necesitan visado para entrar en Luxemburgo. Para los ciudadanos de Australia, Canadá y EE.UU. basta con un pasaporte en regla.

INFORMACIÓN SANITARIA

No hay requisitos especiales de entrada, pero se recomienda hacerse un seguro médico.

HORARIO DE LOS BANCOS

El horario es de 8.30 h. a 12 h. y de 13 h. a 16.30 h. de lunes a viernes. La estación de Luxemburgo también dispone de un servicio bancario abierto de 9 h. a 21 h. los 7 días de la semana.

OFICINAS DE CORREOS

De 8 h. a 12 h. y de 14 h. a 17 h. de lunes a viernes.

HORARIO COMERCIAL

Las tiendas abren de 9 h. a 12 h. y de 13 h. a 18 h. de lunes a sábado, pero cierran los lunes por la mañana.

DESPLAZAMIENTOS

Tren
Los servicios ferroviarios son buenos.

Autobús
Los servicios de autobús son buenos los días laborables, pero muy limitados los domingos.

Automóvil
Se conduce por la derecha. Es necesario ser titular de un permiso de conducir y seguro en regla. Es obligatorio llevar los cinturones de seguridad abrochados tanto en los asientos delanteros como en los traseros y los coches deben transportar un triángulo de advertencia.

Larochette -
Centre Osterbour

45 Osterbour,
L-7622 Larochette.
☎ (352) 837081, 878324
🖷 (352) 878326

Open Dates:	🗓️12
Open Hours:	07.30-10.00; 17.00-22.00hrs
Price Range:	LUF 475-655 € 11.77-16.24 BB inc 🍴
Beds:	75 - 2x^1 14x^2 7x^5 1x^6
Facilities:	♦♦♦ 7x ♦♦♦ 🍴 ᕙ 📺 1 x 🍽 🔟 🅿 📝 🧺 ♿ ⛰ 🌲
Directions:	1N from city centre
🚌	300m
Attractions:	🎣 ⛰ 🚶 ⛷2km

Luxembourg City -
Mansfeld

2 rue du Fort Olisy (Pfaffenthal),
L-2261 Luxembourg.
☎ (352) 226889, 221920
🖷 (352) 223360
📧 luxembourg@youthhostels.lu

Open Dates:	🗓️12
Open Hours:	07.00-02.00hrs
Reservations:	IBN CC
Price Range:	LUF 435-670 € 10.78-16.60 BB inc 🍴
Beds:	274 - 15x^2 8x^4 18x^6 6x^6
Facilities:	♦♦♦ 8x ♦♦♦ 🍴 🔌 ᕙ 📺 🔟 💼 🅿 ♿ ⛰ 🔍
Directions:	1NE from city centre
✈	Findel 5km
A🚌	#9 300m
🚍	Luxembourg 2km
🚌	#9 300m
Attractions:	🚴 🚶

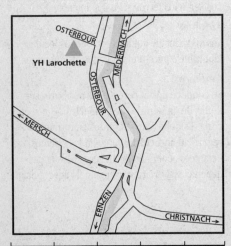

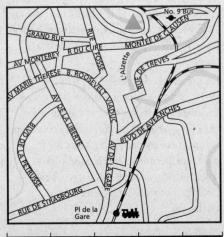

Location/Address	Telephone No. Fax No.	Beds	Opening Dates	Facilities
▲ **Beaufort** 6 rue de l'Auberge, L-6315 Beaufort. **e** beaufort@youthhostels.lu	**t** (352) 836075 **f** (352) 869467	88	01.01–15.01; 16.02–15.11	⍩⍟ 1 SW ✪ ℙ
▲ **Echternach** 9 rue A Duchscher, L-6434 Echternach. **e** echternach@youthhostels.lu	**t** (352) 720158 **f** (352) 728735	130	16.03–15.11; 16.12–31.12	⍥⍥ ⍩⍟ 0.2 W ✪ ℙ
▲ **Eisenborn** Centre de Formation et de Rencontre, 5 rue de la Forêt, L-6196 Eisenborn. **e** eisenborn@youthhostels.lu	**t** (352) 780355 **f** (352) 788459	52	⍟₁₂	⍥⍥ ⍩⍟ Ⓡ 0.5 E ♿ ℙ
▲ **Ettelbrück** - Carlo Hemmer Rue G D Joséphine Charlotte, BP 17, L-9013 Ettelbrück. **e** ettelbruck@youthhostels.lu	**t** (352) 812269 **f** (352) 816935	72	01–15.01; 16.03–15.11; 16–31.12	⍥⍥ ⍩⍟ 1 SW ✪ ℙ
▲ **Grevenmacher** 15 Gruewereck, L-6734 Grevenmacher.	**t** (352) 750222 **f** (352) 759146	54	25.03–30.11	⍥⍥ ⍩⍟ 1 N ℙ
▲ **Hollenfels** 2 rue du Château, L-7435 Hollenfels.	**t** (352) 307037 **f** (352) 305783	103	⍟₁₂	⍥⍥ ⍩⍟ 0.1 W ✪ ℙ
▲ **Larochette** - Centre Osterbour **45 Osterbour, L-7622 Larochette.**	**t** (352) 837081, 878324 **f** (352) 878326	75	⍟₁₂	⍥⍥ ⍩⍟ 1 N ℙ ⍟
▲ **Lultzhausen** rue du Village, L-9666 Lultzhausen.	**t** (352) 839424 **f** (352) 899245	98	16.02–15.11	⍥⍥ ⍩⍟ ✪ ℙ
▲ **Luxembourg City** - Mansfeld (IBN) **2 rue du Fort Olisy (Pfaffenthal),** **L-2261 Luxembourg.** **e** luxembourg@youthhostels.lu	**t** (352) 226889, 221920 **f** (352) 223360	274	⍟₁₂	⍥⍥ ⍩⍟ 1 NE -CC- ✪ ℙ ⍟
▲ **Troisvierges** 24-26 rue de la Gare, L-9906 Troisvierges.	**t** (352) 998018 **f** (352) 979624	64	01.01–14.01; 16.02–31.12	⍥⍥ ⍩⍟ ✪ ℙ
▲ **Vianden** 3 Montée du Château, L-9408 Vianden. **e** vianden@youthhostels.lu	**t** (352) 834177 **f** (352) 849427	90	01–15.01; 16.03–15.11; 16–31.12	⍩⍟ 1 N ✪
▲ **Wiltz** 6 rue de la Montagne, L-9538 Wiltz.	**t** (352) 958039 **f** (352) 959440	72	⍟₁₂	⍥⍥ ⍩⍟ 0.5 S ✪ ℙ ⍟

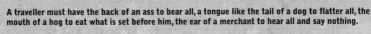

> A traveller must have the back of an ass to bear all, a tongue like the tail of a dog to flatter all, the mouth of a hog to eat what is set before him, the ear of a merchant to hear all and say nothing.

> Un voyageur doit avoir le dos d'un baudet pour tout porter, une langue pareille à une queue de chien pour flatter tout le monde, la gueule d'un cochon pour manger ce qu'on lui sert, l'oreille d'un marchand pour tout entendre et ne rien dire.

> Ein Reisender muß die Haut eines Elefanten haben, um alles zu ertragen, eine zuckersüße Zunge, um allen zu schmeicheln, den Appetit einer neunköpfigen Raupe, um alles zu essen, was man ihm vorsetzt, das Ohr eines treuen Dieners, der alles hört aber nichts sagt.

> El que viaja debe tener la espalda de un mulo para cargar con todo, una lengua como la cola de un perro para alabar a todos, una boca como el hocico de un cerdo para comer todo lo que le pongan, y los oídos de un mercader para oírlo todo y no decir nada.

Thomas Nashe (1567-1601)

HOSTELLING INTERNATIONAL

Make your credit card bookings at these centres
Réservez par carte de crédit auprès des centres suivants
Reservieren Sie per Kreditkarte bei diesen Zentren
Reserve con tarjeta de crédito en los siguientes centros

English

Australia	☎ (2) 9261 1111
Canada	☎ (1) (800) 663 5777
England & Wales	☎ (1629) 581 418
France	☎ (1) 44 89 87 27
Northern Ireland	☎ (1232) 324 733
Republic of Ireland	☎ (1) 830 1766
New Zealand	☎ (9) 303 9524
Scotland	☎ (541) 553 255
Switzerland	☎ (1) 360 1414
USA	☎ (202) 783 6161

Français

Angleterre & Pays de Galles	☎ (1692) 581 418
Australie	☎ (2) 9261 1111
Canada	☎ (1) (800) 663 5777
Écosse	☎ (541) 553 255
États-Unis	☎ (202) 783 6161
France	☎ (1) 44 89 87 27
Irlande du Nord	☎ (1232) 324 733
Nouvelle-Zélande	☎ (9) 303 9524
République d'Irlande	☎ (1) 830 1766
Suisse	☎ (1) 360 1414

Deutsch

Australien	☎ (2) 9261 1111
England & Wales	☎ (1629) 581 418
Frankreich	☎ (1) 44 89 87 27
Irland	☎ (1) 830 1766
Kanada	☎ (1) (800) 663 5777
Neuseeland	☎ (9) 303 9524
Nordirland	☎ (1232) 324 733
Schottland	☎ (541) 553 255
Schweiz	☎ (1) 360 1414
USA	☎ (202) 783 6161

Español

Australia	☎ (2) 9261 1111
Canadá	☎ (1) (800) 663 5777
Escocia	☎ (541) 553 255
Estados Unidos	☎ (202) 783 6161
Francia	☎ (1) 44 89 87 27
Inglaterra y Gales	☎ (1629) 581 418
Irlanda del Norte	☎ (1232) 324 733
Nueva Zelanda	☎ (9) 303 9524
República de Irlanda	☎ (1) 830 1766
Suiza	☎ (1) 360 1414

IBN INTERNATIONAL BOOKING NETWORK

Netherlands

PAYS-BAS
NIEDERLANDE
PAISES BAJOS

**Stichting Nederlandse Jeugdherberg Centrale,
Professor Tulpstraat 2,
1018 HA Amsterdam,
Netherlands.**

❶ (31) (20) 5513155(*information*), ❶ (31) (20) 6392929 (**ŧŧŧ**)
❸ (31) (20) 6390199
www.njhc.org

Office Hours: Monday-Friday, 10.00-16.00hrs or by
❶ Monday-Friday, 09.00-17.00hrs

A copy of the Hostel Directory for this Country can be obtained from:
The National Office

Capital:	Amsterdam	**Population:**	15,423,000
Language:	Dutch	**Size:**	40,844 sq km
Currency:	Fl (guilders)	**Telephone Country Code:**	31

Netherlands

Ameland▲
Terschelling▲
Texel▲
Grou▲
Sneek
Scheemda▲
Heeg▲

NETHERLANDS

Egmond▲
Bakkum▲
Heemskerk▲
Hoorn
Orvelte▲
Meppel
Haarlem▲
Amsterdam
Amsterdam (2)
Noordwijk▲
Nijverdal▲
Soest
Gorssel▲
Den Haag
Bunnik▲
Apeldoorn▲
Rotterdam
Elst
Arnhem
Doorwerth
Dordrecht▲

GERMANY

Bergen op Zoom
Chaam▲
Domburg▲

Valkenswaard▲

BELGIUM

Maastricht▲

N

50   100   150   KMS
0
50   MLS

English

NETHERLANDS HOSTELS

From the bustle of Amsterdam to the tranquillity of the islands, there are 34 Youth Hostels in the Netherlands to choose from. All hostels are participating in Hostelling International's Assured Standards Scheme; see page 4 for details.

Where no opening dates are indicated, hostels are open all year.

The overnight fee varies according to grade and season. Expect to pay in the region of FL 22.50-38.75 including breakfast (10.21-17.58 ECU). Linen hire FL 7.00 although hostellers can bring their own to keep costs down. Family rooms do have different prices.

Category	1/1-1/3 1/11-31/12 Fl	1/3-1/7 1/9-1/11 Fl	1/7-1/9 & public hols Fl
I	22.50	23.50	25.50
II	25.50	27.00	29.25
III	28.00	29.25	31.50
IV + linen	34.25 (1/10-1/4)	38.75 (1/4-1/10)	

PASSPORTS AND VISAS

Citizens of nearly all European countries do not need a visa for a stay of up to three months. All you need is a valid passport and in many cases even a national identity card. Canadians do not require a visa but nationals of other countries outside Europe should check before travelling.

HEALTH

For citizens of the EU the Netherlands provides free medical treatment and prescribed medicine. Presentation of an E111 form, obtainable from your own social security office is sufficient. For citizens outside the EU medical insurance is recommended.

BANKING HOURS

Normal banking hours are 09.00-17.00hrs, Monday to Friday.

POST OFFICES

Post offices are normally open Monday to Friday 09.00-17.00hrs. Some larger post offices are also open on Saturday morning.

SHOPPING HOURS

Most shops are open Monday to Friday 09.00-18.00hrs, and Saturday 09.00-17.00hrs. Late night shopping: Thursday or Friday until 21.00hrs.

TRAVEL

Air

By air, most travellers fly through Amsterdam's Schiphol airport. International flights also serve the airports at Rotterdam, Eindhoven and Maastricht.

Rail

A Netherlands Railways inter-city network links major cities, while smaller towns are served by what the Dutch refer to as 'stop' trains. Trains are clean, comfortable and run on time.

Bus and Trams

Buy a 'Strippenkaart', valid for buses, trams and metros nationwide. Available from newsagents, tobacconists, stations and VVV offices.

Ferry

The major ferry ports are Rotterdam, Hoek van Holland and Ymuiden. French and Belgian ports also provide connections.

Driving

The Netherlands has an excellent highway system which links smoothly to the major European autoroutes north, south and east.

Français

AUBERGES DE JEUNESSE NEERLANDAISES

De la ville affairée d'Amsterdam aux îles tranquilles, vous pouvez choisir parmi 34 auberges de jeunesse aux Pays-Bas. Toutes les auberges participent au Plan Hostelling International pour la Garantie des Normes en auberge (voir page 13 pour plus de détails).

Si aucune date d'ouverture n'est précisée, cela veut dire que les auberges sont ouvertes toute l'année.

Le prix de la nuitée varie selon la catégorie de l'auberge et la saison. Une nuit vous coûtera entre 22,50 et 38.75 FL, petit-déjeuner compris (€10.21-17.58). La location de draps coûte 7.00FL bien qu'il soit possible aux ajistes d'apporter les leurs dans un souci d'économie. Les prix sont différents pour les chambres familiales.

Catégorie	1/1-1/3 1/11-31/12 Fl	1/3-1/7 1/9-1/11 Fl	1/7-1/9 et jours fériés Fl
I	22,50	23,50	25,50
II	25,50	27,00	29,25
III	28,00	29,25	31,50
IV+draps	34,25 (1/10-1/4)	38,75 (1/4-1/10)	

PASSEPORTS ET VISAS

Les citoyens de presque tous les pays européens n'ont pas besoin de visa pour un séjour de trois mois maximum. Un passeport valide sera suffisant, et bien souvent, une carte d'identité nationale fera l'affaire. Les Canadiens n'ont pas besoin de visa mais il est conseillé aux citoyens d'autres pays en dehors de l'Europe de vérifier avant leur départ.

SOINS MEDICAUX

Les Pays-Bas offrent aux citoyens de la CE un traitement médical et des médicaments sur ordonnance gratuits. Le formulaire E111, disponible auprès du bureau de votre sécurité sociale, sera suffisant. Il est conseillé aux citoyens de pays n'appartenant pas à la CE de souscrire à une police d'assurance maladie.

HEURES D'OUVERTURE DES BANQUES

Les banques sont normalement ouvertes de 9h à 17h du lundi au vendredi.

BUREAUX DE POSTE

Les bureaux de poste sont normalement ouverts du lundi au vendredi de 9h à 17h. Certains bureaux plus importants ouvrent aussi le samedi matin.

HEURES D'OUVERTURE DES MAGASINS

La plupart des magasins sont ouverts du lundi au vendredi de 9h à 18h, et le samedi de 9h à 17h. Ils sont ouverts jusqu'à 21h le jeudi ou le vendredi.

DEPLACEMENTS

Avions
La plupart des passagers aériens passent par l'aéroport Schiphol d'Amsterdam. Des vols internationaux desservent aussi les aéroports de Rotterdam, Eindhoven et Maastricht.

Trains
Un réseau interurbain, géré par Netherlands Railways, relie les grandes villes, et les villes plus petites sont desservies par ce que les Hollandais appellent des trains 'stop'. Ils sont propres, confortables et à l'heure.

Autobus et Trams
Achetez une carte 'Strippenkaart', valide pour les autobus, les trams et réseaux de métro dans tout le pays. Vous la trouverez en vente dans les maisons de la presse, les bureaux de tabac, les gares et les bureaux VVV.

Ferry-boats

Les ports principaux d'où partent les bateaux sont Rotterdam, Hoek van Holland et Ymuiden. Des ports français et belges assurent aussi des liaisons.

Automobiles

Les Pays-Bas ont un excellent réseau routier, bien relié aux principales autoroutes européennes au nord, au sud et à l'est.

Deutsch

NIEDERLÄNDISCHE JUGENDHERBERGEN

In der lebhaften Stadt Amsterdam oder auf den ruhigen Inseln - in den Niederlanden können Sie aus 34 Jugendherbergen wählen. Alle Herbergen sind dem Konzept der "Zugesicherten Standards" des Hostelling International angeschlossen (siehe Seite 20).

Wenn keine Öffnungszeiten angegeben sind, ist die Herberge ganzjährig geöffnet.

Die Übernachtungen unterscheiden sich im Preis entsprechend der Saison und des Standards. Es ist mit einem Preis von ungefähr 22,50-38,75 Fl (einschließlich Frühstück) zu rechnen (10,21-17,58 €). Die Gebühr für Bettwäsche beträgt 7,00 Fl. Es ist aber auch möglich, eigene mitzubringen, um die Übernachtungskosten niedrig zu halten. Die Preise für Familienzimmer sind verschieden.

Kategorie	1/1-1/3 1/11-31/12 Fl	1/3-1/7 1/9-1/11 Fl	1/7-1/9 und Feiertage Fl
I	22,50	23,50	25,50
II	25,50	27,00	29,25
III	28,00	29,25	31,50
IV & Bettwäsche	34,25 (1/10-1/4)	38,75 (1/4 – 1/10)	

PÄSSE UND VISA

Staatsangehörige fast aller europäischen Länder brauchen für einen Aufenthalt von bis zu drei Monaten kein Visum. Ein gültiger Reisepaß genügt, und in vielen Fällen reicht sogar ein Personalausweis aus. Kanadier brauchen kein Visum, aber Staatsbürger anderer, nicht europäischer Länder sollten sich vor Antritt ihrer Reise nach den Bestimmungen erkundigen.

GESUNDHEIT

Staatsbürger der EU werden in den Niederlanden kostenlos von einem Arzt behandelt und brauchen auch für verschriebene Arzneimittel nichts zu bezahlen. Es genügt die Vorlage eines Formulars E111, das Sie bei Ihrer Sozialversicherungsbehörde erhalten können. Staatsbürgern aus Ländern außerhalb der EU wird empfohlen, eine Krankenversicherung abzuschließen.

GESCHÄFTSSTUNDEN DER BANKEN

Banken sind normalerweise montags bis freitags von 09.00-17.00 Uhr geöffnet.

POSTÄMTER

Postämter sind normalerweise montags bis freitags von 09.00-17.00 Uhr geöffnet. Einige größere Postämter sind auch am Samstagvormittag geöffnet.

LADENÖFFNUNGSZEITEN

Die meisten Geschäfte sind montags bis freitags von 09.00-18.00 Uhr und samstags von 09.00-17.00 Uhr geöffnet. Donnerstags oder freitags schließen sie erst um 21.00 Uhr.

REISEN

Flugverkehr

Die meisten Flugreisenden fliegen über den Amsterdamer Flughafen Schiphol. Auch die Flughäfen Rotterdam, Eindhoven und Maastricht sind auf internationalen Flugverkehr eingestellt.

Eisenbahn
Das Inter-City-Netz der niederländischen Eisenbahn verbindet alle größeren Städte, während in die kleineren Städte die sogenannten 'Stop'-Züge fahren. Die Züge sind sauber, bequem und pünktlich.

Busse und Straßenbahnen
Eine 'Strippenkaart' gilt landesweit für alle Busse, Straßenbahnen und U-Bahnen. Sie kann bei Zeitungs- und Tabakwarenhändlern, auf Bahnhöfen und in VVV-Geschäftsstellen gekauft werden.

Fähren
Die wichtigsten Fährhäfen sind Rotterdam, Hoek van Holland und Ijmuiden. Französische und belgische Häfen bieten auch gute Verbindungen.

Autofahren
Die Niederlande haben ein ausgezeichnetes Straßennetz mit nahtloser Anbindung an die wichtigsten europäischen Autobahnen in nördlicher, südlicher und östlicher Richtung.

Español

ALBERGUES JUVENILES NEERLANDESES

De la bulliciosa Amsterdam a las tranquilas islas, en los Países Bajos existen 34 albergues juveniles entre los que elegir. Todos los albergues participan en el Plan de Normas Garantizadas (véase la página 28 para más información). Los albergues que no tienen fechas de apertura en la lista están abiertos todo el año.

El precio de una noche depende de la categoría del albergue y de la temporada, y oscila entre 22,50 y 38,75 florines (10,21-17,58 Euros), desayuno incluido. Las sábanas cuestan 7 florines, pero los alberguistas pueden traerse las suyas para más economía. Las habitaciones familiares tienen precios diferentes.

Categoría	1/1-1/3 1/11-31/12	1/3-1/7 1/9-1/11	1/7-1/9 y días feriados
	Fl	Fl	Fl
I	22,50	23,50	25,50
II	25,50	27,00	29,25
III	28,00	29,25	31,50
IV+sábanas	34,25 (1/10-1/4)	38,75 (1/4-1/10)	

PASAPORTES Y VISADOS

Los ciudadanos de casi todos los países europeos no requieren visado para una estancia de menos de 3 meses. Sólo necesitan un pasaporte en regla y, en muchos casos, basta con el documento nacional de identidad. Los canadienses no necesitan visado, pero los ciudadanos de países no europeos deberán informarse antes de salir de viaje.

INFORMACIÓN SANITARIA

Los Países Bajos proporcionan asistencia médica y medicamentos recetados gratuitamente a los ciudadanos de la UE. Para ello, basta con presentar el impreso E111, que usted puede solicitar en las oficinas de la Seguridad Social de su país. Se recomienda a los ciudadanos de países que no pertenezcan a la UE hacerse un seguro médico.

HORARIO DE LOS BANCOS

El horario habitual es de 9 h. a 17 h. de lunes a viernes.

OFICINAS DE CORREOS

Las oficinas de correos abren normalmente de lunes a viernes de 9 h. a 17 h. Algunas oficinas más grandes también abren los sábados por la mañana.

HORARIO COMERCIAL

La mayoría de las tiendas abren de lunes a viernes de 9 h. a 18 h. y los sábados de 9 h. a 17 h. Los jueves o viernes abren hasta las 21 h.

DESPLAZAMIENTOS

Avión

La mayoría de los turistas que viajan a los Países Bajos en avión pasan por el aeropuerto de Schiphol, en Amsterdam. Los aeropuertos de Rotterdam, Eindhoven y Maastricht también son internacionales.

Tren

La red de trenes rápidos interurbanos de la compañía ferroviaria neerlandesa enlaza las grandes ciudades, mientras que a las poblaciones más pequeñas se llega con los trenes que los neerlandeses llaman "con paradas" (trenes "stop"). Los trenes están limpios y son cómodos y puntuales.

Autobús y Tranvía

Compre una tarjeta "Strippenkaart", válida para autobuses, tranvías y metros de todo el país, en venta en las papelerías, estancos, estaciones y oficinas de VVV.

Ferry

Los principales puertos de ferrys se encuentran en Rotterdam, Hoek van Holland e Ymuiden. Los puertos franceses y belgas también ofrecen enlaces entre países.

Automóvil

Los Países Bajos cuentan con una excelente red de autopistas que enlazan sin problemas con las principales autopistas europeas al norte, sur y este del país.

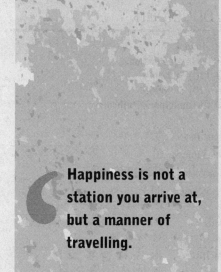

Happiness is not a station you arrive at, but a manner of travelling.

Le bonheur n'est pas une gare à laquelle on arrive, plutôt une façon de voyager.

Glück ist nicht die Endstation, sondern die Reise selbst.

La felicidad no es una estación a la que uno llega, sino una forma de viajar.

Margaret Lee Runbeck

Amsterdam -
Vondelpark

Zandpad 5,
1054 GA Amsterdam.
☎ (20) 5898999
✆ (20) 5898955
✉ fit.vondelpark@njhc.org

Open Dates:	🗓
Open Hours:	⏱
Reservations:	**R** (IBN) ECC=
Price Range:	Hfl 34.25-38.75
	€ 15.54-17.58 BB inc 🍴
Beds:	476 - 6x¹🛏 17x²🛏 34x⁴🛏 1x⁵🛏
	34x⁶🛏 9x⁶🛏
Facilities:	🚹 75x 🚻 🍽 ☕ 🏛 🛗 5 x 🍴
	🧳 8 ♿ ℹ 👕 ♻ 🎪

Directions:

✈	Schiphol 10km
A🚌	NZH 197, 370, Interliner ap Leidseplein
🚂	Amsterdam CS 3km
🚊	1, 2, 5 ap Leidseplein

Attractions: 🚲

Amsterdam -
Stadsdoelen

Kloveniersburgwal 97,
1011 KB Amsterdam.
☎ (20) 6246832
✆ (20) 6391035

Open Dates:	01.03-31.12
Open Hours:	⏱
Reservations:	**R** (IBN) ECC=
Price Range:	Hfl 25.50-29.25
	€ 11.57-13.27 BB inc 🛗
Beds:	184 - 9x⁶🛏
Facilities:	🍽 ☕ 🏛 📺 🛗 🧳 8 ℹ 👕 🔍

Directions:

✈	Schiphol 10km
🚂	Amsterdam CS 1.5km
🚊	9, 16, 24, 25 500m ap Munt
U	Nieuwmarkt 500m

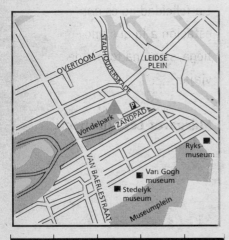

Apeldoorn

Asselsestraat 330,
7312 TS Apeldoorn.
📞 (55) 3553118
📠 (55) 3553811

Open Dates:	🗓
Open Hours:	07.00-24.00 hrs
Reservations:	ⓡ 𝖢𝖢
Price Range:	Hfl 28.00-31.50
	€ 12.71-14.29 BB inc 🍽
Beds:	117 - 3x²🛏 1x³🛏 16x⁴🛏 6x⁶🛏
	1x⁶🛏
Facilities:	👥 16x 👬 🍽 🍺3 x🍷 ▢ 🔒
	🅿 🐾 ⛏

Directions:

✈	Schiphol 95km
🚂	Apeldoorn 3km
🚌	4, 7 ap Chamavenlaan

Attractions: ⛰ 🚴 ⛵1.5km

Arnhem - Alteveer

Diepenbrocklaan 27,
6815 AH Arnhem.
📞 (26) 4420114
📠 (26) 3514892

Open Dates:	🗓
Open Hours:	07.00-24.00 hrs
Reservations:	IBN 𝖢𝖢
Price Range:	Hfl 28.00-31.50
	€ 12.71-14.29 BB inc 🍽
Beds:	200 - 4x²🛏 1x³🛏 12x⁴🛏 1x⁵🛏
	3x⁶🛏 15x⁶🛏
Facilities:	👥 15x 👬 🍽 🍺 👥 📺4 x🍷
	🔒 🖼 🔒 🅿 📋 🦽 🚲 ⛰ 🟢 🐾
	⛏ 👥

Directions:	4NW from city centre
✈	Schiphol 110km
🚂	Arnhem 2.5km
🚌	3 ap Ziekenhuis Rijnstaete

Attractions: ⛰ 🚴 ∪1km ⚓1km ⛵1.5km

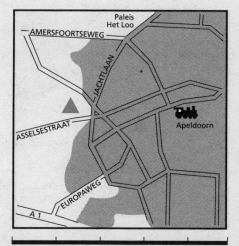

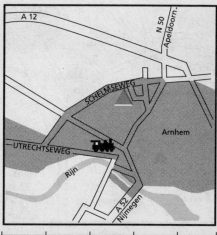

Bakkum

Heereweg 84,
1901 ME Bakkum.
☎ (251) 652226
🛈 (251) 670027

Open Dates: 🗓	
Open Hours: 07.00-24.00 hrs	
Reservations: CC	
Price Range:	Hfl 25.50-29.25
	€ 11.57-13.27 BBinc 🎫
Beds:	152 - 6x 1x 13x
Facilities:	🧑‍🦽 🚻 5x 🚻 🍽 🍺 📷 📺
	3 x 🍽 8 🅿 📋 🛁 ♨ ⛰ 🔍 ▦

Directions:

✈	Schiphol 40km
🚂	Castricum 3.5km
🚌	NZH 164 ap At Hostel

Attractions: 🌳 🔍 3km ⚲ 🚶 ∪ 5km 🏊 3km

Bunnik

Rhijnauwenselaan 14,
3981 HH Bunnik.
☎ (30) 6561277
🛈 (30) 6571065

Open Dates: 🗓	
Open Hours: 07.00-00.30 hrs	
Reservations: CC	
Price Range:	Hfl 28.00-31.50
	€ 12.71-14.29 BBinc 🎫
Beds:	140 - 1x 1x 6x 1x
	9x 5x
Facilities:	🚻 6x 🚻 🍽 🍺 📷 📺 3 x 🍽
	8 🅿 📋 🛁 ♨ ⛰ 🔍 ▦ 👥
	⛲

Directions:

✈	Schiphol 55km
🚂	Utrecht CS 5Km; Bunnik 3km
🚌	From Utrecht CS 40, 41, 43 500m ap Rhijnauwen YH

Attractions: 🌳 🏊 3km

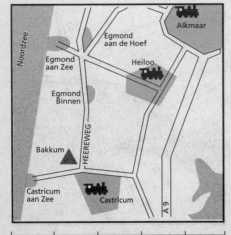

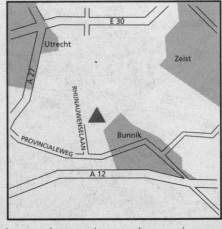

Den Haag

Scheepmakersstraat 25-27,
2515 VA Den Haag.
☎ (70) 3157888
🖷 (70) 3157877
✉ denhaag@njhc.org

Open Dates:	🔟
Open Hours:	🕐
Reservations:	IBN CC
Price Range:	Hfl 34.25-38.75 € 15.54-17.58 BB inc 🍽
Beds:	220 - 12x² 24x 6x 8x
Facilities:	👪 24x 👪 🍽 ☕ 🛏 TV 📷 🧺 3 x 🍷 📺 🖼 📠 📱 P 🛗 ♿ 🎪

Directions:

✈	Schiphol 46km
⛴	Hoek van Holland (Ferrys to Great Britain) 25km
🚆	Den Haag Hollands Spoor 400m; Den Haag Centraal 1km
🚋	1,9,12,16 ap Rijswijkse Plein

Attractions: 🔍 3km 🚲

Egmond

Herenweg 118,
1935 AJ Egmond.
☎ (72) 5062269
🖷 (72) 5067034

Open Dates:	01.03-01.11 (🔟 👪)
Open Hours:	07.00-24.00 hrs
Price Range:	Hfl 25.50-29.25 € 11.57-13.27 BB inc 🍽
Beds:	132 - 4x² 31x⁴
Facilities:	👪 31x 👪 🍽 ☕ 🛏 TV 1 x 🍷 🖼 P 🛗 ♿ ✂ 🎪

Directions:

✈	Schiphol 25km
🚆	Heiloo 3km, Castricum 3km
🚌	from Heiloo NZH 166, from Castricum NZH 164 ap At hostel

Attractions: 🔍 3km 🚲 ∪ 🏊 2km

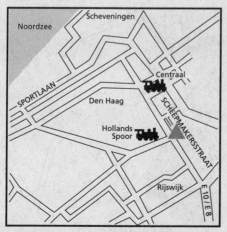

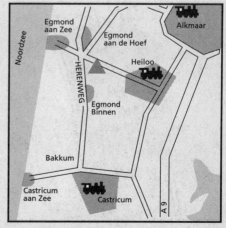

Haarlem

Jan Gijzenpad 3,
2024 CL Haarlem.
☎ (23) 5373793
🖶 (23) 5371176

Open Dates:	22.03-31.12 (🖼️ 👬)
Open Hours:	07.00-24.00hrs
Reservations:	**R** **CC**
Price Range:	Hfl 28.00-31.50 € 12.71-14.29 BB inc ⊠
Beds:	126 - 17x⁴🛏 7x⁶🛏 2x⁶🛏
Facilities:	♿ 👬 🍴 ☕ 👥 📺 1 x 🍷 📷 💼 8 🅿 ℹ️ 🎿 🧺

Directions:

✈	Schiphol 15km
🚂	Santpoort-Zuid 500m, Haarlem 3km
🚌	2 ap Haarlem Youth Hostel

Attractions: 🔍7km 🏊5km ⛵5km

Heemskerk

Tolweg 9,
1967 NG Heemskerk.
☎ (251) 232288
🖶 (251) 251024

Open Dates:	20.03-30.10 (🖼️ 👬)
Open Hours:	07.00-24.00 hrs
Price Range:	Hfl 28.00-31.50 € 12.71-14.29 BB inc ⊠
Beds:	212 - 1x¹🛏 9x²🛏 1x³🛏 5x⁴🛏 1x⁶🛏 12x⁶🛏
Facilities:	👬 5x 👬 🍴 ☕ 📺 3 x 🍷 📷 8 🅿 ℹ️ 🎿 ⚓ 🔍 🧺 🏤

Directions:

✈	Schiphol 25km
🚂	Beverwijk 2km
🚌	74 300m ap Jan van Kuikweg

Attractions: 🦆 🔍5km 🚴 ⛷500m 🏊500m ⛵1km

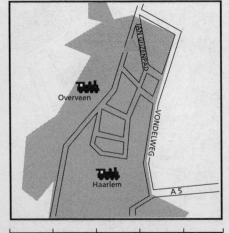

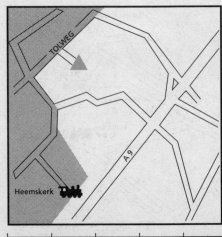

Maastricht -
De Dousberg

**Dousbergweg 4,
6216 GC Maastricht.**
☎ (43) 3466777
✆ (43) 3466755

Open Dates:	🖻
Open Hours:	07.00-01.00 hrs
Price Range:	Hfl 34.25-28.75
	€ 15.54-17.58 BB inc 🗐
Beds:	220 - 14x⁴🛏 13x⁶🛏 6x⁶🛏
Facilities:	♿ 🚻 14x 🚻 🍽 ☕ 📺 3 x 🍴 🔲
	🔲 🔢 💲 🅿 ℹ 🔍

Directions:

✈	Schiphol 225km; Maastricht-Aachen 15km
🚇	Maastricht 4km
🚌	55 or 56 ap Dousberg

Attractions: 🚲 ⚲ 🏊

Noordwijk

**Langevelderlaan 45,
2204 BC Noordwijk.**
☎ (252) 372920
✆ (252) 377061

Open Dates:	01.04-31.10 (🖻 🚻)
Open Hours:	08.00-01.00hrs
Reservations:	Ⓡ ⌐CC⌐
Price Range:	Hfl 28.00-31.50
	€ 12.71-14.29 BB inc 🗐
Beds:	130 - 6x⁴🛏 5x⁶🛏 9x⁶🛏
Facilities:	🚻 6x 🚻 🍽 ☕ 🏠 📺 3 x 🍴 🅿
	ℹ 🗐 🔧 🎢 🔍 🎱 🏠

Directions:

✈	Schiphol 35km
🚇	Leiden 15km
🚌	60, 61 ap Brink (30 minutes walk)

Attractions: 🎪 ⛰ 🔍1km 🚲 ∪ 🏊2km

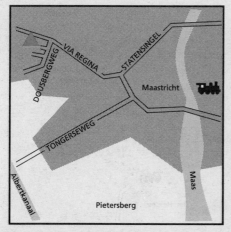

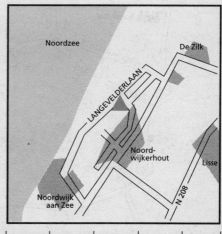

Rotterdam

**Rochussenstraat 107-109,
3015 EH Rotterdam.**
☎ (10) 4365763
🖷 (10) 4365569

Open Dates:	🗓
Open Hours:	07.00-01.00hrs (01.11-29.02: 08.00-24.00hrs)
Reservations:	(IBN) (CC)
Price Range:	Hfl 28.00-31.50 € 12.71-14.29 BB inc ⌂
Beds:	152 - 1x¹ 1x² 1x³ 4x⁴ 1x⁵ 1x⁶ 16x⁶
Facilities:	⁜ 6x ⁜ ⁙ ⌂ ☕ ▦ ⚑ TV ⬚ ◻ ▦ 🔒 ✎ 🖳 ⚘
Directions:	2SW from city centre
✈	Schiphol 95Km; Rotterdam 10km
A🚌	Bus 33 2km
⛴	Europoort 20km
🚂	Rotterdam CS 2km
🚃	4 ap Saftlevenstraat 100m
U	Metro Dijkzigt 100m

Texel - Panorama

**Schansweg 7,
1791 LK Den Burg,
Texel.**
☎ (222) 315441
🖷 (222) 313889

Open Dates:	🗓
Open Hours:	07.30-00.30; 00.30-07.30hrs key service
Reservations:	ⓡ (CC)
Price Range:	Hfl 28.00-31.50 € 12.71-14.29 BB inc ⌂
Beds:	139 - 1x³ 9x⁴ 1x⁵ 12x⁶ 3x⁶
Facilities:	⁜ 10x ⁜ ⁙ ⚑ TV 1 x ☕ 🔒 🅿 ✎ ⚘ ⛺ 🔍 ▦ ⛪
Directions:	
✈	Schiphol 95km
⛴	't Horntje 6km
🚂	Den Helder 10km
🚌	29 ap De Keet

Attractions: ⚲5km 🚲6km ⚲8km ⚓6km

There are 2 hostels in Texel. See following pages.

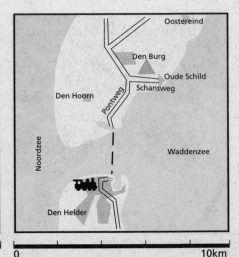

Location/Address	Telephone No. Fax No.	Beds	Opening Dates	Facilities
▲ Ameland Oranjeweg 59, 9161 CB Hollum Ameland.	❶ (519) 555353 ❷ (519) 555355	144	🗓	⛹ 🍴 Ⓡ ♿ 🅲🅲 🅿 🛏 ☕
▲ Amsterdam - Vondelpark ⟦IBN⟧ Zandpad 5, 1054 GA Amsterdam. ✉ fit.vondelpark@njhc.org	❶ (20) 5898999 ❷ (20) 5898955	476	🗓	⛹ 🍴 Ⓡ 🅲🅲 ☕
▲ Amsterdam - Stadsdoelen ⟦IBN⟧ Kloveniersburgwal 97, 1011 KB Amsterdam.	❶ (20) 6246832 ❷ (20) 6391035	184	01.03-31.12	🍴 Ⓡ 🅲🅲 ✦ 🛏 ☕
▲ Apeldoorn Asselsestraat 330, 7312 TS Apeldoorn.	❶ (55) 3553118 ❷ (55) 3553811	117	🗓	⛹ 🍴 Ⓡ 🅲🅲 🅿 🛏 ☕
▲ Arnhem - Alteveer ⟦IBN⟧ Diepenbrocklaan 27, 6815 AH Arnhem.	❶ (26) 4420114 ❷ (26) 3514892	200	🗓	⛹ 🍴 4NW 🅲🅲 🅿 🛏 ☕
▲ Bakkum Heereweg 84, 1901 ME Bakkum.	❶ (251) 652226 ❷ (251) 670027	152	🗓	⛹ 🍴 ♿ 🅲🅲 🅿 ☕
▲ Bergen op Zoom Boslustweg 1, 4624 RB Bergen op Zoom.	❶ (164) 233261 ❷ (164) 239133	176	20.03–30.10 (🗓 ⛹)	⛹ 🍴 Ⓡ 🅲🅲 ✦ 🅿 🛏 ☕
▲ Bunnik Rhijnauwenselaan 14, 3981 HH Bunnik.	❶ (30) 6561277 ❷ (30) 6571065	140	🗓	⛹ 🍴 🅲🅲 🅿 ☕
▲ Chaam Putvenweg 1, 4861 RB Chaam.	❶ (161) 491323 ❷ (161) 491756	133	20.03–30.10 (⛹ 01.04– 01.11)	⛹ 🍴 Ⓡ 🅿 🛏 ☕ 🚶
▲ Den Haag ⟦IBN⟧ Scheepmakersstraat 25-27, 2515 VA Den Haag. ✉ denhaag@njhc.org	❶ (70) 3157888 ❷ (70) 3157877	220	🗓	⛹ 🍴 🅲🅲 🅿 🛏 ☕
▲ Domburg Duinvlietweg 8, 4356 ND Domburg.	❶ (118) 581254 ❷ (118) 583342	112	01.03–01.11 (🗓 ⛹)	⛹ 🍴 Ⓡ 🅲🅲 🅿 ☕
▲ Doorwerth Kerklaan 50, 6865 GZ Doorwerth.	❶ (26) 3334300 ❷ (26) 3337060	104	01.05–31.08 (🗓 ⛹)	⛹ 🍴 Ⓡ 🅿 🛏 ☕
▲ Dordrecht Baanhoekweg 25, 3313 LP Dordrecht.	❶ (78) 6212167 ❷ (78) 6212163	120	🗓	⛹ 🍴 ♿ 🅲🅲 🅿 🛏 ☕
▲ Egmond Herenweg 118, 1935 AJ Egmond.	❶ (72) 5062269 ❷ (72) 5067034	132	01.03-01.11 (🗓 ⛹)	⛹ 🍴 🅿 ☕
▲ Elst Veenendaalsestraatweg 65, 3921 EB Elst.	❶ (318) 471219 ❷ (318) 472460	200	15.06–15.08 (🗓 ⛹)	⛹ 🍴 🅿 🛏 ☕
▲ Gorssel Dortherweg 34, 7216 PT Gorssel.	❶ (573) 431615 ❷ (573) 431832	90	20.03–30.10 (🗓 ⛹)	⛹ 🍴 🅲🅲 ✦ 🅿 🛏 ☕
▲ Grou Raadhuisstraat 18, 9001 AG Grou.	❶ (566) 621528 ❷ (566) 621005	210	🗓 (except Christmas & New Years Eve)	⛹ 🍴 ♿ 🅿 🛏 ☕
▲ Haarlem Jan Gijzenpad 3, 2024 CL Haarlem.	❶ (23) 5373793 ❷ (23) 5371176	126	22.03-31.12 (🗓 ⛹)	⛹ 🍴 Ⓡ ♿ 🅲🅲 🅿 🛏 ☕
The Hague ☞ Den Haag				
▲ Heeg 't Eilân 65, 8621 CT Heeg.	❶ (515) 442258 ❷ (515) 442550	180	20.03–30.10 (🗓 ⛹)	⛹ 🍴 ♿ 🅿 ☕

Location/Address	Telephone No. Fax No.	Beds	Opening Dates	Facilities
▲ **Heemskerk** Tolweg 9, 1967 NG Heemskerk.	❶ (251) 232288 ❺ (251) 251024	212	20.03-30.10 (🔒 ♦♦♦)	♦♦♦ 🍴 P ☕
△ *Hoorn* *Schellinkhouterdijk 1a, 1621 MJ Hoorn.*	❶ *(229) 214256* ❺	*50*	*01.07–01.09*	🍴 P ☕
▲ **Maastricht** - De Dousberg **Dousbergweg 4, 6216 GC Maastricht.**	❶ (43) 3466777 ❺ (43) 3466755	220	🔒	♦♦♦ 🍴 ♿ P 🅾 ☕
▲ **Meppel** Leonard Springerlaan 14, 7941 GW Meppel.	❶ (522) 251706 ❺ (522) 262287	72	17.04–31.08 (♦♦♦ on request)	♦♦♦ 🍴 ☞ P 🅾 ☕
▲ **Nijverdal** Duivenbreeweg 43, 7441 EA Nijverdal.	❶ (548) 612252 ❺ (548) 615372	96	01.04–30.09 (🔒 ♦♦♦)	♦♦♦ 🍴 CC P ☕
▲ **Noordwijk** **Langevelderlaan 45, 2204 BC Noordwijk.**	❶ (252) 372920 ❺ (252) 377061	130	01.04-31.10 (🔒 ♦♦♦)	♦♦♦ 🍴 R CC P ☕
▲ **Orvelte** Zuideresweg 10, 9441 TZ Orvelte.	❶ 593 322263 ❺ 593 322344	39	10.07–19.08	♦♦♦ 🍴 1S 🅾 ☕
▲ **Rotterdam** [IBN] **Rochussenstraat 107-109, 3015 EH Rotterdam.**	❶ (10) 4365763 ❺ (10) 4365569	152	🔒	♦♦♦ 🍴 2SW CC ☞ 🅾 ☕
▲ **Scheemda** Esbörgstraat 16, 9679 ZG Scheemda.	❶ (597) 591255 ❺ (597) 591132	90	01.04–24.10 (♦♦♦04.01–15.12)	♦♦♦ 🍴 ♿ ☞ P ☕
▲ **Sneek** Oude Oppenhuizerweg 20, 8606 JC Sneek.	❶ (515) 412132 ❺ (515) 412188	116	20.03–30.10 (🔒 ♦♦♦)	♦♦♦ 🍴 P 🅾 ☕
▲ **Soest** Bosstraat 16, 3766 AG Soest.	❶ (35) 6012296 ❺ (35) 6028921	140	20.05–29.10 (🔒 ♦♦♦)	♦♦♦ 🍴 CC P 🅾 ☕
▲ **Terschelling** Burg Van Heusdenweg 39, 8881 EE West-Terschelling.	❶ (562) 442338 ❺ (562) 443312	148	🔒	♦♦♦ 🍴 R ♿ CC P 🅾 ☕
△ *Texel* - De Eyercoogh *For information and reservation please contact 'Panorama', Schansweg 7, 1791 LK Den Burg, Texel.*	❶ *(222) 315441* ❺ *(222) 313889*	*102*	*01.07–31.08* *(♦♦♦ 23.04–15.10)*	🍴 P ☕
▲ **Texel** - Panorama **Schansweg 7, 1791 LK Den Burg, Texel.**	❶ (222) 315441 ❺ (222) 313889	139	🔒	♦♦♦ 🍴 R CC P
▲ **Valkenswaard** Past Heerkensdreef 20, 5552 BG Valkenswaard.	❶ (40) 2015334 ❺ (40) 2047932	136	20.03–30.10 (🔒 ♦♦♦)	♦♦♦ 🍴 R P 🅾 ☕

Norway

NORVEGE
NORWEGEN
NORUEGA

Norske Vandrerhjem,
Dronningensgate 26, N-0154 Oslo, Norway.

☏ (47) 23139300
✆ (47) 23139350
e hostels@online.no
www.vandrerhjem.no

Office Hours: Monday-Friday 08.30-16.00hrs

A copy of the Hostel Directory for this Country can be obtained from:
The National Office.

Capital:	Oslo		**Population:**	4,300,000
Language:	Norwegian		**Size:**	324,219 sq km
Currency:	NOK (krone)		**Telephone Country Code:**	47

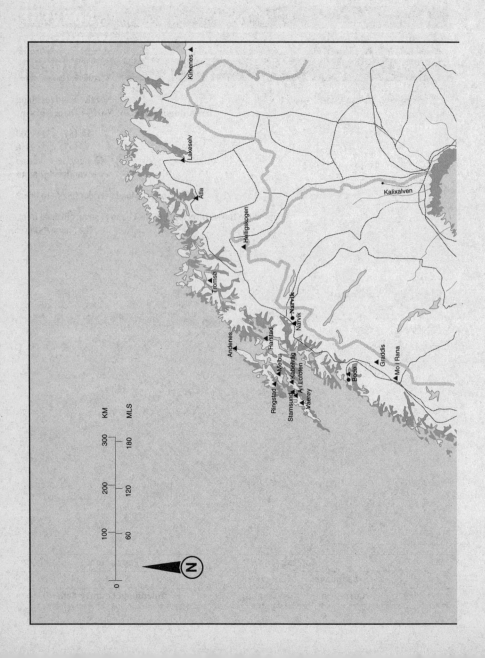

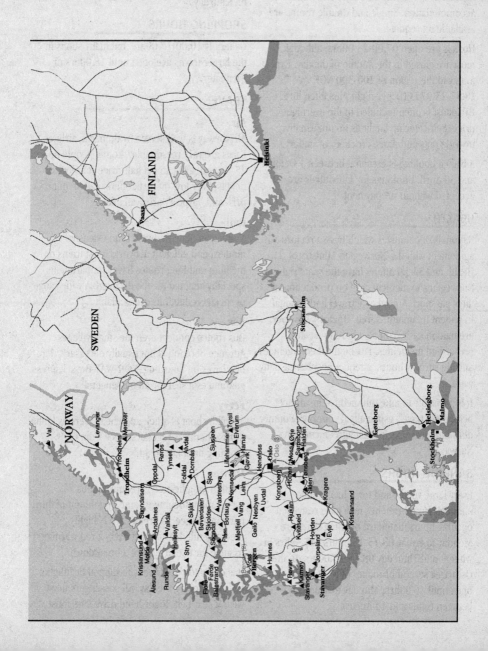

English

NORWEGIAN HOSTELS

All hostels in Norway have excellent family accommodation. Single and double rooms are available on request.

Hostels are open 07.00-23.00hrs, although most are closed in the middle of the day. Expect to pay in the region of 100-300 NOK (8.87-23.07 ECU) per night plus linen hire. Breakfast is often included in the overnight price. Self-catering facilities do not usually provide pots and pans, crockery or cutlery.

Advance booking is essential between 1 October and 30 April. Bookings for individuals are accepted without prepayment.

HEALTH

Nationals of countries which have a reciprocal agreement with the Norwegian Ministry of Health and Social Affairs have the same rights as Norwegians to medical care on production of their passport. Ambulance travel and hospital in-patient treatment is free. Doctors, however, are paid in cash. You also have to pay for prescribed medicines. For medical emergencies outside surgery hours, attend a hospital casualty ward.

It is advisable to take out medical insurance before you travel, especially if your own country does not have a reciprocal agreement with Norway.

BANKING HOURS

Every large village and town has a bank, although rural branches may have restricted opening hours. Standard opening times are Monday to Friday 08.15-15.00hrs (15.30hrs in winter) and Thursday 08.15-17.00hrs. In the Oslo area several branches of NOR Bank are open until 16.00hrs, Monday to Thursday, between 6 July and 14 August.

POST OFFICES

Opening hours vary but are generally from 08.00 or 08.30hrs to 16.00 or 17.00hrs, Monday to Friday, and from 08.00 to 13.00hrs on Saturdays.

SHOPPING HOURS

Generally 10.00-17.00hrs, but many shops in the larger towns are open until 18.00hrs or even later.

TRAVEL

Air

All Norway is well served by domestic airlines. Fares are very reasonable. Young people up to 25 years of age can get half-price standby tickets. Very low off peak offers, called 'mini pris' and 'lavpris', are available.

Rail

Norwegian State Railways is an extensive modern and efficient network. Most trains on medium and long routes have compartments specially adapted for the disabled. A wide range of special reductions are available.

Bus

Bus routes connect even the small villages. Advance booking is not usually necessary. Pay the driver on boarding. NOR-WAY Bussekspress guarantees a seat for all passengers.

Ferry

Travel by boat is quick and cheap. Ferries in the fjords operate a regular service from early morning until late night.

Driving

A full driving licence is required, plus registration documents and a minimum of third party insurance. A green card is highly recommended. You must carry a red warning triangle for use in case of a breakdown.

It is obligatory to drive with dipped headlights on, even during the day. All passengers must wear a seat-belt. Right-hand drive cars must have black adhesive triangles, or clip on beam deflectors, so as not to dazzle oncoming drivers.

Français

AUBERGES DE JEUNESSE NORVEGIENNES

Toutes les auberges norvégiennes ont d'excellentes chambres familiales. Des chambres à un ou deux lits sont disponibles sur demande.

Les auberges sont ouvertes de 7h à 23h, bien que la plupart d'entre elles soient fermées au milieu de la journée. Une nuit vous coûtera entre 100 et 300 NOK (8,87-23,07 Euros), plus location de draps le cas échéant. Le petit déjeuner est souvent inclus dans le prix de la nuitée. Les cuisines à la disposition des voyageurs ne sont en principe pas équipées de casseroles, d'assiettes ni de couverts.

Il est essentiel de réserver à l'avance entre le 1er octobre et le 30 avril. Les individuels peuvent réserver sans avoir à verser d'arrhes.

SOINS MEDICAUX

Les citoyens de pays ayant passé un accord réciproque avec le Ministère Norvégien de la Santé et des Affaires Sociales ont les mêmes droits que les Norvégiens quand il s'agit d'obtenir des soins médicaux, au vu de leur passeport. Les ambulances et les hospitalisations sont gratuites. Toutefois, les médecins sont payés en espèces. Vous devrez aussi payer les médicaments prescrits par le médecin.

Si vous devez voir un médecin en dehors des heures de consultation, il faudra vous rendre à une salle des urgences.

Il est toujours conseillé de souscrire à une police d'assurance maladie avant le départ, surtout si votre pays n'a pas passé d'accord réciproque avec la Norvège.

HEURES D'OUVERTURE DES BANQUES

Tous les grands villages et toutes les villes de Norvège ont une banque, bien que les succursales rurales puissent avoir des horaires réduits. Les heures d'ouverture normales vont du lundi au vendredi, de 8h15 à 15h (15h30 en hiver). Le jeudi, les banques sont ouvertes de 8h15 à 17h. Aux alentours d'Oslo, plusieurs succursales de la banque NOR sont ouvertes jusqu'à 16h, du lundi au jeudi, entre le 6 juillet et le 14 août.

BUREAUX DE POSTE

Les heures d'ouverture varient quelque peu selon les endroits, mais en général, les bureaux de poste ouvrent de 8h ou 8h30 à 16h ou 17h, du lundi au vendredi, et de 8h à 13h le samedi.

HEURES D'OUVERTURE DES MAGASINS

En général, les magasins sont ouverts de 10h à 17h, mais de nombreux magasins dans les plus grandes villes ouvrent jusqu'à 18h00 et même plus tard.

DEPLACEMENTS

Avions
Vu l'étendue du pays, la Norvège est exceptionnellement bien desservie par des lignes intérieures. Les tarifs sont très raisonnables et les jeunes jusqu'à 25 ans peuvent bénéficier de billets en stand-by demi-tarif. Il est possible d'obtenir, pendant la basse saison, des tarifs appelés 'mini pris' et 'lavpris'.

Trains
Les chemins de fer norvégiens ont un réseau très développé, moderne et efficace. La plupart des trains couvrant les moyennes et longues distances offrent des compartiments spécialement équipés pour les personnes

handicapées. De nombreuses réductions spéciales sont disponibles.

Autobus

Les bus desservent même les plus petits villages. En principe, il n'est pas nécessaire de réserver à l'avance. Réglez simplement le conducteur en montant à bord. La compagnie NOR-WAY Bussekspress garantit un siège pour tous ses passagers.

Ferry-boats

Les déplacements par bateau sont souvent les plus rapides et les moins chers. Dans la région des fjords, ils offrent un service régulier et fréquent, depuis très tôt le matin jusque tard le soir.

Automobiles

Les conducteurs doivent être munis d'un permis de conduire et des papiers de leur véhicule, ainsi qu'une assurance au tiers au minimum; la carte verte est fortement conseillée. Il est obligatoire de transporter un triangle de présignalisation, en cas de panne.

Il est obligatoire de conduire en codes, même pendant la journée, et tous les passagers doivent porter une ceinture de sécurité. Les phares des véhicules ayant le volant à droite doivent être munis de triangles noirs adhésifs, souvent fournis par les compagnies maritimes, ou de déflecteurs amovibles, de façon à ne pas éblouir les conducteurs venant en face.

Deutsch

NORWEGISCHE JUGENDHERBERGEN

Alle Herbergen in Norwegen verfügen über ausgezeichnete Familienunterkünfte. Auf Anfrage gibt es Einzel- und Doppelzimmer.

Die Herbergen sind von 07.00-23.00 Uhr geöffnet, die meisten schließen zur Mittagszeit. Es ist mit einem Preis von 100-300 NOK

(8,87-23,07 ECU) pro Nacht zu rechnen, plus einer Mietgebühr für Bettwäsche, wenn erwünscht. Oft ist das Frühstück in dem Übernachtungspreis enthalten. Für Selbstversorger werden normalerweise keine Töpfe oder Pfannen, Geschirr oder Besteck zur Verfügung gestellt.

Zwischen dem 1.Oktober und dem 30.April ist Vorausbuchung erforderlich. Bei Einzelbuchungen wird keine Vorauszahlung verlangt.

GESUNDHEIT

Staatsbürger aus Ländern, mit denen das norwegische Ministerium für Gesundheit und soziale Angelegenheiten ein beiderseitiges Abkommen abgeschlossen hat, haben bei Vorlage ihres Passes den gleichen Anspruch auf ärztliche Behandlung wie Norweger. Die Beförderung mit einem Krankenwagen und stationäre Behandlung in einem Krankenhaus sind kostenlos. Ärzte müssen jedoch in bar bezahlt werden. Man muß auch für verschriebene Arzneimittel selbst aufkommen.

Für Patienten, die außerhalb der Sprechstunden einen Arzt brauchen, gibt es einen Notdienst.

Es empfiehlt sich, vor Antritt der Reise eine Krankenversicherung abzuschließen, besonders, wenn das eigene Land keine gegenseitige Vereinbarung mit Norwegen hat.

GESCHÄFTSSTUNDEN DER BANKEN

In Norwegen gibt es in jedem größeren Dorf und in jeder Stadt eine Bank. Die ländlichen Filialen haben aber oft beschränkte Öffnungszeiten. Normalerweise sind die Banken montags bis freitags von 08.15-15.00 Uhr (15.30 Uhr im Winter) und donnerstags von 08.15-17.00 Uhr geöffnet. In der Gegend von Oslo sind einige Filialen der NOR Bank vom 6. Juli bis 14. August montags bis donnerstags bis 16.00 Uhr geöffnet.

POSTÄMTER

Die Öffnungszeiten der Postämter sind von Ort zu Ort etwas unterschiedlich, aber im allgemeinen sind sie montags bis freitags von 08.00 oder 08.30 Uhr bis 16.00 oder 17.00 Uhr und samstags von 08.00 bis 13.00 Uhr geöffnet.

LADENÖFFNUNGSZEITEN

Normalerweise von 10.00-17.00 Uhr, aber viele Geschäfte in den größeren Städten sind bis 18.00 Uhr oder später geöffnet.

REISEN

Flugverkehr

Norwegen's inländischer Flugverkehr ist gut ausgebaut. Das Fliegen ist sehr preiswert. Junge Leute bis zu 25 Jahren können zum halben Preis ein Standby-Ticket bekommen. Außerhalb der Saison gibt es besonders preisgünstige Flüge zum sogenannten 'mini pris' und 'lavpris'.

Eisenbahn

Norwegen's Staatliche Bahn verfügt über ein gut ausgebautes, modernes und leistungsfähiges Schienennetz. Die meisten Züge haben auf mittleren und langen Strecken behindertenfreundliche Abteile. Bei Fahrpreisen gibt es eine Vielzahl an Sonderermäßigungen.

Busse

Mit dem Bus kann praktisch jedes kleine Dorf erreicht werden. Im allgemeinen braucht man nicht zu reservieren. Man bezahlt einfach beim Fahrer im Bus. NOR-WAY Bussekspress garantiert allen Passagieren einen Sitzplatz.

Fähren

Reisen per Schiff ist schnell und billig. In Fjord-Gebieten verkehren die Fähren regelmäßig vom frühen Morgen bis spät in die Nacht.

Autofahren

Man braucht einen Führerschein und Autopapiere sowie mindestens eine Haftpflichtversicherung. Eine grüne Karte ist sehr empfehlenswert. Man muß ein rotes Warndreieck mit sich führen, das im Falle eines Motorschadens benutzt werden kann.

Man muß auch bei Tag immer mit Abblendlicht fahren, und alle Passagiere müssen einen Sicherheitsgurt tragen. Fahrzeuge mit Rechtslenkung müssen auf ihre Scheinwerfer schwarze Dreiecke kleben oder Strahlablenker aufklemmen, damit entgegenkommende Fahrer nicht geblendet werden.

Español

ALBERGUES JUVENILES NORUEGOS

Todos los albergues noruegos ofrecen excelente alojamiento para las familias y disponen también de habitaciones individuales y dobles para quienes las soliciten.

Los albergues abren de 7 h. a 23 h., aunque la mayoría cierran unas horas al mediodía. Los precios oscilan entre 100 y 300 NOK (8,87-23,07 Euros) por noche y las sábanas, si las necesita, se cobran aparte. El desayuno suele estar incluido en el precio. Las cocinas para uso de los socios no acostumbran tener cazos, sartenes, vajilla ni cubertería.

Del 1º de octubre al 30 de abril es imprescindible reservar con antelación. Se aceptan reservas individuales sin pago previo.

INFORMACIÓN SANITARIA

Los ciudadanos de países que tengan un acuerdo mutuo con el Ministerio Noruego de Sanidad y Asuntos Sociales tienen los mismos derechos que los noruegos a recibir atención médica, previa presentación de su pasaporte. Las ambulancias y las hospitalizaciones son gratuitas, pero los médicos requieren pago en efectivo. También hay que abonar las medicinas recetadas. Si precisa atención médica fuera de horas, le atenderán en urgencias.

Se recomienda hacerse un seguro médico antes de salir de viaje, sobre todo si su país no tiene acuerdo mutuo con Noruega.

HORARIO DE LOS BANCOS

Todas las ciudades y principales pueblos de Noruega tienen un banco, aunque es posible que las sucursales rurales tengan un horario reducido. El horario normal es de lunes a viernes de 8.15 h. a 15 h. (15.30 h. en invierno) y los jueves de 8.15 h. a 17 h. En Oslo y sus alrededores, varias sucursales del banco NOR abren hasta las 16 h. de lunes a jueves del 6 de julio al 14 de agosto.

OFICINAS DE CORREOS

El horario varía un poco de una población a otra, pero por lo general es de 8 h. u 8.30 h. a 16 h. ó 17 h. de lunes a viernes y de 8 h. a 13 h. los sábados.

HORARIO COMERCIAL

Por lo general, las tiendas abren de 10 h. a 17 h., pero, en las ciudades más grandes, muchas de ellas abren hasta las 18 h. e incluso hasta más tarde.

DESPLAZAMIENTOS

Avión

Noruega posee una excelente red de líneas aéreas nacionales. Las tarifas son muy razonables y los jóvenes de hasta 25 años pueden conseguir billetes stand-by (en lista de espera) a mitad de precio. También pueden obtenerse ofertas muy interesantes en temporada baja, denominadas "mini pris" y "lavpris".

Tren

La red de ferrocarriles estatales noruegos es amplia, moderna y eficiente. Casi todos los trenes de mediano y largo recorrido están dotados de compartimientos preparados para uso de disminuidos físicos. Existe toda una gama de descuentos especiales.

Autobús

Incluso los pueblos más pequeños son accesibles en autobús. Normalmente, no es necesario reservar con antelación, basta con pagar al conductor al subir al vehículo. NOR-WAY Bussekspress garantiza un asiento a todos sus pasajeros.

Ferry

Los barcos representan una rápida y económica forma de transporte. En los fiordos los ferrys ofrecen servicios regulares desde primera hora de la mañana hasta última hora de la tarde.

Automóvil

Necesitará su permiso de conducir, la documentación del vehículo y, como mínimo, un seguro contra terceros, aunque es muy recomendable hacerse una carta verde. Deberá transportar un triángulo rojo de advertencia en caso de avería en carretera.

Es obligatorio circular siempre con las luces cortas encendidas, incluso durante el día, y todos los pasajeros deben llevar el cinturón de seguridad abrochado. Los vehículos con volante a la derecha deberán estar provistos de triángulos negros adhesivos o de deflectores en los faros para no deslumbrar a los coches que vengan en dirección contraria.

Bergen - Montana

Johan Blyttsvei 30,
5096 Landås,
Bergen,
Hordaland.
☎ 55208070
✆ 55208075
✉ montvh@online.no

Open Dates:	04.01-20.12 (👪23.12-03.01)
Open Hours:	🕐
Reservations:	**R** IBN CC
Price Range:	NOK140-250 BB inc 🏠
Beds:	266 - 28x² 40x⁴ 10x⁵ 1x⁶
Facilities:	👥 👥 🍴 (B) 📷 TV 🧺 1 x 🍽 🗄 💼 ♿ P 🅿 🔍 📠
Directions:	6 SE from city centre
✈	Bergen 20km
🚆	5km
🚌	Bus #31 200m
Attractions:	🌲 ⛰ 🚲

Kongsberg YH

Vinjesgt 1,
3616 Kongsberg,
Buskerud.
☎ 32732024
✆ 32720534
✉ vh.bergm@online.no

Open Dates:	01.01-23.12; 26-31.12
Open Hours:	07.00-23.00hrs
Reservations:	**R** CC
Price Range:	NOK185-370 BB inc 🏠
Beds:	99 - 1x¹ 3x² 18x⁴ 4x⁵
Facilities:	♿ 👥 22x 👥 🍴 📷 🧺 TV 🧺 5 x 🍽 🗄 💼 ♿ P 🅿 📠 ✨
Directions:	
✈	Torp 100km
🚆	1km
🚌	200m
Attractions:	🌲 ⛰ 🎿 2,5Km 🎿 🏃 ⛵ 🏊 1km

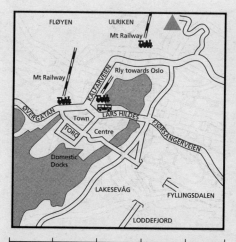

0	4km

0	1km

Kristiansand -
Tangen

Skansen 8,
4610 Kristiansand,
Vest-Agder.
☎ 38028310
✆ 38027505
✉ hostlkrs@online.no

Open Dates:	15.01-15.12
Open Hours:	07.00-23.00hrs
Reservations:	ⓡ ⒸⒸ
Price Range:	NOK170-395 ᴮᴮⁱⁿᶜ 🏠
Beds:	183 - 15x²🛏 31x🛏 5x⁵🛏
Facilities:	♿ 👬 36x 👬 🍽 ☕ 🛌 📺 ⎙ 📷 🅿 ⓘ 🚲 ♨

Directions:

✈	20km
⛴	1.2km
🚂	1.4km
🚌	400m

Attractions: ⊙ 🏊 50m

Lillehammer -
SkyssStasjonen

Jernbanetorget 2,
2609 Lillehammer,
Oppland.
☎ 61262566
✆ 61262577
✉ lillehammervandrerhjem@c2i.net

Open Dates:	15.01-30.11
Open Hours:	08.00-12.00; 17.00-22.00
Price Range:	NOK170-350 ᴮᴮⁱⁿᶜ
Beds:	94 - 7x²🛏 20x🛏
Facilities:	♿ 👬 👬 🍽 ☕ 🛌 📺 1 x ⚲ ⎙ 🧺 ▣ 🅿 ⓘ

Directions:

⛴	1km
🚂	5m
🚌	5m

Attractions: 🎿 ⛷

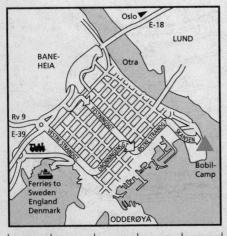

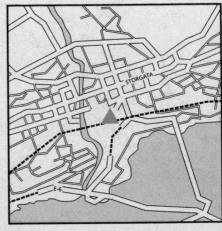

0 ————————— 2.1km

Oslo -
Haraldsheim

Haraldsheim,
Haraldsheimvn 4,
0409 Oslo.
☎ **22222965, 22155043**
🖶 **22221025**
✉ **bjorn.sveinungsen@os.telia.no**

Open Dates:	02.01-22.12
Open Hours:	♫
Reservations:	**R** **IBN** **CC**
Price Range:	NOK165-270 **BB** inc ⛺
Beds:	270 - 8x² 63x⁴
Facilities:	†††
	63x ††† ⑪ ✠ ⚎ TV ☁3 x🍴
	⊡ 🖼 🎱 P 🚼 ⚑ /\ 🔥 ▦
Directions:	5 NE from city centre
✈	Gardermoen 45km
🚂	Oslo S.
🚌	Ekspress 100m
🚃	Kjelsås 1km
Attractions:	🏛 🚶 ⚲1km ⛷2.5km

Sarpsborg -
Tuneheimen

Tuneveien 44,
1710 Sarpsborg,
Østfold.
☎ **69145001**
🖶 **69142291**
✉ **tuneheim@online.no**

Open Dates:	01.01-23.12; 26-31.12
Reservations:	**CC**
Price Range:	NOK135-265
Beds:	91 - 3x¹ 3x² 1x³ 16x⁴
	3x⁵
Facilities:	††† ††† ⑪ ✠ TV 3 x🍴 ⊡ P 🚼
Directions:	
🚂	2km
🚌	Ekspress 100m
Attractions:	⚲2km ⛷500m

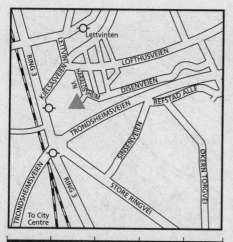

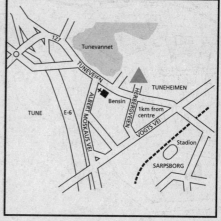

0   600m

Trondheim -
Rosenborg

Weidemannsvei 41,
7043 Trondheim,
Sør-Trøndelag.
- ☎ 73874450
- ❶ 73874455
- ✉ tr-vanas@online.no

Open Dates: 03.01-18.12

Open Hours: 07.00-24.00hrs

Reservations: **R** **CC**

Price Range: NOK170-370 ▦

Beds: 208 - 2x^1🛏 7x^2🛏 23x^4🛏 20x^6🛏

Facilities: ♦♦♦ 50x ♦♦♦ ⑩ (BD) ☞ 🏠 📺
2 x🍴 ▣ 🖼 ⚒ 🅿 ⓘ 🖥 ♻
⚐ ⛩

Directions:

✈	35km
A🚌	600m
⛴	2km
🚃	2km
🚌	Ekspress 300m

Attractions: 🐎 ⛰ ⊕ ⛷ 18Km ⚓ ⚲ ∪6km
⚲3km ⚤2km

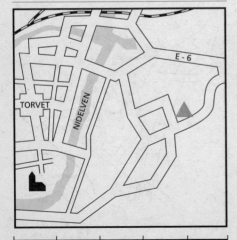

Voss

Evangerveien 68,
5700 Voss,
Hordaland.
- ☎ 56512017, 56512205
- ❶ 56510837
- ✉ voss-hostel@voss.online.no

Open Dates: 03.02-31.03; 25.05-19.09

Open Hours: ◷

Reservations: **R** **CC**

Price Range: NOK175-225 ▣inc ▦

Beds: 180 - 20x^4🛏 20x^5🛏

Facilities: ♿ ♦♦♦ 40x ♦♦♦ ⑩ (BD) 🏠 📺
1 x🍴 ▣ 🖼 ⚒ 🅿 ⓘ 🖥 ♻ ⚓
⚒

Directions:

✈	Flesland 100km
⛴	700m
🚃	500m
🚌	700m

Attractions: 🐎 ⛰ ⛷ 600m ⚓ ⚲ ⚤

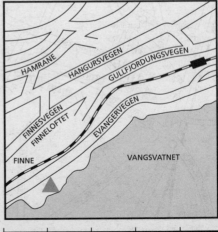

Location/Address	Telephone No. Fax No.	Beds	Opening Dates	Facilities
▲ Å - Lofoten 8392 Sørvågen, Nordland.	☎ 76091121, 76091162 ✆ 76091282	70	▣12	♯♯ ⑩ ⊂cc⊃ ☞ P ⬚
▲ Ålesund YH Parkgaten 14, 6001 Ålesund. ℮ eaaa@online.no	☎ 70115830 ✆ 70115859	48	01.05–30.09	♯♯ ⊂cc⊃ ☞ ⬚
▲ Alvdal YH - Sandli Overnatting Sandli, 2560 Alvdal.	☎ 62487074 ✆ 62487961	31	15.06–20.08	♯♯ ⑩ ☞ P
▲ Åndalsnes - Setnes 6300 Åndalsnes, Møre og Romsdal.	☎ 71221382 ✆ 71226835	89	20.05–10.09	♯♯ ♿ ⊂cc⊃ ☞ P ⬚
▲ Alta YH Midtbakkvn 52, 9511 Alta, Finnmark.	☎ 78434409 ✆ 78434409	59	20.06–20.08	♯♯ 0.8N ⊂cc⊃ ☞ P ⬚
△ *Andenes - Lankanholmen* *Sjøhus,Tusenhjemmet,* *8480 Andenes.*	☎ *76142850;* *76141222* ✆ *76142855*	*14*	*01.06–01.09*	♯♯ ⑩ ⊂cc⊃ ☞ P
▲ Balestrand YH - Kringsjå 6899 Balestrand, Sogn og Fjordane. ℮ skanke@sf.telia.no	☎ 57691303 ✆ 57691670	64	24.06–18.08	♯♯ ⑩ ⊂cc⊃ ☞ P ⬚
▲ Bergen - Montana ⟨IBN⟩ **Johan Blyttsvei 30, 5096 Landås, Bergen,** **Hordaland.** ℮ montvh@online.no	☎ 55208070 ✆ 55208075	266	04.01–20.12 (♯♯ 23.12–03.01)	♯♯ Ⓡ 6SE ⊂cc⊃ ☞ P ⬚
▲ Bergen - YMCA Nedre Korskirkealm 4, 5017 Bergen. ℮ ymca@online.no	☎ 55606050 ✆ 55606051	175	01.05–17.09	♯♯ ⊂cc⊃ ☞ P ⬚ ☕
△ *Bodø - Lokomotivet* *Sjøgt 55, Box 536, 8001 Bodø*	☎ *75645995* ✆ *75646706*	*58*	*04.01–20.12* *Closed Easter*	♯♯ ☞ P ⬚
▲ Borlaug YH 6888 Steinklepp, Sogn og Fjordane.	☎ 91109946, 57668780 ✆ 57668744	50	05.01–20.12	♯♯ ⑩ ⊂cc⊃ ☞ P
▲ Bøverdalen YH 2687 Bøverdalen, Oppland.	☎ 61212064 ✆ 61212064	34	01.06–01.10	♯♯ ⑩ ☞ P ⬚
▲ Dombås - Trolltun 2660 Dombås, Oppland. ℮ vandrerhjem@trolltun.no	☎ 61241500 ✆ 61241330	78	01.01–23.12; 27.12–31.12	♯♯ ⑩ 2NE ♿ ⊂cc⊃ ☞ P ⬚ ☕
▲ Elverum YH - Elverum Hostel & Apartments Meierigt. 28, Box 1311, 2405 Elverum, Hedmark. ℮ elverum.vandrerhjem@c2i.net	☎ 62415567 ✆ 62415600	48	16.06–15.08	♯♯ ⑩ ♿ ⊂cc⊃ ☞ P ⬚
▲ Evje - Setesdal Rafting and Aktivitetssenter, 4735 Evje. ℮ troll.mountain@online.no	☎ 37931177; 91616969 ✆ 37931334	34	01.06–01.10	♯♯ ⑩ Ⓡ ♿ ⊂cc⊃ ☞ P ⬚
△ *Flåm YH* *5742 Flåm.*	☎ *57632121* ✆ *57632380*	*20*	*01.05–30.09*	♯♯ ☞ P ⬚
▲ Florø YH Åsgården Havrenesveien 32 B, 6900 Florø.	☎ 57740689 ✆ 57743820	50	15.06–15.08	♯♯ ⑩ ♿ ⊂cc⊃ ☞ P ⬚

Location/Address	Telephone No. Fax No.	Beds	Opening Dates	Facilities
▲ **Folldal** - Sletten Fjellgard 2584 Dalholen, Hedmark. 📧 fjellgar@online.no	☎ 62493108 📠 62493108	47	10.06–31.08 (👥 🛏12 **R**)	👥 🍽 16W ✆ 🅿 ⬓
▲ **Førde YH** Box 557, 6801 Førde, Sogn & Fjordane. 📧 foerde.camping@c2i.net	☎ 57826500 📠 57826555	32	15.06–1.09 (👥 🛏12)	♿ ⊞CC⊟ ✆ 🅿 ⬓
▲ **Geilo** - Hostel & Sportell Gjeilegutuvn. 1, PB 130, 3581 Geilo, Buskerud. 📧 geilo.vandrerhjem@bu.telia.no	☎ 32090300 📠 32091896	140	01.01–30.04; 01.06–30.09; 01.11–22.12; 27–31.12	👥 🍽 **R** ⊞CC⊟ ✆ 🅿 ⬓
▲ **Gjøvik YH** - Hovdetun Parkveien, 2819 Gjøvik. 📧 hovdetun@ol.telia.no	☎ 61171011 📠 61172602	152	02.01–23.12 (Closed Easter)	👥 🍽 ⊞CC⊟ ✆ 🅿 ⬓
▲ **Graddis YH** Postadresse: 8255 Røkland, Nordland.	☎ 75694341 📠 75694388	26	15.06–30.08	👥 🍽 ✆ 🅿 ⬓
▲ **Halden YH** Box 2110, Brødløs, 1760 Halden.	☎ 69180077 📠 69184005	35	25.06–08.08	👥 🍽 ♿ ✆ 🅿 ⬓
▲ **Hamar YH** - Vikingskipet Motell & Hostel Åkersvikavn. 10, 2321 Hamar. 📧 firmavmv@online.no	☎ 62526060 📠 62532460	138	🛏12	👥 2E ♿ ⊞CC⊟ ✆ 🅿 ⬓
▲ **Harstad YH** Trondenesvn 110, Boks 626, 9486 Harstad, Troms.	☎ 77064154 📠 77065633	101	01.06–20.08	👥 🍽 3N ⊞CC⊟ ✆ 🅿 ⬓
▲ **Hellesylt YH** 6218 Hellesylt, Møre og Romsdal.	☎ 70265128 📠 70263657	54	01.06–01.09	👥 🍽 ✆ 🅿 ⬓
△ *Helligskogen YH - Fjellstue* *Skriv til/ write to John Bertiniussen* *Uranusun. 36, 9143 Skibotn,* *Located Skibotndalen (E8), Troms.*	☎ 77715460 *(Off season* *77633891)* 📠 77715460	40	*20.06–20.08*	👥 🍽 ✆
▲ **Hemsedal YH** 3560 Hemsedal, Buskerud.	☎ 32060315 📠 32060745	80	01.06–15.09	👥 🍽 ⊞CC⊟ ✆ 🅿
▲ **Hønefoss YH** Box 347, 3502 Hønefoss.	☎ 32122903, 93080899 📠 32123614	60	01.06–31.08 (👥 01–15.06; 15–30.08)	👥 🍽 2N ⊞CC⊟ ✆ 🅿 ⬓
△ *Horten - Borre* *Langgrunn, 3190 Horten, Vestfold.*	☎ 33073026	73	*15.06–15.08*	👥 🍽 ✆ 🅿
▲ **Hovden** - Fjellstoge & Vandrerhjem Lundane, 4695 Hovden. 📧 fjellsto@online.no	☎ 37939543 📠 37939818	32	🛏12	👥 🍽 ⊞CC⊟ ✆ 🅿 ⬓
▲ **Kabelvåg YH** - Vågan Folkehøgskole/ Lofoten Sommerhotell 8310 Kabelvåg. 📧 vfhs.skole@nl.telia.no	☎ 76078103, 76070666 📠 76070665	103	10.06–10.08	👥 🍽 ✆ 🅿 ⬓
▲ **Karmøy** - Sandve 4272 Sandve, Rogaland.	☎ 52820040	48	01.06–31.08	👥 🍽 **R** ♿ ✆ 🅿 ⬓
▲ **Kirkenes** - Hesseng Hessengvn 4, Box 30, 9912, Hesseng.	☎ 78996009 📠 78998811	40	20.06–20.08	👥 ♿ ⊞CC⊟ ✆ 🅿 ⬓

Location/Address	Telephone No. Fax No.	Beds	Opening Dates	Facilities
▲ Kongsberg YH Vinjesgt 1, 3616 Kongsberg, Buskerud. ❷ vh.bergm@online.no	❶ 32732024 ❸ 32720534	99	01.01–23.12; 26–31.12	ⅲ ⅉ ℝ ♿ ⅏ ☞ P ⑥
▲ Kragerø YH Lovisenbergvn 20, 3770 Kragerø, Telemark.	❶ 35985700 ❸ 35985701	100	18.06–22.08	ⅲ ⅉ ♿ ⅏ ☞ P ⑥
▲ Kristiansand - Tangen Skansen 8, 4610 Kristiansand, Vest-Agder. ❷ hostlkrs@online.no	❶ 38028310 ❸ 38027505	183	15.01–15.12	ⅲ ⅉ ℝ ♿ ⅏ ☞ P ⑥
▲ Kristiansund - Atlanten Dalav 22, 6511 Kristiansund N, Møre og Romsdal. ❷ resepsjonen@atlanten.no	❶ 71671104 ❸ 71672405	30	01.06–30.09	ⅲ ⅉ ♿ ⅏ ☞ P ⑥
▲ Kviteseid YH - Bræk's 3850 Kviteseid, Telemark.	❶ 35053261 ❸ 35053261	34	26.06–20.08	ⅲ ⅉ ☞ P ⑥
▲ Lakselv - Karalaks Box 74, 9700 Lakselv.	❶ 78461476 ❸ 78461996	50	01.06–01.09	ⅲ ⅉ 7S ♿ ☞ P ⑥
▲ Leira YH - Valdres Folkehøgskule 2920 Leira.	❶ 61359500 ❸ 61359501	74	31.05–08.08	ⅲ ⅉ ☞ P ⑥
△ Levanger YH - Moan 7600 Levanger, Nord-Trøndelag.	❶ 74081638 ❸ 74081638	45	01.05–31.08 (🚉 ℝ)	ⅲ ⅉ ♿ ☞ P ⑥
▲ Lillehammer - SkyssStasjonen Jernbanetorget 2, 2609 Lillehammer, Oppland. ❷ lillehammervandrerhjem@c2i.net	❶ 61262566 ❸ 61262577	94	15.01-30.11	ⅲ ⅉ ♿ ☞ P ⑥
▲ Melbu YH P A Kvaalsgt 5, Box 121, 8459 Melbu, Nordland.	❶ 76157106, 76159130 ❸ 76158382	100	🚉	ⅲ ⅉ ⅏ ☞ P ⑥
▲ Meråker YH - Brenna Camping 7530 Meråker.	❶ 74810234 ❸ 74810300	50	15.06–15.08	ⅲ ⅉ 2E ⅏ ☞ P ⑥
▲ Mjølfjell YH 5700 Voss, Hordaland. ❷ muhas@online.no	❶ 56523150 ❸ 56523151	40	01.03–30.04; 15.06–01.10 (rest of year ℝ)	ⅲ ⅉ ℝ ♿ ⅏ ☞ P ⑥
▲ Mo i Rana - Fageråsen Box 1227, 8602 Mo, Nordland. ❷ mo.vandrehjem@c2i.net	❶ 75150963, 90162135 ❸ 75151530	59	18.05–31.08	ⅲ ⅏ ☞ P ⑥
▲ Molde - Gjestestova Romsdalsgt. 5, 6413 Molde, Møre Og Romsdal. ❷ gjestestova@online.no	❶ 90827732, 71216180 ❸ 71242309	60	15.06–15.08	ⅲ ⅉ ⅏ ☞ P ⑥
▲ Moss - Vansjøheimen Nesparken, 1530 Moss, Østfold.	❶ 69255334 ❸ 69250166	68	01.06–01.09 (02.09–31.05 ℝ)	ⅲ ⅉ ⅏ ☞ P ⑥
▲ Narvik - SSIN Tiurveien 22, 8516 Narvik, Nordland. ❷ postmottak@ssin.no	❶ 76942598 ❸ 76942999	120	23.06–14.08	ⅲ ♿ ⅏ ☞ P ⑥
▲ Nesbyen YH Sutøya Feriepark, 3540 Nesbyen.	❶ 32071397 ❸ 32070111	40	01.05–01.10	ⅲ ⅉ ⅏ ☞ P ⑥

Location/Address	Telephone No. Fax No.	Beds	Opening Dates	Facilities
▲ **Oppdal YH** Sletvold Park Apartments, Gamle Kongevei, 7340 Oppdal.	☏ 72422311 ✆ 72422313	64	🄵	♸ ❄ ⊞ ☞ 🅿 🔘
▲ **Ørje YH** Vågelsbye, 1870 Ørje.	☏ 69811750 ✆ 69811511	30	01.06–01.09	♸ ❄ ☞ 🅿
▲ **Oslo** - Frikirkens Studiesenter Ekeberg Kongsvn.82, PB.23 Bekkelagshogda, N-1109 Oslo.	☏ 22741890 ✆ 22747505	55	01.06–14.08	♸ ℝ 5SE ❄ ⅭⅭ ☞ 🅿 🔘
▲ **Oslo** - Haraldsheim ⒾⒷⓃ **Haraldsheim, Haraldsheimvn 4, 0409 Oslo.** 🅔 bjorn.sveinungsen@os.telia.no	☏ 22222965, 22155043 ✆ 22221025	270	02.01–22.12	♸ ❄ ℝ 5NE ⅭⅭ 🅿 🔘
▲ **Oslo** - Holtekilen Michelets vei 55, 1368 Stabekk. 🅔 holtekil@alfanett.no	☏ 67518040 ✆ 67591230	199	26.05–20.08	♸ ❄ ℝ 9W ⅭⅭ 🅿 🔘
△ *Preikestolen - Jørpeland* *Write to: PB 239, 4000 Stavanger,* *4100 Jørpeland.*	☏ 94531111; 51840200 ✆ 51749111	42	01.06–31.08	♸ ❄ ⅭⅭ ☞ 🅿
△ *Ringstad YH* *8475 Straumsjøen - Vesterålen.*	☏ 76137480 ✆ 76137480	52	01.06–31.08	♸ ☞ 🔘
▲ **Rjukan YH** Birkelandsgt 2, 3660 Rjukan, Telemark.	☏ 35090527 ✆ 35090996	78	🄵	♸ ❄ ❄ ☞ 🅿
▲ **Røros YH** - Idrettsparken Hotel & Hostel Øra 25, 7424 Røros, Sør-Trøndelag.	☏ 72411089 ✆ 72412377	94	🄵	♸ ❄ ⅭⅭ ☞ 🅿 🔘
△ *Røvær YH* *5549 Røvær, Rogaland.*	☏ 52718035, 52718034, 91582226 ✆ 52718048	32	20.06–15.08	♸ ❄ ❄ ☞ 🅿 🔘
△ *Runde YH* *6096 Runde.* 🅔 *runde@runde.no*	☏ 70085916 ✆ 70085870	65	🄵	♸ ⅭⅭ ☞ 🅿 🔘
▲ **Sarpsborg** - Tuneheimen **Tuneveien 44, 1710 Sarpsborg, Østfold.** 🅔 tuneheim@online.no	☏ 69145001 ✆ 69142291	91	01.01-23.12; 26-31.12	♸ ❄ ⅭⅭ ☞ 🅿 🔘
▲ **Sjoa YH** 2670 Sjoa, Oppland. 🅔 sjoa-vh@online.no	☏ 61236200 ✆ 61236014	83	01.05–01.10	♸ ❄ ❄ ⅭⅭ ☞ 🅿 🔘
▲ **Sjusjøen YH** - Fjellheimen 2612 Sjusjøen.	☏ 62363409 ✆ 62363404	89	🄵	♸ ❄ ⅭⅭ 🅿
▲ **Skien YH** Moflatvn 65, 3733 Skien, Telemark.	☏ 35504870 ✆ 35546240	82	🄵	♸ ❄ ❄ ⅭⅭ ☞ 🅿 🔘
△ *Skjolden YH* *6876 Skjolden, Sogn og Fjordane.* 🅔 *kaarbaug@online.no*	☏ 57686615 *Shut:* 57686676 ✆ 57686676	35	01.06–15.09	♸ ❄ ⅭⅭ ☞ 🅿 🔘
△ *Skjåk YH* *2692 Bismo, Oppland.* 🅔 *skjaak.vandrerhjem@c2i.net*	☏ 61214026 ✆ 61214244	53	01.06–01.09	♸ ❄ ☞ 🅿 🔘

Location/Address	Telephone No. / Fax No.	Beds	Opening Dates	Facilities
△ **Sogndal YH** P.b. 174, 6856 Sogndal, Sogn og Fjordane. ✉ sogndal.folkehogskule@vestdata.no	☎ 57672033 🖷 57673145	84	14.06–13.08	
△ **Stamsund YH** - Justad Rorbuer & Hostel P.b.110, 8378 Stamsund, Lofoten, Nordland.	☎ 76089334 🖷 76089739	60	01.01–15.10; 15.12–31.12	
▲ **Stavanger YH** - Mosvangen Henrik Ibsensgt. 21, 4021 Stavanger, Rogaland.	☎ 51872900 🖷 51870630	44	20.05–15.09 (🗓 ♦♦♦)	
▲ **Stryn YH** 6783 Stryn, Sogn og Fjordane. ✉ jonnbein@online.no	☎ 57871106, 57871336 🖷 57871106	60	01.06–31.08	
▲ **Sunndalsøra YH** Trædal, 6600 Sunndalsøra, Møre og Romsdal.	☎ 71691301 🖷 71690555	55	01.01–20.12	
▲ **Tønsberg YH** Dr Blancas gt 22, 3111 Tønsberg, Vestfold. ✉ tonsvand@online.no	☎ 33312848, 33312176 🖷 33312848	102	02.01–22.12	
△ **Tromsø YH** Elverhøy, Gitta Jønsonsv 4, 9012 Tromsø, Troms. ✉ hostels@online.no	☎ 77685319 (Shut 23139300) 🖷 77685319 (Shut 23139350)	50	20.06–18.08	
▲ **Trondheim** - Rosenborg **Weidemannsvei 41, 7043 Trondheim, Sør-Trøndelag.** ✉ tr-vanas@online.no	☎ 73874450 🖷 73874455	208	03.01–18.12	
▲ **Trysil YH** - Kjølen Hotell 2423 Østby. ✉ post@kjolen-hotell.no	☎ 62455100 🖷 62455102	56	🗓	
▲ **Tynset** - Tynset Hotel, Motel & Hostel Brugata 6, 2500 Tynset, Hedmark. ✉ kaare.fiskvik@tynset-hotel.com	☎ 62480600 🖷 62480497	36	🗓 (Christmas, Easter, Whitsun ⓡ)	
▲ **Uvdal YH** 3632 Uvdal, Buskerud.	☎ 32743020, 94218071 🖷 32743020	46	01.06–01.09 (01.09–01.06 ⓡ)	
△ **Værøy YH** - Langodden Rorbu Camping 8063 Værøy, Nordland.	☎ 76095352, 92618477 🖷 76095701	58	01.06–25.08	
▲ **Val YH** 7970 Kolvereid ✉ landbruk@val-landbruk.vgs.no	☎ 74389000 🖷 74389001	28	25.06–15.08	
△ **Valdresflya YH** 2953 Beitostoelen, Oppland.	☎ 94107021 (Shut 22152185)	46	01.06–01.09	
△ **Valldal YH** PB 23, 6210 Valldal, Møre og Romsdal. ✉ no-baeri@online.no	☎ 70257031 🖷 70257315	32	10.06–31.08 (♦♦♦ 🗓)	
▲ **Vang Vandrerhjem i Valdres** 2975 Vang i Valdres	☎ 61367077 🖷 61367470	100	02.01–20.12	
▲ **Voss** **Evangerveien 68, 5700 Voss, Hordaland.** ✉ voss-hostel@voss.online.no	☎ 56512017, 56512205 🖷 56510837	180	03.02–31.03; 25.05–19.09	

Net Savings @Hostelling International

Simply ring us ...

HOSTELLING
INTERNATIONAL

netsavings@hostellinginternational.org.uk

Poland

POLOGNE

POLEN

POLONIA

**Polskie Towarzystwo Schronisk Młodzieżowych,
00-791 Warszawa, ul Chocimska 28,
Poland.**

☎ (48) (22) 8498128
🖷 (48) (22) 8498354

Office Hours: Monday-Friday, 08.00-16.00hrs

Travel Section: "Junior" Travel and "Hostelling Polska" Travel
ul. Chocimska 28, 00-791 Warszawa,
☎ (48) (22) 8498128,
🖷 (48) (22) 8498354

A copy of the Hostel Directory for this Country can be obtained from:
The National Office.

Capital:	Warsaw	**Population:**	38,581,000
Language:	Polish	**Size:**	312,677 sq km
Currency:	Zł (złoty)	**Telephone Country Code:**	48

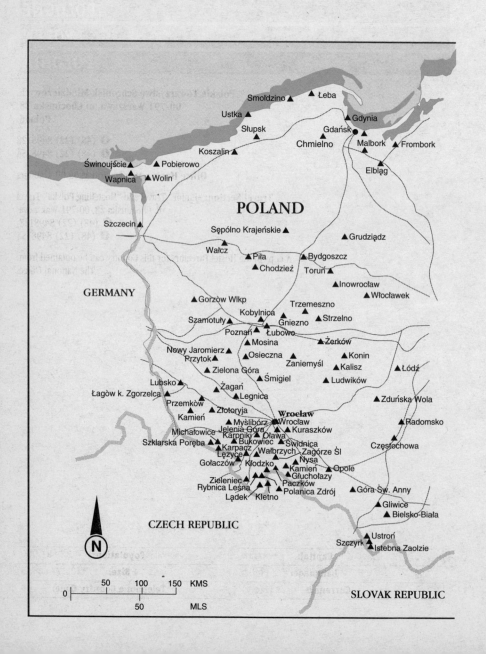

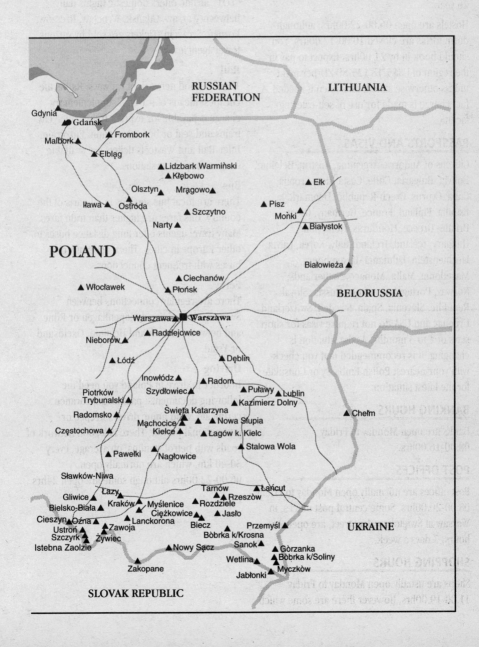

RUSSIAN FEDERATION

LITHUANIA

Gdynia

Gdańsk

Malbork

Elbląg

Frombork

Lidzbark Warmiński

Kłębowo

Olsztyn   Mrągowo

Iława   Ostróda

Szczytno

Narty

Ełk

Pisz

Mońki

Białystok

POLAND

Ciechanów

Włocławek

Płońsk

Białowieża

BELORUSSIA

Warszawa   Warszawa

Radziejowice

Nieborów

Łódź

Dęblin

Inowłódz

Radom

Piotrków Trybunalski

Szydłowiec

Puławy   Lublin

Kazimierz Dolny

Radomsko

Święta Katarzyna

Chełm

Mąchocice   Nowa Słupia

Częstochowa

Kielce

Łagów k. Kielc

Stalowa Wola

Pawełki

Nagłowice

Sławków-Niwa

Łazy

Tarnów

Łańcut

Gliwice

Kraków

Myślenice   Rozdziele

Rzeszów

Bielsko-Biała

Ciężkowice

Jasło

Cieszyn Oźna

Lanckorona

Biecz

Przemyśl

UKRAINE

Ustroń

Zawoja

Bòbrka k/Krosna

Szczyrk

Żywiec

Sanok

Gòrzanka

Istebna Zaolzie

Nowy Sącz

Wetlina

Bòbrka k/Soliny

Zakopane

Jabłonki

Myczkòw

SLOVAK REPUBLIC

English

POLISH HOSTELS

Priority is given to children and students under 26 years.

Hostels are open 06.00-22.00hrs, although dormitories are closed 10.00-17.00hrs. You should book in by 21.00hrs. Expect to pay in the region of US$5-18 (25-80 Zł) per night unless otherwise stated, plus linen if needed. A fuel charge is made for use of self-catering facilities.

PASSPORTS AND VISAS

Citizens of Andorra, Argentina, Austria, Belgium, Bolivia, Bulgaria, Chile, Costa Rica, Croatia, Cuba, Cyprus, Czech Republic, Denmark, Estonia, Finland, France, Germany, Great Britain, Greece, Honduras, Hong Kong, Hungary, Iceland, Ireland, Italy, Korea, Latvia, Liechtenstein, Lithuania, Luxembourg, Macedonia, Malta, Monaco, Netherlands, Norway, Portugal, Romania, Russia, Slovak Republic, Slovenia, Spain, Sweden, Switzerland, Uruguay and USA do not require visas for short stays of 1 to 3 months. As the situation is changing, it is recommended that you check with your nearest Polish Embassy or Consulate for the latest situation.

BANKING HOURS

Banks are open Monday to Friday 08.00-16.00hrs.

POST OFFICES

Post offices are normally open Monday to Friday 08.00-20.00hrs. Some central post offices, in Warsaw at Świętokrzyska Street, are open 24 hours, 7 days a week.

SHOPPING HOURS

Shops are usually open Monday to Friday 11.00-19.00hrs, however there are some which are open 09.00-21.00hrs or on occasion 24hrs, even on Saturday and Sunday.

TRAVEL

Air

"LOT" airline offers domestic flights daily between Warsaw, Gdańsk, Wrocław, Rzeszów, Poznań, Szczecin. Tickets are sold by various travel agencies.

Rail

There is good network of railways. Rail is the cheapest means of travel. A supplementary charge is payable for express trains, inter-city trains and seat or bed reservation. Eurotrain, Inter-Rail and Wasteels tickets are available from main railway stations.

Bus

There are local bus services in all parts of the country. Bus fares are higher than train fares. Many travel agents offer long distance buses to other European cities. There are many city buses with frequent connections.

Ferry

There are regular connections between Świnoujście and Ystad, Copenhagen or Röne and between Gdańsk and Helsinki, Oxelösund or Ystad.

Driving

In order to drive in Poland you need the following documents: passport, insurance certificate, valid home drivers licence or international permit. There is a good network of roads with petrol stations, on average, every 30-40 km, which are normally open 06.00-22.00hrs although some are open 24hrs.

Français

AUBERGES DE JEUNESSE POLONAISES

Priorité est donnée aux enfants et étudiants de moins de 26 ans.

Les auberges sont ouvertes de 6h à 22h, bien que les dortoirs soient fermés entre 10h et 17h. Vous êtes censé prendre possession de votre lit à 21h au plus tard. Une nuit vous coûtera entre 5-18 US$ (25-80 Zł), sauf indication contraire, plus location de draps le cas échéant. Il vous sera demandé une contribution aux frais d'utilisation d'énergie si vous utilisez la cuisine.

PASSEPORTS ET VISAS

Les citoyens d'Andorre, d'Argentine, d'Autriche, de Belgique, de Bolivie, de Bulgarie, du Chili, de Costa Rica, de Croatie, de Cuba, de Chypre, de la République Tchèque, du Danemark, d'Estonie, de Finlande, de France, d'Allemagne, de Grande-Bretagne, de Grèce, du Honduras, de Hong Kong, de Hongrie, d'Islande, d'Irlande, d'Italie, de Corée, de Lettonie, du Liechtenstein, de Lithuanie, du Luxembourg, de Macédonie, de Malte, de Monaco, des Pays-Bas, de Norvège, du Portugal, de Roumanie, de Russie, de la République Slovaque, de la Slovénie, d'Espagne, de Suède, de Suisse, d'Uruguay et États-Unis n'ont pas besoin de visa pour de brefs séjours de 1 à 3 mois. La situation étant en train de changer, nous vous conseillons de contacter votre ambassade ou consulat de Pologne la/le plus proche pour obtenir des renseignements corrects et à jour à ce sujet.

HEURES D'OUVERTURE DES BANQUES

Les banques sont ouvertes du lundi au vendredi de 8h à 16h.

BUREAUX DE POSTE

Les bureaux de poste sont normalement ouverts du lundi au vendredi de 8h à 20h. Certains bureaux principaux, comme celui de Varsovie, situé dans la rue Świętokrzyska, sont ouverts 24 heures sur 24, 7 jours sur 7.

HEURES D'OUVERTURE DES MAGASINS

Les magasins sont en général ouverts du lundi au vendredi de 11h à 19h; toutefois, certains sont ouverts de 9h à 21h ou parfois 24 heures sur 24, même le samedi et le dimanche.

DEPLACEMENTS

Avions

La ligne aérienne "LOT" assure des vols intérieurs journaliers entre Varsovie, Dantzig, Wrocław, Rzeszów, Poznań et Szczecin. Les billets sont en vente dans diverses agences de voyages.

Trains

Le réseau ferroviaire est bon. Le train représente la façon la moins chère de voyager. Un supplément est à payer pour les trains express et les trains rapides interurbains, les réservations de places ou de lits. Les billets Eurotrain, Inter-Rail et Wasteels sont disponibles dans les gares principales.

Autobus

Des services d'autobus locaux desservent toutes les régions du pays. L'autobus est plus cher que le train. De nombreuses agences de voyages offrent des voyages sur grande distance par autobus à destination d'autres grandes villes d'Europe. Il y a de nombreux autobus urbains avec des correspondances fréquentes.

Ferry-boats

Il y a des correspondances régulières entre Świnoujście et Ystad, Copenhague ou Röne et entre Dantzig et Helsinki, Oxelösund ou Ystad.

Automobiles

Pour avoir le droit de conduire en Pologne, il vous faut les documents suivants: passeport, certificat d'assurance, permis de conduire valide ou permis international. Il y a un bon réseau routier, avec des stations-service, en moyenne, tous les 30 - 40 kilomètres, qui sont normalement ouvertes de 6h à 22h, certaines restant ouvertes jour et nuit.

Deutsch

POLNISCHE JUGENDHERBERGEN

Kinder und Studenten unter 26 Jahren werden bevorzugt aufgenommen.

Die Herbergen sind von 06.00-22.00 Uhr geöffnet, aber die Schlafsäle sind zwischen 10.00 und 17.00 Uhr geschlossen. Man sollte bis 21.00 Uhr eintreffen. Sofern nicht anders angegeben, ist mit einem Preis von ca. 5-18 US $ (25-80 Zł) pro Nacht zu rechnen, plus einer Mietgebühr für Bettwäsche, wenn Bedarf für diese besteht. Für die Verwendung der Einrichtungen für Selbstversorger wird eine Brennstoffgebühr erhoben.

PÄSSE UND VISA

Staatsbürger aus Andorra, Argentinien, Belgien, Bolivien, Bulgarien, Chile, Costa Rica, Dänemark, Deutschland, Estland, Finnland, Frankreich, Griechenland, Großbritannien, Honduras, Hongkong, Irland, Island, Italien, Korea, Kroatien, Kuba, Lettland, Liechtenstein, Litauen, Luxemburg, Malta, Mazedonien, Monaco, den Niederlanden, Norwegen, Österreich, Portugal, Rumänien, Rußland, Schweden, der Schweiz, der Slowakischen Republik, Slowenien, Spanien, der Tschechischen Republik, Ungarn, Uruguay, der Vereinigten Staaten und Zypern brauchen für einen kurzen Aufenthalt von 1 bis 3 Monaten kein Visum. Da sich die Situation immer wieder ändert, empfehlen wir Ihnen, sich bei der nächsten Polnischen Botschaft oder dem nächsten Konsulat nach den neuesten Vorschriften zu erkundigen.

GESCHÄFTSSTUNDEN DER BANKEN

Banken sind montags bis freitags von 08.00-16.00 Uhr geöffnet.

POSTÄMTER

Postämter sind gewöhnlich montags bis freitags von 08.00-20.00 Uhr geöffnet. Einige zentrale Postämter in der Świętokrzyska-Straße in Warschau sind jeden Tag 24 Stunden geöffnet.

LADENÖFFNUNGSZEITEN

Die Geschäfte sind gewöhnlich montags bis freitags von 11.00-19.00 Uhr, einige aber auch von 09.00-21.00 Uhr und manche gelegentlich 24 Stunden geöffnet, selbst samstags und sonntags.

REISEN

Flugverkehr

Die Fluggesellschaft "LOT" bietet täglich Inlandsflüge zwischen Warschau, Danzig, Breslau, Rzeszów, Posen und Stettin. Flugtickets werden von verschiedenen Reisebüros verkauft.

Eisenbahn

Es gibt ein gutes Schienennetz. Die Eisenbahn ist das billigste Verkehrsmittel. Für Expreßzüge, Intercityzüge und Platz- oder Bettenreservierungen ist ein Zuschlag zu bezahlen. Eurotrain, Inter-Rail und Wasteels-Tickets werden auf Hauptbahnhöfen verkauft.

Busse

In allen Landesteilen gibt es einen örtlichen Busverkehr. Die Fahrpreise für Busse sind höher als die für die Eisenbahn. Viele Reisebüros verkaufen Fahrkarten für Fernverkehrsbusse in andere europäische Städte. Es gibt viele städtische Busse mit häufigem Verkehr.

Fähren

Zwischen Swinemünde und Ystad, Kopenhagen oder Rönne und zwischen Danzig und Helsinki,

Oxelösund oder Ystad gibt es einen Linienverkehr.

Autofahren

Wer in Polen autofahren will, braucht folgende Dokumente: einen Reisepaß, ein Versicherungszertifikat, einen gültigen Führerschein des eigenen Landes oder einen internationalen Führerschein. Es gibt ein gutes Straßennetz, und die Entfernung zwischen den Tankstellen beträgt im allgemeinen 30-40 km. Tankstellen sind gewöhnlich von 06.00-22.00 Uhr, manche sogar 24 Stunden, geöffnet.

Español

ALBERGUES JUVENILES POLACOS

Los albergues dan prioridad a los niños y estudiantes menores de 26 años.

Están abiertos de 6 h. a 22 h., aunque los dormitorios cierran de 10 h. a 17 h., y es necesario presentarse antes de las 21 h. para registrarse a la llegada al albergue. Los precios oscilan entre 5 y 18 $USA (25-80 Zł) por noche, a menos que se indique otra tarifa, y las sábanas, si las necesita, se cobran aparte. Si desea cocinar usted mismo, tendrá que contribuir al coste del combustible que se utilice para la cocina.

PASAPORTES Y VISADOS

Los ciudadanos de Alemania, Andorra, Argentina, Austria, Bélgica, Bolivia, Bulgaria, República Checa, Chile, Chipre, Corea, Costa Rica, Croacia, Cuba, Dinamarca, República Eslovaca, Eslovenia, España, Estados Unidos, Estonia, Finlandia, Francia, Gran Bretaña, Grecia, Honduras, Hong Kong, Hungría, Irlanda, Islandia, Italia, Letonia, Liechtenstein, Lituania, Luxemburgo, Macedonia, Malta, Mónaco, Noruega, Países Bajos, Portugal,

Rumanía, Rusia, Suecia, Suiza y Uruguay no necesitan visado para estancias cortas de 1 a 3 meses. Dados los cambios que se están produciendo, se recomienda informarse en la embajada o consulado polacos más cercanos sobre los requisitos vigentes.

HORARIO DE LOS BANCOS

Los bancos abren de lunes a viernes de 8 h. a 16 h.

OFICINAS DE CORREOS

Las oficinas de correos suelen abrir de lunes a viernes de 8 a 20 h. Algunas oficinas centrales, como la de Varsovia, situada en la calle Świetokrzyska, están abiertas las 24 horas del día, los 7 días de la semana.

HORARIO COMERCIAL

El horario de las tiendas es normalmente de lunes a viernes de 11 h. a 19 h., si bien algunas abren de 9 h. a 21 h. y, en algunos casos, las 24 horas del día, sábados y domingos inclusive.

DESPLAZAMIENTOS

Avión

La aerolínea LOT ofrece vuelos nacionales diarios entre Varsovia, Gdańsk (Danzig), Wroclaw, Rzeszów, Poznań y Szczecin. Los billetes pueden comprarse en las agencias de viajes.

Tren

Existe una buena red ferroviaria y el tren es el medio de transporte más económico. Tendrá que abonar un suplemento para los trenes expresos y los trenes rápidos interurbanos, así como para las reservas de asientos o camas. Los billetes Eurotrain, Inter-Rail y Wasteels pueden adquirise en las principales estaciones ferroviarias.

Autobús

Hay servicios locales de autobús por todo el país. El autobús es más caro que el tren.

Muchas agencias de viajes ofrecen viajes de largo recorrido en autobús con destino a otras ciudades europeas. Los servicios urbanos son numerosos con correspondencias frecuentes.

Ferry

Hay servicios regulares entre Świnoujście e Ystad, Copenhague o Röne, y entre Gdańsk (Danzig) y Helsinki, Oxelösund o Ystad.

Automóvil

Para conducir en Polonia se necesitan los siguientes documentos: pasaporte, póliza de seguros y permiso de conducir nacional o internacional en regla. Existe una buena red de carreteras, con gasolineras más o menos cada 30-40 km. que suelen estar abiertas de 6 h. a 22 h. y algunas las 24 horas del día.

> The service we render to others is really the rent we pay for our room on this earth. It is obvious that man is himself a traveller; that the purpose of this world is not "to have and to hold" but "to give and serve." There can be no other meaning.

Le service que l'on rend aux autres est vraiment le loyer que nous payons pour notre chambre sur cette terre. Il est évident que l'homme est lui-même un voyageur; que le but de ce monde n'est pas "d'avoir et de posséder" mais "de donner et servir". Il ne peut y avoir d'autre intention.

Den Dienst, den wir für andere leisten, ist im Grunde die Miete für unseren Platz auf dieser Erde. Offensichtlich ist der Mensch selbst ein Reisender; der Zweck besteht nicht in "besitzen und behalten" sondern "geben und dienen". Eine andere Auslegung gibt es nicht.

El servicio que prestamos a nuestros semejantes es, en realidad, el alquiler que pagamos por nuestra morada en esta tierra. Está claro que el hombre en sí es un viajero; que la razón de ser del mundo no es "tener y guardar", sino "dar y prestar servicio". La vida no puede tener ningún otro sentido.

Sir Wilfred T.Grenfell

Kłębowo - "Świteź"

11-107 Kłębowo k/Lidzbarka
Warmińskiego.
☎ (89) 7662382, 7662360
ℹ (89) 7662381

Open Dates: 🗓

Open Hours: 06.00-23.00hrs

Reservations: Ⓡ

Price Range: USD4.00-8.00 BB inc 🏠

Beds: 180 - 1x¹🛏 3x²🛏 8x³🛏 12x⁴🛏
20x⁵🛏

Facilities: 🏃 24x 🏃 🍽 🚹 📺 🛏1 x 🍴
🖼 ♨ 🅿 ℹ 🧺 ☘ 🏔 ⊗ 🔁
🔍 🏛 🏠 👫

Directions:

✈	Gdańsk 120km
🚢	Gdańsk; Gdynia 120km
🚆	Olsztyn 50km
🚌	PKS from Lidzbark Warmiński 8km

Attractions: 🏕 🚴 🎣 ∪12km 🏊100m

Ustroń-Jaszowiec - "Wiecha"

ul.Stroma 5,
43-450 Ustroń-Jaszowiec.
☎ (33) 8543501, 8542741
ℹ (33) 8543501

Open Dates: 🗓

Open Hours: 06.00-23.00hrs

Reservations: Ⓡ

Price Range: USD6.00-10.00 BB inc 🏠

Beds: 170 - 3x¹🛏 10x²🛏 10x³🛏 10x⁴🛏
11x⁶🛏 1x⁶🛏

Facilities: 🏃 33x 🏃 🍽 📱 🚹 📺 3 x 🍴
🖼 ♨ 🅿 ℹ 🧺 ☘ ⊗ 👫

Directions:

✈	Katowice - Pyrzowice 90km
🚆	Ustroń - Polana 3km
🚌	PKS Ustroń - Polana 3km

Attractions: 🏕 🏔 ⛷1200m 🎣 🏃 ∪15km
🎿800m 🏊500m

Warszawa

ul. Karolkowa 53a,
01-197 Warszawa.
📞 (22) 6328829
📠 (22) 6329746

Open Dates:	🗓️
Open Hours:	06.00-23.00hrs
Reservations:	**R**
Price Range:	USD4.5-20.00 💶
Beds:	180 - 2x🛏️ 4x🛏️ 2x🛏️ 3x🛏️ 12x🛏️
Facilities:	👥 11x 👥 🍽️ 🚿 🏠 📺 🍺1 x🍴 💼 ♿ 8 🅿️ ℹ️ 🧺 ♻️ 🏠

Directions:

✈️	Warszawa - Okęcie 10km
A🚌	Warszawa - Centrum 4km
🚇	Warszawa Centralna 3km
🚌	410, 522, 171 50m ap ul. Wolska
🚃	13, 24, 26 50m ap ul. Wolska
U	Stacja Centrum 4km

Attractions: 🏊5km ⛷️10km

There are 2 hostels in Warszawa. See following pages.

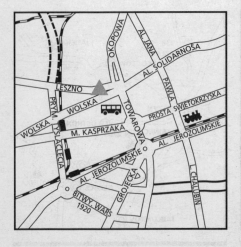

Location/Address	Telephone No. Fax No.	Beds	Opening Dates	Facilities
△ **Białowieża** - *"Paprotka"* ul. Gen. Waszkiewicza 4, 17-230 Białowieża.	☎ (85) 6812560 ✆ (85) 6812560	48		
△ **Białystok** ul. Piłsudskiego 7b, 15-443 Białystok.	☎ (85) 6524250	50		
▲ **Białystok** - "Trzy Sosny" ul. Leśna 20, 16-001 Białystok-Kleosin	☎ (85) 6631311 ✆ (85) 6631311	120		
△ **Biecz** ul. Parkowa 1, 38-250 Biecz.	☎ (13) 4471829	60		
▲ **Bielsko-Biała** - "Bolek i Lolek" ul. Komorowicka 25, 43-300 Bielsko-Biała.	☎ (33) 8227466 ✆ (33) 8227466	92		
△ **Bóbrkak/Krosna** 38-458 Chorkówka.	☎ (13) 4313097	30	01.05–31.10	
△ **Bóbrka k/Soliny** Bóbrka k/Soliny, 38-612 Solina.	☎ (13) 4691861	45	01.07–31.08	
△ **Bukowiec** - "Skalnik" ul. Szkolna 2, 58-532 Kostrzyca.	☎ (75) 7182628 ✆ (75) 7182628	47		
▲ **Bydgoszcz** ul. Sowińskiego 5, 85-083 Bydgoszcz.	☎ (52) 227570 ✆ (52) 227769	100		
△ **Chełm** ul. Czarnieckiego 8, 22-100 Chełm.	☎ (82) 5640022	49		
△ **Chmielno** - "Checz Dlo Wanogów" ul.Gryfa Pomorskiego 33, 83-333 Chmielno.	☎ (58) 6842322 ✆ (58) 6842205	50		
△ **Chodziez** - "Gotyniec" ul. Kochanowkiego 1, 64-800 Chodzież	☎ (67) 2829060	56		
△ **Ciechanów** ul. 17 Stycznia 66, 06-400 Ciechanów.	☎ (23) 6722404, 6724832	35		
△ **Ciężkowice** ul. Św Andrzeja 6, 33-190 Ciężkowice.	☎ (14) 6510119	40		
△ **Cieszyn** ul. Błogocka 24, 43-300 Cieszyn	☎ (33) 8521629	65		
△ **Częstochowa** ul. Jasnogórska 84/90, 42-200 Częstochowa.	☎ (34) 3243121	90	01.07–31.08	
△ **Dęblin** - "Lotnikòw Polskich" ul. 15 Putku Piechoty "Wilków" 5, 08-520 Dęblin	☎ (81) 8830354	52	01.07–25.08	
△ **Elbląg** ul. Browarna 1, 82-300 Elbląg.	☎ (55) 2325670	120	01.07–25.08	
△ **Ełk** ul. Sikorskiego 7a, 19-300 Ełk.	☎ (87) 5102514	45	01.07–31.08	
▲ **Frombork** - "Copernicus" ul. Elbląska 11, 14-530 Frombork.	☎ (55) 2437453 ✆ (55) 2437453	120		
△ **Gdańsk** ul.Wałowa 21, 80-858 Gdańsk.	☎ (58) 3012313 ✆ (58) 3012313	100		
▲ **Gdańsk** ul. Grunwaldzka 244, 80-226 Gdańsk-Wrzeszcz.	☎ (58) 3411660	180		
▲ **Gdańsk** ul. Kartuska 245, 80-125 Gdańsk.	☎ (58) 3024187 ✆ (58) 3024187	152		

Location/Address	Telephone No. Fax No.	Beds	Opening Dates	Facilities
△ Gòrzanka 38-613 Wołkowyja	❶ (13) 4692577	50		
△ Gdynia ul. Morska 108C, 81-216 Gdynia.	❶ (58) 6270005 ❶ (58) 6270005	130		
△ Gliwice ul Żwirki Wigury 85, 44-100 Gliwice	❶ (32) 2302525, 2302882	80		
△ Głuchołazy Powstańców Śląskich 33, 48-340 Głuchołazy.	❶ (77) 4391756, 4391547	50		
△ Głuchołazy ul. M. Sktodowskicj 9, 48-340 Głuchołazy.	❶ (77) 4391340	100	01.07–25.08	
△ Gniezno ul. Pocztowa 11, 62-200 Gniezno.	❶ (61) 4262780 ❶ (61) 4262780	75		
△ Góra Św. Anny ul. Szkolna 1, 47-154 Góra Św. Anny.	❶ (77) 4615473	50.		
△ Gorzòw Wielkopolski ul.St.Wyszyńskiego 8, 66-400 Gorzòw Wlkp.	❶ (95) 7227470 ❶ (95) 7227470	70		
△ Gołaczów ul.Górska 1, Gołaczów k/Kudowy, 57-343 Lewin Kłodzki.	❶ (74) 8662813 ❶ (74) 8661629	47		
△ Grudziądz ul. Gen. Hallera 37, 86-300 Grudziądz.	❶ (51) 4620204 ❶ (51) 4625808	156		
▲ Iława ul. Mierosławskiego 6, 14-200 Iława.	❶ (89) 6486464	80		
△ Inowrocław ul.Poznańska 345a, 88-100 Inowrocław.	❶ (52) 3537222	70	28.06–28.08	
△ Inowłódz ul. Spalska 5, 97-215 Inowłódz.	❶ (44) 7101122	32	01.07–31.08	
△ Istebna Zaolzie - "Zaolzianka" 43-470 Istebna 563	❶ (33) 8556049	100		
△ Jabłonki - "Pod Jelonkiem" 38-606 Baligród.	❶ (13) 4684026, 4684296	45		
△ Jasło ul. Czackiego 4, 38-200 Jasło.	❶ (13) 4463464	25	01.07–31.08	
△ Jedlina Zdròj - "Ad-ew-ka" ul. Kłodzka 81, 58-330 Jedlina Zdròj	❶ (74) 8455235, 8455507	35		
△ Jelenia Góra - "Bartek" ul. Bartka Zwycięzcy 10, 58-500 Jelenia Góra.	❶ (75) 7525746 ❶ 7525746	56		
△ Kalisz ul. Wał Piastowski 3, 62-800 Kalisz.	❶ (62) 7572404	52		
△ Kamień - "Halny" Kamień k/ Świeradowa, 59-870 Mirsk.	❶ (75) 7834336	60		
△ Karpacz - "Liczyrzepa" ul. Gimnazjalna 9, 58-540 Karpacz.	❶ (75) 7619290 ❶ 7619290	66		
▲ Kazimierz Dolny - "Pod Wianuszkami" ul. Puławska 64, 24-120 Kazimierz Dolny.	❶ (81) 8810327 ❶ (81) 8810327	64		

Location/Address	Telephone No. Fax No.	Beds	Opening Dates	Facilities
▲ Kazimierz Dolny - "Straznica" ul. Senatorska 23a, 24-120 Kazimierz Dolny	☎ (81) 8810427	50		⁑ ⁙ Ⓡ ♂ P ◱ ☕
△ *Kielce - "Wędrownik"* *ul. Szymanowskiego 5, 25-361 Kielce.*	☎ *(41) 3423735* ⓕ *(41) 3423735*	*60*		⁑ ⁙ Ⓡ ♂ P
▲ Kłębowo - "Świteź" 11-107 Kłębowo k/Lidzbarka Warmińskiego.	☎ (89) 7662382, 7662360 ⓕ (89) 7662381	180		⁑ ⁙ Ⓡ ♂
△ *Kletno* *Kletno 8, 57-550 Stronie Śl.*	☎ *(74) 8141358*	*40*		Ⓡ ♂ P
△ *Kłodzko* *ul. Nadrzeczna 5, 57-300 Kłodzko.*	☎ *(74) 8672524*	*50*		⁑ Ⓡ ♂ P
△ *Kobylnica - "Syrenka"* *ul. Poznańska 50, 62-006 Kobylnica.*	☎ *(61) 8485836*	*50*		⁑ Ⓡ ♂ P ☕
△ *Konin-Gosławice* *ul. Leopolda Staffa 5, 62-505 Konin Gosławice.*	☎ *(63) 2427235* ⓕ *(63) 2455126*	*60*		⁑ Ⓡ ♂ P
△ *Koszalin - "Gościniec"* *ul. Gnieźnieńska 3, 75-735 Koszalin.*	☎ *(94) 3426068*	*80*		⁑ Ⓡ ♂ P
▲ Kraków - "Oleandry" ul. Oleandry 4, 30-060 Kraków.	☎ (12) 6338822, 6338920 ⓕ (12) 6338920	350		⁑ ⁙ Ⓡ ♂ P ☕
△ *Kraków* *ul. Kościuszki 88, 30-114 Kraków.*	☎ *(12) 4221951*	*110*		Ⓡ ♂ P
△ *Kraków* *ul. Szablowskiego 1C, 30-127 Kraków.*	☎ *(12) 6372441*	*230*	*01.07–25.08*	⁑ ⁙ Ⓡ ♂ P ☕
△ *Kuraszków* *Kuraszków 50, 55-035 Oborniki Ślaskie*	☎ *(71) 3102571*	*50*		Ⓡ ♂ P
△ *Lądek Zdrój - "Skalniak"* *Stójków 36, 57-540 Lądek Zdrój.*	☎ *(74) 8146645*	*30*		⁑ Ⓡ ♂ P
△ *Łagów - "Łużyce"* *ul. Leśna 4, 59-910 Łagów.*	☎ *(75) 7715908*	*40*		⁑ Ⓡ ♂ P ☕
△ *Łagów k/Kielc* *ul. Szkolna 1a, 27-430 Łagów.*	☎ *(41) 3074104*	*48*		⁑ Ⓡ ♂ P
△ *Lanckorona* *ul.Kazimierza Wielkiego 1, 34-143 Lanckorona.*	☎ *(33) 8763589*	*80*		⁑ ⁙ Ⓡ ♂ P
△ *Łańcut* *ul. Mickiewicza 3, 37-100 Łańcut.*	☎ *(17) 2252961*	*22*	*01.07–25.08*	⁑ ♂ P
▲ Łazy Łazy, 32-048 Jerzmanowice.	☎ (12) 3895208	61		⁑ Ⓡ ♂ P
△ *Łeba* *ul. Kopernika 2, 84-360 Łeba*	☎ *(59) 8661482*	*100*		⁑ ⁙ Ⓡ ♂ P ☕
△ *Łeba - "Chaber"* *Łeba, ul.Turystyczna 1, 84-360 Łeba.*	☎ *(59) 8661435* ⓕ *(59) 8662435*	*120*		⁑ Ⓡ P
△ *Lębork* *ul. Kossaka 103, 84-300 Lębork.*	☎ *(59) 621905*	*50*	*01.07–31.08*	⁑ ♂ P
▲ Legnica ul. Jordana 17, 59-220 Legnica.	☎ (76) 8625412	60		⁑ ⁙ Ⓡ ♂ P

Location/Address	Telephone No. Fax No.	Beds	Opening Dates	Facilities
▲ Łęzyce - "U Anny" Łęzyce 41, 57-340 Duszniki-Zdròj	☎ (74) 8669301, 8669202	100	🏠12	♟ ⑩ Ⓡ ♿ ☞ P ☕
△ Lidzbark Warmiński ul. Szkolna 3, 11-100 Lidzbark Warmiński.	☎ (89) 7672444	60	01.07–31.08	♟ ☞ P
▲ Łódź ul. Legionów 27, 91-069 Łódź.	☎ (42) 6330365 🖷 (42) 6302377	83	🏠12	♟ Ⓡ ☞ P ⊚
△ Lublin ul. Długosza 6, 20-054 Lublin.	☎ (81) 5330628 🖷 (81) 5330628	80	🏠12	♟ Ⓡ ☞ P
△ Łubowo 62-260 Łubowo 12.	☎ (61) 4275299	68	🏠12	♟ Ⓡ ☞ P
△ Lubsko ul.Dąbrowskiego 6, 68-300 Lubsko.	☎ (68) 3720398 🖷 (68) 3721167	45	🏠12	♟ Ⓡ ☞
△ Ludwików 63-422 Antonin Ludwików.	☎ (62) 7348178	30	01.07–25.08	Ⓡ ☞ P
△ Mąchocice Mąchocice-Scholasteria, 26-001 Masłòw.	☎ (41) 3112165	32	🏠12	♟ Ⓡ ☞ P
△ Malbork ul. Żeromskiego 45, 82-200 Malbork.	☎ (55) 2722408	56	🏠12	♟ ⑩ Ⓡ ☞ P
▲ Milicz-Sławoszowice ul. Kolejowa 28, 56-300 Milicz-Sławoszowice	☎ (71) 3840480 🖷 (71) 3841767	30	🏠12	♟ ⑩ Ⓡ ♿ ☞ P ☕
△ Mońki ul. Ełcka 36, 19-100 Mońki	☎ (85) 7162638, 7162595 🖷 7162638, 7162595	40	🏠12	♟ ⑩ Ⓡ ☞ P ☕
△ Mosina ul. Topolowa 2, 62-050 Mosina.	☎ (61) 8132734	44	01.07–31.08	♟ ☞ P
△ Mrągowo ul.Wojska Polskiego 2, 11-700 Mrągowo.	☎ (89) 7412712	60	01.07–31.08	♟ ☞ P
△ Myczkòw Myczkòw, 38-610 Polańczyk.	☎ (13) 4692005	30	01.07–31.08	☞ P
△ Myślenice ul. Sobieskiego 1, 32-400 Myślenice.	☎ (12) 2720677	80	01.07–25.08	☞ P
△ Myślibòrz Myślibòrz, 59-422 Piotrowice.	☎ (76) 8708886	46	🏠12	♟ Ⓡ ☞ P
△ Nieborów Al. Legionòw Polskich 92, 96-416 Nieborów.	☎ (46) 8385694 🖷 8385694	25	01.07–25.08	☞ P
△ Nowa Słupia - "Pod Pielgrzymem" ul. Świętokrzyska 64, 26-006 Nowa Słupia.	☎ (41) 3177016	60	🏠12	♟ Ⓡ ☞ P
△ Nowy Jaromierz Nowy Jaromierz, 64-220 Kargowa.	☎ (68) 3525027, 3525142	35	🏠12	Ⓡ ☞ P
△ Nowy Sącz Al.Batorego 72, 33-300 Nowy Sącz.	☎ (18) 4423897	50	🏠12	♟ Ⓡ ☞ P
△ Nysa - "Pod Ziębickim Lwem" ul. Moniuszki 9/10, 48-300 Nysa.	☎ (77) 4333731	60	🏠12	♟ Ⓡ ☞ P
△ Oława ul. Ks. Kutrowskiego 31a, 55-200 Oława.	☎ (71) 3133156	50	🏠12	♟ Ⓡ ☞ P

Location/Address	Telephone No. Fax No.	Beds	Opening Dates	Facilities
▲ **Olsztyn** ul. Kopernika 45, 10-512 Olsztyn.	☎ (89) 5276650 ✆ (89) 5276650	80	ⁱ²⁷	ⅈⅈ ⓡ ⚲ 🅿
△ *Opole* ul. Struga 16, 45-073 Opole.	☎ (77) 4543352	50	01.07–25.08	ⅈⅈ ⚲ 🅿
▲ **Osieczna** - "Morena" ul. Kopernika 4, 64-113 Osieczna.	☎ (65) 5350134	60	ⁱ²⁷	ⅈⅈ 🍴 ⓡ ⚲ 🅿
△ *Ostróda* ul.Kościuszki 5, 13-100 Ostróda.	☎ (89) 646563	80	01.07–25.08	⚲ 🅿
△ *Paczków* - "Pod Basztą" ul. Kołłątaja 9, 48-370 Paczków.	☎ (77) 4316441	50	ⁱ²⁷	ⅈⅈ ⓡ ⚲
△ *Pawełki* ul. Główna 14, 42-718 Kochcice.	☎ (34) 3533716	40	ⁱ²⁷	ⅈⅈ ⓡ ⚲ 🅿
△ *Piła* - "Staszicówka" AL. WP 45, 64-920 Piła.	☎ (67) 2132583	40	ⁱ²⁷	ⅈⅈ ⓡ ⚲ 🅿
△ *Piotrków Trybunalski* ul. Broniewskiego 16, 97-300 Piotrków Trybunalski.	☎ (44) 6470905	47	ⁱ²⁷	ⅈⅈ ⓡ ⚲ 🅿
△ *Pisz* ul. Gizewiusza 10, 12-200 Pisz.	☎ (87) 5232027	24	01.07–31.08	ⓡ ⚲ 🅿
△ *Płońsk* ul. Sienkiewicza 8, 09-100 Płońsk.	☎ (23) 6622844	49	ⁱ²⁷	ⅈⅈ ⓡ ⚲ 🅿 ☕
▲ **Pobierowo** ul. Mickiewicza 19, 72-404 Pobierowo.	☎ (931) 64243 ✆ (931) 64243	60	ⁱ²⁷	ⅈⅈ ⓡ ⚲ 🅿
△ *Polanica Zdrój* ul. Chopina 4, 57-320 Polanica-Zdrój	☎ (74) 8681503, 8681344	45	ⁱ²⁷	ⅈⅈ 🍴 ⓡ 🅿 ☕
△ *Poznań* ul. Drzymały 3, 60-613 Poznań	☎ (61) 8485836 ✆ (61) 8485836	90	ⁱ²⁷	ⅈⅈ 🍴 ⓡ ⚲ 🅿 🖥 ☕
△ *Poznań* ul. Berwińskiego 2/3, 60-765 Poznań.	☎ (61) 8664040 ✆ (61) 8664040	52	ⁱ²⁷	ⅈⅈ ⓡ ⚲ 🅿
△ *Poznań* - "Hanki" ul. Biskupińska 27, 60-463 Poznań.	☎ (61) 8221063 ✆ (61) 8221063	70	ⁱ²⁷	ⅈⅈ 🍴 ⓡ ⚲ 🅿 🖥
△ *Przemków* ul. Głogowska 27, 59-325 Przemków.	☎ (76) 8319465	60	ⁱ²⁷	ⅈⅈ ⓡ ⚲ 🅿
▲ **Przemyśl** - "Matecznik" ul.Lelewela 6, 37-700 Przemyśl.	☎ (16) 6706145	54	ⁱ²⁷	ⅈⅈ 🍴 ⓡ ⚲ 🅿
▲ **Przytok** 66-003 Zabór	☎ (68) 3209698, 3209690	42	ⁱ²⁷	ⅈⅈ 🍴 ⓡ ♿ ⚲ 🅿 🖥 ☕
▲ **Puławy** ul. Włostowicka 27, 24-100 Puławy.	☎ (81) 8883656, 8863367 ✆ (81) 8883656	110	ⁱ²⁷	ⅈⅈ 🍴 ⓡ ⚲ 🅿
△ *Radom* ul. Miła 18, 26-600 Radom.	☎ (48) 40560	40	ⁱ²⁷	ⅈⅈ ⓡ ⚲ 🅿
△ *Radomsko* ul.Piastowska 21, 97-500 Radomsko.	☎ (44) 6834495	50	01.07–31.08	⚲ 🅿
△ *Radziejowice* ul.Sienkiewicza 6, 96-325 Radziejowice.	☎ (46) 8577111	30	ⁱ²⁷	ⅈⅈ ⓡ ⚲ 🅿

Location/Address	Telephone No. Fax No.	Beds	Opening Dates	Facilities
▲ **Rozdziele** 32-731 Żegocina.	☏ (14) 6133087	54	🏠	👪 🆁 ✂ 🅿
△ *Rybnica Leśna* Rybnica Leśna 54, 58-352 Unisław Śląski.	☏ (74) 8451591	44	🏠	🍴 🆁 ✂ 🅿
▲ **Rzeszòw** Rynek 25, 35-064 Rzeszòw.	☏ (17) 8534430	100	🏠	👪 🆁 ✂ 🅿 ☕
△ *Sanok* ul. Konarskiego 10, 38-500 Sanok.	☏ (13) 4630925	66	01.07–31.08	👪 ✂ 🅿
△ *Sępòlno Krajeńskie* ul. Hallera 29, 89-400 Sępòlno Krajeńskie.	☏ (52) 3882686, 3882051	30	01.07–25.08	✂ 🅿
▲ **Sławkòw Niwa** ul. Niwa 45, 42-533 Sławkòw.	☏ (32) 2931100	60	🏠	👪 🍴 🆁 ✂ 🅿
△ *Słupsk* ul. Deotymy 15a, 76-200 Słupsk.	☏ (59) 8424631	88	01.07–25.08	👪 🅿
▲ **Śmigiel** ul. M. Konopnickiej 5, 64-030 Śmigiel.	☏ (65) 5180279	60	🏠	👪 🆁 ♿ ✂ 🅿 ⬛
△ *Smołdzino* 76-214 Smołdzino.	☏ (59) 8117321	40	01.07–25.08	👪 🍴 ✂ 🅿
△ *Stalowa Wola* ul. Podleśna 15, 37-450 Stalowa Wola.	☏ (15) 8421772	40	01.07–25.08	👪 ✂ 🅿
△ *Strzelno* ul. Parkowa 10, 88-320 Strzelno.	☏ (52) 3189568	35	01.07–25.08	👪 ✂ 🅿
▲ **Świdnica** ul. Muzealna 4, 58-100 Świdnica	☏ (74) 8537148, 8520480 ☏ (74) 8533578	44	🏠	👪 🍴 🆁 ✂ 🅿 ⬛ ☕
△ *Święta - Katarzyna* ul. Kielecka 45, 26-013 Święta Katarzyna.	☏ (41) 3112206	45	🏠	🆁 ✂ 🅿
△ *Świnoujście* ul.Gdyńska 26, 72-600 Świnoujście.	☏ (91) 3270613	120	🏠	👪 🆁 ✂ 🅿
△ *Szamotuły* ul.Obornicka 12, 64-500 Szamotuły.	☏ (61) 2921165 ☏ (61) 2921165	44	🏠	👪 🆁 ✂ 🅿
▲ **Szczecin** - "Elka-Sen" ul.3 Maja 1a, 70-214 Szczecin.	☏ (91) 4335604 ☏ (91) 4335604	44	🏠	👪 🆁 ✂ 🅿 ☕
▲ **Szczecin** ul. Monte Cassino 19a, 70-467 Szczecin.	☏ (91) 4224761 ☏ (91) 4235696	130	🏠	👪 🆁 2NW ⟨CC⟩ ✂ 🅿
△ *Szczyrk - "Hondrasik"* ul. Sportowa 2, 43-370 Szczyrk.	☏ (33) 8178933	68	🏠	👪 🆁 ✂ 🅿
△ *Szklarska Poręba - "Wojtek"* ul. Piastowska 1, 58-585 Szklarska Poręba.	☏ (75) 7172141 ☏ (75) 7172141	73	🏠	👪 🆁 ✂ 🅿
△ *Szydłowiec* ul. Kolejowa 26a, 26-500 Szydłowiec.	☏ (48) 6170137	30	🏠	👪 🆁 ✂ 🅿
△ *Tarnòw* ul. Konarskiego 17, 33-100 Tarnòw.	☏ (14) 216916	44	🏠	🆁 ✂ 🅿
△ *Toruń* ul. Św. Józefa 26, 87-100 Toruń.	☏ (56) 6544107 (56) 6544580	30	🏠	👪 🆁 ✂ 🅿

Location/Address	Telephone No. Fax No.	Beds	Opening Dates	Facilities
△ *Trzemeszno* *ul. Wyszyńskiego 3, 88-340 Trzemeszno.*	☎ *(52) 3154031*	*50*	*01.06–30.09*	††† ♂ P
△ *Ustka* *ul.Jagiellońska 1, 76-270 Ustka.*	☎ *(59) 8145317,* *8145081*	*55*	🗓	††† R ♂ P
▲ Ustroń-Jaszowiec - "Wiecha" **ul.Stroma 5, 43-450 Ustroń-Jaszowiec.**	☎ (33) 8543501, 8542741 ✆ (33) 8543501	170	🗓	††† ꛂ R ♂ P
△ *Wałbrzych - "Daisy"* *ul. Markoniego 1, 58-302 Wałbrzych.*	☎ *(74) 8477942*	*60*	🗓	††† R ♂ P
△ *Wałcz* *Al.Zdobywcòw Wału Pomorskiego 76,* *78-600 Wałcz.*	☎ *(67) 2582749*	*31*	*01.07–25.08*	††† ♂ P
△ *Wapnica* *ul. Jodłowa 3, 72-517 Wapnica.*	☎ *(91) 3284106*	*70*	*01.07–25.08*	♂ P
▲ **Warszawa** **ul. Karolkowa 53a, 01-197 Warszawa.**	☎ (22) 6328829 ✆ (22) 6329746	180	🗓	††† ꛂ R ♂ P
△ *Warszawa* *ul. Smolna 30, 00-375 Warszawa.*	☎ *(22) 8278952* ✆ *(22) 8278952*	*120*	🗓	††† R ♂ P
▲ **Wetlina** 38-608 Wetlina	☎ 6	56	🗓	††† ꛂ R ♂ P ☕
▲ Włocławek - "Kujawiak" ul. Mechaników 1, 87-800 Włocławek.	☎ (54) 2362410	48	🗓	††† ꛂ R ♂ P
△ *Wolin* *ul. Spokojna 1, 72-500 Wolin.*	☎ *(91) 3261790*	*50*	*01.07–25.08*	♂ P
▲ **Wrocław** ul. Kiełczowska 43, 51-315 Wrocław.	☎ (71) 3457396, 3457399 ✆ (71) 3457399	100	🗓	††† ꛂ R ♂ P
△ *Wrocław* *ul.Kołłątaja 20, 50-007 Wrocław.*	☎ *(71) 3438856* ✆ *(71) 3438856*	*47*	🗓	††† R ♂ P
▲ Zagórze Śląskie - "Gwarek" ul. Główna 17, 58-321 Jugowice	☎ (74) 8453383	47	🗓	††† ꛂ R ♂ P ☕
▲ Zakopane - "Szarotka" ul. Nowotarska 45, 34-500 Zakopane.	☎ (18) 2013618, 2066203 ✆ (18) 2066203	270	🗓	††† ꛂ R ♂ P
△ *Zaniemyśl* *ul. Poznańska 28, 63-020 Zaniemyśl.*	☎ *(61) 2857289*	*45*	🗓	††† R ♂ P
△ *Zawoja* *34-223, Zawoja-Wilczna.*	☎ *(33) 8775106*	*38*	🗓	††† R ♂ P
▲ Zduńska Wola - "Czekay" ul.Dolna 41, 98-220 Zduńska Wola.	☎ (43) 8232440, 8232374	81	🗓	††† R ♂ P ☕
△ *Zieleniec - "Adamski"* *Zieleniec 68, 57-350 Duszniki Zdrój.*	☎ *(74) 8660435,* *8660425*	*32*	🗓	††† R ♂ P
△ *Zielona Gòra* *ul. Wyspiańskiego 58, 65-036 Zielona Góra.*	☎ *(68) 3270840* ✆ *(68) 3270840*	*129*	🗓	††† R ♂ P
△ *Złotoryja* *ul. Kolejowa 2, 59-500 Złotoryja.*	☎ *(76) 8783674*	*56*	🗓	††† R ♂ P

Location/Address	Telephone No. Fax No.	Beds	Opening Dates	Facilities
▲ **Żagań** ul.X Lecia Pl 19/21, 68-100 Żagań	☏ (68) 3773235 📠 (68) 3772456	40	🗓	👬 Ⓡ ⚲ Ⓟ
△ **Żerków** ul. Cmentarna 8, 63-210 Żerków.	☏ (62) 7403015	30	🗓	👬 Ⓡ ⚲ Ⓟ
△ **Żywiec - "Pod Grojcem"** ul Słonki 4, 34-300 Żywiec.	☏ (33) 8612639	73	🗓	👬 Ⓡ ⚲ Ⓟ

YOUTH HOSTEL ACCOMMODATION
OUTSIDE THE ASSURED STANDARDS SCHEME

Location/Address	Telephone No. Fax No.	Beds	Opening Dates	Facilities
Michałowice "Złoty Widok", ul.Kolonijna 14, 58-572 Michałowice.	☏ (75) 7553344	46	🗓	👬 🍽 Ⓡ ⚲ Ⓟ
Myślenice ul. Zdrojowa 16, 32-400 Myślenice.	☏ (12) 2721163	100	🗓	👬 🍽 Ⓡ Ⓟ ☕
Nagłowice 28-362 Nagłowice	☏ (41) 3814518, 3814382	32	🗓	👬 🍽 Ⓡ ♿ ⚲ Ⓟ ☕
Poznań - im PE Strzeleckiego ul. Głuszyna 127, 61-329 Poznań.	☏ (61) 8788461 📠 (61) 8788461	88	🗓	👬 🍽 Ⓡ Ⓟ
Strużnica - "Sokolik" 58-515 Karpniki	☏ (75) 7137224	40	🗓	👬 🍽 Ⓡ Ⓟ ☕
Szczytno - "Pod Kasztanem" ul. Pasymska 7, 12-100 Szczytno.	☏ (89) 6243992	50	🗓	👬 Ⓡ ⚲ Ⓟ
Wrocław - "Piast" ul.Piłsudskiego 98, 50-017 Wrocław.	☏ (71) 3430033, 3430034 📠 (71) 3437893	140	🗓	👬 🍽 Ⓡ Ⓟ ☕
Zielona Gòra ul. Długa 13, 65-401 Zielona Gòra	☏ (68) 3202237, 3202571	49-	🗓	👬 🍽 Ⓡ ⚲ Ⓟ ☕

The journey is difficult, immense. We will travel as far as we can, but we cannot in one lifetime see all that we would like to see or to learn all that we hunger to know.

Le voyage est difficile, immense. Nous voyagerons aussi loin que le le pourrons, mais il ne nous sera pas possible, dans une vie, de voir tout ce que nous voudrions voir ni d'apprendre tout ce que nous avons soif de connaître.

Die Reise ist unheimlich kompliziert. Wir reisen so weit wie möglich, können aber in einem Leben nicht all das sehen, was wir gerne möchten oder das lernen, wonach wir Hunger verspüren.

El camino es largo y difícil. Iremos lo más lejos posible, pero en el espacio de una vida nunca podremos ver todo lo que queremos ver, ni aprender todo lo que ansiamos aprender.

Loren Eiseley

Portugal

PORTUGAL
PORTUGAL
PORTUGAL

MOVIJOVEM - Agência de Turismo Jovem
Cooperativa de Interesse Público e Responsabilidade Lda,
Av Duque d'Ávila 137, 1069-017 Lisbon, Portugal

☎ (351) (21) 313 88 20
🖷 (351) (21) 353 59 82 (Board)
🖷 (351) (21) 352 86 21 and 352 14 66 (Travel Dept.)
ⓔ movijovem@mail.telepac.pt
www.sejuventude.pt

Opening Hours: Monday-Friday, 09.00-13.00hrs
14.00-18.00hrs

A copy of the Hostel Directory for this Country can be obtained from:
The National Office.

Capital:	Lisboa	**Population:**	10,500,000
Language:	Portuguese	**Size:**	92,082 sq km
Currency:	PTE (Portuguese Escudos)	**Telephone Country Code:**	351

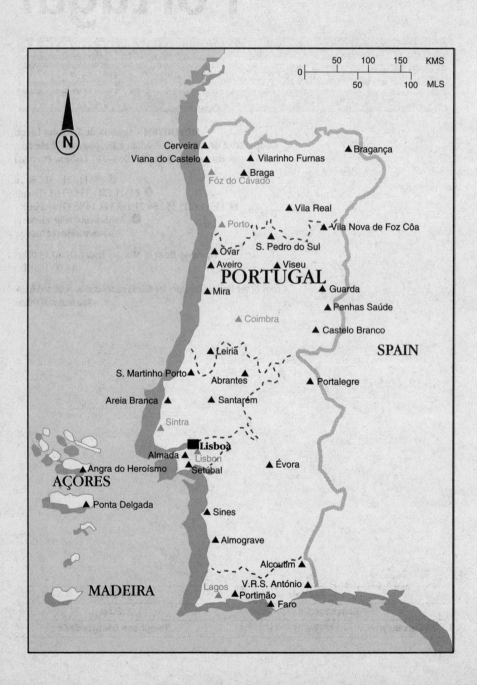

50   100   150   KMS
0
50   100   MLS

N

Cerveira ▲
Viana do Castelo ▲   ▲ Vilarinho Furnas   ▲ Bragança
                             ▲ Braga
Fóz do Cávado

                             ▲ Vila Real

▲ Porto   ▲ Vila Nova de Foz Côa

▲ Ovar   S. Pedro do Sul ▲
▲ Aveiro   ▲ Viseu
                         PORTUGAL
▲ Mira   ▲ Guarda

                          ▲ Penhas Saúde
▲ Coimbra
                          ▲ Castelo Branco

                                        SPAIN
        ▲ Leiria

S. Martinho Porto ▲
                ▲ Abrantes
Areia Branca ▲   ▲ Santarém   ▲ Portalegre

    Sintra

        ■ **Lisboa**
Almada ▲   Lisbon
        ▲ Setúbal   ▲ Évora
▲ Angra do Heroísmo
AÇORES

▲ Ponta Delgada   ▲ Sines

                               ▲ Almograve

                                    Alcoutim ▲
MADEIRA   Lagos   V.R.S. António ▲
                        ▲ Portimão
                             ▲ Faro

English

PORTUGUESE HOSTELS

Hostels are generally open 24hrs although most usually close during part of the day for cleaning. Receptions are normally open 09.00-12.00; 18.00-24.00hrs. If telephoning the hostel please only do so during the reception opening times. The maximum length of stay at any one hostel is 8 consecutive nights, although this rule can be waived at the discretion of the warden. Expect to pay in the regionof 1200-2900 (5.92-14.32 ECU) escudos per night including bedlinen and breakfast. Meals are available, with prices ranging from 250 escudos for a snack to 900 escudos for lunch or dinner. All advance bookings should be made through the Portuguese Association national office.

PASSPORTS/VISAS

Many foreign visitors do not require a visa to visit Portugal provided they do not intend to stay for longer than 60-90 days. Please check before travelling.

HEALTH

Principal residential areas have hospitals and clinics which provide a 24 hour emergency service. Other places usually have clinics open 08.00-20.00hrs.

In Portugal, look for the word 'Farmácia'. They are open 09.00-13.00hrs and 15.00-19.00hrs weekdays and 09.00-13.00hrs on Saturdays. There is always a chemist on duty for emergencies and details can be found in the local press, from telephone operators and in chemists shop windows.

BANKING HOURS

Money changing is exclusive to banks, open to the public 08.30-15.00hrs, Monday to Friday. During the summer, Christmas and Easter, you can change money throughout the day in main tourist areas, frontiers and airports. Travellers cheques and credit cards are accepted in Portugal.

POST OFFICES

Post Offices are normally open 09.00-18.00hrs, Monday to Friday.

TRAVEL

Rail

Eurail and Inter-Rail cards are valid but a supplement must be paid on express trains. The Portuguese Railway Information Desks at Lisbon, Porto and Coimbra are open between 08.00 and 20.00hrs.

Bus

Portugal's bus network provides a fast and frequent service.

Ferry

There are frequent fast services in 4 major locations: Tagus River (from Lisbon to several localities); Setubal to Troia, Vila Nova de Cerveira to Spain and Vila Real de Santo António to Spain.

Driving

The rule of the road in Portugal is drive on the right. When driving seat belts must be worn. Unless otherwise indicated, vehicles coming from the right have priority. Sign posting conforms to the international code. Speed limits are 50 kmph in built up areas, 90 kmph on the open road and 120 kmph on motorways.

The legal alcohol limit for drivers is below 0.5 grammes per litre. Penalties can be either a heavy fine, confiscation or withdrawal of licence.

Français

AUBERGES DE JEUNESSE PORTUGAISES

Les auberges sont en général ouvertes 24h sur 24 bien que la plupart soient fermées une partie de la journée pour nettoyage. L'accueil est d'ordinaire ouvert de 9h à 12h et de 18h à 24h. Si vous téléphonez à une auberge, veuillez ne le faire que pendant les heures d'ouverture de la réception. La durée maximale d'un séjour dans une auberge est de 8 nuits consécutives, bien que ceci reste à la discrétion du directeur. Une nuit vous coûtera entre 1200 et 2900 ESC (5.92-14.32 ECU), draps et petit déjeuner compris. Il y a un service de repas et les prix varient entre 240 ESC pour un casse-croûte et 900 ESC pour le déjeuner ou le dîner. Toutes les réservations doivent être faites auprès du bureau national de l'Association portugaise.

PASSEPORTS ET VISAS

De nombreux visiteurs étrangers n'ont pas besoin de visa pour visiter le Portugal, du moment où ils ne comptent pas y rester plus de 60 à 90 jours. Veuillez vérifier avant votre départ.

SOINS MEDICAUX

Les zones résidentielles principales sont équipées d'hôpitaux et de cliniques qui assurent un service d'urgences jour et nuit. Les autres zones ont en principe des cliniques ouvertes de 8h à 20h.

Au Portugal, cherchez le mot "Farmácia". Les pharmacies sont ouvertes de 9h à 13h et de 15h à 19h en semaine et de 9h à 13h le samedi. Il y a toujours une pharmacie de garde pour les urgences et vous trouverez leur adresse dans la presse locale, en appelant les standardistes du service téléphonique et en regardant la notice dans la vitrine des pharmacies.

HEURES D'OUVERTURE DES BANQUES

Le change de devises ne se fait que dans les banques, qui sont ouvertes au public de 8h30 à 15h, du lundi au vendredi. En été, à Noël et à Pâques, il est possible de changer de l'argent tout au long de la journée dans les principales régions touristiques, aux frontières et dans les aéroports. Les chèques de voyage et les cartes de crédit sont acceptées au Portugal.

BUREAUX DE POSTE

Les bureaux de poste sont normalement ouverts de 9h à 18h du lundi au vendredi.

DEPLACEMENTS

Trains

Les cartes Eurail et Inter-Rail sont valides mais il faut payer un supplément pour les trains express. Les bureaux de renseignements des chemins de fer portugais à Lisbonne, Porto et Coimbra sont ouverts entre 8h et 20h.

Autobus

Le réseau d'autobus portugais assure un service rapide et fréquent.

Ferry-boats

Il y a des services rapides et fréquents dans 4 endroits principaux: sur le Tage (de Lisbonne vers plusieurs régions); à Setubal à destination de Troia, à Vila Nova de Cerveira à destination de l'Espagne et à Vila Real de Santo António à destination de l'Espagne.

Automobiles

La conduite se fait à droite au Portugal. Le port des ceintures de sécurité est obligatoire. Sauf indication contraire, les véhicules venant de la droite ont priorité. Les panneaux de signalisation routière sont conformes à la signalisation internationale. Les limites de vitesse sont de 50 km/h dans les agglomérations, 90 km/h à l'extérieur des agglomérations et 120 km/h sur les autoroutes.

La limite légale d'alcool dans le sang pour les conducteurs est de 0,5 grammes par litre. Les contraventions peuvent être soit une forte amende, soit la confiscation ou le retrait du permis.

Deutsch

PORTUGIESISCHE JUGENDHERBERGEN

Die Herbergen sind normalerweise 24 Stunden geöffnet. Einige Häuser sind aus Reinigungszwecken tagsüber geschlossen. Der Empfang ist normalerweise von 09.00-24.00 Uhr geöffnet. Telefonisch sollte man sich nur während der Empfangszeiten an eine Jugendherberge wenden. Der Höchstaufenthalt in einer Herberge ist auf 8 aufeinanderfolgende Nächte beschränkt. Es liegt jedoch im Ermessen des Verwalters, auf die Einhaltung dieser Vorschrift zu verzichten. Es ist mit einem Preis von 1200-2900 Esc pro Nacht (5.92-14.32 ECU), einschließlich Bettwäsche und Frühstück, zu rechnen. Mahlzeiten sind auch erhältlich. Die Preise variieren zwischen 250 Esc für einen Imbiß und 900 Esc für das Mittag- oder Abendessen. Alle Voranmeldungen sind über die Geschäftsstelle des portugiesischen Verbandes vorzunehmen.

PÄSSE UND VISA

Die meisten ausländischen Reisenden brauchen für den Besuch Portugals kein Visum, sofern sie nicht länger als 60-90 Tage im Land bleiben wollen. Bitte erkundigen Sie sich vor der Abreise.

GESUNDHEIT

In den wichtigsten Wohnbereichen gibt es Krankenhäuser und Kliniken, die einen 24-stündigen Notdienst bieten. An anderen Orten sind Kliniken von 08.00-20.00 Uhr geöffnet.

Schauen Sie sich in Portugal nach dem Wort 'Farmácia' um. Sie sind werktags von 09.00-13.00 Uhr und von 15.00-19.00 Uhr und samstags von 09.00-13.00 Uhr geöffnet. Für Notfälle hat immer ein Apotheker Notdienst. Nähere Einzelheiten stehen in der Ortspresse oder sind im Schaufenster von Apotheken angeschlagen. Auch die Fernsprechvermittlung erteilt Auskunft.

GESCHÄFTSSTUNDEN DER BANKEN

Geld kann nur auf Banken umgetauscht werden, die für die Öffentlichkeit montags bis freitags von 08.30-15.00 Uhr geöffnet sind. Im Sommer, an Weihnachten und an Ostern kann Geld in den wichtigsten Fremdenverkehrsgebieten, an den Grenzen und auf Flughäfen den ganzen Tag über umgetauscht werden. Reiseschecks und Kreditkarten werden in Portugal ebenfalls angenommen.

POSTÄMTER

Postämter sind gewöhnlich montags bis freitags von 09.00-18.00 Uhr geöffnet.

REISEN

Eisenbahn

Eurail- und Inter-Rail-Karten gelten in Portugal, aber für Expreßzüge muß ein Zuschlag bezahlt werden. Die Informationsstellen der portugiesischen Eisenbahn in Lissabon, Porto und Coimbra sind zwischen 08.00 und 20.00 Uhr geöffnet.

Busse

Das Busnetz von Portugal bietet einen schnellen und häufigen Verkehr.

Fähren

Von 4 Hauptorten aus gibt es einen schnellen und häufigen Fährenverkehr: auf dem Tajo (von Lissabon an mehrere Orte); von Setúbal nach Troia ; von Vila Nova de Cerveira nach Spanien und von Vila Real de Santo António nach Spanien.

Autofahren.

In Portugal herrscht Rechtsverkehr. Sicherheitsgurte müssen getragen werden. Wenn nichts anderes angegeben, haben Fahrzeuge, die von rechts kommen, Vorfahrt. Die Beschilderung entspricht den internationalen Gepflogenheiten. Das Tempolimit beträgt in geschlossenen Ortschaften 50 Stundenkilometer, auf Landstraßen 90 Stundenkilometer und auf Autobahnen 120 Stundenkilometer.

Die zulässige Alkoholgrenze liegt für Fahrer unter 0,5 g pro Liter. Zuwiderhandlungen werden entweder mit einer hohen Geldstrafe, Beschlagnahme oder Entzug des Führerscheins bestraft.

Español

ALBERGUES JUVENILES PORTUGUESES

Los albergues abren generalmente las 24 horas del día, pero la mayoría suelen cerrar parte del día para la limpieza. La recepción suele estar abierta de 09.00 a 12.00 horas y de 18.00 a 24.00 horas. Si desea llamar al albergue, se ruega hacerlo solamente durante el horario de apertura de la recepción. La estancia máxima en cualquier albergue es de 8 noches consecutivas, si bien esta norma puede no aplicarse a discreción del encargado. Los precios oscilan entre 1.200 y 2.900 escudos (5,92-14,32 Euros) por noche incluyendo sábanas y desayuno. Se sirven comidas, cuyos precios varían entre 250 escudos por un bocadillo hasta 900 escudos por el almuerzo o la cena. Todas las reservas anticipadas deben hacerse a través de la oficina nacional de la Asociación portuguesa.

PASAPORTES Y VISADOS

Los ciudadanos de numerosos países no necesitan visado para entrar en Portugal siempre que no tengan previsto quedarse en el país más de 60-90 días. Se ruega confirmarlo antes de salir de viaje.

INFORMACIÓN SANITARIA

Las principales áreas residenciales tienen hospitales y clínicas con un servicio de urgencias abierto las 24 horas del día. Otros lugares suelen tener clínicas abiertas de 08.00 a 20.00 horas.

En Portugal busque la palabra 'Farmácia'. Están abiertas de 09.00 a 13.00 horas y de 15.00 a 19.00 horas los días laborables, y de 09.00 a 13.00 horas los sábados. Siempre hay una farmacia de guardia para las urgencias. Para información sobre estas, consulte la prensa local, telefonistas y carteles colocados en los escaparates de las farmacias.

HORARIO DE LOS BANCOS

El cambio de moneda sólo puede hacerse en los bancos, abiertos al público de 08.30 a 15.00 horas de lunes a viernes. En verano, Navidad y Semana Santa se puede cambiar moneda durante todo el día en las principales zonas turísticas, fronteras y aeropuertos. En Portugal se aceptan los cheques de viajero y las tarjetas de crédito.

OFICINAS DE CORREOS

Las oficinas de correos suelen abrir de 09.00 a 18.00 horas de lunes a viernes.

DESPLAZAMIENTOS

Tren

Las tarjetas Eurail e Inter-Rail son válidas, pero hay que pagar un suplemento en los expresos. Los Mostradores de Información de CP (compañía ferroviaria portuguesa) de Lisboa, Porto y Coimbra abren de 08.00 a 20.00 horas.

Autobús

La red de autobuses de Portugal presta un servicio rápido y frecuente.

Ferry

Hay servicios rápidos y frecuentes en 4 puntos del país: en el río Tajo (de Lisboa a varias localidades); de Setubal a Troia, de Vila Nova de Cerveira a España y de Vila Real de Santo António a España.

Automóvil

En Portugal se circula por la derecha. Hay que llevar puesto el cinturón de seguridad. A menos que se indique lo contrario, se da prioridad a los vehículos que vengan de la derecha. La señalización de tráfico cumple con el código internacional. Los límites de velocidad son de 50 km/h en las zonas edificadas, 90 km/h en carretera y 120 km/h en las autopistas.

El límite legal de alcoholemia para conductores es de menos de 0,5 gramos por litro. La sanción por infringir esta norma puede ir desde una multa importante, a la confiscación o retirada del permiso de conducir.

> **If you start now, you will know a lot next year that you don't know now, and that you will not know next year, if you wait.**
>
> Si tu commences maintenant, tu sauras beaucoup de choses l'année prochaine que tu ne sais pas aujourd'hui et que tu ne sauras pas l'année prochaine, si tu attends.
>
> **Mach' Dich heute auf den Weg, dann wirst Du im nächsten Jahr eine Menge mehr als heute wissen, aber im nächsten Jahr dies nicht wissen, wenn Du wartest.**
>
> Si empiezas hoy, el año que viene sabrás muchas cosas que hoy no sabes y que no sabrás el año que viene si tardas en empezar.
>
> **The William Feather Magazine**

Lisbon

Pousada de Juventude de Lisboa,
Rua Andrade Corvo 46,
1050-009 Lisboa.
☎ (21) 3532696
🖷 (21) 3537541

Open Dates:	🗓
Open Hours:	🕐
Reservations:	**R** IBN
Price Range:	PTE 1900-2900
	€ 9.48-14.46
	BB inc 🍴
Beds:	164 - 9x^2🛏 17x^4🛏 13x^6🛏
Facilities:	♿ 🕿 2x 🕿 🍴 ☕ ⛺ 📺 📖
	🌄 1 x 🍷 📷 🔟 ⬇ 🅿 ℹ 🎣 ⊘ 🎡
Directions:	6N from city centre
✈	Lisbon 10km
A🚌	91 (Aerobus) 50m
⛴	Lisbon 8km
🚂	Santa Apolónia 10km
🚌	44, 45, 90 50m ap Picoas
U	Picoas 50m
Attractions:	🚶 🏊 1km ⛵ 3km

There are 2 hostels in Lisbon. See following pages.

Porto

Rua Paulo da Gama 551,
4169-006 Porto.
☎ (22) 6177257
🖷 (22) 6177247

Open Dates:	🗓
Open Hours:	🕐
Reservations:	**R** IBN
Price Range:	PTE 1900-2500
	€ 9.48-12.47
	BB inc 🍴
Beds:	164 - 24x^2🛏 29x^4🛏
Facilities:	♿ 🕿 🕿 🍴 ☕ ⛺ 📺 🌄 1 x 🍷
	📷 🔟 ⬇ 🅿 ℹ 🎣 ⊘
Directions:	7SE from city centre
✈	SÁ Carneiro 20km
A🚌	36, 56 20km
🚂	São Bento 8km
🚌	35 100m ap Paulo da Gama 100m
Attractions:	🚲 2km 🚶 ⛵ 500m

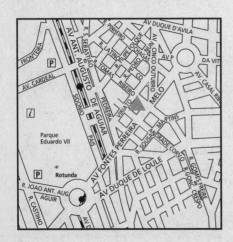

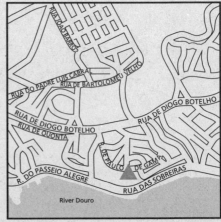

Location/Address	Telephone No. Fax No.	Beds	Opening Dates	Facilities
▲ Abrantes - Abrantes Av. Dr. Francisco Sá, Carneiro, 2200 Abrantes.		80	🔲12	⚐ P
△ *Alcoutim* *8970 Alcoutim.*	☎ *(281) 546004* ✆ *(281) 546004*	*54*	🔲12	0.5N ⚐ P
▲ Almada Quinta do Bucelinho-Pragal-Almada, 2800 Almada.	☎ (21) 2943491/ 2943492 ✆ (21) 2943497	120	🔲12	2E P
▲ Almograve Almograve - 7630 Odemira.	☎ (283) 640000 ✆ (283) 647035	100	🔲12	⚐ P
▲ Angra Do Heroísmo Negrito, S.Mateus, 9700 Angra Do Heroísmo, Ilha Terceira-Açores.	☎ (295) 642095 ✆ (295) 642096	62	🔲12	1SW CC P
△ *Areia Branca* *Praia da Areia Branca, 2530 Lourinhã.*	☎ *(261) 422127* ✆ *(261) 422127*	*116*	🔲12	P
△ *Aveiro* *Rua das Pombas, Apartado 182, 3810 Aveiro*	☎ *(234) 420536* ✆ *(234) 382395*	*52*	🔲12	2NW P
△ *Braga* *Rua de Santa Margarida 6, 4710-306 Braga.*	☎ *(253) 616163* ✆ *(253) 616163*	*62*	🔲12	2NE P
▲ Bragança - Bragança Forte de S.João (near Câmara Municipal) 5300 Bragança.	☎ (273) 304600 ✆ (273) 326136	96	🔲12	⚐ P
△ *Castelo Branco* *Rua Dr. Francisco José Palmeiro,* *6000 Castelo Branco*	☎ *(272) 323838* ✆ *(272) 326950*	*64*	🔲12	2E P
▲ Coimbra IBN Rua Henriques Seco 14, 3000-145 Coimbra.	☎ (239) 822955 ✆ (239) 821730	70	🔲12	3NW ⚐ P
▲ Évora Rua Miguel Bombarda 40, 7000-919 Évora	☎ (266) 744848 ✆ (266) 744843	90	🔲12	P
△ *Faro* *Rua da PSP, 8000 Faro*	☎ *(289) 826521* ✆ *(289) 826521*	*56*	🔲12	1.5SW ⚐ P
▲ Foz do Cávado IBN Alameda Bom Jesus - Fão, 4740 Esposende	☎ (253) 981790 ✆ (253) 981790	83	🔲12	⚐ P
△ *Guarda* *Av. Alexandre Herculano, 6300 Guarda*	☎ *(271) 224482* ✆ *(271) 224482*	*56*	🔲12	1N P
▲ Lagos IBN Rua Lançarote de Freitas 50, 8600-605 Lagos.	☎ (282) 761970 ✆ (282) 769684	62	🔲12	0.5N ⚐
▲ Leiria Largo Cândido dos Reis 9, 2400-112 Leiria.	☎ (244) 831868 ✆ (244) 831868	52	🔲12	⚐
▲ Lisbon - Parque Das Nações Via De Moscavide, Lote 47101, 1800 Lisboa	☎ (21) 8920890 ✆ (21) 8920891	92	🔲12	10NE ⚐ P
▲ Lisbon IBN **Pousada de Juventude de Lisboa,** **Rua Andrade Corvo 46, 1050-009 Lisboa.**	☎ (21) 3532696 ✆ (21) 3537541	164	🔲12	6N
▲ Lisbon - Catalazete - Catalazete IBN Estrada Marginal (near Inatel), Catalazete, 2780 Oeiras	☎ (21) 4430638 ✆ (21) 4419267	94	🔲12	⚐ P

Location/Address	Telephone No. Fax No.	Beds	Opening Dates	Facilities
Lisboa ☞ **Lisbon**				
▲ **Mira** - PJ de Mira Pousada de Juventude de Mira, Parque de Campismo de Jovens, 3070 Praia de Mira.	☎ (231) 471275 ✆ (231) 471275	58	🔲	††† ⑩ Ⓡ 7E ☞ P ☕
△ *Mira - Mira Youth Camping Park* *Parque de Campismo de Jovens,* *3070 Praia de Mira.*	☎ *(231) 471275* ✆ *(231) 471275*	*500*	*15.06–15.09*	⑩ Ⓡ 7E ☞ P
Oporto ☞ **Porto**				
▲ **Ovar** Av D Manuel I (Est Nac 327) 3880 Ovar.	☎ (256) 591832 ✆ (256) 591832	84	🔲	††† ⑩ Ⓡ 7NW ♿ P ☕
▲ **Penhas da Saúde** Serra da Estrela, 6200 Covilhã.	☎ (275) 335375 ✆ (275) 335375	108	🔲	††† ⑩ Ⓡ ♿ ☞ P ☕
▲ **Ponta Delgada** Rua S.Francisco Xavier, 9500 Ponta Delgada, Ilha S.Miguel-Açores.	☎ (296) 629431 ✆ (296) 629431	92	🔲	††† Ⓡ 0.2E P
△ *Portalegre* *Estrada do Bonfim, Apartado 2, 7300 Partalegre*	☎ *(245) 330971* ✆ *(245) 202665*	*52*	🔲	Ⓡ 1.5E P
△ *Portimão* *Lugar do Coca Maravilhas,* *8500-320 Portimão.*	☎ *(282) 491804* ✆ *(282) 491804*	*180*	🔲	††† ⑩ Ⓡ 4N ☞ P ☕
▲ **Porto** ⟦IBN⟧ **Rua Paulo da Gama 551, 4169-006 Porto.**	☎ (22) 6177257 ✆ (22) 6177247	164	🔲	††† ⑩ Ⓡ 7SE ♿ ☞ P
△ *Santarém* *Av. Grupo Forcados Amadores de Santarém, 1.*	☎ *(243) 391914* ✆ *(243) 391914*	*36*	🔲	Ⓡ 1N ♿ P
△ *Setúbal* *Largo José Afonso, 2900 Setúbal*	☎ *(265) 534431* ✆ *(265) 532965*	*64*	🔲	Ⓡ 1E P
△ *São Martinho-Alfeizerão* *Estrada Nacional 8, 2460 Alfeizerão.*	☎ *(262) 999506* ✆ *(262) 999506*	*62*	🔲	††† ⑩ Ⓡ 2NE ☞ P
▲ **Sines** Estrada da Floresta - Edificio E, 7520-137 Sines.	☎ (269) 635361 ✆ (269) 635361	104	🔲	††† ⑩ Ⓡ 1NE ♿ P ☕
▲ **Sintra** ⟦IBN⟧ Stª Eufémia, S. Pedro de Sintra, 2710 Sintra.	☎ (21) 9241210 ✆ (21) 9241210	58	🔲	††† ⑩ Ⓡ 4S ♿ P
▲ **S.Pedro Do Sul** Termas De S.Pedro Do Sul, 3660 S.Pedro Do Sul.	☎ (232) 724543/ 4 ✆ (232) 724541	134	🔲	††† ⑩ Ⓡ ♿ P ☕
▲ **Viana Do Castelo** - Viana Do Castelo Rua da Arçogoza (Zona da Azenha D.Prior), 4900 Viana do Castelo.	☎ (258) 820870 ✆ (258) 820871	82	🔲	††† ⑩ Ⓡ ♿ ☞ P 🅾 ☕
△ *Vila Nova de Cerveira* *Largo 16 de Fevereiro 21,* *4920 Vila Nova de Cerveira.*	☎ *(251) 796113* ✆ *(251) 796113*	*56*	🔲	††† Ⓡ 0.3NE ☞ P
▲ **Vila Nova De Foz Côa** Caminho Vicinal, Currauteles, No 5, 5150 Vila Nova De Foz Côa.	☎ (279) 768190 ✆ (279) 768191	84	🔲	††† ⑩ Ⓡ ♿ ☞ P 🅾 ☕
△ *Vila Real* *Rua Dr Manuel Cardona, 5000 Vila Real*	☎ *(259) 373193* ✆ *(259) 374744*	*64*	🔲	Ⓡ 1.5W ♿ P

Location/Address	Telephone No. Fax No.	Beds	Opening Dates	Facilities
△ *Viseu* *Portal do Fontelo, Carreira dos Carvalhos,* *3500 Viseu*	☎ *(232) 420620* ✆ *(232) 420620*	*70*	▥12	Ⓡ 2NW ♿ ✇ Ⓟ
△ *Vila Real de Santo António* *Rua Dr. Sousa Martins, 40,* *8900 Vila Real de Santo António*	☎ *(281) 544565* ✆ *(281) 544565*	*56*	▥12	ⅢⅢ Ⓡ ✇ Ⓟ ▯
▲ **Vilarinho das Furnas** Parque Nacional do Gerês, São João do Campo, 4840 Terras do Bouro.	☎ (253) 351339 ✆ (253) 351339	180	▥12	ⅢⅢ �ⓄⅠ Ⓡ Ⓟ ▯

Travel, instead of broadening the mind, often merely lengthens the conversation.

Voyager, plutôt que d'élargir l'esprit a tendance simplement à rallonger la conversation.

Anstatt zu bilden, bietet Reisen oft lediglich mehr Stoff zur Unterhaltung.

A menudo, en vez de ampliar los horizontes de las personas, lo único que hacen los viajes es alargar la conversación.

Elizabeth Drew

Net Savings @ Hostelling International

The advantages are clear

HOSTELLING INTERNATIONAL

netsavings@hostellinginternational.org.uk

Scotland

ECOSSE
SCHOTTLAND
ESCOCIA

**Scottish Youth Hostels Association,
7 Glebe Crescent, Stirling,
FK8 2JA, Scotland.**

Central Reservations Service
☎ (44) (08701) 553255
🖷 (44) (1786) 891350
✉ reservations@syha.org.uk
CRS Hours, 08.00-20.00hrs

The National Office ☎ (44) (1786) 891400
🖷 (44) (1786) 891333
✉ info@syha.org.uk
www.syha.org.uk.

Office Hours: Monday-Friday, 08.45-17.00hrs

Travel Section: c/o Scottish Youth Hostels Association
7 Glebe Crescent, Stirling,
FK8 2JA, Scotland.

☎ (44) (1786) 891301

A copy of the Hostel Directory for this Country can be obtained from:
The National Office.

Capital:	Edinburgh	**Population:**	5,112,100
Language:	English	**Size:**	78,781 sq km
Currency:	£ (Sterling)	**Telephone Country Code:**	44

Scotland

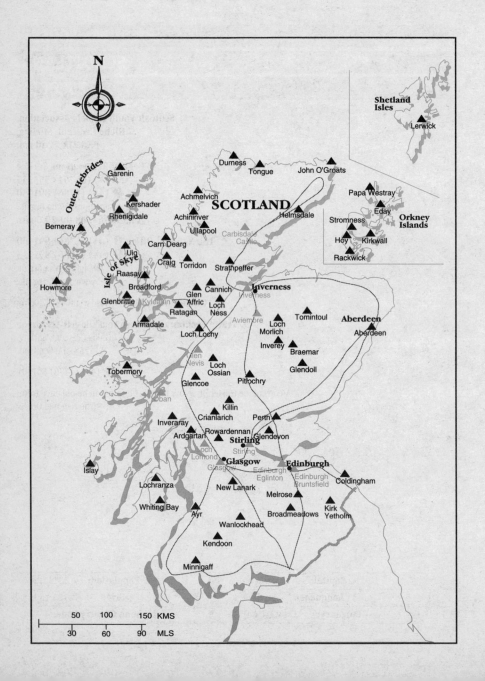

N

Shetland Isles
Lerwick

Outer Hebrides

Garenin

Durness
Tongue
John O'Groats

Achmelvich
Kershader
Rhenigidale
Achininver
SCOTLAND
Helmsdale

Papa Westray
Stromness
Eday
Orkney Islands
Hoy
Kirkwall
Rackwick

Berneray
Ullapool
Carbisdale Castle

Howmore
Carn Dearg
Uig
Craig Torridon
Strathpeffer
Isle of Skye
Raasay
Broadford
Cannich
Inverness
Inverness
Glenbrittle
Glen Affric
Loch Ness
Armadale
Ratagan
Tomintoul
Aberdeen
Loch Lochy
Loch Morlich
Aberdeen
Aviemore
Inverey
Braemar
Tobermory
Glen Nevis
Loch Ossian
Glendoll
Glencoe
Pitlochry
Oban

Killin
Crianlarich
Perth
Inveraray
Rowardennan
Glendevon
Ardgartan
Stirling
Islay
Stirling
Loch Lomond
Glasgow
Edinburgh
Glasgow
Edinburgh
Edinburgh
Bruntsfield
Coldingham
Lochranza
New Lanark
Eglinton
Whiting Bay
Melrose
Ayr
Broadmeadows
Kirk Yetholm
Wanlockhead
Kendoon
Minnigaff

| 50 | 100 | 150 | KMS |
| 30 | 60 | 90 | MLS |

English

SCOTTISH HOSTELS

More than 80 Scottish Youth Hostels offer a wonderful selection of places to stay, from a Highland castle to remote loch-side or island locations. There are hostels in all major cities, generally in historic buildings. Hostels form an ideal base for the activities this varied country can offer, and many offer activity programmes.

You can book all hostels through the Central Reservation Service (CRS). Expect to pay from £6.00-£16.50 (price includes bed linen).

All the Scottish Youth Hostel Association's hostels meet the Hostelling International Assured Standards, and the entries in this section are graded accordingly (see page 4 for details).

Standard grade hostels ▲ are open 07.00-23.45hrs although some may only offer access to limited facilities between 11.00-17.00hrs ie a common room and toilets. Check when booking. Certain hostels have more facilities and are open all day 07.00-02.00hrs (latest booking-in time 23.15hrs).

Simple hostels △ generally in remote and beautiful locations have less facilities and usually close between 10.30-17.00hrs.

Most hostels offer discounts on local attractions/facilities, which you can claim with your Hostelling International card.

At some hostels meals are only available for groups by arrangement. Please check with individual hostels.

PASSPORTS AND VISAS

You will need a valid passport. Not many visitors now require visas but do check in advance.

HEALTH

An international Certificate of Vaccination is not required to enter the UK, but check if one is needed for re-entry into your own country.

Visitors are only eligible for free **emergency** treatment at National Health Service Accident and Emergency departments of hospitals. If you are admitted to hospital as an in-patient you will be asked to pay unless you are a national of an EC country, resident in any member country, or a national or resident of a country which has a reciprocal health care agreement with the UK. You are therefore strongly advised to take out adequate insurance cover before travelling to Britain.

BANKING HOURS

Generally open weekdays 09.30-16.30hrs. Closed on Saturdays, Sundays and Public Holidays.

POST OFFICES

Open weekdays 09.00-17.30hrs and Saturdays 09.00-12.30hrs. They are closed on Sundays and Public Holidays.

SHOPPING HOURS

Most shops are open Monday-Saturday 09.00-17.30hrs. Some newsagents and food stores open from as early as 07.30hrs until as late as 20.00hrs, or 22.00hrs in well populated areas.

TRAVEL

Rail

There are main railway stations in Edinburgh and Glasgow with services to most parts of mainland Scotland.

Bus

Travel by national bus services is economical and there is access to all parts. In more remote areas the Royal Mail operates Postbuses which carry passengers as well as delivering post.

Ferry

There are ferry services to all populated Scottish islands. The two main operators are Caledonian MacBrayne on the west coast and P&O Ferries on the north coast.

Driving

Driving is on the left side. The national speed limit is 60 mph, increasing to 70mph on motorways. In built up areas the limit is usually 30mph. In remote areas single track roads with passing places can be expected, and drivers should not impede other road users.

Français

AUBERGES DE JEUNESSE ECOSSAISES

Plus de 80 auberges écossaises vous offrent un choix fabuleux de lieux de séjour, qu'il s'agisse d'un château dans les Highlands ou d'un endroit isolé sur les bords d'un loch ou sur une île. Il existe des auberges dans toutes les grandes villes, généralement dans des monuments historiques. Les auberges écossaises sont une base idéale pour pratiquer toutes les activités que ce pays varié est en mesure d'offrir. De nombreux établissements proposent d'ailleurs leurs propres programmes d'activités.

Vous pouvez réserver dans toutes nos auberges grâce au Service Central de Réservation (Central Reservation Service, CRS).

Les tarifs vont de £6.00 à £16.50, draps compris.

Toutes les auberges de L'Association Ecossaise des Auberges de Jeunesse satisfont aux exigences du Plan de Garantie des Normes en Auberge et chacune d'entre elles a été classée en conséquence (voir page 13 pour plus de détails).

Toutes les auberges de catégorie standard ▲ sont ouvertes entre 7h00 et 23h45, bien que certains établissements ne permettent qu'un accès limité (c.à.d. à une salle commune et des toilettes), entre 11h00 et 17h00. Vérifiez à la réservation.

Certaines auberges disposent d'installations plus sophistiquées et sont ouvertes toute la journée, de 7h00 à 2h00 (dernier délai pour l'enregistrement: 23h15).

Les auberges 'simples' △ , généralement situées dans des endroits aussi isolés que beaux, sont moins équipées et sont habituellement fermées entre 10h30 et 17h00.

La plupart de nos auberges offrent des réductions sur les attractions et animations touristiques locales, qu'il vous sera possible d'obtenir grâce à votre carte d'adhérent Hostelling International.

PASSEPORTS ET VISAS

Les voyageurs doivent être munis d'un passeport valide. De nos jours, peu de visiteurs doivent être en possession d'un visa mais il est préférable de vérifier à l'avance.

SOINS MEDICAUX

Il n'est pas nécessaire d'être muni d'un certificat international de vaccination mais il vous est conseillé de vérifier qu'il ne vous en faudra pas un pour rentrer dans votre pays. Les visiteurs ne peuvent bénéficier que d'un traitement **d'urgence** gratuit dans les services d'accidents et d'urgence des hôpitaux de la Sécurité Sociale. Si vous êtes hospitalisé, il vous faudra payer à moins d'être un citoyen d'un pays de l'UE, de résider dans un pays membre ou d'être un citoyen ou de résider dans un pays ayant passé un accord médical réciproque avec le Royaume-Uni. Il vous est donc fortement conseillé de souscrire à une police d'assurance avant votre départ pour la Grande-Bretagne.

HEURES D'OUVERTURE DES BANQUES

Les banques sont en général ouvertes en semaine de 9h30 à 16h30. Elles sont fermées le samedi, le dimanche et les jours fériés.

BUREAUX DE POSTE

Ils sont ouverts en semaine de 9h à 17h30 et le samedi de 9h à 12h30. Ils sont fermés le dimanche et les jours fériés.

HEURES D'OUVERTURE DES MAGASINS

La plupart des magasins sont ouverts du lundi au samedi de 9h à 17h30. Certaines maisons de la presse et certains magasins d'alimentation sont ouverts à partir de 7h30 jusqu'à 20h, et dans les secteurs très peuplés, certains restent ouverts jusqu'à 22h.

DEPLACEMENTS

Trains

Les gares principales d'Edimbourg et de Glasgow assurent des services qui desservent la plupart des régions de l'Ecosse continentale.

Autobus

Les services nationaux de bus sont bon marché et desservent toutes les régions. Dans les régions plus isolées, le Royal Mail (service des postes) utilise des "bus postaux" (Postbuses) qui transportent des passagers tout en assurant la distribution du courrier.

Ferry-boats

Les bateaux desservent toutes les îles peuplées d'Ecosse. Les deux compagnies principales sont Caledonian MacBrayne sur la côte ouest et P & O Ferries sur la côte nord.

Automobiles

La conduite est à gauche. Les limitations de vitesse sont de 95km/h sur les routes nationales et de 110km/h sur les autoroutes. La vitesse dans les agglomérations est en principe limitée à 45km/h. Dans les régions isolées, il est fréquent de trouver des chemins à une seule voie où ont été aménagés des aires de croisement pour véhicules; les conducteurs doivent donc être courtois envers les autres usagers de la route.

Deutsch

SCHOTTISCHE JUGENDHERBERGEN

Mehr als 80 Jugendherbergen des Schottischen Jugendherbergsverbandes (SYHA) bieten Reisenden eine große Auswahl an Unterkunftsmöglichkeiten - von einem Schloß im schottischen Hochland bis zu einer abgelegenen Herberge am See oder auf einer Insel. Es gibt Jugendherbergen in allen Großstädten, meist in historischen Gebäuden. Herbergen sind ein idealer Ausgangspunkt für die Freizeitgestaltung, die dieses verschiedenartige Land bietet sowie für eine Vielzahl von Aktivprogrammen.

Buchungen für alle Herbergen können über den Zentralen Reservierungsdienst (CRS) vorgenommen werden. Es ist mit einem Preis von 6.00 £ -16.50 £, einschließlich Bettwäsche, zu rechnen.

Alle Herbergen des Schottischen Jugendherbergsverbandes stehen im Einklang mit den 'Zugesicherten Standards' des Hostelling International. Die Kategorien sind aus der jeweiligen Eintragung ersichtlich (siehe Seite 20 für Einzelheiten).

Jugendherbergen mit normalen Standards ▲ sind von 07.00-23.45 Uhr geöffnet, obwohl manche zwischen 11.00 und 17.00 Uhr nur eingeschränkten Zugang bieten, z.B. zum Gemeinschaftsraum und zu den Toiletten. Erfragen Sie dies bitte bei Ihrer Buchung. Bestimmte Jugendherbergen bieten zusätzliche Leistungen an und sind ganztägig von 07.00-02.00 Uhr (Anmeldungen spätestens um 23.15 Uhr) geöffnet.

Jugendherbergen einfachen Standards △ sind meist in entlegenen und landschaftlich schönen Standorten anzutreffen. Sie verfügen über eine einfache Ausstattung und sind gewöhnlich zwischen 10.30 und 17.00 Uhr aufgrund von Personalkosten geschlossen. Mit der Hostelling International Mitgliedskarte sind auch häufig Vergünstigungen bei verschiedenen örtlichen Attraktionen und Einrichtungen verbunden.

PÄSSE UND VISA

Sie brauchen einen gültigen Reisepaß. Ein Visum wird nur noch von wenigen Reisenden benötigt. Sie sollten sich aber im voraus erkundigen.

GESUNDHEIT

Für die Einreise nach Großbritannien braucht man keine internationale Impfbescheinigung. Sie sollten sich aber erkundigen, ob eine solche Bescheinigung bei der Wiedereinreise in Ihr Heimatland verlangt wird.

Eine Krankenversicherung ist notwendig, da Besucher nur **im Notfall** Anspruch auf kostenlose Krankenhausbehandlung durch die Unfall- oder Notfallabteilung des Staatlichen Gesundheitsdienstes haben. Wenn Sie zur stationären Behandlung in ein Krankenhaus eingeliefert oder an eine ambulante Abteilung überwiesen werden, müssen Sie bezahlen. Es sei denn, Sie sind Staatsbürger eines EG-Landes, oder Sie sind Staatsbürger eines Landes, das mit Großbritannien ein beiderseitiges Abkommen zur Gesundheitspflege hat. Das gilt sogar, wenn die Überweisung von einer Unfall- oder Notfallabteilung veranlaßt wird. Wir raten Ihnen daher sehr, vor Antritt Ihrer Reise nach Großbritannien, eine angemessene Versicherung abzuschließen.

GESCHÄFTSSTUNDEN DER BANKEN

Die Banken sind im allgemeinen werktags von 09.30-16.30 Uhr geöffnet, samstags, sonntags und feiertags geschlossen.

POSTÄMTER

Werktags von 09.00-17.30 Uhr und samstags von 09.00-12.30 Uhr geöffnet, sonntags und feiertags geschlossen.

LADENÖFFNUNGSZEITEN

Die meisten Geschäfte sind montags-samstags von 09.00-17.30 Uhr geöffnet. Einige Zeitungshändler und Lebensmittelgeschäfte sind schon ab 07.30 Uhr geöffnet und schließen erst um 20.00 Uhr. In dicht besiedelten Gebieten sind einige sogar bis 22.00 Uhr geöffnet.

REISEN

Eisenbahn
Hauptbahnhöfe gibt es in Edinburgh und Glasgow mit Verbindungen in die meisten Teile des schottischen Festlands.

Busse
Fahrten mit den landesweit verkehrenden Bussen sind sehr preisgünstig und bieten Zugang in alle Gebiete. In abgelegenen Gebieten werden Postbusse der Royal Mail eingesetzt, die Passagiere und Post befördern.

Fähren
Alle besiedelten schottischen Inseln sind mit der Fähre erreichbar. Die beiden Hauptbetreiber sind "Caledonian MacBrayne" an der Westküste und "P&O Ferries" an der Nordküste.

Autofahren

In Schottland herrscht Linksverkehr. Die zulässige Höchstgeschwindigkeit liegt bei 60 Meilen/h (95 km/h) und auf den Autobahnen 70 Meilen/h (110 km/h). In geschlossenen Ortschaften beträgt das Tempolimit gewöhnlich 30 Meilen/h (45 km/h). In abgelegenen Gegenden muß man mit einspurigen Straßen mit Ausweichstellen rechnen. Autofahrer sollten andere Verkehrsteilnehmer nicht behindern.

Español

ALBERGUES JUVENILES ESCOCESES

Más de 80 albergues juveniles escoceses ofrecen una extraordinaria selección de lugares donde alojarse, desde castillos en las tierras altas (las "Highlands") hasta albergues al borde de remotos lagos (los "lochs") o en las islas. Hay albergues en todas las principales ciudades, situados generalmente en edificios históricos. Los albergues representan una base ideal para disfrutar de todas las actividades que este variado país propone y muchos de ellos organizan programas de actividades.

Es posible reservar en todos los albergues a través del Servicio Central de Reservas (Central Reservation Service o CRS). Una noche le costará entre £6 y £16,50, sábanas incluidas.

Todos los albergues de la Asociación escocesa (la SYHA) cumplen con las normas mínimas garantizadas de Hostelling International y han sido clasificados de acuerdo con las mismas en la guía (véase la página 28 para más información).

Todos los albergues de categoría estándar ▲ abren de 7 h. a 23.45 h., pero es posible que el acceso al edificio en algunos de ellos se vea limitado a la sala común y los aseos de 11 h. a 17 h. Infórmese al reservar. Por otra parte, ciertos albergues cuyas prestaciones son superiores abren todo el día de 7 h. a 2 h. (es posible registrarse hasta las 23.15 h.).

Los albergues de categoría sencilla △, que generalmente se encuentran en lugares remotos y de gran belleza, ofrecen un nivel de servicios inferior y suelen cerrar de 10.30 h. a 17 h. para economizar recursos humanos.

La mayoría de los albergues ofrecen descuentos en el precio de las atracciones turísticas y prestaciones locales, que usted conseguirá presentando su tarjeta Hostelling International.

PASAPORTES Y VISADOS

Se necesita un pasaporte en regla. Actualmente muy pocos visitantes requieren visado, pero infórmese con antelación.

INFORMACIÓN SANITARIA

No es necesario un certificado internacional de vacunación para entrar en el Reino Unido, pero averigüe si necesita uno al regresar a su país. Los visitantes sólo tienen derecho a recibir asistencia médica gratuita **de urgencia** en la sección de Accidentes y Urgencias de los hospitales de la Seguridad Social. Si resulta necesario hospitalizarle, tendrá que pagar a menos que sea ciudadano de un país de la UE, residente en cualquier país miembro, o ciudadano o residente de un país que tenga un acuerdo mutuo de asistencia médica con el Reino Unido. Por lo tanto, es altamente recomendable hacerse un seguro con suficiente cobertura antes de salir de viaje para Gran Bretaña.

HORARIO DE LOS BANCOS

Los bancos abren normalmente los días laborables de 9.30 h. a 16.30 h. y cierran los sábados, domingos y festivos.

OFICINAS DE CORREOS

Las oficinas de correos abren los días laborables de 9 h. a 17.30 h. y los sábados de 9 h. a 12.30 h. Cierran los domingos y días festivos.

HORARIO COMERCIAL

La mayoría de las tiendas abren de lunes a sábado de 9 h. a 17.30 h. Algunas papelerías/kioscos y tiendas de comestibles abren desde las 7.30 h. hasta las 20 h. y hasta las 22 h. en las poblaciones más grandes.

DESPLAZAMIENTOS

Tren

De las principales estaciones ferroviarias de Glasgow y Edimburgo salen trenes para casi toda la Escocia peninsular.

Autobús

Los autobuses nacionales son económicos y recorren todo el país. En las zonas más remotas, los autobuses del Royal Mail que reparten el correo también transportan pasajeros.

Ferry

Hay ferrys a todas las islas escocesas habitadas. Las dos compañías principales son Caledonian MacBrayne en la costa oeste y P&O Ferries en la costa norte.

Automóvil

Se circula por la izquierda. El límite de velocidad nacional es de 60 millas/h (aprox. 95 km/h), 70 millas/h (aprox. 110 km/h) en las autopistas y 30 millas/h (aprox. 45 km/h) normalmente en las zonas urbanizadas. En lugares más remotos, las carreteras suelen ser de vía única con espacios para dejar pasar a los vehículos que vengan en dirección contraria, rogándose a los conductores utilicen dichos espacios y no obstruyan el tráfico.

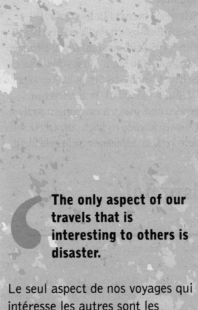

The only aspect of our travels that is interesting to others is disaster.

Le seul aspect de nos voyages qui intéresse les autres sont les désastres qui nous sont arrivés.

Das Einzige, was andere an unseren Reisen interessiert, sind Katastrophen.

Lo único que les interesa a los demás de nuestros viajes son las catástrofes.

Martha Gellman

Aberdeen - The King George VI Memorial Hostel

8 Queen's Rd,
Aberdeen AB15 4ZT.
☎ (1224) 646988

Open Dates:	📅12
Open Hours:	🕐
Reservations:	**R** **CC**
Price Range:	£10.75-£13.25 BB inc 🍽
Beds:	116 - 2x² 13x⁴ 1x⁵ 4x⁶ 3x⁶
Facilities:	♦♦♦ 14x ♦♦♦ 🛏 ⛺ 📺 🔟 💼 🔟 🅿 ℹ 🚽 ✿
Directions:	2W from city centre
✈	Aberdeen 10km
A🚌	Outside hostel
⛴	Aberdeen 2km
🚂	Aberdeen 2km
🚌	14, 15 2km ap Outside hostel
Attractions:	Ⓡ ⚓ 1000m 🎣 ∪ 2km ⚲ 1km ⛵ 1km

Aviemore

25 Grampian Rd,
Aviemore,
Inverness-shire,
PH22 1PR.
☎ (1479) 810345

Open Dates:	📅12
Open Hours:	🕐
Reservations:	**R** **IBN** **CC**
Price Range:	£10.75-£13.25 BB inc 🍽
Beds:	114 - 2x³ 13x⁴ 7x⁶ 2x⁶
Facilities:	♦♦♦ 24x ♦♦♦ 🛏 ⛺ 📺 🔟 💼 🔟 🅿 ℹ 🚽 ✿
Directions:	
✈	Inverness 70km
🚂	Aviemore 400m
🚌	Aviemore 400m ap Train Station
Attractions:	⚑ ⛰ ⚓ 1300m 🎣 🏃 ∪ ⚲ 800m ⛵ 400m

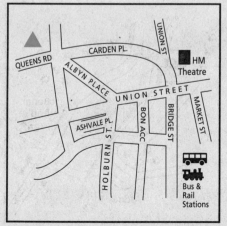

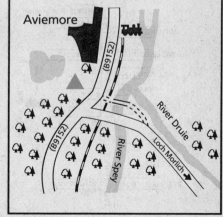

Ayr

5 Craigweil Rd,
Ayr KA7 2XJ.
☎ **(1292) 262322**

Open Dates:	29.01-03.01
Open Hours:	07.00-23.45 hrs
Reservations:	R CC
Price Range:	£8.00-£9.25 📖
Beds:	60 - 2x 🛏 2x 🛏 5x 🛏
Facilities:	👪 2x 👪 🍽 (BD) ☕ 🛋 TV ▢ 🖼 8 P ℹ 🧺 🌿 🎴

Directions:

✈	Prestwick International 15km
A🚌	Ayr Bus Station 1.5km
🚢	Ardrossan 28.5km; Stranraer 8km
🚂	Ayr 1.5km

Attractions: � ∪6.5km ∿1.5km ⚓1.5km

Carbisdale Castle

Carbisdale,
Culrain,
Ardgay,
Ross-shire IV24 3DP.
☎ **(1549) 421232**

Open Dates:	26.02-03.05; 14.05-31.10
Open Hours:	🕐
Reservations:	IBN CC
Price Range:	£11.25-£13.75 BB|inc 📖
Beds:	200 - 1x 🛏 2x 🛏 5x 🛏 14x 🛏
Facilities:	👪 3x 👪 🍽 (BD) ☕ 🛋 TV 1 x 🍷 ▢ 🖼 🏛 8 P ℹ 🌿 ⚲ 🎴

Directions:

✈	Inverness 90km
🚂	Culrain 500m
🚌	Ardgay 7km ap YH

Attractions: ⚙ ⛰ ⚲ ∪15km ∿15km ⚓15km

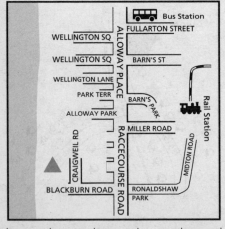

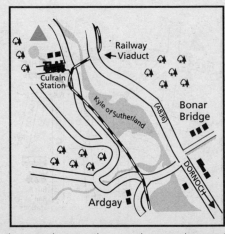

Edinburgh - Eglinton

**18 Eglinton Crescent,
Edinburgh EH12 5DD.**
☎ (131) 3371120

Open Dates:	📅
Open Hours:	🕐
Reservations:	Ⓡ IBN CC
Price Range:	£11.25-£13.75 BB inc 🖥
Beds:	160 - 2x² 9x⁴ 10x⁶ 7x⁶
Facilities:	♦♦♦ 9x ♦♦♦ 🍽 (BD) 🛏 🏷 📺 1 x 🍴 📻 📷 🔒 📁 ♿
Directions:	2W from city centre
✈	Edinburgh International 11km
A🚌	To Haymarket 500m
⛴	Newcastle 400km
🚂	Haymarket 500m
🚌	3, 4, 12, 13, 22, 26, 28, Palmerston 400m ap Haymarket;Palmerston Place

Glasgow

**7/8 Park Terrace,
Glasgow G3 6BY.**
☎ (141) 3323004

Open Dates:	📅
Open Hours:	🕐
Reservations:	Ⓡ IBN CC
Price Range:	£11.25-£13.75 BB inc 🖥
Beds:	138 - 1x² 12x⁴ 4x⁵ 10x⁶ 3x⁶
Facilities:	♦♦♦ 12x ♦♦♦ 🍽 (BD) 🛏 🏷 📺 🍺 1 x 🍴 📻 📷 🏧 🔒 💲 🅿 📁 ♿ ⊙ 🏠
Directions:	2W from city centre
✈	Glasgow International 25km
A🚌	Buchanan Street 2km
🚂	Central 2km
🚌	11, 59 1km ap Woodlands Rd
Ⓤ	Kelvinbridge 2km

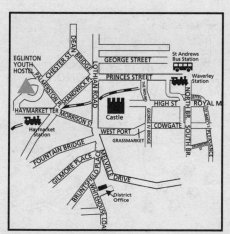

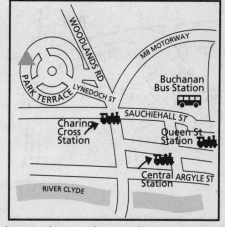

Inverness -
Millburn

Victoria Dr,
Inverness IV2 3QB.
☏ **(1463) 231771**

Open Dates:	🗓
Open Hours:	🕐
Reservations:	**R** IBN CC
Price Range:	£11.25-£13.75 BB inc 🍴
Beds:	166 - 4x² 4x³ 3x⁴ 24x⁶
Facilities:	♐1x ♐ ♐ (BD) 🚿 ♨ TV 1 x🍷 🗄 📷 🔟 P i 🏷 🔥

Directions: 1S from city centre

✈	Inverness 8km
🚂	Inverness 1km
🚌	Inverness 1km ap Bus Station

Attractions: 🏇 🎣3km ⚓3km

Loch Lomond -
Loch Lomond Arden

Alexandria,
Dumbartonshire G83 8RB.
☏ **(1389) 850226**

Open Dates:	🗓
Open Hours:	🕐
Reservations:	**R** IBN CC
Price Range:	£10.75-£13.25 BB inc 🍴
Beds:	160 - 2x² 3x⁴ 1x⁵ 6x⁶ 10x⁶
Facilities:	♐ 4x ♐ ♐ (BD) 🚿 ♨ TV 2 x🍷 🗄 📷 ♨ 🔟 P i 🔥 🔍 🏠

Directions:

✈	Glasgow 24km
🚂	Balloch 3.2km
🚌	ap At driveway

Attractions: 🏇 ⛰ 🎿 ⛳ ⚓3km

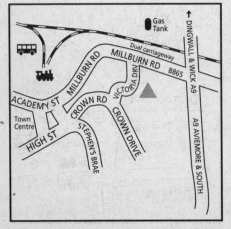

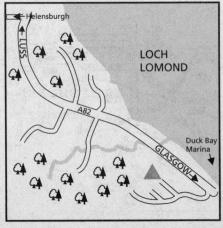

Melrose -
Priorwood

Melrose,
Roxburghshire TD6 9EF.
☎ (1896) 822521

Open Dates:	🗓️
Open Hours:	07.00-23.45
Reservations:	CC
Price Range:	£10.00-£11.25 BB inc 📖
Beds:	86 - 9x⁴ 3x⁶ 3x⁶
Facilities:	👨‍👩‍👧 9x 👨‍👩‍👧 🍽️ (BD) 👕 🛏️ 📺 🔘 💼 🎱 🅿️ ℹ️ 🧺 ♣️

Directions:

✈️	Edinburgh 75km
⛴️	Hull 320km
🚂	Edinburgh 75km

Attractions: 🎣 ⛰️ 🚶 ↺8km ✎1km ⚓6km

New Lanark -
Wee Row

Rosedale St,
New Lanark ML11 9DJ.
☎ (1555) 666710

Open Dates:	🗓️
Open Hours:	07.00-23.45
Reservations:	R CC
Price Range:	£10.00-£11.25 BB inc 📖
Beds:	66 - 2x² 14x⁴ 2x⁵
Facilities:	👨‍👩‍👧 16x 👨‍👩‍👧 🍽️ (BD) 👕 🛏️ 📺 🍺1 x🍷 🔘 💼 ♟️ 🎱 🅿️ ℹ️ 🧺 🏕️ 🏠

Directions:

✈️	Glasgow 59km; Edinburgh 54km
🚂	Lanark 2.5km
🚌	Local Bus 100m

Attractions: 🎣 🚶 ↺ ⚓

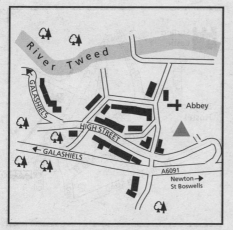

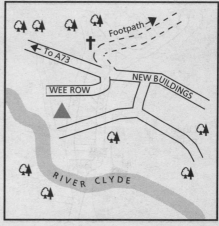

0   500m

0   500m

Oban - Esplanade

Oban,
Argyll PA34 5AF.
📞 **(1631) 562025**

Open Dates: 🗓

Open Hours: ⏱

Reservations: **R** **IBN** **CC**

Price Range: £10.75-£14.25 BB inc 📖

Beds: 154 - 11x4 6x6 6x6

Facilities: 👫 4x 👫 ♂ 🛏 📺 ⬛ 🖼 8
🅿 ℹ 🎦

Directions:

✈	Glasgow 150km
⛴	Oban 1.5km
🚂	Oban 1.5km
🚌	Oban 1.5km

Attractions: 🏕 ⛰ 📷 ⚓1.5km

Stirling - St John St

Stirling FK8 1EA.
📞 **(1786) 473442**

Open Dates: 🗓

Open Hours: ⏱

Reservations: **R** **IBN** **CC**

Price Range: £11.25-£13.75 BB inc 📖

Beds: 126 - 7x2 9x4 12x5 3x6

Facilities: ♿ 👫 24x 👫 🍽 (BD) ♂ 🛏
📺 1 x ⬛ 🖼 🏛 8 🅿 ℹ 🎦
🌿 🏛

Directions:

✈	Glasgow 50km; Edinburgh 50km
🚂	Stirling 1km
🚌	Stirling 1km

Attractions: 🏕 ⛰ 🚶 ∪ ⚲ ⚓

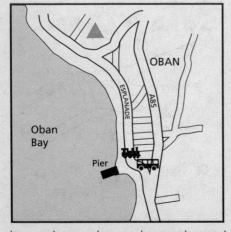

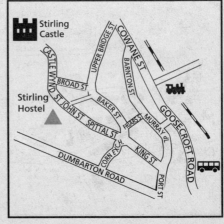

Location/Address	Telephone No. Fax No.	Beds	Opening Dates	Facilities
▲ Aberdeen - The King George VI Memorial Hostel 8 Queen's Rd, Aberdeen AB15 4ZT.	☎ (1224) 646988	116	🗓12	♦♦♦ ⓡ 2W ⌐CC¬ ✇ Ⓟ ⎙
△ Achininver Achiltibuie, Ullapool, Ross-shire IV26 2YL.	☎ (1854) 622254	38	12.05–02.10	⌐CC¬ ✇
△ Achmelvich Recharn, Lairg, Sutherland IV27 4JB.	☎ (1571) 844480	38	03.03–02.10	♦♦♦ ⓡ ⌐CC¬ ✇ Ⓟ
▲ Ardgartan Arrochar, Dunbartonshire G83 7AR.	☎ (1301) 702362	60	28.01–03.01	♦♦♦ ⍾◎⍾ ⓡ ⌐CC¬ ✇ Ⓟ ⎙
▲ Armadale Ardvasar, Sleat, Isle of Skye IV45 8RS.	☎ (1471) 844260	40	31.03–29.10	ⓡ ⌐CC¬ ✇ Ⓟ
▲ Aviemore [IBN] 25 Grampian Rd, Aviemore, Inverness-shire, PH22 1PR.	☎ (1479) 810345	114	🗓12	ⓡ ⌐CC¬ ✇ Ⓟ ⎙
▲ Ayr 5 Craigweil Rd, Ayr KA7 2XJ.	☎ (1292) 262322	60	29.01–03.01	♦♦♦ ⍾◎⍾ ⓡ ⌐CC¬ ✇ Ⓟ ⎙
▲ Braemar Corrie Feragie, Glenshee Rd, Braemar, Aberdeenshire AB35 5YQ.	☎ (1339) 741659	59	🗓12	⌐CC¬ ✇ Ⓟ ⎙
▲ Broadford Isle of Skye IV49 9AA.	☎ (1471) 822442	66	28.01–03.01	♦♦♦ ⓡ ⌐CC¬ ✇ Ⓟ ⎙
△ Broadmeadows Old Broadmeadows, Yarrowford, Selkirk TD7 5LZ.	☎ (1750) 76262	26	31.03–02.10	⌐CC¬ ✇ Ⓟ
▲ Cannich Beauly, Inverness-shire IV4 7LT.	☎ (1456) 415244	54	31.03–29.10	♦♦♦ ♿ ⌐CC¬ ✇ Ⓟ
▲ Carbisdale Castle [IBN] Carbisdale, Culrain, Ardgay, Ross-shire IV24 3DP.	☎ (1549) 421232	200	26.02–03.05; 14.05–31.10	♦♦♦ ⍾◎⍾ ⌐CC¬ ✇ Ⓟ ⎙
▲ Carn Dearg Gairloch, Ross-shire IV21 2DJ.	☎ (1445) 712219	50	12.05–02.10	ⓡ ⌐CC¬ ✇ Ⓟ
▲ Coldingham The Mount, Coldingham, Berwicks TD14 5PA.	☎ (1890) 771298	54	03.03–29.10	♦♦♦ ⌐CC¬ ✇ Ⓟ
△ Craig Diabaig, Achnasheen, Ross-shire IV22 2HE.		16	12.05–02.10	✇
▲ Crianlarich Station Rd, Crianlarich, Perthshire FK20 8QN.	☎ (1838) 300260	75	28.01–03.01	♦♦♦ ⓡ ♿ ⌐CC¬ ✇ Ⓟ ⎙
△ Durness Smoo, Durness, Lairg, Sutherland IV27 4QA.	☎ (1971) 511244	40	31.03–02.10	ⓡ ⌐CC¬ ✇ Ⓟ
▲ Edinburgh - Bruntsfield [IBN] 7 Bruntsfield Crescent, Edinburgh EH10 4EZ.	☎ (131) 4472994	149	🗓12	ⓡ 4W ⌐CC¬ ✇ ⎙
▲ Edinburgh - Central Edinburgh Central YH, Robertsons Close, Cowgate, Edinburgh EH1 1LY.		150	25.06–06.09	♦♦♦ ⓡ 0.1W ⌐CC¬ ✇ ⎙
▲ Edinburgh - Eglinton [IBN] 18 Eglinton Crescent, Edinburgh EH12 5DD.	☎ (131) 3371120	160	🗓12	♦♦♦ ⍾◎⍾ ⓡ 2W ⌐CC¬ ✇ ⎙

Location/Address	Telephone No. Fax No.	Beds	Opening Dates	Facilities
▲ Glasgow (IBN) 7/8 Park Terrace, Glasgow G3 6BY.	☎ (141) 3323004	138	🔲	♟ ❘O❘ R 2W ⊡ECC ☞ P ⊡
△ *Glen Affric* *Allt Beithe, Glen Affric, Cannich, by Beauly, Inverness-shire IV47 7ND.*		26	31.03–29.10	R ☞
▲ Glenbrittle Isle of Skye IV47 8TA.	☎ (1478) 640278	41	31.03–29.10	⊡ECC ☞ P
▲ Glencoe Ballachulish, Argyll PA39 4HX.	☎ (1855) 811219	60	🔲	♟ R ⊡ECC ☞ P ⊡
△ *Glendevon* *Dollar, Clackmannanshire FK14 7JY.*	☎ *(1259) 781206*	36	*31.03–02.10*	♟ ⊡ECC ☞
▲ Glendoll Clova, Kirriemuir, Angus DD8 4RD.	☎ (1575) 550236	45	31.03–29.10	♟ ⊡ECC ☞ P
▲ Glen Nevis (IBN) Fort William, Inverness-shire PH33 6ST.	☎ (1397) 702336	109	🔲	♟ R ⊡ECC ☞ P ⊡
△ *Helmsdale* *Sutherland KW8 6JR.*	☎ *(1431) 821577*	38	*12.05–02.10*	☞
▲ Inveraray Argyllshire PA32 8XD.	☎ (1499) 302454	38	31.03–29.10	♟ ⊡ECC ☞ P
△ *Inverey* *by Braemar, Aberdeenshire AB35 5YB.*	☎ *(1339) 741969*	17	*12.05–02.10*	R ☞ P
▲ Inverness - Millburn (IBN) **Victoria Dr, Inverness IV2 3QB.**	☎ (1463) 231771	166	🔲	♟ ❘O❘ R 1S ⊡ECC ☞ P ⊡
▲ Islay Port Charlotte, Isle of Islay PA48 7TX.	☎ (1496) 850385	42	31.03–29.10	♟ R ☞ P ⊡
▲ John o' Groats Canisbay, Wick, Caithness KW1 4YH.	☎ (1955) 611424	40	31.03–29.10	⊡ECC ☞ P
△ *Kendoon* *Dalry, Castle Douglas, Kircudbrightshire DG7 3UD.*	☎ *(1644) 460680*	34	*31.03–02.10*	☞
▲ Killin Killin, Perthshire FK21 8TN.	☎ (1567) 820546	42	03.03–29.10	⊡ECC ☞ P
▲ Kirkwall Old Scapa Rd, Kirkwall, Orkney KW15 1BB.	☎ (1856) 872243	90	31.03–02.10	♟ R ♿ ⊡ECC ☞ P ⊡
▲ Kirk Yetholm Kirk Yetholm, Kelso, Roxburghshire TD5 8PG.	☎ (1573) 420631	28	31.03–29.10	♟ R ⊡ECC ☞ P
▲ Kyleakin (IBN) Kyleakin, Isle of Skye IV41 8PL.	☎ (1599) 534585	125	🔲	♟ ❘O❘ R ⊡ECC ☞ P ⊡
▲ Loch Lochy South Laggan, Loch Lochy, Spean Bridge, Inverness-shire PH34 4EA.	☎ (1809) 501239	60	31.03–29.10	⊡ECC ☞ P
▲ Loch Lomond - Loch Lomond Arden (IBN) **Alexandria, Dumbartonshire G83 8RB.**	☎ (1389) 850226	160	🔲	♟ ❘O❘ R ⊡ECC ☞ P ⊡
▲ Loch Morlich Glenmore, Aviemore, Inverness-shire PH22 1QY.	☎ (1479) 861238	76	🔲	♟ ❘O❘ R ⊡ECC ☞ P ⊡

Location/Address	Telephone No. Fax No.	Beds	Opening Dates	Facilities
▲ **Loch Ness** Glenmoriston, Inverness-shire IV3 6YD.	☏ (1320) 351274	56	03.03–29.10	††† [CC] ☞ [P]
△ *Loch Ossian* *Corrour, Inverness-shire PH30 4AA.*	☏ *(1397) 732207*	*20*	*31.03–29.10*	[CC] ☞
▲ **Lochranza** Lochranza, Isle of Arran KA27 8HL.	☏ (1770) 830631	68	27.01–03.01	††† [R] [CC] ☞ [P] [O]
▲ **Melrose** - Priorwood **Melrose, Roxburghshire TD6 9EF.**	☏ (1896) 822521	86	[12]	††† [O] [CC] ☞ [P] [O]
▲ **Minnigaff** Newton Stewart, Wigtownshire DG8 6PL.	☏ (1671) 402211	36	31.03–29.10	[CC] ☞ [P]
▲ **New Lanark** - Wee Row **Rosedale St, New Lanark ML11 9DJ.**	☏ (1555) 666710	66	[12]	††† [O] [R] [CC] ☞ [P] [O]
▲ **Oban** - Esplanade [IBN] **Oban, Argyll PA34 5AF.**	☏ (1631) 562025	154	[12]	††† [R] [CC] ☞ [P] [O]
▲ **Perth** 107 Glasgow Rd, Perth PH2 0NS.	☏ (1738) 623658	58	03.03–29.10	††† [R] [2W] [CC] ☞ [P] [O]
▲ **Pitlochry** Braeknowe, Knockard Rd, Pitlochry PH16 5HJ.	☏ (1796) 472308	69	[12]	††† [O] [R] [CC] ☞ [P] [O]
△ *Raasay* *Creachan Cottage, Raasay, Kyle, Ross-shire IV40 8NT.*	☏ *(1478) 660240*	*30*	*31.03–29.10*	[R] ☞ [P]
▲ **Ratagan** Glenshiel, Kyle, Ross-shire IV40 8HP.	☏ (1599) 511243	44	27.01–03.01	♿ [CC] ☞ [P] [O]
▲ **Rowardennan** Rowardennan by Drymen, Glasgow G63 0AR.	☏ (1360) 870259	80	28.01–29.10	††† [O] [R] [CC] ☞ [P] [O]
▲ **Stirling** - St John St [IBN] **Stirling FK8 1EA.**	☏ (1786) 473442	126	[12]	††† [O] [R] ♿ [CC] ☞ [P] [O]
▲ **Strathpeffer** Strathpeffer, Ross-shire IV14 9BT.	☏ (1997) 421532	54	31.03–02.10	[CC] ☞ [P]
▲ **Stromness** Hellihole Rd, Stromness, Orkney KW16 3DE.	☏ (1856) 850589	40	31.03–29.10	[CC] ☞
▲ **Tobermory** Isle of Mull, Argyll PA75 6NU.	☏ (1688) 302481	40	03.03–29.10	[R] [CC] ☞
△ *Tomintoul* *Main St, Tomintoul, Ballindalloch, Banffshire AB37 9HA.*	☏ *(1807) 580282*	*38*	*12.05–02.10*	[R] ☞ [P]
▲ **Tongue** Lairg, Sutherland IV27 4XH.	☏ (1847) 611301	40	31.03–29.10	[CC] ☞ [P]
▲ **Torridon** Achnasheen, Ross-shire IV22 2EZ.	☏ (1445) 791284	60	28.01–29.10	††† [CC] ☞ [P] [O]
▲ **Uig** Uig, Isle of Skye IV51 9YD.	☏ (1470) 542211	58	31.03–29.10	††† [CC] ☞ [P]
▲ **Ullapool** Shore St, Ullapool, Ross-shire IV26 2UJ.	☏ (1854) 612254	56	27.01–03.01	[R] [CC] ☞ [O]

Location/Address	Telephone No. Fax No.	Beds	Opening Dates	Facilities
▲ **Wanlockhead** Lotus Lodge, Wanlockhead, Biggar, Lanarkshire ML12 6UT.	☎ (1659) 74252	28	31.03–02.10	⌐cc⌐ ☞ 🅿
▲ **Whiting Bay** Shore Rd, Whiting Bay, Isle of Arran KA27 8QW.	☎ (1770) 700339	54	03.03–29.10	♦♦ Ⓡ ⌐cc⌐ ☞ 🅿

YOUTH HOSTEL ACCOMMODATION
OUTSIDE THE ASSURED STANDARDS SCHEME

Location/Address	Telephone No.	Beds	Opening Dates	Facilities
Berneray Isle of Berneray, North Uist, HS6 5BQ.		16	🕛	☞
Eday London Bay, Eday, Orkney KW17 2AB.	☎ (01857) 622206	24	01.04–30.09	Ⓡ ☞
Garenin Carloway, Isle of Lewis, HS2 9AL.		14	🕛	☞
Howmore South Uist, HS8 5SH		17	🕛	☞
Hoy Stromness, Orkney KW16 3NJ.	☎ (1856) 873535	26	30.04–11.09	Ⓡ ☞
Kershader Ravenspoint, Kershader, South Lochs, Isle of Lewis, HS2 9QA.	☎ (1851) 880236	14	🕛	☞ ▣
Lerwick Islesburgh House, King Harald St, Lerwick, Shetland ZE1 0EQ.	☎ (1595) 692114	60	31.03–02.10	♦♦ Ⓡ ♿ ☞ 🅿 ▣
Papa Westray Beltane House, Papa Westray, Orkney KW17 2BU.	☎ (1857) 644267	16	🕛	Ⓡ ☞
Rackwick Rackwick Outdoor Centre, Hoy, Stromness, Orkney, KW16 3NJ.	☎ (1856) 873535 Ext 2404	8	11.03–09.09	Ⓡ ☞
Rhenigidale Isle of Harris, HS3 3BD.		11	🕛	☞

Travelling is the ruin of all happiness! There's no looking at a building after seeing Italy.

Le voyage tue le bonheur! Il est impossible d'admirer un bâtiment après voir vu l'Italie.

Reisen ist der Ruin allen Glückes! Nach Italien hat man kein Auge mehr für ein anderes Bauwerk.

Los viajes destruyen nuestra felicidad para siempre. ¿Quién es capaz de admirar un edificio cualquiera después de haber visitado Italia?

Fanny Burney

Slovenia

SLOVENIE
SLOWENIEN
ESLOVENIA

**Počitniška Zveza Slovenije,
Parmova 33, 1000 Ljubljana, Slovenia.**

☎ (386) (61) 1361459
🖷 (386) (61) 1363477
✉ pzs@psdsi.com
www.psdsi.com/pzs/

A copy of the Hostel Directory for this Country can be obtained from:
The National Office.

Capital:	Ljubljana	**Population:**	1,965,986
Language:	Slovene	**Size:**	20,254 sq km
Currency:	Slovene Tolar (SIT)	**Telephone Country Code:**	386

English

YOUTH HOSTELS IN SLOVENIA

There are 5 Youth Hostels located in different parts of Slovenia. The 2 hostels in Ljubljana, where you can visit interesting museums, galleries, festivals and other cultural and sports events, are open 24hrs. Overnight accommodation prices for hostels within the "Assured Standards Scheme" will vary according to location and facilities. The range is from 1886.00 SIT (20 DEM) to 2452.00 SIT (26 DEM) (This price range is accurate at the time of printing, and may be subject to change during the year).

PASSPORTS AND VISAS

You will need a valid passport. An entrance visa is necessary for some countries, please check in advance.

HEALTH

Vaccinations are not required. Major medical centres are open 07.00-19.00hrs; drug stores Monday-Friday 07.00-20.00hrs. Saturday 08.00-13.00hrs. Dial 112 for an ambulance

BANKING HOURS

Monday-Friday 09.00-12.00hrs; 14.00-16.30hrs. Saturday 09.00-12.00hrs.

POST OFFICES

Monday-Friday 08.00-19.00hrs. Saturday 08.00-13.00hrs.

SHOPPING HOURS

Monday-Friday 07.00/08.00-19.00/20.00hrs. Saturday 08.00-13.00hrs.

TRAVEL

Air

Adria Airways run international service link with all major cities in Europe.

Rail

Rail travel is very well developed and inexpensive.

Bus

Bus is a good way to travel between towns.

Driving

Driving is on the right side. Seat belts must be worn and headlights must be on. For help and information dial 987.

Français

AUBERGES DE JEUNESSE

Il y a 5 auberges de jeunesse implantées dans différentes régions du pays. Les deux établissements situés dans la capitale, Ljubljana, où vous pouvez visiter de fascinants musées et galleries d'art, participer ou assister à des festivals ou d'autres manisfestations culturelles et sportives, sont ouverts 24 heures sur 24. Le prix de la nuitée dans les auberges appartenant au "Plan de Garantie des Normes" pourra être compris, selon le lieu et la qualité des prestations offertes, entre 1886.00 SIT (20 DEM) et 2452.00 SIT (26 DEM) (ces chiffres sont corrects à l'heure où nous mettons sous presse mais pourront être ajustés au cours de l'année).

PASSEPORTS ET VISAS

Il vous faudra un passeport valide. Un visa d'entrée est exigé pour les ressortissants de certains pays. Nous vous conseillons donc de vérifier au préalable.

SOINS MEDICAUX

Aucune vaccination n'est requise. Les principaux centres médicaux sont ouverts de 7h à 19h; les pharmacies, du lundi au vendredi, de 7h à 20 et le samedi de 8h à 13h. Composez le 112 pour une ambulance.

HEURES D'OUVERTURE DES BANQUES

Du lundi au vendredi de 9h à 12h et de 14h à 16.30h; le samedi de 9h à 12h.

BUREAUX DE POSTE

Du lundi au vendredi de 8h à 19h; le samedi de 8h à 13h.

HEURES D'OUVERTURE DES MAGASINS

Du lundi au vendredi de 7h/8h à 19h/20h; le samedi de 8h à 13h.

DEPLACEMENTS

Avions
Adria Airways assure un service aérien international vers toutes les grandes villes d'Europe.

Trains
Le réseau de chemins de fer est très étendu et bon marché.

Autobus
Le bus est un très bon moyen de se déplacer de ville en ville.

Automobiles
En Slovénie, la conduite est à droite. Le port de la ceinture de sécurité est obligatoire. Il est également indispensable de rouler en phares. Si vous avez besoin d'assistance ou de plus amples informations, composez le 987.

Deutsch

JUGENDHERBERGEN IN SLOWENIEN

Es gibt 5 Jugendherbergen in verschiedenen Gegenden in Slovenia. Die Jugendherberge Koper ist am Meer, wo Sie ihren Urlaub richtig genießen können. Die Jugendherberge Bezigrad und Tabor sind in der Hauptstadt von Slovenia in Ljubljana, wo Sie interessante Museen, Gallerien, Festivals und andere kulturelle Ereignisse und Sportereignisse besuchen können. Falls Sie die Natur bevorzugen, besuchen Sie unsere komplett wiederhergestellte Jugendherberge Bledec. Die Jugendherberge ist 5 Minuten Gehweg vom See, und Bled kennt man als "die wahre Perle" der slovenischen Skiregion. Die Jugendherberge Rogla bietet Ihnen Winterurlaub an, und die Jugendherberge Maribor ermöglicht Ihnen östliche Teile von Slovenien zu besuchen. Übernachtungpreise schwanken abhängig von Ort und Ausstattung. Die Preisspanne reicht von 1886.00 SIT (20 DEM) bis 2452.00 SIT (26 DEM) (Diese Preisspanne ist bei Drucktermin genau und kann sich während des Jahres ändern).

PÄSSE UND VISA

Sie benötigen einen gültigen Paß, um Slovenien zu besuchen. In einigen Ländern brauchen Sie ein Eintrittsvisum. Bitte erkundigen Sie sich deshalb vor der Abreise.

GESUNDHEIT

Impfungen sind nicht notwendig. Krankenhäuser sind von 17.00-19.00 Uhr geöffnet. Falls Sie einen Krankenwagen brauchen wählen Sie 112. Apotheken sind montags bis freitags von 07.00-20.00 Uhr und samstags von 08.00-13.00 Uhr geöffnet.

GESCHÄFTSSTUNDEN DER BANKEN

Banken sind montags bis freitags von 09.00-12.00 Uhr und 14.00-16.30 Uhr und samstags 09.00-12.00 Uhr geöffnet.

POSTÄMTER

Postämter sind montags bis freitags von 08.00-19.00 Uhr und samstags 08.00-13.00 Uhr geöffnet.

LADENÖFFNUNGSZEITEN

Geschäfte sind montags bis freitags von 07.00 oder 08.00-19.00 oder 20.00 Uhr und samstags von 08.00-13.00 Uhr geöffnet.

REISEN

Flugverkehr
Die Fluggesellschaft Adria Airways bietet internationale Verbindungen mit allen großen Städten Europas an.

Eisenbahn
Es gibt ein sehr gutes Schienennetz in Slovenien, und die Bahn gilt als billiges Verkehrsmittel.

Busse
Der Busverkehr ist eine gute Methode, um von Stadt zu Stadt zu reisen.

Autofahren
Wir fahren auf der rechten Seite in Slovenien. Seit Mai 1998 gibt es neue Tempolimits. 50kmph in geschlossenen Ortschaften, 90kmph auf Landstraßen und 130kmph auf der Autobahn. Sie müssen sich während des Fahrens immer anschnallen und Scheinwerfer benutzen. Das gesetzliche Alkohollimit für Fahrer ist unter 0,5 Gramm pro Liter. Falls Sie Hilfe und Information brauchen, wählen Sie 987.

Español

ALBERGUES JUVENILES ESLOVENOS

En Eslovenia existen 5 albergues juveniles repartidos por el país. Los 2 albergues de Ljubljana, donde podrá visitar interesantes museos y galerías, así como participar en fiestas y demás acontecimientos y actividades culturales y deportivas, están abiertos las 24 horas del día. Los precios por noche en los albergues que se adhieren al "Plan de las Normas Garantizadas" varían según el emplazamiento y las prestaciones ofrecidas. Estos oscilan entre 1.886,00 SIT (20 DEM) y 2.452,00 SIT (26 DEM). (Los precios indicados son correctos al cierre de la edición, pero podrán modificarse durante el transcurso del año).

PASAPORTES Y VISADOS

Es necesario un pasaporte vigente. Los ciudadanos de ciertos países necesitarán un visado de entrada al país - rogamos se informe con antelación.

INFORMACIÓN SANITARIA

No es necesaria ninguna vacuna. Los principales centros médicos abren de 7 h. a 19 h. Las farmacias abren de 7 h. a 20 h. de lunes a viernes y de 8 h. a 13 h. los sábados. Si necesita una ambulancia, marque el 112.

HORARIO DE LOS BANCOS

De lunes a viernes, de 9 h. a 12 h. y de 14 h. a 16.30 h.; los sábados, de 9 h. a 12 h.

OFICINAS DE CORREOS

De lunes a viernes, de 8 h. a 19 h.; los sábados, de 8 h. a 13 h.

HORARIO COMERCIAL

De lunes a viernes, de 7 h./8 h. a 19 h./20 h.; los sábados, de 8 h. a 13 h.

DESPLAZAMIENTOS

Avión
Adria Airways ofrece un servicio aéreo internacional a todas las principales ciudades de Europa.

Tren
Eslovenia disfruta de una extensa y económica red de ferrocarriles.

Autobús
El autobús es una buena forma de desplazarse de una población a otra.

Automóvil
En Eslovenia se conduce por la derecha. Es obligatorio llevar siempre puesto el cinturón de seguridad y los faros encendidos. Si necesita asistencia o información, marque el 987.

Bled - Bledec

Grajska 17,
4260 Bled.
☎ (64) 745251
✆ (64) 745250

Open Dates:	🗓
Open Hours:	07.00-21.00hrs
Reservations:	**R**
Price Range:	2600 SIT € 12.90
Beds:	56 - 1x² 2x³ 6x⁴ 2x⁵ 1x⁶ 1x⁶
Facilities:	🚻 🚻 🍽 ☕ 📺 1 x 🍷 📷 ☺ 🅿 ⓘ 🧺
Directions:	0.5 NE from city centre
✈	Brnik 32km
🚆	Bled 2km
🚌	ap Bled Autobusna Postaja 200m
Attractions:	🌳 ⛰ 🎿 🚶 🔍 🏊

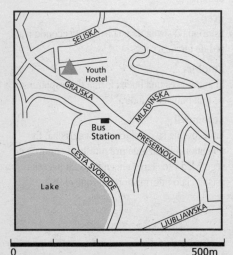

Map showing Youth Hostel, Bus Station, Lake, with streets: Seliska, Grajska, Mladinska, Presernova, Cesta Svobode, Ljubljawska. Scale 0 – 500m.

**John Galt,
in Ayn Rand's Atlas Shrugged:**

" Do not lose your knowledge that man's proper estate is an upright posture, an intransigent mind, and a step that travels unlimited roads.

Ne perdez pas de vue que l'état propre de l'homme est une posture droite, un esprit intransigeant et un pas qui voyage sur une multitude de routes.

Man sollte nie vergessen, daß der Reichtum eines Menschen in folgendem besteht: einer aufrechten Haltung, einem festen Willen und einem festen Schritt, der unzählige Straßen beschreitet.

Nunca olvides que el verdadero ser del hombre es una postura erguida, una mente intransigente y un paso que camina por infinitos senderos. "

Location/Address	Telephone No. Fax No.	Beds	Opening Dates	Facilities
▲ **Bled** - Bledec **Grajska 17, 4260 Bled.**	☎ (64) 745251 🖷 (64) 745250	56	🔟	� 🍽 Ⓡ 0.5NE Ⓟ ◻ ☕
▲ **Koper** Dijaški dom Koper, Cankarjeva 5, 6000 Koper.	☎ (66) 273250 🖷 (66) 273182	35	20.06–20.08 (30 beds); 01.09–20.06 (2 beds)	🍽 Ⓡ Ⓟ ◻
▲ **Ljubljana** - Bežigrad Kardeljeva ploščad 28, 1000 Ljubljana.	☎ (61) 342867 🖷 (61) 342864	200	25.06–25.08	♥♥♥ Ⓡ Ⓟ
▲ **Ljubljana** - Tabor Vidovdanska 7, 1000 Ljubljana. ✉ andrej.cepin@guest.arnes.si	☎ (61) 321067, 321060 🖷 (61) 321060	200	25.06–25.08	♥♥♥ 🍽 Ⓡ Ⓟ
▲ **Maribor** Dijaški dom 26 Junij Maribor, Železnikova 12, 2000 Maribor. ✉ vojteh.stefanciosa@guest.arnes.si	☎ (62) 511800 🖷 (62) 511800	50	01.07–20.08	♥♥♥ 🍽 Ⓡ Ⓟ

It is impossible to travel faster than light, and certainly not desirable, as one's hat keeps blowing off.

Il est impossible de voyager plus vite que la lumière, et ce n'est certainement pas désirable, car on perdrait constamment son chapeau.

Es ist nicht nur unmöglich, schneller als Licht zu reisen, sondern auch unerwünscht, weil einem der Hut ständig wegweht.

Es imposible ir a más velocidad que la luz y, en todo caso, no es aconsejable, ya que se nos volaría constantemente el sombrero.

Woody Allen

Net Savings @ Hostelling International

Don't leave your booking to chance

HOSTELLING INTERNATIONAL ®

netsavings@hostellinginternational.org.uk

Spain

ESPAGNE
SPANIEN
ESPAÑA

Red Española de Albergues Juveniles,
c/ José Ortega y Gasset 71,
Madrid 28006, Spain.

☎ (34) 913477700
📠 (34) 914018160
www.mtas.es/injuve/intercambios/albergues/reaj.html

Office Hours: Monday-Friday, 09.00-14.00hrs

A copy of the Hostel Directory for this Country can be obtained from:
The National Office.

Capital:	Madrid	**Population:**	39,433,942
Language:	Spanish	**Size:**	504,782 sq km
Currency:	Ptas (pesetas)	**Telephone Country Code:**	34

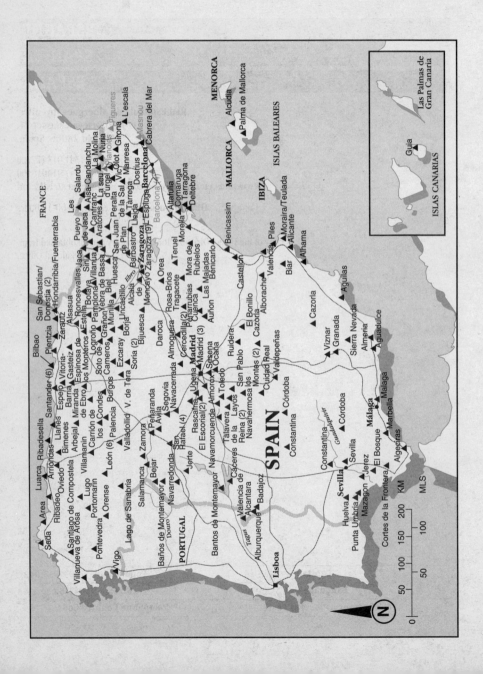

English

SPANISH HOSTELS

Whether on the coast or in the mountains, Spain has 187 Youth Hostels to choose from, including several specialist ski hostels, one in the Canary Islands and two in Majorca. Although there is no upper age limit, those under 26 years have priority. Under 13s are not accommodated except when accompanied by an adult.

Opening times vary but are generally 08.00-22.30hrs in winter, 23.30hrs in summer. You can usually check in any time between 09.30 and 19.00hrs. Overnight accommodation prices for hostels within the Assured Standards Scheme will vary according to location and facilities. The range is from 500-1800 Pts (3.00-10.81 Euros) for under 26 years and 600-2300 Pts (3.60-13.82 Euros) 26 years and over.

Reservations for hostels should be made directly to the Youth Hostel.

PASSPORTS AND VISAS

A passport is required except in the case of EU citizens who only need their Identity Card. Some countries may require a visa so check before you travel.

HEALTH

Medical care is free to nationals of EU countries or those of countries which have a reciprocal agreement with Spain, otherwise it is advisable to take out insurance cover.

BANKING HOURS

Banks are open weekdays 08.30-14.00hrs.

POST OFFICES

Post offices are open weekdays 09.00-14.00hrs.

SHOPPING HOURS

Shops are normally open Monday-Saturday 10.00-13.30hrs and 17.00-20.30hrs.

TRAVEL

Rail

The Spanish railways, RENFE, offer a variety of discounts and reductions for young people under 26 years on their tickets, depending on the day of travel. Eurorail and Inter-Rail cards are valid subject to a supplement on certain fast trains.

Bus

Some bus companies offer a special rate with a discount for young travellers under 26 years of age.

Français

AUBERGES DE JEUNESSE ESPAGNOLES

Sur la côte ou dans les montagnes, l'Espagne a 187 auberges de jeunesse, y compris plusieurs auberges spécialisées dans le ski, une dans les îles Canaries et deux à Majorque. Bien qu'il n'y ait pas d'âge limite supérieur, priorité est donnée aux moins de 26 ans. Les enfants de moins de 13 ans ne sont pas admis à moins d'être accompagnés par un adulte.

Les heures d'ouverture varient mais en général vont de 8h à 22h30 en hiver et jusqu'à 23h30 en été. Vous pouvez en principe arriver entre 9h30 et 19h. Le prix de la nuitée dans les auberges participant au 'Plan de Garantie des Normes' pourra être compris, selon le lieu et la qualité des prestations offertes, entre 500 et 1800 Pts (soit 3,00-10,81 Euros) pour les moins de 26 ans et entre 600 et 2300 Pts (soit 3,60-13,82 Euros) pour ceux qui sont âgés de 26 ans ou plus. Pour réserver, adressez-vous directement à l'auberge en question.

PASSEPORTS ET VISAS

Les passeports sont nécessaires sauf pour les citoyens de l'UE, qui n'ont besoin que d'une carte d'identité. Certains pays peuvent exiger un visa; il est donc prudent de vérifier avant votre départ.

SOINS MEDICAUX

Les citoyens de la CE et ceux venant de pays ayant passé un accord réciproque avec l'Espagne ont droit à des soins gratuits, sinon, il est conseillé de souscrire à une police d'assurance maladie.

HEURES D'OUVERTURE DES BANQUES

Les banques sont ouvertes en semaine de 8h30 à 14h.

BUREAUX DE POSTE

Les bureaux de poste sont ouverts en semaine de 9h à 14h.

HEURES D'OUVERTURE DES MAGASINS

Les magasins sont normalement ouverts du lundi au samedi de 10h à 13h30 et 17h à 20h30.

DEPLACEMENTS

Trains

Les chemins de fer espagnols, RENFE, offrent toute une variété de remises et réductions pour les jeunes de moins de 26 ans sur leurs billets, selon le jour du voyage. Les cartes Eurail et Inter-Rail sont valides, mais un supplément est à payer pour certains trains rapides.

Autobus

Quelques compagnies d'autobus offrent un tarif spécial avec une remise pour les jeunes voyageurs de moins de 26 ans.

Deutsch

SPANISCHE JUGENDHERBERGEN

Ob an der Küste oder in den Bergen, in Spanien hat man die Wahl zwischen 187 Jugendherbergen, darunter mehrere auf Skisport spezialisierte Herbergen, eine auf den Kanarischen Inseln und zwei in Mallorca. Obwohl es keine obere Altersgrenze gibt, werden junge Leute unter 26 Jahren bevorzugt aufgenommen. Kinder unter 13 Jahren werden nicht aufgenommen, es sei denn, sie befinden sich in Begleitung einer erwachsenen Person.

Die Öffnungszeiten sind unterschiedlich, liegen aber im allgemeinen zwischen 08.00 und 22.30 Uhr im Winter und 23.30 Uhr im Sommer. Normalerweise kann man jederzeit zwischen 09.30 und 19.00 Uhr einchecken. Übernachtungspreise für Herbergen innerhalb der "Zugesicherten Standards" unterscheiden sich je nach Gebiet und Ausstattung. Die Preisspanne ist von 500-1.800 Pts (3,00-10,81 Euros) für unter 26-Jährige und 600-2.300 Pts (3,60-13,82 Euros) für 26-Jährige und älter.

Reservierungen müssen direkt bei der Jugendherberge vorgenommen werden.

PÄSSE UND VISA

Für Spanien braucht man einen Reisepaß, ausgenommen davon sind Staatsbürger eines EU-Landes, die nur einen Personalausweis benötigen. Für Reisende aus gewissen Ländern könnte auch ein Visum erforderlich sein. Bitte erkundigen Sie sich deshalb vor der Abreise.

GESUNDHEIT

Für Staatsbürger eines EU-Landes und aus Ländern, mit denen Spanien ein beiderseitiges Abkommen hat, ist die ärztliche Behandlung kostenlos. In anderen Fällen ist es ratsam, eine Versicherung abzuschließen.

GESCHÄFTSSTUNDEN DER BANKEN

Banken sind werktags von 08.30-14.00 Uhr geöffnet.

POSTÄMTER

Postämter sind werktags von 09.00-14.00 Uhr geöffnet.

LADENÖFFNUNGSZEITEN

Die Geschäfte sind gewöhnlich montags bis samstags von 10.00-13.30 Uhr und 17.00-20.30 Uhr geöffnet.

REISEN

Eisenbahn

Die spanische Eisenbahn RENFE bietet je nach Reisetag verschiedene verbilligte Fahrkarten für junge Leute unter 26 Jahren an. Eurorail- und Inter-Rail-Karten sind in Spanien gültig, aber für gewisse Schnellzüge muß ein Zuschlag bezahlt werden.

Busse

Einige Busunternehmen bieten für junge Reisende unter 26 Jahren einen Sondertarif mit verbilligten Fahrpreisen an.

Español

ALBERGUES JUVENILES ESPAÑOLES

Ya sea en la costa o en la montaña, en España existen 187 albergues juveniles entre los que elegir, incluyendo varios albergues especializados en el esquí, uno en las Islas Canarias y dos en Mallorca. Aunque no existe un límite máximo de edad, tienen prioridad los menores de 26 años. No se admiten a menores de 13 años a menos que vayan acompañados de un adulto.

El horario de apertura de los albergues varía, pero suele ser de 8 h. a 22.30 h. en invierno y hasta las 23.30 h. en verano. Normalmente, usted podrá registrarse entre las 9.30 h. y las 19 h.

Los precios por noche en los albergues que pertenecen al "Plan de las Normas Garantizadas" oscilan entre 500 Pts y 1.800 Pts (3,00-10,81 Euros) para los menores de 26 años y entre 600 Pts y 2.300 Pts (3,60-13,82 Euros) a partir de los 26 años, según el emplazamiento y las prestaciones ofrecidas por cada establecimiento.

Para reservar, póngase en contacto directamente con el albergue juvenil.

PASAPORTES Y VISADOS

Es necesario un pasaporte, salvo para los ciudadanos de la Unión Europea, quienes sólo necesitan su Documento Nacional de Identidad. Es posible que los ciudadanos de ciertos países necesiten visado. Por lo tanto, se recomienda hacer las averiguaciones pertinentes antes de viajar.

INFORMACIÓN SANITARIA

La asistencia médica es gratuita para los ciudadanos procedentes de países de la Unión Europea y de otros países que tengan un acuerdo mutuo con España. En los demás casos, se recomienda hacerse un seguro.

HORARIO DE LOS BANCOS

Los bancos abren los días laborables de 8.30 h. a 14 h.

OFICINAS DE CORREOS

Las oficinas de correos abren los días laborables de 9 h. a 14 h.

HORARIO COMERCIAL

Las tiendas suelen abrir de lunes a sábado de 10 h. a 13.30 h. y de 17 h. a 20.30 h.

DESPLAZAMIENTOS

Tren

La red de ferrocarriles españoles RENFE ofrece toda una gama de descuentos para los jóvenes menores de 26 años dependiendo del día en que se viaje. Se aceptan las tarjetas Eurorail e Inter-Rail, pero usted tendrá que abonar un suplemento para viajar en determinados trenes rápidos.

Autobús

Algunas compañías de autobuses tienen una tarifa reducida para los pasajeros menores de 26 años.

Alburquerque -
Castillo de Luna

c/ Castillo,
s/n 06510 Alburquerque (Badajoz).
☎ 924 400041
🛈 924 401523

Open Dates:	🔲
Price Range:	900-1340 ptas € 5.41-8.05
Beds:	8 - 4x² 🛌
Facilities:	👫 🍽️
Directions:	
🚃	3.7km
Attractions:	🏊

Alcudia -
La Victoria

Crta. Cabo Pinar, Km. 4
Alcudia (Mallorca).
☎ 971 545395
🛈 971 545395

Open Dates:	01.03-30.09
Open Hours:	08.00-12.00hrs
Price Range:	1800 pts € 10.81 🍽️
Beds:	120 - 26x⁶ 🛌
Facilities:	👫 🧑‍🤝‍🧑 📺 🔲 🎞️ 8 🅿️ ⅰ 🧩
	🐾 ⛰️ 🕐 🔍 🏛️ 👥
Directions:	
✈️	Son San Juan, Palma de Mallorca 46km
A🚌	Alcudia - Aeropuerto
🚃	Inca 16km
🚌	From Palma - Alcudia
Attractions:	🎎 🏔️ 📷 300m 🚴 🚶 ↻ ⚲

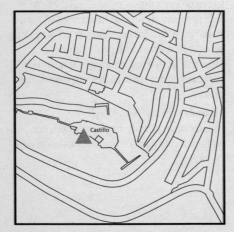

Barcelona - Mare de Déu de Montserrat

Passeig Mare de Déu del Coll 41-51, 08023 Barcelona.
☎ 932 105151
🛈 932 100798

Open Dates:	01.01-24.12; 26-31.12
Open Hours:	07.00-24.00hrs
Reservations:	Ⓡ ⒾⒷⓃ ⒸⒸ
Price Range:	1800-2325 pts € 10.81-13.97 BBinc 🏨
Beds:	183 - 5x2⇥ 2x4⇥ 25x6⇥ 6x6⇥
Facilities:	♿ ♦♦♦ 🍽 ⚑ 📺 📺 1 x 🍴 🗄 💼 🔒 🅿 ⓘ 🍴 🐾 🏍 🔍

Directions:

✈	"El Prat" Barcelona 20km
A🚌	#28 Pza Cataluña
⛴	Barcelona 2km
🚆	Estación-sans (Barcelona 4km)
🚌	25 10m, 28 2m ap Mare de Déu del Coll
Ⓤ	Linea 3 - Green "Valcarca" 500m

Attractions: 🔍 🚴 ∪5km ⚲1km ⚓1km

Benicasim - Argentina

Avda Ferrandiz Salvador 40, 12560 Benicasim (Castellón)
☎ 964 300949; 964302709
🛈 964 300473

Open Dates:	02.02-22.12
Open Hours:	07.00-24.00hrs
Reservations:	Ⓡ
Price Range:	770-1400 pts € 4.62-8.41 🏨
Beds:	140 - 2x2⇥ 1x3⇥ 8x4⇥ 3x6⇥
Facilities:	♿ ♦♦♦ 8x ♦♦♦ ⚑ 📺 ⬛3 x 🍴 🗄 💼 ⓘ 🐾 🏍 🔍 ⬛ 🏠

Directions:

✈	Manises, Valencia 70km
🚆	Benicasim 1.5km
🚌	from Castellón 100m

Attractions: 🔍 🕴 ⚲ ⚓

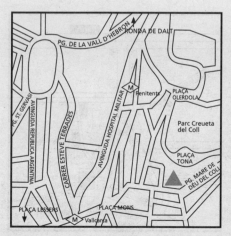

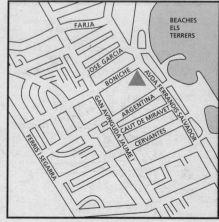

Bilbao -
Bilbao-Aterpetxea

Carretera Basurto-Kastrexana, 70,
48002 Bilbao
☎ 944 270054
📠 944 275479
✉ aterpe@albergue.bilbao.met

Open Dates: 📅

Reservations: **R** CC

Beds: 142

Facilities: ♿ ††† 🍴 📺 ✉ 🧺 ⬚ ⓧ 🅿 ♿ 🔍

Directions:

🚌 58

Attractions: 🚴 🚶

Córdoba -
Plaza Judá Leví S/N.

14003 Córdoba.
☎ 957 290166
📠 957 290500

Open Dates: 📅

Reservations: **R** CC

Price Range: 1600-2135 ptas € 9.61-13.97

Beds: 170 - 44x² 🛏

Facilities: ♿ 🍴 ☕ 🍵 🛏 📺 1 x 🍽 ⊜ ⬚ 🏘

Directions:

�# Cordoba 1.5km

🚌 3, 12, 50m

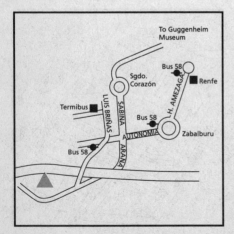

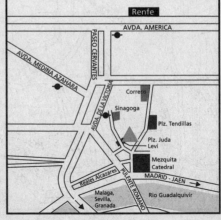

Donostia-San Sebastian - La Sirena

Paseo de Igeldo 25,
20008 Donostia-San Sebastian.
☎ 943 310268, 943 311293
🖷 943 214090
✉ udala.youthostel@donostia.org

Open Dates:	🗓
Open Hours:	08.00-11.00hrs; 15.00-24.00hrs
Reservations:	**R** ⊂CC⊃
Price Range:	1550-1885 pts ᴮᴮⁱⁿᶜ 🗓
Beds:	96 - 1x² 4x⁴ 4x⁶ 5x⁶
Facilities:	♿ ⅲ ⅋ ☞ ♨ 📺 🗓 🖼 ⬩ ℹ ♨ ♨ ⛩
Directions:	2SW from city centre
✈	Hondarribia 20km
A🚌	From City Center of San Sebastian
⛴	Santurtzi 120km
🚆	North Station - San Sebastian 3km
🚌	5, 6, 15, 16, 22, 24, 25, 27 ap Ventaberri or Igeldo
Attractions:	⛳ ⛰ 📷 🚴 🚶 ∪ ᘉ

Figueres - Tramuntana

Anicet de Pagès, 2,
17600 Figueres (Girona)
☎ 972 501213
🖷 972 673808

Open Dates:	01.04-08.12
Reservations:	**R** ⦿IBN⦿
Price Range:	1575-2325 ptas € 9.46-13.97 🗓
Beds:	50 - 1x⁴ 3x⁶
Facilities:	ⅲ ⅋ ☞ ♨ 8 📷 🖾
Directions:	
🚆	Figueres Linea Barcelona-Portbou 800m
🚌	Figueres 100m
Attractions:	🚴 ∪ ᘉ

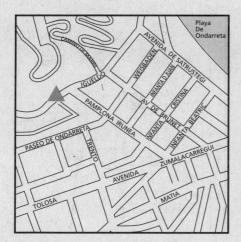

Granada - Albergue Juvenil Granada

Avda Ramon y Cajal 2,
18003 Granada.
☎ 958 284306
🛈 958 285285

Open Dates: 🗓
Open Hours: ◷
Reservations: **R**
Price Range: 1495-1995 ptas € 9.61-12.83
Beds: 150 - 6x¹ 84x² 60x³
Facilities: ♿ ⅲ 🍽 ⛱ TV 🧺 🖼 ⬍ P ⛱ ❄

Directions:

✈	Santa Fé 20km
A🚐	From City Center of Granada
🚂	Granada - "Avda de los Andaluces" 1.5km
🚌	11 ap YH

Attractions: ⛰ ⛷ ⚲1km ⚓1km

Llanes - Juventudes

c/ Celso Amieva 7,
33500 Llanes (Asturias).
☎ 98 5400770
🛈 98 5400770

Open Dates: 🗓
Open Hours: 09.00-13.30hrs; 18.00-20.00hrs
Price Range: 905-1275 ptas € 5.43-7.66 BBinc
Beds: 16 - 8x²
Facilities: ♿ ⅲ 🍽 ⛱ TV 🖼 ⬍ ⬍ ⛱ ❄ ⚒ ⛰

Directions:

✈	Ranón (Avilés) 150km
A🚌	(Alsa) Llanes - Oviedo - Avilés
🚂	F.E.V.E. Oviedo - Llanes 300m
🚌	Oviedo - Llanes (Alsa)

Attractions: ⚲ ⛰ ⚲ ⚲ U ⚲ ⚓1km

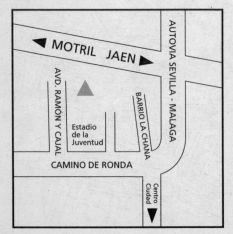

Madrid -
Sta Cruz de Marcenado

**Calle Sta Cruz de Marcenado No 28,
28015 Madrid.**
☎ 915 474532
🛈 915 481196

Open Dates:	🗓
Open Hours:	09.00-20.00hrs
Reservations:	**R**
Price Range:	950-1300 pts € 5.70-7.81 BBinc 🛏
Beds:	72 - 2x^2🛏 6x^4🛏 2x^6🛏 4x^6🛏
Facilities:	♿ 🍽 (B) 👥 📺 🗄 🖼 ⬍ ℹ 👥

Directions:

✈	Barajas 12km
A🚌	Colón - Aeropuerto
🚆	Chamartin 8km
🚌	Circular 1, 2, 44, 133, 21 500m
Ⓤ	Linea 4 - Argüelles 500m

Miranda de Ebro -
Fernán Gonzalez

**c/ Anduva 82,
09200 Miranda de Ebro (Burgos)**
☎ 947 320932
🛈 947 320334

Open Dates:	🗓
Reservations:	**R**
Price Range:	1100-1600 ptas € 6.61-9.61 🛏
Beds:	110 - 13x^1🛏 12x^2🛏 24x^3🛏 1x^6🛏
Facilities:	👥 🍽 🛆 📺 🗄 🗄 8 ⊜ 🅿 🍴

Directions:

🚆	Miranda de Ebro 1.5km

Attractions: ⚲ 🚣

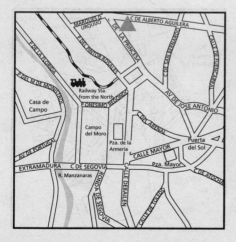

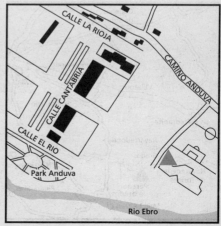

Navarredonda de Gredos - Albergue Juvenil "Navarredonda de Gredos"

Crta. Comarcal C-500 Km 41.5,
05635 Navarredonda de Gredos (Avila)
☎ 920 348005, 920 355095
🖷 920 348005
✉ miguel.angel.ruiz@stec.scj.av.jcyl.es

Open Dates:	🖻
Open Hours:	08.00-24.00hrs
Reservations:	**R** ⊂CC⊃
Price Range:	1,050-1,525 pts BB inc 🗊
Beds:	63 - 3x¹ 20x² 5x⁴
Facilities:	👬
	5x 👬 🍽 ☕ 🚡 📺 📦 1 x 🍴 🗓
	🅿 ℹ ♿ ⛰ 🔍 🏬

Directions:

✈	Barajas 179km
🚂	Avila 64km
🚌	Avila 64km ap YH

Attractions: 🎣 ⛰ 🚶 ∪ 1.5km ⚲ ⛵

Salamanca - Albergue Juvenil "Salamanca"

C/ Escoto 13-15,
37008 Salamanca.
☎ 923 269141, 923 263193
🖷 923 269141
✉ esterra@mmteam.disgumad.es

Open Dates:	🖻
Reservations:	**R**
Price Range:	1500-1800 pts € 9.01-10.81
Beds:	65
Facilities:	♿ 👬 🍽 🚡 🗓 🏬 🅿

Directions:

✈	Barajas (Madrid) 200km
🚂	Salamanca 1km
🚌	1,4, 250m ap Gran Vía & Plaza Mayor

Attractions: 🚴

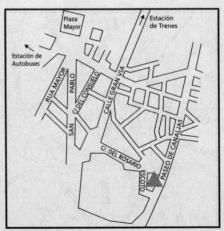

Santiago de Compostela -
Monte do Gozo

Carretera de Santiago-Aeropuerto KM 3, 15820 Santiago de Compostela (A Coruña).
☎ 981 558942
✆ 981 562892

Open Dates:	📅
Open Hours:	🕐
Price Range:	970-1425 pts € 5.82-8.56 BBinc 🏠
Beds:	300 - 38x⁶
Facilities:	👥 🍴 🛏 📺 📦 1 x 🍽 🔲 🖼 ⚒ 🔢 🅿 ℹ️ 🚻 ♨ 🏔 ○ 🔥 ⛺

Directions:

✈	"Lavacolla", Santiago 8km
🚂	Santiago 3km
🚌	#6 5km

Attractions: 🎣 🏔 🚴 🏃 ∪ 🏊

Sevilla

Isaac Peral 2, 41012 Sevilla.
☎ 954 613150
✆ 954 613158

Open Dates:	📅
Open Hours:	🕐
Reservations:	Ⓡ
Beds:	198 - 66x³ 4x⁴
Facilities:	♿ 👥 🍴 🛏 📺 200 x🍽 🖼 ⚒ 🔢 🅱 🚻 ♨

Directions:

✈	San Pablo 10km
A🚌	From City Center
🚂	"Sta Justa" 2km
🚌	34, 6, 35

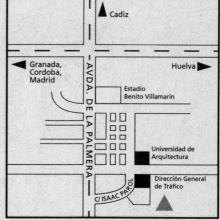

Zaragoza -
Baltasar Gracián

c/ Franco y López 4,
50005 Zaragoza.

☎ 976 551387, 9714967

📠 976 553432

✉ mtmosquera@aragob.es

Open Dates:	01.01-31.07; 01.09-31.12
Reservations:	**R**
Price Range:	1250-1650 pts € 7.51-9.91
Beds:	50 - 1x^1🛏 2x^2🛏 4x^4🛏 1x^6🛏
Facilities:	♿ ⅲ 🍽 (B) 👕 ♨ 📺 🅿 🌿 🔍 🏧

Directions:

✈	Zaragoza
🚆	Zaragoza, El Portillo
🚌	Zaragoza, 22, 38, 24.

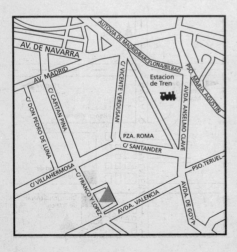

> Know'st thou the land where
> the lemon-trees bloom,
> Where the gold orange glows
> in the deep thicket's
> gloom,
> Where a wind ever soft from the blue
> heaven blows,
> And the groves are of laurel and myrtle
> and rose?
>
> Connais-tu le pays où fleurissent les
> citronniers,
> Où les oranges d'or flamboyent sur leur
> feuillage foncé,
> Où souffle un vent toujours doux venu des
> cieux azurés,
> Et où les vergers sentent la myrte, la rose
> et le laurier?
>
> Kennst Du das Land, wo die Zitronen
> blühen,
> In dunklem Laub die Goldorangen
> glühen,
> Ein sanfter Wind vom blauen Himmel
> weht,
> Die Myrte still und hoch der Lorbeer
> steht?
>
> ¿Conoces la tierra donde los limoneros
> florecen,
> Donde la naranja dorada en el oscuro
> follaje resplandece,
> Donde del cielo azul una brisa siempre
> tenue sopla
> Y en cuyos vergeles crece el
> laurel y el mirto y la rosa?

Goethe (1749-1832)

Location/Address	Telephone No. Fax No.	Beds	Opening Dates	Facilities
▲ **Aguadulce** Campillo del Moro S/N, 04720 Aguadulce (Almeria).	☎ 950 340346 ✆ 950 345855	210	12	👬 ⓣ ⓡ ♿ P
▲ **Aguilas** - Calarreona Ctra. de Vera Km4, 30880 Aguilas (Murcia).	☎ 968 413029 ✆ 968 413029	80	12	ⓣ ⓡ
▲ **Albarracín** - Rosa Bríos Rosa Bríos, c/ Santa María 5, Albarracín 44100 (Teruel).	☎ 978 710005 ✆ 978 641033	70	12	👬 ⓣ ⓡ
▲ **Alborache** - Torre D'Alborache Ctra de Macastre, s/n 46369 Alborache (Valencia).	☎ 962 508123, 962 508124 ✆ 962 508020	116	01.02–17.12	ⓣ ⓡ ♿
▲ **Alburquerque** - Castillo de Luna **c/ Castillo, s/n 06510 Alburquerque (Badajoz).**	☎ 924 400041 ✆ 924 401523	8	12	👬 ⓣ
▲ **Alcalá de Moncayo** c/ Puerta del Lugar s/n, 50591 Alcalá de Moncayo (Zaragoza)	☎ 976 646459 ✆ 976 646459	86	12	👬 ⓣ ⓡ P
▲ **Alcudia** - La Victoria **Crta. Cabo Pinar, Km. 4 Alcudia (Mallorca).**	☎ 971 545395 ✆ 971 545395	120	01.03-30.09	ⓣ P
▲ **Alfaro** Plaza Araña, 26540 Alfaro (La Rioja)	☎ 941 29100 Ext 6202 941 291229	40	12 👬	👬 ⓣ ⓡ
▲ **Algeciras** Ctra. N-340, km 95,600, 11205 Algeciras (Cádiz)	☎ 956679060 ✆ 956679017	100	12	👬 ⓣ ⓡ 8 SE ♿ P
▲ **Alicante** - "La Florida" Avda Orihuela 59, 03007 Alicante.	☎ 965 113044 ✆ 965 282754	184	01.01–30.08; 01.10–31.12	ⓣ ⓡ
▲ **Almería** c/ Isla de Fuerteventura S/N, 04007 Almería.	☎ 950 269788 ✆ 950 271744	164	12	ⓣ ⓡ ♿ P
▲ **Almorox** - "Granja Escuela -Pradoluengo" Camino Cadalso-Pinar, 45900 Almorox (Toledo).	☎ 918 623265, 914 730020	58	12	ⓣ ⓡ
▲ **La Almunia de Doña Godina** - Ramón y Cajal" Avda Laviaga Castillo, La Almunia de Doña Godina (Zaragoza)	☎ 976 600833 ✆ 976 600833	72	12	ⓣ
▲ **Alsasua** - "Sto Cristo de Otadia" Zelai 91, 31800 Alsasua (Navarra).	☎ 948 564814 ✆ 948 564973	70	01.01–10.09; 21.09–23.12	👬 ⓣ ⓡ ♿ CC P
▲ **Altafulla** - "Casa Gran" Placeta 12, 43893 Altafulla (Tarragona)	☎ 977 650779 ✆ 977 650588	65	11.01–22.12	👬 ⓣ ⓡ
▲ **Aratores** - "Santa Maria" Aratores 22860 (Huesca).	☎ 974 348051		12	ⓡ P
▲ **Arbejal** Arbejal 34843 (Palencia).	☎ 979 870174	70	12	👬 ⓣ ⓡ 2 NW P
▲ **Arriondas** c/del Barco, 12. 33540 Arriondas (Asturias).	☎ 985 840334 ✆ 985 841282	12	12	ⓣ P

Location/Address	Telephone No. Fax No.	Beds	Opening Dates	Facilities
▲ Auñon - "Entrepeñas" Poblado de Entrepeñas, 19130 Auñon (Guadalajara).	☎ 949 358415 ✆ 949 222062	64	01.01–30.10; 10–31.12	⑩ R ♿
▲ Avila - "Profesor Arturo Duperier" Av de Juventud s/n, 05003 Avila.	☎ 920 221716 ✆ 920 221716	90	01.07–15.08	⑩ P
▲ Baños de Montemayor - Residencia Juvenil "Joaquin Sama" c/ Calvo Sotelo, s/n, 10750 Baños de Montemayor (Cáceres).	☎ 923 428003	10	01.06–31.08 (Thurs–Sun 01.09–31.05)	� ⑩ R
▲ Barbastro - "Joaquin Costa" Av. Monseñor Escrivá s/n, 22300 Barbastro (Huesca).	☎ 974 311834 ✆ 974 313527	120	🄰	⑩ R
▲ Barcelona - Mare de Déu de Montserrat [IBN] **Passeig Mare de Déu del Coll 41-51, 08023 Barcelona.**	☎ 932 105151 ✆ 932 100798	183	01.01–24.12; 26-31.12	⑩ R ♿ CC P ▣
▲ Barcelona - Hostal de Joves Passeig Pujades 29, 08018 Barcelona.	☎ 933 003104	68	🄰	R ▭ ▣ ☕
▲ Barcelona - Pere Tarrés Numancia 149-151, 08029 Barcelona. ✉ alberg@perelarres.org	☎ 934 102309 ✆ 934 196268	90	03.01–24.12	� ⑩ R ▭ P ▣
▲ Barcelona - Studio Duquesa de Orleans, 56 BIS, 08034-Barcelona.	☎ 932 050961 ✆ 932 050900	40	01.07–30.09	� ⑩ R ▣ ☕
▲ Barría - Monasterio de Barría 01208 Barriá (Araba).	☎ 945 317132 ✆ 945 181988	200	🄰	� ⑩ R ♿ ▭ ▣
▲ Béjar - "Llano Alto" El Castañar, 37715 Béjar (Salamanca)	☎ 923 404052 ✆ 923 400702	160	🄰	� ⑩ R P
▲ Benicarló - "Sant Crist del Mar" Avda de Yecla 29, 12580 Benicarló (Castellón).	☎ 964 470836, 963 985900 ✆ 964 460225	80	01.01–30.06, 01.07–15.08, 01.10–31.12 (Closed weekends)	� ⑩ R
▲ Benicasim - Argentina **Avda Ferrandiz Salvador 40, 12560 Benicasim (Castellón)**	☎ 964 300949; 964302709 ✆ 964 300473	140	02.02-22.12	� R ♿ ▣
▲ Biar Llomes de la Mare de Deu, 6 03410 Biar (Alicante).	☎ 965 810875 ✆ 965 810875	68	🄰	⑩ R ▣
△ *Biel* *Avda. de la Mina, s/n. Biel,* *50619 (Zaragoza).*	☎ 976 669001 ✆ 976 669001	26	🄰	R ▣
△ *Bijuesca* *c/Virgen III, 12, 50316 Bijuesca (Zaragoza).*	☎ 976 847292	63	🄰	⑩ R ▣
▲ Bilbao - Bilbao-Aterpetxea **Carretera Basurto-Kastrexana, 70, 48002 Bilbao** ✉ aterpe@albergue.bilbao.met	☎ 944 270054 ✆ 944 275479	142	🄰	� ⑩ R ♿ CC P ▣

Location/Address	Telephone No. Fax No.	Beds	Opening Dates	Facilities
▲ **Boñar** - Pardomino Avda de Asturias No. 13, 24850 Boñar (León)	☎ 987 741581, 987 735510 ✆ 987 741581	100	📅	††† ¶⊙¶ Ⓡ 1N Ⓟ ⊡
△ *Borja - "Santuario de la Misericordia"* *Santuario de la Misericordia,* *50540 Borja (Zaragoza).*	☎ *976 867844,* *976 714797* ✆ *976 714049*	*45*	*01.01–30.11*	Ⓡ ✦ ⊡
▲ **El Bosque** c/Molino de Enmedio S/N, 11670-El Bosque (Cádiz)	☎ 956 716212 ✆ 956 716258	79	📅	¶⊙¶ Ⓡ ♿
▲ **Brañavieja** - "Estación de Invierno Alto Campoo" Brañavieja (Santander)	☎ 908 309133	42	01.01–31.08; 01.10–31.12	¶⊙¶ ✦ Ⓟ ⊡
▲ **Burgos** - "Gil de Siloe R.J." Avda General Vigón s/n, 09006 Burgos.	☎ 947 220362 ✆ 947 220362	108	01.07–15.08	††† ¶⊙¶ Ⓡ ♿ Ⓟ ⊡ ☕
▲ **Cabrera de Mar** - "Torre Ametller" Veinat de Sta Elena d'Agell, Cabrera de Mar, 08349 Barcelona.	☎ 937 594448 ✆ 937 500495	150	12.02–24.12; 27–31.12	††† ¶⊙¶ Ⓡ ♿ Ⓟ ⊡
△ *Candanchu - "Albergue Aysa Candanchu"* *Puerto de Somport-Aysa-Candanchu-* *22889 Huesca.*	☎ *974 373023*	*40*	*01.12–30.05;* *01.07–15.10*	††† ¶⊙¶
△ *Canfranc* *Estación, Plaza del Pilar 2-3,* *22880 Canfranc (Huesca).*	☎ *974 293025* ✆ *974 293040*	*35*	*01.01–31.05;* *01.07–31.12*	Ⓡ ✦ ⊡
▲ **Caracenilla** - Peñarrubias c/ Consuelo, 4, 16540.- Caracenilla (Cuenca).	☎ 969 272711, 969 272652	30	📅	††† ¶⊙¶ Ⓡ Ⓟ ⊡
▲ **Carrión de los Condes** - Rio Carrion Plaza Marcelino Champagnat, No 1, 34120 Carrion de los Condes (Palencia).	☎ 979 881063 ✆ 979 881063	150	📅	††† Ⓡ ⌐CC┐ ✦ Ⓟ ⊡ ☕
▲ **Castellón de la Plana** - El Maestrat Av Hnos Bou 26, 12003 Castellón de la Plana.	☎ 964 220457, 964 223543 ✆ 964 237600	90	01.01–30.07	††† ¶⊙¶ Ⓡ
▲ **Castellón de la Plana** - Mare de deu del Lledó c/ Orfebres Santalínea 2, 12005 Castellón de la Plana.	☎ 964 254096, 964 254392 ✆ 964 216677	90	01.01–31.08	¶⊙¶ Ⓡ
▲ **Cazorla** Pza Mauricio Martínez 6, 23470 Cazorla (Jaén).	☎ 953 720329 ✆ 953 720203	97	📅	¶⊙¶ Ⓡ ♿
▲ **Cercedilla** - Alvaro Iglesias Puerto de Navacerrada, Cercedilla 28470 Madrid.	☎ 918 523887 ✆ 918 523891	92	02.01–15.08; 16.09–30.12	¶⊙¶ Ⓡ Ⓟ
▲ **Cercedilla** - Villa Castora Cta de las Dehesas s/n, Cercedilla, 28470 Madrid.	☎ 918 520334 ✆ 918 522411	80	02.01–15.08; 01.10–30.12	††† ¶⊙¶ Ⓡ
▲ **Cercedilla** - Las Dehesas Crta de las Dehesas s/n, Cercedilla, 28470 Madrid.	☎ 918 520135 ✆ 918 521836	72	02.01–15.08; 01.10–30.12	¶⊙¶ Ⓡ ♿ Ⓟ

Location/Address	Telephone No. Fax No.	Beds	Opening Dates	Facilities
▲ **Chipiona** Pinar de la Villa s/n, 11550 Chipiona (Cádiz)	☎ 956 371480 ✆ 965 371480	216	Easter & Summer (♦♦♦ 🗓)	♦♦♦ ⑩ ℝ
▲ **Ciudad Real** - Albergue Juvenil Orea Ctra Toledo s/n, 13080 Cíudad Real.	☎ 926 690241 ✆ 949 836435	120	🗓	♦♦♦ ⑩ 🚹 ℙ
▲ **Constantina** c/ Cuesta Blanca S/N, 41450 Constantina (Sevilla).	☎ 955 881589 ✆ 955 881619	93	🗓	⑩ ℝ 🚹
▲ **Comaruga** - Sta Maria del Mar Av Palfuriana 80, 43880 Comaruga (Tarragona).	☎ 977 680008 ✆ 977 682959	180	01.02–30.11	♦♦♦ ⑩ ℝ ⊡ ℙ 🔲
▲ **Córdoba** - Plaza Judá Leví S/N. **14003 Córdoba.**	☎ 957 290166 ✆ 957 290500	170	🗓	⑩ ℝ 🚹 ⊡ 🚲 ☕
▲ **Cortes de la Frontera** Crta A373, Villamartín - Puerto del Espino Km, 51 600 Cortes de la Frontera (Málaga)	☎ 954 277087 ✆ 954 277462	120	01.07–31.12 (only weekends)	⑩ ℙ 🔲
▲ **A Coruña** - Albergue Juvenil, Gandarío Playa de Gandarío, 15167 Sada (A Coruña).	☎ 981 791005 ✆ (81) 794217	300	🗓	⑩ ℙ
▲ **A Coruña** - Marina Española Corbeiroa, Sada (A Coruña).	☎ 981 620118	110	🗓	⑩ ℙ
△ *Daroca - Albergue Juvenil Daroca* *c/ Cortes de Aragón, 13,* *50360 Daroca (Zaragoza).*	☎ *976 800129,* *976 801268* ✆ *976 800362*	*60*	🗓	⑩ ℝ ℙ
▲ **Deltebre** - Mn. Antoni Batlle Avda de les Goles de l'ebres s/n, 43580 Deltebre (Tarragona).	☎ 977 480136 ✆ 977 481284	120	🗓	♦♦♦ ⑩ ℝ 🚹 🚲 ℙ 🔲
▲ **Donostia-San Sebastian** - La Sirena **Paseo de Igeldo 25,** **20008 Donostia-San Sebastian.** 📧 udala.youthostel@donostia.org	☎ 943 310268, 943 311293 ✆ 943 214090	96	🗓	⑩ ℝ 2SW 🚹 ⊡ 🚲 🔲
▲ **Donostia-San Sebastian** - Ulia-Mendi Parque de Ulia, Paseo de Ulia 299, 20013 Donostia-San Sebastian. 📧 udalayouthostel@donostia.org	☎ 943 310268, 943 311293 ✆ 943 214090	60	🗓	⑩ ℝ 5NE ℙ 🔲
▲ **Dosrius** - Mas Silvestre Veinat d'en Rimbles 14, 08319 Dosrius (Barcelona).	☎ 937 955014 ✆ 937 955199	160	01.01–06.01; 27.02–08.12; 26.12–31.12	⑩ ℝ ℙ
▲ **Empúries** - L'Escala Les Coves, 41, 17130 L'Escala (Girona).	☎ 972 771200 ✆ 972 771572	68	02.01–31.09; 16.10–20.12	⑩ ℝ ℙ
▲ **Espejo** Ctra. de Barrio, 1, 01423 Espejo (Araba)	☎ 947 351150 ✆ 945 181988	116	🗓	ℝ 🚲 ℙ 🔲
▲ **L'Espluga de Francolí** - Jaume I Les Masies s/n, 43440 L'Espluga de Francolí (Tarragona).	☎ 977 870356 ✆ 977 870414	160	🗓	♦♦♦ ⑩ ℝ 🚹 ℙ
▲ **Espinosa** - Espinosa de los Monteros Carretera de Baranda S/N, 09560 Espinosa de los Monteros (Burgos).	☎ 947 143660 ✆ 947 120449	60	🗓	⑩ 0.6N ℙ 🔲 🚲

Location/Address	Telephone No. Fax No.	Beds	Opening Dates	Facilities
▲ **Estella** - Oncineda Monasterio de Irache S/N, 31200 Estella (Navarra).	☎ 948 555022 ✆ 948 551745	150	▣	⑪ ⓡ ♿ ℗ ▤
▲ **Ezcaray** - Molino Viejo Camino de los Molinos s/n, 26280 Ezcaray (La Rioja).	☎ 941 354197	49	▣	⑪ ⓡ
▲ **Figueres** - Tramuntana [IBN] **Anicet de Pagès, 2, 17600 Figueres (Girona)**	☎ 972 501213 ✆ 972 673808	50	01.04-08.12	⑪⑪ ⑪ ⓡ ☞ ☕
Fuenterrabia ☞ **Hondarribia**				
▲ **Girona** - Cerveri de Girona Ciutadans 9, 17004 Girona.	☎ 972 218003 ✆ 972 212023	100	▣	⑪⑪ ⑪ ⓡ ♿ ▤
▲ **Granada** - Albergue Juvenil Granada **Avda Ramon y Cajal 2, 18003 Granada.**	☎ 958 284306 ✆ 958 285285	150	▣	⑪ ⓡ ♿ ℗
▲ **Grañón** - Ermita el Carrasquedo Crta Cordorales, s/n 26259 Grañón (La Rioja).	☎ 941 746000	40	01.01–15.09; 01.10–31.12	⑪⑪ ⓡ
▲ **Guía** - Albergue Juvenil San Fernando Av Juventud s/n, Sta Maria de Guía, Gran Canaria.	☎ 928 550827 ✆ 928 882728	87	▣	⑪⑪ ⑪ ⓡ ℗ ▤
▲ **Hondarribia-Fuenterrabia** - "Juan Sebastian Elkano" Subida al Faro, No. 7, 20280 Hondarribia, Gipuzkoa. ✉ juv.hondarribia@gazteria.gipuzkoa.met	☎ 943 641550 ✆ 943 640028	20	01.02–31.10; 01–31.12	⑪⑪ ⑪ ℗
▲ **Huelva** Avenida Marchena Colombo 14, 21004 Huelva.	☎ 959 253793 ✆ 959 253499	128	▣	⑪ ⓡ ♿
△ *Jaca - Escuelas Pías* *Avda Perimetral s/n, 22700 Jaca (Huesca).*	☎ *974 360536* ✆ *974 362559*	*150*	*01.01–30.09; 01–31.12*	⑪ ⓡ ▤
▲ **Jerez de la Frontera** Avda Carrero Blanco 30, 11408 -Jérez de la Frontera (Cádiz).	☎ 956 143901 ✆ 956 143263	120	▣	⑪ ⓡ ♿ ℗
▲ **Jerte** - Emperador Carlos V Crta. Plasencia-Avila, KM 38, Valle del Jerte, Jerte (Cáceres)	☎ 927 470062	10	01.06–31.08 (Fri–Sun 01.09–31.05)	⑪⑪ ⑪ ⓡ 5S ℗
▲ **Layos** - El Castillo de Layos c/ Conde de Mora s/n, Layos (Toledo).	☎ 925 376585 ✆ 913 572564	120	▣	⑪ ⓡ ℗
▲ **Lekároz** - Albergue Juvenil Baztan 31795 Lekároz (Navarra).	☎ 948 581804 ✆ 948 581838	80	10.01–30.09	⑪⑪ ⑪ ⓡ ♿ ℗ ▤
▲ **León** - Infanta Doña Sancha C/ Corredera 4, 24004 León.	☎ 987 203414, 987 203459 ✆ 987 251525	124	01.07–15.08	⑪ ♿ ▤
▲ **León** - Consejo de Europa Paseo del Parque 2, 24005 León.	☎ 987 200206, 987 202969	97	01.07–15.08	⑪ ▤ ☕
▲ **León** - Miguel de Unamuno San Pelayo 15, 24003 León.	☎ 987 233010, 987 233203 ✆ 987 233010	60	01.07–30.09	⑪⑪ ⑪ ⓡ ℗ ▤

Location/Address	Telephone No. Fax No.	Beds	Opening Dates	Facilities
▲ **Lés** - "Matacabos" Sant Jaume s/n, 25540 Lés, Val D'Aran (Lleida).	☎ 973 648048 ✆ 973 648352	46	🗓	ⅲ ⑩ Ⓡ
▲ **Llanes** - Juventudes c/ Celso Amieva 7, 33500 Llanes (Asturias).	☎ 98 5400770 ✆ 98 5400770	16	🗓	⑩ ᕼ
Lleida ☞ **La Seu d'Urgell**				
▲ **Lleida** - Sant Anastasi Rambla d'Aragó 11, 25003 Lleida.	☎ 973 266099 ✆ 973 261865	120	🗓	ⅲ ⑩ Ⓡ 🗗
▲ **Logroño** - Residencia Universitaria c/ Caballero de la Rosa 38, 26004 Logroño.	☎ 941 291145	92	01.07–30.09	⑩ Ⓡ 🗗
▲ **Loredo** Bajada Playa de Loredo s/n, 39140 Loredo (Cantabria)	☎ 942 504160, 919 464221	48	01.01–31.08; 01.10–31.12	🗗
▲ **Luarca** - Fernán Coronas El Villar S/N, 33700 Luarca (Asturias).	☎ 98 5640676 ✆ 98 5640557	18	🗓	⑩ Ⓟ
▲ **Lugo** - Eijo Garay c/ Pintor Corredoira 4, 27002 Lugo.	☎ 982 220450 ✆ 982 230524	100	01.07–30.09	ⅲ Ⓡ Ⓟ 🗗
△ *Lugo - Hermanos Pedrosa R.J.* *Pintor Corredoira 2, 27002 Lugo.*	☎ *982 221090*	*100*	*01.07–30.09*	⑩ Ⓟ
▲ **Madrid** - "San Fermín" Avda de las Fuentes, 36, 28041 Madrid.	☎ 911 920897 ✆ 911 924724	60	🗓	⑩ ᕼ ✂ Ⓟ 🗗 ☕
▲ **Madrid** - Richard Schirrman Casa de Campo, 28011 Madrid.	☎ 914 635699 ✆ 914 644685	132	🗓	⑩ Ⓡ ᕼ Ⓟ 🗗 ☕
▲ **Madrid** - Sta Cruz de Marcenado **Calle Sta Cruz de Marcenado No 28, 28015 Madrid.**	☎ 915 474532 ✆ 915 481196	72	🗓	Ⓡ ᕼ 🗗
▲ **Las Majadas** - Los Callejones Plaza Mayor s/n, 16142 Las Majadas (Cuenca).	☎ 969 283050 ✆ 969 283121	60	🗓	⑩ Ⓡ
▲ **Málaga** Plaza Pio XII 6, 29007 Málaga.	☎ 952 308500, 952 308500 ✆ 952 308504, 952 308504	110	🗓	⑩ Ⓡ ᕼ
▲ **Manresa** - Del Carme Pl del Milcentenari de Manresa, s/n 08240 Manresa (Barcelona).	☎ 938 750396 ✆ 938 726838	71	06.01–07.08; 29.08–21.12	ⅲ ⑩ Ⓡ ᕼ ✂ Ⓟ
▲ **Marbella** Calle Trapiche 2, 29600 Marbella (Málaga).	☎ 952 771491 ✆ 952 863227	142	🗓	⑩ Ⓡ ᕼ Ⓟ
▲ **El Masnou** - Josep Ma Batista i Roca ⟨IBN⟩ Av dels Srs Cusí i Furtunet 52, 08320 El Masnou (Barcelona).	☎ 935 555600 ✆ 935 400552	84	11.01–07.12	⑩ Ⓡ ᕼ Ⓟ
▲ **Mazagón** Cuesta de la Barca S/N, 21130 Mazagón (Huelva).	☎ 959 536262	132	🗓 (ⅲ Only except Easter & Summer)	⑩ Ⓡ ᕼ
▲ **Miranda de Ebro** - Fernán Gonzalez **c/ Anduva 82, 09200 Miranda de Ebro (Burgos)**	☎ 947 320932 ✆ 947 320334	110	🗓	ⅲ ⑩ Ⓡ ✂ Ⓟ 🗗

Location/Address	Telephone No. Fax No.	Beds	Opening Dates	Facilities
▲ **La Molina** - Mare de Déu de les Neus Ctra de Font Canaleta, 17537 La Molina (Girona).	☎ (72) 892012 🖷 (72) 892050	148	01.01–23.12; 26–31.12	♦♦ ⑩ ℝ ℙ ⬚
▲ **Moraira-Teulada** - La Marina Camino Campamento 31, 03724 Moraira-Teulada (Alicante).	☎ 966 492030, 966 492044 🖷 966 491051	130	🗓	♦♦ ⑩ ℝ ⛷ ⬚
▲ **Morella** - Francesc de Vinatea 12300 Morella (Castellón).	☎ 964 160100 🖷 963 985900	60	🗓	♦♦ ⑩ ⛷ ℙ
▲ **Munilla** - Hayedo de Santiago c/ Cipriano Martinez 29, 26586 Munilla (La Rioja).	☎ 941 394213	50	🗓	⑩ ℝ
▲ **Navamorcuende** - El Chortalillo Camino de la Tablada s/n, 45630 Navamorcuende, (Toledo.)	☎ 925 811186	136	🗓	⑩ ℝ ⬚
▲ **Navarredonda de Gredos** - Albergue Juvenil "Navarredonda de Gredos" **Crta. Comarcal C-500 Km 41.5, 05635 Navarredonda de Gredos (Avila)** ℮ miguel.angel.ruiz@stec.scj.av.jcyl.es	☎ 920 348005, 920 355095 🖷 920 348005	63	🗓	♦♦ ⑩ ℝ ⊞CC⊟ ℙ ⬚ ☕
▲ **Nogueira de Ramuin** - A Penalba Nogueira de Ramuin, 32004 Orense.	☎ 988 201127	30	01.01–30.06; 01.10–31.12	⑩ ⬚
▲ **Nogueira de Ramuin** - Monasterio de San Estevo de Rivas do Sil Nogueira de Ramuin, 32004 Orense.	☎ 988 201127	32	01.01–30.06; 01.10–31.12	⬚
▲ **Olot** - Torre Malagrida Passeig de Barcelona 15, 17800 Olot (Girona).	☎ 972 264200 🖷 972 271896	76	🗓	♦♦ ⑩ ℝ ⛷ ⊞CC⊟ ⬚
▲ **Orea** - Albergue el Autillo Llano Hoz Seca, 19311 Orea (Guadalajara).	☎ 949 836470 🖷 948 836470	70	🗓	⑩ ℙ
△ *Orense* - *Florentino López Cuevillas Arturo Perez Serantes 2, 32005 Orense.*	☎ *988 252412,* *988 252451*	*60*	*01.07–30.09*	⑩ ℙ
▲ **Oviedo** - Ramon Menéndez Pidal Avda Julian Clavería 14, 33006 Oviedo.	☎ 98 5232054 🖷 98 5233393	6	🗓	⑩ ℙ
▲ **Palencia** - Escuela Castilla R.J. Avenida de San Telmo S/N, 34004 Palencia.	☎ 979 721475, 979 721650	65	Closed for repairs	♦♦ ⑩ ⚲ ℙ ⬚ ☕
▲ **Palencia** - Residencia Victorio Macho Doctor Fleming S/N, 34004 Palencia.	☎ 979 720462, 979 747300	42	01.07–15.08	♦♦ ⑩ ⬚
Las Palmas ☞ **Guía**				
▲ **Palma de Mallorca** - Playa de Palma Calle Costa Brava, 13 - Sometines-El Arenal, 07610 Palma de Mallorca.	☎ 971 260892 🖷 971 262012	80	🗓	♦♦ ⑩
▲ **Pamplona** - Fuerte del Principe Goroabe 36; 31002 Pamplona-Iruña (Navarra).	☎ 948 291206 🖷 948 290540	15	01.01–30.06; 01.08–31.12	⑩ ℝ [0.5 SE] ⛷ ℙ ⬚
▲ **Peñaranda de Bracamonte** - Resid. "Diego de Torres y Villarroel" c/ Severo Ochoa 4, 37300 Peñaranda de Bracamonte (Salamanca).	☎ 923 540988, 923 296000 🖷 923 540988	50	🗓	♦♦ ⑩ ℝ

Location/Address	Telephone No. Fax No.	Beds	Opening Dates	Facilities
▲ Peralta de la Sal - Escuelas Pias Plaza Escuelas Pias No 1. 22513 Peralta de la Sal (Huesca).	☎ 974 411031	80	▥	⚇ ⊫ ℝ ✆ ℙ ▣
▲ Pesquera - Fernandez de Los Rios 39491 Pesquera (Cantabria)	☎ 942 778614	42	▥	▣
▲ Piles - Mar i Vent Doctor Fleming s/n, 46712 Piles (Valencia).	☎ 962 831748, 963 985900 ☎ 962 831121	89	02.02–16.12	⚇ ⊫ ℝ ♿ ▣
▲ Planoles - Pere Figuera (IBN) Ctra de Neva Prat Cap Riu S/N, 17535 Planoles, Girona.	☎ 972 736177 ☎ 972 736431	170	▥	⚇ ⊫ ℝ ♿ ℙ
▲ Plentzia - A.J. Plentzia Ibiltokia 1, 48620 Plentzia (Bizkaia).	☎ 946 771866 ☎ 946 773041	12	08.01–22.12	⚇ ⊫ ℝ ♿
▲ Poble Nou Del Delta - L'Encanyissada Poble Nou Del Delta, 43549 Amposta (Tarragona).	☎ 977 742203 ☎ 977 742709	50	07.01–01.04; 14.09–25.12	⚇ ⊫ ℝ
▲ Poo de Llanes - Fonte del Cai Carretera General, 33500 Poo de Llanes (Asturias).	☎ 985 400205 ☎ 985 401019	10	▥	⊫ ✆
▲ Punta Umbría Avenida Océano 13, 21130 Punta Umbria (Huelva).	☎ 959 311650 ☎ 959 314229	102	▥	⊫ ℝ ♿
▲ Queralbs - Pic de Áliga c/ Núria, 17534 s/n Queralbs (Girona).	☎ 972 732048 ☎ 972 732048	138	▥	⚇ ⊫ ℝ
▲ Rascafria - Los Batanes Rascafria, 28740 Madrid.	☎ 918 691511 ☎ 918 690125	122	02.01–15.08; 01.10–30.12	⚇ ⊫ ℝ ♿ ℙ
△ Ribadeo - A Devesa 27700 Ribadeo, Lugo.	☎ 982 123300	75	15.06–30.08	⚇ ℝ ℙ ▣
▲ Ribadesella - "Roberto Frassinelli" c/ Ricardo Cangas, s/n 33560-Ribadesella (Asturias)	☎ 985 861380	6	Easter, Summer & Christmas	⚇ ✆
▲ Roncesvalles - Roncesvalles Orreaga Real Colegiata, Roncesvalles (Navarra).	☎ 948 760307 ☎ 948 760362	65	01.01–31.10; 01–31.12	⊫ ℝ ⫽CC⫽ ℙ ▣
▲ Ruidera - Alonso Quijano CTRA. de las Lagunas, s/n. 13249 Ossa de Montiel (Albacete).	☎ 926 528053	80	▥	⚇ ⊫ ℙ
▲ Ruiloba - "Gargantia" B.ª La Iglesia, s/n 39527 Ruiloba (Cantabria)	☎ 942 720172, 908 285167	40	▥	ℙ ☞
▲ San Martin de Castañeda Ctra. Lago Sanabria, San Martin de Castañeda, 49361 Zamora.	☎ 980 622083, 980 622062 ☎ 980 622053	80	▥	⊫ ℙ ▣
▲ Salamanca - Albergue Juvenil"Salamanca" C/ Escoto 13-15, 37008 Salamanca. ℮ esterra@mmteam.disgumad.es	☎ 923 269141, 923 263193 ☎ 923 269141	65	▥	⚇ ⊫ ℝ ♿ ℙ ▣
▲ Salardú - Era Garona CTRA. de Vielha, 25598 Salardú, Lleida.	☎ 973 645271 ☎ 973 644136	180	▥	⚇ ℝ ♿ ⫽CC⫽ ℙ ▣

Location/Address	Telephone No. Fax No.	Beds	Opening Dates	Facilities
△ *San Juan del Plan* - *El Molin* 22367 San Juan del Plan, Huesca.	☎ *974 506208,* *974 506097* 🖷 *974 506208*	*22*	🗓	🅿 ☕
▲ **San Lorenzo del Escorial** - Sta Maria Buen Aire Finca de la Herreria s/n, San Lorenzo de el Escorial, 28200 Madrid.	☎ 918 903640 🖷 918 903792	88	02.01–15.08; 01.10–30.12	¶⊙¶ Ⓡ 🅿
▲ **San Lorenzo del Escorial** - El Escorial c/ Residencia 14, San Lorenzo de El Escorial, 28200 Madrid.	☎ 918 905924 🖷 918 900620	85	02.01–15.08; 01.10–30.12	♦♦ ¶⊙¶ Ⓡ ♿ 🗓 ☕
▲ **San Pablo de los Montes** - Baños del Sagrario c/ Peña del Soto, 36, 45120 San Pablo de los Montes (Toledo).	☎ 608 913968	300	🗓	¶⊙¶ Ⓡ 👟 🗓
▲ **San Rafael** Paseo de San Juan, s/n 40410 San Rafael (Segovia).	☎ 921 171457, 921 417384	65	🗓	¶⊙¶ Ⓡ
▲ **San Rafael** - El Recreo c/ Pinar No. 1, 40410 San Rafael (Segovia)	☎ 921 171900 🖷 921 171900	72	🗓	♦♦ ¶⊙¶ Ⓡ ♿ ⌐CC¬ 🅿
San Sebastian ☞ **Donostia**				
▲ **San Vicente del Monte** 39592 San Vicente del Monte (Cantabria)	☎ 919 464193	50	🗓	🗓
▲ **Santiago de Compostela** - Monte do Gozo **Carretera de Santiago-Aeropuerto KM 3, 15820 Santiago de Compostela (A Coruña).**	☎ 981 558942 🖷 981 562892	300	🗓	¶⊙¶ 🅿 🗓
▲ **Segovia** - Emperador Teodosio Avda Conde de Sepúlveda s/n, 40006 Segovia.	☎ 921 441111, 921 441047	80	01.07–15.08	♦♦ ¶⊙¶ Ⓡ ♿ 🗓
▲ **Seseña** - Sta Maria del Sagrario Ctra de Andalucía Km 36, 200, 45224 Seseña Nuevo (Toledo).	☎ 918 936152 🖷 918 936152	55	01.01–14.09; 21.10–31.12	¶⊙¶ 🅿
▲ **La Seu d'Urgell** - La Valira Joaquin Viola 57, 25700 La Seu d'Urgell (Lleida).	☎ 973 353897 🖷 973 353874	100	🗓 (except 24–25.12)	¶⊙¶ Ⓡ ♿ 🅿 🗓
▲ **Sevilla** **Isaac Peral 2, 41012 Sevilla.**	☎ 954 613150 🖷 954 613158	198	🗓	¶⊙¶ Ⓡ ♿
▲ **Sierra Nevada** C/ Peñones, 22. 18196 Sierra Nevada (Granada).	☎ 958 480305 🖷 958 481377	214	🗓	¶⊙¶ Ⓡ ♿ 🅿
▲ **Sin** - Tella Sin Calle Unica, s/n 22366 SIN (Huesca).	☎ 974 506212	48	🗓	¶⊙¶
▲ **Siresa** - "Albergue Juvenil del Nucleode las Escuelas de Siresa" c/Reclusa, s/n, Siresa-22790 (Huesca).	☎ 976 615283, 619 561004 🖷 976 615283	53	🗓	¶⊙¶ 👟 🗓
▲ **Solorzano** - Albergue Juvenil Gerardo Diego B-° Quintana, s/n 39739 Solorzano (Cantabria)	☎ 942 676342, 919 464220	60	01.01–31.08; 01.10–31.12	👟 🗓

Location/Address	Telephone No. Fax No.	Beds	Opening Dates	Facilities
▲ **Soncillo** Avda Alejandro Rodriguez Valcarcel s/n 09572 Soncillo (Burgos).	☎ 947 7153024, 947 153080	60	🔒	� ♦♦ ⦿ R
▲ **Soria** - Antonio Machado R.J. Plaza José Antonio 1, 42003 Soria.	☎ 975 220089	100	01.07–15.08	♦♦ ⦿
▲ **Soria** - Juan A. Gaya Nuño Paseo de San Francisco 1, 42003 Soria.	☎ 975 221466	118	01.07–15.08	⦿ ♿
▲ **Soto de Cameros** - Hospital San Jose c/ San Jose s/n, 26132 Soto de Cameros (La Rioja).	☎ 941 291100 ✆ 941 256120	46	🔒	⦿
▲ **Talavera de la Reina** - Albergue Juv. Talavera Carretera de Cervera km 3,5, 45600 Talavera de la Reina (Toledo).	☎ 925 709482, 925 709588, 925 810409 ✆ 925 709588	100	🔒	♦♦ ⦿ 35S P ◻
▲ **Tàrrega** - Residencia Ca N'Aleix Plaça Del Carme, 5, Tarrega (Lleida).	☎ 973 313053 ✆ 973 500037	110	07.01–01.08; 26.08–23.12	♦♦ ⦿ R
△ *Teruel - Luis Buñuel* *Ciudad Escolar s/n, 44003 Teruel.*	☎ *978 602223,* *978 601719*	*160*	*01–31.07;* *01–30.09*	♦♦ ⦿ R
▲ **El Toboso** - El Quijote Avda. Castilla-La Mancha, 12, 45820.- El Toboso (Toledo).	☎ 925 197398	50	🔒	♦♦ ⦿ ECC ◻
▲ **Toledo** Castillo de San Servando, Toledo.	☎ 925 224554	46	01.01–15.08; 15.09–31.12 (Closed Easter & Christmas)	☞ P ◻
▲ **Tragacete** - San Blas 16150 Tragacete (Cuenca).	☎ 969 289131 ✆ 969 178866	64	🔒 (♦♦♦ Only)	⦿ R P
▲ **Ugena** - La Chopera Camino de Yuncos S/N. 45217 Ugena (Toledo).	☎ 925 592741 - 916 414422	200	🔒	♦♦ ☞ P ◻
▲ **Uña** - La Cañadilla c/ Egido 23, 16152 Uña (Cuenca)	☎ 969 281332, 969 281464 ✆ 969 281332	30	🔒	⦿ R
▲ **Uncastillo** - Ayllon c/ Mediavilla 30, 50678 Uncastillo (Zaragoza).	☎ 976 679400 ✆ 976 679497	50	🔒	⦿ R ☞ ◻
▲ **Undués de Lerda** c/ Herrería, 50689 Zaragoza	☎ 948 88105, 689 488745 ✆ 948 888105	56	01.03–30.01	♦♦ ⦿ ☞ P ◻ ☕
▲ **Valdeavellano de Tera** C/Soledad S/N 42165 Valdeavellano de Tera (Soria).	☎ 975 233042 ✆ 975 240002	80	🔒	⦿ R
▲ **Valdepeñas** - El Cañaveral Crta Comarcal de Valdepeñas/San Carlos del Valle, s/n 13300 Valdepeñas (Ciudad Real)	☎ 926 338255, 926 322804, 926 322516 ✆ 926 322808	48	🔒	☞ P ◻
▲ **Valencia de Alcántara** - Sta Mª de Guadalupe Puerto Roque, 10500 Valencia de Alcántara (Cáceres).	☎ 927 584059	10	01.06–31.08 (Thurs–Sun)	♦♦ ⦿ R ♿ P

Location/Address	Telephone No. Fax No.	Beds	Opening Dates	Facilities
▲ **Valladolid** - Rio Esgueva c/ Cementerio 2, 47011 Valladolid.	☏ 983 251550, 983 340044	80	🔒12	††† ⬛
▲ **La Vecilla "Santa Catalina"** Finca Santa Catalina, 24840 La Vecilla (León)	☏ 987 741212 🖷 987 741212	80	🔒12	††† ⊺⬤⊺ **R** ♿ ⵗ P ⬛ ☕ ⬤
▲ **Vic** - Canonge Collel Avgd D'Olimpia S/N, 08500 Vic (Barcelona).	☏ 938 894938	156	06.01–21.12	††† ⊺⬤⊺ **R** ♿ ⟨CC⟩ P ⬛
Vitoria ☞ **Gasteiz**				
▲ **Vigo** - Altamar c/ Cesáreo González 4, 36210 Vigo (Pontevedra).	☏ 986 290808	80	01.07–30.09	††† ⊺⬤⊺
▲ **Villalba de la Sierra** - Casa Flores c/ Constitucion 28, 16140 Villalba de la Sierra (Cuenca)	☏ 969 281250	20	🔒12	⊺⬤⊺ ⵗ ⬤
▲ **Villamanín** Plaza del Ayuntamiento S/N 24680 Villamanín (León).	☏ 987 598243, 987 236500	54	🔒12	††† ⊺⬤⊺ **R** P
▲ **Villanúa** Camino de la Selva S/N, 22870 Villanúa (Huesca).	☏ 974 378016, 976 293025 🖷 974 378016, 976 293040	100	🔒12	††† ⊺⬤⊺ **R** P
▲ **Vitoria-Gasteiz** - Carlos Abaitua Escultor Isaac Diez, S/N 01007 Vitoria-Gasteiz (Araba). ✉ abaitua@clienteeuskaltel.es	☏ 945 148100 🖷 945 148100	20	15.01–15.08; 01.09–31.12	⊺⬤⊺ **R** ♿ P
▲ **Viveiro (Lugo)** - Area Playa de Area - Viveiro, 27837 Vivero (Lugo).	☏ 982 560851	120	01.07–30.08	††† **R**
▲ **Viznar** Camino de Fuente Grande S/N, 18179 Viznar (Granada).	☏ 958 543307 🖷 958 543448	108	🔒12	⊺⬤⊺ **R** ♿ P
▲ **Yeste** - Arroyo de la Sierra Valle del Tus, 02480 Yeste (Albacete).	☏ 967 574127	45	🔒12	††† ⊺⬤⊺ **R** ♿ ⟨CC⟩ ⵗ P ☕ ⬤
▲ **Zamora** - Doña Urraca c/ Villalpando No. 7, 49002 Zamora	☏ 980 512671 🖷 980 512759	115	01.07–15.08	††† ⊺⬤⊺ **R** 0.4NW ♿ P ⬛
▲ **Zaragoza** - Baltasar Gracián c/ **Franco y López 4, 50005 Zaragoza.** ✉ mtmosquera@aragob.es	☏ 976 551387, 9714967 🖷 976 553432	50	01.01-31.07; 01.09-31.12	††† ⊺⬤⊺ **R** ♿ ⵗ P
▲ **Zarautz** - Monte Albertia San Inazio 25, 20800 Zarautz, Gipuzkoa ✉ juv.zarautz@gazteria.gipuzkoa.met	☏ 943 132910 🖷 943 130006	25	01–31.01; 01.03–30.09	††† ⊺⬤⊺♿ P

Location/Address	Telephone No. Fax No.	Beds	Opening Dates	Facilities

YOUTH HOSTEL ACCOMMODATION
OUTSIDE THE ASSURED STANDARDS SCHEME

Location/Address	Telephone No. Fax No.	Beds	Opening Dates	Facilities
Botaya - Casa del Herrero Botaya - 22711 (Huesca).	☎ 974 359853	48	🗓	ⅲ ⅓❘ Ⓡ P
Mora de Rubielos c/San Esteban, 28 44400 Mora De Rubielos (Teruel).	☎ 978 800311 📠 978 806050	59	🗓	⅓❘ Ⓡ ⌂ P 🔲
Yebra de Basa - Santa Orosia c/La Iglesia, 22610 Yebra de Basa (Huesca).	☎ 974 480823	26	🗓	ⅲ Ⓡ P

Is it not pleasant to learn with a constant perseverance and application? Is it not delightful to have friends coming from distant quarters?

N'est-il pas agréable d'apprendre avec persévérance et application constantes? N'est-il pas charmant d'avoir des amis venus de loin?

Ist es nicht erfreulich, mit ständiger Ausdauer und gleichbleibendem Eifer zu lernen? Ist es nicht wunderbar, Freunde zu haben, die aus fernen Landen kommen?

¿No es acaso un placer aprender con constante empeño y aplicación? ¿No es acaso un deleite recibir a amigos procedentes de tierras lejanas?

Confucius

Sweden

SUEDE

SCHWEDEN

SUECIA

**Svenska Turistföreningen (STF),
Stureplan 4, PO Box 25,
101 20 Stockholm, Sweden.**

📞 (46) (8) 4632100
📠 (46) (8) 6781958
📧 info@stfturist.se
www.stfturist.se

Office Hours: Monday-Friday, 09.00-17.00hrs

A copy of the Hostel Directory for this Country can be obtained from:
The National Office.

Capital:	Stockholm	**Population:**	8.8 million
Language:	Swedish	**Size:**	449,964 sq km
Currency:	SEK (1 Krona/*crown* = 100 öre)	**Telephone Country Code:**	46

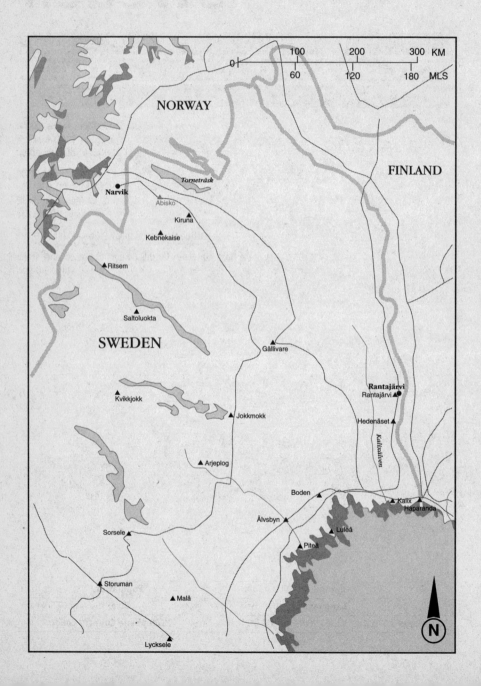

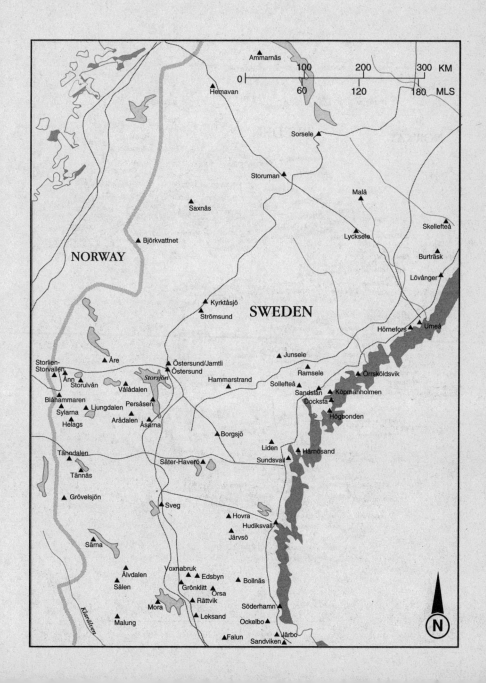

NORWAY

SWEDEN

Ammarnäs

100   200   300 KM
0
Hemavan   60   120   180 MLS

Sorsele

Storuman

Malå

Saxnäs

Skellefteå

Björkvattnet

Lycksele

Burträsk

Lövånger

Kyrktåsjö
Strömsund

Hörnefors   Umeå

Junsele

Åre   Östersund/Jamtli
Östersund
Storlien-   Hammarstrand   Ramsele   Örnsköldsvik
Storvallen   Storsjön   Sollefteå
Ann   Storulvån   Sandslån   Köpmanholmen
Vålådalen   Docksta
Blåhammaren   Persåsen
Sylarna   Ljungdalen   Högbonden
Helags   Arådalen   Åsarna

Borgsjö

Liden
Tänndalen   Härnösand
Säter-Haverö   Sundsvall
Tännäs

Grövelsjön

Sveg

Hovra
Hudiksvall
Järvsö

Sårna

Voxnabruk
Älvdalen   Edsbyn   Bollnäs
Sälen   Grönklitt
Orsa
Mora   Rättvik
Söderhamn
Leksand
Ockelbo
Klarälven   Malung
Falun   Järbo
Sandviken

N

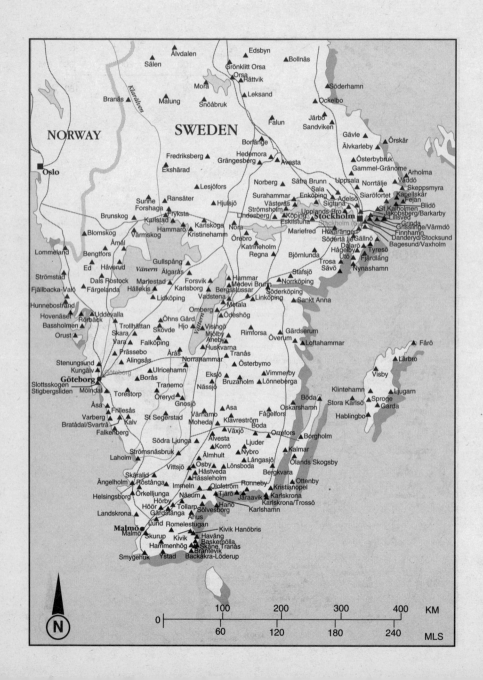

NORWAY

SWEDEN

Oslo

Älvdalen
Sälen
Edsbyn
Bollnäs
Grönklitt Orsa
Orsa
Rättvik
Mora
Leksand
Söderhamn
Branäs
Malung
Snöåbruk
Ockelbo
Fredriksberg
Hedemora
Grängesberg
Avesta
Falun
Järbo
Sandviken
Gävle
Örskär
Ekshärad
Älvkarleby
Österbybruk
Gammel-Gränome
Arholma
Lesjöfors
Norberg
Sätra Brunn
Uppsala
Norrtälje
Väddö
Surahammar
Sala
Skeppsmyra
Ransäter
Enköping
Adelsö
Siaröfortet
Kapellskär
Surne
Fejan
Forshaga
Västerås
Sigtuna
St Kalholmen
Blidö
Hjulsjö
Strömsholm
Köping
Upplands-Bro
Jakobsberg/Barkarby
Tryksta
Lindesberg
Eskilstuna
Stockholm
Lillsved
Brunskog
Karlstad
Karlskoga
Nora
Mariefred
Hökarängen
Grinda
Blomskog
Hammaro
Kristinehamn
Örebro
Södertälje
Gällnö
Glissinge/Värmdö
Finnhamn
Värmskog
Katrineholm
Dalarö
Bagesund/Vaxholm
Danderyd/Stocksund
Åmål
Regna
Hägelöya
Utö
Tyresö
Lommeland
Bengtfors
Gullspång
Björnlunda
Trosa
Utö
Fjärdlång
Ed
Håverud
Vänern
Älgarås
Stafsjö
Sävö
Nynäshamn
Strömstad
Dals Rostock
Marlestad
Forsvik
Hammar
Norrköping
Fjällbacka-Valö
Färgelanda
Hällekis
Karlsborg
Bergslussar
Medevi Brunn
Söderköping
Hunnebostrand
Lidköping
Vadstena
Linköping
Sankt Anna
Hovenäset
Uddevalla
Omberg
Motala
Rörbäck
Öhns Gård
Ödeshög
Bassholmen
Trollhättan
Hjo
Visingö
Rimforsa
Gårdserum
Orust
Skara
Skövde
Mjölby
Överum
Loftahammar
Fårö
Vara
Falköping
Aneby
Huskvarna
Tranås
Prässebo
Åras
Norranammar
Österbymo
Lärbro
Stenungsund
Alingsås
Eksjö
Vimmerby
Visby
Kungälv
Ulricehamn
Bruzaholm
Lönneberga
Göteborg
Borås
Tranemo
Nässjö
Böda
Klintehamn
Ljugarn
Slottsskogen
Mölndal
Toréstorp
Öreryd
Gnosjö
Oskarshamn
Stora Karlsö
Sproge
Garda
Stigbergsliden
Åsa
Åsa
Fågelfors
Hablingbo
Frillesås
St Segerstad
Värnamo
Klavreström
Varberg
Moheda
Boda
Orrefors
Borgholm
Bratådal/Svartrå
Växjö
Falkenberg
Södra Ljunga
Älvesta
Ljuder
Kalmar
Strömsnäsbruk
Korrö
Nybro
Ölands Skogsby
Laholm
Älmhult
Långasjö
Vittsjö
Osby
Lönsboda
Bergkvara
Skäralid
Hästveda
Ängelholm
Röstånga
Hässleholm
Ottenby
Helsingborg
Örkelljunga
Immeln
Olofström
Ronneby
Kristianopel
Näsum
Tjärö
Hörby
Jaraavik
Karlskrona
Landskrona
Höör
Tollarp
Sölvesborg
Karlskrona/Trossö
Gårdstånga
Karlshamn
Malmö
Lund
Åhus
Romelestugan
Malmö
Kivik
Hanöbris
Skurup
Kivik
Havång
Hammenhög
Baskemölla
Smygehuk
Ystad
Bräntevik
Skåne Tranås
Backåkra-Löderup

100   200   300   400   KM
0
60   120   180   240   MLS

N

English

SWEDISH HOSTELS

All Swedish hostels have excellent facilities for families. Your Hostelling International card also gives you access to STF network of mountain accommodation in Lappland and other areas.

Most hostels are shut 10.00-17.00hrs. Always telephone if you have booked and are going to arrive after 18.00hrs. Members should expect to pay in the region of 75-180 SEK (1 ECU=8 SEK) per night, less for children.

PASSPORTS AND VISAS

Citizens of most Eastern European, African and Asian countries must have a special permit/visa before they are allowed to enter Sweden. Apply for your visa at the Swedish Embassy or Consulate in your country of residence.

HEALTH

If you become ill or have an accident whilst in Sweden and have to call a doctor, make sure that the doctor is affiliated to försäkringskassan (the Swedish National Health Service). You can also go to the casualty ward at a hospital.

BANKING HOURS

Banks are normally open Monday to Friday between 09.30 and 15.00hrs. There are also offices to change money near the railway stations and airports of key cities.

SHOPPING HOURS

Most shops are open 09.00-18.00hrs on weekdays and 09.00-13.00hrs on Saturdays .

TRAVEL

Air

Major cities and towns throughout Sweden are linked by an efficient network of services operated mainly by SAS (Scandinavian Airlines) and some other domestic airlines.

Rail

Swedish State Railways (SJ) provides a highly efficient network of train services covering the entire country.

❶ SJ: (46) (8) 6967540 calling from abroad – within Sweden (020) 757575 for more information.

Coach

Sweden has an excellent network of express coach connections between larger towns and cities in southern and central Sweden and between Stockholm and the coastal towns in the north. The main operator is Swebus but several other companies operate a network of weekend coach services.

Ferry

There are ferry services between Sweden and Germany, Great Britain, Denmark, Norway, Finland, Poland, Estonia and Russia.

Driving

The road network in Sweden is extensive and well maintained with toll-free motorways. Seat belts must be worn by the driver and all passengers. Dipped headlights are obligatory when driving, both by day and by night.

Swedish regulations on drinking and driving are strictly enforced, and costly fines are imposed on any motorists who are found to be driving under the influence of alcohol or other stimulants.

Français

AUBERGES DE JEUNESSE SUEDOISES

Toutes les auberges suédoises sont très bien équipées pour accueillir les familles. Votre carte internationale vous donnera accès au réseau STF d'hébergement en montagne en Laponie et dans d'autres régions.

La plupart des auberges sont fermées entre 10h et 17h et vous êtes prié de bien vouloir téléphoner si vous avez réservé et si vous devez arriver après 18h. Une nuit vous coûtera entre 75 et 180 KRS (1 ECU=8 KRS), moins pour les enfants.

PASSEPORTS ET VISAS

Les citoyens de la plupart des pays d'Europe de l'est, ainsi que des pays d'Afrique et d'Asie doivent être munis d'un permis/visa spécial pour entrer en Suède. Pour obtenir un visa, adressez-vous à l'Ambassade ou au Consulat de Suède dans votre pays.

SOINS MEDICAUX

Si vous tombez malade ou êtes victime d'un accident en Suède, et si vous deviez appeler un médecin, assurez-vous qu'il est affilié à försäkringskassan (la sécurité sociale suédoise). Vous pouvez aussi vous rendre au service des urgences d'un hopital.

HEURES D'OUVERTURE DES BANQUES

En principe, les banques sont ouvertes du lundi au vendredi de 9h30 à 15h. Il y a aussi des bureaux où l'on peut changer de l'argent, près des gares et des aéroports des grandes villes.

HEURES D'OUVERTURE DES MAGASINS

La plupart des magasins sont ouverts de 9h à 18h en semaine et de 9h à 13h le samedi.

DEPLACEMENTS

Avions

Les villes et grandes villes de Suède sont reliées par un réseau de services aériens très efficaces assurés en majeure partie par SAS (Scandinavian Airlines) et par d'autres compagnies.

Trains

Les chemins de fer suédois (SJ) gèrent un réseau ferroviaire extrêmement efficace dans tout le pays. Pour plus d'informations ☎ SJ:

(46) (8) 6967540 depuis l'étranger et (020) 757575 depuis la Suède.

Cars

La Suède a un excellent réseau de services express reliant les grandes villes du sud et du centre du pays, ainsi qu'entre Stockholm et les villes côtières du nord. La compagnie principale est Swebus, mais d'autres compagnies assurent un service de cars pendant le weekend.

Ferry-boats

Il existe des traversées entre la Suède et l'Allemagne, la Grande-Bretagne, le Danemark, la Norvège, la Finlande, la Pologne, l'Estonie et la Russie.

Automobiles

Le réseau routier est étendu et bien entretenu, et les autoroutes sont gratuites. Le port des ceintures de sécurité est obligatoire pour tous les occupants du véhicule. Il est obligatoire de rouler en codes, de jour comme de nuit.

Les lois concernant l'alcool au volant sont appliquées de façon très stricte et de très fortes amendes sont imposées aux conducteurs appréhendés sous l'influence de l'alcool ou d'autres stimulants.

Deutsch

SCHWEDISCHE JUGENDHERBERGEN

Alle schwedischen Herbergen haben ausgezeichnete Einrichtungen für Familien. Sie werden mit Ihrer Hostelling International-Karte in allen Bergunterkünften in Lappland und anderen Gebieten aufgenommen.

Die meisten Herbergen sind zwischen 10.00 und 17.00 Uhr geschlossen. Rufen Sie immer an, wenn Sie gebucht haben und erst nach 18.00 Uhr ankommen. Mitglieder haben mit einem Preis von ca. 75-180 skr (1 ECU=8 skr) pro Nacht, für Kinder weniger, zu rechnen.

PÄSSE UND VISA

Staatsbürger der meisten osteuropäischen, afrikanischen und asiatischen Länder müssen sich eine spezielle Genehmigung bzw. ein Visum beschaffen, ehe Ihnen die Einreise nach Schweden gestattet wird. Ihr Visum beantragen Sie bei der Schwedischen Botschaft oder beim Schwedischen Konsulat in Ihrem Heimatland.

GESUNDHEIT

Wenn Sie in Schweden krank werden oder einen Unfall erleiden und einen Arzt rufen müssen, sollten Sie sich vergewissern, daß der Arzt der 'försäkringskassan' (der allgemeinen Krankenkasse in Schweden) angeschlossen ist. Sie können sich auch in der Ambulanz eines Krankenhauses behandeln lassen.

GESCHÄFTSSTUNDEN DER BANKEN

Die Banken sind montags bis freitags von 09.30 bis 15.00 Uhr geöffnet. In der Nähe von Bahnhöfen und Flugplätzen gibt es in größeren Städten auch Wechselstuben.

LADENÖFFNUNGSZEITEN

Die meisten Geschäfte sind werktags von 09.00-18.00 Uhr und samstags von 09.00-13.00 Uhr geöffnet.

REISEN

Flugverkehr

Größere Städte sind über ein effizientes Flugverkehrsnetz, das hauptsächlich von SAS (Scandinavian Airlines) und anderen inländischen Fluggesellschaften betrieben wird, miteinander verbunden.

Eisenbahn

Die Schwedische Staatliche Eisenbahn (SJ) bietet im ganzen Land einen überaus leistungsfähigen Eisenbahnverkehr. Für weitere Informationen: ✆ SJ: (46) (8) 6967540 für Anrufe aus dem Ausland – innerhalb Schwedens (020) 757575.

Busse

Schweden verfügt über ein ausgezeichnetes Expreß-Busnetz, das größere Städte in Süd- und Mittelschweden miteinander verbindet und Stockholm an die Küstenstädte im Norden anbindet. Der Hauptbetreiber ist "Swebus". Es gibt aber noch mehrere andere Unternehmen, die am Wochenende einen Busverkehr anbieten.

Fähren

Zwischen Schweden und Deutschland, Großbritannien, Dänemark, Norwegen, Finnland, Polen, Estland und Rußland gibt es einen Fährverkehr.

Autofahren

Schweden hat ein sehr umfangreiches und gutes Straßennetz mit gebührenfreien Autobahnen. Alle Insassen müssen einen Sicherheitsgurt tragen. Man muß sowohl bei Tag als auch bei Nacht mit Abblendlicht fahren.

Die schwedischen Vorschriften über Alkohol am Steuer werden streng eingehalten. Wer unter dem Einfluß von Alkohol oder anderen Stimulanzien ein Kraftfahrzeug führt, hat mit einer hohen Geldstrafe zu rechnen.

Español

ALBERGUES JUVENILES SUECOS

Todos los albergues suecos cuentan con excelentes instalaciones para las familias. Su tarjeta Hostelling International le da derecho a utilizar la red de albergues de montaña STF de Laponia y de otras zonas.

Casi todos los albergues están cerrados de 10 h. a 17 h. Avise por teléfono al albergue si tiene reserva y piensa llegar más tarde de las 18 h. Una noche le costará entre 75 y 180 coronas suecas (1 Euro = 8 coronas suecas), menos para los niños.

PASAPORTES Y VISADOS

Los ciudadanos de casi todos los países de Europa del Este, África y Asia deben conseguir un permiso especial/visado para entrar en Suecia. Solicítelo en la embajada o el consulado suecos del país donde usted viva.

INFORMACIÓN SANITARIA

Si usted se pone enfermo o tiene un accidente durante su estancia en Suecia y se ve obligado a llamar a un médico, asegúrese de que este pertenece al "försäkringskassan" (la Seguridad Social sueca). También puede acudir a urgencias en cualquier hospital.

HORARIO DE LOS BANCOS

Los bancos suelen abrir de lunes a viernes de 9.30 h. a 15 h. También hay casas de cambio cerca de las estaciones de ferrocarril y los aeropuertos de las ciudades más importantes.

HORARIO COMERCIAL

Casi todas las tiendas abren de 9 h. a 18 h. de lunes a viernes y de 9 h. a 13 h. los sábados.

DESPLAZAMIENTOS

Avión
Las grandes ciudades de Suecia están unidas por una eficaz red aérea operada principalmente por SAS (Scandinavian Airlines) y algunas otras compañías de vuelos nacionales.

Tren
Los ferrocarriles nacionales de Suecia (SJ) ofrecen una excelente red de servicios en todo el país. Para más información, contacte con SJ llamando al ❶ (46)(8) 6967540 desde el extranjero y (020) 757575 desde Suecia.

Autocar
Suecia cuenta con una excepcional red de autocares directos que unen las ciudades y centros urbanos más importantes del sur y centro de Suecia, así como Estocolmo y las ciudades costeras del norte. La compañía principal es Swebus, aunque otras empresas también tienen servicios los fines de semana.

Ferry
Existen servicios de ferry entre Suecia y Alemania, Gran Bretaña, Dinamarca, Noruega, Finlandia, Polonia, Estonia y Rusia.

Automóvil
La red de carreteras de Suecia es muy amplia, está bien mantenida y las autopistas son gratuitas. El conductor y todos los pasajeros deben llevar el cinturón de seguridad abrochado. Es obligatorio circular con las luces encendidas día y noche.

La legislación sueca es muy estricta en materia de conducción bajo la influencia del alcohol o de otros estimulantes y se imponen fuertes multas.

Göteborg -
Slottsskogen

**Slottsskogen,
Vegagatan 21,
41311 Göteborg.**
☎ (31) 426520
✆ (31) 142102
✉ mail@slottsskogenvh.se

Open Dates:	🗓
Open Hours:	08.00-12.00hrs; 15.00-22.00hrs
Reservations:	Ⓡ ⊂CC⊃
Price Range:	SEK 95-130 🏷
Beds:	140 - 16x🛏 2x🛏 16x🛏 2x🛏 2x🛏
Facilities:	👥 20x 🚻 🍴 🛁 🏠 📺 🗄1 x🍺 🔲 💼 ♿ 🅿 ℹ 💈

Directions:

✈	Landvetter 25km
🚢	Stena Line & Seacat 800m
🚆	Central Station 2km
🚌	50, 51, 87, 210, 703, 705 200m ap Olivedalsgatan/Linnéplatsen 200m
🚋	1, 2 200m ap Olivedalsgatan 200m

Attractions: 🚲

Göteborg -
Stigbergsliden

**Stigbergsliden 10,
41463 Göteborg.**
☎ (31) 241620
✆ (31) 246520
✉ vandrarhem.stigbergsliden@swipnet.se

Open Dates:	🗓
Open Hours:	08.00-10.00hrs; 16.00-22.00hrs
Reservations:	⊂CC⊃
Price Range:	SEK 110-150 🏷
Beds:	90 - 1x🛏 10x🛏 1x🛏 14x🛏 1x🛏 1x🛏
Facilities:	♿ 🚻 16x 🚻 🍴 🛁 📺 🗄 ♿ 🔲 🅿 💈 🔍 🏠

Directions:

✈	Landvetter 25km
A🚌	Central Station 3km
🚢	Stena/Seacat 300m, Skandiahamnen 3km
🚆	Central Station 3km
🚋	Brunnsparken 3, 9, 4 300m ap Stigbergstorget 50m

Attractions: 🚲

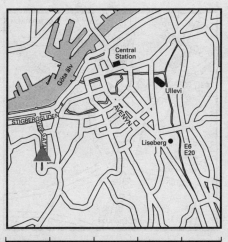

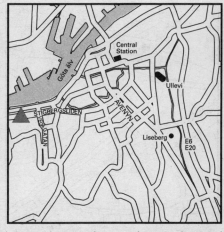

0   8.5km   0   8.5km

Malmö

STF Vandrarhem Malmö,
Backavägen 18,
21432 Malmö
☏ (40) 82220
ⓘ (40) 510659

Open Dates:	11.01-17.12
Open Hours:	08.30-10.00hrs; 16.00-18.00hrs
Reservations:	Ⓡ
Price Range:	SEK 125 🏧
Beds:	157 - 9x^2 4x^3 28x^4 4x^5
Facilities:	⚲ 45x ⚲ 🍴 ♿ ⛟ 📺 ⬛ 🅿 ⚓

Directions:

✈	Sturup 30km
A🚌	Södervärn 2km
⛴	Limhamn 6km, Malmö 4km
🚂	Malmö 4km
🚌	#21 500m ap Vandrarhemmet

Stockholm -
af Chapman/Skeppsholmen

11149 Stockholm.
☏ (8) 4632266
ⓘ (8) 6117155
ⓔ info@chapman.stfturist.se

Open Dates:	🗓
Open Hours:	🕐
Reservations:	Ⓡ ⒾⒷⓃ ⒸⒸ
Price Range:	SEK 110-170 🏧
Beds:	290 - 20x^2 13x^3 22x^4 1x^5 8x^6 8x^6
Facilities:	♿ ⚲ 36x ⚲ 🍴 ♿ ⛟ 📺 ⬛ 🧳 ♨ 🔒 ⬆ 🅿 ♻

Directions:

✈	Arlanda 40km
A🚌	City Terminal 2km
🚂	Central Station 2km
🚌	#65 100m ap af Chapman
Ⓤ	Kungsträdgården 500m

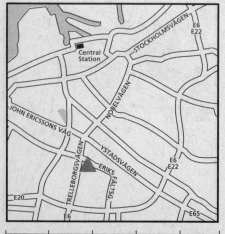

A - Central Station
B - Town Hall
C - The Opera
D - Parliament
E - Royal Castle
F - National Museum
G - Modern Museum

0   7km

0   2.2km

Stockholm - Långholmen

Kronohäktet,
Box 9116,
10272 Stockholm.
☎ (8) 6680510
✆ (8) 7208575
e vandrarhem@langholmen.com

Open Dates:	🗓
Open Hours:	🕐
Reservations:	**R** **CC**
Price Range:	SEK 155 🛏
Beds:	254 - 71x^2🛏 11x^3🛏 13x^4🛏
Facilities:	♿ ⚄ 30x ⚄ 🍽 ☕ 🍺 📺 📺 5 x🍷 🗄 💼 ⚒ 8️⃣ ⬆ 🅿 ⓘ ⛽ 🐾 ⛰ 🏠 🎴

Directions:

✈	Arlanda 40km
A🚌	City Terminal 3km
🚂	Central Station 3.5km
🚌	#4, ap Långholmsg 700m
Ⓤ	Hornstull 700m
Attractions:	🔎

Stockholm - Zinkensdamm

Zinkens väg 20,
11741 Stockholm.
☎ (8) 6168100
✆ (8) 6168120

Open Dates:	🗓
Open Hours:	🕐
Reservations:	**R** **CC**
Price Range:	SEK 140-180 🛏
Beds:	466 - 7x^1🛏 45x^2🛏 22x^3🛏 73x^4🛏 1x^6🛏
Facilities:	♿ ⚄ 148x ⚄ 🍽 ☕ 🍺 🍺 📺 📺 2 x🍷 🗄 💼 8️⃣ ⬆ 🅿 ⓘ ⛽ 🐾 🏠

Directions:

✈	Arlanda 40km
A🚌	City Terminal 3km
🚂	Central Station 3km
Ⓤ	Zinkensdamm 500m
Attractions:	🔎 🚴

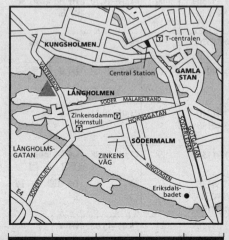

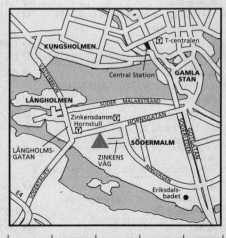

Location/Address	Telephone No. Fax No.	Beds	Opening Dates	Facilities
▲ **Åhus** STF Vandrarhem Åhus, Stavgatan 3, 29631 Åhus	☏ (44) 248535 ✆ (44) 247718	32		
▲ **Älgarås** STF Vandrarhem Älgarås, Box 102, 54502 Älgarås	☏ (506) 40450 ✆ (506) 40237	26		
▲ **Alingsås** STF Vandrarhem Alingsås, Villa Plantaget, 44134 Alingsås	☏ (322) 636987 ✆ (322) 633229	42		
▲ **Älmhult** SFT Vandrarhem Älmhult, Sjöstugan, 34394 Älmhult	☏ (476) 71600 ✆ (476) 12632	24	01.05–01.09	
▲ **Älvdalen** STF Vandrarhem Älvdalen, Tre Björnar, Dalgatan 31, 79631 Älvdalen. ✉ trebjornar@telia.com	☏ (251) 10482 ✆ (251) 10482	32		
▲ **Alvesta** STF Vandrarhem Alvesta, Hamrarnavägen 3, 34232 Alvesta ✉ eksalen@hotmail.com	☏ (472) 12700 ✆ (472) 12701	50		
▲ **Älvkarleby** STF Vandrarhem Älvkarleby, Laxön, 81494 Älvkarleby	☏ (26) 82122 ✆ (26) 72861	66	01.01–20.12	
▲ **Älvsbyn** STF Vandrarhem Älvsbyn, Nyfors 1, 94236 Älvsbyn	☏ (929) 55630 ✆ (929) 10527	56		
▲ **Åmål** STF Vandrarhem Åmål, Gerdinsgatan 7, 66237 Åmål ✉ lokrantz@home.se	☏ (532) 10205 ✆ (532) 10205	48		
▲ **Ammarnäs** STF Vandrarhem, Ammarnäs, Box 21, 92075 Ammarnäs.	☏ (952) 60045 ✆ (952) 60251	44		
▲ **Ängelholm** STF Vandrarhem Ängelholm, Magnarp 174, 26083 Vejbystrand	☏ (431) 452364 ✆ (431) 452364	60	01.04–31.10	
▲ **Ånn** STF Vandrarhem Ånn, Ånn 2467, 83015 Duved	☏ (647) 71070 ✆ (647) 71070	33		
▲ **Arådalen** STF Vandrarhem Arådalen, Västra Arådalen, 84031 Åsarna, Jämtland.	☏ (687) 14054	18	19.06–29.08	
▲ **Arjeplog** STF Vandrarhem Arjeplog, Lyktan, Lugnetvägen 4, 93090 Arjeplog.	☏ (961) 61210 ✆ (961) 10150	30	01.05–30.11	
▲ **Årås** STF Vandrarhem Årås, Kölingared, 56593 Mullsjö.	☏ (515) 91151	28	17.06–13.08	
▲ **Åre** STF Vandrarhem Åre, Brattlandsgården, 83010 Undersåker	☏ (647) 30138, (10) 6905885 ✆ (647) 30138	66		
▲ **Åsa** STF Vandrarhem Åsa, Kuggavik, 43031 Åsa.	☏ (340) 651285	21	15.05–15.08	

Location/Address	Telephone No. Fax No.	Beds	Opening Dates	Facilities
▲ **Asa-Lammhult** STF Vandrarhem Asa, 36030 Lammhult	☎ (472) 263110, 263003	35	🛏	👫 Ⓡ ♿ ☞ 🅿 📷
▲ **Åsarna** STF Vandrarhem Åsarna, Box 245, 84031 Åsarna	☎ (687) 30230 🖷 (687) 30360	85	🛏	👫 🍽 ⧉CC⧉ ☞ 🅿 📷
▲ **Avesta** STF Vandrarhem Avesta, Älvbrovägen 33, 77435 Avesta.	☎ (226) 80623 🖷 (226) 80623	36	🛏	👫 ☞ 🅿 📷
▲ **Backåkra** STF Vandrarhem Backåkra/Löderup, Kustvägen, 27645 Löderup, Skåne.	☎ (411) 526080	70	07.06–31.08	👫 🍽 Ⓡ ☞ 🅿
▲ **Baskemölla** STF Vandrarhem Baskemölla, Simrishamn, Tjörnedalavägen 81, 27294 Simrishamn.	☎ (414) 26173 🖷 (414) 26054	56	🛏	👫 🍽 ♿ ☞ 🅿 📷
▲ **Bassholmen** STF Vandrarhem Bassholmen, c/o Fritidskontoret, 45181 Uddevalla.	☎ (522) 651308 🖷 (522) 16080	38	14.06–06.08	👫 🍽 Ⓡ ☞ 🅿
▲ **Bengtsfors** STF Vandrarhem Bengtsfors, Gammelgården, 66631 Bengtsfors	☎ (531) 61075 🖷 (531) 61075	50	15.05–15.08	👫 🍽 ☞ 🅿
▲ **Bergkvara** STF Vandrarhem Bergkvara, Storgatan 66, 38542 Bergkvara.	☎ (486) 26040 🖷 (486) 26004	60	🛏	👫 🍽 ⧉CC⧉ ☞ 🅿 📷
▲ **Bergs Slussar** STF Vandrarhem Bergs Slussar, S-59061 Vreta Kloster	☎ 013 60330	26	01.05–26.09	👫 Ⓡ ♿ ⧉CC⧉ ☞ 🅿 📷 ☕
▲ **Björkvattnet** STF Vandrarhem Björkvattnet, Björkvattnet 1425, 83090 Gäddede	☎ (672) 23024 🖷 (672) 23024	38	🛏	👫 Ⓡ ☞ 🅿
▲ **Björnlunda** STF Vandrarhem Björnlunda, Box 81, 64050 Björnlunda	☎ (158) 20014, 20702	13	10.06–27.08	👫 🍽 ☞ 🅿
▲ **Blomskog** STF Vandrarhem Blomskog, 67292 Årjäng.	☎ (573) 31035	34	22.05–26.09	👫 🍽 ☞ 🅿 📷
▲ **Böda** STF Vandrarhem Böda, Mellböda, 38074 Löttorp	☎ (485) 22038 🖷 (485) 22198	165	01.06–15.08	👫 🍽 Ⓡ ⧉CC⧉ ☞ 🅿 📷
▲ **Boda** STF Vandrarhem Boda, Bolet 5, 36065 Boda Glasbruk ✉ anita.braneus@emmaboda.mail.telia.com	☎ (481) 24230 🖷 (481) 24006	45	01.05–31.10	👫 ⧉CC⧉ ☞ 🅿
▲ **Boden** STF Vandrarhem Boden, Fabriksgatan 6, 96131 Boden	☎ (921) 13335 🖷 (921) 13335	33	🛏	☞ 🅿 📷 ☕
▲ **Bogesund/Vaxholm** STF Vandrarhem Bogesund/Vaxholm, 18593 Vaxholm	☎ (8) 541 32240	60	🛏	👫 🍽 ♿ ⧉CC⧉ ☞ 🅿 📷 ☕
▲ **Bollnäs** STF Vandrarhem Bollnäs, Lenninge 6003, 82191 Bollnäs.	☎ (278) 23092 🖷 (278) 23092	50	🛏	👫 🍽 ☞ 🅿 📷

Location/Address	Telephone No. Fax No.	Beds	Opening Dates	Facilities
▲ **Borås** STF Vandrarhem Borås, Box 440 22 Sjöbo 4, 50004 Borås	☎ (33) 353280 ✆ (33) 140582	44	🏠	♛ 🍴 ☞ 🅿 🗑
▲ **Borgholm** STF Vandrarhem Rosenfors, Södra vägen 7, 38736 Borgholm	☎ (485) 10756 ✆ (77878)	103	30.04–15.09	♛ 🍴 Ⓡ ☞ 🅿
▲ **Borgsjö** STF Vandrarhem Borgsjö, Borgsjöbyn, 84197 Erikslund.	☎ (690) 20075	30	15.06–15.08	♛ 🍴 ☞
▲ **Borlänge** STF Vandrarhem Borlänge, Kornstigen 23A, 78452 Borlänge ✉ vandrarhem@borlange.se	☎ (243) 227615 ✆ (243) 16411	75	02.01–23.12; 27–30.12	♛ 🍴 ᖴᑕᑕ ☞ 🅿 🗑
▲ **Branäs** STF Vandrarhem Branäs, Box 28, 68060 Sysslebäck ✉ info@branas.se	☎ +46 (564) 35200 ✆ +46 (564) 43260	40	16.05–23.10	♛ Ⓡ ♿ ᖴᑕᑕ ☞ 🅿 🗑
▲ **Bråtadal/Svartrå** STF Vandrarhem Bråtadal/Svartrå, 31060 Ullared	☎ 0346 23343 ✆ 0346 33014	45	15.03–15.12	♛ 🍴 Ⓡ ♿ ☞ 🅿 🗑
▲ **Brantevik** STF Vandrarhem Brantevik, Råkvlle Gård, Gislövsvägen 12, 27234 Brantevik	☎ (414) 22006	20	01.06–15.09	♛ Ⓡ ♿ ☞ 🅿
▲ **Brunskog** STF Vandrarhem Brunskog, Bergamon, 67194 Edane	☎ (570) 52141 ✆ (570) 52149	70	🏠	♛ 🍴 Ⓡ ☞ 🅿
▲ **Bruzaholm** STF Vandrarhem Bruzaholm, Wäduren AB, Eksjövägen 13, Box 25, 57034 Bruzaholm. ✉ nave@telia.com	☎ (381) 20200 ✆ (381) 20200	38	🏠	♛ 🍴 ♿ ᖴᑕᑕ ☞ 🅿 🗑
▲ **Burträsk** STF Vandrarhem Burträsk, Hembygdsgården, Box 72, 93721 Burträsk	☎ (914) 55013, 10287 ✆ (914) 55070	38	🏠	♛ Ⓡ ☞ 🅿
▲ **Dals Rostock** STF Vandrarhem, Dals Rostock, Kroppefjälls Fritidscenter, 46450 Dals Rostock.	☎ (530) 20360 ✆ (530) 20345	54	🏠	♛ 🍴 Ⓡ ☞ 🅿 🗑
▲ **Docksta** STF Vandrarhem Docksta, 87033 Docksta ✉ kustladan@telia.com	☎ (613) 13064, 40391 ✆ (613) 40391	80	🏠	♛ 🍴 Ⓡ ᖴᑕᑕ ☞ 🅿 🗑
▲ **Ed** STF Vandrarhem Ed, Strömstadsvägen 18, 668 31 Ed	☎ (534) 10191	54	15.05–31.08	♛ ☞ 🅿 🗑
▲ **Edsbyn** STF Vandrarhem Edsbyn, Hogagatan 15, 82894 Edsbyn.	☎ (271) 34462 ✆ (271) 34176	36	🏠	♛ 🍴 Ⓡ ☞ 🅿
▲ **Ekshärad** STF Vandrarhem Ekshärad, Klarälvsvägen 35, Pilgrimen, Box 105, 68050 Ekshärad.	☎ (563) 40590	22	🏠	♛ 🍴 ☞ 🅿

Location/Address	Telephone No. Fax No.	Beds	Opening Dates	Facilities
▲ Eksjö STF Vandrarhem Eksjö, Österlånggatan 31, 57580 Eksjö ✉ vandrarhem@eksjo.se	☎ (381) 36180 ✆ (381) 17755	55	▣12	⋔ CC ⛣ P
▲ Enköping STF Vandrarhem Enköping, Bredsand, 74591 Enköping	☎ (171) 80066	48	▣12	⋔ 6S ♿ ⛣ P
▲ Eskilstuna STF Vandrarhem Eskilstuna, Vilsta Sporthotell, 63229 Eskilstuna. ✉ vilsta.sporthotell@swipnet.se	☎ (16) 513080 ✆ (16) 513086	40	▣12	⋔ ♿ CC ⛣ P ▣
▲ Fågelfors STF Vandrarhem Fågelfors, Värdshuset Bruksgården, Bruksgatan 65, 570 75 Fågelfors.	☎ (491) 51250 ✆ (491) 51255	36	19.06–13.08 (14.08–18.06 Ⓡ only)	⋔ Ⓡ CC ⛣ P
▲ Falkenberg STF Vandrarhem Falkenberg, Näset, c/o Turistbyrån, Box 293, 31123 Falkenberg ✉ falkenberg.tourist@mailbox.calypso.net	☎ (346) 17111, (346) 17410 ✆ (346) 14526	40	▣12	⋔ ⊺⊙ Ⓡ 6SE ⛣ P ▣
▲ Falköping STF Vandrarhem Falköping, Lidgatan 4, 52132 Falköping	☎ (515) 85020 ✆ (515) 10043	46	▣12	⋔ ⊺⊙ Ⓡ ⛣ P ▣
▲ Falun STF Vandrarhem Falun, Vandrarvägen 3, 79143 Falun ✉ stf.falun@falun.mail.telia.com	☎ (23) 10560 ✆ (23) 14102	140	05.01–20.12	⋔ ⊺⊙ Ⓡ 4E ⛣ P
▲ Fårö STF Vandrarhem Fårö, Fårögården, 62035 Fårösund	☎ (498) 223639	46	20.05–31.08	⋔ ⊺⊙ Ⓡ ⛣ P
▲ Färgelanda STF Vandrarhem Färgelanda, Dagsholm, 45892 Färgelanda.	☎ (528) 19990 ✆ (528) 19999	60	01.06–31.08	⋔ ⊺⊙ Ⓡ ♿ ⛣ P ▣
▲ Fjällbacka/Valö STF Vandrarhem Fjällbacka, Valö, 45071 Fjällbacka	☎ (525) 31234	12	02.05–25.08	⋔ Ⓡ ⛣ ▣
▲ Forshaga STF Vandrarhem Forshaga, Slottet, Folkets Hus, Slottsvägen 9, Box 76, 66722 Forshaga.	☎ (54) 873040, 873051 ✆ (54) 870780, 873053	20	15.05–15.09	⋔ ⊺⊙ CC ⛣ P ▣
▲ Forsvik STF Vandrarhem Forsvik, Bruksvägen 11, 54673 Forsvik.	☎ (505) 41137	49	01.06–31.08	⋔ ⛣ P
▲ Fredriksberg-Säfsen STF Vandrarhem Fredriksberg, Ludvikav 13, 770 10 Fredriksberg.	☎ (591) 20565 ✆ (591) 20776	40	▣12	⋔ ⊺⊙ Ⓡ ♿ CC ⛣ ▣
▲ Frillesås STF Vandrarhem Frillesås, Vallersvik, Box 64, 43030 Frillesås.	☎ (340) 653000 ✆ (340) 653551	42	29.05–27.08	⋔ ⊺⊙ CC ⛣ P ▣
▲ Fryksta/Kil STF Vandrarhem Fryksta, Box 193, 66525 Kil	☎ (554) 40850 ✆ (554) 13772	40	▣12	⋔ ⊺⊙ ♿ ⛣ ▣

Location/Address	Telephone No. Fax No.	Beds	Opening Dates	Facilities
▲ **Gällivare** STF Vandrarhem Gällivare, Barnhemsv 2, Andra Sidan, 98239 Gällivare.	☏ (970) 14380 🖷 (970) 16586	110		
▲ **Gammel-Gränome** STF Vandrarhem Gammel-Gränome, Stavby, 74794 Alunda	☏ (174) 13108	27		
▲ **Garda** STF Vandrarhem Garda, Kommunhuset, 62016 Ljugarn	☏ (498) 491391 🖷 (498) 491181	30	07.01–20.12	
▲ **Gärdserum** STF Vandrarhem, Gärdserum, 59797 Åtvidaberg	☏ (120) 20134 🖷 (120) 20037	25	01.05–01.09	
▲ **Gårdstånga** STF Vandrarhem Gårdstånga, Flyingevägen Gårdstånga, 24032 Flyinge.	☏ (46) 52087 🖷 (46) 2110873	36	01.02–22.12	
▲ **Gävle - I** STF Vandrarhem Gävle, Södra Rådmansgatan 1, 80251 Gävle	☏ (26) 621745 🖷 (26) 615990	72		
▲ **Gävle - II** STF Vandrarhem Gävle Engeltofta, Bönavägen 118, 80595 Gävle, Gästrikland.	☏ (26) 96160, (26) 96063, 🖷 (26) 96055	74	01.05–31.08	7NE
▲ **Gnosjö** STF Vandrarhem Gnosjö, Fritidsgården Träffpunkten, 33580 Gnosjö	☏ (370) 331115 🖷 (370) 331110	33		
▲ **Göteborg** STF Vandrarhem Kungälv, Färjevägen 2, 44231 Kungälv, Bohuslän. 📧 johan.lenander@mailbox.hogia.net	☏ (303) 18900 🖷 (303) 19295	50	15.04–15.09	15N
▲ **Göteborg** - Slottsskogen **Slottsskogen, Vegagatan 21,** **41311 Göteborg.** 📧 mail@slottsskogenvh.se	☏ (31) 426520 🖷 (31) 142102	140		
▲ **Göteborg** - Stigbergsliden **Stigbergsliden 10, 41463 Göteborg.** 📧 vandrarhem.stigbergsliden@swipnet.se	☏ (31) 241620 🖷 (31) 246520	90		
▲ **Göteborg** IBN STF Vandrarhem Mölndal, Torrekulla Turiststation, 42835 Kållered. 📧 info@torrekulla.stfturist.se	☏ (31) 7951495 🖷 (31) 7955140	140		
Gothenburg ☞ **Göteborg**				
▲ **Grängesberg** - Bergsmansgården STF Vandrarhem Grängesberg, Bergsmansgården, Hårdtorpsvägen 15, 77240 Grängesberg	☏ (240) 21830 🖷 (240) 21830	45	10.06–29.08	
▲ **Grisslinge/Värmdö** STF Vandrarhem Grisslinge/Värmdö, Mörtnäsvägen 25, 13936 Värmdö	☏ (8) 570 20083 🖷 (8) 570 21269	48	15.05–15.09	

Location/Address	Telephone No. Fax No.	Beds	Opening Dates	Facilities
▲ Grönklitt STF Vandrarhem Grönklitt, 79498 Orsa ❸ fritid@orsa-gronklitt.se	❶ (250) 46200 ❸ (250) 46111	40	▣12	♦♦♦ ⓨⓞⓛ ⸠CC⸠ ☞ P ⬚
▲ Gullspång STF Vandrarhem Gullspång, Affärshuset Laxen, 57430 Gullspång	❶ (551) 20786 ❸ (551) 20277	36	▣12	♦♦♦ ⓨⓞⓛ Ⓡ ☞ P ⬚
▲ Hablingbo STF Vandrarhem Hablingbo, Hablingbo, 62011 Hardhem	❶ (498) 487070 ❸ (498) 487095	32	01.05–30.09	♦♦♦ ⓨⓞⓛ ⸠CC⸠ ☞ P ⬚ ⬛
▲ Hågelby STF Vandrarhem Hågelby, Hågelbygård, 14743 Tumba. ❸ hagelbyparken@hagelby.se	❶ (8) 53062020 ❸ (8) 53062020	28	▣12	♦♦♦ ⓨⓞⓛ Ⓡ ⸠CC⸠ ☞ P ⬚
▲ Hällekis STF Vandrarhem Hällekis, Falkängen, Falkängsvägen, 53374 Hällekis	❶ (510) 540653 ❸ (510) 540085	100	▣12	♦♦♦ ⓨⓞⓛ ☞ P
▲ Hammarö STF Vandrarhem Hammarö, Skoghall Djupsundsvägen 1, 66334 Skoghall	❶ (54) 510440 ❸ (54) 518158	80	07.06–08.08	♦♦♦ ⓨⓞⓛ ☞ P ⬚
▲ Hammenhög STF Vandrarhem Hammenhög, Skolgatan 20, 27650 Hammenhög.	❶ (414) 440095 ❸ (414) 440041	72	15.05–15.09	♦♦♦ ⓨⓞⓛ ⸠CC⸠ ☞ P
▲ Hammarstrand STF Vandrarhem Hammarstrand, Hotell, 84070 Hammarstrand.	❶ (696) 10780 ❸ (696) 55790	34	01.06–31.08	♦♦♦ ⓨⓞⓛ ☞ P
▲ Hanö STF Vandrarhem, Hanö, 29407 Sölvesborg	❶ (456) 53000	24	▣12	♦♦♦ Ⓡ ☞ P
▲ Hargebaden/Hammar STF Vandrarhem Hargebaden/Hammar, Hargebaden, 69694 Hammar	❶ (583) 770556	40	15.04–15.09	♦♦♦ ⓨⓞⓛ ☞ P
▲ Härnösand STF Vandrarhem Härnösand, Volontären 14, 87162 Härnösand.	❶ (611) 10446	70	11.06–06.08	♦♦♦ ⓨⓞⓛ ☞ P ⬚
▲ Haparanda STF Vandrarhem Haparanda, Strandgatan 26, 95331 Haparanda	❶ (922) 61171 ❸ (922) 61784	45	▣12	♦♦♦ ⓨⓞⓛ ♿ ⸠CC⸠ ☞ ⬚
▲ Hässleholm STF Vandrarhem Hässleholm, Hässleholmsgården 303, 28135 Hässleholm ❸ hassleholmsgarden.hassleholm@swipnet.se	❶ (451) 268234 ❸ (451) 268232	35	▣12	♦♦♦ ☞ P ⬚
▲ Hästveda STF Vandrarhem Hästveda, Hembygdsparken, Box 97, 28023 Hästveda	❶ (451) 30273 ❸ (451) 30864	35	01.04–31.10	♦♦♦ Ⓡ ♿ ☞ P ⬚
▲ Haväng STF Vandrarhem Haväng, Skepparpsgården, 27737 Kivik	❶ (414) 74071 ❸ (414) 74073	50	01.05–15.09	♦♦♦ ⓨⓞⓛ Ⓡ ☞ P
▲ Håverud STF Vandrarhem Håverud, Museiv 3, 46472 Håverud	❶ (530) 30275, 30745	38	▣12	♦♦♦ Ⓡ ☞ ⬚

Location/Address	Telephone No. Fax No.	Beds	Opening Dates	Facilities
▲ **Hedemora** STF Vandrarhem Hedemora, Hälla, Hällavägen, 77630 Hedemora	☎ (225) 711350 ✆ (225) 711350	47	▣	♦♦♦ �🍽 🛏 🅿 ▣
▲ **Helsingborg** STF Vandrarhem Helsingborg,KFUM Nyckelbo Scoutstigen, 25284 Helsingborg	☎ (42) 92005 ✆ (42) 91050	30	01.05–30.09	♦♦♦ 🍽 ⓡ ♿ 🛏 ▣
▲ **Hemavan** STF Vandrarhem Hemavan, FBU-gården, Box 163, 92066 Hemavan. @ info@fbu.to	☎ (954) 30002 ✆ (954) 30510	48	15.06–30.09	♦♦♦ 🍽 ⌐cc⌐ 🛏 🅿 ▣
▲ **Hjo** STF Vandrarhem Hjo, Stadsparken, 54433 Hjo	☎ (503) 10085	47	01.05–31.08	♦♦♦ 🛏 🅿 ▣
▲ **Hjulsjö** SFT Vandrarhem Hjulsjö, Mårtensbo Gård, 712 91 Hällefors. @ martensbo@stockholm.mail.telia.com	☎ (587) 62102 ✆ (587) 62102	30	01.05–31.08	♦♦♦ ⓡ 25 SE 🛏 🅿 ▣
▲ **Högbonden** STF Vandrarhem Högbonden, Fyrvaktarbostaden, Sund 1688, 870 33 Docksta	☎ (613) 23005 ✆ (613) 42119	30	01.06–30.09	♦♦♦ ⓡ 🛏 🅿 ☕
▲ **Hökensås** STF Vandrarhem Hökensås, Kyrkbyn, 56693 Brandstorp.	☎ (502) 50350, 50013 ✆ (502) 50024	25	22.06–31.08	♦♦♦ ⓡ ⌐cc⌐ 🛏 🅿
▲ **Hörby** STF Vandrarhem Hörby, Kursgården i Hörby, 24292 Hörby.	☎ (415) 14830 ✆ (415) 14328	40	07.06–15.08	♦♦♦ 🍽 🛏
▲ **Höör** STF Vandrarhem Höör, Backagården, Stenskogen, 24391 Höör.	☎ (413) 25510 ✆ (413) 25956	48	▣	♦♦♦ 🍽 ⓡ ⌐cc⌐ 🛏 🅿 ▣
▲ **Hörnefors** STF Vandrarhem Hörnefors, Sundelinsvägen 62, 91020 Hörnefors.	☎ (930) 20480	40	01.06–31.08	♦♦♦ ♿ 🛏 🅿 ▣
▲ **Hovenäset** STF Vandrarhem Hovenäset, Box 110, 45601 Kungshamn	☎ (523) 37463	34	08.06–16.08	♦♦♦ ⓡ ♿ 🛏 🅿 ▣
▲ **Hovra** STF Vandrarhem Hovra, 82042 Korskrogen.	☎ (651) 767092 ✆ (651) 767092	30	▣	♦♦♦ ♿ 🛏 🅿 ▣
▲ **Hudiksvall** STF Vandrarhem Hudiksvall, Malnbaden, Box 19, 82421 Hudiksvall.	☎ (650) 13260 ✆ (650) 13260	36	▣	♦♦♦ ⌐cc⌐ 🛏 🅿 ▣
▲ **Hunnebostrand** STF Vandrarhem Hunnebostrand, Gammelgården, 45046 Hunnebostrand.	☎ (523) 58730	82	01.05–30.09	♦♦♦ 🍽 ⓡ 🛏 🅿 ☕
▲ **Huskvarna** STF Vandrarhem Huskvarna, Odengatan 10, 56132 Huskvarna	☎ (36) 148870 ✆ (36) 148840	98	▣	♦♦♦ 🍽 ♿ ⌐cc⌐ 🛏 ☕
▲ **Immeln** SFT Vandrarhem Immeln, Pl 2338, 28063 Sibbhult	☎ (44) 96090 ✆ (44) 96090	30	▣	♦♦♦ ♿ ⌐cc⌐ 🛏 ▣

Location/Address	Telephone No. Fax No.	Beds	Opening Dates	Facilities
▲ Jakobsberg/Barkarby STF Vandrarhem Jakobsberg/Barkarby, Kaptensvägen 7, 17738 Järfälla ✉ vandrarhemmet.majorskan@swipnet.se	☎ (8) 4457270 ✆ (8) 4457273	60		††† R 1W ⊂⊂⊃ ☞ P ⊚ ☕
▲ Järbo STF Vandrarhem Järbo, Britta Zachrisson, Vandrarhemsvägen 4, 81195 Järbo	☎ (290) 70151	30		††† R ☞ P ⊚
▲ Järnavik STF Vandrarhem Järnavik, Gula Huset, Box 19, 37010 Bräkne-Hoby	☎ (457) 82200 ✆ (457) 82201	26		R ♿ ☞ P ⊚ ☕
▲ Järvsö STF Vandrarhem Järvsö, Harsagården, Harsa, 82040 Järvsö. ✉ info@harsa.se	☎ (651) 49511 ✆ (651) 49590	28		††† ⓘ⊙⓵ ⊂⊂⊃ ☞ P ☕
▲ Jokkmokk STF Vandrarhem Jokkmokk, Åsgård, Åsgatan 20, 96231 Jokkmokk	☎ (971) 55977 ✆ (971) 55977	50		††† ⓘ⊙⓵ R ⊂⊂⊃ ☞ P
▲ Junsele STF Vandrarhem Junsele, Kullberg 3031, 88037 Junsele	☎ (621) 30000 ✆ (621) 30000	46		††† ⓘ⊙⓵ 12N ☞ P ⊚
▲ Kalix STF Vandrarhem Kalix, Grytnäs Herrgård, Box 148, 95222 Kalix	☎ (923) 10733	37	15.06–20.08	††† ☞ P
▲ Kalmar STF Vandrarhem Kalmar, Rappeg 1, 39230 Kalmar ✉ info@hotellsvanen.se	☎ (480) 12928 ✆ (480) 88293	84		††† ⓘ⊙⓵ 1N ⊂⊂⊃ ☞ P ⊚ ☕
▲ Kalv STF Vandrarhem, Kalv, Erikslund 2, 51261 Kalv	☎ (325) 51000 ✆ (325) 51083	27	15.05–15.08	††† ☞ P
▲ Karlsborg STF Vandrarhem Karlsborg, Ankarvägen, 54630 Karlsborg	☎ (505) 44600 ✆ (505) 44600	84	01.06–31.08	††† R ☞ P
▲ Karlshamn STF Vandrarhem Karlshamn, Surbrunnsvägen IC, 374 39 Karlshann. ✉ stfturistkhamn@hotmail.com	☎ (454) 14040 ✆ (454) 14040	72		††† R 0.3NE ⊂⊂⊃ ☞ P ⊚
▲ Karlskoga STF Vandrarhem Karlskoga, Grönfeldtsudden, 69141 Karlskoga	☎ (586) 56780	92		††† ⓘ⊙⓵ ♿ ☞ P ⊚
▲ Karlskrona/Trossö STF Vandrarhem Karlskrona/Trossö, Drottninggatan 39, 37132 Karlskrona ✉ trosso.vandrarhem@karlskrona.mail.telia.com	☎ (455) 10020 ✆ (455) 10020	45		††† ♿ ☞ P
▲ Karlskrona STF Vandrarhem Karlskrona, Ruthensparre, Bredgatan 16, 37122 Karlskrona. ✉ turistbyran@karlskrona.se	☎ (455) 10020 ✆ (455) 10020	54	16.06–15.08	††† R ☞ P ⊚

Location/Address	Telephone No. Fax No.	Beds	Opening Dates	Facilities
▲ **Karlstad** STF Vandrarhem Karlstad, Ulleberg, 65342 Karlstad	☎ (54) 566840 ✆ (54) 566042	102	10.01–15.12	ⅲ ⑩ 🅙 ☞ 🅿
▲ **Katrineholm** STF Vandrarhem Katrineholm, Stora Djulö, 64192 Katrineholm	☎ (150) 10225 ✆ (150) 10225	43	01.06–31.08	ⅲ ⑩ Ⓡ 3S ☞ 🅿 ⓞ
▲ **Kiruna** STF Vandrarhem Kiruna, Bergmästaregatan 7, 98133 Kiruna	☎ (980) 17195 ✆ (980) 17195	88	🔓	ⅲ ⑩ Ⓡ ⫴CC⫴ ☞ 🅿 ⓞ
▲ **Kivik** STF Vandrarhem Kivik, Tittutvägen, 277 30 Kivik.	☎ (414) 71195 ✆ (414) 70050	35	🔓	ⅲ ⑩ Ⓡ ☞ 🅿
▲ **Kivik/Hanöbris** STF Vandrarhem Kivik Hanöbris, Eliselundsvägen 6, 27730 Kivik	☎ (414) 70050 ✆ (414) 70050	40	15.06–15.08	ⅲ Ⓡ ☞ 🅿
▲ **Klavreström** STF Vandrarhem Klavreström, Malmvägen 1, 36072 Klavreström ✉ stfvhem.klavrestroem@swipnet.se	☎ (474) 40944 ✆ (474) 40944	70	🔓	ⅲ ⑩ Ⓡ 🅙 ☞ 🅿 ⓞ
▲ **Klintehamn** STF Vandrarhem Klintehamn,Pensionat Warfsholm, Box 56, 62020 Klintehamn	☎ (498) 240010, (708) 445302 ✆ (498) 241411	50	21.01–19.12	ⅲ Ⓡ ☞ 🅿
▲ **Köping** STF Vandrarhem Köping, Ågärdsg 2D, 73132 Köping	☎ (221) 24495 ✆ (221) 24495	40	10.01–09.12	ⅲ Ⓡ ☞ 🅿 ⓞ
▲ **Köpmanholmen** STF Vandrarhem Köpmanholmen, Köpmanholmsvägen 2, 89340 Köpmanholmen.	☎ (660) 223496	36	15.05–15.09	ⅲ Ⓡ ☞ 🅿 ⓞ
▲ **Korrö** STF Vandrarhem Korrö, 36024 Linneryd (5km S Linneryd on route 122).	☎ (470) 34249 ✆ (470) 34556	87	01.04–30.09	ⅲ ⑩ ☞ 🅿
▲ **Kristinehamn** STF Vandrarhem Kristinehamn, Kvarndammen, 68100 Kristinehamn	☎ (550) 88195 ✆ (550) 12393	16	01.05–30.08	ⅲ ⑩ ☞ 🅿 ⓞ
▲ **Kvikkjokk** STF Vandrarhem Kvikkjokk, Kvikkjokk Fjällstation, 96202 Kvikkjokk	☎ 0971 21022 ✆ 0971 21039	60	18.03–01.05; 17.06–10.09	ⅲ ⑩ Ⓡ ⫴CC⫴ ☞ 🅿 ⓞ ⫿
▲ **Kyrktåsjö** STF Vandrarhem Kyrktåsjö, Tåsjödalens Pl 1525, 83080 Hoting	☎ (671) 713510	20	01.06–30.08	ⅲ Ⓡ ☞
▲ **Laholm** STF Vandrarhem Laholm, Tivolivägen 4, 31230 Laholm	☎ (430) 13318 ✆ (430) 15325	68	🔓	ⅲ ⑩ Ⓡ ⫴CC⫴ ☞ 🅿 ⓞ
▲ **Landskrona** STF Vandrarhem Landskrona, St Olovsgatan 15, 26136 Landskrona	☎ (418) 12063 ✆ (418) 13075	45	10.01–10.12	ⅲ ⑩ ☞ 🅿
▲ **Långasjö** STF Vandrarhem Långasjö, Stallgatan, 36195 Långasjö	☎ (471) 50310	43	🔓	ⅲ Ⓡ 🅙 ☞ 🅿

Location/Address	Telephone No. Fax No.	Beds	Opening Dates	Facilities
▲ Lärbro STF Vandrarhem Lärbro, Kappelshamnsvägen 10, 620 34 Lärbro 🅔 bokning@grannen.nu	☎ (498) 225033	120	15.05–31.08	⑂ ⊞CC⊟ ⚹ 🄿 🄾 ☕
▲ Leksand STF Vandrarhem Leksand, Källberget, Parkgården, Box 3051, 79335 Leksand	☎ (247) 15250 ✆ (247) 10186	80	🖻	⑂ 2.5S ⚹ 🄿 🄾
▲ Lesjöfors STF Vandrarhem Lesjöfors, Esperanto Gården, Stiftelsevägen 1, 68096 Lesjöfors	☎ (590) 30909 ✆ (590) 30309	58	🖻	⑂ 🍽 ♿ ⚹ 🄿
▲ Liden STF Vandrarhem Liden, Larmvägen 2, Box 35, 86041 Liden.	☎ (692) 10567	50	01.06–31.08	♿ ⚹ 🄿 🄾
▲ Lidköping STF Vandrarhem Lidköping, Gamla Stadens Torg Nicolaigatan 2, 53132 Lidköping	☎ (510) 66430	52	08.11–16.09	⑂ 🍽 ⚹ 🄿 🄾
▲ Linköping STF Vandrarhem Linköping, Klostergatan 52A, 58223 Linköping	☎ (13) 149090 ✆ (13) 148300	84	11.01–20.12	⑂ 🍽 Ⓡ ♿ ⚹ 🄿
▲ Ljuder STF Vandrarhem Ljuder, Grimsnäs Herrgård, 36053 Skruv	☎ (478) 20400 ✆ (478) 20400	70	01.04–30.09	⑂ Ⓡ ♿ ⚹ 🄿 🄾
▲ Ljugarn STF Vandrarhem Ljugarn, Strandridaregården, 62016 Ljugarn	☎ (498) 493184 ✆ (498) 482424	31	15.05–31.08	⑂ Ⓡ ⚹ 🄿
▲ Ljungdalen STF Vandrarhem Ljungdalen, Dunsjögården, Box 15, 84035 Ljungdalen	☎ (687) 20285 20364 (15.10-23.6)	40	🖻	⑂ ⚹ 🄿 🄾
▲ Loftahammar STF Vandrarhem Loftahammar, Trillin, Trillinvägen 3, Box 57, 59095 Loftahammar	☎ (493) 61110 ✆ (493) 61929	25	🖻	⑂ 🍽 ♿ ⊞CC⊟ ⚹ 🄿 🄾
▲ Lommeland STF Vandrarhem Lommeland, Råsshult, Pl 3135 Röd Lommeland, 45293 Strömstad	☎ (526) 42027 ✆ (526) 42020	57	20.05–01.09	⑂ ⚹ 🄿 🄾
▲ Lönneberga STF Vandrarhem Lönneberga, Lönneberga vägen, 57794 Silverdalen	☎ (495) 40036 ✆ (495) 40175, (070) 6192851	55	🖻	⑂ 🍽 Ⓡ ⚹ 🄿
▲ Lönsboda STF Vandrarhem Lönsboda, Tranebodavägen 12, 28070 Lönsboda	☎ (479) 21525 ✆ (479) 21525	18	🖻	⑂ 🍽 Ⓡ ⚹ 🄿
▲ Lövånger STF Vandrarhem Lövånger, Lövångers Kyrkstad, Box 13, 93010 Lövånger. 🅔 info@lovangerskyrkstad.se	☎ (913) 10395 ✆ (913) 10759	80	🖻	⑂ 🍽 ⊞CC⊟ ⚹ 🄿
▲ Luleå STF Vandrarhem Luleå, N:a Gäddvik, Örnviksvägen 87, 97594 Luleå.	☎ (920) 252325 ✆ (920) 252419	68	🖻	⑂ 🍽 ⊞CC⊟ ⚹ 🄿 🄾

Location/Address	Telephone No. Fax No.	Beds	Opening Dates	Facilities
▲ **Lund** STF Vandrarhem Lund, Tåget Vävaregatan 22, Bjeredsparken, 22237 Lund.	☎ (46) 142820 ✆ (46) 320568	108	10.01–17.12	ŤŤŤ ĭⓄĭ 0.1 NW ☞ P
▲ **Lycksele** STF Vandrarhem Lycksele, Duvan i Lycksele AB, Storg 47, 92132 Lycksele.	☎ (950) 14670 ✆ (950) 10233	40	14.06–14.08	ŤŤŤ ĭⓄĭ CC ☞ P
▲ **Malå** STF Vandrarhem Malå, Hotellgatan 10, 93070 Malå.	☎ (953) 14291 ✆ (953) 14291	24	01.06–31.08	♿ ☞
▲ **Malmö** **STF Vandrarhem Malmö, Backavägen 18, 21432 Malmö**	☎ (40) 82220 ✆ (40) 510659	157	11.01-17.12	ŤŤŤ ĭⓄĭ Ⓡ ☞ P ⓘ
▲ **Malung** STF Vandrarhem Malung, Vallerås Turistgård, Mobyn PL 1448, 78233 Malung.	☎ (280) 14040 ✆ (280) 41057	46	🗓	ŤŤŤ ĭⓄĭ ☞ P
▲ **Mariefred** STF Vandrarhem Mariefred, Röda Korsets idé och utbildningscenter, 64781 Mariefred.	☎ (159) 36100 ✆ (159) 12350	70	15.06–15.08	ŤŤŤ ĭⓄĭ 1 W CC ☞ P ⓘ
▲ **Mariestad** STF Vandrarhem Mariestad, Hamngatan 20, 54230 Mariestad	☎ (501) 10448	60	🗓	ŤŤŤ Ⓡ ☞ P
▲ **Medevi Brunn** STF Vandrarhem Medevi Brunn, Medevi Brunn, 59197 Motala	☎ (141) 91100 ✆ (141) 91532	50	06.06–10.08	ŤŤŤ ĭⓄĭ CC ☞ P
▲ **Mellbystrand** STF Vandrarhem Mellbystrand, Kustvägen 152, 31261 Mellbystrand.	☎ (430) 25220 ✆ (430) 15325	37	01.06–31.08	ŤŤŤ Ⓡ ☞ P ⓘ
▲ **Mjölby** STF Vandrarhem Mjölby, Hembygdsgården, Norrgårdsgatan 14, 59541 Mjölby	☎ (142) 10016	48	07.01–21.12	ŤŤŤ Ⓡ ☞ P ⓘ
Mölndal ☞ **Göteborg**				
▲ **Moheda** STF Vandrarhem Moheda, Kursgården Kronobergshed, 34036 Moheda	☎ (472) 40052 ✆ (472) 40135	46	🗓	ŤŤŤ Ⓡ ☞ P ⓘ
▲ **Mora** STF Vandrarhem Mora, Målkull Ann's, Vasagatan 19, 79232 Mora. ✉ ann@maalkullann.se	☎ (250) 38196 ✆ (250) 38195	62	🗓	ŤŤŤ ĭⓄĭ ♿ ☞ P
▲ **Motala** STF Vandrarhem Motala, Skogsborgsgatan 1, 59152 Motala, Östergötland. ✉ skogsborg@mbox301.swipnet.se	☎ (141) 57436 ✆ (141) 57435	60	18.05–14.08	ŤŤŤ ĭⓄĭ Ⓡ ♿ ☞ P ☕
▲ **Nässjö** STF Vandrarhem Nässjö, Sörängens Folkhögskola, Rågången 4, 571 38 Nässjö.	☎ (380) 10645 ✆ (380) 19076	50	08.06–13.08	ŤŤŤ ĭⓄĭ ☞ P ⓘ
▲ **Näsum** STF Vandrarhem Näsum, Klagstorpsvägen 80-20, 29594 Näsum.	☎ (456) 20188 ✆ (456) 24640	22	15.06–15.08	ŤŤŤ ĭⓄĭ ♿ ☞ P ☕

Location/Address	Telephone No. Fax No.	Beds	Opening Dates	Facilities
▲ Nora STF Vandrarhem Nora, Tåghem, Box 52, 71322 Nora.	☎ (587) 14676 ✆ (19) 312711	64	01.05–15.09	♦♦ �🍴 Ⓡ ☞ P ⓓ
▲ Norberg STF Vandrarhem Norberg, Gruvbyn Klackberg, 73891 Norberg.	☎ (223) 20247 ✆ (223) 23704	50	🄓	♦♦ 2NW ☞ P ⓓ
▲ Norrahammar STF Vandrarhem Norrahammar, Spånhultsvägen 19, 56231 Norrahammar.	☎ (36) 61075 ✆ (36) 61078	35	🄓	♦♦ �🍴 Ⓡ 9S � & CC ☞ ☕
▲ Norrköping STF Vandrarhem Norrköping, Turistgården, Ingelstadsgatan 31, 60223 Norrköping	☎ (11) 101160 ✆ (11) 186863	87	11.01–16.12	♦♦ �🍴 & CC ☞
▲ Norrköping STF Vandrarhem Norrköping, Abborreberg, Lindö, Box 7100, 60007 Norrköping	☎ (11) 319344 ✆ (11) 319146	60	01.05–15.09	♦♦ �🍴 5E CC ☞ P ☕
▲ Norrtälje STF Vandrarhem Norrtälje, Brännäsgården, Bältartorpsgatan 6, Box 803, 76128 Norrtälje.	☎ (176) 71569 ✆ (176) 71589	32	13.06–18.08	♦♦ �🍴 ☞
▲ Nybro STF Vandrarhem Nybro, Vasagatan 22, 38232 Nybro, Småland.	☎ (481) 10932 ✆ (481) 12117	100	01.03–31.10	♦♦ �🍴 & CC ☞ P
▲ Nynäshamn STF Vandrarhem Nynäshamn, Nickstabadsvägen 15, 14943 Nynäshamn.	☎ (8) 52020834	42	🄓	♦♦ Ⓡ ☞ P
▲ Ockelbo STF Vandrarhem Ockelbo, Perslundavägen 18, 81630 Ockelbo ✉ obbk@ockelbo.se	☎ (297) 55691 ✆ (297) 55990	28	🄓	♦♦ Ⓡ & ☞ ⓓ
▲ Ödeshög STF Vandrarhem Ödeshög, Hembygdsgården, Södra Vägen 63, 59931 Ödeshög	☎ (144) 10700 ✆ (144) 10700	55	15.05–25.08	♦♦ �🍴 Ⓡ & ☞ P ⓓ
▲ Öhns Gård STF Vandrarhem Öhns gård, Odensåker, 54015 Väring.	☎ (500) 441317 ✆ (500) 441210	50	🄓	♦♦ �🍴 & ☞ P ⓓ
▲ Ölands Skogsby STF Vandrarhem Ölands Skogsby, 38693 Färjestaden	☎ (485) 38395 ✆ (485) 38324	70	28.04–31.08	♦♦ �🍴 CC ☞ ⓓ
▲ Olofström STF Vandrarhem Olofström, Tåkasjövägen 36, 29337 Olofström.	☎ (454) 99499 ✆ (454) 99499	72	13.06–16.08	Ⓡ 1N ☞ P ⓓ
▲ Omberg STF Vandrarhem Omberg, Stocklycke, 59993 Ödeshög	☎ (144) 33044	55	16.01–14.12	♦♦ �🍴 Ⓡ & ☞ P
▲ Örebro STF Vandrarhem Örebro, Fanjunkarevägen 5, 70365 Örebro. ✉ vandrarhemmetorebro@usa.net	☎ (19) 310240 ✆ (19) 310256	112	01.01–20.12	♦♦ Ⓡ 1N & CC ☞ P ⓓ

Location/Address	Telephone No. Fax No.	Beds	Opening Dates	Facilities
▲ Öreryd Hestra STF Vandrarhem Öreryd, 33027 Hestra.	☎ (370) 337035 ✆ (370) 337008	27	🔢	♨ Ⓡ ♿ ᴄᴄ ☞ P ⊡
▲ Örnsköldsvik STF Vandrarhem Örnsköldsvik, Pl 1980, 89440 Överhörnäs 🅔 sodersten@ebox.tninet.se	☎ (660) 70244	30	🔢	♨ 🍴 Ⓡ 8W ᴄᴄ ☞ P ⊡
▲ Orrefors STF Vandrarhem Orrefors, Box 28, Backabyggningen, Silversparregatan 14, 38040 Orrefors.	☎ (481) 30020 ✆ (481) 30020	64	01.05–01.09	♨ ᴄᴄ ☞ ⊡
▲ Orsa STF Vandrarhem Orsa, Box 95, 79422 Orsa.	☎ (250) 42170 ✆ (250) 42365	68	🔢	♨ 🍴 1E ♿ ☞ P ⊡
▲ Orust STF Vandrarhem Orust, Tofta gård, Stocken, 47492 Ellös	☎ (304) 50380	68	01.05–15.09	♨ Ⓡ ☞ P ⊡
▲ Osby STF Vandrarhem Osby, c/o Stora Hotellet, V Järnvägsgatan 17 28331 Osby	☎ (479) 31830 ✆ (479) 16222	30	22.06–10.08	♨ 🍴 ᴄᴄ ☞ P
▲ Oskarshamn STF Vandrarhem Oskarshamn, Åsavägen 8, 57234 Oskarshamn	☎ (491) 88198 ✆ (491) 81045	130	🔢	♨ 🍴 ☞ P ⊡
▲ Österbybruk STF Vandrarhem Österbybruk, Stråkvägen 3, Box 76, 74822 österbybruk.	☎ (295) 21570 ✆ (295) 20050	36	🔢	♨ 🍴 Ⓡ ☞ P ⊡
▲ Österbymo STF Vandrarhem Österbymo, Ydregården, 57060 Österbymo	☎ (381) 60103 ✆ (381) 60999	20	01.05–30.09	♨ 🍴 ☞ P
▲ Östersund STF Vandrarhem Östersund, Södra Gröngatan 36, 83135 Östersund	☎ (63) 139100, (63) 34130	58	19.06–10.08	♨ Ⓡ ☞ P
▲ Östersund/Jamtli STF Vandrarhem Östersund/Jamtli, Museiplan, Box 482, 83123 Östersund.	☎ (63) 105984	30	🔢	♨ 1N ☞ P ⊡
▲ Ottenby STF Vandrarhem Ottenby, Näsby, 38065 Degerhamn	☎ (485) 662062 ✆ (485) 662161	146	🔢	♨ 🍴 Ⓡ ♿ ☞ P ⊡
▲ Överum STF Vandrarhem Överum, Källarbacken 2, Box 19, 59096 Överum	☎ (493) 30302, (70) 6742621	26	🔢	♨ ☞ P
▲ Persåsen STF Vandrarhem Persåsen, Persåsen 3370, 83024 Oviken 🅔 info@persasen.com	☎ (643) 40180 ✆ (643) 40105	27	24.06–20.08	♨ 🍴 ♿ ᴄᴄ ☞ P ⊡
▲ Piteå STF Vandrarhem Piteå, Storgatan 3, 94131 Piteå.	☎ (911) 15880 ✆ (911) 15880	35	🔢	♨ ♿ ☞ P
▲ Prässebo STF Vandrarhem Prässebo, Pl 3606, 46012 Prässebo	☎ (520) 667024	32	15.05–31.08	♨ Ⓡ ♿ ☞ P

Location/Address	Telephone No. Fax No.	Beds	Opening Dates	Facilities
▲ **Ramsele** STF Vandrarhem Ramsele, Prästbordet 1000, 88040 Ramsele	☻ (623) 10167 ✆ (623) 10167	36	15.06–15.08	♔♖ ⑂Ⓡ ♿ ☞ Ⓟ ⓾
▲ **Ransäter** STF Vandrarhem Ransäter, Geijersvägen 1, 68493 Ransäter	☻ (552) 30050	18	01.05–31.08	♔♖ ☞ Ⓟ
▲ **Rättvik** STF Vandrarhem Rättvik, Centralgatan, 79530 Rättvik ⓔ rattviksparken@rattviksparken.fn.se	☻ (248) 10566 ✆ (248) 56113	104	⑂	♔♖ ⑂ ♿ ⒸⒸ ☞ Ⓟ ⓾
▲ **Rantajärvi** STF Vandrarhem Rantajärvi, Rantajärvi 78, 957 94 Övertorneå ⓔ stfvandrarhen@camprautajarvi.se	☻ (927) 23000 ✆ (927) 23123	38	01.06–31.08	♔♖ ⑂ ♿ ☞ Ⓟ ⓾
▲ **Regna** STF Vandrarhem Regna, Regnagården, 64010 Högsjö.	☻ (151) 70127 ✆ (151) 70127	40	⑂	♔♖ ⑂Ⓡ ☞ Ⓟ
▲ **Rimforsa** STF Vandrarhem Rimforsa, Kalvudden, 59041 Rimforsa. ⓔ kalvudd@algonet.se	☻ (494) 20137	25	01.06–15.08	♔♖ ⑂Ⓡ ☞ Ⓟ
▲ **Romelestugan** STF Vandrarhem Romelestugan, Box 47, 24013 Genarp	☻ (46) 55073, 55138	26	⑂	♔♖ ⑂Ⓡ ☞ Ⓟ
▲ **Ronneby** STF Vandrarhem Ronneby, Övre Brunnsvägen 54, 37236 Ronneby.	☻ (457) 26300 ✆ (457) 26300	104	07.01–17.12	♔♖ ⑂ ☞ Ⓟ
▲ **Rörbäck** STF Vandrarhem Rörbäck, Bokenäs, v Rörbäck 29, 45196 Uddevalla.	☻ (522) 650190 ✆ (522) 650190	54	01.05–30.09	♔♖ Ⓡ ☞ Ⓟ
▲ **Röstånga** STF Vandrarhem Röstånga, Röstånga Gästgivaregård, Marieholmsvägen 2, 26024 Röstånga. ⓔ info@rostongagastgivaregard.se	☻ (435) 91370 ✆ (435) 91619	36	⑂	⑂ ♿ ⒸⒸ ☞ Ⓟ ⧫
▲ **Sala** STF Vandrarhem Sala, Sofielund, Mellandammen, 73336 Sala	☻ (224) 12730	28	⑂	♔♖ Ⓡ ♿ ☞ Ⓟ
▲ **Sälen** STF Vandrarhem Sälen, Gräsheden, Box 58, 78067 Sälen	☻ (280) 82040 ✆ (280) 82045	62	⑂	♔♖ ⑂Ⓡ ☞ Ⓟ ⓾
▲ **Sandslån/Kramfors** STF Vandrarhem Sandslån, Sandslån 3144, 87052 Nyland.	☻ (612) 50541 ✆ (612) 50006	80	15.05–15.09	♔♖ ⑂Ⓡ ☞ Ⓟ
▲ **Sandviken** STF Vandrarhem Sandviken, Skogsfruvägen 22, 81141 Sandviken. ⓔ stf.vandrarhem@sandviken.se	☻ (26) 251915 ✆ (26) 259865	69	02.01–20.12	♔♖ ⑂ ☞ Ⓟ

Location/Address	Telephone No. Fax No.	Beds	Opening Dates	Facilities
▲ **Sankt Anna** STF Vandrarhem Sankt Anna, Gamla Färjeläget, 61498 St Anna. ⊜ yngre.andersson@mbox301.swipnet.se	☎ (121) 51312	32	01.06–31.08	♦♦♦ ⓘⓞⓘ ⌐ 🅿 ⊡
▲ **Särna** STF Vandrarhem Särna, Björkhagen, Box 535, 79090 Särna	☎ (253) 10308	25	ⓖ₁₂	♦♦♦ ⓘⓞⓘ Ⓡ ⌐ 🅿 ⊡
▲ **Särna** STF Vandrarhem Särna, Turistgården, Sjukstugev 4, 79090 Särna ⊜ alpen.utreckling@swipnet.se	☎ (253) 10437 ❻ (253) 10437	37	ⓖ₁₂	♦♦♦ ⓘⓞⓘ ECC⊟ ⌐ 🅿 ⊡
▲ **Säter-Haverö** STF Vandrarhem Säter-Haverö, Haverö Hembygdsgård, Säter, 84193 Östavall	☎ (690) 30137	14	05.06–15.08	♦♦♦ ⌐ 🅿
▲ **Sätra Brunn** STF Vandrarhem Sätra Brunn 73326, Sala.	☎ (224) 54600 ❻ (224) 54601	43	01.05–30.09	♦♦♦ ⓘⓞⓘ ECC⊟ ⌐ 🅿
▲ **Saxnäs** STF Vandrarhem Saxnäs, Kultsjögården Box 6, 91088 Marsfjäll	☎ (940) 70044 ❻ (940) 70189	52	ⓖ₁₂	♦♦♦ ⓘⓞⓘ ECC⊟ ⌐ 🅿
▲ **Sigtuna** STF Vandrarhem Sigtuna, Kyrkans utbildningscentrum, Manfred Björkquists allè 12, Box 92, 19322 Sigtuna	☎ (8) 59258478 ❻ (8) 59258384	60	26.06–06.08	♦♦♦ ⓘⓞⓘ ECC⊟ ⌐ 🅿
▲ **Skåne Tranås** STF Vandrarhem, Skåne Tranås, Helgonavägen, 27392 Tomelilla	☎ (417) 20330 ❻ (417) 20330	88	ⓖ₁₂	♦♦♦ ⓘⓞⓘ Ⓡ ⌐ 🅿 ⊡
▲ **Skara** STF Vandrarhem Skara, Vasaparken, 53232 Skara	☎ (511) 12165, 63619 ❻ (511) 63656	65	ⓖ₁₂	♦♦♦ ⓘⓞⓘ ♿ ECC⊟ ⌐ 🅿 ⊡
▲ **Skäralid - Klippan** STF Vandrarhem, Skäralid, PL 750, 26070 Ljungbyhed	☎ (435) 442025 ❻ (435) 442383	29	ⓖ₁₂	♦♦♦ Ⓡ ⌐ 🅿
▲ **Skövde** STF Vandrarhem Skövde, Billingens Stugby & Camping, Alphyddevägen 54133 Skövde.	☎ (500) 471633 ❻ (500) 471044	18	ⓖ₁₂	♦♦♦ ⌐ 🅿 ⊡
▲ **Skurup** STF Vandrarhem Skurup, Bruksgatan 3, 27435 Skurup	☎ (411) 536061 ❻ (411) 536061	32	14.06–20.08	♦♦♦ ⓘⓞⓘ ⌐ 🅿 ⊡
▲ **Smygehuk** STF Vandrarhem Smygehuk, Kustvägen, P1 314, 23178 Smygehuk. ⊜ smygehuk.vh@telia.com	☎ (410) 24583 ❻ (410) 24509	43	ⓖ₁₂	♦♦♦ ⓘⓞⓘ Ⓡ ⌐ 🅿
▲ **Snöå Bruk** STF Vandrarhem Snöå Bruk, 78051 Dala Järna. ⊜ stf.vandrarhem@snoabruk.se	☎ (281) 24018 ❻ (281) 24045	91	ⓖ₁₂	♦♦♦ ⓘⓞⓘ ⌐ ⊡
▲ **Söderhamn** STF Vandrarhem Söderhamn, Mohedsvägen 59, 82692 Söderala	☎ (270) 425233 ❻ (270) 425326	35	26.05–31.08	♦♦♦ ⓘⓞⓘ 15W ECC⊟ ⌐ 🅿

Location/Address	Telephone No. Fax No.	Beds	Opening Dates	Facilities
▲ Söderköping STF Vandrarhem Söderköping, Mangelgården, Skönbergagatan 48, 61430 Söderköping	☏ (121) 10213	36	01.06–31.08	♦♦♦ ⓡ ♿ ☛ 🅿
▲ Södertälje STF Vandrarhem Södertälje, Tvetagården, 15192 Södertälje	☏ (8) 55098025 🖷 (8) 55098471	54	01.02–16.12	♦♦♦ ⦿ 6SW ☛ 🅿
▲ Södra Ljunga STF Vandrarhem Södra Ljunga, 34191 Ljungby	☏ (372) 16011 🖷 (372) 16160	50	ⓒ	♦♦♦ ⦿ ☛ 🅿 ⊡
▲ Sollefteå STF Vandrarhem Sollefteå, Björklunden, Övergård 7006, 88193 Sollefteå.	☏ (620) 15817 🖷 (620) 15917	26	ⓒ	♦♦♦ ⦿ ☲CC☲ ☛
▲ Sölvesborg STF Vandrarhem Sölvesborg, Ynde Byväg 22, 29492 Sölvesborg. 🅔 yndegarden@solvenet.se	☏ (456) 19811 🖷 (456) 19449	60	ⓒ	♦♦♦ ⦿ 3NW ☛ 🅿 ⊡
▲ Sorsele STF Vandrarhem Sorsele, Torggatan 1-2, 92070 Sorsele	☏ (952) 10048 🖷 (952) 55281	24	10.06–31.08	♦♦♦ ⦿ ⓡ ☛ 🅿 ⊡
▲ Sproge STF Vandrarhem Sproge, Mattsarve Sommargård, Sproge, 62020 Klintehamn	☏ (498) 241097 🖷 (498) 241097	48	01.05–31.08	♦♦♦ ⦿ ☛ 🅿
▲ Stafsjö STF Vandrarhem Stafsjö, Störningsväg 8, 61895 Stafsjö.	☏ (11) 393384 🖷 (11) 393343	28	11.01–20.12	♦♦♦ ♿ ☲CC☲ ☛ ⊡
▲ Stensjö STF Vandrarhem Stensjö, 37034 Holmsjö.	☏ (455) 92310 🖷 (455) 92114	24	01.06–31.08	♦♦♦ ⦿ ☛ 🅿 ☕
▲ Stenungsund STF Vandrarhem Stenungsund, Tollenäs, Pl 6109, 44491 Stenungsund.	☏ (303) 82120 🖷 (303) 770485	50	15.04–15.10	♦♦♦ ⦿ ⓡ ♿ ☛ 🅿
▲ Stockholm - af Chapman/Skeppsholmen ⒾⒷⓃ 11149 Stockholm. 🅔 info@chapman.stfturist.se	☏ (8) 4632266 🖷 (8) 6117155	290	ⓒ	♦♦♦ ⦿ ⓡ ♿ ☲CC☲ ☛ 🅿 ⊡
▲ Stockholm STF Vandrarhem Backpackers Inn, Box 9116, 10272 Stockholm.	☏ (8) 6607515 🖷 (8) 6654039	300	27.06–10.08	♦♦♦ ⦿ 🅿
▲ Stockholm STF Vandrarhem Hökarängen, Martinskolan, Munstycksvägen 18, 12357 Farsta.	☏ (8) 941765 🖷 (8) 6041646	46	21.06–08.08	♦♦♦ ⦿ 3SW ♿ ☛ 🅿 ☕
▲ Stockholm - Långholmen Kronohäktet, Box 9116, 10272 Stockholm. 🅔 vandrarhem@langholmen.com	☏ (8) 6680510 🖷 (8) 7208575	254	ⓒ	♦♦♦ ⦿ ⓡ ♿ ☲CC☲ ☛ 🅿 ⊡
▲ Stockholm - Zinkensdamm Zinkens väg 20, 11741 Stockholm.	☏ (8) 6168100 🖷 (8) 6168120	466	ⓒ	♦♦♦ ⦿ ⓡ ♿ ☲CC☲ ☛ 🅿 ⊡ ☕

Location/Address	Telephone No. Fax No.	Beds	Opening Dates	Facilities

Hostels in the Archipelago /
AJ dans l'archipel/JH im Archipel/Albergues en el archipiélago

Location/Address	Telephone No. Fax No.	Beds	Opening Dates	Facilities
▲ **Adelsö** STF Vandrarhem Adelsö, 17892 Adelsö.	☎ (8) 56051450 ✆ (8) 56051400	30	15.06–31.08	⚄ ⓣⓞⓛ ⓡ ☞ ℗ ⓐ
▲ **Arholma** STF Vandrarhem, Arholma 162, 76041 Arholma.	☎ (176) 56018	34	🔟	☞ ℗
▲ **Blidö** STF Vandrarhem Blidö, Blidö Wärdshus AB, Stämmarsund 1429, 76017 BLIDÖ.	☎ (176) 82299 ✆ (176) 82232	60	🔟	⚄ ⓣⓞⓛ ⓡ ⓖ ⒸⒸ ☞ ℗ ⓐ 🐾
▲ **Dalarö** STF Vandrarhem Dalarö, Lotsen Tullbacken 4, 13054 Dalarö	☎ 08 50151636 ✆ 08 50151636	8	🔟	50 SE ☞ ℗ ⓐ
▲ **Fejan** STF Vandrarhem Fejan, 76015 Gräddö.	☎ (176) 43031 ✆ (176) 43205	53	01.05–30.09	ⓣⓞⓛ ☞ ℗
▲ **Finnhamn** STF Vandrarhem Finnhamn, Finnhamns Friluftsområde, Box 84, 13025 Ingmarsö.	☎ (8) 54246212 ✆ (8) 54246212	80	🔟	⚄ ⓡ ⒸⒸ ☞
▲ **Fjärdlång** STF Vandrarhem, Fjärdlång, 13054 Dalarö.	☎ (8) 50156092	36	07.06–26.09	⚄ ⓡ ☞ ℗
▲ **Gällnö** STF Vandrarhem Gällnö, 130 33 Gällnö by	☎ (8) 57166117 ✆ (8) 57166288	31	01.05–30.09	⚄ ⓡ ☞
▲ **Grinda** STF Vandrarhem Grinda, Grinda Friluftsområde, Södra Bryggan, 10005 Stockholm 1.	☎ (8) 54249072 ✆ (8) 54249345	44	01.05–15.10	⚄ ⓡ ☞
▲ **Kapellskär** STF Vandrarhem Kapellskär, Pl 985, Riddersholm, 76015 Gräddö	☎ (176) 44169 ✆ (176) 239046	36	🔟	⚄ ⓡ ☞ ℗
▲ **Lillsved** STF Vandrarhem, Lillsved 13990, Värmdö.	☎ (8) 54138530 ✆ (8) 54138316	148	01.06–31.08	⚄ ⓣⓞⓛ ☞ ℗
▲ **Örskär** STF Vandrarhem Örskär, Örskärs Fyrplats, 74071 Öregrund ⓔ orskars.vandrarhem@telia.com	☎ (173) 34021 ✆ (173) 34011	18	01.05–30.09	⚄ ⓡ ☞ 🐾
▲ **Sävö** STF Vandrarhem Sävö, Lotsplatsen, Ekviken, 61075 Västerljung.	☎ (156) 40346 ✆ (156) 40346	32	🔟	⚄ ☞ ℗
▲ **Siaröfortet** STF Vandrarhem Siaröfortet, Box 75, 18403 Ljusterö.	☎ (8) 54242149 ✆ (8) 54242149	32	01.05–30.09	⚄ ⓡ ☞
▲ **Skeppsmyra** STF Vandrarhem Skeppsmyra, Pensionat Lyckhem, 76042 Björkö. ⓔ lyckhem@algonet.se	☎ (176) 94027 ✆ (176) 94044	40	🔟	⚄ ⓣⓞⓛ ⓡ ⒸⒸ ☞ ℗ ⓐ
▲ **Stora Kalholmen** STF Vandrarhem Stora Kalholmen, c/o Rubin, Hummelmora väg, 13990 Värmdö	☎ (8) 54246023 ✆ (8) 57160125	22	10.06–20.08	⚄ ⓡ ☞ ℗

Location/Address	Telephone No. Fax No.	Beds	Opening Dates	Facilities
▲ Tyresö STF Vandrarhem Tyresö, Prinsvillan, Kyrkvägen 3, 13560 Tyresö	✆ (8) 7700304 ✆ (8) 7700355	42	🛏️	♦♦ Ⓡ ⚿ 🅿
▲ Utö STF Vandrarhem Utö, Gruvbyn, 13056 Utö	✆ (8) 50157660 ✆ (8) 50157265	44	🛏️	♦♦ 🍴 Ⓡ ⒸⒸ ⚿ 🅿 ⊡
▲ Väddö/Älmsta STF Vandrarhem Väddö, Älmsta, Box 9, 76040 Väddö	✆ (176) 50078	31	30.06–13.08	♦♦ ⚿ 🅿
▲ Stora Karlsö STF Vandrarhem Stora Karlsö, 62020 Klintehamn.	✆ (498) 240500, 240567 ✆ (498) 245260	28	01.05–31.08	♦♦ 🍴 Ⓡ ⚿ 🅿
▲ Stora Segerstad STF Vandrarhem Stora Segerstad, 33021 Reftele. ✉ segerstad.naturbruksgymnasium @educ.itjkpg.se	✆ (371) 23200, 23209, (070) 5567551 ✆ (371) 23210	56	12.06–12.08	♦♦ 🍴 ⚿ 🅿
▲ Stocksund/Danderyd STF Vandrarhem Danderyd, Stocksunds hamn, 18278 Stocksund.	✆ (8) 853507 ✆ (8) 852251	40	15.06–15.08	♦♦ 🍴 ⚿ 🅿 ⊡
▲ Storuman STF Vandrarhem Storuman, Hotell Toppens annex, Blåvägen 238, 92331 Storman	✆ (951) 77700 ✆ (951) 12157	24	01.06–31.08	♦♦ 🍴 ⒸⒸ ⚿ 🅿
▲ Storvallen-Storlien STF Vandrarhem Storvallen, Box 119, 83019 Storlien Jämtland. ✉ info@storvallen.km.scout.se	✆ (647) 70050 ✆ (647) 70050	46	🛏️	♦♦ 🍴 ♿ ⚿ 🅿 ⊡
▲ Strömsholm STF Vandrarhem Strömsholm, Sofielundsvägen 33, 73040 Kolbäck	✆ (220) 43774 ✆ (220) 24187	32	15.06–15.08	♦♦ ♿ ⚿ 🅿 ⊡
▲ Strömsnäsbruk STF Vandrarhem Strömsnäsbruk, Fågelvägen 2, 28733 Strömsnäsbruk ✉ hostel.g@swipnet.se	✆ (433) 20050 ✆ (433) 20970	55	🛏️	♦♦ 🍴 Ⓡ ⒸⒸ ⚿ 🅿 ⊡
▲ Strömstad STF Vandrarhem Strömstad, N Kyrkogatan 12, 45230 Strömstad	✆ (526) 10193 ✆ (70) 8410195	76	12.01–17.12	♦♦ 🍴 Ⓡ ⚿ 🅿
▲ Strömsund/Tullingsås STF Vandrarhem Strömsund, Tullingsås, PL 6173, 83392 Strömsund	✆ (670) 30088, (70) 2056173 ✆ (670) 30088	70	🛏️	♦♦ 🍴 Ⓡ ♿ ⚿
▲ Sundsvall STF Vandrarhem Sundsvall, N Stadsberget, 85640 Sundsvall	✆ (60) 612119 ✆ (60) 617801	150	🛏️	♦♦ 🍴 Ⓡ ⚿
▲ Sunne STF Vandrarhem Sunne, Hembygdsvägen 7, 68631 Sunne	✆ (565) 10788	71	🛏️	♦♦ 🍴 ⚿ 🅿

Location/Address	Telephone No. Fax No.	Beds	Opening Dates	Facilities
▲ **Surahammar** STF Vandrarhem Surahammar, Stationsvägen 2, 73531 Surahammar	☎ (220) 33008, (10) 6686474	68	01.04–30.09	♦♦♦ ⦿ ⓡ ☛ ℗ ⎙
▲ **Sveg** STF Vandrarhem Sveg, Hotell Härjedalen, Vallarvägen 11, 84233 Sveg	☎ (680) 10338	50	⓬	♦♦♦ ⓡ ☛ ℗
▲ **Tännäs** STF Vandrarhem Tännäs, Tännäsgården, Box 4, 84094 Tännäs. ✉ tannasgarden@harjedaten.mail.telia.com	☎ (684) 24067 ✆ (684) 24067	30	⓬	♦♦♦ ⦿ ⌐CC⌐ ☛ ℗ ☕
▲ **Tänndalen** STF Vandrarhem Tänndalen, Skarvruets fjällhotel, 84098 Tänndalen.	☎ (684) 22111 ✆ (684) 22311	49	⓬	♦♦♦ ⦿ ⓡ ⌐CC⌐ ☛ ℗
▲ **Tingstäde** STF Vandrarhem Tingstäde, Box 73, 62033 Tingstäde	☎ 0498 274333 ✆ 0498 274830	26	01.05–31.08	♦♦♦ ♿ ☛ ℗
▲ **Tjärö** STF Turiststation Tjärö, 37010 Bräkne Hoby. ✉ info@tjaro.stfturist.se	☎ (454) 60063 ✆ (454) 39063	100	01.05–12.09	♦♦♦ ⦿ ⓡ ⌐CC⌐ ☛ ℗ ☕
▲ **Tollarp** STF Vandrarhem Tollarp, Box 33, Lundgrensväg 2, 29010 Tollarp.	☎ (44) 310023 ✆ (44) 312304	60	15.06–15.08	♦♦♦ ⦿ ☛ ℗ ⎙
▲ **Torestorp** STF Vandrarhem Torestorp, Solbergavägen 2, 51193 Torestorp.	☎ (320) 55141 ✆ (320) 55143	37	01.05–15.09	⦿ ⓡ ♿ ☛
▲ **Tranås** STF Vandrarhem Tranås, Hembygdsgården, 57339 Tranås	☎ (140) 15166	35	⓬	♦♦♦ ⓡ ☛ ℗
▲ **Tranemo** STF Vandrarhem Tranemo, Tranan, Smedsgatan 2, 51431 Tranemo	☎ (325) 76710, (70) 4690275 ✆ (325) 76710	42	⓬	♦♦♦ ⦿ ⓡ ♿ ☛ ℗ ⎙
▲ **Trollhättan** STF Vandrarhem Trollhättan, Gulavillan, Tingvallavägen 12, 46132 Trollhättan	☎ (520) 12960 ✆ (520) 12960	40	⓬	♦♦♦ ⦿ 3W ⌐CC⌐ ☛ ℗
▲ **Trosa** STF Vandrarhem Trosa, Stensunds folkhögskola, 61991 Trosa	☎ (156) 53200 ✆ (156) 53222	15	14.06–13.08	♦♦♦ ⦿ ☛ ℗ ⎙
▲ **Uddevalla** STF Vandrarhem Uddevalla, Gustafsberg 124, 45191 Uddevalla	☎ (522) 15200 ✆ (522) 511798	55	15.06–16.08	♦♦♦ ⦿ 6SW ☛ ⎙
▲ **Ulricehamn** STF Vandrarhem Ulricehamn, STF VH, 52390 Ulricehamn	☎ (321) 10550 ✆ (321) 14802	40	⓬	♦♦♦ ⦿ 2N ☛ ℗
▲ **Umeå** STF Vandrarhem Umeå, Västra Esplanaden 10, 90326 Umeå. ✉ stfumea.vandrarhem@swipnet.se	☎ (90) 771650 ✆ (90) 771695	100	03.01–20.12	♦♦♦ ⦿ ⌐CC⌐ ☛ ⎙

Location/Address	Telephone No. Fax No.	Beds	Opening Dates	Facilities
▲ **Upplands-Bro** STF Vandrarhem Upplands-Bro, Säbyholm, Naturbruksgymnasiet, 19791 Bro	☎ (8) 58242481 🖷 (8) 58242693	40	10.06–09.08	�037 ☞ 🅿 🗇 ☕
▲ **Uppsala** STF Vandrarhem Uppsala, Sunnersta Herrgård, Sunnerstavägen 24, 75651 Uppsala	☎ (18) 324220	84	🔳32	♂♂ 🍴 6S ☞ 🅿
▲ **Vadstena** STF Vandrarhem Vadstena, Skänningegatan 20, Box 28, 59221 Vadstena.	☎ (143) 10302 🖷 (143) 10404	65	🔳32	♂♂ ⓡ ᴄᴄ ☞ 🅿 🗇
▲ **Vålådalen** STF Vandrarhem Vålådalen, 83012 Vålådalen. ✉ info@valadalen.stfturist.se	☎ (647) 35300 🖷 (647) 35353	37	🔳32	♂♂ 🍴 ᴄᴄ ☞
▲ **Vara** STF Vandrarhem Vara, Folkhögskolan, Badhusgatan, Box 145, 53481 Vara	☎ (512) 10838 🖷 (512) 31200	35	19.06–06.08	♂♂ 🍴 ⓡ ♿ ☞ 🅿 🗇
▲ **Varberg** STF Vandrarhem Varberg, Vare 325, 43291 Varberg	☎ (340) 41173 🖷 (340) 41600	43	🔳32	♂♂ 7S ☞ 🅿
▲ **Värmskog** STF Vandrarhem Värmskog, 67195 Klässbol	☎ (570) 461134	28	15.06–31.08	♂♂ 🍴 ☞ 🅿 🗇
▲ **Värnamo** STF Vandrarhem Värnamo, Tättingvägen 1, 33142 Värnamo. ✉ smalandsagenturer@varnamo.mail.telia.com	☎ (370) 19898 🖷 (370) 18235	89	17.01–22.12	♂♂ 🍴 ⓡ ♿ ᴄᴄ ☞ 🅿 🗇
▲ **Västerås** STF Vandrarhem Västerås, Lövudden Hotell & Konferens, 72591 Västerås.	☎ (21) 185230 🖷 (21) 123036	72	02.01–23.12	♂♂ 🍴 5SW ᴄᴄ ☞ 🅿 🗇
▲ **Växjö** STF Vandrarhem Växjö, Evedals Brunn, 35263 Växjö	☎ (470) 63070 🖷 (470) 63216	65	11.01–15.12	♂♂ 🍴 ⓡ 6NE ☞ 🅿 🗇
▲ **Vimmerby** STF Vandrarhem Vimmerby, Hörestadhult, 59800 Vimmerby	☎ (492) 10225	27	01.06–31.08	♂♂ 4E ☞
▲ **Visby** STF Vandrarhem Visby, Alléskolan, Gamla A7 Området, 62182 Visby.	☎ (498) 269842 🖷 (498) 204290	99	12.06–11.08	♂♂ 🍴 ♿ ☞ 🅿 🗇
▲ **Visingsö** STF Vandrarhem Visingsö, Tunnerstad, 560 34 Visingsö.	☎ (390) 40191, (705) 794315 🖷 (390) 40191	29	🔳32	♂♂ ᴄᴄ ☞ 🅿
▲ **Vittsjö** STF Vandrarhem Vittsjö, Lehultsväg 13, 28022 Vittsjö.	☎ (451) 22087 🖷 (451) 22488	30	01.05–31.08	♂♂ 🍴 ⓡ ☞ 🅿
▲ **Voxnabruk** STF Vandrarhem Voxnabruk, Voxnadalens Kanot, Voxna 21, 82893 Voxnabruk.	☎ (271) 41150, (70) 5737871 🖷 (271) 43080	28	🔳32	♂♂ 🍴 ⓡ ☞ 🅿 🗇

Location/Address	Telephone No. Fax No.	Beds	Opening Dates	Facilities
▲ **Ystad** STF Vandrarhem Ystad, Kantarellen, Sandskog, Fritidsvägen, 27160 Ystad 🄴 ystad.kantarellen@home.se	☎ (411) 66566, (708) 577995 🄵 (411) 10913	104	🖭	⫯ⵏ ⵢⵓⵍ ⵙ 🅿 ▣

MOUNTAIN CENTRES /
Centres de Montagne / Berggzentren / Centros de Montaña

(For further information, contact STF / *Pour de plus amples renseignements, s'adresser à la STF / Nach weiteren Angaben STF fragen / Para más información, diríjase a la STF*)

Location/Address	Telephone No. Fax No.	Beds	Opening Dates	Facilities
▲ **Dalarna** - Grövelsjön MC 79091 Idre. 🄴 info@grovelsjon.stfturist.se	☎ (253) 23090 🄵 (253) 23225	150	27.12–09.01; 12.02–02.05; 17.06–24.09	ⵢⵓⵍ ⵙ 🅿
▲ **Härjedalen** - Helags MC 84035 Ljungdalen.	☎ (687) 20150 🄵 (687) 20150	72	19.02–01.05; 23.06–24.09	ⵙ
▲ **Jämtland** - Blåhammeren MC 83015 Duved. 🄴 info@blahammaren.stfturist.se	☎ (647) 70120 🄵 (647) 70637	52	19.02–01.05; 24.06–17.09	ⵢⵓⵍ ⵙ
▲ **Jämtland** - Storulvån MC 83015 Duved. 🄴 info@storulvan.stfturist.se	☎ (647) 72200 🄵 (647) 74026	140	19.02–01.05; 24.06–17.09	ⵢⵓⵍ ⵙ 🅿
▲ **Jämtland** - Sylarna MC 83015 Duved. 🄴 info@sylarna.stfturist.se	☎ (647) 75010 🄵 (647) 75012	100	19.02–01.05; 25.06–17.09	ⵙ
▲ **Jämtland** - Vålådalen MC 83012 Vålådalen. 🄴 info@valadalen.stfturist.se	☎ (647) 35300 🄵 (647) 35353	230	20.12–24.04; 24.06–17.09	ⵢⵓⵍ ⵙ 🅿
▲ **Lappland** - Abisko MC 98107 Abisko. 🄴 info@abisko.stfturist.se	☎ (980) 40200 🄵 (980) 40140	330	26.02–07.05; 01.06–17.09	ⵢⵓⵍ ⵙ 🅿
▲ **Lappland** - Kebnekaise MC 98129 Kiruna. 🄴 info@kebnekaise.stfturist.se	☎ (980) 55000 🄵 (980) 55048	196	04.03–07.05; 17.06–10.09	ⵢⵓⵍ ⵙ
▲ **Lappland** - Ritsem MC 98299 Gällivare. 🄴 info@ritsem.stfturist.se	☎ (973) 42030 🄵 (973) 42050	40	03.03–07.05; 16.06–08.10	ⵙ 🅿
▲ **Lappland** - Saltoluokta MC 98299 Gällivare. 🄴 info@saltoluokta.stfturist.se	☎ (973) 41010 🄵 (973) 41013	97	10.03–02.05; 16.06–23.09	ⵢⵓⵍ ⵙ

Mountain Huts/ *Cabanes de Montagne/*
Berghütten/ Cabañas de Montaña

(For further information, contact STF / *Pour de plus amples renseignements, s'adresser à la STF / Nach weiteren Angaben STF fragen / Para más información, diríjase a la STF*)

Most of these mountain huts are far from roads and railways and are situated near rough tracks; these tracks cover more than 4,700km, the best known being Kungsleden, in Lappland. 💬 100-220 SEK.

La plupart de ces cabanes de montagne sont loin des routes et des chemins de fer et se trouvent près de sentiers primitifs; ces sentiers couvrent plus de 4700km - le mieux connu est Kungsleden, en Laponie. 💬 *100-220 SEK.*

Die meisten dieser Berghütten sind weit von einer Straße oder Bahnlinie abseits an Wanderwegen gelegen; diese erstrecken sich über mehr als 4700km - der bekannteste ist Kungsleden, in Lappland. 💬 *100-220 SEK.*

La mayoría de las cabañas de montaña están alejados de las carreteras y de los ferrocarriles yse se encuentran cerca de senderos agrestes que cubren más de 4.700km - el más conocido es el Kungsleden, en Laponia. 💬 *100-220 SEK.*

Lappland

Pältsa
Kårsavagge
Abiskojaure
Unna Allakas
Alesjaure
Tjäktja
Vistas
Nallo
Sälka
Tarfala
Hukejaure
Sitasjaure
Singi

Kaitumjaure
Teusajaure
Vakkotavare
Vaisaluokta
Akka
Kutjaure
Sitojaure
Aktse
Pårte
Pieskehaure
Vaimok
Sämmarlappa

Tarrekaise
Njunjes

Aigert
Serve
Tärnasjöstugan
Syterstugan
Viterskalet
Bleriken

Jämtland

Anaris
Lunndörren
Vålåvalen

Stensdalen
Gåsen

Härjedalen

Helags
Fältjägarn
Skedbro
Rogen

Dalarna

Storrödtjärn

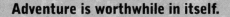

> **Adventure is worthwhile in itself.**
>
> L'aventure elle-même en vaut la peine.
>
> **Abenteuer allein lohnt sich.**
>
> La aventura merece la pena por la experiencia en sí.
>
> **Amelia Earhart**

HOSTELLING
INTERNATIONAL

Make your credit card bookings at these centres
Réservez par carte de crédit auprès des centres suivants
Reservieren Sie per Kreditkarte bei diesen Zentren
Reserve con tarjeta de crédito en los siguientes centros

English

Australia	☎ (2) 9261 1111
Canada	☎ (1) (800) 663 5777
England & Wales	☎ (1629) 581 418
France	☎ (1) 44 89 87 27
Northern Ireland	☎ (1232) 324 733
Republic of Ireland	☎ (1) 830 1766
New Zealand	☎ (9) 303 9524
Scotland	☎ (541) 553 255
Switzerland	☎ (1) 360 1414
USA	☎ (202) 783 6161

Français

Angleterre & Pays de Galles	☎ (1692) 581 418
Australie	☎ (2) 9261 1111
Canada	☎ (1) (800) 663 5777
Écosse	☎ (541) 553 255
États-Unis	☎ (202) 783 6161
France	☎ (1) 44 89 87 27
Irlande du Nord	☎ (1232) 324 733
Nouvelle-Zélande	☎ (9) 303 9524
République d'Irlande	☎ (1) 830 1766
Suisse	☎ (1) 360 1414

Deutsch

Australien	☎ (2) 9261 1111
England & Wales	☎ (1629) 581 418
Frankreich	☎ (1) 44 89 87 27
Irland	☎ (1) 830 1766
Kanada	☎ (1) (800) 663 5777
Neuseeland	☎ (9) 303 9524
Nordirland	☎ (1232) 324 733
Schottland	☎ (541) 553 255
Schweiz	☎ (1) 360 1414
USA	☎ (202) 783 6161

Español

Australia	☎ (2) 9261 1111
Canadá	☎ (1) (800) 663 5777
Escocia	☎ (541) 553 255
Estados Unidos	☎ (202) 783 6161
Francia	☎ (1) 44 89 87 27
Inglaterra y Gales	☎ (1629) 581 418
Irlanda del Norte	☎ (1232) 324 733
Nueva Zelanda	☎ (9) 303 9524
República de Irlanda	☎ (1) 830 1766
Suiza	☎ (1) 360 1414

IBN INTERNATIONAL BOOKING NETWORK

Switzerland

SUISSE
SCHWEIZ
SUIZA

**Schweizer Jugendherbergen,
Schaffhauserstrasse 14, Postfach 161,
CH 8042 Zürich, Switzerland.**

📞 (41) (1) 3601414
📠 (41) (1) 3601460
📧 bookingoffice@youthhostel.ch
www.youthhostel.ch

Office Hours: Monday-Friday, 08.00-12.00hrs and 13.00-18.00hrs

A copy of the Hostel Directory for this Country can be obtained from:
The National Office.

Capital:	Bern	**Population:**	7,096,800
Language: French/German/Italian/Romansh		**Size:**	41,285 sq km
Currency:	CHF	**Telephone Country Code:**	41

Switzerland

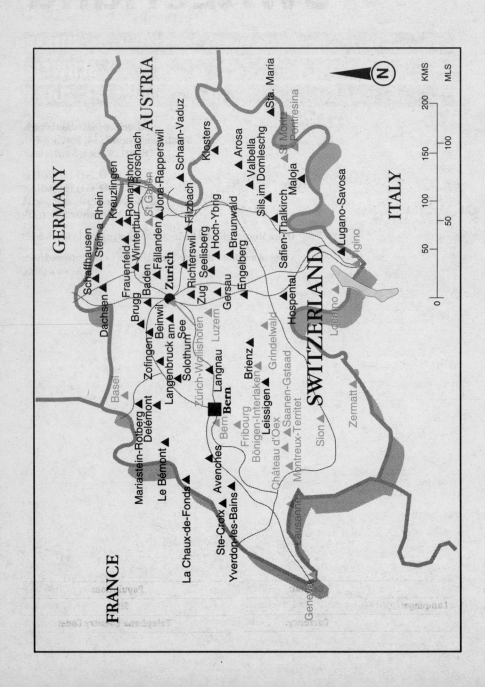

English

SWISS HOSTELS

Swiss Youth Hostels are renowned for their quality and are all participating in Hostelling International's Assured Standards Scheme (see page 4 for details), whether a tranquil lakeside location or a base for your annual ski-ing trip. Many hàve family rooms.

In most Swiss Youth Hostels you must check out by 10.00hrs on day of departure and have checked in by 22.00hrs on day of arrival. Opening times vary, so check with the hostel or get hold of a copy of the Swiss guide.

Expect to pay in the region of CHF 18.00-30.00 per night including bed linen and breakfast. Breakfast is not included in hostels with prices below CHF 18.00.

PASSPORTS AND VISAS

Many visitors require only a valid passport to enter Switzerland, but you should contact the nearest Swiss embassy for details.

BANKING HOURS

Banks are open Monday to Friday 08.30-12.00hrs and 14.00-17.00hrs.

POST OFFICE

Post offices are open Monday to Friday 07.30-12.00hrs and 13.30-18.00hrs. They are also open on Saturdays 08.30-11.00hrs.

SHOPPING HOURS

Shops are open Monday to Friday 08.00-12.00hrs and 13.30-18.30hrs, Saturday 08.00-16.00hrs. In big cities shops do not tend to close at lunch time.

TRAVEL

Rail
Rail travel is regular and efficient. Eurail and Inter-Rail cards are valid, though only on state-run railways.

Bus
The Swiss bus service is both regular and efficient.

Driving
An international driving licence is required.

Français

AUBERGES DE JEUNESSE SUISSES

Les auberges de jeunesse suisses sont réputées pour leur qualité et participent toutes au Plan Hostelling International pour la Garantie des Normes en auberge (voir page 13 pour plus de détails), qu'elles soient situées au bord d'un lac tranquille ou qu'elles servent de base pour vos vacances de sports d'hiver annuelles. Beaucoup disposent de chambres familiales.

Dans la plupart des auberges suisses, les visiteurs doivent quitter leur chambre à 10h et en prendre possession à 22h. Les heures d'ouverture varient; il est donc conseillé de vérifier auprès de l'auberge ou d'obtenir un exemplaire du guide suisse.

Une nuit vous coûtera entre CHF 18,00 et CHF30,00, petit déjeûner et draps compris. Le petit-déjeûner n'est pas compris lorsque la nuitée n'atteint pas les CHF 18,00.

PASSEPORTS ET VISAS

Un passeport valide sera suffisant pour de nombreux visiteurs mais il est prudent de vérifier auprès de l'Ambassade suisse la plus proche pour plus de détails.

HEURES D'OUVERTURE DES BANQUES

Les banques sont ouvertes du lundi au vendredi de 8h30 à 12h et de 14h à 17h.

BUREAUX DE POSTE

Les bureaux de poste sont ouverts du lundi au vendredi de 7h30 à 12h et de 13h30 à 18h. Ils sont aussi ouverts le samedi de 8h30 à 11h.

HEURES D'OUVERTURE DES MAGASINS

Les magasins sont ouverts du lundi au vendredi de 8h à 12h et de 13h30 à 18h30. Le samedi, ils ouvrent de 8h à 16h. Dans les grandes villes, les magasins ont tendance à ne pas fermer pour midi.

DEPLACEMENTS

Trains

Le système ferroviaire fonctionne bien et les trains sont réguliers. Les cartes Eurail et Inter-Rail sont valides seulement sur les réseaux gérés par l'état.

Autobus

Le système d'autobus suisse fonctionne bien et les bus sont réguliers.

Automobiles

Les conducteurs doivent être munis d'un permis de conduire international.

Deutsch

SCHWEIZER JUGENDHERBERGEN

Die Schweizer Jugendherbergen sind für ihre Qualität bekannt und sind am Konzept der 'Zugesicherten Standards' beteiligt (siehe Seite 20 für Einzelheiten). Das gilt sowohl für die Jugendherbergen an ruhigen Seen als auch für die von Skiläufern benutzten Jugendherbergen. Viele haben Familienzimmer.

In den meisten Schweizer Jugendherbergen gelten folgende check-in und -out-Zeiten:
Check-in: vor 22.00 Uhr
Check-out: bis 10.00 Uhr am Abreisetag.
Die Öffnungszeiten sind unterschiedlich. Erkundigen Sie sich daher bei der jeweiligen Jugendherberge, oder besorgen Sie sich ein Exemplar des Schweizer Verzeichnisses.

Die Preise sind zwischen 18,00-30,00 CHF pro Nacht, einschließlich Bettwäsche und Frühstück. In Jugendherbergen mit Preisen unter 18,00 CHF ist das Frühstück nicht eingeschlossen.

PÄSSE UND VISA

Viele Besucher brauchen für die Einreise in die Schweiz nur einen gültigen Reisepaß. Erkundigen Sie sich aber bitte bei der nächsten Schweizer Botschaft.

BANKEN

Banken sind von Montag bis Freitag von 08.30-12.00 Uhr und von 14.00-17.00 Uhr geöffnet.

POST

Postämter sind von Montag bis Freitag von 07.30-12.00 Uhr und von 13.30-18.00 Uhr geöffnet. Sie sind auch am Samstag von 08.30-11.00 Uhr geöffnet.

LADENÖFFNUNGSZEITEN

Die Geschäfte sind von Montag bis Freitag von 08.00-12.00 Uhr und von 13.30-18.30 Uhr und am Samstag von 08.00-16.00 Uhr geöffnet. In Großstädten sind die Geschäfte im allgemeinen länger geöffnet.

REISEN

Eisenbahn

Die Züge sind pünktlich, und die Eisenbahnverbindungen sind gut. Eurail- und Inter-Rail-Karten sind in der Schweiz nur auf staatlich betriebenen Strecken gültig.

Busse

In der Schweiz gibt es gute Busverbindungen und einen regelmäßigen Busverkehr.

Autofahren

Es wird ein internationaler Führerschein verlangt.

Español

ALBERGUES JUVENILES SUIZOS

Los albergues juveniles suizos son reconocidos por su calidad y todos participan en el Plan de Hostelling International de Normas Garantizadas (véase la página 28 para más información), ya sea que se encuentren al lado de un tranquilo lago o en una estación de esquí. Muchos de ellos disponen de habitaciones familiares.

En la mayor parte de los albergues juveniles suizos hay que dejar el albergue antes de las 10 h. y registrarse antes de las 22 h. El horario de apertura varía, por lo que se recomienda confirmarlo con el albergue deseado o hacerse con un ejemplar de la guía suiza.

Los precios oscilan entre 18,00 y 30,00 francos suizos por noche incluyendo sábanas y desayuno. No obstante, este último no está incluido en el precio de la estancia si éste es menos de 18,00 francos suizos.

PASAPORTES Y VISADOS

La mayoría de los visitantes sólo necesitan un pasaporte válido para entrar en Suiza, pero se recomienda dirigirse a la embajada suiza más cercana para confirmarlo.

HORARIO DE LOS BANCOS

Los bancos abren de lunes a viernes de 8.30 h. a 12 h. y de 14 h. a 17 h.

OFICINAS DE CORREOS

Las oficinas de correos abren de lunes a viernes de 7.30 h. a 12 h. y de 13.30 h. a 18.00 h. También abren los sábados de 8.30 h. a 11 h.

HORARIO COMERCIAL

Las tiendas abren de lunes a viernes de 8 h. a 12 h. y de 13.30 a 18.30 h., los sábados de 8 h. a 16 h. En las grandes ciudades, las tiendas suelen permanecer abiertas durante la hora del almuerzo.

DESPLAZAMIENTOS

Tren

Los trenes son frecuentes y rápidos. Las tarjetas Eurail e Inter-Rail son válidas, pero sólo en los servicios estatales.

Autobús

El servicio de autobús suizo es bueno y rápido.

Automóvil

Se necesita un permiso de conducir internacional.

Basel

St. Alban-Kirchrain 10,
4052 Basel.
☏ (61) 2720572
f (61) 2720833
e basel@youthhostel.ch

Open Dates:	03.01-22.12
Open Hours:	High Season. 07.00-10.00; 14.00-24.00hrs, Low Season. 07.30-10.00; 14.00-23.00hrs
Reservations:	**R** **IBN** **CC**
Price Range:	from CHF 26.10 **BB**inc 🍽
Beds:	197 - 1x¹ 12x² 3x³ 6x⁴ 5x⁶ 14x⁶
Facilities:	♿ � 11x � 🍴 🛏 📺 📖 1 x 🍷 🔒 🔢 ⬆ ✒ 🎣 ♨
Directions:	1 SE from city centre
✈	Basel - Mulhouse 7km
🚂	Basel 1.5km
🚋	2 500m ap Kunstmuseum
Attractions:	✎2km ⚓1.5km

Bönigen-Interlaken

Aareweg 21,
Am See,
3806 Bönigen (Bern).
☏ (33) 8224353
f (33) 8232058
e boenigen@youthhostel.ch

Open Dates:	18.12-09.01; 23.01-13.11
Open Hours:	High Season. 07.00-10.00; 14.00-23.30hrs, Low Season. 07.00-10.00; 16.00-23.00hrs
Reservations:	**R** **IBN** **CC**
Price Range:	from CHF 22.50 **BB**inc 🍽
Beds:	150 - 1x³ 6x⁴ 10x⁶ 3x⁶
Facilities:	666 6x 666 🍴 🛏 📺 📖2 x 🍷 🔒 🔢 🅿 📖 🎣 🎿 ⛰ ♨ 🏔 🏠
Directions:	
✈	Zürich 150km
🚂	Interlaken-East 1.8km
🚌	1+3 500m ap Lütschinenbrücke
Attractions:	⚑ ⛰ 🚴 ⛷ 2200m 🎿 🎿 ∪3km ✎3km ⚓300m

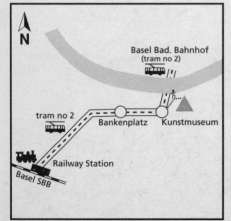

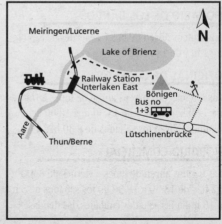

Grindelwald

Weid 12,
Terrassenweg,
3818 Grindelwald (Bern).
☎ (33) 8531009
📠 (33) 8535029
✉ grindelwald@youthhostel.ch

Open Dates:	01.01-10.04; 13.05-30.10; 18-31.12
Open Hours:	06.30-09.30; 15.00-24.00hrs
Reservations:	**R** **IBN** **CC**
Price Range:	from CHF 26.00 **BB** inc 🍴
Beds:	125 - 4x² 15x⁴ 2x⁵ 6x⁶ 1x⁶
Facilities:	♿ ♟ 15x ♟ 🍴 ♨ 📺 🍴 1 x ⛾ 🔲 🔢 🅿 📋 🍴 ♫ ⛰ ♦ ♠
Directions:	1 NW from city centre
✈	Zürich 170km
🚂	Grindelwald 1km
🚌	4 100m ap Terrassenweg-Gaggi Säge
Attractions:	♦ ⛰ ♦ 1km ♦ ⛷ 2200m ⛸ ♀ ∪ 20km ♦ 1km ♨ 500m

Locarno - Palagiovani

Via Varenna 18,
6600 Locarno (Ticino).
☎ (91) 7561500
📠 (91) 7561501
✉ locarno@youthhostel.ch

Open Dates:	🔢
Open Hours:	High Season. 08.00-10.00; 15.00-23.30hrs, Low Season. 08.00-10.00; 16.00-22.30hrs
Reservations:	**R** **IBN** **CC**
Price Range:	from CHF 28.50 **BB** inc 🍴
Beds:	188 - 54x² 14x⁴ 4x⁶
Facilities:	♟ 13x ♟ 🍴 ♨ 📺 3 x ⛾ 🔲 🔢 🔢 📋 🍴 ♫ ♦
Directions:	1.5 W from city centre
✈	Agno 35km
🚂	Locarno 1.5km
🚌	31, 36 50m ap Cinque Vie
🚋	Centovalli-Bahn 200m ap St. Antonio
Attractions:	♦ ♦ 1km ♦ ♀ ∪ 10km ♦ 1.5km ♨ 1.5km

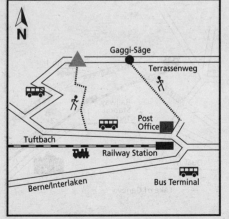

0   4km   0   2km

Lucerne

am Rotsee,
Sedelstr 12,
6004 Lucerne (Lucerne).
☏ (41) 4208800
🖷 (41) 4205616
✉ luzern@youthhostel.ch

Open Dates:	🗓️
Open Hours:	High Season. 07.00-10.00; 14.00-24.00hrs, Low Season. 07.30-09.30; 16.00-24.00hrs
Reservations:	**R** **IBN** **CC**
Price Range:	from CHF 28.00 BB inc 🍴
Beds:	194 - 8x² 4x³ 18x⁴ 9x⁶ 2x⁶
Facilities:	👫 👫 🍽 👥 📺 1 x ☕ 🔒 📷 🔟 🅿 📋 🧺 ♨ 🐾 👼
Directions:	2N from city centre
✈	Zürich 50km
🚂	Lucerne 2km
🚌	1/18/19 500m ap Schlossberg/ Jugendherberge/Rosenberg
Attractions:	🌳 🎿 2km 🚶 ⛷ 5km ⛷ 2km ⛵ 2km

Montreux-Territet

Passage de l'Auberge 8,
1820 Montreux-Territet (Vaud).
☏ (21) 9634934
🖷 (21) 9632729
✉ montreux@youthhostel.ch

Open Dates:	01.02-30.11
Open Hours:	High Season. 07.00-10.00; 16.00-23.00hrs, Low Season. 07.30-09.30; 17.00-22.00hrs
Reservations:	**R** **IBN** **CC**
Price Range:	from CHF 27.00 BB inc 🍴
Beds:	112 - 5x² 6x⁴ 9x⁶ 3x⁶
Facilities:	♿ 👫 6x 👫 🍽 👥 📺 2 x ☕ 🔒 📷 🔟 🅿 📋 🧺 ♨ 🐾
Directions:	2E from city centre
✈	Geneva 100km
⛴	Port de Territet 150m
🚂	Montreux 2km
🚌	1 100m ap Territet
Attractions:	🌳 ⛰ 🎿 1km 🚶 ⛷ 10km ⛷ 500m ⛵ 1km

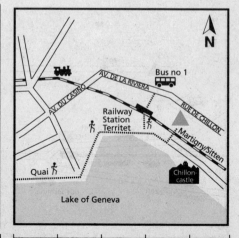

0	3km
0	2.5km

St. Gallen

Jüchstrasse 25,
9000 St. Gallen (St. Gallen).
📞 (71) 2454777
📠 (71) 2454983
✉ st.gallen@youthhostel.ch

Open Dates:	06.03-12.12
Open Hours:	07.00-09.30; 17.00-22.30hrs
Reservations:	**R** IBN CC
Price Range:	from CHF 21.50 BB inc 🍽
Beds:	88 - 6x² 4x⁴ 10x⁶
Facilities:	♿ ♦♦♦ 8x ♦♦♦ 🍽 🚪 📺 🛒 2 x 🍴 🔲 🔟 🅿 🛈 🛒 ♣ ⛰ 🔍 🏠

Directions:

✈	Zürich 80km
🚂	St. Gallen 1.5km
🚌	1 500m ap Singenberg
🚋	Trogenerbähnli 800m ap Schülerhaus

Attractions: 🏞 🚶 🔍8km ⛵2km

St. Moritz Bad

Stille,
Via Surpunt 60,
7500 St. Moritz Bad (Graubünden).
📞 (81) 8333969
📠 (81) 8338046
✉ st.moritz@youthhostel.ch

Open Dates:	🗓
Open Hours:	Summer. 07.00-10.00; 16.00-22.00hrs, Winter. 07.30-10.00; 17.00-22.00hrs, 01-30.11. 07.30-09.00; 17.00-19.30hrs.
Reservations:	**R** IBN CC
Price Range:	from CHF 28.50 BB inc 🍽
Beds:	190 - 14x² 42x⁴
Facilities:	♦♦♦ 42x ♦♦♦ 🍽 🚪 📺 3 x 🍴 🔲 🔟 🅿 🛈 🛒 ♣ 🔍 🏠

Directions: 2S from city centre

✈	Zürich 220km
🚂	St. Moritz 2km
🚌	Postauto 300m ap Hotel Sonne

Attractions: 🏞 ⛰ 🚴 ⛷3300m 🎿 🚶 ∪1km 🔍1km ⛵800m

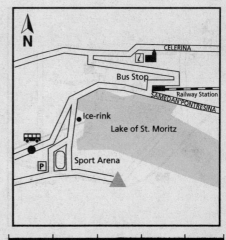

Solothurn

Landhausquai 23,
"Am Land",
4500 Solothurn (Solothurn).
☏ (32) 6231706
🖷 (32) 6231639
📧 solothurn@youthhostel.ch

Open Dates:	19.01-20.11
Open Hours:	High Season. 07.30-10.00; 16.30-22.30hrs, Low Season. 08.00-10.00; 17.00-22.00hrs
Reservations:	® ⊂CC⊃
Price Range:	from CHF 24.00 ᴮᴮⁱⁿᶜ 🛒
Beds:	92 - 4x³🚪 2x⁵🚪 4x⁶🚪 5x⁶🚪
Facilities:	♿ � 6x ♦♦♦ 🍴 👥 📺 🍷1 x 🍷 🔒 🔢 ⇅ ⓘ 🔌 🎴

Directions:

✈	Zürich 80km
🚆	Solothurn 500m
Attractions:	🚲 🏃 ∪2km ⌕2km 🏊1km

Zermatt

Winkelmatten,
3920 Zermatt (Wallis).
☏ (27) 9672320
🖷 (27) 9675306
📧 zermatt@youthhostel.ch

Open Dates:	01.01-07.05; 18.06-01.11; 17-31.12
Open Hours:	High Season. 06.30-10.00; 16.00-23-00hrs, Low Season. 07.00-09.30; 16.30-22.30hrs
Reservations:	® ⟦IBN⟧ ⊂CC⊃
Price Range:	from CHF 27.50 ᴮᴮⁱⁿᶜ 🛒
Beds:	138 - 1x²🚪 2x⁴🚪 1x⁶🚪 12x⁶🚪
Facilities:	♦♦♦ ♦add 🍴 👥 🍷3 x 🍷 🔒 📷 🔢 ⓘ 🔌 🎿 ⛰ 🥾

Directions:	⟦0.8 SE⟧ from city centre
✈	Geneva 235km
🚆	Zermatt 800m
🚌	Ortsbus 100m ap Luchre
Attractions:	🌄 ⛰ 🚲 🎿 3800m 🏃 ∪5km ⌕600m 🏊500m

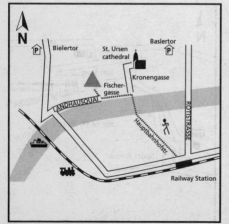

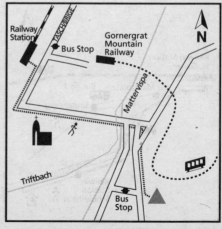

0			1.5km

0			2km

Zürich

**Mutschellenstr 114,
8038 Zürich (Zürich).**
📞 (1) 4823544
📠 (1) 4801727
📧 zuerich@youthhostel.ch

Open Dates:	🗓
Open Hours:	🕐
Reservations:	Ⓡ IBN CC
Price Range:	from CHF 28.50 BBinc 🍴
Beds:	315 - 5x¹🛏 1x²🛏 8x⁴🛏 46x⁶🛏
Facilities:	♿ 👪 4x 👪 🍴 🛋 📺 2 x 🍷 🔘 📷 🏧 🔒 ⬆ Ⓟ ⓘ 🧺 🐾 🔍
Directions:	3SW from city centre
✈	Zürich 8km
🚆	Zürich 4km
🚌	33 ap Jugendherberge
🚋	7 350m ap Morgental
Ⓤ	1/8 Zürich-Wollishofen 500m
Attractions:	🏛500m ⛷1km ⚓500m

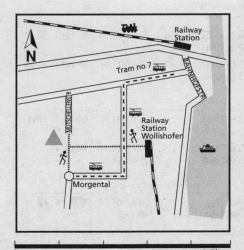

> **We think of travel as a matter of place, when in fact, place is a matter of people."**

On a tendance à penser que voyager est une question de lieu alors qu'en fait, le lieu est une question de personnes.

Wir sehen Reisen als eine Frage des Ortes, aber tatsächlich ist ein Ort eine Frage der Menschen.

Creemos que los viajes tienen que ver con lugares, cuando en realidad los lugares tienen que ver con gente.

Sonny Landreth

Location/Address	Telephone No. Fax No.	Beds	Opening Dates	Facilities
▲ **Arosa** Seewaldweg, 7050 Arosa (Graubünden).	☎ (81) 3771397 ✆ (81) 3771397	155	18.06–23.10; 11.12–17.04	⑩
▲ **Avenches** rue du Lavoir 5, 1580 Avenches (Vaud).	☎ (26) 6752666 ✆ (26) 6752717	76	15.04–17.10	⑪ ⑩ 〔CC〕 🅿 ⓞ
▲ **Baden** Kanalstr 7, 5400 Baden (Aargau). ⓔ baden@youthhostel.ch	☎ (56) 2216736 ✆ (56) 2217660	88	16.03–23.12	⑩ 〔CC〕 ☞ 🅿 ⓞ
▲ **Basel** 〔IBN〕 **St. Alban-Kirchrain 10, 4052 Basel.** ⓔ basel@youthhostel.ch	☎ (61) 2720572 ✆ (61) 2720833	197	03.01–22.12	⑪ ⑩ ⓡ 〔1 SE〕 ♿ 〔CC〕 ⓞ
▲ **Beinwil am See** Seestrasse 71, 5712 Beinwil am See (Aargau). ⓔ beinwil@youthhostel.ch	☎ (62) 7711883 ✆ (62) 7716123	98	13.02–12.12	⑪ ⑩ 〔CC〕 ☞ 🅿 ⓞ
▲ **Le Bémont** 2877 Le Bémont (Jura). ⓔ bemont@youthhostel.ch	☎ (32) 9511707 ✆ (32) 9512413	96	02.02–30.11	⑪ ⑩ 〔CC〕 ☞ 🅿 ⓞ
▲ **Bern** 〔IBN〕 Weihergasse 4, 3005 Bern. ⓔ bern@youthhostel.ch	☎ (31) 3116316 ✆ (31) 3125240	186	01–09.01; 25.01–31.12	⑩ ♿ 〔CC〕 ⓞ
▲ **Bönigen-Interlaken** 〔IBN〕 **Aareweg 21, Am See, 3806 Bönigen (Bern).** ⓔ boenigen@youthhostel.ch	☎ (33) 8224353 ✆ (33) 8232058	150	18.12–09.01; 23.01–13.11	⑪ ⑩ ⓡ 〔CC〕 ☞ 🅿 ⓞ
▲ **Braunwald** 'Im Gyseneggli', 8784 Braunwald (Glarus). ⓔ braunwald@youthhostel.ch	☎ (55) 6431356 ✆ (55) 6432435	82	18.12–04.04; 19.06–24.10	⑪ ⑩ 〔CC〕 ☞
▲ **Brienz** Strandweg 10, am See, 3855 Brienz (Bern). ⓔ brienz@youthhostel.ch	☎ (33) 9511152 ✆ (33) 9512260	86	15.04–17.10	⑪ ⑩ 〔CC〕 ☞ 🅿
▲ **Brugg** Schlössli Altenburg, 5200 Brugg (Aargau). ⓔ brugg@youthhostel.ch	☎ (56) 4411020 ✆ (56) 4423820	52	01.03–31.10	⑩ 〔CC〕 ☞ 🅿 ⓞ
▲ **Château-d'Oex** Les Riaux, 1837 Château-d'Oex (Vaud).	☎ (26) 9246404 ✆ (26) 9245843	50	23.12–24.10	⑩ 〔CC〕 🅿 ⓞ
▲ **Dachsen** Schloss Laufen am Rheinfall, 8447 Dachsen (Zürich). ⓔ dachsen@youthhostel.ch	☎ (52) 6596152 ✆ (52) 6596039	87	19.03–15.11	⑩ 〔CC〕 ☞ 🅿
▲ **Delémont** Route de Bâle 185, 2800 Delémont (Jura).	☎ (32) 4222054 ✆ (32) 4228830	80	06.03–31.10	⑪ ⑩ ♿ 〔CC〕 ☞ 🅿 ⓞ
▲ **Engelberg** Berghaus, Dorfstr 80, 6390 Engelberg (Obwalden). ⓔ engelberg@youthhostel.ch	☎ (41) 6371292 ✆ (41) 6374988	150	01.12–18.04; 01.06–18.10	⑩ 🅿
△ *Fällanden* *'Im Rohrbuck', Maurstr 33, 8117 Fällanden (Zürich).*	☎ *(1) 8253144* ✆ *(1) 8255480*	46	28.02–05.12 ⑪ *only*	ⓡ ☞ 🅿

Location/Address	Telephone No. Fax No.	Beds	Opening Dates	Facilities
▲ Figino (IBN) Via Casoro 2, 6918 Figino (Ticino). ✉ figino@youthhostel.ch	☎ (91) 9951151 🖷 (91) 9951070	160	28.02–23.10	♛ ⑩ CC- ☞ P
▲ Filzbach 'Lihn' Blaukreuz Kurs-und Ferienzentrum, 8757 Filzbach (Glarus). ✉ filzbach@youthhostel.ch	☎ (55) 6141342 🖷 (55) 6141707	50	25–12.12	♛ ⑩ & CC- P 🗗
▲ Frauenfeld Rüegerholz, Festhüttenstr 22, 8500 Frauenfeld (Thurgau).	☎ (52) 7213680 🖷 (52) 7213680	40	01–31.01; 01.03–31.10; 29.11–31.12	☞ P
▲ Fribourg (IBN) 2 rue de l'Hôpital, 1700 Fribourg (Fribourg). ✉ fribourg@youthhostel.ch	☎ (26) 3231916 🖷 (26) 3231940	90	26.02–01.11	⑩ & CC- ☞ 🗗
▲ Genève (IBN) 30 rue Rothschild, 1202 Genève (Genève). ✉ geneve@youthhostel.ch	☎ (22) 7326260 🖷 (22) 7383987	350	🗓	⑩ 1S & CC- ☞ P 🗗
▲ Gersau Rotschuo, 6442 Gersau (Schwyz).	☎ (41) 8281277 🖷 (41) 8281263	120	01.03–30.11	♛ ⑩ CC- ☞ P 🗗
▲ Grindelwald (IBN) **Weid 12, Terrassenweg,** **3818 Grindelwald (Bern).** ✉ grindelwald@youthhostel.ch	☎ (33) 8531009 🖷 (33) 8535029	125	01.01–10.04; 13.05–30.10; 18–31.12	♛ ⑩ ® 1NW & CC- P 🗗
Gstaad ☞ **Saanen-Gstaad**				
▲ Hoch-Ybrig Fuederegg, 8842 Unteriberg (Schwyz). ✉ hoch.ybrig@youthhostel.ch	☎ (55) 4141766 🖷 (55) 4142065	86	05.12–05.04; 04.07–24.10	♛ ⑩ CC- ☞
△ *Hospental* *Gotthardstrasse, 6493 Hospental (Uri).* ✉ *hospental@youthhostel.ch*	☎ *(41) 8871889,* 🖷 *(41) 8870902*	*65*	*16.12–05.04;* *16.05–14.10*	⑩ ☞ P 🗗
Interlaken ☞ **Bönigen**				
▲ Jona-Rapperswil 'Busskirch', Hessenhofweg 10, 8645 Jona (St. Gallen). ✉ jona@youthhostel.ch	☎ (55) 2109927 🖷 (55) 2109928	74	30.01–01.11	♛ ⑩ & CC- P
▲ Klosters 'Soldanella', Talstr 73, 7250 Klosters (Graubünden). ✉ klosters@youthhostel.ch	☎ (81) 4221316 🖷 (81) 4225209	84	17.12–12.04; 02.07–18.10	♛ ⑩ CC- P 🗗
▲ Kreuzlingen Promenadenstr 7, 8280 Kreuzlingen (Thurgau). ✉ kreuzlingen@youthhostel.ch	☎ (71) 6882663 🖷 (71) 6884761	97	01.03–30.11	⑩ CC-
▲ La Chaux-de-Fonds Rue du Doubs 34, 2300 La Chaux-de-Fonds (Neuchâtel)	☎ (32) 9684315 🖷 (32) 9682518	80	31.12–05.11	⑩ & CC- ☞ P 🗗
△ *Langenbruck* *Haus Rosengarten, Bärenwilerstr. 10,* *4438 Langenbruck (Baselland).* ✉ *bookingoffice@youthhostel.ch*	☎ *(1) 3601414* 🖷 *(1) 3601460*	*42*	🗓 *♛ only*	® ☞ P

Location/Address	Telephone No. Fax No.	Beds	Opening Dates	Facilities
▲ **Langnau im Emmental** Mooseggstr 32, 3550 Langnau i.E. (Bern).	☎ (34) 4024526	50	18.10–12.02; 22.02–24.09	☞ 🅿
▲ **Lausanne** - Jeunotel [IBN] Ch.du Bois-de-Vaux 36, 1007 Lausanne (Vaud) ✉ lausanne@youthhostel.ch	☎ (21) 6260222 ❶ (21) 6260226	240	🔓12	🍴 ♿ ⌐CC⌐ 🅿 ⓞ
▲ **Leissigen** "La Nichée", Horbacher, 3706 Leissigen (Bern). ✉ leissigen@youthhostel.ch	☎ (33) 8471214 ❶ (33) 8471497	42	30.04–16.10	ⅲ 🍴 ⌐CC⌐ 🅿
Lenzerheide ☞ **Valbella**				
Liechtenstein ☞ **Schaan-Vaduz**				
▲ **Locarno** - Palagiovani [IBN] **Via Varenna 18, 6600 Locarno (Ticino).** ✉ locarno@youthhostel.ch	☎ (91) 7561500 ❶ (91) 7561501	188	🔓12	ⅲ 🍴 ⓡ 1.5W ⌐CC⌐ ⓞ
▲ **Lugano** - Savosa Via Cantonale 13, 6942 Savosa (Ticino). ✉ lugano@youthhostel.ch	☎ (91) 9662728 ❶ (91) 9682363	110	16.03–31.10	ⅲ 🍴 ♿ ⌐CC⌐ ☞ 🅿 ⓞ
▲ **Lucerne** [IBN] **am Rotsee, Sedelstr 12, 6004 Lucerne (Lucerne).** ✉ luzern@youthhostel.ch	☎ (41) 4208800 ❶ (41) 4205616	194	🔓12	ⅲ 🍴 ⓡ 2N ⌐CC⌐ 🅿 ⓞ
▲ **Maloja** Hauptstrasse, 7516 Maloja (Graubünden).	☎ (81) 8243258 ❶ (81) 8243571	100	19.06–04.09; 02–23.10; 18.12–17.04	🍴 ⓡ ⌐CC⌐ ☞ 🅿 ⓞ
▲ **Mariastein-Rotberg** Jugendburg, 4115 Mariastein (Solothurn). ✉ mariastein@youthhostel.ch	☎ (61) 7311049 ❶ (61) 7312724	86	01.03–11.12	🍴 ⌐CC⌐ ☞ 🅿
▲ **Montreux-Territet** [IBN] **Passage de l'Auberge 8, 1820 Montreux-Territet (Vaud).** ✉ montreux@youthhostel.ch	☎ (21) 9634934 ❶ (21) 9632729	112	01.02–30.11	ⅲ 🍴 ⓡ 2E ♿ ⌐CC⌐ 🅿 ⓞ
▲ **Pontresina** [IBN] Langlaufzentrum, 'Tolais', 7504 Pontresina (Graubünden). ✉ pontresina@youthhostel.ch	☎ (81) 8427223 ❶ (81) 8427031	130	18.06–23.10; 10.12–10.04	ⅲ 🍴 ⌐CC⌐ 🅿 ⓞ
Rapperswil-Jona ☞ **Jona-Rapperswil**				
Rheinfall ☞ **Dachsen & Schaffhausen**				
▲ **Richterswil** "Horn", Hornstr 5, 8805 Richterswil (Zürich). ✉ richterswil@youthhostel.ch	☎ (1) 7862188 ❶ (1) 7862193	80	01.03–19.12	ⅲ 🍴 ♿ ⌐CC⌐ 🅿
△ *Romansborn* *Gottfried-Keller-Str 6, 8590 Romansborn (Thurgau).* ✉ *romansborn@youthhostel.ch*	☎ *(71) 4631717* ❶ *(71) 4611990*	*114*	*01.03–31.10*	🍴 🅿
△ *Rorschach* - YH Rorschach Berg *Im Ebnet, 9404 Rorschacherberg (St. Gallen). Postaddress: Seefeldstrasse 5, 9403 Goldach.*	☎ *(71) 8415411*	*20*	*01.04–31.10*	ⓡ ☞ 🅿

Location/Address	Telephone No. Fax No.	Beds	Opening Dates	Facilities
▲ **Rorschach** - YH Rorschach See Churerstrasse 4, 9400 Rorschach.	✆ (71) 8449712 🖷 (71) 8449713	32	01.04–31.10	�
▲ **Saanen-Gstaad** ⒾⒷⓃ Chalet Rüblihorn, 3792 Saanen (Bern). 🅔 saanen@youthhostel.ch	✆ (33) 7441343 🖷 (33) 7445542	76	01.12–31.10	♦♦♦ ⍾⍾ CC
▲ **St. Gallen** ⒾⒷⓃ **Jüchstrasse 25, 9000 St. Gallen (St. Gallen).** 🅔 st.gallen@youthhostel.ch	✆ (71) 2454777 🖷 (71) 2454983	88	06.03–12.12	♦♦♦ ⍾ Ⓡ ♿ CC P
△ *Sta Maria im Münstertal* *Chasa Plaz, 7536 Sta. Maria im Münstertal (Graubünden).*	✆ (81) 8585052 🖷 (81) 8585496	62	22.05–23.10; 18.12–10.04	⍾ CC ✦ P
▲ **Ste-Croix** 18 rue Centrale, 1450 Ste-Croix (Vaud). 🅔 ste.croix@youthhostel.ch	✆ (24) 4541810 🖷 (24) 4544522	58	01.04–30.10	♦♦♦ ⍾ CC ✦
▲ **St. Moritz Bad** ⒾⒷⓃ **Stille, Via Surpunt 60, 7500 St. Moritz Bad (Graubünden).** 🅔 st.moritz@youthhostel.ch	✆ (81) 8333969 🖷 (81) 8338046	190	🗓12	♦♦♦ ⍾ Ⓡ 2S CC P
△ *Safien-Thalkirch* *7109 Thalkirch (Graubünden).*	✆ (81) 6471107 🖷 (81) 6471107	28	01.12–31.10	✦ P
▲ **Schaan-Vaduz** Untere Rüttigasse 6, 9494 Schaan (Fürstentum Liechtenstein).	✆ (75) 2325022 🖷 (75) 2325856	96	01.03–30.11	♦♦♦ ⍾ ♿ P
▲ **Schaffhausen** Belair, Randenstr 65, 8200 Schaffhausen. 🅔 schaffhausen@youthhostel.ch	✆ (52) 6258800 🖷 (52) 6245954	86	01.03–31.10	⍾ CC ✦ P
▲ **Seelisberg** Gadenhaus beim Rütli, 6377 Seelisberg (Uri).	✆ (41) 8201784, 8201274 🖷 (41) 8201784, 8201274	25	01.04–31.10	Ⓡ ✦ P
△ *Sils im Domleschg* *Burg Ehrenfels, 7411 Sils im Domleschg (Graubünden).*	✆ (81) 6511518	40	01.04–31.10 ♦♦♦ only	Ⓡ ✦
▲ **Sion** ⒾⒷⓃ rue de l'Industrie 2, 1950 Sion (Valais). 🅔 sion@youthhostel.ch	✆ (27) 3237470 🖷 (27) 3237438	80	24.12–04.01; 23.01–25.10	⍾ ♿ CC ✦
▲ **Solothurn** **Landhausquai 23, "Am Land", 4500 Solothurn (Solothurn).** 🅔 solothurn@youthhostel.ch	✆ (32) 6231706 🖷 (32) 6231639	92	18.01–21.11	♦♦♦ ⍾ Ⓡ ♿ CC
▲ **Stein am Rhein** Hemishoferstr 87, 8260 Stein am Rhein (Schaffhausen). 🅔 stein@youthhostel.ch	✆ (52) 7411255 🖷 (52) 7415140	121	01.03–31.10	♦♦♦ ⍾ ✦ P
Vaduz ☞ **Schaan**				
▲ **Valbella-Lenzerheide** Voa Sartons 41, 7077 Valbella (Graubünden).	✆ (81) 3841208 🖷 (81) 3844558	115	19.06–24.10; 18.12–18.04	♦♦♦ ⍾ CC P

Location/Address	Telephone No. Fax No.	Beds	Opening Dates	Facilities
△ *Winterthur* *Schloss Hegi, Hegifeldstr 125, 8409 Winterthur (Zürich).*	**☎** *(52) 2423840* **❶** *(52) 2425830*	*48*	*01.03–31.10*	**R** ⚲
▲ **Zermatt** ⌷IBN⌷ **Winkelmatten, 3920 Zermatt (Wallis).** ✉ zermatt@youthhostel.ch	**☎** *(27) 9672320* **❶** *(27) 9675306*	138	01.01–07.05; 18.06–01.11; 17–31.12	††† ⅇ⅃ **R** 0.8SE ⌷CC⌷ ⅆ
▲ **Zofingen** General Guisan-Str 10, 4800 Zofingen (Aargau). ✉ zofingen@youthhostel.ch	**☎** *(62) 7522303* **❶** *(62) 7522316*	60	02.03–14.12	ⅇ⅃ ⌷CC⌷ ⚲ **P**
▲ **Zug** Allmendstr 8, Sportstadion 'Herti', 6300 Zug (Zug). ✉ zug@youthhostel.ch	**☎** *(41) 7115354* **❶** *(41) 7105121*	92	13.03–02.01	ⅇ⅃ ♿ ⌷CC⌷ ⚲ **P** ⅆ
▲ **Zürich** ⌷IBN⌷ **Mutschellenstr 114, 8038 Zürich (Zürich).** ✉ zuerich@youthhostel.ch	**☎** *(1) 4823544* **❶** *(1) 4801727*	315	⌷12⌷	††† ⅇ⅃ **R** 3SW ♿ ⌷CC⌷ **P** ⅆ

Travel is fatal to prejudice, bigotry, and narrow-mindedness.

Voyager porte un coup de grâce au préjugé, au fanatisme et à l'étroitesse d'esprit.

Reisen ist der Todfeind von Vorurteilen, Borniertheit und Engstirnigkeit.

Los viajes son funestos para los prejuicios, el fanatismo y la intolerancia.

Mark Twain (1869)

ADDITIONAL HOSTEL INFORMATION

At the time of printing, no information has been received from the country listed below for this 2000 Edition. We have, therefore, reprinted the information available from the 1999 edition for reference purposes only.

YUGOSLAVIA

Ferijalni savez Jugoslavije,
11000 Beograd, Obilićev venac 4/III,
Yugoslavia (Federal Republic of).

☎ (381) (11) 622-956, 622-584 📠 (381) (11) 322-07-62

Location/Address	Telephone No. Fax No.	Beds	Opening Dates	Facilities
▲ Belgrade (Beograd) - 'M' Beograd Bulevar JNA 56a, Beograd 11000	☎ (11) 3972560, 3972561 📠 (11) 461236	382	🔲12	♦♦♦ 🍴 Ⓡ 5SE ⊂CC⊃ 🖐 P ⊡
△ Belgrade (Beograd) - Lipovička Šuma Lipovica-Barajevo, Beograd.	☎ (11) 8302184 📠 (11) 8302134	40	🔲12	♦♦♦ 🍴 Ⓡ 20S P ⛛
▲ Belgrade (Beograd) - SRC "Pionirski Grad" "Pionirski Grad" Kneza Višeslava 27, 11000 Belgrade	☎ (11) 542166 📠 (11) 559538	40	🔲12	♦♦♦ 🍴 Ⓡ 5S P ⛛
▲ Bijela Hotel "Delfin", 85343 Bijela.	☎ (88) 72215, 72219 📠 (88) 71730	460	🔲12	♦♦♦ 🍴 Ⓡ P ⊡ ⛛
▲ Brezovica "Junior Ski Klub", Brezovica Štrpce	☎ (290) 70155, 70162 📠 (11) 620437	100	🔲12	♦♦♦ 🍴 Ⓡ 0.1S P ⛛
▲ Brus - YH Junior Kopaonik, 37220 Brus.	☎ (37) 833176 📠 (37) 833193	150	🔲12	♦♦♦ 🍴 Ⓡ 2SW P ⛛
△ Buljarice "Toplica", 81352 Buljarice.	☎ (86) 61479 📠 (27) 321035	200	01.07–30.08	🍴 0.5E P ⛛
▲ Kladovo Omladinski Kamp "Djerdap" 19320 Kladovo	☎ (19) 87577, 87983 📠 (19) 81394	350	01.07–30.08	♦♦♦ 🍴 Ⓡ 2W P ⊡ ⛛
△ Kragujevac YGH, 'Sloboda', Ul Lenjinova 1, Kragujevac.	☎ (34) 63035	60	20.07–30.08	🍴 P
△ Novi Sad YH "Ribnjak" Donji Put 79, Novi Sad	☎ (21) 434846, 25339 📠 (21) 52543	52	01.07–30.08	♦♦♦ Ⓡ 3S P
△ Sutomore Ljetovalište FS "Bori i Ramiz", Naselje "Gorelac", 81355 Sutomore.	☎ (85) 72352 📠 (38) 22842	100	01.07–30.08	♦♦♦ 🍴 0.2NW P ⛛
▲ Sutomore - "Lovćen" Hotel - "Lovćen", 85000 Sutomore.	☎ (85) 74444, 74111 📠 (85) 73468	175	🔲12	♦♦♦ 🍴 Ⓡ 0.3NW 🗄 ⊡ ⛛

Location/Address	Telephone No. Fax No.	Beds	Opening Dates	Facilities
△ *Sutomore* Odmaralište Crvenog Krsta, 85000 Sutomore.	☎ (85) 73124, 73608 🖷 (85) 73124	200	01.06–31.08	♦♦♦ ⑩ Ⓡ 0.3 W P 回 ☕
▲ Sutomore Hotel - "Zlatibor", Haselje Haj-Nehaj, 85000 Sutomore.	☎ (85) 73400, 73138 🖷 (85) 13025	250	🖾	♦♦♦ ⑩ Ⓡ 1.5 NW P 回 ☕

‘
The world is a book, and those who do not travel read only one page.

Le monde est un livre et ceux qui ne voyagent pas n'en lisent qu'une seule page.

Die Welt ist ein Buch, und die, die nicht reisen, lesen nur eine Seite.

El mundo es un libro y los que no viajan sólo leen una página.

St Augustine
’

AFFILIATED ORGANIZATIONS

The International Youth Hostel Federation also has Affiliated Organizations in a number of other countries. These are not listed in the main body of the Guide, as they do not fulfil the minimum requirements for full membership, and hostel standards may be outside the assured standards scheme. In some instances, approval has been given for the inclusion of details on their hostel network and/or other relevant information.

Those organizations which are in Europe are as follows:-

ORGANISATIONS AFFILIEES

La Fédération Internationale des Auberges de Jeunesse a également des organisations affiliées dans un certain nombre d'autres pays. Celles-ci ne figurent pas sur la liste des pays dans la partie principale du Guide, car elles ne répondent pas aux exigences minimales régissant l'adhésion de membre à part entière et la conformité de leurs établissements aux Normes Minimales n'est pas garantie. Dans certains cas, la publication de renseignements concernant leurs auberges de jeunesse et/ou d'autres informations utiles a été approuvée.

Les organisations en question en Europe sont les suivantes:-

ANGESCHLOSSENE ORGANISATIONEN

Der Internationale Jugendherbergsverband steht ebenso in Verbindung mit angeschlossenen Organisationen in verschiedenen anderen Ländern. Diese sind jedoch nicht im Hauptverzeichnis angegeben, weil sie zum einen keine vollberechtigten Mitgliedsverbände sind und zum anderen der Standard dieser Herbergen nicht den zugesicherten Normen entspricht. In einigen Fällen konnten jedoch Angaben über JH solcher Verbände sowie andere wesentliche Angaben ins Verzeichnis aufgenommen werden.

Es handelt sich dabei um folgende Organisationen in Europa:-

ORGANIZACIONES AFILIADAS

La Federación Internacional de Albergues Juveniles (IYHF) también posee Organizaciones Afiliadas en otros países. Estas no han sido incluidas en la parte principal de la Guía, ya que no cumplen con los requisitos mínimos necesarios para ser miembros de pleno derecho y es posible que el nivel de calidad de sus albergues no corresponda al garantizado por nuestras normas. En algunos casos, se ha aprobado la publicación de información sobre su red de albergues y/u otros datos pertinentes.

En Europa, estas organizaciones son las siguientes:

ESTONIA:

Eesti Noortehostelite Ühendus, Estonian Youth Hostels Association,
Tatari 39-310, 10134 Tallinn.
☎ (372) 6461455, 6461457
✆ (372) (6) 461595
✉ eyha@online.ee
✉ puhkemajad@online.ee (*Travel*)
http://eyha.jg.ee

LITHUANIA:

Lithuanian Youth Hostels,
PO Box 12, Filaretų St, 17, 2007 Vilnius.
☎ (370) (2) 262660, 254627
✆ (370) (2) 262660, 220149
✉ filaretai@post.omnitel.net

MACEDONIA:

Macedonian Youth Hostel Association,
PO Box 499, Prolet 25, 91000 Skopje.
☎ (389) (91) 239947, 235029
✆ (389) (91) 235029

MALTA:

NSTS,
220 St. Paul St, Valletta VLT 07.
☎ (356) 244983
✆ (356) 230330
✉ salesinb@nsts.org
www.nsts.org

ROMANIA:

Youth Hostel Association Romania,
3400 Cluj-Napoca Str
Clabucet Street Nr 2, Bloc P4, Ap 69
Jud. Cluj.
☎ (40) (64) 186616
✆ (40) (64) 186616
✉ ildi@civitas.org.soroscj.ro

RUSSIA:

Russian YHA,
St Petersburg International Hostel, PO Box 57, St Petersburg 193312.
☎ (7) (812) 2770569, 3298018
✆ (7) (812) 2775102, 3298019
✉ ryh@spb.ru
www.ryh.spb.ru

Blue Chip Travel,
Chistoprudny Blvd 12a, Suite 628, 101000 Moscow.
☎ (7) (095) 9169364/65
✆ (7) (095) 9244968

STAR Travel,
Leningradski pr.80/21, 125178 Moscow.
☎ (7) (095) 7979555
✆ (7) (095) 7979554
✉ star@glasnet.ru

SLOVAK REPUBLIC:

CKM SYTS,
Vysoka 32,
814 45 Bratislava.
☎ (421) (7) 52731018
✆ (421) (7) 52731025
✉ ckmsyts@ckm.sk
www.ckm.sk

TURKEY:

Gençtur Tourism & Travel Agency Ltd,
Prof K Ismail Gurkan Cad No.14 K.4,
Cagaloglu-Sultanahmet, Istanbul.
☎ (90) (212) 5205274/5
✆ (90) (212) 5190864
✉ info@genctur.com
www.genctur.com

Yücelt Interyouth Hostel,
Caferiye Sok No 6/1, Sultanahmet 34400, Istanbul.
☎ (90) (212) 5136150, 5136151
✆ (90) (212) 5127628
✉ info@yucelthostel.com
www.yulcelthostel.com

ESTONIA

Eesti Noortehostelite Ühendus - Estonian Youth Hostels Association,
Tatari 39-310, 10134 Tallinn.
☎ (372) 6461 457, 📠 (372) 6461 595
✉ eyha@online.ee www.eyha.jg.ee

Visas:

A visa may be required for entering Estonia, which in most cases will be valid for Latvia and Lithuania also. A visa is obtainable from an Estonian Embassy. For updated information see our Internet http://eyha.jg.ee or Ministry for Foreign Affairs of Estonia http://www.vm.ee. If you need any visa support we will be happy to provide you with any relevant information or documentation.

Bookings:

If possible, visit our WWW page for update information and/or bookings. Please allow at least a week for dealing with fax/mail bookings. Booking conditions may change - current information in Internet. When requesting information by mail-enclosing IPRC is essential. To make secure, fast and guaranteed bookings pleasebook through our website at http://eyha.jg.ee. If booking through Internet is not possible please contact hostel directly. Groups must book through EYHA office. Credit cards are accepted.

Travel Section:
Balti Puhkemajad,Tatari 39-310, 10134 Tallinn, Estonia
☎ (372) 6461 457 📠 (372) 6461 595
✉ puhkemajad@online.ee www.bpm.jg.ee

Budget travel services for incoming individuals or groups. Accommodation bookings for Estonia, Russia, Latvia, Lithuania and Finland.

Location/Address	Telephone No. Fax No.	Beds	Opening Dates	Facilities
▲ **Tallinn** - "Merevaik" Söpruse Str 182, Tallinn 13424.	☎ (2) 529604	60	📧	††† 🍽 Ⓡ 2 SW 🅿 ☕ 🔌

YOUTH HOSTEL ACCOMMODATION
OUTSIDE THE ASSURED STANDARDS SCHEME

Haapsalu - Paralepa Paralepa, Lääne County.	☎ (5) 106735 📠 (47) 55849	56	01.05–30.08	††† 🍽 Ⓡ 🛏 🅿 🔲 ☕
Harju County - Laulasmaa Laulasmaa, Keila Parish, Harju County.	☎ 6 715521 📠 6 715733	215	📧	††† 🍽 Ⓡ 🅿 ☕
Harju County - Nelijärve Nelijärve 4, Aegviidu, Harju County.	☎ (2) 767382, 6 304350 📠 6 304500	150	📧	††† 🍽 Ⓡ 🅿 🔲 ☕
Kuressaare - Ühishümnaasium Hariduse 13, Kuressaare, Saaremaa.	☎ (45) 54388 📠 (45) 57226	48	📧	††† 🍽 Ⓡ 🅿 ☕
Otepää - Pühajärve Pühajärve Parish, 67406 Valga County.	☎ (76) 55103 📠 (76) 61206	233	📧	††† 🍽 Ⓡ 3 SE 🅿 ☕
Põlva - Taevaskoja Taevaskoja puhkemaja, Taevaskoja sjk, Põlva County.	☎ (79) 92 067	40	📧	††† 🍽 Ⓡ 6 S 🅿 🔲

Location/Address	Telephone No. Fax No.	Beds	Opening Dates	Facilities
Rakvere - Essu Essu, Haljala Parish, Lääne-Viru County.	☎ (32) 92110 🖷 (32) 92110	72	🏠12	♂♀ 🍴 Ⓡ ☞ 🅿 🔲 ☕
Tallinn - 'Gabriel' Kallasmaa 3, Maardu-Tallinn.	☎ 6384161	80	🏠12	♂♀ 🍴 Ⓡ 15E ☞ 🅿 🔲 ☕
Tallinn - Mahtra Mahtra 44, Tallinn.	☎ (2) 218828 🖷 (2) 586765	26	🏠12	♂♀ 🍴 Ⓡ ☞ 🅿 🔲
Tallin - Vikerlase Vikerlase Str.15, 13616 Tallinn.	☎ 6327781 🖷 6327781	60	🏠12	♂♀ 🍴 Ⓡ 6E ☞ 🅿 🔲 ☕
Tartu - Tartu Soola 3, Tartu.	☎ (7) 432091 🖷 (7) 433041	80	🏠12	♂♀ 🍴 Ⓡ 0.1SE ⟨CC⟩ 🅿 🔲

LITHUANIA

Lithuanian Youth Hostels, PO Box 12, Filaretų St, 17, 2007 Vilnius.
☎ (370) (2) 262660, 254627 🖷 (370) (2) 262660, 220149
✉ filaretai@post.omnitel.net

Visas:

Visa free entrance for all main Western countries (Australia, USA, Canada, UK, Sweden, Finland, Norway, Croatia, Hungary, Japan, Poland, Slovenia, Portugal).

Need for visas: Russia & CIS countries, Romania, all African & Asian countries, Latin America (with exception of Ecuador, Venezuela, Columbia).

Location/Address	Telephone No. Fax No.	Beds	Opening Dates	Facilities
▲ **Vilnius** - Filaretai ⟨IBN⟩ Filaretų str 17, Vilnius. ✉ filaretai@post.omnitel.net	☎ (3702) 254627 🖷 (3702) 220149	54	🏠12	1.2E ⟨CC⟩ ☞ 🅿 🔲

YOUTH HOSTEL ACCOMMODATION
OUTSIDE THE ASSURED STANDARDS SCHEME

Klaipeda - Travellers Guesthouse Turgaus 3-4, Klaipeda ✉ oldtown@takas.lt	☎ (3706) 214935, (37085) 33104 🖷 (3706) 214935	10	🏠12	Ⓡ
Labanoras - Bičiulis YH Paprūdės km, Labanoro p.š.t., Švenčionių	☎ (37017) 51543	10	10.05–20.09	Ⓡ 🔲
Vilnius - Old Town YH Aušros Vartu, 20-15A, Vilnius ✉ livijus@pub.osf.lt	☎ (3702) 625357 🖷 (3702) 220305	8	🏠12	0.8S 🔲
Zarasai Šiaulių Gatvė 26, Zarasai		8	15.05–15.09	Ⓡ
Zervynos - Svirnelis YH Zervynos km, Varėnos raj ✉ svirnelis@hotmail.com	☎ (37060) 52720	12	15.05–15.09	Ⓡ

MALTA

NSTS, 220 St Paul Street, Valletta VLT 07.
☎ (356) 244983, 246628 🖷 (356) 230330
✉ salesinb@nsts.org www.nsts.org

Location/Address	Telephone No. Fax No.	Beds	Opening Dates	Facilities
▲ **Bugibba** Crystal Hotel, Triq Il-Halel.	☎ (356) 573022 🖷 (356) 571975	30	01.04–31.10	††† ⑩ Ⓡ 0.1 S ▢ P 回 🍺
▲ **Gozo** St. Joseph Home Hostel, Mgarr Rd, Ghajnsielem, Gozo	☎ (356) 556439 🖷 (356) 556439	50	🗓	††† Ⓡ 0.2 SW
▲ **Lija** University Residence, Robert Mifsud Bonnici St, Lija.	☎ 436168 🖷 434963	250	🗓	††† ⑩ Ⓡ 0.1 E ♿ 🖋 P 回 ☕
▲ **Rabat** YTC bungalow, Buskett, Rabat.	☎ 459445	30	🗓	††† Ⓡ 🖋 P 回
▲ **Sliema** - Gateway Hostel Hibernia House, Depiro St, Sliema.	☎ 333859 🖷 230330	100	🗓	††† ⑩ Ⓡ 0.3 W 🖋 P 回 🍺
▲ **St Julian's** Pinto Guest House, Sacred Heart Ave, St Julians.	☎ 313897 🖷 319852	30	01.04–31.10	††† ⑩ Ⓡ 0.5 SW P 回 🍺

RUSSIA

Russian Youth Hostels, St. Petersburg International Hostel,
3rd Sovetskaya Ulitsa, 28, St. Petersburg, 193036, Russia.
☎ (7) (812) 3298018 🖷 (7) (812) 3298019
✉ ryh@ryh.spb.ru www.ryh.ru

Visas:
Visa is required. IBN voucher not sufficient to receive visa. Only RYH visa support allows guest to obtain a tourist visa from the Russian consulate. Consulate requires passport, 3 passport photos and consular fees. Visa Support is valid for in-transit and reserved hostel dates + 2 weeks to allow travel flexibility. We can extend tourist visas for 3 days only. For more information see the Internet: www.spb.ru/ryh

Bookings & Visa Support:
Fax or e-mail each guest's full legal name; citizenship; birth date; passport number and expiration date; hostel dates; date of entry/exit - into/from Russia; IBN voucher number and fax number. Booking confirmation and/or visa support will be faxed to you next work day. If using IBN, visa support and fax fees are payable upon arrival.

International Bookings:
Russian Youth Hostels, (to Russia via Finnish post), PO Box 8, SF-53501, Lappeenranta, Finland.
☎ (7) (812) 3298018 🖷 (7) (812) 3298019
✉ ryh@ryh.spb.ru

Travel Services:

Sindbad Travel, 3rd Sovetskaya Ulitsa, 28, St. Petersburg, 193036, Russia.
☎ (7) (812) 3278384, **✆** (7) (812) 3298019
✉ sindbad@sinbad.spb.ru

IBN booking center for hostels in Russia and worldwide; full-service student and youth budget travel agency; discounted air, rail, bus and sea tickets.

Location/Address	Telephone No. Fax No.	Beds	Opening Dates	Facilities
▲ **St Petersburg** - International Hostel (IBN) 3rd Sovetskaya Str. 28 **✉** ryh@ryh.spb.ru	**☎** (812) 3298018 **✆** (812) 3298019	50	🗓	⍤ ⵢ R 0.5SW ☂ P ⊙

ADDITIONAL HOSTEL INFORMATION

At the time of printing, no information has been received from the country listed below for this 2000 Edition. We have, therefore, reprinted the information available from the 1999 edition for reference purposes only.

MACEDONIA

Macedonian Youth Hostel Association, PO Box 499, Prolet 25, 91000 Skopje.
☎ (389) (91) 239947, 235029 **✆** (389) (91) 235029

YOUTH HOSTEL ACCOMMODATION
OUTSIDE THE ASSURED STANDARDS SCHEME

Location/Address	Telephone No. Fax No.	Beds	Opening Dates	Facilities
Ferijalen Dom-Skopje Prolet 25, 91000 Skopje	**☎** (91) 114849 **✆** (91) 235029	46	🗓	⍤ ⵢ P

The Youth Hostel membership card - a synonym for borderless freedom and for one's first steps into the great wide world.

La carte d'adhérent Hostelling International - un synonyme de liberté sans frontière et de premiers pas à la découverte du monde.

Der Jugendherbergsausweis - ein Synonym für grenzenlose Freiheit, für die ersten Schritte hinaus in die große, weite Welt.

El carné de alberguista es sinónimo de libertad sin fronteras, de puerta de entrada al mundo entero.

Die Zeit Magazine

WHAT IS FIYTO ?

FIYTO

Ever since its inception in 1951, the aim of FIYTO has been to promote educational, cultural and social travel among young people.

In its fifty year history, FIYTO has become the largest and most influential organisation in the youth travel industry. Towards the mainstream travel and tourism community, international, governmental and non-governmental organisations, FIYTO advocates the special identity of young travellers and their right to affordable travel and travel-related services.

FIYTO is today the premier trade association for youth travel and tourism, a rapidly growing segment of the travel industry. Today we represent the unique interests of an estimated 20% of the tourism population. Our nearly 400 Members account for a turn-over of more than 8 billion US Dollars, serve some 16 million young travellers annually and sell over 9 million air- and surface tickets. FIYTO Members can be found in over 70 countries on all continents.

FIYTO is an open, world-wide, non-political and non-sectarian organisation. Non-profit and for-profit companies, public and private, retailers, wholesalers, buyers, sellers and suppliers are all represented in the FIYTO membership.

FIYTO is an affiliate member of the World Tourism Organisation (WTO) and a member of the Pacific Asia Travel Association (PATA). FIYTO enjoys operational relations with UNESCO, the United Nations Educational, Scientific and Cultural Organisation.

For qualified companies, actively engaged in incoming or outgoing youth travel, FIYTO provides the pre-eminent professional forum to trade, exchange information and advance the interests of the young traveller.

For more information on FIYTO please contact:

FIYTO, Bredgade 25H
1260 Copenhagen K, Denmark
E-mail: mailbox@fiyto.org
www.fiyto.org

International Student Travel Confederation (ISTC)

The International Student Travel Confederation (ISTC) is a not-for-profit association of student travel organisations. Together, they develop international opportunities for students and young travellers.

The associations are active in the areas of student travel services—international identity cards, student flights, surface travel, work exchange programmes and insurance. ISTC members are the world's student travel specialists, committed to making travel affordable and accessible to students.

Since 1967, the ISTC has maintained a relationship with UNESCO, the United Nations Educational, Scientific and Cultural Organisation, to promote student travel and international understanding.

International Student Identity Card Association

The ISIC Association oversees the worldwide distribution, promotion and development of the International Student Identity Card (ISIC) through 5,000 offices in more than 90 countries. The ISIC is the **only** internationally recognised proof of full-time student status providing worldwide, photo identity documentation for student travellers. The ISIC makes thousands of discounts available to students. The ISIC Help Line provides 24-hour emergency assistance. ISIConnect offers cardholders a worldwide communications package. UNESCO endorses the ISIC and recognises it as the unique document for student mobility.

International Student Surface Travel Association

Through ISSA, student travel organisations from around the globe co-operate to develop rail, bus, and ferry travel opportunities for students.

Student Air Travel Association

SATA members negotiate special airline fares for students with more than 125 major airlines.

International Association of Student Insurance Services

IASIS develops and promotes insurance programmes especially for travelling students.

International Association of Educational and Work Exchange Programmes

IAEWEP is active in providing short-term international work exchange opportunities. More than 50,000 students and youth participate in work and voluntary service programmes worldwide each year.

For more information about the ISTC and its member Associations, contact: ISTC, PO Box 15857, 1001 NJ Amsterdam, The Netherlands, or on-line at **http://www.istc.org.**

... help us to implement our assurance of standards at hostels by writing to us or by using the reply slip in this Guide to tell us what you think of our hostels.

Just tick the boxes to indicate how well the hostel did in the five areas, and remember to let us have your comments on how you found your stay.

Simply put your reply in an envelope and post to us at the address shown on the slip.

NOUS AIMERIONS CONNAITRE VOTRE OPINION...

... aidez-nous à mettre en place les normes garanties dans nos auberges en nous faisant part de ce que vous pensez d'elles, soit en nous écrivant, soit en remplissant la fiche prévue à cet effet que vous trouverez dans ce guide.

Il vous suffira de cocher les cases pour évaluer la performance de l'auberge dans les cinq domaines indiqués, sans oublier d'ajouter vos observations sur votre séjour.

Envoyez-nous votre fiche sous enveloppe, à l'adresse indiquée dessus.

WIR MÖCHTEN IHRE MEINUNG HÖREN...

... helfen Sie uns, unsere zugesicherten Standards zu gewährleisten, indem Sie uns wissen lassen, was Sie von unseren Herbergen halten. Bitte schreiben Sie uns oder benutzen Sie dazu die am Ende dieses Führers beigefügte Antwortkarte.

Kreuzen Sie bitte Ihre Beurteilung für die jeweilige Kategorie in dem entsprechenden Kästchen an, und vergessen Sie nicht, uns Ihren Kommentar über Ihren Aufenthalt mitzuteilen.

Ihre Antwort ganz einfach in einen Umschlag stecken und an die auf der Antwortkarte angegebene Adresse schicken.

QUEREMOS SABER LO QUE USTED OPINA...

... ayúdenos a implementar nuestras normas garantizadas en los albergues. Escríbanos, o haga uso de las hojas provistas en la Guía, para comunicarnos lo que piensa de nuestros albergues.

Sólo tiene que marcar las casillas según la opinión que le merezca el albergue en lo que respecta a los cinco apartados de consulta. No olvide añadir comentarios sobre su estancia en el recuadro de las observaciones.

Envíe su comunicación en un sobre dirigido a la dirección indicada.

we want to hear from YOU....

TELL US WHAT YOU THINK!

DITES-NOUS CE QUE VOUS EN PENSEZ!
SAGEN SIE UNS IHRE MEINUNG!
¡DIGANOS LO QUE OPINA!

Hostel Name-Address/
Nom de l'Auberge-Adresse/
Name der Jugendherberge
Anschrift/
Nombre y Dirección del Albergue

City/Ville/Stadt/Ciudad

Country/Pays/Land/País

Date(s) stayed/*Dates du séjour/*
Daten des Aufenthaltes/
Fechas de la Estancia

Please return to:
INTERNATIONAL YOUTH HOSTEL FEDERATION,
1st Floor, Fountain House, Parkway, Welwyn Garden City,
Hertfordshire AL8 6JH. ENGLAND

Welcome/*Accueil/*
Aufnahme/*Recibimiento*

Comfort/*Confort/*
Komfort/*Comodidad*

Cleanliness/*Propreté/*
Sauberkeit/*Limpieza*

Security/*Sécurité/*
Sicherheit/*Seguridad*

Privacy/*Intimité,*
Privatsphäre/*Intimidad*

COMMENTS/*COMMENTAIRES/***BEMERKUNGEN/***OBSERVACIONES*

Name/*Nom/*
Name/*Nombre*

Address/*Adresse/*
Anschrift/*Dirección*

... help us to implement our assurance of standards at hostels by writing to us or by using the reply slip in this Guide to tell us what you think of our hostels.

Just tick the boxes to indicate how well the hostel did in the five areas, and remember to let us have your comments on how you found your stay.

Simply put your reply in an envelope and post to us at the address shown on the slip.

NOUS AIMERIONS CONNAITRE VOTRE OPINION...

... aidez-nous à mettre en place les normes garanties dans nos auberges en nous faisant part de ce que vous pensez d'elles, soit en nous écrivant, soit en remplissant la fiche prévue à cet effet que vous trouverez dans ce guide.

Il vous suffira de cocher les cases pour évaluer la performance de l'auberge dans les cinq domaines indiqués, sans oublier d'ajouter vos observations sur votre séjour.

Envoyez-nous votre fiche sous enveloppe, à l'adresse indiquée dessus.

WIR MÖCHTEN IHRE MEINUNG HÖREN...

... helfen Sie uns, unsere zugesicherten Standards zu gewährleisten, indem Sie uns wissen lassen, was Sie von unseren Herbergen halten. Bitte schreiben Sie uns oder benutzen Sie dazu die am Ende dieses Führers beigefügte Antwortkarte.

Kreuzen Sie bitte Ihre Beurteilung für die jeweilige Kategorie in dem entsprechenden Kästchen an, und vergessen Sie nicht, uns Ihren Kommentar über Ihren Aufenthalt mitzuteilen.

Ihre Antwort ganz einfach in einen Umschlag stecken und an die auf der Antwortkarte angegebene Adresse schicken.

QUEREMOS SABER LO QUE USTED OPINA...

... ayúdenos a implementar nuestras normas garantizadas en los albergues. Escríbanos, o haga uso de las hojas provistas en la Guía, para comunicarnos lo que piensa de nuestros albergues.

Sólo tiene que marcar las casillas según la opinión que le merezca el albergue en lo que respecta a los cinco apartados de consulta. No olvide añadir comentarios sobre su estancia en el recuadro de las observaciones.

Envíe su comunicación en un sobre dirigido a la dirección indicada.

We want to hear from YOU....

TELL US WHAT YOU THINK!

DITES-NOUS CE QUE VOUS EN PENSEZ!
SAGEN SIE UNS IHRE MEINUNG!
¡DIGANOS LO QUE OPINA!

Hostel Name-Address/
Nom de l'Auberge-Adresse/
Name der Jugendherberge
Anschrift/
Nombre y Dirección del Albergue

City/Ville/Stadt/Ciudad

Country/*Pays/***Land/***País*

Date(s) stayed/*Dates du séjour/*
Daten des Aufenthaltes/
Fechas de la Estancia

Please return to:
INTERNATIONAL YOUTH HOSTEL FEDERATION,
1st Floor, Fountain House, Parkway, Welwyn Garden City,
Hertfordshire AL8 6JH. ENGLAND

Welcome/*Accueil/*
Aufnahme/*Recibimiento*

Comfort/*Confort/*
Komfort/*Comodidad*

Cleanliness/*Propreté/*
Sauberkeit/*Limpieza*

Security/*Sécurité/*
Sicherheit/*Seguridad*

Privacy/*Intimité,*
Privatsphäre/*Intimidad*

COMMENTS/*COMMENTAIRES/*BEMERKUNGEN/*OBSERVACIONES*

Name/*Nom/*
Name/*Nombre*

Address/*Adresse/*
Anschrift/*Dirección*

DISCOUNTS & CONCESSIONS

Hostelling International Membership enables you to claim discounts and concessions on everything from travel and museums, to eating and entertainment! The top discounts are included here – for the full story check out the Global Discounts Database at **www.iyhf.org.** Simply present your Hostelling International Membership Card to claim a discount – and begin recovering the cost of Membership!

Discounts are sorted by **Country**. Within each country, discounts are listed alphabetically by **City** – national discounts are listed first. Within each city, discounts are listed by **Discount Category** – Entertainment ✆, General ✪, Museums and Culture ✆, Retail ✆, or Travel ✈. For each discount, we list: discount provider's name, address and telephone number, along with a brief description of the discount available.

Please note: The information about discounts has been supplied by the Youth Hostel Associations of each country represented. Every effort has been made to ensure that this information is correct, and Hostelling International can accept no responsibility for any inaccuracies or for changes subsequent to publication.

REMISES ET RÉDUCTIONS

Votre adhésion à Hostelling International vous permet de profiter de nombreuses remises et réductions sur presque tout, des transports aux entrées de musées en passant par la restauration et les spectacles! Seuls les avantages les plus importants sont cités ci-après – pour la liste complète, faites donc un tour sur notre site Internet, **www.iyhf.org**, où vous trouverez notre base de données mondiale des remises. Présentez votre carte d'adhérent Hostelling International pour bénéficier d'une réduction et commencez à amortir le coût de votre adhésion!

Les différents avantages que l'on vous propose sont d'abord répertoriés par **Pays** puis en ordre alphabétique par **Ville** – les offres qui sont valables à l'échelle nationale sont en tête de liste. Elles sont ensuite classées par **Catégorie** – Voyages ✈ *(Travel)*, Magasins et Restaurants ✆ *(Retail)*, Spectacles et Activités ✆ *(Entertainment)*, Musées et Culture ✆ *(Museums and Culture)* ou Général ✪. Pour chaque remise, nous fournissons le nom de l'entité qui la propose, son adresse et numéro de téléphone, ainsi qu'un bref descriptif de l'offre en question.

Remarque: Les renseignements sur ces remises nous sont communiqués par l'Association d'Auberges de Jeunesse de chaque pays représenté. Tout a été mis en oeuvre pour s'assurer que ces données sont correctes mais Hostelling International ne peut accepter aucune responsabilité pour toute inexactitude ou tout changement intervenant ultérieurement à la publication du présent ouvrage.

RABATTE & ERMÄßIGUNGEN

Die Mitgliedschaft bei Hostelling International sichert Ihnen Anspruch auf Rabatte und Ermäßigungen bei Reisen und Museen, in der Gastronomie und Unterhaltung! Die Top-Preisnachlässe sind hier enthalten – für einen kompletten Überblick schauen Sie in die Datenbank für internationale Rabatte *(Global Discounts Database)* unter **www.iyhf.org**. Legen Sie einfach Ihre Hostelling International Mitgliedskarte vor, um einen Nachlaß in Anspruch zu nehmen – und fangen Sie an, den Mitgliedsbeitrag wieder einzuholen!

Die Rabatte sind nach **Ländern** *(Country)* und innerhalb jedes Landes nach **Städten** *(City)* in alphabetischer Reihenfolge geordnet. Die nationalen Preisnachlässe *(National)* sind zuerst aufgeführt. Sie sind für jede Stadt nach **Rabattkategorien** *(Discount Category)* – Unterhaltung ♭ *(Entertainment)*, Allgemeines ✪ *(General)*, Museen und Kultur ♨ *(Museum and Culture)*, Einzelhandel 🏛 *(Retail)* sowie Reisen ✈ *(Travel)* – systematisiert. Für jeden Nachlaß ist, neben dem Namen des Anbieters, dessen Adresse und Telefonnummer, eine kurze Beschreibung des verfügbaren Rabattes *(Discount Discription)* aufgeführt.

Bitte beachten Sie: Die Informationen über die Rabatte wurden von den Jugendherbergsverbänden jedes aufgeführten Landes zur Verfügung gestellt. Wir haben alles unternommen, um sicherzugehen, daß diese Informationen korrekt sind. Hostelling International kann keine Verantwortung für jegliche Ungenauigkeiten oder Änderungen im Anschluß an die Veröffentlichung übernehmen.

OFERTAS Y DESCUENTOS

Su afiliación a Hostelling International le permite disfrutar de ofertas y descuentos de todo tipo: en los transportes y entradas de museo, restaurantes y espectáculos – ¡la lista es interminable! A continuación se relacionan los descuentos más importantes solamente. Si desea verlos todos, consulte nuestra Base de Datos Mundial de Descuentos *(Global Discounts Database)* en Internet en **www.iyhf.org**. Para conseguir un descuento, no tiene más que presentar su tarjeta de socio de Hostelling International – y así ir amortizando el coste de la misma.

Los descuentos están clasificados en primer lugar por **país** y en segundo lugar por **ciudad o población**, ambos en orden alfabético. Los que son válidos a nivel nacional aparecen primero y todos están ordenados por **categoría**, a saber: Viajes ✈ *(Travel)*, Tiendas y Restaurantes 🏛 *(Retail)*, Actividades Recreativas ♭ *(Entertainment)*, Museos y Cultura ♨ *(Museums and Culture)*, y General ✪. Para cada uno de ellos, se indica el nombre de la organización o compañía que concede el descuento, su dirección y número de teléfono, y una breve descripción del mismo.

Importante: La información sobre estos descuentos nos ha sido suministrada por la Asociación de Albergues Juveniles de cada país representado. Hemos hecho todo lo posible por asegurarnos de que los datos son correctos y Hostelling International no se responsabiliza de ninguna inexactitud ni de ningún cambio que se produzca en fecha posterior a la publicación de la presente guía.

Explanation of Symbols

✪ General	✪ Général	✪ Allgemeines	✪ General
♭ Entertainment	♭ Spectacles et Activités	♭ Unterhaltung	♭ Actividades Recreativas
🏛 Retail		🏛 Einzelhandel	🏛 Tiendas y Restaurantes
♨ Museums and Culture	🏛 Magasins et Restaurants	♨ Museen und Kultur	
✈ Travel	♨ Musées et Culture	✈ Reisen	♨ Museos y Cultura
	✈ Voyages		✈ Viajes

ARGENTINA

BARILOCHE

Cumbres Patagonia S.R.L
Villegas 222

10% off land excursions. 10% off rental cars. 5% off adventure trips. 5% off local activities

MENDOZA

Betancourt Rafting
Ruta Pananericana y Río Cuevas. Barrio Trapiche. Godoy Cruz

☎ 0361 4 390229   10% off rafting

TILCARA

Tilcara Mountain Bikes
Belgrano 700

25% off mountain bike rental

AUSTRALIA

NATIONAL

IMAX

World's biggest Screen in Sydney, Melbourne, Brisbane and Adelaide. Free popcorn and soft drink (valued at over $6). Present your YHA member card at the IMAX Theatre ticket counter to collect your free small popcorn and small Pepsi voucher with every valid IMAX theatre ticket purchased. Not valid with any other offer. One voucher per YHA Member card presented.

Geo

☎ 02 9900 5375 or
03 9555 7377
✉ hallmark@halledit.com.au

25% off the normal subscription rate for Geo magazine (normal rate $29 per year; $55 per 2 years).

Travel Clinics Australia

☎ 1300 369 359

10% off vaccines, medications and travel health products, a free Travellers Pocket Guide and International Vaccination Certificate (value $6.95) with first consultation. Clinics in every state.

YHA Travel Insurance

5-10% nationwide discount on all Australian and overseas travel insurance policies at all YHA Membership and Travel Centres.

Lonely Planet Guides

🏠	10-15% off when purchased at YHA Membership and Travel Centres

Mountain Designs

🏠 ☎ 07 3252 8894	10% off all outdoor and travel equipment (sale and discounted items excluded). Call 07 3252 8894 for your nearest store.

Paddy Pallin

🏠 ☎ 1800 805 398	10% discount for cash, 7% for credit card purchases over $50 for all outdoor and travel equipment (does not apply to sale items). Stores all over Australia. Call 1800 805 398 for a free catalogue or mail order.

Snowgum

🏠	10% off normal price of all outdoor and travel equipment. Over 20 locations throughout Australia.

Avis Australia

✈ ☎ 136 333	A minimum of 30% off standard rates and a further 5% off promotional rates (excludes commercial vehicles). Conditions apply. Quote discount number P081600 when making a reservation.

Budget Rent-A-Car

✈ ☎ 1300 362 848 (reservations)	Average discount of 30%. Rent a small manual car for seven days for $55 per day. Call reservations and quote BCD number E013609

Countrylink Rail

✈	10% off NSW Discovery Pass

Hertz Australia

✈ ☎ 13 30 39	Up to 35% off standard car hire rates. To access these rates please call 13 30 39 and quote Customer Discount Programme (CDP) number 317961. Quote your Qantas Frequent Flyer number when booking to receive 5 Qantas Frequent Flyer Points for every dollar spent.

McCafferty's Coaches

✈	10% discount on all McCafferty's passes and point to point tickets. 15% discount on passes and point to point tickets when purchased outside Australia.

Network Rentals

✈ ☎ 1800 077 977	Up to 35% off standard vehicle hire rates through any of 100 offices throughout Australia. Call nation-wide freecall 1800 077 977 to arrange further details.

Oz Experience

✈	5% discount on selected Oz and Kiwi Experience passes in Australia and New Zealand.

ADELAIDE

SA Cricket Association

✎ ☎ 08 8300 3853	25% off all Adelaide Oval tours

ALICE SPRINGS

Ballooning Downunder
✈ ☎ 08 8952 8855 — 20% off 30 minute or 60 minute flight

Sahara Tours
✈ ☎ 08 8952 8855 — 5% off when booked direct

BLUE MOUNTAINS - KATOOMBA

Abercrombie Caves
☎ 02 6368-8603 — 50% off camping permits

BRISBANE

Double Jaunt Tandems
☎ 07 3255 0047 — 20% of hourly rate.

CAIRNS

Great Diving Adventures
☎ 07 4051 1368 — 10% off dive courses, certified and resort diving

CANBERRA

Hire-a-Guide
☎ 02 6288 7894 — 15% off plus souvenir book

DARWIN, KAKADU & LITCHFIELD

Kakadu Downunder
✈ ☎ 08 8981 2560 — 10% off 3 day Kakadu tours

GOLD COAST

Bungee Downunder
☎ 07 5536 7644 — $15 off jump; $5 off T-shirt

Cable Ski World
☎ 07 5537 6300 — 20% off all activities

HOBART

Maritime Museum of Tasmania
☎ 03 6224 2111 — $1 off entry

MELBOURNE

Rialto Tower's Observation Deck
☎ 03 9629 8222 — 15% off adult entry

Victorian Winery Tours

📞 03 9670 9611 — 20% off standard rate day tours

Mexican Hacienda Restaurant

📞 03 9489 7524 — 30% discount on meal (Mon to Thurs)

Victorian Harley Rides

📞 03 9670 9611 — up to 15% off tours

PERTH

The Stables Yanchep

📞 08 9561 1606 — 20% off selected horse rides

Net Chat

📞 08 9228 2011 — 10% off Internet access

The Moon Cafe

📞 08 9328 7474 — 50% off all pastas

PORT CAMPBELL

Shipwreck Coast Scenic Flights

📞 019 634 520 — 20% off flight

PORT MACQUARIE

Macquarie Mountain Tours

📞 02 6585 9242 — 20% off for 2 or more

QUEENSLAND

Queensland Rail

📞 07 3236 1680 — 10% off adult economy seat, economy and first class berths

SUNSHINE COAST

Under Water World

📞 07 5444 8088 — 20% off admission

SYDNEY

AMP Tower

📞 02 9231 1000 — 20% Discount on adult admission plus free VIP Discount Shopping Card

Sega World Sydney

📞 02 9273 9273 — 20% off, unlimited rides pass, adults and children

Berta Opal Company

📞 02 9552 6388 — 40% off purchases

Gray Line

✈ ☎ 02 9261 1111 — 20% off Sydney day tours

Red Terra Tours

✈ ☎ 02 9261 1111 — 10% for direct booking Olympic park site tour

TASMANIA

Tasmanian Redline Coaches

✈ ☎ 1300 360 000 — 20% off all main road route services

WHITSUNDAYS

Forget the World Cruises

✈ ☎ 07 4946 6312 — 10% off illusions day trip

AUSTRIA

EBENSEE

Wassersportzentrum Peter Gigl
Strandbadstraße 12

☼ ☎ 06133 63 81 — 10% discount on all diving courses
   ☎ 06133 63 86

Bootsverleih Stadlmann
Strandbadstraße 46a

✈ ☎ 06133 88 04 — 25% discount on half-daily and daily tickets

HALLEIN DÜRRNBERG

Salinen Tourismus GmbH
Ramsamerstraße 3

🏰 ☎ 06245 85 285 — Admission for ATS 95 instead of 195
   ☎ 06245 85 285-18

INNSBRUCK

Tiroler Volkskunstmuseum
Universitätsstraße 2

🏰 ☎ 0512 58 43 02 — Admission at student's discount for ATS 35 instead of 60
   ☎ 0512 58 43 70

SALZBURG

Mozart's Geburtshaus
Getreidegasse 9

🏰 ☎ 0662 84 43 13 — Membership card holder gets group discount
   ☎ 0662 84 06 93

Salzburg VELOactive
Willibald Hauthaler Straße 10

✈ 🕿 0662 43 55 95-0   10% discount on bike hire
   📠 0662 43 55 95-22

WIEN

Vienna's English Theatre
Josefsgasse 12

✒ 🕿 01 402 12 60   20% discount on all tickets
   📠 01 408 80 83

Beethoven Gedenkstätte
Probusgasse 6

🏛 🕿 01 37 54 08   Admission ATS 10 instead of 25

Schubert Geburtshaus
Nußdorferstraße 54

🏛   ATS 10 instead of 25

DDSG Blue Danube Schiffahrt GmbH
Friedrichstraße 7

✈ 🕿 01 588 80-0   10% discount on round trips within Vienna and Wachau
   📠 01 588 80-440

BELGIUM

NATIONAL

Grote Routepaden
Nationwide

🏛   15% discount on maps and guidebooks for long distance walking and cycling

Eurolines
Nationwide

✈   10% discount

CANADA

NATIONAL

Cathay Pacific Airways
Nationwide

✈ $150 off the Asia Pacific Pass

Greyhound Lines of Canada

✈ ☎ 403 265-9111 (Calgary)   10% off all regular fares
403 413-8747 (Edmonton)

Rent-a-Wreck

✈ ☎ 1 800 327 0116 $25 off weekly rental

BANFF

Luxton Museum of the Plains Indian
1 Birch Avenue

🏛 ☎ 403 762-2388   40% discount on admission

Hydra River Guides

✈ ☎ 403 762-4554   20% discount on white-water rafting day trips- includes transportation and gear

CALGARY

Calgary Tower
101-9 Avenue SW

✍ ☎ 403 266-7171   Group rate admission for individuals

Calgary Canoe Club
6449 Crowchild Trail SW

🏪 ☎ 403 246-5757   15% discount on reservoir canoe rentals

CELISTA

Impulse Ventures
Box 82

✈ ☎ 250 955-6177   10% off all fishing, sightseeing cruises and murder mystery dinner cruises on Shuswap Lake

EDMONTON

Edmonton Space & Science Centre
11211-142 Street

🏛 ☎ 403 452-9100   50% discount on an individual. Day pass admission

Blackbyrd Myoozik
10442 Whyte (82nd) Ave.

🏪 ☎ 403 439-1273   15% off all used CD's, Vinyl and Cassettes. 10% off all new CD's, Vinyl & Cassettes

Bytes Internet Café
1668 Bourbon Street, West Edmonton

🏪 ☎ 403 444-7873   20% off all regular internet rates, food and beverages (excluding liquor)

KAMLOOPS

Kamloops Wildlife Park
Box 698

🛏 ☎ 250 573-3242 — 25% off adult and youth admission

KANANASKIS

Mountain Gallery

🏬 ☎ 403 591-7610 — 15% off regular priced goods

Peregrine Sports & Rentals

🏬 ☎ 403 591-7453 — 15% off all rentals

MONTRÉAL

Aromate d'Asie
Mackay Street

🏬 — Special Menu for HI members

Croixe Bleue
4008 rue St. Denis

🏬 ☎ 514 844-0287 — 10% discount on travel insurance (contact: Tourisme Jeunesse)

NANAIMO

Bungy Zone
Box 399 Station "A"

✎ ☎ 250 753-5867 — 20% off jump

La Creperie Sunporch Restaurant
139 Bastion Street

🏬 ☎ 250 753-7531 — 20% off all food purchases

NIAGARA FALLS

Kanata Native Indian Show

✎ — 50% off regular adult fare

NORDEGG

Bighorn Canyon Llama Tracks

✈ ☎ 403 729-3814 — 20% off day trips

QUÉBEC

Croisières AML
124 rue Saint-Pierre

🏬 ☎ 418 692-1159 — 10% on cruises from Québec City

Excursions touristiques les tours de Vieux-Québec

✈ ☎ 418 664-0460 — 10% discount on all tours

TORONTO

Historic Fort York

25% off

Nike Shop & Athelet's World
Eaton Centre

15% off regular price merchandise

VANCOUVER

REO Rafting Adventure Resort
#355 - 535 Thurlow Street

☎ 604 684-4438   10% - 20% discount off whitewater rafting and other adventure packages

Budget Rent-A-Car
855 Kingsway

☎ 604 668-7000   15% off regular rates (time and kilometre only)

VICTORIA

Suze Lounge and Restaurant
515 Yates Street

☎ 250 383-2829   15% off food

Midnight Sun Tours
PO Box 355

☎ 250 652-5955   10% off all tours.

Seacoast Expeditions
45 Songhees Rd

☎ 250 383-2254   30% discount on regular 3 hour adult fare

CHILE

NATIONAL

Reifschneider
Nationwide

15% discount on developing film, 10% discount off fuji films, 5% discount off general items

SANTIAGO

Escuela de Idiomas Violeta Parra
Ernesto Pinto Lagaguirre 362-A

☎ 7358240   20% discount off classes in Spanish, German, English and French
🌐 2298246
✉ vioparra@chilesat.net

Cafe Virtual
Alameda 145

| 🏧 ☎ 6386846 | 10% discount on spending. 25% discount on Internet |

COSTA RICA

SAN JOSÉ

Academia Latinoamericana de Español
Avenida 8, calles 31 y 33, Apdo.1280-2050 San Pedro de Montes de Oca

✪ ☎ 506 224 99 17	15% discount on all Spanish Courses
📠 506 225 81 25	
✉ recajhi@spl.racsa.co.cr	

CZECH REPUBLIC

PRAGUE

Národni museum / National museum + branch offices

| 🏛 | 35% discount for members under 26 years - especially groups booked via KMC. |

DENMARK

AALBORG

Nordjyllands Kunstmuseum
Kong christians alle 50, 9000 Aalborg

| 🏛 ☎ +45 9813 8088 | 50% discount |

Eurolines
J.F. Kennedys plads 1, 9000 Aalborg

| ✈ ☎ +45 9934 4488 | 10% discount on all tickets |

BRORUP

Museet på Sonderskov
Sonderskovgårdsvej 2, 6650 Brorup

| 🏛 ☎ +45 7538 3866 | Two for the price of one |

CHRISTIANSFELD

Genforenings og grænsemuseet
Koldingvej 52, 6070 Christiansfeld

| 🏛 ☎ +45 7557 3003 | 25% discount |

ESBJERG

Esbjerg Museum
Torvegade 45, 6700 Esbjerg

🏰   ☎ +45 7512 7811   20% discount

FREDERIKSVÆRK

Frederiksværk Bymuseum
Torvet 18-20, 3300 Frederiksværk

🏰   ☎ +45 4772 0605   50% discount

KOBENHAVN K

Guinness World of records museum
Ostergade 16, 1100 Kobenhavn K

🏰   ☎ +45 3332 3183   DKK 5.00 discount

ODENSE

Jernbanemuseet
Dannebrogsgade 24, 5000 Odense

🏰   ☎ +45 6612 3265   50% discount

ENGLAND & WALES

CHESTER

Martin Mere Wildfowl Trust

🖎   20% discount

Mouldsworth Motor Museum

🏰   20% discount

CITY OF LONDON

St Pauls Cathedral

🏰   £1 off Adult admission on presentation of full valid
membership card

HAMPSTEAD HEATH

London Aquarium

🖎   £2.00 off admission fee on production of valid membership
card

Madame Tussaud's

🖎   £1.50 off admission and no queuing if you buy a ticket at the
hostel

LINCOLN

Sherwood Forest	
▉	£1 discount

MANCHESTER

Manchester United Tour	
▨	10% discount

ROTHERHITHE (DOCKLANDS)

Catamaran Cruises	
▨	20% discount on return trip from Charing Cross to Greenwich Pier
Thames Barrier	
▨	70p discount for Adults; 40p for OAP's and children
Imperial War Museum	
▉	£1 discount for Adults & OAP's; 50p for children

ESTONIA

TALLINN

Insurance company "Inges"
  "Balti Puhkemajad" or "Inges KIndlustus", Raua 35

✪	☎ 372 6410436	5% off Travel Insurance
	✆ 372 6410438	

FINLAND

NATIONAL

Cruises to the Coast
  Nationwide

✈	10-20% discount on normal rates on most cruises off the coast and on most lake routes and cruises. Season in summertime. Tickets usually on board

Europcar Interrent
  Nationwide

✈	☎ 9 751 553 00	10% discount on car hire and mileage rates

FRANCE

NATIONAL

Eurolines
Nationwide

✈ 3% discount

BOULOGNE SUR MER

Horse riding center Honvault

🏇 20% discount

Ascalt canoe kayak

✈ 10% discount

BOURGES

Bourge's Museums

🏰 All museums in Bourges - Free entrance

MONTPELLIER

Le Comptoir du disque (CD, Music)

🏬 20% discount

PARIS

Tour Montparnasse

✈ 5% discount

Vedettes de Pont Neuf (Cruises on La Seine)

✈ 5% discount

VERDUN

World Peace Center (museum)

🏰 30% discount

IRELAND, REP OF

NATIONAL

Avis Car Rental

✈ ☎ 01 605 7500   10% discount

Eurodollar

✈ ☎ 01 844 4927   10% discount

Irish Cycle Hire
Drogheda

✈ ☎ 0404 41067 | 10% discount

Irish Ferries

✈ ☎ 01 855 2222 | 20% discount on Adult Foot passengers on the Irish Sea and Direct from France

Lough Swilly
Letterkenny or Derry

✈ ☎ 074 29400 or 0807504 262017 | 50% discount

Malone Car Rental

✈ ☎ 01 670 7888 | 10% discount

Windsor Group

✈ ☎ 1800 51 58 00 | 10% discount

CO KERRY

Kenmare Heritage Centre
Kenmare

🏰 ☎ 064 41233 | 10% discount

CO ROSCOMMON

Strokestown Famine Museum
Strokestown

🏰 ☎ 078 33013 | 20% Discount

CORK

Cork City Gaol
Sundays Well

🏰 ☎ 021 305 022 | 10% discount

DUBLIN 2

Dublin Castle
Dame Street

🏰 ☎ 01 677 7510 | Student Discount

ISRAEL

NATIONAL

Tarmil Shop
Nationwide

✪ | Society for the Protection of Nature - Countrywide. 7% discount on equipment

EILAT

Coral Sea Divers (diving services)

🏸 **☏** 07 6370337 — 10% discount. For guests at Eilat Youth Hostel

Sea Jeeps

🏸 **☏** 07 6375528 — 10% discount. For guests at Eilat Youth Hostel

MITZPCH RIMON

Hai Rimon

🏰 **☏** 07 6588493 — Two tickets for the price of one - Hai Rimon. Purchase tickets at the Youth Hostel

PURIYAH

Abu Kayak

🏸 **☏** 06 6750050 — 10% discount. Purchase tickets at Youth Hostel

TEL AVIV CENTRAL

Eretz Yisrael Museum

🏰 **☏** 03 6415244 — 20% discount

ITALY

NATIONAL

Sixt Agency (Rent a Car)
Nationwide

✈ **☏** 1670/18668 (toll-free) — Sixt Agency offices are in every Italian city and airport and offer 30% discount on their fees. For further information please call the toll free number stated

ASSISI

Assisi Youth Hostel

🏰 50% discount for visiting: Roman Forum, Picture Gallery, Rocca Maggiore, Perkins Museum. For further information, please ask at the Youth Hostel in Assisi.

ROME

Teatro Belli

🏸 **☏** 06 5894875 / 5897094 — 50% ticket discount for Members + Chaperon

JAPAN

NATIONAL

Japan Rent-a-Car

🏨	☎ 03-3356-3900 (Tokyo)	20% discount off the basic rate (except for "joyful JSS,JS" class car)

Nara Bank (headquarters & all 23 branches)

🏨	☎ 0120-39-3800 (Nara headquarters - free dial)	50% discount off travellers check issue commission

Sanyo-do

🏨	☎ 03-3580-3410 (head office)	Suitcase 20% off, Backpacks 15% off, Small travel goods 5% off

Sogo department stores

🏨	☎ 03-3284-6711 (Tokyo - Yurakuo-cho)	5% discount for over ¥1,000 purchase. "Shopping ticket" should be purchased in advance at GAISHO-salon. (As for Osaka & Kobe Sogo, they are available at YH information center)

Nissan Rent-a-Car

✈	☎ 03-5424-4123 (Tokyo)	20% discount off the basic rate (except for at Station Rent-a-Car & Service cars)

ASAKUSA

Asakusa Hana-yashiki amusement park

🖌	☎ 03-3842-8780	30% discount off amusement ticket (¥1,000)

BIEI-CHO

Bibagyu guide no Yamagoya

✪	☎ 0166-95-2277	15% discount off outdoor tours (except for canoe & rafting)

MORIOKA

Wanko soba (noodle)

🏨	☎ 019-622-2252	10% discount off Wanko soba (noodle) available at each branch

NIHONMATSU

Tohoku Safari park

🏨	☎ 0243-24-2336	10% discount off the entrance fee

KOREA

NATIONAL

Cho Heung Bank
Int'l Dept, of Cho Heung Bank, 14, Namdaemunro-1ga, Jung-ku, Seoul

✆ +82 2 733-2000 (Seoul) | Special exchange rate: 10won (Korean currency) off per 1 US dollar

SEOUL

Chongdong Theater
8-11, Chong-dong, Jung-ku, Seoul

✆ +82 2 773-8960 | 20% off on admission

LUXEMBOURG

CLERVAUX

Museum of Battle of the Ardennes
Montée du Château, L9712 Clervaux

✆ +352 92 96 56
✆ +352 92 56 58 | LUF 20.-per person. contact M. Kieffer F.

LUXEMBOURG

CD-Rom Land SA
14A, rue Notre-Dame, L-2240 Luxembourg

✆ +352 46 01 46 | LUF 50.-per hour Internet surf + 5% software. Contact M. F. Muller

Walkman Sightseeing-Tour
2, rue du Fort Olisy, L-2261 Luxembourg

✆ +352 22 68 89
✆ +352 22 30 60 | LUF 50.-per person.

MACEDONIA

SKOPJE

Olimpiski Bazen
bul. Koco Racin bb, Skopje

✆ +389-91-114-143 | Discount 30%

Muzej na Makedonija
Kurciska bb, Skopje

✆ +389-91-221-973 | 60% discount

NETHERLANDS

NATIONAL

GWK

✪	25% discount on transaction costs for cash currency exchange at any of the 65 GWK outlets, situated at main railway stations and border crossings

Budget Rent a Car

✈ 📞 0800 0537 (toll free in The Netherlands)	10% discount on car rental. Ask for Budget traveller (1 or 2 days) or Budget World Travel Plan (from 3 days)

NEW ZEALAND

NATIONAL

YHA Travel
Nationwide

✪ 📞 09 379 4224	5%-30% off. Specialists for all your travel needs. Ask for details about the wide range of discounts on your domestic or international travel plans.

Air New Zealand
Nationwide

✈ 📞 0800 737 000 (freephone)	50% off when flying standby. Members must have a current Hostelling International Membership Card, an International passport and inbound and outbound international air tickets under the members' name

Air Safaris

✈ 📞 0800 806 880 (freephone)	The spectacular 50 minute "Grand Traverse" of Mount Cook and the glaciers departs regularly form Lake Tekapo, Glentanner Park and Franz Josef

Ansett NZ
Nationwide

✈ 📞 0800 267 388 (freephone)	50% standby fares. Members must have a current Hostelling International Membership Card and inbound and outbound international air tickets under the members' name

Intercity Coachlines
Nationwide

✈ 📞 09 913 6100	20% off standard adult fares. Explore New Zealand on our extensive network of coach services. Available to all members on Intercity Services Nationwide

Magic Travellers Network
Nationwide

✈ 📞 09 358 5600 📠 09 358 3471 📧 info@magicbus.co.nz	5% off New Zealand's number one transport network for the independent adventurous traveller. Passes are valid for six months

Mount Cook Landline
Nationwide

✈   ☎ 0800 800 287, 7 days | 30% off standard adult fares. Discount applies to adult fares exceeding $20.00 one way

Newmans Coach Lines
Nationwide

✈   ☎ 09 309 9738 | 20% off standard adult fares. Discount applies to adult fares exceeding $20.00 one way. Ticketing may be done on day of travel

Rent-a-Dent Quality Rental Vehicles
Nationwide

✈   ☎ 0800 736 823 (freephone) | 5% off brochure rate upon production of your YHA card. 30 branches Nationwide. Save with our competitive rates

Shoestring Rentals (NZ) Ltd
Nationwide

✈   ☎ 03 385 3647 | 10% off cars in Christchurch, Wellington, Picton, Auckland, Queenstown & Dunedin. Free pick up, delivery, AA coverage. Free maps and info

Tranz Scenic Unique Train Journeys
Nationwide

✈   ☎ 0800 802 802 (freephone) | 30% off standard adult fares on Tranz Scenic Services nationwide. Can not be used in conjunction with any other discount

NORWAY

NATIONAL

Hertz
Nationwide

✈   ☎ +47 80 03 20 00 | 10% discount on excellent local, weekend and holiday tarifs. Remember to give the agreement number CDP 858545 when you book your car. You must be aged 25 or more to qualify

Nor*Way Bussekspress
Nationwide

✈   ☎ +47 81 54 44 44/+ 47 23 00 24 40 | A discount of NOK 50 on the Osterdal and Nordfjord express coaches. The discount is calculated as a part payment for full fare passengers travelling more than 300km. The discount is granted on presentation of the membership card when entering the coach.

ALVDAL

Alvdal Hostel

🏛 | 50% discount on admission to teh Husantun rural museum (valid only if staying more than one night)

BERGEN

Ulriksbanen cable car

✈ | 33% discount

DOMBÅS

Dovrefjell Aktivitetssenter

15% on canoeing, rafting, musk ox tours, elk safaris, mountain-climbing etc

Budsfjord Gårds Farm Museum

20% discount on standard ticket price

ELVERUM

Elverum Youth Hostel

10% discount on guided fishing trips on the Glomma river, fishing from boat or bank

EVJE

Troll Moutain AS

10% discount on rafting and safaris

HARSTAD

Trondenes Historiske Senter

25% discount on standard ticket price

OSLO

Båtservice AS

50% discount on boat trips where food is not included in the ticket

SJOA

Heidal Rafting AS

10% discount on rafting, glaciering, canyoning etc.

SKIEN

Skien Fritidspark

50% discount on day ticket (swimming, tennis, volleyball, etc)

STRYN

Stryn Sommerski (summer skiing centre)

10-15% discount on ski pass for downhill, snowboarding and cross country skiing

TRONDHEIM

Ringve Musikkhistorik Museum

Ringve Music History Museum : 50% discount

VAL

Namsen Lakseakvarium

Namsen Salmon Aquarium: 25% discount on ticket price

SOUTH AFRICA

CAPE TOWN

World of Birds
⊕ ☎ 021 790 2730	Africa's largest bird park offers you landscaped walks through more than 100 averies with over 3000 birds and animals. Less R5 on normal entrance fee of R22

Contiki Tours
✈ ☎ 021 424 2511	10% discount on all of Contiki's African tours. The tours include Mamibia, Botswana, Zimbabwe and East Africa. Also included are their South Africa Tours. Bookings must be made through the HISA office in Cape Town

DURBAN

The Grass Hopper
✈ ☎ 031 306 6585 or 031 304 5346 ✉ grasshopper@saol.com	5% discount on the purchase of any ticket. Bus service route leaves from Jo'burg/Pretoria and goes to Cape Town via Swaziland, Zululand, Durban, Transkei and the Garden Route

JEFFREYS BAY

Breakers Restaurant
23 Diaz Road
⌂ ☎ 0423 293 1975	10% discount

UNITED STATES OF AMERICA

ASTORIA

Columbia River Maritime Museum
1792 Marine Drive, Oregon
⚓ ☎ 503 325 2323	$1 off regular adult admission

BOSTON

Designs for Living Café
55 Queensberry Street
⌂ ☎ 617 536 6150	Net Café with internet access; 20% off all food and beverage

Enterprise Rent-A-Car
800 Boylston Street
✈ ☎ 617 262 8222	15% car rental discount with hostel receipt or HI membership card

Peter Pan Bus Lines
1776 Main Street
✈ ☎ 800 237 8747	10% discount with HI card for travel between Hartford, New York City, Philadelphia, Baltimore, and Washington DC

BUFFALO

Studio Arena Theatre
710 Main Street, New York

🖋   ☎ 716 856 5650 $10 on a "rush" basis, available one hour before
      ✉ studio@pce.net   performance, based on availability. Recommend calling box
                       office in advance

Pettibones Grille
275 Washington Street, New York

🍴   ☎ 716 846 2100   20% discount on your entire bill. Dine-in only

CANNON BEACH

Clean Line Surf Shop
171 Sunset Blvd, Oregan

🍴   ☎ 503 436 9726   10% off surf package rental, including full wet suit, boots,
                       gloves, swim fins, and a choice of surfboard or boogie board

CHICAGO

Trattoria Caterina
616 S Dearborn

🍴   ☎ 312 939 7606   20% off. Must present membership card before ordering

DEADWOOD

Alkali Ike Tours
PO Box 652, South Dakota

✈   ☎ 605 578 3147   10% off ticket price for Deadwood tour

HILL CITY

Sylvan Rocks Climbing School and Guide Service
89 Elm PO Box 600, South Dakota

🖋   ☎ 605 574 2425 $10 off any beginner group class
      ✉ info@sylvanrocks.com

HONOLULU

Reef Trekkers Hawaii
PO Box 8899, Hawaii

🖋   ☎ 808 943 0588   Complimentary rental dive gear, transportation, snacks and
      ✉ dive@reeftrekers.com   drinks on all our dive charters

KISSIMMEE

Boggy Creek Airboat rides
2001 E. Southport Road, and 3702 Big Bass Road, Florida

🖋   ☎ 407 933 4337 & $2.00 off adult airboat tour
      407 344 9550
      ✉ info@bcairboats.com

Kissimmee Water Sports
4914 West Irlo Bronson Memorial Hwy, Florida

🏄   ☎ 407 396 1888   Water Skiing, wake boarding $10 off regular rates

---

Vacation Works Inc
4838 West US 192, Florida

☺   ☎ 1800 396 1883 or   Free Orlando Access card for discounts at attractions,
     407 396 1883   restaurants, shopping and much more. Save up to $500.00
     ✉ tickets@orlandovisitor.com

The Netkafee
22 Broadway, Florida

🏧   ☎ 407 943 7500 $2.00 off first hour of computer/internet use. Limit 1 per
     ✉ custserv@netkaffee.com   person. May not be combined with any other offer.

NORTH CONWAY

Cranmore Sports Center
PO Box 1640, New Hampshire

☺   ☎ 603 356 6301 $2 off of daily guest pass or daily climbing wall pass

---

Sports Outlet Ski Shops
Main Street, New Hampshire

🏧   ☎ 603 356 3133 $20 per day bike rentals

Freedom Rent-A-Car
PO Box 2245, New Hampshire

✈   ☎ 603 447 3873   Unlimited mileage, $33 per day, must be 25 years of age,
                   insurance is $8 for 1,000 deductible if needed. 8% rental
                   tax applies. Pick up can be arranged Mon-Fri 8.00-3.30.

OHIOPYLE

Wilderness Voyageurs Inc
PO Box 97, Pennsylvania

🏄   ☎ 800 272 4141   10% discount on Whitewater Rafting, canoes, bikes and raft
     ✉ rafting@wilderness-   rentals
     voyageurs.com

ORLANDO

Gatorland
14501 S Orange Blossom Trail, Florida

🏄   ☎ 407 855 5496 or   20% discount off regular admission rates. Offer valid for up
     1800 393 JAWS   to 6 people in the party. Offer not valid with any other
     ✉ info@gatorland.com   coupons or discounts

PHILADELPHIA

Mad Mex
3401 Walnut Street (The Shoppes at Penn)

📠 ☎ 215 382 2221
    ✉ madmex-philly@madmex.com

10% off your bill. Not valid with any other specials, discounts or promotions

PITTSBURGH

Mattress Factory Museum of Art
500 Sampsonia Way

🏰 ☎ 412 231 3169
    ✉ info@mattress.org

$1.00 off admission, and 10% off merchandise in museum

Casbah
339 S Highland Street

📠 ☎ 412 661 5656
    ✉ casbah@bigburrito.com

10% off your bill. Not valid with any other specials, discounts or promotions

Golden Triangle Bike Rentals
416 Woodrift Lane

📠 ☎ 416 655 0835
    ✉ goldentrianglebikes@yahoo.com

10% discount on bike rentals

SACRAMENTO

Bike Sacramento
1050 Front Street, California

📠 ☎ 916 444 0200

Get around town or bike the Jedediah Smith River Trail with 25% off all bike rentals

SEASIDE

Seaside Aquarium
200 N Promenade, Oregon

🛶 ☎ 503 738 6211

Half price admission with HI Membership

SEATTLE

Upper Left-Hand Corner Kayak Tours
10823 NE 60th Street

🛶 ☎ 425 828 4772
    ✉ roger@kayak-wa.com

20% discount on half-day and full-day sea kayaking tours in the Seattle area. Beginners and experienced kayakers are welcome. All equipment provided.

SIMSBURY

Bicycle Cellar
532 Hopmeadow Street, Connecticut

📠 ☎ 860 658 1311

10% off on repairs and accessories (cannot be used on previous purchases or sales items)

◄ ENGLISH

HOW TO USE THE SIGNS

❶ OPEN THIS FLAP

❷ TURN TO THE COUNTRY IN WHICH YOU ARE INTERESTED

❸ COMPARE THE SIGNS FOR EXPLANATION

◄ FRANÇAIS

COMMENT INTERPRETER LES SYMBOLES

① OUVRIR CE VOLET

② REPORTEZ-VOUS AU PAYS QUI VOUS INTERESSE

③ COMPAREZ LES SIGNES POUR EN AVOIR L'EXPLICATION

◄ DEUTSCH

ANLEITUNG ZUR BENUTZUNG DER ZEICHEN

❶ ÖFFNEN SIE DIESES FALTBLATT

❷ SUCHEN SIE DAS LAND ÜBER WELCHES SIE AUSKÜNFTE HABEN MÖCHTEN

❸ VERGLEICHEN SIE DIE ZEICHEN AUF DER KLAPPE MIT DENEN DES LANDES

◄ ESPAÑOL

COMO UTILIZAR LOS SIMBOLOS

① ABRA ESTA SOLAPA

② BUSQUE EL PAIS QUE LE INTERESA

③ COMPARE LOS SIMBOLOS PARA OBTENER SU EXPLICACION

Cover Design and Hostelling International advertisements by Big Design, London.
Inside Front Cover, pages 1-32 & "We want to hear from you" pages by Elanders (UK)
Limited.

IYHF acknowledges the help of Member Associations in providing photographs for contents
page and pages 1-32.

In pursuance of the Environmental Charter adopted by IYHF's 39th International Conference,
this book has been produced using only paper from environment-friendly sources. The Nordic
Council of Ministers decided in November 1989 to introduce common Nordic environmental
labelling of products. Today, the 'Swan' is the only existing environmental label for printed
matter in Europe. The criteria is set with this main target area:

The effect on the environment is minimised within the production process.

The product itself:

This product is 100% recyclable.

The ink, varnish and glue does not contain chemicals classified as environmentally
hazardous according to EU directives.

The paper used is produced with low environmental impact (emissions) not with
chemicals classified as environmentally hazardous according to EU directives.

Published in 1999 by
International Youth Hostel Federation
Secretariat, 1st Floor, Fountain House, Parkway, Welwyn Garden City,
Hertfordshire, AL8 6JW, England
Registered under the Charity Act in England.

Distributed in the United Kingdom by World Leisure Marketing
… and through Hostelling International outlets worldwide.
"Hostelling International" is the brand name of Youth Hostelling Worldwide

HOSTELLING
INTERNATIONAL